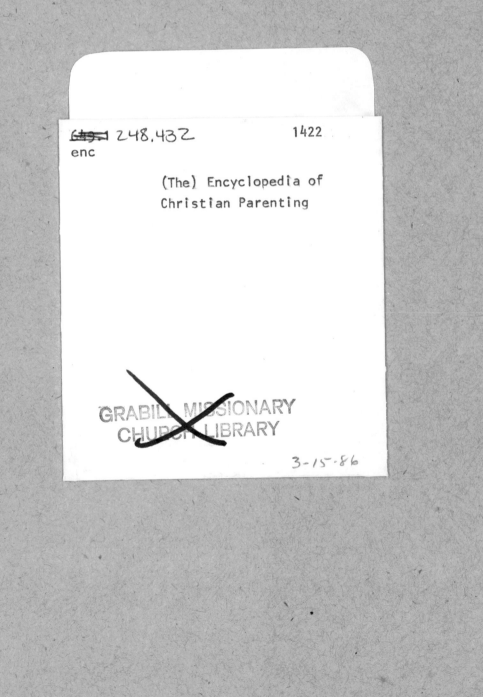

The Encyclopedia of Christian Parenting

The Encyclopedia of Christian Parenting

Fleming H. Revell Company
Old Tappan, New Jersey

Scripture quotations identified NEB are from *The New English Bible.* © The Delegates of the Oxford University Press and the Syndics of the Cambridge University Press 1961 and 1970. Reprinted by permission.

Scripture quotations identified TEV are from the *Good News Bible*—Old Testament: Copyright © American Bible Society 1976: New Testament: Copyright © American Bible Society 1966, 1971, 1976.

Scripture quotations identified TLB are from The Living Bible, copyright © 1971 by Tyndale House Publishers, Wheaton, Illinois. Used by permission.

Acknowledgments continued on page 11.

Library of Congress Cataloging in Publication Data
Main entry under title:
The Encyclopedia of Christian parenting.
    Includes bibliographies and index.
    1. Parenting—Religious aspects—Christianity—Dictionaries.
HQ755.8.E52   649′.1′0321   82-562
ISBN 0-8007-1276-5   AACR2

Contents

Foreword

Many books and articles on child raising are available today. This encyclopedia brings together in one volume valuable parenting information, which includes original material as well as carefully selected items from published sources. Always putting emphasis on a careful blend of the practical and spiritual, we have attempted to cover matters most likely to be of concern in the everyday lives of responsible Christian parents.

Included are articles in the general areas of emotional and physical health, personality, behavior, learning, spiritual training, family relationships and activities, and more. In a collection of concentrated information such as this, articles sometimes serve, basically, as introductions to the topics. Of special value, then, are the reading lists following most sections, referring the reader to selected works in the field for further amplification.

It is our aim in this work to provide a comprehensive but readable reference book of information, sound advice, and direction for persons who are seeking to become better informed in order to fulfill their roles as Christian parents in the very best way possible.

THE PUBLISHER

Acknowledgments

We are grateful to Leslie R. Keylock, who did the original compilation of the material in this volume. An ordained Baptist minister, he is a writer, editor, and a consultant for religious and inspirational paperbacks for the New American Library.

Acknowledgment is made to the following for permission to reprint copyrighted material:

ABINGDON: Excerpts from UNDERSTANDING YOUR FAITH by H. Newton Malony. Copyright © 1978 by Abingdon. Used by permission.

JAY E. ADAMS: Excerpts from *The Big Umbrella*.

AUGSBURG PUBLISHING HOUSE: Excerpts from LIVING WITH DYING by Glen W. Davidson (Augsburg Publishing House, 1975). Excerpts from WHY AM I SHY? by Norman B. Rohrer and S. Philip Sutherland (Augsburg Publishing House, 1978).

BAKER BOOK HOUSE: Excerpts from FOCUS ON FAMILY LIFE by Gladys M. Hunt. Copyright © 1970 by Gladys M. Hunt and used by permission of Baker Book House.

ELIZABETH C. BAKER-SMITH: Excerpts from *The Impact of Illness on the Family and the Ministry of the Christian Community*.

BRIGHAM YOUNG UNIVERSITY PRESS: Excerpts from *Dear Mom and Dad* by Barbara J. Taylor (Brigham Young University Press, 1978).

BROADMAN PRESS: Excerpts from *Evelyn Duvall's Handbook for Parents* by Evelyn Duvall (Nashville: Broadman Press 1974) pp. 24–35, 127–136. Used by permission. Excerpts from *Bridging the Generation Gap* by William L. Self (Nashville: Broadman Press 1970) pp. 41–52. Used by permission.

CHRISTIAN HERALD BOOKS: Excerpts from *Lure of the Cults* by Ronald M. Enroth.

GARY R. COLLINS: Excerpts from EFFECTIVE COUNSELING and MAN IN MOTION.

CONCORDIA PUBLISHING HOUSE: Excerpts from YOU AND YOUR RETARDED CHILD by Nancy Roberts © 1974 Concordia Publishing House. Used by permission.

DAVID C. COOK PUBLISHING CO.: Excerpts from *TV: Friend or Foe?* by Paul Borgman, David C. Cook Publishing Co., 1979. Excerpts from *Understanding Suicide* by William L. Coleman, David C. Cook Publishing Co., 1979.

CREATION-LIFE PUBLISHERS: Excerpts from *The Battle for Creation* by Henry M. Morris and Duane T. Gish, Creation-Life, 1976.

JOAN DAVES: Excerpts from A PARENT'S GUIDE TO CHILDREN'S EDUCATION by Nancy Larrick, copyright © 1963 by Nancy Larrick. Reprinted by permission of Joan Daves.

DOUBLEDAY & COMPANY, INC.: Excerpts from "Being a Father Today" by Richard E. Wolf; and other excerpts from THE NEW ENCYCLOPEDIA OF CHILD CARE & GUIDANCE, edited by Sidonie Matsner Gruenberg. Copyright © 1954, 1956, 1959, 1963, 1967, 1968 by Doubleday & Company, Inc. Reprinted by permission of the publisher. Excerpts from THE PARENTING ADVISOR, edited by Frank Caplan, copyright © 1976, 1977 by the Princeton Center for Infancy and Early Childhood. Reprinted by permission of Doubleday & Company, Inc.

DUKE UNIVERSITY PRESS: Excerpts from *Child Safety Is No Accident* by Jay M. Arena and Miriam Bachar, copyright 1978 Duke University Press (Durham, N.C.).

DR. ALICE GINOTT: Excerpts from *Between Parent and Child* by Haim G. Ginott.

GROLIER EDUCATIONAL CORP.: Excerpts from *All Children Want to Learn* by Lorena Fox, copyright © 1954 by The Grolier Society, Inc.

HARVEST HOUSE PUBLISHERS: Excerpts from PARENTS: GIVE YOUR KID A CHANCE by Ken Poure and Dave Stoop, Harvest House Publishers, Eugene, Oregon 97402.

HAWTHORN PROPERTIES (Elsevier-Dutton Publishing Co., Inc.): Excerpts from *Parents on Trial* by David Wilkerson, © 1967 by David Wilkerson.

HOLT, RINEHART AND WINSTON, INC.: Excerpts from PHYSICAL EDUCATION: A PROBLEM-SOLVING APPROACH TO HEALTH AND FITNESS by Perry B. Johnson, Wynn F. Updyke, Donald C. Stolberg and Maryellen Schaefer. Copyright © 1966 by Holt, Rinehart and Winston, Inc. Reprinted by permission of Holt, Rinehart and Winston, CBS College Publishing.

LONGMAN GROUP LIMITED: Excerpts from *How We Can Help Children to Pray* by E. E. Read Mumford. Used by permission.

LONGMAN INC.: Excerpts from INDIVIDUAL DIFFERENCES IN THE CLASSROOM by R. Murray Thomas and Shirley M. Thomas. Copyright © 1965 by Longman Inc. Reprinted with permission of Longman Inc., New York.

LUTHERAN CHURCH IN AMERICA: Excerpts from *Bible and Doctrine for 3's to 5's* by Eleanor Zimmerman. Copyright 1963, Lutheran Church Press. Used by permission.

McGRAW-HILL BOOK COMPANY: Excerpts from SAFETY EDUCATION by A. E. Florio and G. T. Stafford, copyright © 1962. Used by permission. Excerpts from INTRODUCTION TO THE GIFTED by Gertrude Hildreth, copyright © 1966. Used by permission.

NAVPRESS: Excerpts from *Honesty, Morality and Conscience* by Jerry White, NavPress, Colorado Springs, Colo. (1979). Used by permission.

PAULIST PRESS: "Forgiveness . . . A Painful Truth" by Clarice Flagel and "Can We Ever Do Anything As a Family" by Kevin and Rita Cronin are reprinted from *Christian Parenting: The Adolescent*, © 1979 by The Missionary Society of St. Paul the Apostle in the State of New York. Used by permission of Paulist Press. "Valuing Who We Are: Self-Esteem for Our Children and Ourselves" by Maureen Miller is reprinted from *Christian Parenting*, © 1979 by The Missionary Society of St. Paul the Apostle in the State of New York. Used by permission of Paulist Press. "Someone Special" by Brigid O'Donnell is reprinted from *Christian Parenting: The Young Child*, © 1979 by The Missionary Society of St. Paul the Apostle in the State of New York. Used by permission of Paulist Press.

PUBLICATIONS INTERNATIONAL, LTD.: Excerpts from EMERGENCY FIRST AID used by permission.

FLEMING H. REVELL COMPANY: Excerpts from *Do You Know Where Your Children Are?* by John Benton copyright © 1981 by John Benton. Excerpts from *How To Be Happy Though Young* by Darien B. Cooper copyright © 1979 by Darien B. Cooper. Excerpts from *Hide or Seek* by Dr. James Dobson copyright © 1974, 1979 by Fleming H. Revell Company. Excerpts from *Teenage Rebellion* by Truman E. Dollar and Grace H. Ketterman copyright © 1979 by Truman E. Dollar and Grace H. Ketterman. Excerpts from *A Crowded Church* by Eugene Dolloff, copyright © 1946 by Fleming H. Revell Company; © 1974 by Eugene Dolloff. Excerpts from *You Can Be Financially Free* by George Fooshee, Jr., copyright © 1976 by George Fooshee, Jr. Excerpts from *People in Process* by Maxine Hancock copyright © 1978 by Maxine Hancock. Excerpts from *The People You Live With* by O. Quentin Hyder, M.D., copyright © 1975 by Fleming H. Revell Company. Excerpts from *Money* by David J. Juroe copyright © 1981 by David J. Juroe. Excerpts from *How to Teach Your Child About Sex* by Grace H. Ketterman, M.D., copyright © 1981 by Grace H. Ketterman, M.D. Excerpts from *The Complete Book of Baby and Child Care for Christian Parents* by Grace H. Ketterman, M.D., and Herbert L. Ketterman, M.D., copyright © 1982 by Grace H. Ketterman,

M.D., and Herbert L. Ketterman, M.D. Excerpts from *The Battle for the Mind* by Tim LaHaye copyright © 1980 by Tim LaHaye. Excerpts from *Family Devotions With School-Age Children* by Lois E. LeBar copyright © 1973 by Fleming H. Revell Company. Excerpts from *Dr. Messenger's Guide to Better Health* by David L. Messenger, M.D., copyright © 1981 by David L. Messenger, M.D. Excerpts from *Adolescence Is Not An Illness* by Bruce Narramore, Ph.D., copyright © 1980 by Bruce Narramore. Excerpts from *Whatever Happened to the Human Race* by Francis A. Schaeffer and C. Everett Koop, M.D., copyright © 1979 by Franky Schaeffer V Productions, Inc. Excerpts from *How to Help Your Child Survive and Thrive in Public School* by Cliff Schimmels copyright © 1982 by Cliff Schimmels. Excerpts from *Design for Christian Marriage* by Dwight Hervey Small copyright © 1959 by Fleming H. Revell Company. Excerpts from *The Single Parent* by Virginia Watts copyright © 1976 by Fleming H. Revell Company. Excerpts from *Intended for Pleasure* by Ed Wheat, M.D., and Gaye Wheat copyright © 1977 by Fleming H. Revell Company; © 1981 by Ed Wheat and Gaye Wheat.

FRANKY SCHAEFFER V PRODUCTIONS: Excerpts from *Whatever Happened to the Human Race?* by Francis A. Schaeffer and C. Everett Koop, M.D., copyright © 1979 by Franky Schaeffer V Productions. Used by permission.

SIMON & SCHUSTER: Excerpts from EFFECTIVE PARENTING by Joan Beck. Copyright © 1976 by Joan Beck. Reprinted by permission of SIMON & SCHUSTER, a Division of Gulf & Western Corporation.

CHARLES C THOMAS, PUBLISHER: Excerpts from QUESTIONS AND ANSWERS ON STUTTERING by Dominick A. Barbara, 1965. Courtesy of Charles C Thomas, Publisher, Springfield, Illinois.

UNIVERSITY OF TORONTO PRESS: Excerpts from *Paediatric Allergy and Clinical Immunology (as applied to Atopic Disease)* by Cecil Collins-Williams.

TYNDALE HOUSE PUBLISHERS, INC.: Excerpts from THE STRONG-WILLED CHILD by Dr. James Dobson. Published by Tyndale House Publishers, Inc. © 1978. Used by permission.

VICTOR BOOKS: Excerpts from SAY IT WITH LOVE by Howard G. Hendricks, Victor Books, 1972. Excerpts from CONQUERING FAMILY STRESS by J. Allan Petersen, Victor Books, 1978. Excerpts from 200 YEARS—AND STILL COUNTING by Wesley R. Willis, Victor Books, 1978. Excerpts from THE FAMILY THAT LISTENS by H. Norman Wright, Victor Books, 1978.

VISION HOUSE PUBLISHERS, INC.: Excerpts from HOW TO BE A PEOPLE HELPER by Dr. Gary Collins used by permission. Copyright © 1976 by Vision House Publishers, Santa Ana, California 92705. All rights reserved.

WORD BOOKS: Excerpts from *Learning to Love* by Lewis T. Bird and Christopher R. Reilly, copyright © 1971, pp. 65–73; used by permission of Word Books, Publisher, Waco, Texas 76796. Excerpts from *Deliver Us From Fear* by Eileen Guder, copyright © 1976, pp. 9–24, used by permission of Word Books, Publisher, Waco, Texas 76796. Excerpts from *Violence* by Peter W. Macky, copyright © 1973, pp. 121–123; used by permission of Word Books, Publisher, Waco, Texas 76796.

H. NORMAN WRIGHT: Excerpts from *In-Laws, Outlaws*.

ZONDERVAN PUBLISHING HOUSE: Excerpts from PRINCIPLES OF PERSONALITY BUILDING FOR CHRISTIAN PARENTS by C. B. Eavey copyright © 1952 by Zondervan Publishing House. Used by permission. Excerpts from HOW TO WIN OVER DEPRESSION by Tim LaHaye copyright © 1974 by The Zondervan Corporation. Used by permission.

The Encyclopedia of Christian Parenting

A

ABORTION

OUR REASONS against abortion are logical as well as moral. It is impossible for anyone to say when a developing fetus becomes viable, that is, has the ability to exist on its own. Smaller and smaller premature infants are being saved each year! There was a day when a 1000-gram preemie had no chance, now 50 percent of preemies under 1000 grams are being saved. Theoretically, there once was a point beyond which technology could not be expected to go in salvaging premature infants—but with further technological advances, who knows what the limits may be! The eventual possibilities are staggering.

The logical approach is to go back to the sperm and the egg. A sperm has twenty-three chromosomes; even though it is alive and can fertilize an egg, it can never make another sperm. An egg also has twenty-three chromosomes, and it can never make another egg. Thus, we have sperm that cannot reproduce and eggs that cannot reproduce unless they get together. Once the union of a sperm and an egg occurs and the twenty-three chromosomes of each are brought together into one cell that has forty-six chromosomes, that one cell has all the DNA (the whole genetic code) that will, if not interrupted, make a human being.

Our question to a pro-abortion doctor who would not kill a *newborn* baby is this: "Would you then kill this infant a minute before he was born, or a minute before that, or a minute before that, or a minute before that?" At what point in time can one consider life to be worthless and the next minute precious and worth saving?

Having already mentioned the union of sperm and egg to give forty-six chromosomes, let us briefly review the development of a baby. At twenty-one days, the first irregular beats occur in the developing heart, long before the mother is sure she is pregnant. Forty-five days after conception, electroencephalographic waves can be picked up from the baby's developing brain.

By the ninth and tenth weeks, the thyroid and the adrenal glands are functioning. The baby can squint, swallow, and move his tongue. The sex hormones are already present. By twelve or thirteen weeks, he has fingernails; he sucks his thumb and will recoil from pain. His fingerprints, on the hands which have already formed, will never change throughout his lifetime except for size. Legally, it is understood that an individual's fingerprints distinguish him as a separate identity and are the most difficult characteristic to falsify.

In the fourth month the growing baby is eight to ten inches long. The fifth month is a time of lengthening and strengthening. Skin, hair, and nails grow. Sweat glands come into being; oil glands excrete. This is the month in which the mother feels the infant's movements.

In the sixth month the developing baby responds to light and sound. He can sleep

17

and awaken. He gets hiccups and can hear the beat of his mother's heart. Survival outside the womb is now possible. In the seventh month the nervous system becomes much more complex. The infant is about sixteen inches long and weighs about three pounds. The eighth and ninth months see a fattening of the baby.

We do not know how anyone who has seen the remarkable films of the intrauterine development of the human embryo can still maintain that the product of an abortion consists of just some membranes or a part of the woman's body over which she has complete control—or indeed anything other than a human life within the confines of a tiny body. At the very least we must admit that an embryo is not simply an extension of another person's body; it is something separate and uniquely irreplaceable. Another good reason we should not view the unborn baby as an extension of the woman's body is that it did not originate only from the woman. The baby would not exist without the man's seed.

We are convinced that the reason the Supreme Court decision for abortion-on-demand never came to grips with the issue of the viability of the human fetus is that its viability (that is, ability to live outside the womb on its own) is really not the important point.

Viable or not, the single-celled fertilized egg will develop into a human being unless some force destroys its life. We should add that biologists take the uniform position that life begins at conception; there is no logical reason why the pro-abortionist should try to arrive at a different definition when he is talking about people, the highest form of all biological creatures. After conception, no additional factor is necessary at a later time. All that makes up the adult is present as the ovum and the sperm are united—the whole genetic code!

There are three commonly used techniques for abortion. The technique used most often to end early pregnancies is called the D & C or *dilation and curettage.* . . . An alternate method which is used during the same period of pregnancy is called *suction abortion.* . . .

Later in pregnancy, when the D & C or suction abortion might produce too much bleeding in the expectant mother, doctors employ the second most common abortion technique, called the *saline abortion,* or "salting out". . . . If abortion is decided on too late to be accomplished by either a D & C, suction, or saline procedure, physicians resort to a final technique called *hysterotomy.*

There are many unpleasant spin-offs from the basic ugliness of the abortion scene. One is that fewer babies are available for adoption. More childless couples remain childless. This seems especially ironic when one considers that many abortions are being performed very late in term and that a prospective mother could, with little more physical trauma, wait to deliver a normal child at full term and give it up for adoption. That this is not done more often raises the question as to whether in certain cases the mother-to-be does not have an instinctive attachment to the unborn child. That she anticipates the sorrow the separation will bring—and would rather kill the child than lose it—testifies to the fact that the mother knows subconsciously that she has in her womb something more than the mere glob of protoplasm the abortionist would have her believe she is carrying.

Obviously, many more babies are unwanted early in pregnancy than is the case later in pregnancy or after birth. It is the ready availability of abortion-on-demand, when a pregnant woman first has that natural question about how well she can handle a pregnancy, that leads to the tremendous number of abortions. This can be put in personal terms by asking people, "If abortion-on-demand had been available to your mother when she first heard she was pregnant with you, would you be here today?"

Recently several local and state abortion regulations have stipulated that some time must elapse between the woman's decision to abort and the actual procedure. The Akron ordinance passed in March 1978 is the prototype for such legislation. Such legislation does not ban abortion (a ban that would be unconstitutional at the present time), but it does impose some controls. The Akron regulation requires that parents of pregnant girls under eighteen be notified before an abortion is performed. The ordinance also requires that a woman receive counseling by a physician about the results of abortion and that at least twenty-four hours must pass before the abortion can be performed. This provision of course gives a woman more time to think through a hasty decision, so that there will be less chance that she will regret it later.

Current sexual mores, sexually permissive life-styles, and the breakdown of the family demand abortion. At the same time the availability of abortion contributes to a change in our sexual mores, our permissive life-styles, and general family breakdown—truly a vicious cycle. The changes in the technical aspects of medicine are almost staggering. It is said that about 90 percent of the current body of medical knowledge has been learned in the last twenty-five years. We can only regret that ethical views of the medical profession, and of society in general, have not kept pace with the technological advances.

We need to think seriously about the aborted human beings who have been deprived of a chance to live, but we also need to consider with sympathy and compassion the women being turned into "aborted mothers"—bereft mothers—bitter in some

cases, hard in some cases, exceedingly sorrowful in other cases. It is unfair not to make the options clear. To tell a pregnant woman that a few hours or a day in the hospital or clinic will rid her of all her problems and will send her out the door a free person is to forget the humanness of women who are now mothers. With many of the women who have had abortions, their "motherliness" is very much present even though the child is gone.

Abortion does not end all the problems; often it just exchanges one set for another. Whether or not one believes in the reality of guilt is *not* the question at this point. One of the facts of being a human being is that in spite of the abnormality of human beings and the cruelty of their actions, there still exist the hopes and fears, the longings and aspirations, that can be bundled together in the word *motherliness*. To stamp out these feelings is to insure that many women will turn into the kind of hard people they may not want to be. For others, it is a bewildering nightmare to be overwhelmed with longings for the baby to be back in them and to be able to complete that which had begun. To assume that all women will want to abort—and to give flat advice without explaining the very real problems some aborted mothers have—is cruelty in the wrappings of blasé and glib kindness.

Second, abortion is not a "Roman Catholic issue." This must be emphasized. Those who favor abortion often try to minimize the arguments of those who oppose it by conveying the idea that only the Roman Catholic Church is against abortion. We must indeed be glad for the Roman Catholics who have spoken out, but we must not allow the position to be minimized as though it is a "religious" issue. It is not a religious issue.

This line of attack has been carried so far that some lawyers want to rule out the entrance of Congress and the courts into the discussion at all, on the basis that it is only a Roman Catholic issue and therefore a violation of the separation of church and state. The issue, however, is not "divided along religious lines," and it has nothing to do with the separation of church and state.

The issue of the humanness of the unborn child is one raised by many people across a vast spectrum of religious backgrounds, and, happily, also by thousands who have no religion at all. A picture in the *International Herald Tribune* on January 25, 1978, showed a Washington protest march on the fifth anniversary of the Supreme Court decision that restricted the rights of states to regulate and thereby curtail the spread of abortion. The most outstanding sign being carried read: IF MY MOM DIDN'T CARE—I MIGHT NOT BE HERE—THANKS, MOM! The young girl carrying that sign did not have to be religious to paint and carry it; all she needed was to be glad she was not aborted. And the right of that girl to express her views on life and death to those who represent her in the democratic process and to be heard in the courts depends only on her being a citizen of the United States. Abortion is not a religious issue. It is a human issue!

Christians and others who wish to see an end to inhumanities, in compassion and love must offer alternative solutions to the problems. What we are about to suggest does not by any means exhaust the inventory of practical proposals we must put forward—and for which we must sacrifice our own personal peace and affluence. Such a list would be impossible to complete, so we will just give examples.

Churches and other groups opposed to abortion must be prepared to extend practical help to both the unmarried woman who is pregnant and the married woman who may be faced with the question of abortion. Merely to say to either one, "You must not have an abortion"—without being ready to involve ourselves in the problem—is another way of being inhuman.

The unmarried woman may need a place to stay. Time should be taken to tell her about the many couples who cannot have babies and who long to have a child to adopt. She will certainly need counsel about how to care for her child if she decides to keep the baby. Pleasant institutions should be available for unmarried women awaiting the birth of a baby, but each person who does not believe that abortion is right should personally be prepared to offer hospitality, financial aid, or other assistance.

Have you ever welcomed an unwed mother in your home for the months before her baby was born? Are there babies now growing happily in homes that adopted them, or living with their mothers who have a changed outlook on life and death because of the months spent in your home? Hospitality, for a great number of us, should include some period of time in our lives when we care for a pregnant woman in her waiting months.

For married women facing the problems that prompt them to consider abortion, support from a church can be a critical factor. If a mother must work, why shouldn't the church provide for her child's care? Surely such an arrangement could be worked out as an expression of the community which the church is supposed to be. The church might provide a child-care center on its own premises (too many of our churches are only one-purpose buildings) or church members might take a child into their own families for a certain number of hours each week.

We are not trying to propose a universal formula, but to emphasize that saying that abortion is wrong immediately confronts us with a challenge to be willing to share in the consequences which our advice brings. For Christians who adhere to the truth of the Bible, the importance of doing what it teaches is imperative. We are to be compassionate about people's physical needs.

—From Francis A. Schaeffer and C. Everett Koop, M.D., *Whatever Happened to the Human Race?* Old Tappan, N.J.: Fleming H. Revell Co., 1979.

FOR FURTHER READING:

Bajema, Clifford E. *Abortion and the Meaning of Personhood.* Grand Rapids: Baker Book House, 1974.

Brown, Harold O. *Death Before Birth.* Nashville: Thomas Nelson, Inc., 1977.

Martin, Walter. *Abortion: Is It Always Murder?* Santa Ana, Calif.: Vision House Publishers, 1977.

Shoemaker, Donald P. *Abortion, the Bible and the Christian.* Grand Rapids: Baker Book House, 1977.

ACCIDENT PREVENTION

FAR AHEAD of any of the children's diseases, accidents today are the leading cause of death in childhood. In the United States about 14,000 children lose their lives each year in accidents of various kinds. It is a sad fact that more than a third of these deaths occur in the home. Every home is different, of course, and there is no check list to cover all possible hazards. But part of the answer, at least, lies in greater awareness of the most common danger spots on the part of parents and other adults who live with children. The vital problem of preventing accidents has two main parts. One consists of removing all possible danger spots from the home:

Cuts: Keep knives (a knife rack high on the wall is useful), broken or sharp-edged toys, pointed scissors, and other sharp tools out of the reach of small children, who can be given blunt, rounded scissors for their own use.

Burns: When in use, turn handles of pots and pans so that they do not project into the room. Even with this, young children should be taught not to go too near the stove when things are cooking there. One can establish a "cooking line" not to be crossed. Screen the fireplace when in use. Don't leave matches or cigarette lighters where young children can reach them. Loose wires and frayed cords are dangerous. Unused electric outlets are hazards where there is a small child who might stuff metal objects into them. "Dummy" plugs can be used to avoid shock.

Poisoning: Keep medicine chest in careful order. Medicines that are no longer used should be removed and all others should be clearly labeled and read each time before using. Keep medicines containing poisons in a special place out of the reach of children. Remember that some of the most ordinary household items—kerosene, gasoline, cleaning fluids, shoe polish, insecticides—contain poisonous substances, and that a bottle of aspirin looks like candy to a young child. Check before repainting toys or a crib to make sure paint does not contain lead. Do not leave child in a gas- or oil-heated room with all windows closed. A little child must simply be kept away from the countless small objects that he might try to swallow or to stuff into his nose and ears.

Falls: Don't wax floors too highly; wipe up spilled liquids immediately. Provide a rubber mat in the bathroom and a soft mat on the floor nearby. Tack down scatter rugs or place slip-proof mats under them; mend frayed rugs. Make sure that the rails on a child's bed, crib, or playpen are secure. Fasten window screens tightly and, on the upper floors, use guards or bars in addition to the screens. In a home with a small child there should be gates at the top and bottom of the stairs, and the adult should hold onto the banister when carrying him. Check to see that a youngster's new shoes are not too slippery for running and climbing. "Clutter" is the most common cause of tripping. Toys and shoes, bikes and roller skates, cleaning pails and garden rakes—all such things should be put away when not in use.

Guarding against accident possibilities is the first step parents take toward keeping children safe. The second step is to teach them how to take care of themselves—at home, on the playground, on country roads and city streets.

Learning to Climb: Small children must, of course, be kept from climbing to high or dangerous places. As soon as they are able, however, they should be shown places where they can climb—both indoors and outdoors—so that they can develop their physical capacities and self-assurance.

Learning About Sharp Tools: From an early age boys and girls need to develop skill and judgment in handling tools. Though three- and four-year-old children should use rounded scissors, at about five they can start handling some adult tools—large needles, small hammers, and saws. For a long time these are used only under the supervision of a grown-up until the child has gradually learned to handle them with skill and self-confidence.

Learning About Fire and Electricity: Parents need to impress on their children the fact that fire is not a plaything. Children must also learn *never* to touch a light switch or other electric appliance when their hands or any part of their bodies are

wet. But fire and electricity, too, are tools that must be mastered. Boys and girls should not grow up afraid to light a stove, make a campfire, or change a fuse. They can be taught by example and practice to do all such things competently.

Learning About Water: If possible, every child should be given the chance to splash and wade when he is little, to learn to swim before the age of eight or nine. Never leave young children alone near the water, however (or in the bathtub). Don't allow older children—no matter how well they swim— to break the safety rule of never going swimming alone.

Learning About Traffic: Motor vehicles are the leading single cause of accidents in childhood. Boys and girls need to learn how and when to cross streets (grown-ups cannot set a good example if they themselves disobey traffic lights) and where and how to ride their bicycles.

Schools are doing an excellent job in safety education. Parents should follow up by seeing that their children do not play in streets that have traffic. Not only toddlers but school-age children, too, need space to run and climb, to roller-skate and play ball. Even in crowded cities, however, it is possible to find playgrounds and other suitable play areas. For older adolescents who begin to drive, it is important to develop the attitude that a car is not merely a social convenience but a powerful instrument and something in which they should take pride by acquiring (through good driving instruction) the needed skill, experience, and sense of responsibility.

In general, preventing accidents to children is up to the adults. They can do a good job if they take pains to protect small children, to make homes safe, to set a good example in safety habits, and to guide growing children toward an attitude of common sense, confidence, and responsibility.

—From *The New Encyclopedia of Child Care and Guidance*. Garden City, N.Y.: Doubleday & Co., 1968.

A Safe-Home Check List

Yes   No

____   ____   1. Is the area around your driveway free from shrubs, trees, and other obstructions that would prevent a clear view by a person driving a car in or out of your driveway?

____   ____   2. Are handrails provided for any stairway of three or more steps that leads to an entrance to your house?

____   ____   3. Are entrances to the house adequately lighted?

____   ____   4. Is the porch or terrace, if it is more than 10 inches above ground, protected by a firm railing?

____   ____   5. Are clotheslines higher than head level and located away from normal paths of travel across the yard?

____   ____   6. Is the child's outdoor play area located within clear view of the kitchen window?

____   ____   7. Is the child's indoor play area located away from the normal path of traffic through the house?

____   ____   8. Do inside stairs have a firm and continuous handrail?

____   ____   9. Are stairs well lighted, with a light switch located at both the top and the bottom of the stairway?

____   ____   10. Is the bottom basement step painted white?

____   ____   11. Is there sufficient headroom (6 feet 8 inches) on all stairs?

____   ____   12. Is the stair covering firmly tacked down?

____   ____   13. Are the top and bottom of the staircase free of small rugs?

____   ____   14. Are all small rugs in the house laid on nonskid materials?

____   ____   15. Are floors thinly waxed and thoroughly polished to prevent slipping?

____   ____   16. If small children live in the house, are bar gates installed at the top and bottom of the stairs?

____   ____   17. Is furniture so placed that it does not hinder free movement around the room?

____   ____   18. Do doors swing into rooms and not into halls or other normal traffic lanes?

____   ____   19. Is there a tight-fitting screen before the open fireplace?

____   ____   20. Are all cords run along the wall, not under rugs or furniture?

____   ____   21. Are light cords short (not more than 7 feet) and firmly connected to the wall to preclude the possibility of tripping over them?

____   ____   22. Are all wall sockets fitted with guards to prevent children from inserting a finger or a piece of metal into a socket?

____   ____   23. Is all electric wiring properly installed by a reputable electrician?

____   ____   24. Is all electrical equipment of the type recommended by the National Electrical Code and Underwriters' Laboratories, Inc.?

___ ___ 25. Is all electrical equipment regularly inspected, and is any part that is found defective promptly replaced?

___ ___ 26. Are there sufficient outlets for all appliances to prevent overloading the wires?

___ ___ 27. Are all fuses of proper amperes (usually 15 amperes)?

___ ___ 28. Are master switches or multiple-control switches placed at the entrance to each of the principal rooms?

___ ___ 29. Are all portable electrical appliances, such as the washing machine, grounded to the nearest water (not gas) pipe?

___ ___ 30. Are all electrical fixtures or controls in the bathroom located beyond arm's reach from the sink, tub or shower, and any metal objects?

___ ___ 31. Are all electrical appliances, such as pressing or curling irons, fans, heaters, and so on, disconnected when not in use?

___ ___ 32. Is there an insulating link in the chain of all pull-type electric sockets?

___ ___ 33. Are the locations of the various shutoffs for electricity, gas, and water known to all adult members of the family?

___ ___ 34. Are all low-silled bedroom windows barred or screened to protect children from falling out?

___ ___ 35. Are bunk beds equipped with a bar to prevent children from falling out?

___ ___ 36. Is the rule "No smoking in bed" always obeyed?

___ ___ 37. Are all kitchen shelves within easy reach? If not, is a safe and sturdy stepladder kept handy?

___ ___ 38. Are all curtains located near a gas stove of nonflammable material? If not, are they securely fastened to prevent them from blowing over the flame?

___ ___ 39. Are all knives and other sharp tools kept in a special drawer out of the reach of children?

___ ___ 40. Is the kitchen can opener of the kind that leaves no rough edges?

___ ___ 41. If grease or water is spilled on the floor, is it promptly wiped up to remove the danger of slipping?

___ ___ 42. Are all stove-burner controls out of the reach of young children?

___ ___ 43. Is the gas stove equipped with a gas pilot in good working order?

___ ___ 44. Is there a recently inspected fire extinguisher in the kitchen?

___ ___ 45. Are safety matches used, and are all matches kept out of the reach of children?

___ ___ 46. Is there adequate storage space for all kitchen equipment?

___ ___ 47. Is there adequate storage space for tools, toys, bicycles, the lawn mower, screens, storm windows, sewing equipment, etc?

___ ___ 48. Is the bathtub or shower equipped with a strong grip rail?

___ ___ 49. Is a nonskid rubber bath mat used in the tub or shower?

___ ___ 50. Do all members of the household know where the nearest fire alarm is or how to telephone the fire department in case of fire?

___ ___ 51. Are all poisons kept in a special cabinet, properly marked, and out of the reach of children?

___ ___ 52. Is an approved first-aid kit readily available?

___ ___ 53. Are flammable materials, such as oily rags, kept in a closed metal container?

____ ____ 54. Are such flammable materials as tissue paper, excelsior, and old paper boxes properly stacked in the basement away from the furnace while awaiting disposal?

____ ____ 55. Is the attic free of such flammable materials as wrappings and newspapers that might be subject to spontaneous combustion?

____ ____ 56. Are ashes collected in a metal container?

____ ____ 57. Are furnace, chimney, and flues cleaned regularly?

____ ____ 58. Is home dry cleaning done outdoors with a nonflammable fluid?

____ ____ 59. Are all flammable fluids, such as kerosene or gasoline, kept outside and stored in properly marked containers?

____ ____ 60. Is there a special storage place for toys, and do children return them to that place when they are through using them?

____ ____ 61. Are guns unloaded, dismantled, and stored in a locked cabinet?

____ ____ 62. Are chimneys inspected above and below the roof at regular intervals, and is any loose mortar or cement properly restored?

____ ____ 63. Are all minor injuries incurred around the house given prompt first-aid treatment?

—From A. E. Florio and G. T. Stafford, *Safety Education*. New York: McGraw-Hill Book Co., 1962.

ADOLESCENCE

DO YOU WANT your kids to grow up? I sure did! I didn't want them sitting around my house the rest of their lives. And we let them know it. Now we didn't shove them out—don't get me wrong. We just dropped subtle little hints now and then. Like when Sandra was in the twelfth grade, we'd ask her quite regularly what she was going to do when she graduated. Once she said, "Sometimes I get the feeling you want me to move out." And we smiled back at her and replied, "You're right."

We started our program when our kids first became teenagers. Kids look forward to that day. So we made it special. We had what we called a "growing-up" party or a spiritual "bar mitzvah." And from that point on we recognized them as young men or young women.

Our oldest wanted us to allow her to go out on dates, even before she was a teenager. I assured her that was impossible, at least before she became a teenager. Then I realized that was only six months in the future. So I said, "Sandra, let me be your first date." She got very excited, but then she stopped and asked, "Really? You mean you'd take me out?" I informed her that not only would I take her out, but that we would go "top drawer."

So we had six months to get ready and we made a big to-do about it all. When her birthday arrived, her Mom took her down to the hairdresser and had Sandra's hair all done up fancy. Then she helped her with some make-up and some fancy toilet water. Of course, a new dress and some pantyhose and little high heels finished the job. She was beautiful. I borrowed a friend's Cadillac and bought Sandra a corsage and off we went.

What an evening! We went to a nice restaurant and had our picture taken by a waterfall. Every so often we pull out the picture and all of us just crack up. Great memories!

Anyway, while we were finishing our dinner, I said, "Sandra, I know you want to grow up, and your mom and I want to do everything we can to help you." Then I pulled out my pen and drew a box on the paper napkin. "Honey," I continued, "now you're a teenager, and we want to give you some new freedoms. I'm going to put some things inside this box and they will become your responsibility. You know how to take care of your room. But from now on this will be your responsibility. We believe you can handle it; so we're not going to say another word about your room to you. If you want to live in a pigpen, you can live in a pigpen." And her eyes got big as she realized I meant it.

Then I added, "Now here's what we're going to do with the box. When you turn fourteen, we want to give you a bigger box with more responsibilities and with more freedoms as well. And when you're fifteen, a bigger box, and so on until you're eighteen, there will be no box. You'll be free. Do you understand?" And my beautiful little thirteen-year-old daughter said, "Yes, Daddy."

That's how we started using what we called the "Poure boxes," or the "birthday boxes," with our kids. There is a difference between the kind of permissiveness these boxes imply and the permissiveness that precedes the teen years. With progressive permissiveness, everything you put into the box as your child's responsibility is his *total responsibility*. So you need to be careful what you put into the box. You see, prior to the boxes, if I told one of my kids to take out the trash and he didn't take it out, then I took it out. But when the kids hit the teen years, there was a new dimension of responsibility added—total responsibility in progressively larger areas of life.

The hook is that whatever goes into the fourteen-year-old box is completely dependent upon how well the child took care of his thirteen-year-old responsibility. And you have a whole year to work things out and discuss what goes into the next year's box.

So what do you put inside the box? Well, that's between you and your teen. Mark, my youngest, was very well organized. Giving him the responsibility for his bedroom would be no challenge at all. So on his thirteenth birthday we put a big M in his box. That stood for money. Up to that point we had given him a little allowance each week and his lunch money every day. But when he turned thirteen, that all stopped. Instead, we gave him five one-dollar bills every Monday. Note—not Saturday, but Monday; otherwise he'd never make it past the weekend. Mark's task was to regulate his own budget. He did it beautifully.

And along with the responsibility, you also put some freedoms into the box. David, our middle guy, wanted to drive the car when he turned sixteen. So when he turned fifteen, I drew his box and put a big G in it for grades. I said, "David, I want you to get your grade point average up to 3.0, and I want you to get at least a 90 percent in your driver's education class. That's going to be your responsibility this year."

Do you know what he did? He got a 3.6 grade point average—higher than ever before or since. But because it was his responsibility, he made it. Kids respond to these long-range challenges if they know that their freedoms and privileges are related to them. And all the time, you are building responsibility into their lives.

If children aren't allowed to act responsibly, their character development is going to be stunted. It's just like tying your arm to your side for six weeks so you can't use it or move it. You'd have to work on strengthening it again. It is the same with responsible behavior. Your kids need to work on strengthening that characteristic early. Responsibility cannot be strengthened unless it is used. And that's the purpose of progressive permissiveness.

Another item we put into the box was the time the kids had to be home. This illustrates beautifully one of the advantages of progressive permissiveness. When my children were thirteen, they had to be in at 10:00 in the evening. (Of course, exceptions were made for special occasions.) Each year we added 30 minutes extra to the time they could spend on their night out. By the time they got to be seventeen, the magic hour was midnight. Of course, at eighteen, there were no boxes or time limits.

Say you have two teenagers and your thirteen-year-old says, "Why can Bobby stay out till 11:30 when I have to be in at 10:00?" "Easy," you answer. "When you get to be Bobby's age, you can stay out until 11:30—you'll have that freedom." Of course, you can set your own times and traditions (rules) to fit your own family. But the boxes work!

There was another tradition we had in our family concerning the curfew. If the kids were supposed to be home by 11:30 and they didn't make it until 12:00, we'd knock 30 minutes off their next outing. Unless, of course, they had problems and phoned.

When Sandra was dating the guy she eventually married, they played the time-game to the letter. When she was seventeen, they arrived home at the stroke of midnight. We started calling her Cinderella because she was so exact. It was wild. Then on her eighteenth birthday, I took her out and talked with her and gave her total freedom—she could come home any time she wanted. Guess what they did? They were home at 10:30 or 11:00 every time! How hard they must have tried to stay out until midnight before. And after they had their freedom, they proved the value of progressive permissiveness. Their freedom didn't go to their heads.

What if your child flunks his box? Well,

then you simply erase the next year's box and redraw the previous year's box. If it were my kid, I'd say something like, "Well, you know it's really not our fault. It's yours. You didn't take care of this simple responsibility like we KNEW you could; so we can't give you any more freedom." Here again, the burden of responsibility is on his shoulders.

But I think you'll find that kids rise to the challenge. In fact, with Sandra, we didn't know what to put into her box when she turned sixteen. She was doing such a good job. So we suggested, "Sandra, why don't you put some things down on a piece of paper that you would like as freedoms, and we'll try to think of some corresponding responsibilities for your birthday."

Well, the next day we got a little note that said, "The only thing I would like to have is the freedom to choose where I go on my dates, even church." And that was all. Melba and I looked at each other and sort of gulped because we didn't really know what she meant by all that. I said, "Well, she's done a good job each year. . . ." So we asked the Lord to give us some guidance that night. The next morning we still felt Sandra could handle it; so on her birthday we said, "You're on."

Oh, that was a shaky feeling. She was only sixteen and it was her choice to go anywhere she wanted to go. She still had her time limit and we had to check out who she went out with, but she could go anywhere.

We were two weeks into the deal when she got a telephone call from one of her girl friends. Her friend wanted her to go to a Friday Nighter, a school-sponsored dance, down in what is now called Narc Park. It's "doper's heaven" in our town. Sandra leaned around the corner and said, "Daddy, my friend wants me to go to the Friday Nighter. May I?" I was sitting there reading my paper, and from behind the pages I said, "Honey, you just ask the Lord what you should do. Remember on your birthday we told you that you have the freedom to go where you want to go. So you just ask the Lord and whatever He says to you is fine with us." And before I could congratulate myself on the fine job I had done in handling that one, Sandra let out a squeal and said into the phone, "I'll go, I'll go, I'll go." She didn't even take time to ask the Lord.

Oh, I wanted to pull rank on her so bad I could taste it. I had to bite my tongue to keep quiet. She came by and leaned over my paper to give me a kiss—I was still staring at the paper, not seeing a single word—and then she said, "Good-bye, Daddy." You can believe that she knew what was going on inside her dad! She knew me like the back of her hand. And she knew I was steaming inside. But I just sat there silent.

"Would you pick us up at eleven?" she asked sweetly as she got to the door. "Yeah, I'll pick you up," I answered glumly. And off she went while I sat there with my paper covering up my agony.

About this time I heard some footsteps coming into the room. Ah, here was Melba—my wife and helpmate, my tower of strength. But not a sound came from her mouth. I was still sitting there looking at my paper and I could see through that little opening at the bottom. I saw my wife's two feet, and she was shifting her weight back and forth on them. Nonverbal language—I knew I had problems. So I slowly, very slowly, let the paper come down until our eyeballs met across the top of the page. She was standing there with her hands on her hips, waiting. And as soon as our eyeballs met, she said, "Big box, BIG DEAL!"

Oh, I tell you, leadership is lonely. I don't remember what I said or did, but I do remember that Sandra called in less than an hour and I almost shouted with joy when I heard her ask, "Daddy, would you come and get me? This place is weird." My heart was

soaring as I told Melba. She let out a little squeal of delight as I ran to the car and took off to get our daughter.

All the way to the park, I thought to myself, "Now which sermon should I use on her?" And as I turned the last corner, I had one all picked out. But then the Spirit of God told me something. How do I know when God's talking to me? Very simple. When God tells me something, it's always diametrically opposite of what I have just decided. And this time He said, "Poure, keep your mouth shut!" I'd never say that to myself!

So when Sandra jumped into the car, I simply said, "Hi." And we drove on towards home. Finally, she couldn't take it any longer. Her mouth is even more gregarious than mine. And when I didn't give her a sermon, she asked, "Well, Daddy, don't you want to know what happened?" I responded calmly, "Sure, Honey, if you want to talk about it." And all the way home I listened as she related what she saw, the influence it had on her, and her reaction to it all. But what I really heard were some personal convictions. Melba and I both learned that night that God can lead our kids to conclusions, convictions, and standards, just as He does us, if we'll give Him a chance.

I know it's kind of scary, but I believe the only way for parents to survive the adolescent years is to have this kind of confidence. Sure we have had our defeats. We've wept in the night wishing we could undo some of our kids' mistakes. I will do everything I can as a parent to help my kids, but their behavior is their own responsibility.

Some parents play the blame-game if their kids have problems. We all make mistakes and many times we could do better. But I believe God is at work in every situation. Sometimes all you can do is pray that your kids make it. Peer pressures can be so great that kids will mess themselves up in spite of everything their parents do. But if the pattern is correct—if you begin with restrictiveness and move to progressive permissiveness—you're giving your kids the best chance they can have.

You say your son or daughter is already fifteen, and you wonder if it's too late to begin with the boxes? I don't think it is. Just sit down and explain to your kids that you're interested in seeing them grow up. Tell them that you have discovered something that has helped some other kids and you're going to use it in your family. Then draw the boxes and work out a fair exchange of responsibilities for freedoms. Be consistent as you work it out together. Now let's consider what it means to build character during these permissive years.

—From Ken Poure and Dave Stoop, *Parents: Give Your Kid a Chance*, Eugene, Ore.: Harvest House Publishers, 1977.

FOR FURTHER READING:

Dobson, James C. *Preparing for Adolescence.* Santa Ana, Calif.: Vision House Publishers, 1978.

Dollar, Truman E., and Ketterman, Grace H. *Teenage Rebellion.* Old Tappan, N.J.: Fleming H. Revell Co., 1980.

Wiersbe, Warren. *Be a Real Teen.* Evanston, Ill.: Moody Press, 1971.

Witte, Kaaren. *Angels in Faded Jeans.* Minneapolis: Bethany Fellowship, 1979.

Wright, N. Norman, and Johnson, Rex. *Building Positive Parent-Teen Relationships*, Eugene, Ore.: Harvest House Publishers, 1978.

ADOPTION

FIRST LET'S DISCUSS the possibility of adoption as an answer to your desire to have children. Adoption has made a marvelously happy family life possible for many childless people in times past. It may answer certain questions or doubts some of you experience about having children. For example, some couples who have a serious sense of responsibility about overpopulation, believe they can help other children in need of a home and parents, and fulfill their need for children at one and the same time.

The availability of children for adoption, however, has decreased dramatically in the past decade. Due to freely available contraceptives and the legalization of abortions, but mainly due to the removal of social stigma against unwed parenthood, there are few babies to be found for adoption. To be sure, there are some and, tragically, "black-marketing" (selling babies) has become all too common. But the average waiting time in this country for adopting an infant is about three and a half years.

Older Children

More easily found, however, are older children. Many of these were children of unwed mothers who desperately tried to care for them and couldn't. They had to give them up. Some of these babies, due to the immense stress and inexperience of their young mothers, received a less-than-ideal start in life, and thus present special needs and handicaps. Many times these can be overcome. But the first eighteen months are crucial ones in a child's habit patterning and development. We may wish that a toddler were just as easy to accept, love, and raise as an infant, but that simply is not so, especially when he has been neglected or abused. We may empathize and care about the heroic young mothers, too, but that doesn't change the facts, either. In many large cities, one out of every five births is to a teenage mother—most of whom are unmarried. Rarely have they gained the maturity and experience it takes to successfully parent a child.

Handicapped Children

There are many adoptable children of two or three years. There are also a number who have various physical or emotional handicaps who may be adopted. Many of these require costly medical attention and certainly need parents who can manage to honestly accept and love them as they are. They demand a fine balance in empathy and concern, but firmness and consistency in expecting them to help overcome the handicap as fully as possible.

Children From Overseas

There also are children from other countries who need parents. After the Korean War, there were many Korean children, fathered by American servicemen, who were brought to America for adoption. This has continued with full-blooded Koreans, half-American Vietnamese, as well as children from various other countries. The death rates in some impoverished countries leave a disproportionate number of orphans, and there are several adoption agencies which can help you find such children. There is, unfortunately, a great length of red tape to untangle in bringing such a child to this country.

Children of Other Races

In many communities, there is still some racial prejudice. This is tragic but true. So before you decide on adopting a child of another race, be careful that you are doing him a favor. Sound out your friends, neighbors, schools, and church. See if they will accept, love, and help you raise this special child with sincerity. If not, you may even move to

a community that is more democratic. A child may be better off in poverty in his own country than to live in prosperity yet suffer the rejection of prejudice.

Go to a Recognized Agency

We strongly recommend, if you want to adopt a child, that you go to a *recognized* child-placement agency. Your minister or family doctor can help you locate such a place. They will work with you to discover just the sort of child whom you can honestly love and accept. And they will try to find such a child. Acceptance as an adoptive family by such an agency is not a pass-fail selection. It is a process of matching what you parents have to offer with the exact child who needs that—to the joy and fulfillment of both.

The Legalities

Be clear about the legal process of adoption. Most states issue a new birth certificate at the time of adoption, and seal the one on which the biological parents' names are inscribed. Such names are very difficult to obtain. Now there is a widespread movement to liberalize the release of information about biological parents. *Again, let me remind you that such information belongs to those other parents as well as the child, and it may not be wise or kind to dig into it.*

Telling the Child He's Adopted

If you decide to adopt a child, there are several ideas you must consider. First, how and when should you tell him he is adopted? If he is older or of another nationality, he may well know from the start that he is adopted. If not, you will want to tell him before he hears from someone else. For some reason, it is shocking to a child to learn that his parents did not give birth to him.

In a well-meant effort to save children from such a shock, adoptive parents many years ago tried very hard to keep children from finding out that they had been adopted. Fortunately, that practice gave way to a better one (in our opinion). Adoptive parents started, when the child was one year of age, to have a biological birthday celebration and an adoptive anniversary party. They would explain to this small child about their search for him and how very much they loved and wanted him. This helped the child to view his adoption as a happy event. It is likely that some parents overplayed this, and perhaps a more ideal plan is to simply begin to explain as soon as the parents wish.

Have Information About Biological Parents

Adoptive parents need to understand their feelings about not having a child of their own. They must get over any sense of failure, inferiority, or guilt if they are to be free to be really confident parents. In the case of adoption, *it is also urgent that adoptive parents know something and feel comfortable about the child's biological parents.* Sooner or later, many adoptive children become curious about their background. They will want to know how their mothers or fathers looked, what they did for a living, what their interests were, and rarely spoken, but extremely important: *Why did they give us away?*

Curiosity Not Rejection

When adoptive parents see such interest as a rejection of themselves, they will be hurt. Often they unconsciously bristle defensively and create an unnecessary chasm between themselves and their child. This is understandable, since such questions often

begin during adolescence when there will be some rebelling in any family. Please understand, however, that such curiosity is natural. You need not take it as a wish to replace you. Discuss their concerns openly, and tell them all you can about their biological parents. Tell them especially of the heroic love that prompted them to release the child to a family who could provide what they could not. Let us assure you that starting early to give as much information as is desired and appropriate can prevent problems later. You need to find out as much as you can about the biological parents without identifying them. Any condemnation or judgment on your part—no matter how bad their behavior may have been—will be subtly but definitely conveyed to your child. And he is likely, with time, to feel that he may have inherited or acquired some of that badness. Find a way to feel loving and grateful to those people for giving you your special child. You will just as certainly convey that positive feeling to him, and he can grow in the self-esteem that is so important to healthy personality development.

Search for "Birth" Parents

Another important issue involves the fact that it is becoming increasingly possible for adoptive children to find their "birth" parents. Courts are often willing to open records and even help trace parents once the child has reached a legal age. We believe this decision bears careful consideration. Such a search is often an outgrowth of the philosophy that one should have the right to anything he wants. We personally disagree with this idea. Having worked with several hundreds of unwed mothers and their families, Dr. Grace understands the pain they experienced through conceiving, bearing, and releasing the child. Laboriously, most of them worked through profound pain and grief and only slowly put it to rest. To be reminded of that period of their lives is not necessarily a useful thing or a happy ending. Marital problems and resentments and confusion by later children may result from the sudden appearance of an earlier child.

Perhaps a trusted intermediary could find out if the "birth" parents wish to rediscover the child. At any rate, it seems, they need a vote in the matter. If they choose to remain unknown, the adopted child and his parents will need to respect that choice and resolve their grief. It may be that this will draw them even closer to each other.

The glamorized television depiction of happily reunited families may be extremely deceptive. American people have become quite gullible and they may believe, even unconsciously, that every case will have such a happy ending. That is not true. If you were adopted and cannot find your biological parents, remember that it is not life threatening to grieve; accept limits over which you have no power.

Adoptive Children and Emotional Problems

Still another consideration regarding the adoption of children demands a look at statistics. Significantly more adoptive children have serious emotional problems than do biological children. There are several theories but no proven facts about why this is true. It seems logical to assume that some of it comes from what we've just discussed—the unconscious rivalry of adoptive parents with the biological parents—even when the latter are unknown. Children, so prone to manipulate adults in favor of their own wishes in all circumstances, may (knowingly or not), encourage such competition and then become the victims of the outcome. Perhaps they just feel that something must have been wrong with them to make their birth parents give them away, or they may feel that they were

an undue burden upon these parents. In some cases with which I have worked, all of the above factors played a role.

If you have an adopted child or plan to have one, do remember such issues. Don't worry over them, but if your child seems sad or preoccupied regarding his background, invite him to discuss it openly. Accept his feelings; comfort and reassure him. It may be useful to have a few visits with a counselor to be sure things are right, or to set them right if your own help doesn't seem to be doing the job with your adopted child.

An adoption by loving and secure parents can create a delightful family. Children need parents and a home, and if you need and want children, I hope you can find each other and live happily ever after!

—From Grace H. Ketterman, M.D., and Herbert L. Ketterman, M.D., *The Complete Book of Baby and Child Care for Christian Parents*. Old Tappan, N.J.: Fleming H. Revell Co., 1982.

FOR FURTHER READING:

Dennis, Muriel, ed. *Chosen Children*. Westchester, Ill.: Good News Publishers, 1978.

Miles, Judith M. *Journal from an Obscure Place*. Minneapolis: Bethany Fellowship, 1978.

Wheeler, Bonnie. *Of Braces and Blessings*. Chappaqua, N.Y.: Christian Herald Books, 1981.

AGGRESSIVENESS

THE QUALITY of aggressiveness is generally regarded as being not too admirable or worthy of encouragement. Some believe that if it could be eliminated in childhood, war would disappear. The description "He's too aggressive" is usually applied in criticism of a person who is too self-assertive and pushing. But "He's not aggressive enough" is also used critically, and parents of a boy, especially, often become worried if he doesn't show enough of this quality.

Aggressiveness is then an essential ingredient of personality. It is the inner urge of a living being to grasp at food or to attack an obstruction or an enemy. A baby is aggressive when he reaches for food or a rattle or his mother's finger. The same urge leads him to struggle until he can turn himself over, pull himself to his feet, walk, and climb. A child without any aggressiveness would not only be unable to keep possession of a toy on the playground; he also would not grow beyond infant helplessness.

Children differ widely in the vigor with which they go after things; this can be seen even in tiny infants. One will grasp at a dangled toy while another waits for it to be put into his hand. They react as variously in the early years. One child dashes an offending toy to the ground, while another stands and cries. One kicks and screams at restraints and another meekly submits. Personality differences largely determine the child's first responses to such situations. But his experience in the early years, especially with the ways in which his parents restrain him, will affect his personality in the future.

Aggressiveness in the first two years of a child's life takes the form of asserting himself, of taking or asking for what he wants, of learning to manage himself and trying to manage things and people around him.

The toddler, however, begins to run into obstacles. His own childish limitations of strength and ability frustrate him. Things resist him: drawers and doors won't open, blocks won't balance, the tricycle won't climb the curb. And grown-ups balk him; his mother and father stop him from doing some things and try to make him do others. When his aggressiveness meets an obstacle, he may react in several ways. He may try to obey his mother because he wants her to be pleased with him. He may stop vainly tugging at the

tricycle and try pushing it up instead. Or he may get angry, burst into howls of rage, even kick the offending tricycle.

A great deal depends on how his reaction is received, particularly his "disobedient" or angry reaction. He can be made to obey and to suppress his actions out of fear of punishment or scolding or fear that his mother will not love him. But then the aggressiveness and the anger at its frustration only disappear from the surface. They are buried, to come out in other forms in later life.

The child needs to express whatever he feels when he feels it. According to his age and experience, it is not "bad" or "naughty" to strike back at whatever gets in the way of his struggle to grow, to move forward; but he has to learn ways of showing his anger that are acceptable to adults. He cannot be allowed to hit and destroy, but there is no real reason why he cannot protest in other ways, even though some of them are noisy or inconvenient. He can safely blow off some steam by crying or shouting and still learn that aggressiveness in some directions—such as snatching other children's toys or riding his tricycle in the living room—may be impractical or undesirable.

A child can be too aggressive in ways that are obviously extreme. A child who fights with other children more than he plays with them, who consistently teases other children or tortures pets, is probably troubled by anxious and unhappy feelings. He is angry—at what, he doesn't know—and he is taking out his anger where he can. Such a child probably also feels unloved and unappreciated. Obviously punishments only make these feelings worse. It does not help the little girl who tears her dolls apart and pulls the puppy's tail to tell her she is "bad." She needs kindly understanding and some effort to discover if possible what is really making her angry. The child cannot, of course, tell what the trouble is; she does not even know. Often the arrival of a new baby or some other situation that seems to deprive the child of parents' time and attention brings about such behavior.

Too little aggressiveness in a child is also troubling, though usually it is less obvious. It is not natural for a healthy child to be always obedient and docile. Some rebellion, some resistance now and then, is to be expected. When a child always meekly gives in, it is time to look for reasons. Often the too obedient child has aggressive feelings but is deeply afraid of expressing his feelings. For a great variety of reasons, not always easy to trace, a child who has every reason to feel loved and secure may be uncertain or even timid. Instead of being shocked or disapproving, parents can really feel relieved when one day such a child answers back or fights for his rights instead of giving up. Children who never rebel need encouragement in speaking up for what they want and in expressing their opposition.

A healthy aggressiveness need not always show itself as a readiness to fight, even for cause, or a bold frontal attack on a problem or an opponent. Some gentle, soft-spoken people are thoroughly effective in getting what they really want and defending their own and others' rights. Children also go through stages of more and less outwardly aggressive behavior. Aggressiveness in a child is not something for parents to fear or repress as dangerous so long as it is not usually expressed in a way that hurts others or the child himself either physically or in his feelings. It is an essential quality of a competent, self-reliant, self-confident individual, a force not to be quenched but to be guided.

—From *The New Encyclopedia of Child Care and Guidance*. Garden City, N.Y.: Doubleday & Co., 1968.

FOR FURTHER READING:

Augsburger, David N., Jr., *Anger and Assertiveness in Pastoral Care*. Philadelphia: Fortress Press, 1979.

AGING PARENTS

The Christian Responsibility

So strongly does the New Testament feel about the responsibility of the Christian to care for members of his own family that it says the person who fails in this area ". . . has denied the faith and is worse than an unbeliever" (1 Timothy 5:8 NEB).

Aging parents, especially widows, are mentioned explicitly. "If a Christian man or woman has widows in the family, he must support them himself . . ." (1 Timothy 5:16 NEB). "But if a widow has children or grandchildren, then they should learn as their first duty to show loyalty to the family and to repay what they owe to their parents and grandparents; for this God approves" (1 Timothy 5:4 NEB).

There are, of course, cultural differences between the first and twentieth centuries. Social security and such other government assistance as Medicare and Medicaid have given the elderly greater financial independence from their children. The New Testament was written in the context of what sociologists call the "extended family," in which children, parents, grandparents, and other family members all lived together. Today, by way of contrast, the typical family is the "nuclear family," consisting of two parents and their children.

These cultural differences modify slightly, but do not change, the Christian's responsibility to care for his aging parents. But how is he to do it?

Practical Questions

As long as both parents are alive, they tend to live together by themselves as a separate family, even when one member, usually the man, becomes an invalid.

When one spouse, again usually the father, dies, the Christian family is confronted with its Christian responsibility for the surviving parent. Where possible, such a question should be discussed with the other members of the immediate family.

Should mother stay in her present home? Or will that have too many memories for her and harm her emotionally? If she stays, who will do the repairs and upkeep on the house? If she agrees to sell the house, where should she go? Should she stay with one of us? What problems might that create? How will the other members help out financially, if that is necessary? Or should she move to an apartment? Or is her health such that she should be in a nursing home?

These are some of the questions responsible Christian children will want to ask, especially when the death of one parent seems imminent. As often as possible, these questions should be discussed sensitively with the one who is expected to survive. In cases in which that person is stubborn, senile, or so used to depending on her husband that she is unable to handle such decisions, however, such an approach may not be possible.

Suppose the decision is reached that your mother, or mother-in-law, will stay with you. You as a Christian parent need to be alert for adjustment problems. It will not be easy for a new widow, after being independent, cooking and taking care of a house for half a century or more, to adjust to her new life as part of your family. Nor will it be easy for members of your family to adjust to the presence of a grandparent.

At the same time, you need to welcome the advantages that an aging parent can bring to your home. Much has been written about the stresses experienced by parents in the nuclear family. The aging parent can help take some of the burden off the shoulders of the parents. With a built-in babysitter, parents can schedule time out for dinner together away from the children and their constant demands.

What happens when the aging parent becomes invalid or senile? It is at this point that the question of nursing-home care is usually raised—though it should have been discussed and a nursing home tentatively selected years before (*see* Opal Hutchins Sollenberger's excellent *I Chose to Live in a Nursing Home*). Of course, if one parent does not work out of the home, the question may be postponed. But with over half the nation's wives and mothers employed outside the home, this is increasingly less of an option.

Practical Solutions

When an aging parent moves in with you, an effort needs to be made to make the adaptation as smooth as possible. If he has loved gardening, turn over certain responsibilities to him. If the widow has cooked all her life, discuss with her the idea of taking over cooking responsibilities certain days of the week.

Experts in aging note that those who have many hobbies and interests tend not to get senile. College courses at lowered tuition rates are available in many communities. The University of Kentucky's model "Donovan Program" for retired persons is being adopted in many regions of the country. Christian women can become more involved in volunteer community and church work. And with fewer responsibilities, the aging parent can pray as he has never been able to before.

Family devotions after the evening meal could occasionally include such passages as

Exodus 20:12; Leviticus 19:32; Psalms 71:9; Proverbs 16:31; 20:29; Ecclesiastes 4:13, 14; 12:1–7; Isaiah 46:3, 4; and 1 Timothy 5:1–16.

But moving in with children is not the only solution. In some areas of the country "mother-daughter" houses are popular. In such an arrangement, the mother has her own apartment with its own entrance in the daughter's home.

Or a widow may choose to stay in her own home. One woman we know decided to take in roomers and even a boarder or two her own age.

With the percentage of the population over the age of 65 having risen from 4 percent in 1900 to 8 percent in 1953 and 11 percent today, it is not surprising that the number of nursing homes has burgeoned dramatically. Scandal shrouded some nursing homes in the 1970s when greedy, unscrupulous speculators saw an opportunity to make a lot of money from them.

But today Christian nursing homes sponsored by a number of evangelical denominations are countering the bad image. Representative of these are the Fairhaven Christian Home in Rockford, Illinois (Evangelical Free Church); Calvary Fellowship Homes in Lancaster, Pennsylvania (Reformed Presbyterian Church—Evangelical Synod and Orthodox Presbyterian Church); Shell Point Village in Fort Myers, Florida (Christian and Missionary Alliance); and Brookside Manor Home in Overbrook, Kansas.

Living with aging parents will probably be part of God's plan for most Christian families. There are responsibilities. But there are also benefits.

—LESLIE R. KEYLOCK

FOR FURTHER READING:

Anderson, Margaret J. *Your Aging Parents.* St. Louis: Concordia Publishing House, 1979.

Sollenberger, Opal Hutchins. *I Chose to Live in a Nursing Home.* Elgin, Ill.: David C. Cook Publishing Co., 1980.

ALCOHOL

THE DRINKING of alcoholic beverages has become increasingly accepted in American life.

It is, therefore, perhaps not surprising that the evangelical Christian community is not of one mind on the topic.

Many Christians insist that the only correct position is total abstinence. They point out that as much as 10 percent of the population has severe problems with alcohol, that about half of all traffic accidents involve a drinking driver, and that billions of dollars are lost to business each year because of absenteeism related to alcoholic beverages. For biblical support they cite "Wine is a mocker, strong drink is raging; and whosoever is deceived thereby is not wise" (Proverbs 20:1). If Jesus criticized the evil servant who began "to eat and drink with the drunken" (Matthew 24:49), how much more would He oppose Christians doing the same when the art of distillation has so greatly increased the alcoholic content of many alcoholic beverages.

Other evangelical Christians are equally ardent in their insistence that the Bible teaches moderation, not total abstinence. They point out that the wine Jesus drank, for example, at the wedding in Cana of Galilee, was unquestionably alcoholic (John 2:10). While recognizing the serious social problems that result from excessive drinking, they argue that such excesses result from the psychological and spiritual weakness of those who drink too much. They maintain that to demand total abstinence from the 90 percent who have no problems with drinking is unrealistic and unenforceable. The person who becomes an alcoholic has spiritual and psychological needs that lie behind his alcoholism; *they* need to be tackled, not the drinking he turned to to escape from his problems.

Each Christian family must settle this question for itself. Christian parents who believe in total abstinence need to discuss their position with the members of their family, perhaps during family devotions after the evening meal. Christian parents who believe in moderation need to discuss their position in a similar way. They need to make clear to their children that the Bible does not approve of the excessive drinking that is sometimes admired as smart or sophisticated in some high-school circles. Their children need to know that it is the insecure and unloved teenager who usually abuses alcohol by drinking until he is high or drunk. Schools will usually have programs on the dangers of excessive drinking.

Christian parents who use alcohol need to keep their Christian stewardship in mind. Alcoholic beverages are expensive. Heavy expenses in this area take away from better uses of their money.

And although wine was drunk in biblical times, "hard liquor" as we know it was not. Given the problems that are connected with excessive drinking in biblical times, many Christians will want to abstain from hard liquor, even if they occasionally drink wine at home or on social occasions.

If your teenager somehow has a problem with drinking, see that he gets professional help. Your pastor will be able to suggest places where he can get aid.

—LESLIE R. KEYLOCK

FOR FURTHER READING:

Lyles, John S. *Youth and Alcoholic Beverages.* Atlanta: John Knox Press, 1967.

Mehl, Duane. *You and the Alcoholic in Your Home.* Minneapolis: Augsburg Publishing House, 1979.

Wilkerson, Don. *Fast Track to Nowhere.* Old Tappan, N.J.: Fleming H. Revell Co., 1979.

ALLERGIES

THERE IS NO such thing as a "non-allergic person." Although only about 10 percent of people manifest major allergy (i.e., eczema, urticaria, hay fever, or asthma) some time in their lives, and 50 percent of people manifest either major allergy or minor allergy (allergic manifestations other than these included in major allergy) some time in their lives, these manifestations can come on at any age. Since any child is potentially allergic, it is intelligent to protect him from unnecessary risks which may bring on serious and perhaps prolonged allergic symptoms and even disability.

This can be done by:

1. Breast feeding
2. Using evaporated cow's milk instead of bottled milk
3. Avoiding occasional feedings of cow's milk in the newborn period
4. Delaying the introduction of highly allergenic foods into the infant's diet, e.g., egg, fish, peanuts
5. Introducing foods singly so that the cause of allergic symptoms can be recognized
6. Introducing foods in a well-cooked (hypoallergenic) form
7. During intestinal upsets avoiding new, raw, or lightly cooked foods
8. Avoiding highly allergenic environment. No horseback riding for a highly allergic child
9. Maintaining dust-free room for an infant with eczema to minimize his chance of developing respiratory allergy

10. Avoiding highly allergenic medications such as penicillin unless there is a definite indication
11. Giving medications orally when possible
12. Restricting the diet of the pregnant woman who has had one allergic child
13. Treating allergic symptoms early before the disease (e.g., asthma) is far advanced
14. Treating hay fever early to prevent pollen asthma

—From Cecil Collins-Williams, *Paediatric Allergy and Clinical Immunology (as Applied to Atopic Disease)*. Toronto: University of Toronto Press, 1973.

ALLOWANCES

IN THE MODERN HOME, spending money—like food and clothes—is given to a child as a matter of course, because he is a member of the family. An allowance is not a reward for good behavior nor a payment for chores. It is an educational device that has a distinct purpose: to provide experience in the use of money by exercising choices and assuming responsibilities. Therefore, oversupervision of an allowance would defeat its purpose. What is required is a general policy which stipulates the expenditures the allowance is expected to cover: carfare, lunches, school supplies, etc. As the child grows older the allowance is increased to include additional expenses and responsibilities: membership dues, the cost of entertainment and clothing accessories, etc.

Abuses of an allowance can be expected. Some children will mismanage the budget and spend too much too soon. The abuses should be discussed with the child in a businesslike manner in order to arrive at mutually agreed solutions. In repeated cases of instant spending, it may be necessary to divide

the allowance and give it to the child twice or thrice a week. The allowance itself should not be used as a club over the child's head to exert pressure for achievement or obedience. It should not be withheld in times of anger, or increased arbitrarily in times of good mood.

What is a fair allowance? There is no universal answer to this question. The allowance should fit our budget. Regardless of neighborhood standards, we should not be pushed into allowing more than we can afford comfortably. If the child protests, we can tell him sincerely and sympathetically, "We wish we could give you a larger allowance but our budget is limited." This is a better approach than trying to convince the child that he does not really need more money.

Money, like power, can be easily mishandled by the inexperienced. An allowance should not be greater than the child's capacity to manage it. It is better to start with a small allowance, which can be adjusted from time to time, than to overburden the child with too much money. The allowance might be started when the child begins attending school and has learned to count money and make change. One condition is essential to an allowance: the small sum of money left after the fixed expenditures should be the child's own to save or to splurge.

—From Haim G. Ginott, *Between Parent and Child.* New York: Macmillan Publishing Co., 1965.

AMBITION

THE STRONG DESIRE to gain position, recognition, or power is a form of self-seeking that is definitely a part of growing up. Ambition takes different forms, depending on the traditions and culture in which one lives, but also, for any individual child, depending upon his family—its status and means.

Children's early ambitions are largely determined by what they see others do, by what they hear praised or admired. It is natural for children to emulate their parents at one stage and the older boys and girls they come to know at another. They find their models among their agemates on the playground and in school. When they are old enough to hear stories read or to see movies and television, they discover new heroes and heroines and pick new models. When they are able to read, their horizon broadens and their dreams of glory keep shifting with the levels of their understanding.

Changing interests result in part from disappointment and disillusion, for while parents may praise a good try at acting like a space man or a movie star, each child discovers that some of his friends are able to do even better than he. A child cannot win every athletic contest and every hand-to-hand fight. The best that parents can do is to encourage a child in whatever he tries while helping him to accept the failures for what they are—a part of learning about his limitations. At the same time they can suggest other worthwhile activities that are within the range of his abilities and interests. Although the childish values and strivings are eventually outgrown, many children need help in discovering what is most worthwhile to them.

Some children set their goals in terms of what they can do easily and well, without any sense of rivalry and also without much concern about the value of their efforts. However excellent their achievements may turn out to be, such individuals are in effect withdrawing themselves not merely from competition but from the life around them. A scholarly monk or a fine painter or a creative scientist can justify himself by the purity

of his motives, for he strives for excellence for its own sake.

Parents sometimes complain that a boy or girl lacks ambition. This usually means that the child has failed to become sufficiently interested in any one aspect of life to want to do something about it. He may have experienced too many frustrations in efforts already made, or the competition may have been too great. He may have dreams that seem utterly unattainable, that could not be understood or appreciated. In some cases, bodily conditions may account for indifference or lack of purpose.

A child who is considered "too ambitious" may be one whose energies have not found sufficient outlets and is eager to be noticed.

Parents have their own ambitions and ideas and often would like to fulfill themselves in the achievements of their children, especially if they have themselves been frustrated. They can be most helpful if they treat each child as a distinct person and try to find the best use for his combination of talents and shortcomings.

—From *The New Encyclopedia of Child Care and Guidance.* Garden City, N.Y.: Doubleday & Co., 1968.

ANGER

CHRISTIAN PARENTS are often confused about anger. The Bible tells them that anger should be eliminated from their lives: "Have done with spite and passion, all angry shouting and cursing, and bad feeling of every kind" (Ephesians 4:31 NEB). But at the same time they read secular newspaper and magazine articles that speak of a child's "right to be angry" and warn of the danger of "bottled-up anger."

What does the Bible actually say about

anger? And how does the Christian parent handle anger in his children—and in himself?

Biblical Teaching

When the Bible speaks of "laying aside" all anger (Colossians 3:8), it seems to be saying that both sudden outbursts of anger and long-term, inward, seething anger should *ideally* be avoided.

Yet psychologists know that anger is one of the earliest human emotions to develop in the infant. God created us with the capacity to be angry. Jesus at one point is said to have looked at some Jewish religious leaders "... with anger and sorrow at their obstinate stupidity ..." (Mark 3:5 NEB). The Living Bible nicely paraphrases this as "... angrily, for he was deeply disturbed by their indifference to human need. ..."

The Bible also seems to recognize that anger may not always be wrong. "If you are angry, do not let anger lead you to sin," it says, "do not let sunset find you still nursing it ..." (Ephesians 4:26 NEB).

What the Bible is saying, in brief, is that anger is wrong when it represents an impulsive eruption at the frustration of our will, and when it is nursed and becomes a grudge.

Jesus' anger was of a different kind. He was angry at the indifference of the Pharisees to the physical ailment of a man in a synagogue. Although it is not explicitly stated, Jesus may also have been angry at the cupidity of the moneychangers in the temple. He was angry in that case that human greed could turn a faith that demanded righteousness into a way of robbing people to get rich.

Anger is justified when it expresses opposition to the inhumanity and greed of other people. It is not justified when it simply expresses reaction to the frustration of our personal whims and hopes.

Anger in Children

Your child will express his anger in different ways at different ages. The infant's howl is his way of letting you know he is in pain. He may want food, he may need changing, or he may have a diaper pin sticking into him. The anger disappears when the pain disappears.

The toddler and young child express their anger in the form of temper tantrums, which may involve kicking, crying, or screaming. These may occur when they are taken away from something they enjoy, for example, when they have to come in for supper from playing with their friends. Gradually they learn that anger is not necessary, because they can return to their game later. The toddler may also strike another child, though he soon learns that the chances are pretty good he'll get hit back. Calm reasoning with the child is called for, though it may take time before the child understands you. The proper response to an outburst of "I hate you" is neither severe reprimand nor approval of his outburst. He will forget it sooner than you will.

Anger in the adolescent expresses itself in new forms. In place of tantrums are loudness of voice, use of the fist, and bad language. Teenagers often give vent to what psychologists call *displacement*. They may, for example, slam a door to express anger at you. They may withdraw to their room to sulk. At this age the ability to nurse a grudge also emerges.

Parents need to relax their control of their adolescent children gradually. They need to explain that it is wiser to overcome the frustration than to give vent to their anger. Teenagers are notorious for their inability to evaluate the seriousness of disagreements. Fights with brothers and sisters over trivia are common. Adolescents need to learn that some things are not worth getting mad about. A good Bible verse for adolescents—and their parents!—is "Keep your temper under control; it is foolish to harbor a grudge" (Ecclesiastes 7:9 TEV).

The Angry Parent

Our children's behavior can easily make us angry at times. Fortunately, children learn quickly just how much they can get away with before Mom or Dad will become angry. They also learn to imitate us. Volatile children are produced by volatile parents. The ideal for the parent is reasonable anger with love. The mature adult leader is often one who has learned to control his temper in tense situations. The Bible holds such a man up as a model of the righteous man.

—LESLIE R. KEYLOCK

FOR FURTHER READING:

Augsburger, David, N., Jr. *Anger and Assertiveness in Pastoral Care*. Philadelphia: Fortress Press, 1979.

Davis, Drew. *On the Other Side of Anger*. Atlanta: John Knox Press, 1979.

Hart, Archibald D. *Feeling Free*. Old Tappan, N.J.: Fleming H. Revell Co., 1979.

Skoglund, Elizabeth. *To Anger with Love*. New York: Harper and Row Publishers, 1977.

Wright, H. Norman. *The Christian Use of Emotional Power*. Old Tappan, N.J.: Fleming H. Revell Co., 1974.

ANXIETY

CHILDREN'S FEARS, like adults', fall into two main groups: normal fears of real and immediate dangers, and fears—more properly called anxieties—of imaginary dangers. For example, it is quite normal for children to be afraid of hurting themselves by a fall if they find themselves high up in a tree. But if a child is terrified of climbing anything at all and frightened by every little casual tumble, this is no longer normal fear; it is anxiety.

Anxieties are common in the early years of childhood, and even infants seem to have them. Many babies who during their first half year don't seem to mind at all when their parents go out, suddenly, at about seven to ten months, develop an anxiety when they leave. A baby may now begin to cry as soon as his mother puts on her hat. His perception has developed to the point where he notices that she is leaving him, where he has beome aware of the difference in his relationships to his mother and to strangers, but not to the point where he is sure that she will return. Playing the simple game of peek-aboo can help him gain confidence in the feeling that "Mother-goes-away-but-comes-back-again." The age-old delight of the infant in this game comes essentially from this need to assure himself that he can actually make what is lost (his mother's face) return again. It is only recently that we have found out that most babies are subject to this phase of anxiety at about eight months; being aware, parents can be extra careful at this time so that the anxiety may pass more quickly. If, for example, they have planned to be away from home at the time their baby begins to show fearfulness when they leave, it would be wise to postpone the trip until he has passed out of this anxiety stage.

In varying degrees most children seem to go through periods when they are afraid of dangers that do not really threaten them, such as the doctor, the policeman, animals, death, being left alone. They may also be frightened of creatures of their own inventing. To understand childhood anxieties parents need to know that these menacing fantasy figures and other imaginary threats represent, at least in part, the child's belief that he somehow deserves to be punished. Even though his parents are kind and loving, a four-year-old can't help feeling that it is wrong of him to be so jealous of the baby or to have a strong impulse to do something "bad" of which his parents (and therefore his own conscience) will not approve. As children gradually gain mastery over their antisocial impulses and as their sense of reality grows through greater knowledge of life, anxieties tend either to fade or to disappear.

A child's ability to become less anxious as he grows older, to grow stronger and more secure, depends mainly on his relation to his mother and father. He needs to believe that they will go on loving him no matter what he feels or does. This kind of trust is fundamental to the success of any immediate practical measures toward reducing a child's anxiety.

There are practical ways, too, in which parents may help. It is important, for example, to go to a child who calls in the night because he has had a bad dream or is afraid of something and reassure him with a little quiet conversation and some affectionate patting. And the child who asks for it can be given the comfort of a small night light. The most ineffective thing to do is to shame a child about his fears; this will only confirm his belief that his parents are dissatisfied with him. Reasoning, too—trying to "talk him out of it"—is apt to be futile. Imaginary fears are terribly painful, and it's best to treat the child as if he were frightened by something "real." Above all, parents need to be patient and reassuring.

Parents can also help if they encourage everything that promotes the child's sense of competence in day-to-day living. He needs to learn as many skills as he is ready for, and he needs a chance to be as independent as he possibly can be. Simple, everyday things like learning to dress himself, to manage his food himself, give a preschool child both new skills and new independence. And especially he needs to gain a feeling of mastery over the situations where he has been insecure. For example, a child's fear of the dark or of going to bed often breaks out at a time following some anxiety-producing experience—going to the doctor for an inoculation, perhaps. The mother who recognizes this might encourage her child to "play inoculation." A child will usually like to do this over and over again with a doll or toy animal—and this time he is the doctor who gives the shot instead of being the passive recipient. Being actively in control gives him a sense of mastery in place of anxiety.

In such ways, speedy, sympathetic action on the part of parents may help resolve these early childhood anxieties and prevent their lasting into the later years. But there are times when it isn't easy to do; this is especially true in later childhood as the child's personality grows more complex. Anxieties about school, for instance, can be so troublesome that sometimes a child refuses to go. It is important to get him back as quickly as possible, even if his mother has to stay in school with him until he feels ready to let her leave. But this is just the beginning. Most of the time parents can sense worry in their youngsters, but it is harder to establish the reason for it. What events, real or fancied, caused the anxiety in the first place? The child's answers alone cannot be relied on to reveal the real issue. Is one of the boys teasing him too much? Does he feel unpopular? Does he perhaps resent being away at school while the new baby stays home with mother? Is he afraid of not keeping up with the others in his work? Sometimes the teacher can help parents appraise the school situation.

When the child reaches adolescence, he begins to be anxious about new and more generalized things. "What do I want to do? How do I measure up? Will someone fall in love with me? Why don't Mom and Dad seem to understand?" and so forth. Experience and knowledge of the world—the things that only time can bring—eventually help to clear up these worries.

In the meantime, however, a basic sense of security fostered throughout the years by his parents' affection, confidence in him, and guidance forms the best bulwark against anxiety. Adults sometimes heighten children's anxiety by wanting always to know the "reason." The more surely parents learn to understand the language of childhood, the more effective their help will be. Often children can't put into words just what it is that's troubling them. Yet, as parents grow more experienced and aware, they can recognize clues in their children without probing and perhaps discover some recent event that may account for the outcropping of anxiety.

If the clue doesn't come to light, however, parents can still help even if they are not aware of the hidden cause. But when anxieties seem severe and persist over a long period, it may be helpful to consult with a trained person who has seen many children and parents through the same circumstances.

Children who have been given quiet, comforting reassurance plus a chance to reenact the frightening experience as the active rather than the passive person, who have not been shamed about their imaginary fears, who have been helped to work out each anxious phase as it occurs, stand the best chance of becoming mature adults without anxieties carried over from childhood.

—From *The New Encyclopedia of Child Care and Guidance.* Garden City, N.Y.: Doubleday & Co., 1968.

FOR FURTHER READING:

Buchanan, Jerreal. *Who's Calling My Name?* Nashville: Broadman Press, 1977.

Collins, Gary. *Overcoming Anxiety.* Santa Ana, Calif.: Vision House Publishers, 1975.

Jeremiah, James T. *God's Answers to Your Anxieties.* Grand Rapids: Baker Book House, 1979.

Kennedy, Larry W. *Down with Anxiety.* Nashville: Broadman Press, 1979.

Narramore, Clyde M. *How to Win Over Nervousness.* Grand Rapids: Zondervan Publishing House, 1976.

B

BABYSITTERS

THE BABYSITTER is an important member of most households these days. We know that everybody is happier if parents can get out with each other now and then. Couples need to continue to enjoy community affairs and personal interests after the baby is born. We know, too, that sometimes children are better off at home than being dragged around from store to store.

Regardless of how long or how often you use a sitter, she must be someone who can be trusted. It is best if you use the same or few persons. Both sitter and children are more at ease when they know each other. When you hire anyone who will have more or less regular contact with your children, ask for references and a current physical examination, including a test for tuberculosis. Teenagers often have these tests at school.

The first time ask the sitter to arrive well before you expect to leave so that all can become acquainted. Even if you expect the child to be asleep while you are away, be sure he knows the sitter. The soundest sleeper has a way of awakening on such occasions. Then both the child and the sitter have a harder time because the child is frightened by the stranger and your unexpected absence.

Such an episode can start persistent sleeping difficulties. Once frightened, the child may waken crying night after night, or refuse to go to bed, until he finally becomes reassured that he can trust you again.

By the time a child is 2 or 3, after he and the sitter have become old friends, he can be told ahead of time that you are going out. Put him to bed, and he'll be able to remember that you'll be gone.

Many young couples band together as a club to exchange sitting for each other. A volunteer secretary keeps track of the hours. By this plan many different mothers and fathers may be used, but the problem presented by the changing faces will be offset, somewhat, because they usually have other contacts with the child and are also apt to be familiar with the home routines.

Teenagers do a lot of babysitting. They may or may not be experienced with the ways of young children and feel more confident if you take the time to show them how you feed, diaper, and care for your child. For that matter, any sitter, old or young, appreciates full information about your ways of doing things. As the child grows older, he's sure to announce "mother always does it this way," or "mother lets me have that." If you've talked your ways over with her, the sitter will be able to distinguish fact from the child's understandable wish to try her out.

Among the items a sitter likes to know are: Does the child expect food or drink before bed? What time does he go to bed? Is he supposed to have any medicine? Should he have any medicine if he asks for it? What is his favorite toy? How do you arrange the covers? Does he go to the bathroom during the evenings? Where may he play—indoors and out?

In addition, the sitter should have other information: what is the telephone number where you, or some responsible person, can be reached; the telephone number of your doctor, and the fire department. How do you regulate the heat? Are there any extra jobs you have in mind? How about snacks, use of radio or TV? Do or don't you permit the sitter to have companions? What time do you return? If you are to be delayed more than 15 minutes, phone. People who are otherwise conscientious about promptness are frequently careless in their commitments to sitters.

—From *Your Child From 1 to 6*. Washington: U.S. Department of Health, Education and Welfare, 1969.

FOR FURTHER READING:

Branson, Mary Kinney. *The Basics of Babysitting*. Nashville: Broadman Press, 1976.

BED-WETTING

MOST CHILDREN of four or five, or even older, wet occasionally when they are excited or upset or when they are too much absorbed in their play. Enuresis means regular wetting that persists well beyond the age of five or so, when most children have stopped, or a recurrence of regular wetting after a child has had grown-up toilet habits for some time. Different youngsters achieve bladder control at widely varying ages. Some are dry during the day at two years, others at three. Some are completely dry day and night at three and a half, others at four or five.

Many things can cause a temporary lapse: for example, illness or anxiety, disturbance about moving to a new home, or difficulty in adjusting to nursery school or kindergarten. When new experiences become a "load," one of the first features of maturity to be sacrificed may be bladder control. Sometimes the wetting occurs only at night. If a child is ordinarily happy and active, enuresis usually stops when conditions once more approach normal. Meanwhile, making sure the child voids just before going to bed and reducing the amount of fluids he consumes toward evening may help if handled casually, without making an issue of the matter, and if the child does not feel deprived. Some parents find, too, that there is less likely to be a wet bed if the youngster is taken to the toilet during the night. However, the more important step is to alleviate any feeling of shame or concern he might have by letting the youngster know casually that many children wet occasionally.

When at any age a youngster not only loses bladder control but must urinate much more frequently than usual, a doctor should be consulted. This is especially so if the child complains of a burning sensation around the genitals. He may have a bladder or kidney infection that can be treated with modern drugs.

When enuresis persists, the causes have usually taken root over a period longer than some specific situation like anxiety about moving to a new home. It takes longer, too, to eliminate the disturbance. A youngster may feel that he was rushed into grown-up toilet habits, that he wasn't given enough time to enjoy being a baby. Unconsciously he asks to be taken care of by having his clothes and bedding changed in the middle of the night. If his mother and father have the patience and understanding to make these changes without disapproval and give him more of their time and affection, his enuresis may disappear. But when parents have no idea what the cause might be, persistent bed-wetting beyond the age of five or so needs the counsel of someone trained to help with emotional problems.

In determining the significance of enuresis, however, a child's state of health and general development should be kept in mind. It would not be considered enuresis, for instance, if there was something about the size or shape of the four- or five-year-old's bladder that made it harder to retain a large amount of urine until the morning.

A casual, unblaming attitude toward enuresis is probably the most useful measure in trying to help a child overcome it. Important, too, is building a youngster's confidence in himself and in his parents' love for him. Asking a young daughter's suggestions for the dinner menu, sharing a son's enthusiasm for clay modeling or cowboys, having a special story hour won't immediately result in a child's staying dry. But such measures go a long way toward relieving his general tension, making him happier and more relaxed.

—From *The New Encyclopedia of Child Care and Guidance.* Garden City, N.Y.: Doubleday & Co., 1968.

FOR FURTHER READING:

Azrin, Nathan H. *A Parent's Guide to Bedwetting Control.* New York: Simon and Schuster, Inc., 1980.

BEHAVIOR PROBLEMS

MOST PARENTS wonder at some time or other whether their child isn't having problems that are different from those of other children. They often ask themselves, "Is this the sort of thing all children go through, or is this a serious problem?" Parents are aware, of course, that all children pass through difficult periods and that this doesn't make them "problem children." The name is, in itself, a misnomer, because we no longer think of a disturbed child as a "problem child" but rather as a child with problems. Yet parents do speak in terms of a problem child and wonder whether their children do or do not fit into this category. When, then, should a child be considered a problem child? Are there any valid criteria?

To understand whether children's problems are more or less normal or really serious, we have first to understand—as in all other aspects of child development—the underlying basis of their behavior. Children behave the way they do for definite reasons, though these may not always seem reasonable to grown-ups. When a little girl of three, for example, who has been quite adept at feeding herself begins suddenly—when the new baby comes—to demand that she be fed by her mother, it is not hard for most parents to realize that she is doing so because she's jealous of all the attention the new baby is receiving. But often we have to seek deeper to find the roots of a child's behavior. Children, and young children in particular, cannot tell us in words what troubles them, and besides, it may not be something in the immediate environment but something that happened a long time ago. Often the objective insight that parents can get from a doctor, a public health nurse, a teacher, or a counselor in a family-guidance clinic can be of great help in understanding a child's difficulties.

When parents are seriously worried, when they think that their child may possibly have deep problems, there are a few simple signposts that may be used to gauge in a general way whether such special consultation or guidance is required. The three main points they might consider are (1) whether the child's "problem behavior" has persisted too long, so that they can no longer think of it as something he will obviously grow out of, but rather as something not in keeping with his present stage of development; (2) whether

47

the child is acting in a way that is appropriate to the circumstances he finds himself in; (3) whether his behavior is in keeping with his temperament.

Let us examine the first of these signposts. Is the child's behavior in keeping with his age and with his stage of development? Though we remember that children vary enormously in the time schedule at which they attain new skills and accomplishments, is this child acting his age, so to speak? The mother of Bobby, for example, didn't worry too much when he followed her around everywhere at the age of two or so. But when he is still tagging her heels at five, isn't she right in assuming that her son hasn't achieved the independence to be expected at his age?

Normally one may expect children to progress from stage to stage more or less as others do, in a fairly universal development sequence. This progress may not always be apparent since it is usually accomplished with alternating spurts and leveling-off periods when there is often little outward sign of change. The significant question is how long these periods of apparent time-marking last, not measured in days or weeks, but rather judged against the whole picture of the child's development and the way he compares with other children in general. It is also important to discover (and usually outside help will be needed) the real quality of these periods of little progress. Do they indicate that the child just hasn't developed enough to be ready to move ahead? Or is he stuck at one stage, for emotional reasons that are usually not clear either to him or to his parents, because he cannot use the abilities that are there?

We are discussing here, of course, only those children whose basic equipment is normal and healthy. If a child between one and two, for example, doesn't use his simple playthings to push and bang, to touch and explore, he is apparently not reaching out into the world around him as one would expect. He would seem to be stuck in his development. A child who had wet his clothes in the daytime when he was three and still does at night when he is five or six is one who is not moving toward self-control in a way that his age and stage of development would warrant. Children of normal intelligence who have been given every good chance to develop the usual school skills but who haven't done so are probably stuck, too, because they're apparently unable to move forward in the same way as other children their age. Where there is no physical basis for these difficulties, marked failure in any functioning—in eating, sleeping, toilet training; in play (when a child shows no interest first in objects and later in other children) or in schoolwork—can be considered a symptom of some disturbance that has interrupted the child's progress and blocked his growth. Sometimes these symptoms occur singly, sometimes in many combinations. The causes may be quite different from child to child and usually a trained person is needed to detect them.

The second point we should like to clear up: Is the child behaving according to the circumstances he finds himself in? It is not unusual, for example, for a child of three or four (even though he has been dry at night for some time) to wet his bed after a new baby has been added to his family. This change in behavior suggests that he is reacting to the emotional stress of the new circumstances he finds himself in, impelled by his feelings to behave like the baby whose presence he resents. Once his parents understand the reason for his slipping back to infancy, they can help him weather this crisis by being sympathetic.

Or, in another situation, we would expect any older child to be profoundly distressed at the loss of his father, for example. On the other hand, if the same child reacted in a similarly intense way to a minor deprivation, such as having his parents leave for a weekend trip, then we might have reason to be concerned. In other words, exaggerated feelings, feelings that seem out of keeping with the reality of the situation, are often signs of disturbance beneath the surface. Continuing and apparently unwarranted fears, strong moods that don't change with the circumstances, excessive withdrawal and daydreaming even when there are interesting things happening all around—these things have to be given special consideration.

The third point we should like to have insight into: Is the child behaving in a way that is more or less in keeping with his temperament and general makeup? We know that children differ widely in their personality, heredity, and environment, each contributing a share in creating a unique individual. Parents recognize a child's special quality quite early—they know "what he's like." When a child's behavior therefore, changes radically, and continues to be different from what it usually was, this may be a symptom of inner upset. A happy child, for instance, who becomes irritable and moody, an alert youngster who becomes apathetic and loses interest in what is going on—such behavior tells us that the youngsters are probably in emotional trouble.

Such changes are usually the result of complex factors that take much skill to unravel at any age, but at adolescence the causes are particularly hard to determine since this is the time when the behavior of all young people undergoes some change. The special pressures at this period create tensions that are expressed in sudden outbursts of irritability and quick changes of mood. Some of the behavior is "normal" and to be expected; only when it persists for a long time and with high intensity is it a cause for special concern.

The last question we have to ask ourselves is not really a behavior criterion, but it is important. We want to know whether we have really and honestly tried all the obvious commonsense methods of handling the child's problem. If a girl of fifteen, for example, who had previously been friendly begins to refuse to go to parties, the cause may be as simple as that her friends have nicer clothes than she has and she is ashamed to go out in what she owns. But there are many situations that cannot be solved by common sense, and we must be aware when this is the case. Parents try to do their best to provide children with the physical comfort, understanding, and affection they need. Parents also need to understand something of children's usual psychological growing pains and how to help them to pass through them. But parents are not doctors or therapists. When things have definitely gone wrong they should not be reluctant about seeking professional help. More and more parents today are making use of professional guidance when it is available, consulting an expert about their child's behavior in the same way they consult a doctor about their child's physical problems. Sometimes the consultation is well worthwhile if only because it serves to set at rest any fears that are unfounded.

—From *The New Encyclopedia of Child Care and Guidance.* Garden City, N.Y.: Doubleday & Co., 1968.

Common Behaviors of Concern to Parents

Many behavior difficulties are normal reactions to growing up. Some behaviors of concern to parents include head banging, pica (non-food nibbling), the use of a security blanket, thumb-sucking, temper tantrums, breath holding, stuttering, shyness, destructiveness, and dawdling. These behaviors are nothing to be worried about and normally disappear within a few months. It is important for parents not to become unduly alarmed at their child's behavior and perhaps create a real problem out of what may be a normal occurrence at a particular age and stage. Parents can try to recognize some of the reasons for their child's behavior without resorting to labels, such as "stubborn" or "sloppy." In spotting and understanding the causes of behavior, parents can ease and sometimes remedy the situation for their child.

Head Banging, Head Rolling, and Jouncing

Toward the second half of the first year babies sometimes take to banging their heads hard and rhythmically against their crib, rolling their heads from side to side, or they may get on hands and knees and jounce against their heels in a steady rhythm.

Head banging is especially disturbing and frightening to parents. They are afraid that their baby will hurt herself and sometimes imagine that she is lacking in normal intelligence. Even when they are reassured that this banging will not injure the brain and that it is not a sign of any kind of mental abnormality, they may find it nerve-racking to listen to the constant thudding.

Why do babies do this? No one seems to know for sure. Many babies do not go directly to sleep, but first seem to go through a short period of tenseness. Head banging, head rolling, and jouncing, like thumb-sucking, may be the baby's way of handling tension before falling asleep.

If your baby bangs his head, you can line the crib with quilted padding so he will not bruise himself. Try padding the outside of the crib if head banging causes the crib to thump against the wall. An infant who bangs his head may need more cuddling and stimu-

lation than he is getting. Scolding the baby and/or trying to restrain him physically are likely only to make him more tense. It will probably not be long before he outgrows this behavior. Your baby may get over it even sooner if you can relax, cuddle, and generally enjoy him.

For head banging, you might try a radio tuned to an all-music station (if possible start with music that approximates the rhythm of the banging). The ticking of a metronome or the beat of music may satisfy your baby and eliminate head banging for a while anyway. Sometimes a warm bath right before bedtime will have the effect of relaxing your baby so that she will go right to sleep.

Tics

A tic is an uncontrollable, persistent muscle spasm, such as eye blinking, shoulder shrugging, facial grimacing, neck twisting, throat clearing, sniffing, dry coughing, etc. The motion always takes the same form. A tic may last on and off for weeks or months and go away for good or a new one may take its place.

Generally a tic develops as the result of some anxiety with which a child is unable to deal. For example, bottled-up resentment, too much pressure at home, reaction against constant disapproval. Tics seem to develop more commonly in tense children. A child may copy a tic from another child, but he would not have picked it up if he were not already tense.

A child should not be scolded or corrected on account of a tic. Since a tic is beyond the child's control, it cannot be reasoned or disciplined away. The remedy is to discover and try to relieve the basic cause of the child's anxiety. If no physical cause is found and the symptom persists after the parents have made every effort to make the child's home life relaxed and agreeable, her school and/or social life satisfying, and their own attitude undemanding, then consultation with a trained counselor is suggested.

Pica—Non-food Nibbling

Pica is a condition in which the child continually eats things that are generally considered inedible—paint, plaster, dirt, dust, paper, etc. Often pica is highly selective; one child will confine his nibbling to chips of paint while another child is partial to strands of wool from a blanket, still another will eat dirt from the back yard. Some of the substances are harmless, while others (paint and plaster, for example) are prominent causes of lead poisoning.

Pica is not too well understood. In some cases, the child may be trying to compensate for some lack in his diet or for an inability to utilize certain nutritional elements. It may merely be a habit that has persisted since infancy (when children will put practically anything into their mouths). In some cases, pica may be a sign of an emotional disturbance.

Pica usually does not go on beyond the age of five, but if you find that your child is an habitual non-food nibbler, she should be checked by her pediatrician for any damage the ingested material may have caused and to determine the cause of her behavior.

Security Objects

Many babies develop an attachment to a favorite blanket or toy. Such an object becomes a concrete security link for the child who is encountering new situations and should be made available. Most parents do not look upon this kind of attachment as being objectionable when they view it prop-

erly as fulfilling their child's emotional needs.

Thumb-sucking

Thumb-sucking is a normal reflex behavior. In fact, it has been proved that thumb-sucking occurs in utero. Some parents react negatively to this behavior because it mistakenly represents to them their failure to satisfy their child's basic needs. Current research suggests that contented, happy babies suck their thumbs and the habit usually is outgrown well before the age of four or five (thereby precluding damage to permanent teeth, which do not come in until about the age of five or six).

Temper Tantrums and Breath Holding

These are common behavior patterns in one- to three-year-olds, but not as easily ignored or even tolerated as is thumb-sucking. Suddenly a child goes into a tantrum, performing usually in front of an audience. The causes are varied—fatigue, frustration, seeking attention, etc. Parents should try to "keep their cool" during these outbursts since adult screaming will only serve to reinforce the child's behavior.

Stuttering

Stuttering (or stammering) is quite common in young children when they are first beginning to talk. At this time speaking is new to children and they cannot keep up with their thoughts. Often children become frustrated and tense as they grope for the words to express themselves, which then causes them to repeat phrases. In some instances, the reverse is true; these children talk faster than they can think, thus producing repetitions of words and letters until their thoughts catch up with their tongues. Sometimes stuttering develops when the child is under too much pressure or when there are anxieties with which he cannot deal, such as a move to a new home or the departure of a close relative.

Shyness

Sometimes shyness bothers parents, but in young children occasional shyness is often a sign that the child has become more aware of the world around her and has learned that new things and situations should be examined carefully before fully accepting them. It is not good to force your child to accept a person or situation before she is ready to do so.

Some children are timid when playing with others, especially if they have had little opportunity for playmates. If your child is being pushed around by her peers, help her stand up for herself (without fighting her battles for her). Teach her how not to be browbeaten by other children. It may be desirable for you to stay with her at first to help her to verbalize her needs if she lacks the words to do it. If her toys are taken, suggest that she go and get them back, but do not get them for her. You might accompany her at first in her quest for lost toys. This way you are helping your child gain independence while letting her know that you are there for reassurance.

Destructiveness

Tearing things down and building things up are common practices for toddlers, who are discovering things around them. In a child's attempt to explore objects and discover their properties, he may take things apart or inadvertently break them. In addition, young children are somewhat clumsy. They usually are not able to manipulate ob-

jects precisely, so they may appear to be careless or destructive.

Some children, however, may destroy things purposefully for a variety of reasons. For example, the child may be angry at his parents and unable to express his anger in other ways. He may be upset over a parental separation or he may be seeking attention. An understanding of why he is behaving destructively helps you to know what to do.

Dawdling

With most children dawdling is merely a result of their imprecise notions of time. When they are absorbed in play, "five more minutes until cleanup time" does not mean much. Therefore, parents should compensate for the toddlers' distractibility by allowing more time than is necessary for the expected cleanup or other activity. Frequent reminders also help.

It is important to stress that the "problem" behaviors of toddlers described here may in fact be normal reactions to growing up. The parents' handling of their child may be an important factor as to whether their child's behavior will become a real problem or whether the child will pass through this stage of development and on to the next plateau of growth.

Childhood Tension

Dr. Brazelton points out (in the Boston Children's Hospital's *Child Health Encyclopedia*) that "tension in children can set the stage for psychosomatic disease later on. There is even recent evidence to suggest that susceptibility to infection may be associated with tension. This may take such forms as respiratory infection in small children, just as parents are about to go away on a trip or move to another city; or lowered resistance from tension in a household. More serious are the complaints associated with stress, such as asthma, eczema, stomach ulcers, and colitis."

The reaction to stress or stimulus takes so many psychological forms that it is impossible to prescribe remedies. But there are certain age-determined physical and psychological symptoms that crop up regularly. By recognizing them as normal and passing signs of development, parents can avoid their becoming serious.

FIRST YEAR

Colic and crying—normally two to three hours a day in the first three months

Spitting up after feedings

Thumb- or finger-sucking

Infrequent bowel movements in a breast-fed baby

Constipation—hard bowel movements which can be softened by changes in diet

Waking at night just prior to developmental spurts

Feeding refusals associated with wanting to feed self at eight months or so

SECOND YEAR

Feeding aberrations—refusing one food after another, eating only one meal a day

Temper tantrums and breath-holding spells

Withholding stools and problems around toilet training—usually from too early and too much pressure to conform

If parents overreact to these symptoms and are punitive or overly strict, are overconcerned, or if they ignore the symptoms, the problem gets unreasonably worse. Doctors often dodge their responsibility by such advice as "He will grow out of it"—some prescribe aspirin. Parents need to establish close communication with their child by attentive listening and helping their child understand the reason for the symptom.

—From Princeton Center for Infancy. *The Parenting Advisor.* Garden City, N.Y.: Anchor Press/Doubleday & Co., 1977.

FOR FURTHER READING:

Aaseng, Rolf E. *Sense and Nonsense: A Word for Teens.* Grand Rapids: Baker Book House, 1976.

Augsburger, David. *So What, Everybody's Doing It.* Evanston, Ill.: Moody Press, 1969.

Krutza, William J., and Dicicco, Philip P. *Youth Faces Today's Issues.* Grand Rapids: Baker Book House.

Price, Eugenia. *Find Out for Yourself.* Grand Rapids: Zondervan Publishing House.

BIBLE READING

THE CENTRALITY of Scripture in the Christian family is a cherished tradition for many of us; but it will only continue if we are faithful in passing it on to our children.

"What should be the distinctives of Christian family life?" Sheila raised the question, one she had been discussing with the other members of her Bible-study group.

I jotted notes on a page in my coil notebook as we tossed ideas back and forth. As I read our list now, picking it out from the doodles and extra notes, I see that we suggested the following areas in which the Christian family should be distinguishable from others:

commitment and fidelity in marriage
servant leadership within home
discipline
hospitality and sharing
restraint and moderation in life-style
priority given to church involvement
sharing of faith, values, and truth through
    Scripture reading and prayer

The last two items on that list constitute the laying of a firm foundation for the spiritual and moral development of our children.

Those of us with small children are members of a "hang loose" generation, with a primary emphasis on "doing your own thing." And there is the danger that we may lose sight of the importance in our own lives and in those of our children of having close bonds with other believers within a church fellowship. As a "community of faith," the church should represent an extension of family life and caring to our children.

Not long ago, the pastor in our local church asked the children, "Why do you come to church?"

Little Wade's hand shot up. "Because it's Sunday and because we like to come," was his answer. And a good one. It expressed church attendance as both a *routine discipline* and a *special joy* in his family's life. And church attendance needs to be both if it is to contribute to our family life. "I'm so glad I'm a part of the family of God," should be a song our children can sing, with a deep, personal understanding of a church fellowship which represents that larger family to him.

But while the church has a very important part to play in Christian family life, the full burden of the transmission of Christian truth and values can never be laid upon it. At best, church activities will only occupy two or three hours each week. So the teaching of the church will be most effective only when it reinforces and reiterates teaching which is going on in the home on a day-to-day basis.

Paul tells Timothy that food is "sanctified by the word of God and prayer" (1 Timothy 4:5 KJV). And so it should be in our homes. Grace before meals is, of course, basic. But mealtimes also provide a natural gathering together of the family when the Scriptures can be read. With our family, breakfast has been the best time for reading and prayer together. The evening meal may be more suitable to others. What is important is that the Bible be read together daily. Scripture reading and prayer together should be a joyful routine in Christian family life.

All the helpful hints on how to have happy family devotions have, I think, made parents feel they have to plan a program in order to share the Scriptures with their children. The sad result is that most just get tired thinking about it—or have a few flops—and quit. It just does not need to be that complicated. "The word of God and prayer": a short passage, a short prayer. That, made a part of at least one meal a day, is far better than an elaborate family worship held once in a while. . . . "Isn't it hard on little children to have to sit through a Bible reading once or twice a day?" many parents ask. "Won't they come to resent it?" Obviously, Bible reading should not be prolonged with little children. My father used to read ten verses ("even if that left him midparagraph," my mother remembers). So Scripture reading was not tediously long. With modern speech translations set out in paragraphs instead of verses, it is easy to read a "thought unit"—a paragraph or two—with children.

I remember being startled when a young minister who had visited my parents' home asked me, "How did you kids feel about having to read the Bible every day?" How did we feel about it? Well, for one thing, we were never asked. It was a part of family life that was as unquestionable as breakfast itself. And my parents made us aware that the Bible was special, a gift that had come to us at great cost. On long winter evenings when we were very young, my mother read us stories such as *Great Was the Company* and *Mary Jones and Her Bible*. Missionary stories gave us a look at cultures untouched by the Gospel. A little history, a little geography: it all helped us value the Scriptures we heard. Our parents' attitude of reverence for the Word and gratitude for its availability became ours.

. . . . .

If our children are to learn to love the Lord, they must learn to love the Word that reveals Him to us. And, let's face it: they will not only be spiritually impoverished but also culturally and intellectually impoverished if we fail to transmit the Bible with all its wealth of precept and principle and story and example to them.

The question of what passages to read with preschoolers is important. Some parents flounder at this point, and finally give up, hopelessly bogged down in genealogies in Numbers! With our preschoolers, we majored on the poetry of Psalms and Proverbs, the wonderful Old Testament stories, and the Gospels. I made a scrapbook of "Proverbs for Little People," with selected proverbs printed beside bright magazine pictures illustrating the message. In another scrapbook, I pasted illustrations for selected Psalms (23, 24, 131, and 148). These books the children quite literally wore out with reading and handling.

The Old Testament stories we read as serializations, a short episode at a time. The stories of David (1 and 2 Samuel) and of Daniel and his friends emerged as favorites, requested over and over again. The "family stories" of Genesis, the stories of the Judges, and of the Prophets Elijah and Elisha (1 and 2 Kings) are also good listening for little children. Of the Gospels, Mark is perhaps the most suitable for very young children, with its fast-paced narrative. But Luke places a much-loved emphasis on the birth and boyhood of our Lord. The other Gospels, too, are interesting—but they have more doctrinal and interpretive content.

Since "All Scripture is God-breathed and is useful for teaching, rebuking, correcting and training in righteousness" (2 Timothy 3:16 NIV), as children grow older they should be given the opportunity to read together the whole Bible. A complete understanding is probably less important than a careful implanting of the Word. For if the Word really takes root in our children's minds, the Holy Spirit can instruct them in its meanings and implications through all the years of their lives.

Beyond the daily routine of Scripture reading, Christian parents will find many opportunities to widen their children's experience with the Bible and its truths. Reading from storybooks and listening to records or tapes with the children are some possibilities. One of our preschoolers has listened, engrossed, to whole books of the Bible on the *Living Bible* cassettes. Role playing and informal dramatizations of many of the stories has been fun. For a few favorite stories I gave the children flannelgraph figures to work with.

The reciprocal of God's speaking to us in His Word is our speaking to God in prayer. And prayer should be an important aspect of Christian family living. Over and above the ritualized patterns of grace before meals and prayer after Bible reading, there are many times for spontaneous prayer.

I recall a day with Cammie-Lou, not yet four, in the "Windless Woods," a favorite little woods on our farm, where the tall trees held out the wind and created a place of complete stillness. The late summer was moving toward fall, and a few colored leaves had already drifted to the ground. Ants scurried at our feet as we sat together on a rot-softened log, peeling the moss back with our fingers. "Let's say thank you to God," Cammie suggested.

"Let's. But let's not shut our eyes. It's too beautiful for that." We prayed together, thanking God for each lovely thing we saw.

And "eyes open" prayers became a part of our family's prayer repertoire.

Several years later, the girls ran in on a fall afternoon with a beautiful little bouquet of field flowers and grasses. They arranged them in a vase. Then Heather Ruth offered a Bambi candle to complete the centerpiece. We sat down at the table, just to look. As Heather lit her candle, the aesthetic delight focused itself on God, the giver of all good gifts. We began to praise the Lord together in song—with both tune and words extemporaneous. I sang a phrase, then one of the children offered a phrase, and round our little fellowship circle we went, praising God for the joy of our family, the beauty of His world, and the love of His Son. We celebrated together the joy of life. And, in the words of C. S. Lewis, our minds "ran back up the sunbeam to the sun."

Our after-bedtime visits with the children usually include informal prayer. Cam most often makes the rounds, sitting on the edge of each bed, visiting with each child individually, and closing with a time of prayer. It is a way of incorporating closeness and love with prayer in an intimate way.

It seemed natural to me to help the children pray about a problem on the spot, to ask forgiveness when they had done wrong, to continuously offer up their praise and thanksgiving. But I found I had to work more consciously at teaching them to pray about the needs of others. Our family's friendship with missionary families has been the main prompting to prayer for missions. We share with our children current prayer letters as they arrive and have special prayer for the needs of that particular missionary or family.

One young mother told me about the prayer program in her home. Their coffee table had a glass top, under which were placed pictures of missionary friends. When prayer time came, each child was invited to choose a missionary to pray for. The child would place his hand over the picture as he prayed for the people. I think this is a beautiful way to teach children to intercede, to identify with the needs of others.

A scrapbook of missionary pictures, maps showing their location, and space for clippings from their letters is another good prayer prompter. A family which supports a foster child in another country can learn to pray for the personal needs of those in our world who are materially deprived. Interceding on behalf of friends and neighbors is something which children can enter into earnestly and simply. Encouraging such prayer helps to develop the attitude of concern and compassion which should mark Christian people.

Talking with God about daily joys, expressing our praise and gratitude, learning to pray in confession of sin, interceding for others; in all of these ways we can help our children to grow spiritually. And as we teach them, we will find ourselves making, again and again, the disciples' request, "Lord, teach us to pray" (Luke 11:1 KJV).

Making time for church attendance, Bible reading, and prayer is a task of primary importance for Christian parents. Not only our food but also the whole of family life should day-by-day be "sanctified by the word of God and prayer" (1 Timothy 4:5).

—From Maxine Hancock, *People in Process*. Old Tappan, N.J.: Fleming H. Revell Co., 1978.

FOR FURTHER READING:

Hunt, Gladys. *Honey for a Child's Heart*. Grand Rapids: Zondervan Publishing House, 1969.

Johnson, Ruth I. *Daily Devotions for Juniors*. Evanston, Ill.: Moody Press.

Mack, Wayne. *How to Read the Bible*. Phillipsburg, N.J.: Presbyterian and Reformed Publishing Co., 1977.

Miles, Mary L. *Devotions for Pre-Teens*. Evanston, Ill.: Moody Press, 1970–1974.

BIRTH CONTROL

IN LIGHT OF the new medical developments in the area of birth control, we need to examine this in some depth. There are many opposing viewpoints, held by profoundly honest people, about using contraception at all. In this chapter we will learn about the more common methods of birth control and their safety and effectiveness. You must decide for yourself which to use and when and how to teach your older children about them.

Birth control is an issue that keeps coming back for resolution. When God created Adam and Eve, He told them, "Be fruitful ... and replenish the earth ..." (Genesis 1:28). Certainly in their day that made sense. A world empty of humans except for the two of them needed some replenishing! In today's world of indescribable poverty, hunger, and overpopulation, however, there is quite the opposite problem. We need fewer people, not more.

The Roman Catholic Church, for its own respected reasons, has devoutly maintained that medical birth control is a sin. Let me define birth control as the use of artificial means to prevent conception, and not the interruption of life after conception. Roman Catholics are permitted to use the rhythm method of birth control, but are strictly forbidden to use other means. This has created a conflict for many sincere Catholics who are forced to choose between economic practicalities and church doctrines. There is an ongoing discussion among Catholic theologians, prelates, and social scientists on this matter.

Common Methods of Birth Control

The first type of birth control we will consider is called the "rhythm method." You will remember that ovulation takes place about midway between a woman's menstrual periods and it is possible to become pregnant only within a very few days after ovulation. To abstain from sexual intercourse, then, would prevent pregnancy. The problem with this method is the erratic nature of ovulation. Sometimes it occurs earlier and sometimes later. There is now the possibility of taking one's temperature every morning before rising. This is called the "basal temperature" and it is one degree higher at the time of ovulation. This knowledge helps the user of this method to be more accurate in timing. It is also known that during ovulation, the degree of acidity and alkalinity of the vaginal area changes. There are simple ways by which a woman may test this, and again, the chance of preventing pregnancy is increased. The rhythm method at best, however, is not a sure one.

The Diaphragm

Another method of birth control is the use of a mechanical barrier over the cervix or the penis. In common use today is the diaphragm, a cuplike structure made of soft rubber and held in shape by a firm rim. It is inserted into the vagina before each sexual contact and left in place for six to eight hours after intercourse. It covers the cervix and prevents the entry of sperm into the womb. It is used with a gelatinous preparation that tends to destroy sperm as well. The diaphragm, to be effective, must be precisely fitted by a physician. This is 96 percent effective in preventing conception.

Prophylactics

Condoms or rubbers have been used by men for many decades. These are also made of soft rubber and are slipped over the penis just before sexual intercourse is completed. Not only do they prevent pregnancy but they also protect men from most venereal diseases. Condoms are about 99 percent effective as a birth-control measure but they are inconvenient and spoil the spontaneity of lovemaking.

Nonprescription Preparations

Various foams, gels, and vaginal suppositories as well as douches have been widely used as a form of birth control. They generally work by killing the sperm cells, washing them out, or preventing them from entering the womb. These preparations can be purchased without a doctor's prescription, are usually harmless, but are not very effective in preventing pregnancy. Often young people experiment with them, falsely thinking that they are safe from a pregnancy.

The Pill

For about three decades, birth control has been possible through hormonal intervention in the form of a pill. By understanding accurately the complex hormone cycle that begins menstruation at puberty, doctors have discovered how to safely prevent the process of ovulation. The ovaries are simply put at rest, until a couple is ready for a child. By stopping "the Pill," as it is commonly called, in a few weeks or months, the woman has reestablished her normal cycle and may become pregnant. This is almost 100 percent effective, is relatively safe, and only requires that a woman never forget her pill. According to her normal cycle, she will take a pill every day for twenty-one days. Upon stopping them, she will have a menstrual period and will again take the pill for twenty-one days. She needs to have regular medical examinations to be sure that she is not having any negative reactions.

The few side effects of the Pill need to be understood. Some women suffer mild nausea and tend to eat more to get rid of that uncomfortable sensation, causing weight gain. Most women gain a few pounds of fluid in their tissues, similar to that just before their menstrual period, and on lower doses, about midway through the month's supply of pills, they may have a little vaginal bleeding, called "breakthrough" bleeding. This means that the doctor needs to adjust the dosage. All of these problems may be solved by medical advice. The much-publicized possibility of blood clots being caused by the Pill is less than the risks of a normal pregnancy. Pills that may stop the manufacture of sperm by men are under study, but are not yet perfected or available.

It is also probable that in the next few months or years, a tiny pellet of the chemical contained in the Pill may be inserted through a tiny incision in the skin, and will slowly release the substance without a person's even having to take a pill!

There is a hormone, commonly called the "morning-after pill," that can destroy the fertilized ovum as long as three days after intercourse. It is especially useful in cases of rape or incest. This pill does not prevent conception and therefore is less desirable than the methods previously mentioned. It also causes such severe nausea and discomfort that it could not be used on a regular basis.

The IUD

The most common method for preventing the implantation of the ovum is the IUD, or intrauterine device. It is a coil of fine plastic that is inserted into the womb. Without injuring the tissues, it moves about just enough to prevent the egg from settling into that soft lining, establishing its nurturing system of blood vessels, and instead it causes the egg to be discharged from the womb. Recently, there has been concern among some medical authorities about the safety of the IUD. Women who use or are considering the use of this method should consult their doctors for more information.

Medical science has studied and perfected

safe methods of birth control. By the use of these proven methods, the sexual enjoyment of a husband and wife may be greatly enhanced. The ability of today's couple to plan the size of their family may enrich the quality of life for everyone.

Family Planning

Some idealistic couples believe that God, who is Lord of all, surely is able to give them only the children He wants them to have. They feel that preventing conception takes away from their total dependence on God. While I believe God can do anything He chooses, I do not often see Him interfering with His own natural laws. In a world as overpopulated as ours, if every couple had a child every year (and that is quite possible), for some twenty years, the problems of world hunger and poverty would multiply beyond correction. Statistics show that in order to even hold the population where it is, without reducing it at all, each family needs to be limited to two children. In the Orient, there are financial motivators by the government that give tax exemptions for two children, but heavy penalties for more than two. It may be socially irresponsible, therefore, for couples to have large families.

John Kepler, scientist and astronomer, said in worship and wonder, "O, God, I am thinking Thy thoughts after Thee." Surely God has inspired scientific progress with amazing rapidity in recent decades. Very few Christians refuse to take antibiotics when they are ill, and because of medical discoveries, life expectancy has doubled in about fifty years. Health and the quality of life have been enhanced immeasurably. Careful family planning seems to belong in the category of increasing the quality of life. It seems responsible and wise to use the means God has provided to plan our families.

Teaching Teens About Contraceptives

Birth-control measures have their disadvantages as well as their advantages. Not only are they effective for married couples but also for singles and those who want to have affairs outside of marriage. The risk of unwanted pregnancies used to serve as a deterrent to such a way of life. Now that people can almost totally prevent such pregnancies or easily abort the rare one that happens, sexual promiscuity is a reality.

So far this chapter has been written for your information as parents. There is a point, however, where you need to teach your older children about contraceptives. They certainly need to know by the time they are considering marriage. But in practicality, they may need to know much sooner.

When we know that almost 50 percent of high-school girls have had sexual intercourse before graduation, we know that at least one out of every two girls needs to understand how to prevent pregnancy. The statistics for boys are even higher. Many thoughtful people are looking hard at teenage sexual practices, and the permissiveness that has allowed such premature activities. Hopefully we can educate our children so well that they will reverse the trends and decide to postpone sex until they are ready for marriage.

Until that day comes, however, you need to speak openly with your children. Encourage them to be responsible enough to avoid sex until marriage, but be aware that they may not. Temptation is present in the form of peer pressure, the media, and the values of today's liberal society. Another level of being responsible means, therefore, that you have provided your children with adequate information about birth control.

You may believe that by teaching your teenager about birth control you are, theoretically, providing him a basis for being sexually active. That will not happen if you

59

have taught him the entire concept of this book. By showing him your own wholesome attitudes, sharing accurate information with him, and developing in him a sense of responsibility, you will finish the cycle of your own maturity. Giving him guidelines about contraception will only complete his sex education.

—From Grace H. Ketterman, M.D., *How to Teach Your Child About Sex.* Old Tappan, N.J.: Fleming H. Revell Co., 1981.

FOR FURTHER READING:

Hughes, Philip. *The Control of Human Life.* Grand Rapids: Baker Book House, 1971.

Spitzer, Walter O., and Saylor, Carlyle L., eds. *Birth Control and the Christian.* Wheaton, Ill.: Tyndale House Publishers, 1969.

Stackley, Muriel, and Friesen, Duane. *Moral Issues in the Control of Birth.* Newton, Kans.: Faith and Life, 1974.

Trobisch, Walter. *Please Help Me! Please Love Me!* Downers Grove, Ill.: Inter-Varsity Press, 1970.

"BLUES" AFTER CHILDBIRTH

IN THE WEEKS after the baby is born, it is not at all unusual for a new mother to have some days of feeling depressed and weepy. Perhaps these so-called "baby blues" are more noticed now that mothers leave the hospital so soon after the baby's birth. They're eager to get home, of course, to take charge of things. But suddenly they feel quite alone. Formerly, the "blues" hit when mother and baby were safe in the hands of experienced hospital staff.

There are many reasons why a feeling of depression is apt to occur. If you find yourself on the verge of tears for no apparent reason, you are actually being quite reasonable.

The "blues" may be no more complicated than the letdown most of us feel after any long-awaited moment has come—and gone. Christmas, for instance. Or, from your childhood, you may be able to recall the all-at-loose-ends feeling when school ended for the summer. Dreams of the vacation never quite lived up to expectations, at first. Later on, life took shape again with the fun of going barefoot, of seemingly endless summer afternoons, of catching fireflies at dusk, of family picnics.

Physical changes within the mother's body may trigger and deepen feelings of depression, too. Since mind and body are so delicately meshed, any profound physical readjustment is bound to be reflected in our feelings and thoughts. Hormones secreted during pregnancy, for one thing, are no longer needed. Then there's the all-worn-out feeling that follows any sudden change in schedule, and the supply of available energy may not match the increased demands of the day—and night.

There are times when real problems must be faced. Sometimes it's a momentary twinge of disappointment in the sex of the baby. She's not the brown-eyed, blond boy you mentally pushed in a baby carriage during the months of pregnancy. Or the baby may not be off to a good start. He may have a physical defect which is an ever-present concern until you can take the measure of it and learn just what it will mean to you, and to the baby. If it has been necessary to leave the baby in the hospital for some time after you have come home, there is the pain of separation, even when you know the baby will be coming home eventually. The empty crib becomes a rebuke that somehow you didn't manage things better, though commonsense tells you that it is not your fault. In such cases, you may find it helpful to talk with your doctor, a visiting nurse, social worker at the hospital, or counselor at your family service agency.

Sometimes new parents feel a touch of mourning or sadness. It is hard to explain the feeling of loss, after you've gained something so real, but it seems to be present for many a man and woman. Partly, it may be loss of the former husband or wife, exchanged for the mother and father you've become. Part may be loss of the freedom you felt was yours before. You haven't quite moved yet into the satisfaction of saying "Johnny already sleeps through the night" or some other conversational newsy item, but you know that the past is gone.

Probably the best way to deal with ordinary baby blues is to be reassured that many mothers have them and they are temporary. Try to keep the days as simple as possible, and ask nothing of yourself beyond the essentials. Treat yourself to all the extra help you can afford. Let thank-you notes and birth announcements wait until you have strength for them. When you can get out, indulge yourself in a trip to the beauty parlor, or whatever makes you feel fresh.

—From *Infant Care*. Washington: U.S. Department of Health, Education and Welfare, 1970.

BOTTLE-FEEDING

Formulas

There are many formulas available today that are chemically identical to mother's milk. The baby's doctor will recommend one that he feels will best suit your baby's needs. The same holds true for bottles and nipples. The ones with collapsible plastic sacks have some advantage in preventing the swallowing of air, but if a baby burps readily, that is not necessarily a factor.

Bottles

Ordinary Pyrex bottles are just fine for feeding your baby. They are cheaper than the disposable plastic-sack type. *But they do need to be sterilized.* You may use a big kitchen pan with a rack on the bottom to prevent breakage, or you may buy a sterilizer. Your doctor will advise you about "terminal sterilization," or just sterilizing the bottles, nipples, and water, and then adding the concentrated formula.

Many child manuals go into great detail on feeding equipment and the mechanical aspects of child rearing. Do look at them if these concerns are important to you. We believe that babies are endowed with great resources by their Creator. And as you learn to relax, watch your baby's signals, and respond to them, you will become good parents. *The equipment is not as important as the people involved.*

Milk Temperature

The temperature of mother's milk, of course, is just right. Bottles should be warmed slightly, so that a drop of milk shaken on your wrist feels lukewarm, or just as warm as your skin. It's better to have the formula a shade too cool than too hot. Many mothers give cold milk, and we see nothing wrong with that. Your baby will thrive on it just as well as warm milk.

Starting the Bottle-Fed Baby

Feeding a bottle to a baby is as easy as the breast, but again, at first it is necessary to get the sucking started. Touching the baby's mouth on the side of his cheek with your finger will trigger his rooting reflex and make his mouth fly open if he is awake and hungry. Stroking his tongue gently with the nipple will start the sucking. Let him take as little or as much as he wants. In newborns this is usually less than three ounces. Do not try to get him to empty the bottle. If there is milk left, it is wonderful to use in cooking so it needn't be wasted. Forcing babies to take more formula than they want can cause spit-

61

ting up. And it may make your baby too fat. And too fat is not healthy. The baby's doctor will tell you if he's gaining too much or too little, so let him worry about that.

If He Won't Take the Bottle

If your baby tires out before he has a reasonable amount of milk, it may be due to being too tired before feeding. He may have cried too hard or waited too long; or the nipple holes may be too small. The only way we found to enlarge the holes in a rubber nipple was to heat a needle red-hot over a stove burner. Hold it firmly with a pair of pliers. Then insert it into one of the existing holes in the nipple and burn it larger. Test the nipple with milk in it. If it is the right size, the milk will drip slowly and steadily out. If it runs out, the hole is too big and that nipple will have to be discarded. Most new-nipple holes are far too small, and the baby will be worn out too soon. It takes only a little time and patience to get it just right.

Signs of Trouble

The importance of feeding and burping is, of course, to nourish a baby and help him be comfortable. Air bubbles, hunger, and cramping due to milk that doesn't agree with a particular baby's digestive system, may all make a baby miserable. And when he is miserable he will cry, as he should, for how else will you know something is wrong? Be careful that every time your baby cries, however, you don't think he is hungry and feed him too much.

Formula Problems

Signs that something is wrong with a new baby's formula include vomiting (not just spitting up, but actual regurgitating of all the stomach contents), diarrhea, (watery or mucus-filled stools that irritate baby's skin and may even contain blood flecks), and a failure to thrive or gain weight. Now it may be that a nursing mother has eaten too many onions, or some food that makes her milk unpleasant. You will discover what these foods are and may easily avoid them while you are nursing.

Formulas may simply be too rich. Diluting them more may help; or the baby may be allergic to cow's milk and may need another type of formula. Be sure to ask your doctor before you change and *don't* change too quickly. It will take several days to get all of the last formula out of a baby's system, before you can evaluate the new one.

—From Grace H. Ketterman, M.D., and Herbert L. Ketterman, M.D., *The Complete Book of Baby and Child Care for Christian Parents*. Old Tappan, N.J.: Fleming H. Revell Co., 1982.

BRAGGING

WE HAVE ALL HEARD small children say, "My Daddy can beat up your Daddy!"

What the young child who brags in this way is in effect saying to himself and others is that he is as strong as the child he is speaking to. In this way he dispels the fear that the other child may be able to hurt him because he may be stronger.

If there is a lot of emphasis on competition and achievement in the home, older children who are not able to meet the demands of the family easily will sometimes cover up their feelings of inferiority by displaying their knowledge or exaggerating their abilities to others.

Parents in such a family need to ask why they are making such difficult demands on their children. It may be their way of making up for personal feelings of inferiority. Paul writes, "Who made you superior to others? Didn't God give you everything you have?

Well, then, how can you boast, as if what you have were not a gift?" (1 Corinthians 4:7 TEV).

Through Jeremiah in the Old Testament, God gives the Christian family the proper balance: "Wise men should not boast of their wisdom, nor strong men of their strength, nor rich men of their wealth. If anyone wants to boast, he should boast that he knows and understands me ..." (Jeremiah 9:23, 24 TEV). If bragging is a problem in the family, this passage might be a good one for family devotions after dinner some evening.

Unless bragging is exaggerated, however, it should not be of concern to the Christian parent. With the passage of time it disappears in most cases.

—LESLIE R. KEYLOCK

BREAST-FEEDING

A NEW MOTHER's breasts automatically prepare her to feed her baby. Whether to breast- or bottle-feed is another big question. You should decide this some time before your baby's birth. Perhaps you did decide but now you want to change your mind. Here are some facts to help you decide.

Mother's milk was made for babies. It is automatically warm and germ-free. It is easily digestible, usually gives babies fewer, less irritating bowel movements, less colic, and is always instantly available. It also contains certain antibodies that help prevent illness in your baby.

Some mothers, however, simply cannot breast-feed. They may have to return to work. Their bodies may not produce enough milk; their nipples may be inverted and make it hard for baby to nurse (though this is not an insurmountable problem). The skin may be tender and an abscess could develop. Perhaps psychologically they just cannot feel

right about nursing. Each mother is different.

Nursing may cause some breakdown of breast tissue and later figure changes may disappoint the wife and husband. In today's breast-conscious society, many couples do seriously consider this fact.

The La Leche League has promoted breast-feeding of infants zealously. And many mothers, having tried it, find it a highly enjoyable experience. Mother and baby find an intimacy that is special, and that is fine. Contacting a local La Leche League chapter through a telephone directory will provide a wealth of information and support.

If, for any reason, a mother decides not to breast-feed her baby or tries it unsuccessfully, she need not feel guilty, or think she is an inadequate mother. The bond of intimacy encouraged in breast-feeding can be just as strong between the bottle-fed baby and mother as the breast-fed one. It is important, however, that a baby be held while he is fed. The warmth and cuddling feed his soul, as the milk does his body. He also needs adequate sucking time. The nipple holes can be adjusted in size to fit each baby's sucking strength and needs—and that is one advantage over breast-feeding.

You, the mother and father, must decide what method of feeding is best for all of you, and then rest in that decision without further doubts or negative feelings. If you choose to bottle-feed, it is a great idea and wonderful experience for father to feed at least one bottle per day. The baby needs to feel warm and cuddled by you, Dad, just as much as by his mother, and this is one way that can be accomplished. Though fathers often feel a little awkward at first, practice will quickly change that. Father's helping with a baby amazingly knits an entire family together as a real unit. Mothers will usually have extra-tender feelings toward fathers who help them in such ways.

Starting the Breast-Fed Baby

Feeding is an instinctive function for all babies. Just put a nipple in their mouths, and they know what to do with it. At first, however (only a feeding or two), they may need help in getting started. For breast-fed babies, hunger will usually cause them to open their mouths and search for the mother's nipple. It is called the "rooting reflex." If your baby is slow about this, stroke the side of his face nearest the breast. This will encourage the baby's readiness to nurse. At first he should nurse only four or five minutes on each side, so the mother's nipples do not become tender. There is little nourishment for the first several days in the mother's milk (called *colostrum* when it is still thin and watery). As the nipple and areola (pigmented area around the nipple) become tougher, and the real milk comes in, the baby may nurse as long as he likes—usually fifteen minutes on one side, and five or ten minutes on the other. Mothers get to know when a breast is empty. The next feeding should start with the breast last used to keep the milk supply balanced, and hence mothers more comfortable.

Care of Breasts

For support and comfort, nursing mothers should wear a special nursing bra. Usually it is necessary to wear a small pad over the nipple to avoid the leaking of milk onto the clothing. It is important, however, to keep the skin dry to prevent irritation and infection.

Rarely such an infection may develop. If you become aware of pain in a local area of a breast, unusual tenderness under the arm, and any fever, call your doctor. This may mean that an abscess is forming. It will need to be promptly treated with antibiotics, and the baby should not nurse from that breast until it is well.

Breast Pump

A breast pump may be used to relieve the pressure in that breast and keep the milk supply ready for nursing, when the infection is well. A breast pump is a special type of a rubber-bulb syringe attached to a container. It fits firmly around the nipple and gently withdraws the milk which goes into the container. If you have an infection, you will want to discard this milk.

Water or Formula

If you are a nursing mother, offer your baby a bottle of water occasionally through the day. Also teach your baby to take formula at times. This frees you a bit more for an occasional time out alone or, hopefully, with your husband. It is important that the two of you keep your relationship close and happy. If your baby refuses formula, you may pump your own breast milk and leave it in a sterile bottle for the sitter to feed the baby while you are gone.

Burping

After a baby has nursed for some ten or fifteen minutes, gently withdraw the nipple and burp him. Burping is the ancient custom of helping an infant expel the air he has swallowed while he was nursing. Breast as well as collapsible-bottle-fed infants swallow less air, but they usually need to rest a bit and may need to burp, too. Putting the baby over the shoulder so the upper abdomen rests on the firm part of the shoulder, and patting him on the lower part of his back, usually will press and jostle the air bubble out—sometimes loudly and sometimes quietly. Another method we found helpful with a hard-to-burp baby is to hold him with the heel of one hand pressing gently into his tummy, while the thumb and forefinger supported the head. Firmly but gently rubbing and patting the back should do the trick. It's fine to try different ways. *It is important to take time.* Babies are good for parents—though trying at times—because they don't know how to hurry. If you will listen to them, you will learn to slow down, too, and may develop calmness and patience you never thought possible.

By the time you burp your baby, he may feel quite content and be nearly asleep. The more relaxed he is, the harder it is to burp, so you may need to stimulate him a little. Then allow him to nurse again to the point of contented fullness. One final burping and a diaper change later, with good fortune, he is ready for his next three- or four-hour nap.

In the hospital, due to necessary routines, a baby must be brought to the mother at scheduled intervals. He may have been awake and hungry earlier, but perhaps has fallen asleep by the time you get him. Don't worry about that. As soon as you get home, you and the baby will establish his own schedule, and he can be fed when he is hungry.

—From Grace H. Ketterman, M.D., and Herbert L. Ketterman, M.D., *The Complete Book of Baby and Child Care for Christian Parents*. Old Tappan, N.J.: Fleming H. Revell Co., 1982.

BUDGET

BUDGETING is planned spending! Doesn't that sound easy? And budgeting *is* easy when you understand its purpose, follow a workable system, and use it to maximize the family income. A family that knows where its money is going can usually make it go farther.

Most of the money you earn in your life, you will spend. You will spend your funds for things you want. Unfortunately, your yearnings will exceed your earnings.

If you follow your wants in your buying, the result will be chaos. If you design your spending, then your dollars can take care of you. With a system you will probably be more satisfied, have more of what you really want, and have less financial problems. Without a strategy money matters will probably cause tension and crisis in your family. Convinced that a budget will benefit your family, you must now build a spending plan for your needs. Estimating expenditures for a year at a time is the place to start. Here's a three-step process to help you:

Our Financial Goals

	Monthly	Annually
1. Tithes and Offerings	____	____
2. Federal Income Tax	____	____
3. State Income Tax	____	____
4. Social Security Tax	____	____
5. Other Taxes (such as City)	____	____
6. Shelter	____	____
7. Food	____	____
8. Clothing	____	____
9. Health	____	____
10. Education	____	____
11. Life Insurance	____	____
12. Gifts	____	____
13. Transportation	____	____
14. Personal Allowances	____	____
15. Vacations	____	____
16. Savings	____	____
17. Household Purchases	____	____
18. Debt Reduction	____	____
19.	____	____
20.	____	____
Total	====	====

Step A   Review the categories on the list, Our Financial Goals. The purpose of estimating your expenditures is to arrive at an annual and monthly figure for each spending category. Are there other categories you need in your budget? Are there categories you do not need? Make any necessary changes on this form, so that it meets your family's requirements.

Step B Fill in the monthly or annual column of each category you are using on Our Financial Goals. The explanations which follow will guide you in arriving at amounts for each spending category. Start with the first item and work through them in order. Remember that a journey of a thousand miles begins with the first step. If you have a monthly estimate, multiply it by twelve for the annual figures. If you have an annual figure, divide it by twelve for the monthly figure. You may need to refer to your checkbook to obtain previous expenditures so you can make accurate estimates of future amounts.

1. Tithes and Offerings—all charitable giving: church, United Way, etc.
2. Federal Income Tax—all amounts withheld, plus estimates paid, plus any amounts due with tax return.
3. State Income Tax—all amounts withheld, plus estimates paid, plus any amounts due with tax return.
4. Social Security Tax—[6.65% of your first $29,700 earned; total for year $1,975.05; same for your spouse. These are 1981 figures.]
5. Other Taxes—taxes on your wages, such as city income taxes.
6. Shelter.
   (a) If renting include rent, heat, lights, telephone, household supplies, appliance repairs, other home-related expenses.
   (b) If buying include house payments, interest, insurance, real-estate taxes, repairs and maintenance, other items listed under renting.
7. Food—grocery-store items, paper goods, cleaning supplies, pet foods. Include all eating-out and carry-out items and school lunches. It may also include entertainment.
8. Clothing—purchases, cleaning, repairs. This may be divided with a separate budget for each family member.
9. Health—health insurance premiums, medical, dental, hospital expenses, drug items, medicines, cosmetics.
10. Education—school expenses, books, lessons, college expenses, uniforms, equipment, subscriptions to newspapers and magazines.
11. Life Insurance—all premiums, whether paid monthly, quarterly, or annually.
12. Gifts—birthdays, anniversaries, special occasions, Christmas, weddings, funerals, office collections, dues for organizations.
13. Transportation—gas, oil, repairs, licenses, personal property tax, insurance. Car payments or an amount set aside to purchase your next car.
14. Personal Allowances—for each family member to spend personally. Hair care, recreation, baby-sitting, hobbies, and children's allowances.
15. Vacations—trips, camps, weekend outings; trips for weddings, funerals, and family visits.
16. Savings—amounts set aside now for future needs.
17. Household Purchases—for major appliances, furniture, carpeting, and major home maintenance such as roofing and painting.
18. Debt Reduction—includes all payments on debt not included in other categories such as: school loans, amounts due relatives, banks, or others.
19. Special Categories—anything tailored to your own needs or desires; this may include a boat, cabin, airplane, or hobby.

Step C After filling in all of the monthly and annual estimates, add the totals. *Wow!* The totals are greater than your income! Right? Right!! If so, you are not unusual. Every budget I've ever seen starts out with wants in excess of income.

Now! The fun and prayers start. What are your needs? What are your wants? Here are some hints and guidelines to help you.

Shelter—not over 30% of your gross income. If gross income is $1,000 monthly, all expenses for shelter should not exceed $300. If you are over in this area, you may need to secure a cheaper living situation in order to balance your budget.

Food—as high as 30% with less than a $700 monthly income to less than 20% for $1,500 income.

Clothing—not over 10% of your income.

Short-term debt—not to exceed 10% of your monthly take-home pay times 18. With a monthly net income of $750 the debt limit would be $75 × 18 = $1,350. This figure would not include a mortgage on your home. The experts all say that you are headed for trouble if your short-term monthly debt payments exceed 20% of your take-home pay. Thus, with a take-home pay of $750, you are in real financial trouble if your monthly payments for debt exceed $150, excluding a home mortgage.

All successful budgets have one thing in common: the outgo is *not* greater than the income! God's guidance is essential as you begin together the painful surgical process of cutting back your spending plans to match your income. Have you prayed? You need God's wisdom. Ask Him for it.

Now, examine each spending category. Ask these questions: Which expenses are essential? Which can you do without? Which can you reduce?

Yes, the surgical process of trimming the family budget is painful. So is the Christian walk! Jesus instructed us clearly about the way we choose in every area of our lives: "Enter by the narrow gate; for the gate is wide and the way is easy, that leads to de-struction, and those who enter by it are many. For the gate is narrow and the way is hard, that leads to life, and those who find it are few" (Matthew 7:13, 14 RSV).

The wide financial path is easy; no money down and an easy-payment plan. Buy what you want when you want it. CHARGE IT! Don't bother with budgets and record keeping. Such thinking maps out the road to de-struction.

God's financial way is hard. Self-denial, discipline, and sacrifice are the marks of a Christian and his money. God's stewardship calls for wise and knowledgeable use of our money. This means a plan and records to help you stay within the plan. God's abundance is not found in overspending what He provides for us, but in His blessing us as we are faithful with what He gives us.

Keep praying and cutting until your expenses are within your income. Remember, if your spending plan won't work on paper, it won't work—period.

—From George Fooshee, Jr., *You Can Be Financially Free*. Old Tappan, N.J.: Fleming H. Revell Co., 1976.

FOR FURTHER READING:

Burkett, Larry. *Your Finances in Changing Times*. San Bernardino, Calif.: Campus Crusade For Christ, 1975.

Gallagher, Neil. *How to Save Money on Almost Everything*. Minneapolis: Bethany Fellowship, Inc., 1978.

Hardisty, George and Margaret. *Honest Questions, Honest Answers*. Eugene, Ore.: Harvest House Publishers, 1977.

Thomason, James C. *Common Sense About Your Family Dollars*. Wheaton, Ill.: Victor Books, 1979.

C

CHEATING

WHEN A BOY OR GIRL cheats at school, parents often feel that they have failed in a most important responsibility—that of developing character and a sense of personal integrity. Cheating is so common among school and even college students, however. . . . Yet we cannot dismiss cheating by saying, "All the kids do it," for the fact remains that one who cheats is not living up to the best in himself. Of course there is a great difference between yielding to occasional temptation and accepting cheating as the way to get along. Certainly parents cannot hold up cheating as a way of life for themselves or for their children.

Children learn early in playing with their friends that cheating doesn't go, and they can carry over this same attitude into their social life—that cheating does not belong in the honest-to-goodness relationships among people in their daily intercourse. As for his schoolwork, any child who is old enough to take tests is old enough to understand that cheating is wrong. This does not call for a lengthy lecture from his parents if they find out that their child has cheated in an exam. They can let him know firmly, whenever the subject comes up, that they know it's wrong, and that they know *he* too knows it's wrong, and that they realize this was a slip—not the taking on of ways they would all be ashamed of.

It is true that parents and teachers often do lay too much emphasis on attaining good grades instead of making clear the purpose of the test in terms of the benefit for the child. A child can understand that the test's value for him is also to get a measure—like taking his temperature or weighing him—to guide those who wish to help him. Confusing means with ends is like caring more for winning than for the fun of a game—and certainly even young children can learn that. In the usual competitive setting, however, a youngster may need help to see that cheating means stealing a rating to which he is not entitled, or that it is like wearing another's badge to impress people falsely.

Another basic source of cheating is the young person's lack of confidence in his own worth. He builds his self-confidence and his self-respect through his successes, so we want him to try out all kinds of tasks and challenges. But if we force him to undertake what is beyond him, the frustrations and humiliations will more likely make him rebel against the whole system. Parents must realize the pressures put upon their children to try for things they cannot possibly achieve [are such] that often many worthy goals can have no real value for them. Reproving a child for his low rating is in many cases as senseless—and confusing—as rewarding a child for attaining a good mark in a task that requires no effort from him at all. Our own confusion between one goal and another may often block a child's growth in self-reliance and dependability.

69

Young children cannot value "honesty" in the abstract, but they can learn the difference between being honest and being sneaky and cheating. We can help a child to develop his own sense of honor by helping him feel respect for himself and have pride in being able to make choices and decisions. We must help him feel respect for what he can do well in developing what we call his "sense of honor." He must experience honor if he is to cultivate it, but he needs, fully as much, to develop a healthy respect for what he himself is and what he is capable of doing.

It is safe to say that when a child is helped to develop real self-respect, when he knows he has the respect and unconditional love of his parents, his sense of honor will develop too. To help a boy or girl take these difficult steps in growing up, parents need, of course, a clear sense of their own values and standards.

—From *The New Encyclopedia of Child Care and Guidance.* Garden City, N.Y.: Doubleday & Co., 1968.

CHURCH ATTENDANCE

LET US NOW give our attention to designating definite ways in which young people can be challenged and enlisted for Kingdom service.

1. *A Profound Religious Belief.* No young person will be impressed by a weak, faltering, spineless religious expression. He wants a faith that is positive, aggressive, victorious, and heroic. Both dogmas and doubts will be quickly rejected. Young folks demand something more than a skim-milk type of religion; they refuse to be satisfied with anything less than the cream of the crop. They literally detest the insipid and vacillating wherever it is found or by whomsoever it may be presented. Faith sufficient to command their allegiance must be deep and exacting.

One of the most effective ways to dampen the ardor of youth with respect to the church is to either say or to imply that to live the Christian life is simple and easy. With simple and easy endeavors young people have no desire to identify themselves. They yearn after the deep and difficult things.

Youth clamors for a religion the details of which have not been fully discovered or interpreted. Hand a young person a book, and say, "The religion of Jesus Christ is completely explained in this," and, nine times out of ten you will have lost a worker in the church. Youth want to face baffling things in religion; they are inspired by the challenge of the impossible; they greatly desire to climb the mountains and search the valleys in their pursuit of the larger truth. Youth look with obvious askance at a religious belief so simple as to be handed on in predigested forms. The deeper it actually is, the more commanding is its appeal.

Ministers frequently err in attempting to cater to their young people by preaching simple platitudes on the popular ideas of the day. This is a sure way to lose young people, both from the congregation and from the church. One of the surest ways to retain youth is to preach about the great facts and verities of religion—always in simple terms. The content of the message should be deep, the form of the message simple and unassuming. This is a great combination, and happy and successful the pastor who can master this commanding method. Young people become rightly resentful when the preacher prostitutes his position and opportunities by discussing trivial subjects. Never should a minister preach down to people, least of all to youth.

In my present congregation there is a man of rich maturity, not only in years but also in spiritual quality, who one day asked, "Did you know good old Dr. B?" "Yes, why?" "Well," said he, "I was brought up as a youngster under his preaching, and he always gave us the strongest meat so simply that even a callow youth could understand and assimilate the truth. I've thanked God many times for that man because his discussions of great truth laid the foundation of that which later was to satisfy my soul."

The preacher of wisdom will never minimize the difficulties which the Scriptures may sometimes present. The very existence of these perplexities will serve to challenge youth even more deeply. Neither should the preacher endeavor to rationalize all the elements of mystery involved in Christian experiences. This attempt will not satisfy the aspirations of youth, for young people will come rather quickly to the place where they can accept on faith many things which they find it impossible to fathom on any intellectual process. One need have little fear for the religious faith of the young if they have the benefits of considerate, sympathetic advisers.

2. *A Commanding Program.* Young people are responsive to the magnetism of great endeavors. Idealistic in the extreme, they refuse to be stirred, or even interested, by small things, to say nothing of joining in such enterprises with zeal and enthusiasm. Youth demand a part in a growing institution, they want to share, and they will, share wholeheartedly in a movement which is big enough to generate the spirit of compulsion.

When the programs of many churches are carefully analyzed we are not surprised that young people are not attracted. On the contrary, we are amazed by the fact that a few young folks, by exercising the spirit of heroic duty, share in these programs, although decidedly bored all the while. This condition never eventuates in success for the Kingdom. It is almost a crime to invite youth to the services and service of a church which fails to offer a program worthy of the ideals of Jesus Christ. They will come, but they come not to stay. Their reaction to anaemic efforts is potentially dangerous, as they are liable to interpret the weak program as typical of that offered by churches generally, and they will have a tendency to wash their hands entirely of such enterprises as being unavailing and totally undeserving of their allegiance.

This often occurs in its financial phase. Subjecting itself to a "hand-to-mouth," unbusinesslike monetary method, a church soon finds its bills unpaid, the result being a church which is a poor financial risk in the community. A church of this type cannot be expected to command the respect and support of young folks. They want no part in a faltering, failing institution. Youth are keen at reasoning—they understand that there is money for other things, even for sports and every sort of luxury. The church which cannot secure sufficient funds to maintain its work with credit is reckoned to have failed, and youth will not ally themselves with failing enterprises. What a challenge for pastors and church officials to see to it once and for all that their churches establish a businesslike financial program.

Again, the matter of attendance upon public worship counts heavily with youth. If more than half of the pews are empty during services young people gain a very unpleasant impression. Young folks want to go to church where people want and do go to church; youth want to rub elbows with the crowds. If large numbers attend church the young people will be deeply and favorably stirred. The old adage proves itself here—"Nothing succeeds like success." An institution which can and does bring together large companies of people attracts youth. Unquestionably, this principle, more than any other, explains the remarkable success of the European youth movements. There is a subtle and compelling magnetism for the young person in large numbers.

The program must be many-sided. Many churches have strong programs, so far as they go, but they stop too soon. More and more, the successful church must touch every arc in the circle of life. The strongest preaching program in America today is not enough in itself. What of the social and recreational aspects of life? What of the opportunities for self-expression? What of the waste which comes to the church which is closed from Sunday morning to Sunday morning? We honor and exalt the worship services of the church, but all should recognize that these can never constitute a well-rounded program, particularly one which can meet the requirements of youth.

The program need not be fully realized in order to command the attention and support of youth, but it must be marked with the elements of boldness, courage, vision, and deep spiritual quality. Were the ideas and ideals of the program completely achieved much of its appeal for youth would be lost. They want to be challenged by difficult tasks, they want to prove the possibility of doing the impossible, they yearn for the call to put their shoulders to the wheel and do some long and heavy pushing.

The church which succeeds in its service to and for youth must give them a large and important place in its program. This feature is of itself the most commanding part of the entire procedure. Young folks rightly want suitable recognition, and in response to this recognition they will serve with renewed ardor and devotion. . . .

3. *Faith in the Fidelity of Youth.* No pastor can ever legitimately hope or expect to enlist youth in any considerable numbers for the church unless in his soul he believes in the essential goodness and fidelity of young people. Very, very frequently this belief should become vocal. A young person ordinarily is as sensitive to the true attitude of his pastor as is a flower to the sunlight. He seems to possess a subtle intuition, a soul perception, a sixth sense—call it by any name you wish—by which to plumb the depths of the older person. If in the heart of this would-be helper he discovers a genuine faith in youth, together with an honest desire to assist young people to find themselves, he will cling to that person, be he pastor or layman, with a devotion stronger than hooks of steel.

There is a profound something, buried in every life, which gladly and gratefully responds to the person who believes in us. We refuse to be disloyal to the confidence placed in us, and, conversely, we have a particular detestation for the man—the traitor—who deliberately proves himself disloyal. This subtle attribute is markedly present in youth. The average young person will ring true as a cathedral bell to one who believes in him.

This fact explains why it is suicidal for the pastor, or any other worker with youth, who takes the occasion to "knock" or discredit young people. Of course, young people are basking today, to a very large extent, in the dangerous light of what many falsely call "the new-found freedom." Admittedly, large numbers of young people are flaming ingloriously. But bitter censure is not the remedy. To say harsh things about a person is usually equivalent to driving him farther away. Every wrong perpetrated—even the wrong of most serious character—is evidence of power misused. Vice is virtue misused. The power to do wrong is the power to do right. The objective of the young people's leader is to turn the river of potential goodness into its rightful and proper channel. The exercise of faith in youth at all times will prove a mighty lever toward the realization of this idea.

Then, too, young people deserve our faith. Every young person secretly pulses with the purpose to scale the summits of worthy achievement. He who retains faith in the inherent fidelity of youth, come what may, goes a long way to buttress this purpose, and also toward solving the problem of youth enlistment.

4. *The Assignment of Definite Tasks.* Young people are aggressive, they want and need action. Youth is the time of greatest activity, both in work and play. Said Farr, "Youth is eminently the fittest season for establishing habits of industry." These words are as pertinent with regard to the church as in any other field. The normal, red-blooded young person will never rest content merely as an observer, he must "jump in and help play the game." Fortunately, there is a wealth of opportunity for this in every church, if the pastor and the officials will permit.

One of the best ways for youth to express itself is that offered by those services of worship in which all the parts are taken by young people. In the church served by the writer this type of program is carried out at least twice each year, sometimes more frequently, and the results are always highly profitable.

We invariably select four young people as the speakers, each being allowed ten minutes for his or her message. We believe four to be better than one or two, in that it gives a larger number place on the program. The pastor assigns the topics, not that he fears what the youthful speakers might say, but to insure some continuity of thought. The four topics discussed in one youth night were:

"What the Bible Means to Me."
"What the Church Means to Me."
"What Christian Service Means to Me."
"What Christ Means to Me."

At another similar meeting the four subjects were:

"How Can Young People Help Other Young People?"
"How Can Young People Benefit the Community?"
"How Can Young People Assist the Pastor?"
"How Can Young People Serve the Church?"

In every instance the speakers work out their messages quite unassisted, and they unfailingly speak well and with considerable wisdom. It is little less than amazing to note the thought and attitude reflected by these presentations. Incidentally, this sort of service will always insure a crowded auditorium.

All the other parts—responsive reading, announcements, dedication of the offering, reading of the Scripture, announcement and leadership in the hymns and the prayer—are taken by other young people. Even richer will be this service if a youth choir can be specially drilled for the occasion. The ushers may be composed of either young men or young women, and the offering should be taken by young people.

Gradually, qualified and promising youth can be assigned work as teachers and workers in the church school. The musical ministry of the church is rich in privilege for young folks, especially if junior and intermediate choruses are maintained, in addition to the senior choir. Thirty to forty young people sing in my junior choir every Sunday morning—they are wedded to church for life.

A large place among the ushers should be found for young men. As rapidly as conditions will warrant, the older young people should be given representation on the boards and committees of the church.

Plays and pageantry present a field of peculiar privilege for the youth of the church. For the most part, the characters should be taken by the young. This affords a rich opportunity for expressional activity.

The distinctively young people's groups,

which are organized in every church, are potentially great developers of youth, and present the privilege of being fully directed by young people. They can be mighty assets by the judicious guidance of self-effacing counselors.

Special projects for community betterment, as well as individual services for the sick and shut-ins, should always be the order for the church-school classes. Visits to hospitals, institutional homes, and other like places are thrilling and blessed experiences for the young.

Christmas caroling, and the other seasonal opportunities for service seldom find youth hesitant—they love to serve, the more, the better. Every encouragement should be given by the pastor.

Then, too, we should not overlook the many manual tasks connected with the church which can and will command the attention and ability of youth if they be informed. Hymn books must be rearranged, tables must be set up, taken down and put away, many copies of various announcements must be run off on the mimeograph. These are merely suggestive of the opportunities of the manual sort. Youth seldom fail in their response.

Happy is the pastor who finds or makes a task for every group of young people in his church. To do this may compel him to lie awake nights, but the investment produces splendid results. Busy young people are happy young people.

The absence of young folks should be carefully noted and the reason quickly ascertained. All people like to be missed, but this is particularly true of youth. A young person will actually beam with the consciousness that his absence has been noted, and that the pastor "did something about it."

Every year some of the young folks will go away to college. This group must not be forgotten, in fact, they should be peculiarly and frequently remembered. College life brings an undreamed-of environment, and often the experience at the outset is not happy. Every church in a college community should have a competent student counselor who, together with the pastor, will keep in regular touch with the students. At least once a year, preferably on a Sunday afternoon just prior to commencement, the entire group can be brought together for a social and refreshments, after which they should attend the church in a body. Such considerations are deeply valued by practically every student.

These various agencies, and others which space will not permit us to mention, should be continually employed for the benefit and development of youth. The church owes this service to its young people, and the church which carries on a program like this will have small difficulty in enlisting youth.

But there is another imperative which must never be lost from view—the future of the church. "The destiny of any nation at any given time," said Goethe, "depends upon the opinions of its young men under five-and-twenty." This fact applies most emphatically to the church. As goes the life of youth, so will and must go the life, the very existence, of the individual church.

—From Eugene Dolloff, *A Crowded Church*. Old Tappan, N.J.: Fleming H. Revell Co., 1946.

FOR FURTHER READING:

DiGiacomo, James, ed. *See You in Church*. Macon, Ga.: Winston Press, 1971.

Hunter, George, 3rd. *The Contagious Congregation*. Nashville: Abingdon Press, 1979.

CLOTHING

THE BIBLE has very little to say about clothing. Jesus tells us we shouldn't worry about clothing and other material wants, especially if they take the place of God's kingdom as our number-one concern in life (Matthew 6:28–33). He also commended those whose social concern led them to do several things for the humblest of His brothers, including clothing them (Matthew 25:36, 40). James warns about paying special attention to the well-dressed person who visited the early house churches and snubbing "the poor man in shabby clothes" (James 2:3 NEB). And Peter places higher importance on the inward beauty of a gentle, quiet spirit than on dress and other forms of outward adornment (1 Peter 3:3).

Clothing children today is comparatively simple to what it used to be. Parents today tend to emphasize comfort and practicality when they buy clothes for their children. The frilly dresses of our grandparents' childhood have been largely replaced by clothing that can be worn often and washed easily.

For winter, lightweight down jackets are more practical and comfortable than the cumbersome winter clothing of the past.

Baby clothing should be purchased a bit on the large size. Otherwise, arms and legs will have to be forced into uncomfortable positions when the baby has gotten a bit bigger.

Be sure you try on all clothing you buy for a child. Complete standardization of sizes has not yet been achieved.

Once a child is in school, and increasingly as he enters adolescence, clothing comes to have psychological values that sometimes overshadow its practical use. Certain brands of sneakers, T-shirts, and jeans become important to the child because "all" his friends are wearing them. (This trait is not absent in adult dressing either, remember!) Parents can become upset by teenage fads. Unless they are patently indecent, however (as the wording on some T-shirts is), parents should allow their children the liberty and security

of conforming to what their peers are wearing. After all, the repelling fad usually fades even faster than did the Edsel! As one writer pointed out, we all conform to the world in which we live to some extent, and a certain amount of conformity is only common sense.

What does the parent do when a child dresses in a way that appears to be indecent? When are blue jeans too tight? When is a blouse unbuttoned too far? The wisest parental role is to suggest as calmly as possible that when an adolescent child dresses in such a way as to draw sexual attention to his or her body, an invitation to further immoral attention is implied.

If the child is open to biblical teaching, some of the verses in the Bible that refer to clothing might be appropriate reading for family devotions.

If the child is going through a rebellious phase, however, it is probably wiser to say as little as possible about dress and to focus on more important issues such as establishing rapport so spiritual commitment can be emphasized first.

When clothing is no longer worn, for whatever reason, it is good Christian stewardship to pass it on to someone else or place it in the clothing bins of the Salvation Army or a similar agency. Some children are so fickle, however, that they lose interest in their clothing selections almost as soon as they have been purchased! In such cases, you may have to insist that a child must wear what he selects for a minimum period of time before getting rid of it.

—LESLIE R. KEYLOCK

COLIC

Still a Puzzle

After all these years of scientific study and discoveries, colic is still a puzzle. We do not know how to cure it, or what causes it. We can describe it, and most people live through it! Colic begins at a few days of age, usually shortly after arrival home from the hospital. Baby cries hard, pulls up his legs as if he has severe abdominal pain, and waves his clenched fists wildly. He usually has excess gas, but it is hard to say this is worse than in a noncolicky child. He may eat frequently but does not seem satisfied or content. He sleeps only fitfully and wakens to cry again. Parents walk the floor, feed the baby, diaper him, give him rectal suppositories to help him expel the gas, and nothing really helps. No medicine or formula change seems to be a magic wand.

Suggestions for Overcoming Colic

So what can you do if you have a baby with colic? Here are some suggestions.

Your Diet. Call your doctor about your diet if you are breast-feeding or a formula change if you use formula. Ask him about any possible medication. The only ones we have are sedatives, and he will usually not want to get your baby "hooked" on them.

Cool It. Work very hard to be calm and soothing. We do know that parents' tensions create tension in babies and feed into a vicious cycle. This may mean that you ask relatives and friends to help out so you can get some sleep.

Act (Sort of) Tough. Set your mind to a bit more calloused attitudes. Once you know your child is well, you really can ignore his crying sometimes. Most parents of colicky babies are always doing something to them. If he's going to cry, why not let him cry in peace and quiet? I have a suspicion that

colic would stop sooner with such a practice. Babies can get into a habit of crying over nothing.

Hurrah for Three Months! Count the days until the end of three months. Most colic goes away by then, and you can recover and enjoy him. Rarely it may last until six months, but don't think about that if your child is three weeks and going strong!

A New Discovery. Very recently, researchers have discovered that some babies will stop crying when they hear a tape recording of their own crying. We cannot vouch for this, but it is an intriguing idea. It must be his own crying—not that of any other infant. If you have a tape recorder, you may experiment with recording your baby's crying and playing it back. By gradually reducing the sound level, you may be able to stop your baby's crying!

—From Grace H. Ketterman, M.D., and Herbert L. Ketterman, M.D., *The Complete Book of Baby and Child Care for Christian Parents*. Old Tappan, N.J.: Fleming H. Revell, 1982.

FOR FURTHER READING:

Spock, Benjamin. *Baby and Child Care.* New York: Pocket Books, Inc., 1980.

White, Burton L. *The First Three Years.* Englewood Cliffs, N.J.: Prentice-Hall, Inc., 1975.

COLLEGE

MANY PARENTS, whatever their own schooling, want their children to have a college education. Most authorities feel that if a young person wants to go to college and is able to, he should do so. It is important to decide, however, whether college fits in with his individual needs and aspirations.

In the past 50 years more and more boys and girls have been made aware both of higher educational standards for employment and of increasing opportunities to meet them. Industry, business, and the professions need men and women with better general education as well as more specialized training than ever before. In some fields of business and the arts a college degree by itself is of less value than technical, art, music, or other special schooling.

The general value of a college education in individual development should not, of course, be minimized. Special training undertaken too soon may be narrowing and hampering, not only in the broad sense but also in the furtherance of a special or professional interest. More and more young men and women attend junior college for two years of general education before getting special training for a vocation of their choice.

Sometime before the junior year of high school the young person would do well to talk the matter over with teachers and school advisers and then sit down with the family to think through together the question of whether to go to college. His parents' ideas on the subject, and the reasons for them, need to be expressed although they may not accord with the youngster's own view. Parents can help him to clarify his own ideas of what he hopes to gain from college.

Does he want to go because his best friend is going, because it promises good fun or is the thing to do? Or does he genuinely want a chance to learn more about the world, to mature in his thinking and develop his capacities, and either to find the field of his future work or pursue one already chosen?

Does the family income warrant college? The fees for tuition and board at private colleges vary widely. Athletic, health, and activity fees and books and supplies add to college expense. Provisions for laundry, pocket money, recreation, travel, and of course wardrobe will vary with the individual.

Relatively few young people are entirely barred from a college education because of lack of money, provided their earnings are not needed at home. State universities, and in some cases city colleges, require only low fees from residents. A college may be near enough for the student to live at home, thus saving dormitory expense, or not so far that travel is a sizable item.

All colleges offer scholarships, job assistance, and loans to deserving students. They do not, however, encourage a student to come if he must earn so large a part of his expenses as to leave too little time for college work. Some scholarships are regional, some competitive, and some are awarded outright for academic or other special qualifications, but most require that real financial need be shown. A college may also award scholarships for reasons not related to the applicant as an individual: to bring to the college students from certain geographical areas or those in certain fields of study.

Many boys and girls genuinely want and can benefit from a college experience even though their school averages do not meet scholarship standards. On the other hand, it is unwise for a family to undertake a financial burden that may impose undue sacrifice on the parents or other children.

When a state or other low-fee college is not the answer, young people sometimes find it a good idea to work for a year or so and save for college. The experience of many studying under the G.I. Bill of Rights has shown that the time spent at college may be more profitable for those who come to it with greater maturity. Many young people who must earn their own living entirely, and perhaps contribute to the family as well, have achieved college and even graduate or professional degrees at their own pace, in evening or extension courses.

Most educators believe that the choice of a college should be the student's own. Parents are wise to advise and then let the young person decide. A parent's alma mater may have sentimental appeal but is not necessarily the best choice for son or daughter. When financial considerations permit, the student should be the one to weigh whether to live at home or away, whether to choose a coeducational college, whether a large university or a small college will best suit his individual interests. Some colleges enjoy a special reputation for the quality of the work done in certain subjects—for example, in science, the arts, or languages.

Different institutions serve different needs. Some of the older colleges traditionally prepare students for graduate or professional study. Certain colleges emphasize a combination of vocational with general education within the four, and in some cases five, years required for a bachelor's degree; practical work experience is in some cases part of the curriculum. The large universities offer a spread of opportunities for the individual's choice. Some of the small private colleges, with fewer students and a more individual approach on the part of teachers and administration, are concerned with each student's whole development as well as with his meeting objective academic standards. Tests, interviews, and numerous opportunities for informal acquaintance help teachers to learn the student's individual capacities and guide him toward their realization.

A full list of institutions of higher learning in the United States, information on vocational schools, and a bulletin on scholarships and financial aid can be obtained by writing to the United States Office of Education in Washington, D.C. 20202. High school advisers will help narrow the choice. Each college supplies on request a catalogue listing faculty, facilities, an estimate of expenses, and descriptions of the courses of study; entrance requirements are also given and warrant careful attention. The college admissions office or dean will give further information on request.

When it is feasible, applicants are asked to visit the college for an interview. Some colleges send interviewers to large cities to see applicants by appointment. It is helpful, when possible, to talk to alumni or undergraduates of the college in which one is interested.

Applications for admission, and at the same time for scholarships, are generally made at least a year before high school graduation, and it is wise to apply to several colleges.

Entrance Examinations are scheduled by the College Entrance Examination Board for several dates during the year at high schools and other points accessible to most candidates. Certain colleges require other tests. Notification of acceptance is generally received by May.

Aside from specific courses to meet specific interests, it is safe to say that a worthwhile education can be had at any college or university on the accredited lists of the seven regional accrediting organizations. It is seldom that the college finally chosen can meet every preliminary criterion. Occasionally a student wants to transfer after a year to another college, and if his reasons are sound he should be permitted to make the change. In general, however, students quickly develop loyalty and interest for the college they have chosen.

—From *The New Encyclopedia of Child Care and Guidance*. Garden City, N.Y.: Doubleday & Co., 1968.

FOR FURTHER READING:

Benjamin, Barbara. *The Impossible Community*. Downers Grove, Ill.: Inter-Varsity Press, 1978.

Seabough, Ed. *So You're Going to College*. Nashville: Broadman Press.

COMMUNICATION

Understand Their Needs and Feelings. Homes are coming apart because their members are; that is, everyone moves within his separate orbit and home becomes the filling station where we check the gas and chassis for replenishment and repair, but we don't spend much time there. We are like ships passing in the night, and very little life flows from one member to another.

As a marriage and family counselor, I encounter some very interesting cases. Some time ago a boy was picked up by a police squad car, and the first thing he said to the officer was, "You aren't going to tell my old man, are you?"

He replied, "I'd be interested in hearing why you don't want your father to know."

"I'll tell you," he answered. "He's not interested in me; he's too busy."

When the policeman called the father about his son, the irate response was: "What in the world are you calling me for?"

The case was referred to me, and it was my privilege to lead the father to Jesus Christ. He became a different person, and he became concerned about his family problems.

He came to my office one day and said, "OK, now what do I do? Let's put this thing back together."

"Friend, this is going to take time," I warned him. "You can't decimate the bridges for fifteen years and rebuild them overnight. What does your son like to do?"

He had to think for a long time but finally came up with, "He likes to go fishing."

I said, "OK, why don't you plan a fishing trip with him?"

He went home and in typical adult fashion announced: "Son, next week we are going fishing."

The boy looked him in the eye and said, "You're going fishing. I've already got some things planned."

The father blew his top. He gave the boy a portion of his mind he couldn't really afford to lose, and the son countered very calmly: "A number of years ago I wanted to go fishing, and you were too busy. Now you want to go fishing, and I'm too busy. What's your problem?"

The father came back to my office like a whipped dog to find out what he could do. He was so low he began to realize he must trust God to do what he himself could not. He could appreciate the fact that his family needed to understand each other, not just talk at each other.

Sometimes I encounter a family where communications are so frozen that I get them all in my office and we start a conversation. I only allow one person to talk at a time and after one expresses himself, I ask another member: "Now tell me what you heard him say." And we stick to that until everyone in the group can say back to the satisfaction of the speaker what he said. It's painful and time-consuming, but it's amazing how for the first time they begin to hear what the individual is really saying. Then they have the possibility of communicating.

Some parents thoroughly involve their children in the father's work. I was in a home of a Chicago executive and had wonderful fellowship with the whole family. In the kitchen I saw the walls plastered with the advertising of the executive's company and I said, "Well, you do have a promotional program here."

"No," he replied. "That's my ministry. We pray for that as a family."

That's vastly different from the family that speaks of the factory or the office or what-have-you as the "monster" that is supposedly ruining their lives.

Enjoy Life with Them. In Deuteronomy 6:7 there are two key terms which spell out the nature of parental education. One is teach (that's formal, structured). The other is talk (that's informal, situational). A good parent uses both kinds of instruction, realizing that informal times together are actually teaching situations, for good or ill.

Do you take the time and make the effort to have fun in your home? Do your kids enjoy their home? To me, the poorest representative of Jesus Christ is the Christian who doesn't know what it is to enjoy life. Many of us are so glum we look as if we're on the road to hell instead of the road to heaven. The only people in the world today who are in a position to laugh and rejoice are those who are secure in Jesus Christ!

I can remember in the early days of my family recreation we started out with a tent. My wife was not exactly the tenting type, but it's amazing what you can get used to. Now that my children are pretty well grown, it is interesting to ask what they remember most. The two boys remember when they and I stayed in a pup tent—talk about to-getherness, it was wall-to-wall!

Before we went to bed that night, I looked to the west and said, "Hey, fellows, you'd better dig those trenches deep around the edge; it looks like we may get some rain." Well, we got nine inches of rain in four hours. And we ended up two miles down the creek drying ourselves out under a shelter and talking about the Lord and His protective hand. Back in Dallas, we found out later, 13 people died that night from the storm. You know, that lesson in God's protection

wasn't sermon number 293 in my file; that was real life, and it communicated!

One of the great fun times in our home has been the Friday night "Hendricks Talent Theater." We would put old clothes and junk in a bag and drag them out for an unrehearsed drama. Television was boring beside our production. I came out of those experiences with my ribs sore from laughing. Have you ever examined the atmosphere of your home and asked, "How attractive is it?" You say, "I'm so glad you asked; we just finished decorating it. Man, we've got wall-to-wall carpeting, coordinating drapes."

No, I didn't ask you that—that's your junk. I asked you, "How attractive is your home?" I go into many Christian homes today and frankly I am repelled. They are covered over with legalism. There is what I call a suffocating fog of moralism, and every time the kid moves we're nailing him to the floor. Every time he turns around we're cramming something down his throat. "All right, let's get together; we're going to have Bible study now." Not too long ago, one dear lady blew her cork in the midst of the family worship. She shouted at the kids, "Shut up; you ought to hear what God has to say!" Some of us say shut up so many times, our children are like the kid who was eight years old before he discovered his name was not Shut Up. What are you like to live with?

We had two students at the seminary from a home in California that has sent all its children into Christian work. Sometime ago I was with one of them and I asked: "What do you remember most about your father?"

He thought for a minute and then said, "Two things stand out in my mind, and they're quite contrasting. The first thing is getting up early in the morning for a paper route and seeing my father on his knees praying. That made a profound impression on me. The second thing is his rolling on the floor in laughter with us kids!" What a combination—on the floor in prayer and on the floor in laughter! By the way—what will your children remember you for?

Live Honestly Before Them. The atmosphere of the home inculcates Christian truth more effectively than the words we speak. The attitude of truthfulness, for example, is more caught than taught. A student asked me sometime ago what I thought was the most important trait for my children to gain. I told him I'd have to think about that awhile, and I came to the conclusion that if I had to choose only one characteristic for my children it would be honesty. I want children who are honest to God, to other people, and honest with themselves. And I realized it is most likely to be conveyed through example.

The phone rings. It's for Tom. Tom's wife, Mary, asks, with her hand securely covering the mouthpiece, "Tom, are you here?"

Tom deceitfully replies, "No, I'm not here!"

Now, you can tell your child all you want about honesty, but you are teaching him to be a first-class liar.

I find that young people from Christian homes are rebelling most over phoniness and lack of reality, not from having parents who are not perfect. I find that the parent who is honest enough to admit "Buddy, I goofed: I apologize" comes over like horseradish.

Let's suppose that I were to tell you I sell the best hair restorer lotion in existence—it's guaranteed. You take another look at my bald head and go into hysterics. Should I blame you? But this is what is happening in many Christian homes. Parents are trying to teach truth and love for God when they don't possess them. If the reality of Jesus Christ has not gripped you, you cannot pass it on to your children. I sometimes think we might communicate Christ better to our

children if we were deaf and dumb because we would realize how much we need Jesus Christ helping us.

I have trouble with this, too. I can understand that I need the control of the Holy Spirit to address a crowd, or to witness, or to teach a Bible Class. But who needs the control of the Spirit for playing a game with the kids? Paul says, "Whatsoever you do in word or in deed, do all in the name of the Lord Jesus" (Colossians 3:17). There's only one way we can do that, and that's under the Spirit's control.

When I had the privilege of speaking to 8,000 people at a Sunday School convention in California my students told me they'd be praying for me. I felt it, and the good results were obviously from God. Then I caught a plane back to Dallas. After my wife welcomed me back, she got down to reality and said, "Honey, I've got bad news for you. The sewer has broken."

"Did you call the repairman?"

"Four times. He says it's caved in."

"Well, let's get it fixed."

"He said it will cost $425 to dig a trench out to the alley."

"Not $425! I'll dig it myself."

So I enlisted my son—he's a physical fitness buff—and we went to work. If you've ever dug in Texas gumbo, you know it's like concrete. We got out six or eight feet and discovered the pipe was going in a downward direction! We dug in again, and finally we came to the break—sure enough, it was caved in. We stood there in the trench meditating and suddenly someone flushed the toilet!

Was the Holy Spirit with me in that soggy trench—as He had been when I was speaking to 8,000 people about Christian truth? If not, I don't have much to talk about. If the Holy Spirit doesn't control your temper at the office or your tongue when you're around godless people, then we shouldn't talk about having the fullness of the Spirit. He has to work in the nitty-gritty of life, or He isn't working in us.

Some of my toughest tests come at home—after God has used me in a public ministry to other people. And the more you try to live distinctly for Jesus Christ, the more you will understand what reality is—because you'll face the basic issues and find you can't handle them except in Jesus power.

"Whom the Lord loves, He chastens." Is God disciplining you? He loves you, and He has saved you so you may be conformed to the image of His Son. We remember that even Jesus learned obedience by the things that He suffered. Your children have a great need for adequate models—are you one? Neither am I—that's why the Lord is working on us.

Express Love for Them. Another thing we parents can work on is expressing our love for one another. I hope you're not ashamed to express your love in front of your children. The best thing a father can do for his son is to love his son's mother; the best thing a mother can do for her daughter is to love her daughter's father. In this context the children learn to give and receive love for each other. And you'll never develop a pervert in this kind of environment.

Maybe you get all shook up over your kids fighting. My counsel as a veteran referee is: don't sweat it. Our two girls and two boys had some knock-down, drag-out skirmishes—the Civil War all over again. They are now in their teens and twenties, and I dare anyone to scowl at my daughter when her brother is around. They are so close that tears roll down their faces when they greet one another at an airport, and they couldn't care less what others think of their affection.

How do you develop love? It comes over a period of time and as a product of a pattern.

We can do a lot of things to encourage the expression of love.

Birthdays have always been significant in our home. I remember when my girls were learning to cook, and the younger one decided she would make doughnuts for Bob's birthday. They turned out like rocks—every time you'd swallow a bit you could hear the splash. But Bob ate the last one of those doughnuts, hugged his sister, and said, "Man, what a cook you are, Bev."

Recently I had a thrilling experience in an unexpected place. I was in an opulent home—probably in the $500,000 class. It belongs to a man who told me: "I ended up at the top of my field but at the bottom of life." Then he found Jesus Christ as his Saviour, and he and his wife began studying the Word to find out how the Lord wanted them to train their children.

I went into their gorgeous living room and almost got lost in the living room rug—felt like I might get a severe case of mink rash on the spot. Interior decorators have convinced us that a living room has to have a center of interest, but right in the center of that lovely room was a peanut butter jar holding wilted daisies. I found out that her son had picked them for her on his way home from school, and I said, "I bet they have a lot of meaning to you."

She beamed and said, "That's the most wonderful thing in this room."

My wife taught me that a relationship is far more important than a clean home. We can have a *Better Homes and Gardens* layout and a *Mad* family life. The floor can be quickly cleaned after little feet have muddied it, but bruised relationships are not so easily restored.

Occasionally I have had the assignment of going into an exclusive home in Dallas and telling the parents that the court has decided to put away their child permanently. When these people have no internal resources, they come unglued at the seams. We had one boy in custody who drove the most expensive brand sports car in America and a monthly allowance of $475. He had just about everything except parents who gave of themselves. The stuff you buy never substitutes for you; there is no substitute for a personal, loving relationship in the family.

You know what I have to do? People call me on the phone. "Prof, will you come over and preach to us?"

"No, I'm awfully sorry, I won't."

Well, I've learned to say, "I'm otherwise engaged," which, being interpreted, means, "I'm going to stay home."

A few years ago I used to be a little more direct. Somebody would call up and say, "Would you come over and preach for us?"

"No, I'm awfully sorry, I can't come that night."

"How come?"

"I'm going to stay home and play with my kids."

"You mean you're not coming to preach to us?"

"No, I'm not coming to preach to you."

Somebody says, "Oh, that's how liberalism gets started in the seminary." And if I listen to that kind of garbage I could lose my whole family in the process. We must not allow anybody to control our lives except the Spirit of God, and there is no conflict between duty and Christian experience. Your call to be a parent is not in conflict with your call to be a Christian. If it is, you should have remained a celibate!

I don't know what my kids will remember me for. I hope they will be able to remember me as a father who loved them and enjoyed them. I believe the greatest challenge confronting Christian fathers today is to become articulate concerning our faith so we can communicate it to our children. Our homes should be laboratories for instructing our children formally and informally. Homes should be training grounds for developing habit patterns that serve Jesus Christ. And then we'll avoid the tragedy described in Judges 2:10—a generation arose which knew not the Lord.

—From Howard G. Hendricks, *Say It With Love*. Wheaton, Ill.: Victor Books, 1972.

FOR FURTHER READING:

Balswick, Jack. *Why I Can't Say I Love You*. Waco, Tex.: Word Books, 1978.

Howard, J. Grant. *The Trauma of Transparency: A Biblical Approach to Interpersonal Communication*. Portland: Multnomah Press, 1979.

Iversen, Rachel. *Talking Together with Young Children*. Ventura, Calif.: Regal Books, 1978.

Narramore, Clyde M. *How to Build Bridges to Other People*. Grand Rapids: Zondervan Publishing House.

Webber, Robert E. *God Still Speaks*. Nashville: Thomas Nelson, Inc., 1980.

CONFLICT

A CONFLICT is said to exist when a person entertains two desires that apparently cannot be reconciled. When one of the desires is very much stronger than the other, the conflict is usually resolved by the choice of the more powerful one. It is when the opposing drives are relatively equal in strength and importance that the choice becomes most difficult and the conflict most painful.

Conflicts both serious and trivial occur all through life. A toddler who is presented with a new rubber ball has to decide whether to play with it now or to put it aside and continue with his favorite occupation—building with blocks. A school child may earnestly wish to earn high marks by doing his homework, and at the same time want to go out and play with his friends after school.

There are other, more deep-seated conflicts that may beset children. A child of parents who are given to frequent quarrels or who are separated, still wants to love and be loved by both mother and father. Yet if his mother makes him feel that by loving his father he will lose some of her love and approval, he is likely to feel torn in his loyalties. In such a situation, the child will probably be unable to resolve the conflict, particularly because he is not consciously aware of what is troubling him.

The resolution of conflicts is the heart of healthy growth. For it is by making choices and deciding upon courses of action that the youngster shapes his life pattern, and his capacity for making wise decisions will determine the degree of his maturity.

—From *The New Encyclopedia of Child Care and Guidance.* Garden City, N.Y.: Doubleday & Co., 1968.

FOR FURTHER READING:

Augsburger, David. *Caring Enough to Confront.* Ventura, Calif.: Regal Books, 1980.

Ahlem, Lloyd H. *How to Cope: With Conflict, Crisis, and Change.* Ventura, Calif.: Regal Books, 1978.

Hatfield, Mark O. *Conflict and Conscience.* Waco, Tex.: Word Books, 1971.

Scanzoni, John. *Love and Negotiate: Creative Conflict in Marriage.* Waco, Tex.: Word Books, 1979.

Self, William L. *Bridging the Generation Gap.* Nashville: Broadman Press, 1971.

COUNSELING

HEALTHY MARRIAGE has been described as "at once the most demanding and the most potentially rewarding" of all human relationships. As husband and wife, two adults merge their separate lives into an intimate and complex union which the Bible describes as good and honorable (Proverbs 18:22; Hebrews 13:3).

Mergers, however, are not always smooth. Often there are disagreement, distrust and misunderstanding before the two parties begin to function as a unit. The merger of two people in marriage can be likened to the coming together of two great rivers. For many miles the waters share the same riverbed, but only slowly is there a mixture so that the two become one. In most marriages this is a long, slow process. Some never achieve a mutually satisfying union, and for others the merger comes only when a counselor is present to guide.

The Need for Marriage Counseling. As you read these words, hundreds of thousands of marriages—many probably in your own community—are sick and dying. Couples who went to the altar with high hopes and eager expectations have seen their marriages degenerate into tired friendship or a long drawn-out war. The reasons for this marital disharmony are both numerous and complex, but some of the more common include the following:

Lack of Communication. Marriage counselors consistently report that couples who aren't getting along are often unable to communicate. Sometimes there is open quarreling, sometimes sullen silence, but always there is inability to honestly share feelings and ideas about significant issues. . . . I met with a young couple who were on the verge of divorce. When they entered my office together, neither said much but both showed a lot of nonverbal hostility, mostly in the form of contemptuous glances at each other. Since we weren't getting far with them both in the room, I separated them and talked with each alone. When the spouse was absent, each spoke freely and gave the same message: "We can't talk about anything. All we do is shout and scream or give each other the silent treatment." To improve communication the partners must learn to transmit clear messages and to listen carefully. By patiently watching a couple as they interact, the counselor can often see where communication is breaking down; but to improve future interaction is a hefty assignment, especially when the couple doesn't particularly want to improve their communication.

Immaturity. Very often couples begin marriage with unrealistically high expectations, only to be disappointed and disenchanted when the relationship does not turn out as they had hoped. This realization can be cause for working harder at the marriage and making it a mutually satisfying experience. Planning new experiences together, having a cause for living, making opportunities for intimacy, ritualizing romantic occasions, and continuing to spend time interacting with each other are ways that have been suggested for maintaining the relationship.

For many couples, however, the disenchantment does not lead to increased efforts; instead, it encourages immature behavior that puts further strain on the marriage. Unreasonable demands, lack of consideration for the spouse's feelings, blaming the other for one's own faults, impulsive behavior, irresponsibility, intemperance, increased rigidity in one's attitudes, and an overdependency on the parents are all indications of immaturity. Sometimes a person will develop an overdependence on the hoped-for intervention of God and refuse to work at the realities of the problems which exist. All of these attitudes take time to overcome. People don't mature in a day, and even with the understanding guidance of a counselor, a marriage built on immaturity will have a long slow road to improvement.

Failure to Take Marriage Seriously. Several months ago an advertisement appeared in a psychological journal showing a young bride in her wedding dress. Underneath was the caption: ". . . till divorce do us part." It hasn't quite come to this yet, the advertisement proclaimed, "but almost as many marriages are ended by divorce as by death."

According to the Bible, marriage is a lifelong institution, but many people today fail to accept this view. They see marriage as an arrangement of convenience which lasts "for the forseeable future" and to be terminated at will by either or both of the parties involved. Even among married couples there may be many who feel no responsibility to remain faithful to their spouse. In one recent survey, for example, over 20,000 readers of *Psychology Today* magazine (most of whom are over 30 and well educated) answered questions about marriage and sex. Eighty percent of the respondents thought that extramarital sex was acceptable, and 40 percent of the men and 36 percent of the women had engaged in this behavior. With this loose view of the sanctity of sex, and with divorce so widely accepted and so easily attained, there is less willingness for couples to work at a marriage and to insure its growth and survival. If things aren't going well, one can always get a divorce and find somebody better.

Perhaps this attitude has developed because Western man has such a distorted view of love. Ask any couple why they plan to get married and the most common response is: "Because we are in love." If they later decide to get a divorce, one of the stated reasons is likely to be: "We don't love each other anymore." The Scriptures instruct husbands to love their wives (Ephesians 5:25) and wives to love their husbands (Titus 2:4), but what does this mean? Popular ballads, poems and movies glorify love but the term is used so broadly that it is almost meaningless.

In regard to the marital relationship, the

Bible gives two examples of what love should be like: First, husbands should love their wives as Christ loved the church (Ephesians 5:25–27). The love of Christ is unselfish, and without strings attached. As described in 1 Corinthians 13, Christian love is patient, kind, and free of jealousy, envy, boasting, pride, grudges, rudeness or self-glorification. It is a giving relationship which involves loyalty and concern for the object of one's love. This kind of love cannot be "turned on" at will, nor is it something we "fall into or out of." Love is a growing relationship which, for Christians, is an outward expression of the love of Christ in a life. Marital love is also to be similar to self-love. Men should love their wives, the Scriptures say, as they love themselves (Ephesians 5:28–33). This can hardly be consistent with the casual way in which some people view the marriage bond.

Unhealthy Need Fulfillment. In any successful marriage, the participants will have certain needs fulfilled. The need for love, security, respect, acceptance, safety, and sexual fulfillment in marriage, for example, is so important, that one counselor has defined a happy marriage as "one in which there is a relatively high degree of mutual need satisfaction," and an unhappy marriage as one with much need frustration. Sometimes marriages experience difficulty because one or both of the partners have needs that are not being met. In such cases, communication of the lack of fulfillment is important, and the partners can work—perhaps with the help of a counselor—to make the relationship more mutually need-satisfying.

In some marriages this is difficult to accomplish, especially if the normal needs are exaggerated to an excessive degree. When a person has an insatiable need to feel secure and be assured of acceptance; an intense desire to cling or to be dependent on someone else; a strong need to dominate, to hurt or to

stand aloof; a perpetual urge for sex; or some similar intense desire, we conclude that his needs are neurotic and that the marriage is unhealthy. Improvement in such marriages is unlikely unless there is long-term counseling accompanied by patience and understanding on the part of the mate.

The Goals of Marriage Counseling. In his contacts with married couples, the church leader can help in two important ways: he can guide in the building and improving of a marriage, and he can counsel with those who are having marital conflicts. Briefly stated, these are the two basic goals of marriage counseling. In both cases, the counselor is attempting to help the partners improve their relationships with each other and with God.

These two broad goals can be subdivided into more specific aims. The counselor should try, during the course of his counseling to:

—reopen lines of communication between the couple and to encourage the expression of feelings.

—encourage understanding of each person's own attitudes, goals, needs and views of marriage as well as those of one's spouse.

—help couples accept each other and stop trying to reform and transform each other.

—help the couple work together at translating their new understanding and acceptance into appropriate action so that the relationship is improved.

—interrupt the vicious cycle of mutual retaliation.

—be less demanding and more responsible in relating to each other.

—encourage commitment to Christ and a familiarity with the biblical guidelines for marital stability.

Family Counseling. We live in a period when the family is changing drastically. No longer the tightly knit unit that it once was, the family is, in the opinion of some, becoming less and less important in our culture. While this analysis may be true in many respects, the family still fulfills some unique and crucial roles in Western society. It is the accepted channel for childbirth; it provides shelter and protection; it educates, especially in the early years; it largely determines one's status in life; it gives religious instruction and determines whether or not a child will be in contact with the church; it guides in recreational activities; and it provides the love and affection which are necessary for survival and development. Families differ in the efficiency with which they do all of this, and they differ in the ability of the members to get along with one another. But in spite of its problems and changes, the family is still a core part of the society.

The many problems of the modern family have been summarized and analyzed in a number of books and articles. The birth of a deformed or unwanted child, the delinquency of a teenager, the demands of an aging parent, the death of a loved one, the "empty nest" when the last child gets married, the serious illness of a family member, the loss of family income—these and other events put stress on the family and demand some kind of readjustment. This becomes especially difficult when family members are unable to communicate, cannot agree on values, or lack respect for one another.

To deal with problems such as these, counselors traditionally worked with individual family members. Over the years, however, it became more and more apparent that something more was needed because the value of individual counseling was often undermined when the counselee went back into the turmoil of a family in conflict. To meet this problem, some counselors began to work with the family as a group. In counseling, the family members (of school age and above) meet together to discuss their mutual problems, to increase mutual understanding, and to learn how to improve communication.

The church leader may find himself involved in a simple form of family counseling whenever he makes a pastoral call. In more formal counseling the family might come to the church to meet together with the counselor. In this situation it is sometimes good to talk briefly with the parents alone, and briefly with the children alone, but most of the time should be spent with the whole family meeting together. Each family member should be given the opportunity to talk about the family problems from his perspective. At first this is likely to be threatening to the participants, but as the counselor encourages openness and is himself a model of good communication, the discussion becomes freer. As with all pastoral counseling, the group leader may suggest that the family should consider one or two relevant Bible passages, and there is value in encouraging prayer together.

Summary. In a study conducted several years ago, college men and women were asked what they expected would bring the greatest satisfaction in life. Sixty percent of the men and 87 percent of the women replied, "Family relations." Apparently most young people in our society look forward to marriage and a family of their own, although many are later disappointed. The problems of marriage lead one out of three couples to get a divorce, and numerous others live together in frustration and family misery.

In his counseling, the church leader will likely spend more time dealing with marriage and family problems than with any other issue. Before marriage, couples should be guided in their preparation for life together. After the wedding, newlyweds can be helped in their adjustments to marriage and subsequent parenthood. When problems arise, the church leader can work to heal broken relationships and stimulate better communication between the husband, wife and other members of the family. All of this takes time, effort and skill, but the end result can be family units which function smoothly and are committed to following and serving Jesus Christ.

—From Gary Collins, *Effective Counseling*. Carol Stream, Ill.: Creation House, 1972.

FOR FURTHER READING:

Adams, Jay E. *The Big Umbrella*. Grand Rapids: Baker Book House, 1976.

Collins, Gary R. *Christian Counseling*. Waco, Tex.: Word Books, 1980.

Crabb, Lawrence J. *Effective Biblical Counseling*. Grand Rapids: Zondervan Publishing House, 1977.

Solomon, Charles R. *Counseling with the Mind of Christ*. Old Tappan, N.J.: Fleming H. Revell Co., 1977.

Skoglund, Elizabeth. *You Can Be Your Own Child's Counselor*. Ventura, Calif.: Regal Books, 1978.

CRAWLING

WHEN THEY ARE ABOUT eight months to a year old babies begin to "travel." One hitches along on his buttocks, another crawls on hands and knees, a third slithers backward, another scuttles about on all fours. As with any other step in their growth and development, some babies start earlier, some later.

All growing things need space, and the creeper has special need for it. He needs freedom to practice his new achievement, to develop muscles coming into use. He needs it to develop mentally, too, for his creeping ventures give wider range and stimulus to his curiosity. He may send a ball some distance across a room, then creep intently after it— possibly sideways. This is his sole goal—but when he nears it, he can be completely taken up with a minute piece of lint lying nearby. Everything in the new world that opens up because he can move about is subject to scrutiny and consideration.

A new phase for the baby always means a new phase for his mother and father. Besides being one of delight and humor, this is also a "putting things out of reach" period for parents. Until the baby begins to pull himself up, such precautions usually apply only to things on floor level: small objects that he may pick up and decide to test for taste; electrical outlets that must be covered; tippy chairs or floor lamps that may be pulled over easily. Precautionary measures may take a few minutes' careful survey and labor, but there is reward in the baby's obvious glee over space to roam in. Playpens and fenced-off areas are helpful during those times when no one can watch over the baby.

Overalls are called for now to protect small overworked knees and because creeping is also the beginning of getting zestfully dirty. The happiest solution for parent and child is to let the grime accumulate until bedtime. There's no need for overconcern, either, about the dirty fingers that the baby puts in his mouth. By the time he is old enough to creep he has developed a good deal of resistance to germs.

—From *The New Encyclopedia of Child Care and Guidance*. Garden City, N.Y.: Doubleday & Co., 1968.

CREATIVITY

ALONG WITH THE WORD *love*, *creativity* is one of the most overused words of our day. Everything's coming up creative—especially high-priced toys. It's the catchword on a half dozen psychologies and a baker's dozen of religious innovations. I am not all that wild about creativity if all it means is doing something different every day. But I am deeply interested in the native creativity of children—a creativity that has brightened my life for the past ten years.

Human creativity—the kind of creativity that is needed desperately now in all of the arts and sciences and technologies—is finding new ways of putting existing components together to make a whole. That's all. The child who turns the laundry basket upside down over himself (preferably when it is empty) and becomes a fearsome lion in the zoo is being creative. He has seen another way of composing the components to make a new configuration. The child who takes a cardboard box and with flow pen, glue, and imagination converts it into a car or a stove or a television set is being creative. The child who sits at a typewriter and composes a letter to his grandmother is being creative.

Creativity is something which develops through a number of phases as the preschool child grows. (All of the phases I delineate are overlapping, of course, with gradual shading into the next phase. And the ages I suggest are only rough estimates based on my own observations.)

From age six months to one year, the child's creativity is mostly seen in manipulating his own body or the immediate things he uses: playing with his hands; finding new ways to pull himself to a stand; learning to retrieve his bottle. From one to three years, creativity takes two main forms: creative use of words to manipulate the environment, and imaginative play. Children's early free-art forms reach their peak during the fourth year. Then a sense of representationalism sets in—a desire to make the picture conform to the thing—and the free drawing of happy faces or brightly colored circles gives way to more difficult and less frequently successful attempts to draw representationally.

At about age five, children become interested in crafting things: making candles, cookies, wall hangings. You name it, they'll make it. Their interest switches from art for art's sake to craft for function's sake. This tendency grows with the child. At about six years of age, the compulsion to make things that are real, working, and functional seems to reach its early peak. The pleasure Mitchell got one day from cutting a piece of plywood to a size I needed for fixing a magazine rack was greater than the pleasure he now gets out of drawing a picture. He wants what he is making to be functional—a difficult desire to bring to realization in our technological era.

The parental role in the face of this natural outpouring of childhood creativity is fourfold: (1) to *recognize* developing creative abilities; (2) to *stimulate* creativity; (3) to *facilitate* the child's imaginative projects; and (4) to *respond* to the child's products.

1. Recognize developing creative abilities.
"Oh, my, you have such talented children," one mother sighs to another.

"What a talented family," another comments.

And in Christian circles, we have become so sensitive about the words *gifts* and *talents* that we are not sure whether we should be complimented or reproached. The idea has been communicated that "gifts" given by the Holy Spirit are entirely different from native abilities or learned skills because they are entirely supernatural. However, a close study of the Word of God reveals that this is not necessarily so. And understanding how gifts and talents relate to each other is important if we are to place a value on ascertaining our children's talents and giving opportunities for their development.

A case study to consider is the young man Timothy. Paul speaks to Timothy about the responsible use of a gift: ". . . kindle afresh the gift of God which is in you through the laying on of my hands" (2 Timothy 1:6 NAS). But, before Paul ever laid eyes, let alone hands, on Timothy, there was considerable preparation. In 2 Timothy 1:5, we find that the faith had been lived out before him by his mother and his grandmother. In 2 Timothy 3:14, 15, we learn that the Word of God had been carefully and soundly taught to him. In Acts 16:1, 2, we find that he was using this background plus native leadership ability to build a sound reputation for Christian living and leadership among the brethren. So, when Paul laid his hands on Timothy and the Holy Spirit endowed him with a special gift for the ministry, he was confirming and empowering a set of natural abilities and carefully taught behaviors.

Or, if you wish, look at Paul. We learn that God separated Paul to Himself from birth (Galatians 1:15). When Ananias laid hands on Paul to ordain him for the service to which God had set him apart, the zeal was already there (Acts 9:17). The training in Old Testament Scriptures was already there. The native leadership ability was already there. The education and training was already there. And God, by His Holy Spirit, took hold of this many-talented man and filled him, and made all that knowledge and zeal and training and ability a gift to His Body, the Church.

Doesn't this make the childhood years exciting and interesting? Instead of waiting passively with the idea that God will someday drop a gift on your children, you recognize that God had His hand on each child from before birth. Genes and chromosomes are just as surely counted as the hairs of the head. Your child is equipped with the potential necessary for his part in God's program.

How, practically, do we discover our children's abilities? And how do we help prepare them for use in God's work?

(a) Watch your children. There is no substitute for really knowing your children. What activities do they most often choose to do, given a free choice? A two-year-old I know already loves to take apart and put together Lego blocks. She has an interest in building and in putting things together, which suggests a mechanical bent. It will be interesting to watch it develop. "Having then gifts differing . . ." is an apparent condition even when children are very young (Romans 12:6 KJV). It takes time spent really seeing your children. It takes supportive encouragement together with noncontrolling interest in their activities to really discover what they like to do.

(b) Be supportive of all natural abilities. Do not be more supportive of artistic bents than of mechanical ones; more interested in a flair for math than a flair for poetry. Give all abilities your enthusiastic encouragement. Don't narrow the channel on your child. If he shows a flair in some area, encourage it. But do not act as though that is the only ability the child has. Encourage breadth of development. Your children may well be ten-talent people if you give them a chance to discover all of their abilities. Don't assume that your talents will be your children's—or insist that they should be. But be aware of hereditary possibilities and cultivate interests as your children show them.

(c) Accept development and change. Don't be surprised if a natural artistic flair seems to dry up. Recognize that if there is strong artistic talent it will flourish again. Keep opening doors in as many directions as you can, at the same time giving thorough training in at least one area of ability for several years.

(d) Don't wait until you see a big talent to offer training. Many parents say, "Well, we'll let Johnny start piano lessons, and if he shows a talent, we'll let him keep at it." That is really not good enough. Johnny may not mature into his ability for several years. Or he may not have a great deal of natural ability, but with training may gain a very worthwhile skill as well as the discipline of practice. When we started Geoffrey on piano lessons at age five, we wondered if perhaps he was tone deaf. He had never sung the songs at Sunday school. In fact, he seemed quite disinterested in vocal music. But music lessons were available, and we felt he would enjoy a music ability in his adult years. Now, to our great delight and considerable surprise, Geoffrey is displaying a talent and promise in music that is exciting.

2. Stimulate. In the early stages, the best stimulation to creativity is to enter into imaginative play with children; to help them unlock their world with words; to praise their innovative play or art. Supplying toys and helping the child see or create in new ways may be important, but need not be expensive. Looking at and reading books together and going for walks help to stimulate the child to *see*—and that is absolutely basic to creativity. "Originality," said Woodrow Wilson, "is simply a fresh pair of eyes." Those eyes the child has; you can help him to see in new ways. Suggesting activities will be a part of your parental role as stimulator.

The greatest stimulus of all will be parents who value "doing" and "being" above "having." Such a parental attitude will be reflected in creative children.

3. Facilitate. You facilitate your child's creativity by following up the child's choice of activity and making it possible. You may have to say, "We don't have those materials, but what we can substitute is. . . ." You may have to say, "That would need too much help and I'm busy this morning, but you do something else and we'll work on that

project this afternoon." You should encourage children to projects which need a minimum of your supervision and help. Complicated crafts which require endless adult intervention are not for preschoolers. Avoid them. Children's sense of self-worth is enhanced by the "I can do it myself" feeling.

You will facilitate creativity by supplying materials and a work space suitable to the child's projects. You may have to take a few minutes to help the child round up essential materials or decide upon satisfactory substitutes—another creative activity—but time spent in finding the crayons and glue and paper is repaid in a period of meaningful activity.

Facilitating includes developing an attitude of tolerance toward the "mess" which goes with children's doings. I recall a housekeeper who worked for me for two days while I substitute taught. I came home to find the house shining and the children neat and tidy. I thought she was a dream come true—until my four-year-old told me how the day had gone. "After lunch, she put away all our toys and crayons and things and made us watch TV. She wouldn't let me have scissors or anything! She said, 'That would make a mess.' " Such an attitude was foreign to our kids who were allowed to use the kitchen or living room for their many projects with only two conditions. One was that they cleaned up one activity before embarking on another. The other was that, when the day's end came, they helped with a complete pickup.

Facilitating may also include removing some distractions: turning off the TV, sending neighbor kids home, putting baby in bed or playpen. And, of course, as the child matures, facilitating means taking the time to teach the necessary skills for increasingly interesting creative design.

While you go about your work, you may have to stop to help a child with a problem in his project, to answer a question, to spell a word (or a dozen of them), to untangle a knotted thread. All are worth your time. Your interest and time will bear fruit in your child's creative flowering.

4. Respond. The child brings you the finished project. It doesn't resemble the item shown in the craft book. Be glad. Glue is dripping from the sheet. Wipe it up quickly. But note the boldness, the freshness of color, or just a sincerity of effort—well worth your encouragement and praise!

Respond with genuine interest: "How did you make the tree look so old?" With questions concerning content: "Why does the little girl look so sad?" With praise, always: "Your picture is lovely," or "That was a hard project and you felt like quitting. But don't you feel good now that it's done?" Respond with encouragement. "That's so nice that I think you should do another one." Respond with display: "Let's hang this picture right here where our friends can see it, too." Respond with use: "I like that card so much I'm going to send it to Grandma for her birthday." Respond with delight: "I would never have seen it that way. What an interesting picture."

Do not hold up unreasonable standards. Judge your child's work as a child's work, and don't let perfectionism become the stumbling block to his growth. Encourage sincerity, effort, originality, beauty, or interest.

Your response to your child's efforts will be the greatest stimulus you could possibly make to more creative effort on his part. Your enthusiasm builds your child's confidence in his own creative work. Whether or not your child becomes an artist or a writer or a poet is beside the point. We need more creative housewives and more creative bank managers. We need, desperately, people who can see new ways of approaching old and difficult problems in society as a whole. We need creative Christians. God has planted the creative potential within our children. It is our duty—and what a joyous one—to let that creativity flourish in our homes.

—From Maxine Hancock, *People in Process.* Old Tappan, N.J.: Fleming H. Revell Co., 1978.

FOR FURTHER READING:

Campbell, David P. *Take the Road to Creativity and Get Off Your Dead End.* Allen, Tex.: Argus Communications, 1977.

Ezell, Suzanne and Mancil. *Being Creative.* Nashville: Broadman Press.

Howe, Reuel L. *Creative Years.* New York: Seabury Press.

Larrick, Nancy. *A Parent's Guide to Children's Education.* New York: Trident Press, 1963.

CRISIS

AS WE GO THROUGH LIFE, all of us at times encounter crises. The death of a loved one, the birth of a deformed child, the breakdown in a marriage, the failure to be accepted into college, the occurrence of an automobile accident—all these are among those events of life that shake us and can make us feel threatened, anxious, confused, and depressed.

Stated somewhat formally, a crisis is any event or series of circumstances which threatens a person's well-being and interferes with his routine of daily living.

Most of us move along from day to day, meeting the problems and challenges of life in a more or less efficient manner. Periodically, however, a situation arises which is so novel and threatening that our usual ways of handling problems no longer work. Suddenly we are forced to rely on new and untried methods to deal with the tension that has come into our lives.

In the past people usually turned to relatives on such occasions, seeking their advice and accepting their help and sympathy. In many parts of the world this still takes place, but in North America things are different. We are a mobile people who move frequently and are often far away from family members who could give the greatest support in times of crisis. In the absence of relatives, therefore, we turn to neighbors, friends, fellow church members, and pastors. These are the people who are on the scene at the moment of crisis and are best able to help.

The Major Kinds of Crises

Crises can be divided into two broad categories. Developmental crises are those which occur at predicted times as we journey through life. Facing the first day in school, coping with adolescence, adjusting to marriage, dealing with the insecurities of middle age, adapting to retirement—all of these are crisis situations which require extra effort on the part of an individual and his family. Such crises may be very severe, but they usually are predictable in advance and are resolved as the individual learns to adjust to a new stage in life.

Accidental crises, as the name implies, are much less predictable, and as a result they often hit with greater force. A sudden loss of status or possessions, the traffic death of a loved one, the unexpected ending of an engagement, the sudden loss of a job—any of these can put extreme demands on an individual and create confusion as he ponders what to do next.

Reacting to Crises. Usually the person under crisis turns first to his habitual ways of dealing with problems. Very soon, however, he discovers that the old coping devices don't work. The initial tension is still there, but in addition the person feels a sense of frustration and confusion because of his inability to cope. At this point all of one's inner resources are mobilized. The person tries a number of trial-and-error methods to deal with the problem, he draws on his reserves of physical strength, he racks his brain to think of creative new ways for dealing with the situation, and he learns to accept or make the best of circumstances which cannot be changed. If all of this fails and the problem continues, the person eventually collapses, either physically or mentally or both. Very often this is what happens in a so-called nervous breakdown. There are no more resources or stamina left for coping with the stress. The person gives up exhausted, withdraws into a world of unreality, or persists irrationally in some behavior which may deny the problem but does nothing to solve it.

The Uniqueness of Each Crisis. Every crisis situation is unique. The circumstances, personalities, and psychological makeup of the people involved; one's past experience (or lack of it) in handling crises; the availability of others who can help—all of these influence what happens in a given crisis situation. It is difficult to predict what any individual, including ourselves, might do in a crisis. Some people collapse almost immediately, while others discover that they have tremendous inner reserves which enable them to cope with even prolonged periods of intense crisis.

Some characteristics, however, seem to be very common. There is, for example, *anxiety,* which sometimes causes the person to make a poor judgment, which then adds to the problems. Often there is a sense of *helplessness.* The person doesn't know what to do and often feels ashamed because he cannot be more self-reliant. A *dependence on others* is often inevitable, but this can also create problems. Sometimes the person feels guilty for being so dependent, frustrated with his inability to make decisions, and angry because other people are running his life. This all contributes to a *loss of self-esteem* because the person feels vulnerable and not in control. *Anger* over the whole situation is a common emotion which is sometimes hidden but often directed to others—including the people who are trying to help. In his frustration the person in a crisis doesn't know who to be mad at, so he lashes out against those who are closest and most likely to stick with him in spite of the anger. Sometimes there is anger at God followed by feeling of guilt. Often there is also a *decreasing efficiency* in our daily behavior. Ruminating on the problem, worrying about what will happen next, questioning why it happened in the first place—these all take time, energy, and attention which normally would be directed to other activities.

Coping in a Crisis. In many respects a crisis is more than an increase in tension or an upset in our daily pattern of living. A crisis represents a turning point which has a bearing on one's future adjustment and mental health. If we are able to cope with the crisis, to adapt to our new circumstances, or to find efficient ways for solving the crisis problem, then we have developed a greater self-confidence and experience, which will help us deal more effectively with future crises. If, on the other hand, a person is unable to cope, there are feelings of failure or incompetence which spill over the next crisis and make it even harder to adapt in the future.

According to one psychiatrist, it is common in crises for a person to both mobilize his own inner resources and to seek help from the people around him. Others see these signs of increasing tension and are stimulated to come to the distressed person's assistance. Professional counselors can help here, but the best helpers are those whom the person in crisis already knows, respects, and loves. The closer we are to the person in crisis—the more we are aware of the situation—the more likely we are to be called on and the easier it is for us to intervene on our own initiative. It is clear, therefore, that the family and the church are of crucial importance in crisis counseling. How an individual relates to those around him will determine to a considerable degree how successful he will be in finding a solution which, in turn, will promote or hamper his future mental health. . . .

When sickness, death in the family, financial losses, marital strife, and other crises come along, the counselor's goal is to help the person to avoid unhealthy behaviors, feelings, or thoughts and to focus instead on that which is healthy and constructive.

To do this the crisis counselor must be geographically near the person in crisis (it is difficult to help someone across the country), immediately available (even if this means in the middle of the night), mobile (so that we can go to the person in need, especially when he or she cannot come to us), and flexible in counseling methods. Professional counselors who maintain rigid office hours often fail to meet these criteria and are thus less effective in crisis situations than are family members, friends, neighbors, church members, and ministers. The latter can be especially helpful in times of crisis because they symbolize hope and theological stability to a person in the midst of discouragement and great uncertainty.

Crisis Intervention. There can be no standard formula or cookbook approach for helping a person in crisis. There are some things, however, which can be done in almost every case.

Make Contact

It is difficult to be very effective in crisis counseling if the helper is half a country (or even half a block) away from the helpee. As Christians we believe that we can intervene from afar through prayer, and this must not be overlooked, but whenever possible we should also show personal concern by our presence, warmth, and willingness to listen. The sooner we can be there, the more likely we are to help.

Reduce Anxiety

Contrary to some popular beliefs, this is not done by encouraging the helper to think about something else. To take an extreme example, if at a funeral home we find ourselves talking to a surviving mate about baseball or the stock market, we may be avoiding the reality of death in order to reduce our own anxiety. But this doesn't work very well with people who are in crises. They often want to talk about the situation, describe what happened, think back to happier times before the crisis, and feel free to express their emotions of sadness, grief, remorse, or anger.

At such times the helper can demonstrate calmness, concern, and acceptance. He can bring the comfort of the Scriptures and pray with the helpee, making sure, however, that these are not gimmicks to keep everyone from talking about the hurt and expressing feelings.

If the helper doesn't know much about the situation, he or she will want to find out, if possible, when the crisis started and what went on before it began. In so doing we can sometimes spot the source of the trouble and begin to deal with it. If a person says, for example, "Everything was going great for me until I started college," we might be able to assume that there is something in the college setting that is causing the crisis symptoms.

Sometimes anxiety-reduction will involve bearing the brunt of the helpee's anger, helping him to see his problem, commending him for steps already taken to face the crisis, and helping him to see that all is not hopeless. This, of course, can backfire if done improperly. Romans 8:28, for example, can be stated in a glib fashion which angers the helpee, especially if he feels that the verse-quoter has not taken the time to really understand the situation.

When several people are involved in a crisis, it helps if you can deal with the most anxious person first and send away the curious onlookers. Several years ago our family saw a little boy get hit by a car. As my wife, who is a nurse, applied first aid and talked calmly to the distressed mother, an older brother appeared on the scene. In an agitated manner he yelled, "Mommy, is Jimmy going to die?" Immediately the whole scene got tense until my wife assured the older brother that Jimmy would probably be okay and then suggested that the mother might want a coat or sweater over her shoulders as she rode in the ambulance. The older brother ran off to get the sweater and the situation calmed down considerably.

Focus on the Issues

In the midst of a crisis it is easy to see a mass of issues all of which seem to be overwhelming. The helper can do several things at this point. First, he or she can help the person in crisis to explore the present situation by describing his feelings, thoughts, and plans (if he has any), his view of the events that have taken place, and his efforts to solve the problem. This is a process of sorting out the problems one at a time, finding out what is threatening and seeing what has been done or might be done about the situation.

At some time there needs to be a narrowing down of what the real problems are, an inventory of the person's resources (what money, ability, people, and opportunities are available), a listing of the different alternatives that the person has before him, and an evaluation of each of these. If the helpee has not raised all of the alternatives, raise a few yourself. For each alternative, try to decide with the helpee what is feasible, what will really help with the problem, and what is easiest to accomplish.

I visited the tornado area of a city in which a number of homes had been damaged. One house was completely destroyed except for one wall, which was still standing. Across the wallpaper, in bold black letters, someone had written "The Richardsons will build again!" Following the crisis their alternative had been decided!

Remember that people in crises are often very suggestible, so we must be careful not to push for our own solutions. We must also help people to be realistic and practical. The last thing a person in crisis needs is to add failure to his other problems. Indeed, the fear of further failure is what immobilizes many people in times of crisis, and they need help and encouragement in deciding to act.

In helping with a crisis the helper can do much to mobilize church or community aid. Massive prayer support can not only sustain a person through a crisis, but it is also an encouraging demonstration that people really care. To this there sometimes can be added the more tangible help about which James writes: "If a brother or sister is without clothing and in need of daily food, and one of

you says to them, 'Go in peace, be warmed and be filled,' and yet you do not give them what is necessary for their body, what use is that?" (James 2:15, 16). Faith in Jesus Christ, and commitment to Him, should at times manifest itself by helping people in a tangible way, with money, supplies, babysitting, helping around the house, or other down-to-earth assistance.

Encourage Action

Sometimes, with or without help, a person will decide on some course of action but will then be afraid to move ahead with the plan. Here is where a helper can encourage the helpee to acquire skills, if these are needed, and to stick with him as he takes action. One must be careful not to be doing things for the helpee all the time. It is easy for all of us to sit back, to "let somebody else do it," and then to complain about the quality of the service. The person in crisis needs to be helped to help himself. He needs to evaluate his actions with the counselor's help and, if necessary, to come up with different or better alternatives when an earlier plan is unsuccessful.

All of this assumes, of course, that the helper and helpee are the only ones involved in meeting the crisis situation. We should remember, however, that most crises begin with a series of environmental events or circumstances. Very often the most effective way to take action in a crisis is to change the environment. To help the counselee get another job, to mobilize the community to help rebuild a house or provide for medical expenses, to counsel with relatives or friends who may have been causing much of the stress in the first place—these are all ways in which we can reduce the force of the crisis by making an intervention in the environment.

Help With Acceptance

Paul Tournier suggests in one of his books that acceptance is the first step toward dealing with a serious problem. Sometimes a crisis will bring permanent change. The death of a loved one, the destruction of property, or the discovery of a terminal illness, for example, are all events which must be accepted and dealt with. To do otherwise is to deny the problem and to delay its solution until later.

Acceptance, like healing, takes time. Often it involves a painful, conscious thinking about the situation, an expressing of feelings, a readjustment of one's life-style, a building of new relationships, and a planning for the future. Acceptance may involve risks and potential failure. It is more successful when we are surrounded by sincere, patient, helpful friends, and when we know in a personal way the Savior who told us to come to Him with our burdens, to cast them on Him, and to experience the peace and guidance that give us real hope and stability during times of crisis (Matthew 11:28, 29; Psalms 55:22, 32:8). We should remember, however, that when a person casts his burden on the Lord, the Lord may sustain him through other human beings. . . .

Jesus as a Crisis Counselor. A familiar example of crisis counseling is recorded in John 11. It involves a terminal illness, personal danger, and the loss of a loved one.

When Lazarus of Bethany became seriously ill, his sisters sent a message to Jesus: "Lord, behold, he whom You love is sick."

According to the Biblical account, Jesus loved Lazarus, Mary, and Martha. Perhaps more than anyplace else, their home near Jerusalem was a place where Jesus could relax. And yet, instead of hurrying to their

need, he sat around for two days. Jesus, of course, knew what was going on in Bethany, and He even used the crisis to teach the disciples (vv. 4, 9–15) before they realized that Lazarus' illness was terminal.

The disciples, however, were facing a crisis of their own. Jesus' life was in danger, and so were theirs, because of their association with a wanted man (vv. 8, 16). To appear in public was to risk violent death, but when Jesus told them that Lazarus was dead they agreed to accompany the Lord to Bethany.

When they arrived, the scene was one of great sadness. A number of friends had come to comfort the sisters in their loss, but when Martha heard that Jesus was coming she left the house and went down the road to meet Him. Notice how Jesus handled the situation:

—He explained what was happening to the confused disciples (vv. 4, 14, 15).
—He let Martha express her feelings and confusion (vv. 21, 22).
—He reassured her in a calm manner and instilled hope (vv. 23, 25, 26).
—He pointed her to the Person of Christ (v. 25).
—He let Mary express her feelings, feelings which might have contained some anger (v. 32).
—He did not stop people from grieving but, on the contrary, expressed His own sorrow (vv. 33–36).
—He calmly bore the hostility of many of the saddened mourners (v. 37), even though it deeply moved Him (vv. 37, 38).

Then Jesus took action—action which changed the sadness into joy, brought glory to God, and caused many people to believe in Christ (vv. 38–45). On this occasion Jesus did not send the observers away, as He had at the raising of Jairus' daughter, but by calling Lazarus from the grave He demonstrated conclusively His victory over death, the greatest of all crises. A few days later, when He Himself was executed, Jesus approached the cross with calmness and then rose again. Little wonder that the Apostle Paul could shout to the Corinthians that death had been swallowed up in victory and that believers had certainty of a life after death, a life with Christ Himself (1 Corinthians 15:51–58).

It is true that none of us can bring a dead person back to life, as Jesus did, but it is also true that as crisis helpers we can employ each of the other techniques that Jesus used during this crisis in Bethany. Even without the resurrection of Lazarus, the crisis in Bethany would have served a useful purpose. Jesus tried to convince the disciples of this (John 11:4), but they obviously didn't get the message until later.

Crisis Helping Today. The same is true of most crises today. They are painful, traumatic experiences, but they can also be growing experiences which provide good opportunity for learning. I remember the words of a friend who once remarked, "We never have problems around here—we just have opportunities!"

According to Dr. Gene W. Brockopp of the Suicide Prevention and Crisis Service in Buffalo, New York, crises can be both helpful and therapeutic. They often throw a person into such a state of tension that there is a breakdown of defenses, a strong willingness to change, and an unusual openness to the suggestions of a counselor. If the helpee is able to mobilize his resources and solve his problems, there is an increase in his confidence and self-esteem. Sometimes crises teach the person to look more objectively at problems when they arise and to solve them more efficiently. All of this contributes to his mental well-being and psychological stability. It might be added that crises also have a way of alerting people to spiritual issues and teaching them to lean more fully on the Christ who called Lazarus out of the grave. Everyone doesn't react this way, of course. Some get critical and angry with God, but others look back to crises as a turning point in their spiritual development.

As we have seen, however, people in crises are often confused, suggestible, guilty, and self-condemning. Very often they feel so hopeless about a situation that they contemplate suicide as one of their most viable alternatives. In dealing with such people, it would be easy for a helper to play on the person's guilt and manipulate him into making some kind of spiritual decision which he may later regret, resent, and repudiate.

The Spiritual Implications of a Crisis. When faced with the death of Lazarus and the dangers to His own life, Jesus did not deny the spiritual implications of what was happening. He used the situation to teach spiritual truths, to show how to cope with crises, and to demonstrate the power of God in the lives of His children. Notice, however, that in pointing to the spiritual He did not play on people's emotions, nor did He rob them of their freedom to doubt (John 11:16), to criticize (v. 37), to resist (vv. 46–53), or to turn to Him and believe (v. 45).

God uses crises to bring people to Himself. He uses crises to help Christians grow and to mature as disciples. Our task as people helpers is to be open to the leading of the Holy Spirit, trusting that He will show us when and how to bring spiritual issues into our crisis-helping in a way that will draw the helpee closer to the Lord and ultimately bring glory to God.

—From Gary Collins, *How to Be a People Helper.* Santa Ana, Calif.: Vision House Publishers, 1976.

98

FOR FURTHER READING:

Ahlem, Lloyd H. *How to Cope with Conflict, Crisis and Change*. Ventura, Calif.: Regal Books, 1978.

Petersen, J. Allan. *Conquering Family Stress*. Wheaton, Ill.: Victor Books, 1978.

CRYING

THERE'S AN OLD FOLKSONG that asks: "How can you have a baby with no cryin'?" It's a good line to remember when you start out life with a baby, for there's sure to be some.

Often a baby will settle on a certain time of day to "sound off." This is apt to be the late afternoon, or early evening, when the household is more active and everybody is busy—and tired. Daddy comes home, dinner must be prepared, other children are more demanding. Sometimes you may be able to switch around the feeding or the hour you bathe the baby, and persuade him to pick out another—and more convenient—time of day to fuss. But you may just have to put up with it for a month or so. As he becomes able to amuse himself, use up energy in other ways, and his body processes become more settled, the fussy periods will taper off.

If your baby cries a good deal, however, he should be checked by a doctor. If he's bottle fed, sometimes a change in the formula is helpful, although usually a baby will adapt himself to any standard milk mixture. The doctor may suggest more food, or less; he may find other physical causes for the baby's distress.

Often babies who cry a good deal for no reason that can be discovered are the most active, vigorous babies. Quieter ones may spend more time lying awake but are still, sucking their fingers or a pacifier. A husky, healthy infant may be telling you how to run the world, just to let off steam.

At first, you may feel each time the baby cries that he's hungry. He is apt to try to ease any pain or discomfort by stuffing a fist into his mouth, or by making sucking movements since these have brought him pleasure. This convinces you that it must be hunger. If it has been a couple of hours since a feeding, or if he took but little at his most recent feeding, food may be the answer. It's worth trying to rule out other things, though, for not all cries are from hunger and inexperienced parents may tend to overfeed the baby. The obvious things to check are whether or not he's wet (although lots of babies don't mind soaked diapers a bit); or has a pin sticking in him (they hardly ever do, but it's worth looking); or is thirsty, cold, or in an uncomfortable position. Maybe he just needs to hear your voice, or be patted to remove an uncomfortable air bubble.

Sometimes the baby will cry briefly, and settle down if left alone. And some regularly fuss for 10 minutes or so as they are going off to sleep. If you rush in to pat or prod, you postpone sleeping even longer.

—From *Infant Care*. Washington: U.S. Department of Health, Education and Welfare, 1970.

CULTS

CULTS CAPITALIZE on the human need for association, for belonging, for family. Many of the new religious movements which are communal in style actually become surrogate families for their members. Leaders are sometimes referred to as "spiritual parents" or "parents in the Lord." So strong is the influence of the cult that a member's natural parents are usually relegated to an inferior status, sometimes totally rejected.

The severing of all ties with one's family is an integral part of the process of psychological kidnaping which new members undergo.

If parents and other family members can be recast into the role of agents of Satan or viewed as representatives of the corrupt old order, the young recruit is even more effectively bonded to the cult. At best, parents are tolerated and pitied, at worst scorned and abandoned.

An ex-member of Faith Tabernacle tells how the leadership of that cult used Scripture to reinforce their view that all contacts with parents and close relatives must be cut off. "We were taught that even Jesus said that your worst enemies are those of your own household. Your parents are back in the kindergarten stage of church. They may be Christians, but they are hindering you from going on with God." Members were told that the "cutting off" process could include insults and hate letters directed at parents. "In so doing we were told that all our bridges would be completely burned and family members would never accept us back if we ever did decide to leave." Another example of a not-so-subtle control mechanism.

In several new religious groups where families are present, there have been reports of child abuse and neglect. Children are raised communally with their age peers in organizations like Synanon and the Hare Krishna movement. A former member of Faith Tabernacle reports that a particularly pretty little girl—just learning to talk—was forced to repeat "I ugly, I ugly" over and over so that she would not develop pride. In the same cult, teenage children were forced to slap their parents who were being disciplined by the group.

Numerous instances of marriages being broken up by cult leaders have been reported to the writer. The adversarial impact of cult membership on marriage and the family is illustrated by this incredible statement by David Berg, prophet of the Children of God:

God breaks up marriages in order that he might join each of the parties together to himself. He rips off wives, husbands or children to make up his bride if the rest of the family refuses to follow. He is the worst "ripper-offer" of all. God is the greatest destroyer of home and family of anybody! . . . If you have not forsaken your husband or wife for the Lord at some time or another, you have not forsaken all.

This diabolical undercutting of the God-ordained institution of the family is one of the most tragic by-products of the emergence of extremist cults. In addition to the parents and other family members themselves, perhaps only those of us who have counseled or have had sustained contact with parents of cult members can comprehend the magnitude of the problem. The heartache, the anxiety, the feelings of hopelessness and frustration which these parents feel must surely be one of the major tragedies of our day. The plight of parents was dramatized by the events in Jonestown, although many thousands of parents continue to face uncertainty and uneasiness over the ultimate fate of their children enmeshed in scattered new-age cults, some of which have received little attention in the media.

Not all parents are worried about their offspring's involvement in new religious movements. Some see the dramatic personality changes which have occurred in their sons and daughters as an improvement over past association in the drug scene or counterculture. Other young people caught up in the cults have no real family to relate to outside the group. Even if they wanted to leave the cultic life, they have few, if any, resources or caring contacts "on the outside" to assist them in the resocialization process. After years of developing strong dependency ties to the sect, it is difficult—if not frightening—for an individual to actually follow through on a decision to leave.

What alternatives exist for concerned parents who have a son or daughter in an extremist cult? They can patiently wait it out, hoping that someday something will occur in the group itself or in the mind of the member which will trigger a voluntary exit. For parents who occasionally see their child and maintain some degree of contact, this can be a very painful period. The months and years go by and with them educational and career opportunities which probably never will be recouped. Parents see the best, most productive years of a young person's life essentially wasted in a cult. Even more trying is the experience of parents who see the mental and physical health of their children impaired and are powerless to do anything about it. All too frequently parents echo the lamentation of Jeremiah: "Those I cared for and reared, my enemy has destroyed" (Lamentations 2:22).

A much more precarious and controversial option for parents of a cult member is to go the route of deprogramming. This word became a part of the American vocabulary a few years ago when Ted Patrick began snatching cult members away from their groups. Patrick put each cultist through intense, emotional sessions designed to force them to think on their own and then, it was hoped, decide to leave the cults.

Parents who see no other way to retrieve a son or daughter from an extremist group have elected to hire deprogrammers and essentially kidnap their own children. Parents hope that this forced separation from the cult combined with the input of the deprogramming team (which usually includes young people who have been members of the group in question) will have the desired impact. The process can take a few hours or a few days, and it can be very expensive for the parents, who must pay the fees charged by the deprogrammers, their transportation and expenses, as well as the motel bills for the actual site of the deprogramming.

The morality of involuntary deprogramming and the techniques involved in the process have been the subjects of much heated debate in the media and elsewhere. "Its definition and connotation are largely dependent on who and what you read and who and what you choose to believe. There are conflicting reports with regard to the purposes, procedures and personnel involved in deprogramming. . . . Depending on one's perspective, deprogrammers are viewed as either 'latter day vigilantes' or courageous rescuers of ensnared youth."

Because they have lost members as a result of deprogramming, the cults have been very vocal in their denunciation of the practice, calling it a violation of the principle of religious liberty through forced confinement and the use of "mental torture." Victor Paul Wierwille, the leader of The Way, views deprogramming as a "scheme invented by the Devil, fostered by some denominational churches troubled by unsound doctrine and dwindling congregations, and supported by unwary parents distressed by the neuroses of our times." Cults tend to define all attempts to dissuade an individual from cultic membership—whether that attempt is in a voluntary or involuntary context—as deprogramming.

Many ex-cult members view their deprogramming favorably; others have major reservations about the tactics and techniques employed, not questioning the motives or sincerity of the deprogrammer. Still others return to the cults. For them, the process was unsuccessful, and the alienation from parents is greater than before. A flurry of lawsuits involving both parents and deprogrammers has not resolved the controversy.

There are many deprogrammers still active in the United States, despite costly legal battles and mixed reaction in the press. Their fees vary as much as their techniques. Few if any professionals are directly involved in deprogramming activities. Some deprogrammers operate in association with rehabilitation programs—usually small and constantly facing legal and financial trouble. Most deprogrammers, if involved in rehabilitation work at all, focus on the physical, social, and psychological needs of ex-members; hardly any attempt is made to meet the spiritual needs of people. A few evangelical Christians identify themselves as deprogrammers and attempt to fill the spiritual vacuum remaining after someone leaves a cult with a positive witness to the redeeming work of Jesus Christ.

In some states parents are able to obtain a legal conservatorship with the aid of professional (usually medical) and legal effort. After making a case that their son or daughter (regardless of age) is in physical or mental danger or is incompetent, the parents obtain a court order giving them custody of the child for a stipulated period of time. They are then legally free to obtain the services of a counselor, clergyman, psychologist, psychiatrist, or deprogrammer to assist in the "recovery" or "rescue" procedure.

Critics charge that both deprogramming and conservatorship procedures are subject to abuse. The question has been raised about who decides which groups are indeed "cults" and whether conservatorship laws might be used by parents wishing to extract a child from a marginal or even mainstream religious group. There are non-Christian parents, for example, who consider Jews for Jesus and Campus Crusade for Christ to be cultic. Where is the line drawn? On the other hand, supporters of deprogramming and conservatorships argue that abuse is rare because parents and society can distinguish between truly destructive cults and "legiti-

mate" religious organizations, whether large or small. Supporters point to the successes of deprogramming and state that it is the *only* method which effectively deals with the thoroughly brainwashed cultist.

Many ex-cult members are grateful that their parents intervened and had them deprogrammed. "These people say that they had felt themselves powerless to carry out their desire to leave because of psychological and social pressure from companions and officials inside. They often speak of a combination of guilt over defecting and fear of the cult's retaliation—excommunication if they tried."

Christian parents must approach with caution any procedure which might involve the use of force and illegal acts. However, to parents who have tried everything short of force, including prayer, and who have seen no results and have little prospect of regaining a son or daughter, that advice is of small comfort. It is my opinion, nevertheless, that patience and prayer combined with a hopeful and sustained love—despite the desperately trying circumstances—is an appropriate Christian response.

Parents who decide against some type of deprogramming must make every attempt to keep channels of communication open with their children. While they need not disguise their honest feelings about cult leaders and cult practices, they should seek to keep to a minimum those discussions which lead to confrontation and further alienation. Wisdom and discernment as well as the strength and help of the Holy Spirit are continuing prerequisites for Christian parents with children in such groups. Parents must be fully informed about cults and may wish to counsel with a pastor or other Christian professional who is knowledgeable in this area. They will also want to avail themselves to the resources provided by the various parent's organizations—such as the Citizens

Freedom Foundation—which are active in most sections of the United States.

What can parents do to prevent and ward off the possibility of their children's involvement in cults and aberrational Christian movements? Because of the seductive and satanic nature of false religion, there is probably no infallible insurance available, even after young people have been alerted. Christian parents who have conscientiously done their best, with God's help, in rearing children who then join cults often suffer tremendous guilt. They constantly ask, "Where did we go wrong?" As we have seen, the reasons young people join new religious groups are varied and complex. In particular cases parents undoubtedly have played a role in the situation. In other instances, young people from what appear to be "model" families become involved in cults.

Still, one of the best protections against the possibility of cultic involvement is a strong, supportive, loving family in which communication is open and honest and in which children develop early a positive self-image and a healthy sense of autonomy. A secure young person who thinks for himself and yet values and accepts advice from adults is less likely to feel the need to search out a rigidly authoritarian group for direction. Parents who listen to and relate to a young person as an adult-in-the-making will win the confidence of their children.

Christian parents who wish to prevent the loss of a son or daughter to cultic religion must be prepared to work hard at cultivating meaningful, loving, and flexible relationships within the family unit. Young adults need affirmation and acceptance, not merely toleration or routine attention. They need positive Christian role models—people who can be authoritative without being authoritarian.

Most important, parents need to encourage their children to have a firm faith in Christ as personal Savior and a biblical understanding of that faith. People—whether young or old—who seek after "new truth" frequently have little of the "old truth." A person who has firmly established his own values and goals in the framework of his own Christian faith is not likely to find cultic alternatives appealing.

—From Ronald M. Enroth, *The Lure of the Cults*. Chappaqua, N.Y.: Christian Herald, 1979.

FOR FURTHER READING:

Boa, Kenneth. *Cults, World Religion and You*. Wheaton, Ill.: Victor Books, 1977.

Enroth, Ronald M. *Youth, Brainwashing and the Extremist Cults*. Grand Rapids: Zondervan Publishing House, 1977.

Martin, Walter. *The Rise of the Cults*. Irvine, Calif.: Vision House Publishers, 1977.

Petersen, William J. *Those Curious New Cults*. New Canaan, Conn.: Keats Publishing, Inc., 1975.

Robertson, Irvine G. *What the Cults Believe*. Evanston, Ill.: Moody Press, 1966.

Spittler, Russell. *Cults and Isms*. Grand Rapids: Baker Book House, 1973.

CURIOSITY

BEFORE A CHILD is old enough to ask a question, he shows his wonder as he follows an object with his eyes, as he turns toward a sound. He handles everything he can grasp, including parts of his own body: he rubs, he pulls, he squeezes. He puts things in his mouth and licks and bites them. He examines his mother's earring and his father's nose, and tastes his father's necktie or coat button.

The child's wonder and curiosity delight his parents and other adults, but they also make trouble for his mother in the early years. The toddler often hears his first "No! No!" when he is sampling scraps from the floor, pulling at lamp cords or a tablecloth, prying into closets or drawers, darting through open doors. Someone has to snatch objects out of his reach and keep him from going out of bounds. From the time he is able to move about on his own, the child forces his parents to choose almost from moment to moment between letting him find things out for himself and saving him and others, as well as the furniture and furnishings, from more or less serious hurt. In every situation parents want to give the child a chance to explore and investigate—but must keep him within reasonable limits. When the toddler, taken along to the supermarket, wants to stop at every window, to watch the steam shovel dig or a coal truck unload, or when he stops to make experiments with his shadow, the mother thinks of the dinner she has to get started and she tries to find a way to expedite the return home.

Parents can enlarge and enrich a child's experience during the preschool years by taking him whenever possible to the shops and stores, to places where building is going on or wherever people are working, to a bridge or a wharf or a firehouse. On a ride in the country they can stop to see cows in the field or chickens in a farmyard. Everything is new to the child and exciting; the young human being constantly wonders about every new object he sees. What's that, how does it work, what does it do, what makes it like that instead of like the already familiar things? But the wondering reaches far beyond the names and workings of the things he sees. The child asks not only, "Where did I come from?" but also, "Who was the first man?" and "What came before that—and then before that?"

The modern school cultivates children's natural wish to learn by taking them on trips to see how a factory works or how a water supply is pumped to the city, and by giving them opportunities to handle and experiment with materials directly. A good teacher encourages boys and girls to follow the lead of their own curiosity into individual projects on which they then report to the class. Each child's wondering is his own, and no school could possibly satisfy the special curiosities of every individual child. As the boys and girls grow older, reading and visits to the museum, free-time projects and hobbies can do a great deal to fill the gaps.

Before they start school, children begin to ply their parents with questions—and very often questions that parents cannot answer. The important thing, however, is to encourage children's curiosity rather than make it seem unimportant. Even when parents and teachers do not know the answers, it is possible to encourage the growth of curiosity by helping children to find ways of getting their answers—from books, experiments, or other sources.

It is possible to discourage children's curiosity by overwhelming them. In response to a mild interest in a chemical process, the present of an elaborate chemical set might do more harm than good, for the sight of that expensive set lying idle in the corner might well make the boy uncomfortable and cautious about expressing curiosity later. Similarly, an elaborate answer that tells a child more than he cares to know may also discourage further inquiries.

Curiosity is of course much more than a convenient practical device for spurring a child's learning. It is one of mankind's most distinctive characteristics. With men and women everywhere, curiosity has been a most dynamic factor in advancing human well-being through the ages.

—From *The New Encyclopedia of Child Care and Guidance.* Garden City, N.Y.: Doubleday & Co., 1968.

D

DANCING

EVANGELICAL PARENTS today have differing views about dancing.

Some insist that dancing has always been connected with immorality and that Christian parents have a duty not only to avoid dancing themselves but also to teach their children that dancing is wrong. For biblical support they will point to the connection between Israel's apostasy in worshiping the golden calf and the dancing that accompanied it (Exodus 32:19). They also note Michal's objection to David's vigorous dancing and jumping before the servant girls of his officials, dressed only in a priestly linen cloth around his waist (2 Samuel 6:14–23).

Others point out, however, that it is apostasy on the one hand and foolish exposure on the other that are criticized, not dancing *per se*. They argue that in the Bible dancing usually has a religious context (Psalms 149:3; 150:4, for example). Usually women danced happily for the Lord while the men rejoiced in other ways (*see* Judges 11:34; 21:21, 23; 1 Samuel 18:6; 21:11; 29:5; Jeremiah 31:13; but see also 2 Samuel 6:5, 14–22). The Gospels, they add, never criticize dancing when they refer to it (Matthew 11:17; 14:6; Mark 6:22; Luke 7:32; 15:25). And with all their concern for morality, the rest of the New Testament books make no reference to dancing.

Dancing today, however, has lost most of its religious overtones. It is still connected with celebration. And, of course, when men and women, young or old, dance together, especially in each other's arms, sexual implications are suggested.

Christian parents are usually first confronted with the question of dancing in school physical education classes. Such classes usually seek to develop the child's God-given love of rhythm in spontaneous ways. Other children, especially girls, want to take ballet lessons, partly because they love the beauty of the ballerina's clothes.

During pre-adolescence and adolescence dancing becomes a way for boys and girls to meet each other and relate to each other socially. Square and folk dances are harmless forms of fun and exercise.

Social dancing has more potential for expressing behavior that Christians find more objectionable. Whether the solution is to prohibit all social dancing or to teach your child that non-Christians will sometimes turn the dance floor into an erotic extramarital affair Christians do not approve of is a decision each set of parents will have to decide.

—LESLIE R. KEYLOCK

DATING

BEFORE WE CONSIDER some of the problems of teenage dating and specific suggestions for parental guidance, let's look at some general contributions we can make to our teenagers' dating experiences. Since dating is both a new form of interpersonal relationship and an exercise of new social skills, we can offer practical instruction they will find useful. Though some teenagers want to find their own way, others will appreciate suggestions from those who have already walked the trail. A good time to begin is at the beginning with the first date.

A casual conversation can introduce the subject of asking a girl for a date. We can let our son know that he should not ask a potential date, "What are you doing Saturday night?" or, "Are you free Saturday evening?" His purpose is not to pry into what she is doing Saturday night! The question should be direct: "Would you like to go to _____ with me on Saturday evening?" This gives opportunity to say an honest *no* or *yes*. It avoids putting her in an awkward spot and may avoid unwanted embarrassment for your son!

Instructions on other courtesies, such as going to the door to meet a date, politely greeting the parents, telling them what time he will return with their daughter, and opening the car door for his companion will go a long way to start dating off pleasantly. Such actions instill confidence in both the girl and her parents for the outing.

If flowers are appropriate for the date, or there are other special hints that can be helpful, we should offer them to sons who are interested. If not, of course, we should leave them to their own devices and let them learn through their own experience.

Daughters need help, just as their male counterparts. On their first date, they may not know how to politely excuse themselves for freshening up. A simple, "Excuse me; I'll be right back" will prevent a long evening! We can suggest that a nice way to end a date is to invite their companion into the house for a few minutes. Parents can greet them

and leave them to themselves for a while. This has many advantages over extended parking in the driveway! Sharing a bit of dessert and conversation in the home promotes the kind of relationship both we and our children want.

What about specific guidelines for our offsprings' dating? Do we let them adopt their own and hope for the best, or do we exercise direct supervision. Ideally, we will have established a good degree of family unity and practiced preparatory training, before our children even reached the teenage years. We will have shown that we approve of fun and excitement, as well as study and work. We will have helped them build friendships with children we believe will have a positive influence by the schools we select, the church we attend, the friends we choose, the neighborhood we live in, and the guidance, training, and example we have been offering for years. We will have carried out a natural process of wholesome sex education so our children are well aware of their bodies' functions and developing a beginning understanding of the meaning of love and the role of sexual intercourse. And we will have shown the way to a personal relationship with Christ and a solid commitment to biblical morality. If we have taken these steps together, entrance into teen dating will not introduce large, new hurdles in the form of dating principles. But we have been talking about the "ideal," which rarely fits a family perfectly.

Interest in dating generally begins during the junior-high-school years—especially for girls. Boys' interests sharpen a little later. I see no good reason for formal, unsupervised dating by seventh- and eighth-grade children. If your son or daughter becomes interested in someone of the opposite sex at this age, let them see each other at school or pal around informally. A natural friendship is healthy—assuming you know and approve of the friend. But at this age, the early adolescent is just not ready for serious dating. Junior highers are often pushed into a social world of dating, sophisticated dress, and older-peer influence which they simply are not ready to handle. Hence the need for specific guidelines and supervision.

When our teenagers reach their freshman and sophomore years of high school (fourteen and fifteen), they are ready to assume some responsibility in dating experience. This doesn't mean that they are ready for regular dating nor that they are abnormal if dating doesn't attract them. But their level of maturity does warrant their trying their wings, if they wish to participate. They will concurrently be extending the informal boy-girl relationships and occasionally having a "real date" at some group event. I would not allow a thirteen- or fourteen-year-old girl, however, to date a seventeen- or eighteen-year-old boy. Even though girls mature more rapidly than boys, the typical freshman girl is not ready to handle the potential intimacies and the responsibilities of dating a boy that much older. I would also not allow a son or daughter this age to go to an unchaperoned party, and I would be hesitant about unchaperoned beach dates. The same goes for any type of trip when another teenager is driving a group of friends. This activity has a big appeal for thirteen- and fourteen-year-olds, but the hazards of reckless driving, negative peer influence, and of "just cruising" make this generally inadvisable at this age.

By the time teenagers reach their last two years of high school (ages sixteen to eighteen), they need a great deal more freedom in their dating and social activities in general. At this age, they are mature enough to "single date," to regularly use the family car and, if they feel strongly about it, to date one person steadily. By then parents have had fifteen years to instill positive moral and spiritual values in their children. They have helped develop social skills. And the older teens have the intellectual capacity to see the consequences of their choices and to plan more wisely. Though some parents decide to prohibit their adolescents from "going steady," and some still exert a lot of control, it seems more profitable to influence actions through discussion rather than through arbitrary limits or commands.

—From Bruce Narramore, Ph.D., *Adolescence Is Not an Illness.* Old Tappan, N.J.: Fleming H. Revell Co., 1980.

FOR FURTHER READING:

Butler, John. *Christian Ways to Date, Go Steady, and Break Up.* Cincinnati: Standard Publishing Co., 1978.

Hartley, Fred. *Update.* Old Tappan, N.J.: Fleming H. Revell Co., 1977.

Miles, Herbert J. *The Dating Game.* Grand Rapids: Zondervan Publishing House, 1975.

Poure, Ken, and Stoop, Dave. *Parents: Give Your Kid a Chance.* Eugene, Ore.: Harvest House Publishers, 1977.

DAY-CARE CENTERS AND PRESCHOOL

IF PARENTS ACCEPT the reality that each preschool child requires constant individual attention and daily routines which overburdened mothers or working parents cannot always supply, then quality day-care centers can contribute greatly to strengthening family life. They can fulfill the needs of both the children and the family.

A day-care center is as good as the caretaker who works there. She must earn the trust of her charges by being sensitive to their moods, feelings, and needs. She must always be conscious of how the children respond to what she does with them.

Parental participation is fundamental to a successful operation. Parents and teachers need to exchange information about the child's behavior, his likes and dislikes, and his health on a regular basis.

We have learned at least two things from Head Start: remedial programs must begin before the child is three years of age and the parents must be involved in these programs. A day-care center that provides the child with a good initial learning experience and social stimulation is offering an opportunity that many children would not receive from their mothers. Even if the mother were at home and had the time available, chances are she would not have the educational background to offer her child the stimulation he needs.

Should a mother feel guilty about wanting to send her toddler to a day-care center? Is a day-care center as good as home care? Is day care *only* for working mothers? Dr. Bruno Bettelheim, a distinguished child psychiatrist, disagrees. "I feel that it is too narrow to think of Day-Care Centers merely for mothers who have to work or as therapeutic centers for underprivileged children. Day Care can do a vital job for *all* mothers and *all* children. There is no doubt that mother is the most important person for a child but we are aware of too intense a mother–child attachment. . . . We need to find a better balance between home care and day care. . . . A child feels much better about himself and the world if he spends part of the day in a planned setting that exists only for him."

The real difficulty with day-care centers is not that they separate mother and child, but that there are so few good ones. The modern mother has considerable need for time by herself. If she has her own time, she can more easily and happily relate to her child. A child, too, needs to go his own way.

Syracuse University has set up a day-care center for children beginning at six months of age. The center began as an experiment to show how "culturally determined mental retardation" could be prevented among children from disadvantaged areas. It deliberately tried to stimulate the child's intellectual development by offering a highly individualized type of care. The experiment proved that the children thrive and that their IQ score increased with time (rather than the reverse, which usually happens with these children).

The study also demonstrated that early day-care experience with its attendant separation from the mother does not lead to emotional insecurity. Conversely, inadequate day care may be harmful and nothing is worse than a series of caretakers. A child needs one person to identify with as the mothering figure.

Educators agree that in addition to complying with local safety regulations, a good day-care center should have a cheerful environment, good equipment, and well-trained, loving teachers, as well as:

1. Forty to fifty square feet of indoor space per child.
2. One hundred square feet of enclosed outdoor space per child.
3. A nourishing lunch and frequent snacks available.
4. A place to nap with privacy and a cot for each child.
5. Medical attention at the center, as well as home care when the child is too sick to attend class.
6. Diapers and changing tables.
7. Furniture and toilet facilities adapted to the child's height.
8. Two to three adults available to each group of eight to ten children.
9. Ample storage space for the child's clothes and toys.
10. Mandatory parent participation.

Day Care and Early Education, an informative magazine presenting a broad range of topics to the concerned working mother, is available by writing 2852 Broadway, New York, N.Y. 10025.

Private industry is beginning to enter the day-care field, realizing that providing day care increases their available work force and aids in retaining their employees. Day-care facilities cut down on expensive absenteeism and permit a woman to work full time instead of part time. Without day-care centers, many mothers could not work and as a result would be on welfare.

Expense

Providing good day-care service is expensive, but what better opportunity do we have for offering children of low-income families educational and health facilities where they are most needed?

The federal government makes funds available to state public welfare agencies under Title IV of the Social Security Act. Other funds may be obtained from state and local public welfare agencies.

Princeton Center for Infancy Point of View

Children who are taught how to learn, to use their senses to their best advantage, and to express themselves in their early years are more likely to function successfully in any classroom. In fact, day-care services should be available to all families so a child can have experiences that supplement the ones provided by the home. Our children are our best investment and richest resources!

How to Select a Preschool

In selecting a preschool, parents are sometimes bewildered by the variety of different programs available, as well as the differences in methods, materials, and goals. Many preschools have no "formal information sheets" describing their educational philosophies, so the astute parent must visit the various programs and observe the classes in session. Before making a final selection, you should discuss the program in detail with the teacher. You should not hesitate to ask questions. It is much better to ask questions than to enroll your child in a program you are not comfortable with.

Matching a Preschool Program to Your Child

First of all, the preschool program you select for your child should not conflict greatly with your own philosophy of child rearing. If you tend to be a "permissive" parent, you probably would not choose to enroll your child in a structured preschool program. If you encourage independence, self-discipline, and responsibility, you probably would be unhappy to have your child in a very "permissive" or "anything-is-okay" school. Similarly, you must consider your child's personality and tendencies.

Also, you should consider the number of children in the class, their ages, and the child–adult ratio. How much individual attention does your child need? Most nursery schools use chronological age grouping while many Montessori schools use mixed-age grouping.

In evaluating a preschool, you should look carefully at its program. Is there a daily routine followed by allotted time periods for free play, snack, story time, rest time, etc. or is most of the time unstructured?

Does the teacher insist that all the children join the group during certain activities—group singing, story time or snack time? What is included in the *content* of the curriculum? (Are there science experiments, nature study, animals, pre-reading and pre-math activities, etc.?) Can you judge how much pre-planning takes place? How many new projects are planned and how many trips are taken? Is the program organized into units (farms, community workers, foods, etc.)? Does the program incorporate special events and special visitors?

Are there special teachers to enrich the program (music, science, art, foreign language)? What is the music program: singing, rhythm instruments, Montessori sensory training, Orff and Kodály music methods? What is the structure of the program, formal or informal, i.e., do the teachers instruct the class as a whole? Is a great deal of spontaneous learning taking place?

What are the opportunities for group interaction and for dramatic and social play? This varies with the goals of the particular preschool. Are there opportunities for individual play and concentration? How is snack time handled, as a group social time (everyone altogether) or individually at any time during the preschool day, as in many Montessori programs? How is rest time handled and moving from one activity to the next?

What *values* are stressed in the program: sharing, co-operation, cleanliness, routines, etc.? Are the children encouraged to learn to do things for themselves? Finally, are fathers encouraged to become involved in the program in any way?

The Staff

It is important that you feel some rapport with your child's potential teachers. You should feel comfortable with the way the teachers are handling the children. You should feel satisfied with their "education approach" and their competency.

Do they in any way seem "overwhelmed" by the classroom situation? What are their methods of "discipline," of modifying the

unacceptable behavior of a child? How well do they handle disputes among the children?

Do the teachers interact with the children as individuals or is the majority of their time spent dealing with small groups of children? Are teachers tuned in to the "room as a whole," as well as individual children? Are they warm without "smothering" them with affection? Are they genuine with the children? How do the children respond to the staff?

Discipline and Behavior

What kinds of behavior are encouraged and what are the limits on a child's behavior? How is discipline handled and how effective does it seem? How much pressure is put on the child "conforming," joining the group, and learning to "get along" with the group? Does the teacher allow for a child's individuality? How are the children helped to grow? Do the teachers encourage the children to learn to do things by and for themselves? Do the teachers genuinely listen to the children when they are talking or are they busy "getting something ready" for the next project?

How do the children interact with one another?

Atmosphere

How would you describe the atmosphere in the classroom? Is it chaotic, spontaneous, controlled, or stilted? Do the children seem happy? Do you feel their social, cognitive, and affective needs are being met? Do the children seem bored, restless, or overstimulated by the program?

Physical Equipment and Surroundings

Look carefully at the physical surroundings. Are they clean and inviting? Are the children learning to handle the equipment with respect or are they behaving destructively? Are the books and puzzles accessible and attractive? Are the children encouraged to clean up after themselves; to put their own toys, books, and materials back on the shelves? Is there enough of a *variety* of stimulating materials accessible to meet the changing interests of the children? Are the materials varied during the school year?

Outdoors, is the equipment safe, supervised, adequately spaced, and attractive? Are the children able to move freely from indoors to out or does the group as a whole have an "indoor time" and an "outdoor time"?

Indoors and outdoors, is there opportunity for sand play, water play, and other "messy" activities? Is there a variety of art materials available at all times or only during art "lessons"? Are the art "projects" appropriate for the preschool child or are they teacher-designed to "take home and impress mama and papa"? Is there enough physical space inside, as well as some indoor provision for rainy day, large-muscle exercise and play?

What is the physical arrangement of the room? Are there activity areas: a doll corner, a housekeeping corner, an art area, a place for water and sand play, toys, blocks, puzzles, a workbench, a comfortable book corner, records, child-sized tables and chairs?

No two preschool programs will ever be exactly alike. The most important variable is the teacher. You should feel she is genuinely enjoying her work with young children. You should see whether she acts as a caretaker or as a sensitive person who enters into the play life of the group and enhances the learning. The second most important variable is the physical space and equipment.

—From The Princeton Center for Infancy, *The Parenting Advisor*. Garden City, N.Y.: Anchor Books/Doubleday & Co., 1978.

FOR FURTHER READING:

Reynolds, Jean K., ed. *How to Choose and Use Child Care*. Nashville: Broadman Press, 1980.

Sauerman, Thomas H., and Schomaker, Linda, eds. *Starting a Church-Sponsored Weekday Preschool Program: A Manual of Guidance*. Philadelphia: Fortress Press, 1980.

DEATH AND GRIEF

WE CAN EXPECT to mourn only within the limits of our emotional capacity. When loss is encountered as a child, grieving is a feeling only. When loss is encountered as an adolescent, grieving is both a feeling and a concept. When loss is encountered as an adult, grieving is not only a feeling and a concept, but also evaluated behavior. Following is a brief description of how we develop our capacity for mourning.

The Child's Encounter With Loss. The way a child reacts to loss depends largely on his emotional age. Children feel pain and they suffer emotionally, but they do not have an adult's logic by which to understand the experience. Consequently, their mourning is often abbreviated and left incomplete.

An infant who loses its mother through death or abandonment in the second or third month seems to experience distress when the "mother-figure" is changed, but distress can be relieved so long as the infant's needs are satisfied. But loss experienced between six months and one year registers with more serious distress because the infant has become able to distinguish between what satisfies his needs and who does the satisfying. Should loss occur, the child does not automatically transfer emotional attachment for his mother to someone else.

Loss can be quite a shock to a young child because he has no innate notion that life ever ceases. But before the age of four years, he

111

may begin to ask questions about dying, questions stimulated by the phenomena of autumn, death of a favorite pet, or the loss of a cherished person. His questions assume that there is a reason for everything. While he generally is not interested in the physiological aspects of death, he does want to know, "Where did Grandma go?" "Why?" "How?" He may ask the same questions over and over again. Because he does not have a well-developed conceptual framework by which to interpret the answers, the child's questions seem new to him even though they are redundant to adults.

A child of five is able to see relationships, some causations, and some implications. But he is usually unable to put himself in another person's position; therefore he has great difficulty handling other people's mourning. One family received word of the death of a beloved grandmother. When his parents and two older sisters began to cry, Jimmie did too. But then he began to laugh. Indignantly, his sisters demanded that he explain his behavior. "Well, she will be back, won't she? Why be sad?"

We all have a limited capacity for grieving, but the child is even more limited. Often confused by the seemingly long rituals adults use for grieving, children are usually ready to return quickly to their routine rhythms of living. A child's capacity for dealing with loss is limited.

Denial is a child's initial reaction to loss. His rhythms of mourning are usually broken by periods of denial and "make believe," either that the crisis has never happened, or that he has the magical power to make the deceased come back alive. What impact denial has on his emotional development depends largely on how well people around him react to his behavior. A college student reports that when he returned home from school as a first-grader, he was told that his older sister had "gone away" and would

never come back. Out of bewilderment, he asked questions only to have his parents respond with evasiveness. Finally they ordered him to stop asking anything more. Through the child's thought processes, which tend to be egocentric and concrete, he assumed that he must have done something wrong and that is why his sister went away. He suffered with his unmentionable guilt until he took a course about "death and dying" in college.

The young child evaluates events of loss in terms of what repercussions they have had on him. For the college student whose sister died when he was a first-grader, the repercussion was guilt. For another college student, it was anger. Sarah had been a "dying child." She reports that while she knew something was basically wrong, both from the way that she felt and the way people acted around her, her questions were rebuffed. An embarrassed nurse retorted that she was a "very naughty girl" for asking questions about dying. In her bewilderment, infected by increasing anger, Sarah had the most distorted of fantasies. Sometimes she believed she was being eaten alive by frogs. At other times she pictured the doctors and nurses as wizards and witches who were changing her into an animal. Her mother and father appeared in her dreams as miniature toys, utterly helpless. Sarah alternated between roles of a little girl screaming for their help and of a heroine trying to rescue them. What was happening to her was incomprehensible. She had intense feelings but an inability to interpret the experience. Now as an adult, she works with critically ill children and tries "to help these children have a different ending to their nightmares."

Children use a great deal of fantasy in their efforts to grasp inexplicable phenomena. In the illustrations above, I have focused on children who have experienced loss first hand. But children between the ages of five and puberty also work through notions concerning dying and loss in peer relationships. They speculate and create games. They play at "what it must be like."

. . . . .

If adults don't oppress his initiative, a child's questions concerning death arise out of his curiosity about how change through loss could have occurred. Some children express profound confusion in fantasy and bizarre games. Recent research suggests that all children have some confusion about inevitable and irreversible loss.

Because children have feelings but an incomplete capacity for interpreting the experience that stimulates these feelings, their healing process usually is incomplete until late adolescence or adulthood. But if the child is encouraged to share his emotions and how he perceives them, he learns that he is still acceptable and lovable despite his loss. He can continue to grow emotionally as well as physically.

The Adolescent's Encounter With Loss. The adolescent is able to understand the full implications of dying and the finality of death. He has the capacity for both feeling and interpreting experiences of loss. He has well developed ways for testing reality and has capacities to adapt to the change loss brings. Generally, however, his overt behavior is significantly different from the patterns of mourning among mature adults. Like children, the adolescent tends to overcompensate for his feelings of grief by fantasizing either return of the loved person or power to reverse the loss. The intensity of this contradiction in behavior seems to be in direct proportion to the adolescent's progress in establishing independence from his parents. The more insecure he is in his own identity, the more he tries to over-compensate for his inadequacies.

The normal adolescent, whether having developed a very strong self-concept or a weak one within the family structure, must be able to identify those points that differentiate him from his parents before he can become an autonomous adult. In order to do this, he no longer is dependent on adults as he was as a child. He turns to his peers for identity support. It is from close peer competitors that a boy, for example, can estimate his own prowess—whether his mind is keen, his body is strong, his accomplishments worthy. It is from her peers that a girl learns what is mature and what is immature, even though the peer group's definitions may be quite at odds with those of adults. Hair and clothing styles often reflect the definitions of the peer group. At the very same time, however, the adolescent seemingly needs his parents, or other authority figures, in order to have a mark by which to measure his development into adulthood.

Research on the emotional needs of adolescents in times of crisis suggests that the overwhelming majority fear loss of those closest to them—both their friends and family. And they fear isolation. Unfortunately, at the time an adolescent needs support from his family he also seeks approval of his own peers who often set themselves in opposition to an adult's identity. Competition between peers and parents to influence an adolescent produces conflict under very normal circumstances. This conflict becomes intense in a crisis of loss. The adolescent's signals of needs may be confusing to adults, as, in fact, the adolescent's own feelings are confusing to himself. Both close fellowship and solitude are important for the adolescent in crisis. Every adolescent needs access to adults who are loving and tolerant of his erratic behavior.

In *Growing Up Absurd*, Paul Goodman argues that our society's great indulgence for children makes it difficult for even the most ambitious adolescent to prove himself with real work for real rewards. Those adolescents struggling with disease, who are not permitted by well-meaning adults to struggle with the reality of their disease in ways that seem "real" to them, are either forced back into a posture of infant dependency or into exaggerated rebellion for independence. For an adolescent patient, it is bad enough that he must wrestle with a body deteriorating at the same time that his own peers are filling out in full bloom of maturity, but it is intolerable to have one's sense of worth snatched away either by those the patient loves or with whom he competes.

While adolescents have the capacities for both feeling and conceptualizing experiences of loss, their judgments about the implications of their experiences are often quite immature and their healing may be left incomplete. Often an adolescent treats all loss with the same intensity. When Bob lost his favorite coat, for example, he thought his life was ruined. Mary thought she could never recover when her boyfriend left her, but she was as emotionally distraught over losing her athletic pin. Unlike children, adolescents have the capacity to conceptualize experiences of loss. But unlike adults, they have not had the experience to evaluate their concepts of loss. One mark of maturity is the ability to differentiate degrees of loss.

The adolescent's encounter with loss is far less affected by whether adults respond with exactly the right words as by the "feeling tones" with which they respond. If adults convey to the adolescent their feelings of, or questions about, loss are inappropriate, the adolescent is thwarted in his mourning. Only as he is encouraged to express himself and to evaluate what his loss means to him, can he resolve the conflicts of his experience and thereby be free to move on to discover new concerns, curiosities, and loves of living.

The Adult's Encounter With Loss. By the time many of us reach adulthood, we have

learned that our days are numbered, and we try to use our life wisely. To know that we are mortals does not keep us from feeling the excruciating sting of loss. Hopefully our knowledge does permit us to trust that even though we experience irreversible loss we are given the capacities to go on living. Mature mourning permits us to adapt to change forced by loss.

John Bowlby and C. Murray Parkes identify four phases of healthy mourning: 1) numbness, 2) yearning for the deceased person or lost object, 3) disorganization and despair, and 4) reorganization.

Numbness is a characteristic of emotional shock and is exhibited both by outright denial that loss has taken place and by stupor. Some people may believe that they are functioning normally at time of loss, but objective observation indicates the contrary.

The second phase is characterized by painful yearning for the deceased person or lost object. The mind becomes obsessed with everything that can be recalled about the deceased. Familiar sounds and smells may, at least momentarily, make the mourner believe that their loved one has returned. Anger at being left alone, guilt over omissions in their relationship, and separation from familiar patterns of life shared with another—all these deepen the pain of separation.

The period of disorganization is marked by the struggles of survivors to compensate for the role no longer played by the deceased. In the family constellation, there are problems over who will assume vacated roles. For a surviving spouse, there not only is the need to compensate for former dependence on the deceased but the uncertainty over what degree of independence is either possible or desirable.

Reorganization usually occurs gradually. But some people seem to be relieved of their grief in a relatively short time. In some cultures, the period of reorganization is marked by a ritual, such as a feast on the anniversary of the death, which signals that the period of mourning is over. But what is important is when, in one's heart, the deceased is permitted to be released. Then healing takes place, and one's love may again be directed to others.

Adults who suffer loss of someone close to them sometimes mourn with behavior more appropriate to a child. Analysis usually uncovers unresolved loss from childhood or adolescence, evidence that for some reason the mourning process was left incomplete. Mark is an example.

Mark was thirty-five when his mother died. He appeared to have a stable home life and a satisfying career, but he began to exhibit erratic behavior soon after his mother's funeral. He failed to complete assignments at work, his sleep patterns were disturbed, and he seemed aloof from his family. When Mark came for counseling, he said he was coming to satisfy his family, that there was nothing wrong with him. Yet, even in the first session, he broke down in tears and began to speak of "Auntie." When asked why he called his mother "Auntie," he reacted with surprise. "I don't. That is what I called my aunt." Mark remembered his aunt as a surrogate mother. She had lived next door to his parents, had provided him with a great deal of companionship, and had taken care of him while his mother had been confined to bed with a long illness. Auntie died when Mark was twelve. The occasion of his mother's death stimulated repressed conflict. Mark, as a child, had not been able to understand his aunt's death and in his subconscious, at least, he had tried to keep her within grasp.

Mourning is our natural way of healing from loss. When our grieving process is healthy, we are able to express our feelings,

conceptualize or make sense out of the experience, and we are able to come to a weighted assessment of what the experience means to us. Not every loss will be felt with the same intensity.

Our Encounter With Another's Loss. Even though we may have developed healthy ways for handling loss, we may fall into what I call the "Surrogate Suffering Syndrome" when we encounter another's loss. It is one thing to work through our own feelings of loss; it is quite another to realize that we must let others work through their sense of loss, too. Most of us try to shield our loved ones from suffering, particularly when the one we love is a child. But, as noted above, even children must be able to work through feelings of loss. The following examples demonstrate why.

Two six-year-old children had leukemia. Martha, mother of the first child, had great difficulty handling her own emotions. She was often hysterical, anxious, and guilt-ridden. She conveyed to both her friends and the hospital personnel that no one should permit her child to suffer. "Don't explain anything to him. Don't play with him. Leave him to me." Her child in turn, reflected the emotions and behavior of his mother, largely it seemed because those were the emotions she would accept from him. Each step of therapy was a hassle. Panic seemed to infect the child every time someone came into his room. He was confused and frightened.

Geri, mother of the second child, maintained a sense of composure, courage, and competence even though there were times when she freely cried. She identified times and circumstances when she needed help from others, particularly from her husband, and assumed a healthy dependence on the hospital staff. Her son exhibited similar behavior. Even as he was dying, he insisted that he do some things for himself. Despite the usual side-effects of his disease and therapy, which sometimes lead to disorientation and depression, the patient seemed to have a sense of confidence that he would be taken care of.

For both children, the disease was debilitating. For the first child, there was additional suffering with fears of being unable to cope.

The attempt to shoulder a patient's suffering for him is as futile as it is to try to do his dying for him. The attempt seems to be motivated by a mixture of good will and guilt, love and hostility, service and need to control. Every attempt to be the surrogate sufferer imposes an additional burden of loss on the patient.

Attempts to be another's surrogate sufferer or attempts to stifle our own feelings are not healthy ways to handle loss. Mourning is our natural way for coping with loss. When our grieving process is healthy, we are able to express our feelings, conceptualize or make sense out of the experience, and we are able to come to a weighted assessment of what the experience means to us. "Blessed are those who mourn, for they shall be comforted."

—From Glen W. Davidson. *Living with Dying*, Minneapolis: Augsburg Publishing House, 1975.

FOR FURTHER READING:

Hubbard, David A. *Why Do I Have to Die?* Ventura, Calif.: Regal Books, 1978.

Kübler-Ross, Elisabeth. *On Death and Dying*. New York: Macmillan Publishing Co., 1969.

Miller, Jack S. *The Healing Power of Grief*. New York: Seabury Press, 1978.

Reed, Elizabeth L. *Helping Children with the Mystery of Death*. Nashville: Abingdon Press, 1970.

Swindoll, Chuck. *For Those Who Hurt*. Portland: Multnomah Press, 1977.

DELINQUENCY

IT IS UNLIKELY that there will ever be a real end to my search for the truth about why kids go wrong—or right, but I have reached a point where I can draw a number of conclusions and pass some of my thinking along to other parents. First I would like to ask several questions.

What kind of parent are you? What kind of children are you rearing? Are your kids among the 95 percent of American youngsters who are members of the upbeat generation, whose exploits are reported on honor rolls and in school publications? Or, are they among the delinquent 5 percent whose names are on police blotters and who are included in national crime statistics, who attract a disproportionate amount of attention in newspaper headlines and require enormous expenditures of time and money?

I am grateful to J. Edgar Hoover for reminding us that basically most of our youngsters are honest, and except for those with mental deficiencies, appear to know the basic difference between right and wrong. But we still have the "5 percenters" to plague those who are in the 95 percent bracket. Just glancing at the bare statistics, you might be justified in wondering why there should be so much noise about juvenile delinquency. But if you search further, you will find that federal, state and local governments, church organizations, schools, and private bodies devote millions of dollars a year and countless man-hours to coping with the 5 percent, all at the expense of the 95 percent.

. . . The six basic essentials of good parenthood have become clear, at least to me: love, supervision, discipline, communication, companionship, and religious education. And it seems that if you love your children and can communicate with them, the other qualities that constitute good parenthood will just come naturally.

A recently published study by a prominent psychiatrist showed dramatically that 77 percent of all our problem children come from families without adult supervision, which really means without love. Most of the reports I have read on delinquency by psychologists and sociologists point to a lack of proper communication between parents and children, and therefore also the absence of love.

Few youngsters I have worked with have ever known what it meant to have parents who were really involved in their lives. Their fathers never played ball with them. Their mothers did not bake cookies or cakes for them or make lemonade on hot summer days. PTA meetings were shunned. Sunday was a time for individual pursuits. Mealtimes were not occasions for families to sit down together and talk, but rather ordeals to be rushed through in a hurry. Nobody cared what Jimmy or Susie did after school as long as they were out of the way. There was little interest in progress in school. These youngsters were, for the most part, left alone to shift for themselves. It amazes me when I think of the number of children from homes such as these who somehow have managed to turn out all right. And I have been astonished also when I have seen financially solid homes run just as haphazardly as some of our tenement dwellings.

Most of the youngsters who have turned up at Teen Challenge have gone bad because their parents appeared to be unconcerned about which way they were going in life. Deprived children go wrong. So do children from advantaged homes, but often for different reasons. Too much pressure and over-planning do as much harm to the suburban youth as neglect does to the poor kid in the city.

On learning his child is in trouble, the suburban parent says, "I can't figure it out. We did everything for our child." This parent saw to it that every minute of his child's day was occupied—school, music lessons, dancing lessons, little league sports, club meetings, and tutoring sessions to make sure he got into college. Mom has been the chauffeur, carrying the kids from one activity to another. The parents are in a rat race for status in their community and they have thrust their children into a mouse race, herding, goading, and pressuring their youngsters to be popular, to be successful, to get into the right college. These children are being suffocated, but not by love. With loving concern and communication, the pressures that prompt some kids to steal, smoke marijuana, get drunk, or seek an outlet in illicit sex would not be there.

We parents must learn to be involved in the lives of our children without becoming too involved, without smothering and frustrating them. We have to judge when to withdraw from their activities and stand aside and let nature take its course. We need to allow for personal development and initiative. Children have a way of turning out all right when they are given a chance to explore their own world as long as they are within reach and sound of their loving mothers and fathers.

I learned from my own son that you can go too far in trying to be a pal to your kids. Last summer I decided that I should spend more time with Gary, who was then eight, so I invited him to go bicycle riding with me on three consecutive days. On the third day, after we had ridden about two miles, he pulled off the road and flopped down on the ground.

"How are you doing, pal?" I asked.

"O.K. Daddy, but are you sure you aren't tired?"

I knew something was "bugging" him, so I

dug a little deeper. Eventually he looked embarrassed and blurted it out.

"I've been going with you just so you'd know I still love you," Gary said.

It turned out that he would have preferred to be playing with his friends. You should have seen the expression of relief that swept his face when we started home so he could join his neighborhood pals, who were building a tree house. Now Gary and I spend most of each Monday afternoon together. Both of us plan for it. His friends and my associates know that is Dad's day and we are comfortable together. The rest of the week, both of us are too busy to spend much time together, but it does not matter because Monday is our day.

This is one path to communication between parents and child, but there are others. In our home, and in the homes of a few others I know, parents are always available to answer their children's questions and to talk to them. We encourage them to do their homework, but without ever actually helping them do it. We try to make our dinner table conversation an occasion for a real exchange of ideas. The children, my wife, and I save interesting experiences or problems concerning us all to discuss at the table, and each has his chance to talk. This I find is a rarity in our busy society where everyone is in such a hurry to get to the next order of business of the day that meals are bolted in silence or are the occasion for family fights.

Rules for child-rearing are easy to come by, but I do feel deeply that there are some that are intelligent guidelines for family-living. Before I present these ideas on how to help your kids grow up, however, let me pass on to you a few of the comments I have heard from teen-agers who have talked to me after hearing me speak at meetings. During a recent tour of the larger cities in England, I had a chance to talk to teen-agers

and I learned that youngsters on the other side of the Atlantic have much the same concerns and problems as ours do. Parents everywhere seem to be basically the same, and so are the youngsters.

Here is what a sixteen-year-old boy told me in Bristol: "My folks are good people, but they just aren't with it. They don't know what I have to be to keep up with the crowd, so I'm really two people. They know just one side of me, but they seem satisfied with that. It's easy to fool them."

John, a teen-ager, took me for a walk through Soho, London's counterpart of Greenwich Village. "See all those strip joints?" he observed. "That's where our fathers go for entertainment. Then they go home and lecture to us about bad women. It takes a stupid kid to fall for mockery like that. We've got eyes. Parents should set the right example or keep quiet."

Thousands of miles away, in Los Angeles, a fifteen-year-old girl told me: "If being interested is communication, I'd say my parents do communicate. There are a thousand ways they show their interest. But they let me choose my own religion and faith instead of offering guidance and then regulate my meals and tell me what brand of toothpaste to use. My mother is afraid I will get too emotional about religion, but she sobs over soap operas on television. It just doesn't add up."

Another California teen-ager came to me to tell me she was pregnant. "My folks are sick about it. They think that sex education should have been enough to keep me from getting hung up on a boy. They have always been more worried about me having a baby than about my knowing what real love means. I learned the hard way about the difference between love and lust. I don't think my mother knows how to reach me with sex values."

A nineteen-year-old narcotics addict who

lives in Brooklyn told me how he had been looking in on life from the outside since early childhood. "I remember standing outside Yankee Stadium two years ago and watching all the dads and their kids getting in their cars," he said. "I was high on stuff, but I still remember how I hurt. It wouldn't have taken a ball game to grab me. All it would have taken was a swift kick in the pants or a slap on my face. I wanted someone to really care what happened to me. I don't understand the question about communication and all that, but I understand what it means to sit all night in a cold subway with no one to tell you to come or go, and no one to talk to with respect. . . ."

A fifteen-year-old minister's daughter had this to say: "I think parents want to be in the dark about certain things. Take me, for instance. My dad's a minister and I think he knows I go to Greenwich Village every Friday night. I tell him I'm staying with friends, but he knows I'm running around with two beatniks. He takes me shopping, just to talk, but he never comes right out with it about what I'm doing. He told me he didn't like my long hair but it was up to me to make the choice.

"I've lost my faith. I'm really an atheist in my heart and I'm dropping out of school. My father could have stopped me, but he was afraid he would make me bitter. I know he is really worried about me, and so am I, but I don't know what to do."

A Houston, Texas, minister's son has rebelled by refusing to cut his shoulder-length hair and wear conventional clothes. "My dad says I am incorrigible," he said. "The last time we talked we almost had a fist fight. He traveled for the first seven years of my life and I hardly knew he was alive. Now, all of a sudden, he won't let me breathe without a license.

"My mother just cries and begs me to be good. I'm not really bad. I'm just trying to show them they can't shove me around for no reason at all. When I was twelve I wanted a father I could talk to, but he was never there. Now that I've got my own friends and do a little drinking, he wants to have a heart-to-heart talk with me. It is too late and he knows it, so he's trying to get me to go to Chicago to live with my uncle. That way I won't be an embarrassment to him any more. I'll be out of his way."

Just so no one will think that all children have these problems, let me tell you what a seventeen-year-old Boston boy said. "My dad is an advertising executive and I've got it pretty nice," he told me. "I think I'm well adjusted and I've never been bored. Both Mom and Dad are always busy and I spend summers away from them. I think I'll make it because Dad has always been a friend, not just a father, but a real friend. We talk."

Perhaps an effective way for me to spell out some guidelines on rearing children to go right instead of wrong would be first to use a little reverse psychology and outline ten ways to produce a juvenile delinquent:

1. Keep your children out of sight and silent. Stop their eternal questions and pestering for attention. Turn away their important queries by saying, "You're too young to know," or "Don't bother me with that now." Repress them when they act their age in childish ways.

2. Hound them to be at the top of their class in school. Tell them they have to go to college whether they want to or not. Make a scene whenever they bring home unsatisfactory report cards. Never compliment them on the best work they do; just pick on the poor results. Make sure they feel they are stupid and lazy if they don't make all A's and B's. Put the pressure on them.

3. If you cannot or do not take your children to church, don't bother to send them. Use the excuse that they are too young to understand about God or the church. Tell

them to wait until they are old enough to make up their own minds. Don't let your day of rest be disturbed by having to send your children off to Sunday School.

4. Have your fights in front of your children. Make certain they see and hear everything. Pick on each other within the family circle but be sure to act affectionately toward one another when company comes so that your children will come to know you as phonies, a knowledge that will adversely affect them all the rest of their lives.

5. Don't be too interested in your children's friends. Let them run around with any kids they choose. Take the attitude that if some of their friends are undesirable, your boy or girl will be a good influence on them. Do not be firm about your children's associates and do not make sure that you know at all times where the youngsters are and what they are doing.

6. Demonstrate your love for your children with material things. Fill their pockets with money. Let them buy all the clothes they want. Make sure they get the impression that they do not need to turn to stealing for the things they want because you will give them everything you can. Give your child the things you could not have when you were growing up and then when he gets in trouble you will be able to tell yourself, "There isn't a thing I haven't given that child! I cannot understand why he had to steal."

7. Set a bad example so the children will not want to grow up to be like you! When a father gets drunk periodically, the mother should warn her children against growing up like "the old man." A father should point out to his daughters he hopes they won't turn out the way their mother has—a poor housekeeper and disinterested cook. Cheat a little on your income tax and violate the speed laws and then bawl the kids out whenever they tell a lie or crib in a school examination.

8. Refuse to believe it when you are told your children have done something wrong. Stand up to their teachers when they complain and tell them they must be mistaken. When Junior comes home with a bloody nose, go out and berate his adversary's father without finding out who was to blame for the fight. If you fight your child's battles for him, he may reward you some day with the honor of standing beside him in juvenile court.

9. Don't be too tough on disciplining your children, lest they hate you for it. Ignore their temper tantrums. Never spank them. Bribe them into obedience by threatening to cut down allowances or reduce television time. If that makes them angry, tell them they are acting like delinquents. If you fail to keep threats of punishment they will learn your bark is worse than your bite and become incorrigible.

10. Never discuss the facts of life with your children. Let them learn about sex from their playmates and from pornographic literature they buy or borrow and sneak into the house. Put a taboo on discussions about sex in the home. Let them learn with a little experimenting and then overlook their transgressions. Don't be concerned as long as they know how to keep from having babies. Ignore talk about drug addiction and delinquency as exaggerations and things that never could involve your children.

Follow these rules and your kids are likely candidates to qualify for the delinquent 5 percent. Violate the rules and your chances are high of having decent, upbeat kids.

Teen-agers themselves have given me some positive tips on how to give your kids a chance, and I would like to pass them on to you. In the language of the youngsters themselves, it is colorful jargon indeed, but quite to the point, as you will see:

1. "Keep your cool." Don't lose your temper in every crisis. Don't get excited when things go wrong. Kids need the confidence

only a steady hand and settled soul can offer.

2. "Don't get hung up on a jag that keeps you away from home." Salesmen fathers should keep in touch with their families somehow. Mothers should forego heavy social schedules to be at home to supervise the children. If a mother works, she should make sure someone else is on hand.

3. "Don't get strung out." Stay away from liquor and sleeping pills. Be a square.

4. "Bug me a little." Use strict but loving discipline. Show your kids who is boss. Don't just let them ride out the storms. Help them anchor their ships.

5. "Don't blow your class." Keep the dignity of parenthood. Stay on the pedestal, if your children have put you there. Don't dress, act, and swing the way teen-agers do. Let them know you are an adult.

6. "Light me a candle." Show your children the way to faith. Tell them that God is not dead, sleeping, hiding—or on vacation. Give them the security of a living faith.

7. "Take the world off my shoulders." Share your children's problems. Discuss morals, life and love, eternity, beauty, peace of mind, and values with them. Try to help them understand that the world can be a good place in which to achieve.

8. "Scare the hell out of me." When you catch a child in his first encounter with smoking, drinking, or sex, punish him. Let him know why you are taking punitive action and impress upon him that more stringent measures will be taken if the transgression is repeated. Be certain he understands what he has done wrong and why it is wrong and that you are doing this out of love and concern and not to be vindictive. By all means, do not mete out punishment in anger.

9. "Call my bluff." Let a youngster know once and for all that you mean what you say. Regardless of what threats a teenager makes—to run away, to become a delin-quent, to drop out of school—stand firm and the bluffing will cease.

10. "Be honest with me." Always tell your children the truth. Never keep them in doubt where you stand on any matter. Be truthful and generous in praise, and then when it comes time to criticize, they will believe you and respect your judgment.

The do's and don'ts are simple to describe but they can be difficult to carry out. However, every child, as well as every adult, needs limits and rules to live by. The teenager especially craves reassurance that his parents are interested enough to try to keep him from getting into trouble. And all youngsters need discipline that will enable them to direct their energies into creative channels. All of us have developed behavior patterns based on the behavior patterns of those who cared for us as children. We, in turn, are providing our children with their behavior patterns.

Rather than dwelling further on this subject, perhaps we should all pause now and take stock of ourselves. What are we as parents going to contribute to the development of healthy patterns? What are we doing that may hurt our children? How can we become better parents so we can help our kids to grow up, so we can give them a chance to go right instead of wrong?

You may find your answer sooner than you realize. You may find it in the expression on your child's face and the sound of his voice when you greet him at breakfast tomorrow morning with a kiss or a hug or a pat on the back.

—From David Wilkerson, *Parents on Trial.* New York: Hawthorn Books, 1970.

FOR FURTHER READING:

Frellick, Francis I. *Helping Youth in Conflict.* Philadelphia: Fortress Press, 1968.

McLean, Gordon R. *Man, I Need Help!* Minneapolis: Bethany Fellowship, 1975.

Skoglund, Elizabeth. *Your Troubled Children.* Elgin, Ill.: David C. Cook Publishing Co., 1975.

Williams, L. Weinberg. *Our Runaway.* Valley Forge, Pa.: Judson Press, 1979.

DENTAL CARE

THE CHILD gets two sets of teeth. While only the baby or "milk" teeth are visible during the first 5 years of life, the permanent teeth begin to form in the jaw soon after birth, and are nearly completed by the time a child reaches school age. Whatever nourishment is in the child's body during these 5 years has to be the building material for adult teeth. It is no wonder that dentists emphasize a diet adequate in minerals and vitamins for young children.

Brothers and sisters are apt to be like each other in the time their teeth erupt. Most children cut a tooth by 8 months of age. They will have anywhere from 2 to 10 teeth a year, with 4 to 6 as average. If a 1-year-old has no teeth at all, see the doctor.

Teeth continue to come in—usually in pairs—until the age of 2½ or 3, when all 20 of the first set are in and the child can handle an adult diet. When a tooth is coming in, the child may be irritable or fretful, and may not eat well for a few days. But teething alone rarely accounts for an illness. Because teething goes on for such a long time, it is easy to blame all childhood upsets on cutting a tooth, but it is safer to rule out other causes first.

The first 4 permanent teeth to come through are the 6-year molars which appear sometime between the fifth and seventh birthdays. They come in behind the last baby teeth on both sides of upper and lower jaws, and are sometimes mistaken for temporary teeth. Take good care of the 6-year molars, for they must last the lifetime.

All of the child's teeth are important, however. They enable him to chew his food properly as an aid to digestion. The presence of baby teeth helps to form a proper jaw line. The child's bite, or occlusion of the teeth, is determined largely by his heredity, but premature loss of baby teeth can alter its shape. Therefore, baby teeth need to be examined regularly by a dentist and checked between times if decay appears or a tooth is chipped or broken by a fall. Before age 3, a child can begin to brush his teeth. He'll need reminding and supervision for many years, though.

To be sure that their children have the lifetime benefits of good teeth and sound jaw structure, all parents will want their children to have:

A diet which emphasizes milk, vegetables, and fruits and minimizes sugars and sweets. Too many sweet foods and soft drinks make the child neglect other more essential foods.

Regular check by the dentist beginning at age 2 or 3. With an early start, the child will be able to make friends with his dentist through the examination and cleaning. Cavities will be found early and easily treated. If the first visit is postponed until a later age, the child's introduction to the dentist is apt to be less pleasant.

—From *Your Child From 1 to 6.* Washington: U.S. Department of Health, Education and Welfare, 1969.

FOR FURTHER READING:

Denholtz, Melvin and Elaine. *How to Save Your Teeth and Your Money: A Consumer's Guide to Better, Less Costly Dental Care.* New York: Van Nostrand Reinhold Co., 1980.

Himber, Jacob. *The Complete Family Guide to Dental Health.* New York: McGraw-Hill Book Co., 1978.

Moss, Stephan J. *Your Child's Teeth: A Parent's Guide to Making and Keeping Them Perfect.* Boston: Houghton Mifflin Co., 1979.

DEPRESSION

To our dismay as parents, the tendency to depression sometimes begins at a very early age. The depressed child will usually withdraw and become abnormally quiet and seclusive. He will sulk or hide from group activities at play, hoping someone will notice his pain. Because parents are often the last to recognize depression in their children, their frustration and anger at the child's withdrawal may compound the difficulty before they become fully aware of it.

If the depressed child does not withdraw, he tends to nurse his resentments until they erupt in such erratic behavior that he earns the reputation of being "a problem child." He may break things to get attention, fight with other children, and in general make himself "Peck's bad boy." Such behavior should be interpreted by his parents as a cry for help. He craves love, affection, and reassurance from them, but instead their exasperation at his behavior only amplifies his feeling of rejection. This lowers his self-esteem, increases his anger, and produces further obnoxious behavior.

Statistics indicate that suicide may well accompany such a condition. Because children often live in a fantasy world and through television feed upon violence, they have no comprehension of the finality of death. Therefore, determined to get even with their parents by some act of self-destruction, while at the same time hoping to return to life (as some individuals do on television), depressed children resort to suicide. This is becoming an alarming tragedy of our times. And even if the depressed child escapes self-destruction, he is almost certain to develop the dreadful habit of self-rejection. A negative thinking pattern or failure complex can well leave him emotionally and mentally scarred for life.

The adopted son of a couple caused such concern because of his erratic behavior that his parents came for counseling. Although the boy had developed a reputation in school for being "stupid," "inept," and "bungling," in reality he had an I.Q. in excess of 145 and knew as much about science and electronics as many engineers. By drawing deeply upon spiritual resources and administering unusual love, acceptance and approval, the parents brought that boy out of his tendency to depression.

For every home which has been blessed with children, the following sixteen suggestions may serve as a checklist of children's special needs:

1. Love and affection—The primary cause of depression in children, lack of love and affection from their parents, sets up thought patterns of resentment and self-pity. God has so constructed the mental mechanism of a child that he automatically looks to his parents for affection. A child's emotional need for love matches his physical need for food.

In my opinion, one reason so many adults encounter recurring depression today is that they were not breast-fed as babies. Humanistic man in his determination to effect a way of life independent of God made the mistake of suggesting to young mothers that modern science had produced a substitute for mother's milk. But he failed to take into account that a bottle in a crib is no substitute for a mother's love.

A group of Jewish doctors set up a special clinic in New York for Jewish orphans. They spared no hygienic means to protect the babies from germs, even to using special germ-killing lights, filtering the air, and requiring that attendants put on new sterile uniforms and rubber gloves when feeding the little ones. Much to their horror, they discovered that the mortality rate in their hospital was three times higher than in a similar hospital in Mexico. An investigator was dispatched to find what the Mexican hospital contained which theirs did not. When the report came back, they could hardly believe it! The understaffed Mexican hospital, lacking in registered nurses, unsanitary by New York standards, and totally inadequate according to the rules of modern medicine, adhered faithfully to a rather "odd rule." Every baby was held in the arms of an attendant at feeding time.

As important as the mother's milk is to the child physically, so is the tenderness and reassurance of a mother's love to the child's emotions. I am deeply convinced that the Creator had this vital relationship in mind when He designed both the mother's body and the child's emotions.

All children crave affection, even the most choleric child. If he receives it at this stage, he tends to develop into normality and finds it easy to express affection. The love-starved child will either become cold or develop an obsessive compulsion for affection. When our first child was a preschooler, we boarded children. I will never forget the olive-skinned four-year-old named Carol who lived in our home for one year. She had been abandoned by her mother, no one knew the identity of her father, and she had lived in eight different homes by the time she came to us. I never saw a child who craved so much kissing. Whenever I showered kisses on our Linda, Carol would demand many more—and always insisted that I kiss her squarely on the mouth. Sometimes it took the supernatural love of God to bestow sufficient love upon that child, but I can testify that He supplies that need.

2. Acceptance—The need for acceptance by those closest to us in life is well-known. In fact, many children are afraid they really do not belong to their parents or seem apprehensive lest a mistake was made in bringing them home from the hospital. Not only their relationship with parents in the home, but also their appearance, capabilities, and habits are in need of acceptance. The child who is conscious that he is approved by his parents and was desired by them before his birth is a fortunate child indeed. By contrast, many counselees begin the sad narration of their life story, "I was a mistake; my parents never wanted me in the first place." Such a mental hurdle is very difficult to overcome.

It is a sign of maturity in a parent when he does not react negatively to his child's weaknesses that parallel his own. Most parent-child personality conflicts are caused by the parent's reaction to his own weakness manifested in his child. He hates the thing in himself; consequently, he despises it in his child and overreacts. The child should not be expected to understand that the parent's rejection is not against him personally, but against those traits that remind him of himself. As a child, he will interpret the parent's actions as total rejection.

The mature parent will recognize himself in his child, emotionally, physically and mentally. If he has learned to accept himself, he can easily accept his child. Once having communicated that acceptance, he can lovingly help him toward overcoming his weaknesses.

3. Avoid anger in the home—Destructive anger erupts in many forms, all of which prove harmful to children, who are so self-centered by nature that parental irritation automatically makes them regard themselves as the cause of the upset and the object of the anger. Such anger produces an insecure and resentful child, which as we have seen compounds his negative behavior and

increases his parent's expression of anger. Young parents in particular are very impatient. When confronted with the immature and often exasperating activities of a child, this impatience bursts into harsh language or angry discipline, which only aggravates the child's self-rejection and insecurity and prepares him for self-pity and depression.

4. Open display of parental love in the home—One of the best things parents can do to promote a sense of security and love in a child is to demonstrate love regularly in the home. As a result of the rising divorce rate today, children are forced to choose sides between the two people on earth they love most, mother and father, whose angry outbursts toward each other emotionally confuse the child and cause him to build up defenses against giving himself in love to someone else. If the home disintegrates and he is forced to leave one parent, he may resent the one he accompanies and fantasize about the one he leaves. Remember, the child who watches his mother and father demonstrate affection for each other will develop a predisposition toward security, affection and a good mental attitude.

Looking back on my childhood, I recall being raised during the depression. My father died before my tenth birthday, leaving my twenty-eight-year-old mother a widow with three small children, including my five-year-old sister and my seven-week-old brother. I have never had to deal with a sense of insecurity, largely because I have never known what it is not to be loved. My father had a great capacity to love, and although he was taken from us at an early age, as a child I could understand his absence through death (a sharp contrast to the problem of divorce).

My mother's love for me and her great faith in God always sustained the optimistic idea that no matter what problems arose, a reasonable solution could be found. Every child has a right to such love and acceptance. As I conjure up fond memories of my parents, I especially remember my father coming into the kitchen, putting his arms around my mother, and lifting her three inches off the floor in a warm, affectionate embrace. That scene always gave me a sense of security. Even the memory of that scene made me feel good. Many of the emotional neuroses children reflect today could probably have been avoided had they experienced such obvious demonstrations of their parents' love.

5. Rules for guidelines—Just as a swinging bridge with guardrails is easier to walk across than the same bridge without protection, so every child needs fences or limits set by his parents to direct his behavior. These rules should be simple and well-defined, administered with love. They will constantly change with the age of the child, but whenever you set a rule, prepare for the child to test it, and don't expect him to thank you for it. I have watched children chafe at rules, badger their parents about them, and then, when they have forced their parents to revoke the rule, indicate a loss of respect for the parent.

6. Discipline—what a relief!—Too much parental leniency begets undisciplined children. The Bible makes it very clear that if you spare the rod, you will undoubtedly spoil the child. "Foolishness is bound in the heart of a child; but the rod of correction shall drive it far from him" (Proverbs 22:15). Educators tell us that knowledge accompanied with emotion provides the surest form of learning. A vigorous spanking or other appropriate form of discipline when delivered in love makes a profound impression on the mind of the child. Yes, he may feel rejected at the time, but every child needs to discover that he cannot do some things in life. If he is not exposed to discipline, he will fail to learn many valuable lessons that he desperately

needs to know. In addition, discipline is cathartic. A child can certainly feel true guilt when he has done wrong; consequently, even though his punishment hurts, it provides a welcome mental relief. That is why children are frequently in a good mood shortly after being disciplined. Those who refuse to discipline their children cheat them out of that much-needed alleviation of conscience.

Roger came to live in our home against my better judgment. Still in our twenties, my wife and I were not prepared to cope with a teenager. But the welfare worker assured us that if we didn't take him, he would be sent to a boy's detention home. Caught in the crossfire of parental hostility, he was assigned to his mother but desperately wanted to live with his father.

We got along fine as long as we let Roger do pretty much as he pleased. Gradually we had to assign him some chores as we did our own children. Day after day he got worse. Wantonly destructive, he refused to comply with our minimal standards, becoming verbally abusive and nasty. Then it happened! When my wife asked him to do the dishes one Sunday afternoon, he refused, sassed her back, and became downright insulting.

One of the things I had learned from my father the hard way was that no man worthy of the title would suffer his wife to be verbally or physically abused by anyone—including his own children. Stepping into the kitchen, I demanded that Roger apologize, but he steadfastly refused. When I gave him a choice between a "spanking and an apology," he said, "You wouldn't dare!" That challenge couldn't be passed up—so I took him into the bedroom and administered the rod of knowledge to the seat of learning.

Within fifteen minutes Roger was out in the kitchen talking affectionately and happily. He even pitched in and helped me dry

the dishes. Somehow that spanking taught him we did love him and also cleared his conscience of the heavy load of guilt for his misconduct. Life once again became livable for the whole family.

Contrary to popular opinion, discipline does not crush or stifle a child's spirit when properly administered. Instead, it often creates quite the opposite effect. The child who is disciplined when he is wrong gains the assurance of his parent's love. It is not at all uncommon for the obstreperous child, whose guilt-laden activities make him irrepressible, to become more considerate, obedient and loving after proper discipline. By contrast the undisciplined child will have difficulty in achieving a sense of acceptance.

One factor about parental discipline should be stressed. Parents absolutely must be united on rules and standards of behavior. The child will naturally work one parent against the other, much to the disruption of the family and the breakdown of effective discipline. Disagreement on principles should never be aired in front of the child, but thoroughly discussed until a united position and joint policy statement can be shared with the child, whether both parents are present or absent. I have seen perfectly normal children, particularly in their teen years, turn into maladjusted monsters because the mother let it be understood that as soon as father went off to work, his rules were no longer enforced. Equally as harmful is the immature father who finds he can win the affection of his children by lowering mother's standards. That is a short-term love that sows the bitter seeds of confusion and rebellion.

7. Consistency—thou art a gem!—The most important part of discipline is consistency. This relates not only to individual problems in the life of one child, but also to equal consideration of all the children in the family. Maintain few rules whose violation

results in spanking, but once established, make sure you exact the penalty without hesitation!

8. Be fair—no child is perfect!—Most young people want their day in court. For that reason the parent should project the image that he is willing to discuss the rules. The child always feels better when he has been able to air his feelings in the family court of justice, even when regulations are not altered. Besides, the parent should train his child to reason matters out, not merely respond emotionally.

9. Communicating God's love early—The child raised by Christian parents is most fortunate, for next to parental love, every human being needs to be assured of God's love. Such a message is best communicated by the child's parents early in life. The little Sunday school song, "Jesus loves me, this I know, for the Bible tells me so," sung fervently by young children every week, acts as a source of reassurance to them. In some of their lives, only such reassurance can compensate for the lack of parental love and help to generate a normal attitude toward life.

10. Leading your child to Christ when he is young—Every human being needs to accept Christ as his personal Lord and Savior. The sooner he does that, the better are his chances of avoiding unnecessary pitfalls that induce emotional trauma. He then can develop a mature, confident emotional pattern that helps to prepare him for the uncertain circumstances of life.

11. Guarding against negative thinking—One's thinking pattern is learned early in life. Watch your child carefully for signs of negativism or defeatism. Foster in him the assurance that he can do all things through Christ who strengthens him. Let him understand that today's impossibility may well become tomorrow's achievement. A child must develop the mental attitude espoused by the old adage, "You can learn to do anything if you want to bad enough." But a positive approach to life does not just happen; it results from consistent, patient reassurance on the part of the parent.

A child will never benefit from constant criticism or condemnation. In an airport lounge I recently overheard a parent instructing a second grader how to purchase a paper from a coin-operated newsstand. With a leap of joy the child returned with the paper, obviously expecting his father's approval. His smile instantly turned to dismay and fear as his father berated him publicly for being "stupid." It was yesterday's paper! The father had not learned that family unity and personal responsibility are not promoted by public humiliation.

12. The malady of griping—We have already discovered that griping is very harmful, for verbalized criticism has a way of entrenching negative thoughts not only in the mind of the speaker, but also in the mind of all hearers. Children who go about griping are establishing a predisposition for consistent periods of depression. Refuse to allow your children the luxury of cluttering up your house with criticism.

At fifteen one of our children was a professional griper. No matter what the occasion, he could find something critical or negative to say. Nothing ever pleased him. Finally we decided to take some long overdue parental action. On the basis of 1 Thessalonians 5:18 we showed him that his griping was contrary to the will of God. The first thing he said was, "But . . ." I stopped him and said, "No buts about it! From now on you are not permitted to gripe in this house. We have a happy household here, and we want your help in keeping it that way." Within three weeks we could see definite signs of improvement. That boy today has a different personality than he had then and much better than if we had permitted him to let that habit become more deeply ingrained in his nature.

13. The infirmity of self-pity uncorrected—Self-pity is a natural mental escape pattern for the child who cannot keep up with or compete in an adult world. Even the third child, contending with older brother and sister, tends to struggle with self-pity more than others.

Gentle and consistent instruction in avoiding this tendency will guard the child from a thought pattern that will have to be broken forceably later in life to avoid depression.

14. And be ye thankful—Every Christian should learn that the spirit of thanksgiving brightens drooping spirits and eliminates depression. Children who are taught to be thankful to God first and then to their parents are well on their way to depression-free living. Teach them early to give thanks for food, love, shelter, health, teachers, and friendship. Children have an amazing ability to learn spiritual truths, and it is often easier for them than for adults to understand that God has a plan even in adverse circumstances. Train your child, "In every thing give thanks" (1 Thessalonians 5:18), "and when he is old, he will not depart from it" (Proverbs 22:6).

15. See your child as he is becoming— Most parents tend to view their children as they are rather than as they will become. I can remember looking at my sons and wondering whether they would ever amount to anything. Today I am very proud of two young men. When children are little, picture them on your imagination screen as they are becoming, for then you will empathize with them and sense their latent potential. Otherwise the reality of the present may only illuminate an intemperate, grimy little urchin. Be careful to maintain an attitude of affec-

tion and patience, for a child cannot easily distinguish between his parent's displeasure at him or his deed. Happy is the child whose parents recognize that by God's grace he will grow up to be a well-adjusted, successful adult some day.

16. Setting a good example—The best learning tool for any child is the example of his parents. If they see you indulging in negativism, self-depreciation, or self-pity, they will follow suit. But if you manifest practices conducive to winning over depression, your children will imitate those good habits.

Almost every authority on depression, both modern and ancient, observes that depression seems to run in families. We know two reasons for this: inherited temperament and home training. You cannot control the temperament of your child, but you can govern his training. I am inclined to believe that depression runs in families primarily because children tend to copy the bad habits of their parents. I have long observed that depressed children of depressed-prone parents display similar vocabularies and thinking patterns.

Have you ever heard the expression, "When you talk to him, it's just like talking to his father"? Every parent should ask himself, "If my child grows up to think and talk like me, will he manifest a happy spirit and emotional stability or exhibit those symptoms which anticipate depression?"

—From Tim LaHaye, *How to Win Over Depression.* Grand Rapids: Zondervan Publishing House, 1974.

FOR FURTHER READING:

Barrett, Roger K. *Depression: What It Is and What to Do About It.* Elgin, Ill.: David C. Cook Publishing Co., 1977.

Minirth, Frank B., and Skipper, States. *One Hundred Ways to Defeat Depression.* Grand Rapids: Baker Book House, 1979.

Narramore, Clyde M. *How to Handle Feelings of Depression*. Grand Rapids: Zondervan Publishing House, 1974.

Hart, Archibald D. *Feeling Free*. Old Tappan, N.J.: Fleming H. Revell Co., 1979.

Trobisch, Walter. *Love Yourself*. Downers Grove, Ill.: Inter-Varsity Press, 1976.

DEVOTIONS

To you the Lord has committed the great responsibility of Christian nurture. The Bible says,

Children, obey your parents in the Lord:
    for this is right.
Honour thy father and mother;
    which is the first commandment with
    promise;
That it may be well with thee,
    and thou mayest live long on the earth.
And, ye fathers, provoke not your children
    to wrath:
    but bring them up in the nurture and
    admonition of the Lord.

EPHESIANS 6:1–4

In other words, bring them up with Christian discipline and instruction (ASV), in such training and correction as befits the servants of the Lord approves (Charles B. Williams), raise them by letting the Lord train and correct them (William F. Beck). (The comments by these men may be found in *The New Testament From Twenty-Six Translations* published by Zondervan Publishing House.)

This responsibility cannot be relegated to church or school, though church and school may supplement home training. Only in the home can problems be dealt with when they arise. Only in the home can children see living models of Christ reflecting Him in the midst of daily living. Only in the home are there time and experience enough to mold human nature into Christian character.

The purpose of family devotions is not systematic Bible study but rather it is making the Lord the center of all the activities of daily living. When we see the Lord at work, we rejoice together; when conflicts and frustrations annoy, we discover the Lord's perspective on them. The lack of this kind of interaction is what creates a gap between generations and drives young people into their own inner worlds or away from home. In a family we need to relate to each other in terms of how we are feeling and loving and hurting as well as what we are thinking.

Therefore, ask yourself each day what is the particular need of your family for that day.

As you study the topic of the day before the family gathers, adapt it to your own circumstances. The natural way to begin is to describe the cause for rejoicing or a difficulty until all the members of the family sense its significance. Concentrate on the aspects of the problem that you are now experiencing. After you lead the family in finding the biblical answer, discuss very specifically what you as a family should do about the problem in order to obey the Word. Whenever possible, illustrate from your own daily lives, except of course when a person would be humiliated by the disclosure.

There are usually three parts to the subject for each day:

a. Focusing the problem until the need is keenly felt.

b. Finding the answer to the problem in Scripture.

c. Deciding how to obey the Lord in this matter, and talking to Him about it.

Please don't hurry through the first and third parts as if they aren't really important. Unless the members of your family feel a current need, they won't put forth much energy to find the answer in Scripture; God's truth will just be empty words to them. Too often the Word of God means nothing to us as individuals because it doesn't touch our lives in any way. Don't leave any idea from Scripture up in the air without personal relevance. Unless we make definite plans to do something during the day, it's natural for good intentions to evaporate. If possible, check up on decisions before the day is ended, or at least once a week.

Guide the family in studying their own Bibles rather than telling them what God says. Whenever you come to a question, pause to let the members of the family find the answer in Scripture or think about it or answer from their own experience. It is much easier for all of us to obey God if we ourselves discover the truth rather than listen to someone preach to us. Keep the one idea for each day sharply and clearly focused so that it will stay in your minds all day without being clouded by details, even if they are relevant.

As parents be ready to make changes as the Word speaks personally to you. If you pretend to be perfect, in need of nothing, the children will not dare to reveal their real inner needs. The Word of God deals with the basic problems of human nature. As we grow older our problems become more refined and mature, but we still have the basic problems of human nature. The children will think more rather than less of you if you admit that you will always continue to grow in Christ-likeness. They are quick to detect phoniness. The Word admonishes, "Confess your faults one to another . . ." (James 5:16).

Keep family devotions from becoming routine, which is deadly. You will be training your children in wrong attitudes if this time together is boring or impersonal. Don't get preachy. You can make it the best hour of the day if it becomes a part of life, not apart

from life. If you penetrate the very inner life of your own family, the children will think of devotions as a time to solve their personal problems, to talk over with you their deepest frustrations. Make this time so enjoyable and profitable that no one will want to miss it. You may start with a short period, then extend it as the children get personally involved.

Don't think you've committed a crime if the family can't manage a time together every day. We need the Lord's help and guidance each day, but we can talk to Him as we walk down the street or drive in the car. Cultivate a continual communion with and reliance upon the Lord, yet keep home devotions as regular as possible. And don't think you need to cover a whole subject each day. You might profitably spend one day focusing the problem, another on the scriptural answer, and another deciding how you as a family and as individuals should obey the Word of the Lord. It takes time to relate biblical principles to one's own life. If you have only a few minutes together, it might be well to read a praise psalm, like Psalms 19, 27, 92, 96, 103.

Though many families find it very difficult to get together at any time in the day, perhaps the best time is morning as you start the day, with a discussion at the evening dinner table on how the subject of the morning worked out during the day. Or you can discuss a subject one evening and report how you carried it out the next evening before you talk about the new subject. It is as important to check on progress as to make plans for change. Good intentions will evaporate unless you establish the habit of checking up on them.

Older teens should realize that they should identify with you, the parents, rather than with the younger children. Bible truths are so basic that all ages need to continually work on them as new levels of difficulty come along, yet they are simple enough for children to begin to comprehend. If you have an older teen and a primary child, the teen can sit by the primary to help him find the Bible portions and read a few dominant words, or read to him. The primary cannot be expected to grasp all the details, but he should get the general idea, he will probably want to be present, and he can often draw or cut out or find something that illustrates the subject of the day.

If you have only primary and preschool children, they need Bible truths geared to a lower level and activities that do not require reading.

The purpose of family devotions is that the Lord God may speak a personal word to each of you each day for the living of that day. Then each day can be an exciting adventure with the Maker of the universe! You can be caught up in His great plans and draw upon His power. It is just as important that you continually communicate with Him as it is to talk to your parents and brothers and sisters if you have them. God wants to talk to you about your school, your work, your play, your friends, your thoughts. He is personally interested in everything that affects you because He has given Himself for you so that you can freely give yourself back to Him. Try every day to hear some word from His Book that relates to what you are now doing.

If you are going to have a happy home, each member must be open and honest with each other member. None of us will be perfect until we see the Lord face-to-face, so now all of us want to be growing and changing. Of course, outside your home you will stand up for each other, but inside, in the presence of the Lord who understands us all, we must face reality—things as they are, our weaknesses as well as our strengths. Since there are reasons for everything we do, try to understand each other, help each other, and pray for each other, that each of you may become what you want to be. If you hide in your shell or put on a mask to protect what you don't like about yourself, you become unreal, a phony, hurting rather than helping yourself. It's a wonderful feeling to be free and transparent before God and before men. So be free to rejoice over what God does for you and also free to say I'm sorry when you do wrong.

Of course different ages have different needs, but we all need God's truth and God's help, from parents down to the young child, as soon as he understands what God is saying. When a question makes you think, that question is for you. If a question is evident to all of you, skip it and go on.

Each member of the family should bring his or her own Bible to family devotions. If possible each of you should work in a different version so that you can often read a verse from various versions to give it depth of meaning. Younger children will find it easier to read the paraphrased Living Bible and the New Testament's Good News For Modern Man. It would also be helpful, though not essential, to have handy a chalkboard and chalk to make notes as you go along.

Though Father or Mother leads devotions, all of you should be ready to take your part. God gives younger people as well as older people insight into His higher ways. Parents can learn from children as well as children from parents. If you have your own questions about a subject in the book, don't hesitate to ask them. Home devotions focus on our daily lives, just as they are, difficulties as well as joys. See if you can grow stronger in some way every day.

KEEP CHECKING.

Are we creating an atmosphere of sharing
and discussion of common problems
of concern to us all?

Are we making our discussions personal—
  relating what is happening each day in
  our lives
    to the principles of Scripture?
Do we parents acknowledge that we are
human beings
  with our own problems,
    as well as being responsible to God
    for our home?
Is each child recognized as a special creation of God
  with his own potential
    and place in the family?
Is each child getting actively involved
  in terms of his own daily living?

—From Lois E. LeBar, *Family Devotions with
School-Age Children.* Old Tappan, N.J.: Fleming
H. Revell Co., 1973.

FOR FURTHER READING:

Bock, Lois, and Working, Miji. *Happiness Is a
Family Walk with God.* Old Tappan, N.J.:
Fleming H. Revell Co., 1977.

Johnson, Ruth I. *Devotions for the Family.* (3
vols.) Evanston, Ill.: Moody Press.

Priester, Gertrude A. *Let's Talk About God:
Devotions for Families with Young Children.*
Philadelphia: Westminster Press, 1967.

Webb, Barbara O. *Devotions for Families:
Building Blocks of Christian Life.* Valley Forge,
Pa.: Judson Press, 1976.

Whitehouse, Donald and Nancy. *Pray and
Play: A Guide for Family Worship.* Nashville:
Broadman Press, 1979.

DIET

IT IS BECOMING increasingly difficult to get
adequate nourishment from our food, and
most of us are blissfully unaware of what
foods we put into our mouths. Without realizing it, we deprive ourselves of the proper

nutritional balance the body must have to
function to its full potential. Why do we eat
this way?

Stop for a moment and think about why
you eat what you eat. There are basically
five factors which determine your tastes and
appetites. One, your past cultural training
(from your parents); two, availability of food
products; three, convenience; four, your income level; and five, propaganda from the
food industry.

Eating is something we grow up doing but
thinking very little about. What we eat is
definitely similar to what our parents ate.
What they fed us, we came to adopt as our
own. So often we think that the foods we eat
are what everyone eats, but if you examine
the diets of people around the world, you
will find the diversity is amazing. However,
few countries have diets with the quantities
of refined, processed, and preserved foods
which we Americans consume.

We eat primarily to please our taste buds.
After a child has lived for a year or so, he develops a sweet tooth. He learns that some
foods taste sweet and some don't. Many children hold out, refusing to eat what is set before them, so that they can make it to dessert. Often parents give in and allow their
children to win, because they're fearful if
they "don't eat something" they will get
sick. It is actually better for a child to go
hungry for a meal or two and learn to eat the
right food, than to be pampered and allowed
to develop a taste for junk food.

Almost all of us fall into the rut of eating
foods we like and avoiding those we don't.
We usually have very simple diets which do
not provide the variety and balance necessary for proper nutrition.

Once you realize the body is a chemical
machine which needs the right food chemicals to make it run properly, you will realize
what you eat is *all-important* to your health.

The vitality of the body is measured by its

ability to function, whether it is to think or feel or move. *Energy* is the basis of all of life's functions. Without energy there is no life. All of the processes of life involve motion and energy. Whether it is digesting food or thinking, the body requires energy and motion to do those tasks.

God reveals that the foremost commandment is to "LOVE THE LORD YOUR GOD WITH ALL YOUR HEART, AND WITH ALL YOUR SOUL, AND WITH ALL YOUR MIND, AND WITH ALL YOUR STRENGTH" (Mark 12:30).

Strength implies energy and motion—health and vitality. The essence of "loving God" is to have sufficient strength to function properly.

The body needs seven types of essential food chemicals to support life. They are water, carbohydrates, proteins, fats, minerals, vitamins, and bulk. By "essential" I mean substances or chemicals that cannot be manufactured in or converted from any other source by the body; that is, they must be supplied from outside the body.

1. *Water* is about 55–60 percent of the body by weight; it is our most important and immediate need. The average body functions best on eight glasses of water a day. Water is really the body's only fluid need. Such drinks as milk, coffee, tea, sodas, and juices are not fluid needs; they are taste needs.

2. The second basic food need is found in *complex carbohydrates*, i.e., starches and sugars. These must be eaten whole, natural, and complex, rather than processed, purified, and refined. Refined or "simple" carbohydrates, such as white flour, sugar, cornstarch and corn syrups, sugar gelatins, white rice, peeled potatoes, most processed cereals (dry and instant cooked), are grossly depleted foods. In their natural "complex" form, these are the energy foods that are the basis of all bodily functions. They are our best overall source of energy.

3. The next group is the *amino acids*, which are the building blocks of protein. These are the basic structural substances of the body. There are ten essential amino acids from which thirty other amino acids can usually be made within the body. Only ten of the forty amino acids found in the body are "essential." Essential means the human body is unable to manufacture these within itself. These ten essential acids must be taken into our bodies in sufficient quantities to maintain life. Protein has an all-or-none law. That means all ten of the amino acids must be present in their proper balance, at the same time, for synthesis of protein to occur. Eating six of the essential amino acids for breakfast and four for lunch will not sustain life.

4. The fourth group is the *fats and oils*. These substances are an essential part of cellular structure and metabolism. They are far less essential as an energy storage (that is, fat deposits). Fatty acids are the basic building blocks of all fats and oils. There are only two essential fatty acids, linolenic and linoleic acids.

5. The fifth group is *vitamins*. They function to assist (catalyze) biochemical reactions in cellular metabolism. Those that dissolve in water are the B complexes and vitamin C. They are not stored well in the body. Not having enough of certain vitamins can cause deficiency diseases, like scurvy, beriberi, and pellagra. A, D, E and K are fat soluble and store well.

6. The sixth group is the *minerals*, which are divided into two categories: macro- and micro-nutrient. The macro—those needed in large amounts in the body (more than four grams per adult)—are calcium, magnesium, potassium, sodium, phosphorus and chlorine. The micro-nutrients are iron, zinc, chromium, aluminum, copper, manganese, co-

balt, selenium, iodine, sulphur, molybdenum, vanadium, silicone, and nickel. An important difference between the minerals and most vitamins is that their overuse may be directly toxic to the body. Many of the trace elements can become deadly poisons if overused. Many, like chromium and selenium, are needed only in minute amounts. The toxic minerals are beryllium, cadmium, lead, and mercury.

7. The seventh need is for *bulk*. This includes foods that provide pectin, fiber, cellulose, and mucins. They are necessary for good gastrointestinal-bowel functions and for good peristalsis in the elimination process.

One of the most difficult tasks a parent has to teach his children is to eat properly. This will be especially difficult if your children have become accustomed to sugared cereals, fast-food meals, and highly sugared bakery products. Children learn by example. If we want to foster good nutrition, it is going to be up to us to put it in front of them; but it takes more than just putting the right food on their plates.

One parent, alone, cannot improve a family's nutrition very successfully. Both parents must know what good nutrition is and decide this is what they want for their children and themselves. Parents can't expect to have a double standard of expecting the children to have a certain diet, while they go out and "live it up" or sneak junk food in for themselves. Working together, both parents can cooperate and teach their children how to eat the right foods.

Generally, the wife carries the burden of bringing in the proper foods, because she usually does the shopping, plans and prepares the meals. Throw out both the sugar and the sugar bowl. You don't have to have sweet things to eat. You can learn to like many foods that aren't sweetened with refined carbohydrates.

If your children are still in the cradle, your task will be comparatively simple, since they are not used to processed products. It will be easy for you to introduce them to good foods. If they have grown to teenagers and have not incorporated good nutrition into their way of life, your task will be much more difficult, because they have lived in an atmosphere of poor nutrition all their lives. This will take a selling job, but even a teenager can understand that by avoiding refined carbohydrates and other depleted foods, he will have more energy, less skin problems, less sickness, a clearer mind, and a stronger body.

Have a counseling session with your kids. Explain the harm that junk foods cause; explain how much better it will be for them to have proper nutrition. Anyone can learn to "like" new foods. They can learn to enjoy munching on carrot or celery sticks in place of candy bars. They can learn to eat nuts and fruit instead of cookies, cake, and sweet rolls.

Breakfast can be a problem, if your children have learned to demand the sugared cereals. You can cook whole-grain and cracked-grain cereals and serve them with a little honey and milk and cinnamon. Adding fruit to the cereal should take the place of adding sugar or artificial sweeteners. There are puffed rice, whole grain granolas, shredded wheat, puffed corn, and many other prepared cereals that do not contain sugar or other refined carbohydrates. "Long-cook cereals" are better than the instant-cook variety because they are less processed. Eggs and vegetables should also be introduced to your children, as other breakfast possibilities.

Lunches can also be a problem. The lunches served at school usually provide few vegetables. Home-prepared lunches allow for much more nutritious variety. When they eat at their friends' houses, or are served refreshments at church, they will receive cookies and punch and other items that are definitely depleted. Train your children on a consistent basis. Help them identify "junk food" items and how to avoid them.

—From David L. Messenger, M.D. *Dr. Messenger's Guide to Better Health.* Old Tappan, N.J.: Fleming H. Revell Co., 1981.

A DAILY GUIDE TO FOODS NEEDED BY CHILDREN AND THEIR FAMILIES

type of food		each day
MILK GROUP		
Milk	Children under 9	2 to 3 cups.
	Children 9–12	3 or more cups.

Dairy products such as:

Cheddar cheese, cottage cheese, and ice cream.................... May be used sometimes in place of milk.

VEGETABLE-FRUIT GROUP .... 4 or more servings.

Include—

A fruit or vegetable that contains a high amount of vitamin C: Grapefruit, oranges, and tomatoes (whole or in juice), raw cabbage, green or sweet red pepper, broccoli, and fresh strawberries.

A dark green or deep yellow vegetable or fruit for vitamin A: You can judge fairly well by color—dark green and deep yellow: broccoli, spinach, greens, cantaloupe, apricots, carrots, pumpkin, sweet potatoes, winter squash.

Other vegetables and fruits, including potatoes.

MEAT AND MEAT SUBSTITUTES .... 2 or more servings.

Include—

Meat, poultry, fish, or eggs .... 1 or more servings.

Dried beans or peas, peanut butter, and nuts can be used as meat substitutes.

BREADS AND CEREALS .... 4 or more servings.

Whole grain, enriched, or restored bread and cereals or other grain products such as corn meal, grits, macaroni, spaghetti, and rice.

PLUS OTHER FOODS

To round out meals and to satisfy appetite, many children will eat more of these foods, and other foods not specified will be used, such as—butter, margarine, other fats, oils, sugars, and unenriched refined grain products. These "other" foods are frequently combined with the suggested foods in mixed dishes, baked goods, desserts, and other recipe dishes. They are a part of daily meals, even though they are not stressed in the food plan.

—From *Your Child From 6 to 12.* Washington: U.S. Department of Health, Education and Welfare, 1966.

FOR FURTHER READING:

Baker, Yvonne. *From God's Natural Storehouse.* Elgin, Ill.: David C. Cook Publishing Co., 1980.

Josephson, Elmer A. *God's Key to Health and Happiness.* Old Tappan, N.J.: Fleming H. Revell Co., 1976.

Renwick, Ethel H. *Let's Try Real Food: A Practical Guide to Nutrition and Good Health.* Grand Rapids: Zondervan Publishing House, 1976.

Rohrer, Norman and Virginia. *How to Eat Right and Feel Great.* Wheaton, Ill.: Tyndale House Publishers, 1977.

DISCIPLINE

God's Discipline. Human beings have two basic needs: discipline and love. Discipline without love is tyranny. Love without discipline is sentiment. The goal of discipline is always maturity. This is why God disciplines us. He gives us a pattern for personal discipline and for disciplining our children in the way He cares for us.

Hebrews 12:5–11 discusses God's discipline. The King James version uses the word chastens and chastisement, which is defined as punishment in contemporary English. Discipline is a better translation; however, punishment is inevitably part of correcting our wayward tendencies. We are told not to lose courage when we are punished by God, nor to regard His discipline lightly. For,

1. Discipline gives security. God cares enough about us to train us so that our behavior becomes what it should be. It is a proof that He loves us.

2. Discipline is for our good. At the time it seems painful rather than pleasant (v. 10) but God has in mind that we should share His holiness.

3. Discipline yields the fruits of righteousness to those who are trained by it (v. 11). Discipline is training for righteous living. God has a high goal in mind for His children. He is not afraid to use discipline to see the goal accomplished.

Parental Discipline. Parental discipline helps transfer the fruit of God's discipline into the lives of our children. Parents are God's chosen agents, and in a sense stand in God's place until the child is older. Parents are not God; however they are responsible to Him. A parent can say to a child, "Learn to obey me now, so you will know how to obey God later." Wise discipline provides a secure environment in which to grow up. Someone cares. Someone knows what the standard is.

Child psychologists believe that discipline is necessary for mental health. It makes us feel terribly insecure not to know where the fences which surround our lives are located. It's frightening because it may mean no one knows. Where may you run? How far may you go? Teen-agers have made open pleas in youth panels and in letters to newspaper advice columns asking for ground rules, because they know that these mean "someone cares about me."

The Book of Proverbs contains abundant instructions on raising children. Proverbs 19:18 says, "Discipline your son while there is hope; do not set your heart on his destruction."

Proverbs 29:17 reads, "Discipline your son, and he will give you rest; he will give delight to your heart."

Proverbs 22:6 tells us to "Train up a child in the way he should go, and when he is old he will not depart from it."

Train a child while he is young. Take into consideration his whole person. Do not let him go his own way, yet at the same time give him an adequate view of self. Our goal is not to break the child's spirit but to channel it. Punishment for disobedience is a fact in God's economy. Our children should learn that we uphold this standard. But discipline is far more creative, less one-sided than this. It is building into the life some concept of self-esteem, the ability to choose wisely and a respect for the authority of God.

Wise discipline requires special help from God. Some children are crushed by strong words; others respond only to a spanking. A spanking doesn't phase others; they need to be denied choice privileges. We need always to remember that children are people, that love and discipline go together, and that our goal is maturity.

We discipline because it is right to do so, because we are concerned about righteousness. While anger is not an adequate motive for discipline, I am inclined to think that it is not always wrong to be aroused to anger over our children's disobedience.

Recently I heard a father tell of his son's repeated lack of response to his mother's call to come upstairs. Five, six times—still no response. The father finally stopped his gentle urgings that his son obey and spanked the boy all the way up the stairs to the mother. Sensitive to his anger, the father later apologized to the boy. I am quite sure the father was more sensitive than the boy. The son had a sense of justice; he knew he deserved it. The father would have done well to have acted sooner. There will be times when we need to apologize for our behavior to our children—and we must do this. But anger at their behavior which brings about just discipline is not necessarily one of those times.

Ground rules for discipline. Here are some ground rules for disciplining children:

1. Keep your word. Make no idle threats or promises. Be careful that you don't make unimportant negatives for the child to lash out against, which will force you to back down on your word. Don't make promises you don't expect to keep. Then insist that their word be kept as carefully as yours.

2. Don't harangue. It's hard to find the off-switch on some mothers once they get started scolding. Bringing up every past wrong in the course of the scolding defeats the child and leaves the feeling that nothing is ever forgotten. Speak carefully and mean what you say.

My nephew once remarked, "My mother gets her point across to us just by giving us the old hairy eyeball!" Which was his way of saying, "We know her standards, and all it takes is a look from her."

3. Don't argue. Have a discussion, perhaps, as the child grows older. But if you give in to arguing, whining, and crying, you'll have plenty of it to cope with. Parents generally get from their children what they ask for. Some parents put up with a great deal of needless inconvenience, which is of no benefit to the child, because they insist on too little. Children understand more than we think!

4. Be just. Children have an acute sense of fair play. If punishment is involved, make it fit the situation. You are teaching what is morally and socially important. If you treat careless milk-spilling in the same way you treat telling a lie, you make milk-spilling and lie-telling of the same moral importance. And they are not!

5. Teach your child the importance of a genuine admission of guilt. "I'm sorry" are perhaps the hardest words in the English language to say but these words are most easily learned when the child is small. Don't ever accept glibness in their usage, however.

I remember taking our three-year-old to the neighbor's house with the firm instruction that he was to address her by name, look at her face while he spoke, and tell her he was sorry for picking her prize tulips. It never occurred to him or to me that he wouldn't do exactly what I had said he should. It was very important to me to train him to look someone in the eye and say, "I'm sorry." How cowardly are the foot-shufflers, who look the other way, while they mumble out an apology with the sincerity of a fish!

6. Teach your child that forgiveness is real. Let him know you face common sinnerhood together, but teach him by your example that you know what forgiveness is all about.

7. Discuss situations which reflect on life's values whenever you can as the child grows older, so that he can construct his own value structure. Let him help make decisions. The goal is maturity. On unimportant matters, be prepared to let him make a few mistakes as a learning process. Make it easy for him to admit poor judgment and give him confidence to try again.

8. Go to God regularly for help and wisdom. Then act confidently, with a strong note of certainty. He who hesitates finds reluctant obedience. Pray daily that your children's hearts will be available to the promptings of the Holy Spirit.

We discipline our children because it is the loving thing to do. God has a high standard for them, and we uphold this standard. We are agents in building character, in curbing the traits that would lead to folly. We discipline our children so they can learn to discipline their own lives. We do this more effectively if they can see that we, also, have learned this. Our goal is maturity and self-control. We want them to know what is valuable.

Discipline opens up a life of freedom to those trained by it. Real freedom is freedom to choose what is right. The undisciplined person is pushed about by life. He often is a slave to himself, to his own lack of self-control.

Discipline yields peaceable fruits of righteousness in our lives and in the lives of our children. It is the password to freedom; it gives delight to the heart.

—From Gladys M. Hunt, *Focus on Family Life.* Grand Rapids: Baker Book House, 1970.

FOR FURTHER READING:

Barber, Bill. *Discipline and the Young Child.* Ventura, Calif.: Regal Books.

Dobson, James C. *Dare to Discipline.* Wheaton, Ill.: Tyndale House Publishers, 1977.

Holt, Dave and Pat. *How Not to Raise Cain.* Wheaton, Ill.: Victor Books, 1978.

Naylor, Phyllis R. *Getting Along in Your Family.* Nashville: Abingdon Press, 1976.

Treadwell, M. A. *The Discipline of Raising Children.* Eugene, Ore.: Harvest House Publishers, 1977.

DISEASES OF CHILDHOOD

Diseases and Disorders

The following brief descriptions of common diseases and disorders give background information needed by parents as they live with children—children and their spots, runny noses, and wheezes. Of course, such information does not replace the doctor's diagnosis of your child. And, while the list may look alarming, no child contracts them all.

The disorders are grouped so parents can look up any group of symptoms, not as they would be in a medical textbook.

Allergies

What Are They?   When a person is sensitive to a normally harmless substance, he has an allergy. If he receives more of the irritant than he can tolerate, he will show an allergic reaction. An allergy may look like a cold, an upset stomach, a skin disease or a number of other disorders.

There is such a variety of allergic reactions that a series of tests are usually necessary to determine their true nature. Allergies are not infections and cannot be "caught" or given to anyone else. While seldom fatal, they cause discomfort and inconvenience— mild to severe—and can lead the way to infections.

A child with an allergy should be under the care of a doctor who will, by means of tests, trial diets, and changes in the child's surroundings try to determine what the child is sensitive to.

What Causes Allergies? A child may inherit a tendency to allergy, but his reaction to a substance may differ from the reaction of his parents, or, he may be allergic to quite different substances. Any child may develop an allergy, however. Climate, season, degree of exposure, state of mind and other factors seem to contribute to the frequency and intensity of reaction. And the reaction itself may change or disappear as the child grows older. Frequently the doctor will study the child's whole life—the stresses and tensions he lives with—as well as specific irritants in order to get at the cause.

A person may be allergic to certain foods (such as eggs, chocolate, strawberries, milk, fish); to fine particles which are breathed (dust, pollen, feathers); to irritants which he touches (poison ivy, dog or cat hair, wool, glue, soap, detergent); to drugs which are taken by mouth or injections (sedatives, antibiotics, antitoxins); or to germs which are released in the body by an infection.

Sometimes it is relatively easy to find the cause and eliminate it from the child's life so that he gets complete relief. In other cases, the child is sensitive to so many things or to such widely present or obscure substances

that the particular offenders cannot be eliminated.

Some common allergic reactions are:

Asthma, an irritation of the bronchial tubes, narrows the air passages and produces mucus so there is difficulty in breathing. The child wheezes and coughs in an alarming fashion. It may be worse when the child lies down, and he has to sleep propped up. Attacks frequently occur at night, and will vary considerably with the season of the year. Sometimes a cold precedes an asthmatic episode.

Hay fever resembles the common cold, with sneezing, itching and weeping eyes, and a stuffed-up head caused by swelling of the membranes of the nose. It is usually caused by pollens of weeds, grasses, and trees and therefore, unlike a cold, usually comes only at regular seasons of the year. It is rarely seen in children under 3 years of age.

Eczema is a red, thickened rough patch on the skin, frequently on the cheeks, folds of skin at the elbow and behind the knee. It will itch, and scratching causes oozing which forms crusts. While it is not contagious, the open sores may readily become infected.

Hives are itching, raised welts on the skin which resemble large mosquito bites. They usually appear and disappear suddenly. The child with hives can be made more comfortable by applying ice to the welts, or giving a warm soda bath (1 cup of baking soda for a small tub).

Child Who is Under-par

If a child tires quickly, is pale and listless, and lacks the bounce you expect, something is wrong although no sign of acute illness develops. Chronic ill health and lack of vitality have various causes. Until you know the source, you can't treat the condition effectively. Don't buy special foods and tonics. Get a physical checkup for the child. Then, if the doctor prescribes something special, you'll know you're treating your child's specific needs.

The child who lacks energy and seems run down may be suffering from:

A chronic infection which drains him of vitality.

Lack of sufficient rest. Slow down the pace of the child's day, plan for a mid-day rest, and arrange an earlier bedtime. It may do wonders for him, and you, too!

Anemia, lack of sufficient red coloring matter (hemoglobin) in the blood. Anemia may occur when a child loses a great deal of blood or has had a severe illness. Unless the loss is severe, he'll build new red blood cells in time, but the doctor may feel that a transfusion of whole blood is necessary to replenish the supply quickly. Or the doctor may prescribe iron as a medicine. Otherwise, good general care is all that is needed, with special emphasis on foods rich in iron, such as meats (especially liver, kidney, and heart), egg yolk, green leafy vegetables, whole-grain and enriched bread and cereals, molasses, raisins and other dried fruits.

Anemia may also be caused by disease which destroys the blood, by faulty diet, or by an inherited condition. In each case, the cause will determine the treatment.

Poor nourishment. In some instances, a child is run down because the foods he eats fail to supply his body with energy and the building substances he needs. If he receives a faulty diet, correct this by offering foods from the list on page 135. In rare instances, a child's body is unable to use the materials present. Your doctor will have to prescribe for such a condition.

Emotional problems. A child who lives in a tense, unhappy home is sure to suffer deeply. So much of his energy is bound up in worry and distress, he is apt to tire readily and care little about play. Even his posture will show dejection. Sometimes a child may be disturbed by problems and you have no idea why.

If you suspect that your child is trying to handle emotional problems which are beyond him—and you—don't hesitate to seek professional help. Your doctor, or a social worker in a family agency, may be the one to start with. You may wish to seek psychiatric aid through a child guidance clinic.

Colds and Other Respiratory Infections

During the preschool years, children seem to get a discouraging number of coughs and colds and sore throats. There is an array of possibilities: croup, aching or running ears, flu, grippe, swollen glands and so on. Some are named for the part involved: laryngitis, tonsillitis, adenoiditis, bronchitis, pharyngitis. Many mothers feel as if they can name them all. It is some help to know that the child will be less susceptible as he grows older and will have less severe reaction to those which he does get.

You never know at the beginning what you're dealing with. What looks at first like a simple running nose may become in a day or two a common childhood disease with typical eruption, chickenpox for instance. It may be the first sign of a more serious infection. Or it may, despite a furious onset with high fever or a convulsion, settle down to be an ordinary cold. Many times children produce their own typical response to infection. One will get croup every time. Another never does, but screams with earache.

About all a parent can do is to decide that every cold and cough and sore throat deserves the safest treatment. Check with the doctor, and keep in touch with him as symptoms change. He'll decide whether he needs to see the child. Keep the child indoors, in bed if there's fever, and unroll all the tender-loving care routine you know so well.

In this way, you're going to avoid complications which can result when a slight infection opens the way for a more serious one.

Be wary of nose drops or cough medicines without a doctor's instructions. These will not cure the infection. Keep the child comfortable, with grease or cream under his nose to prevent soreness; keep the room warm but not overheated; add moisture to the air if you feel it will help; and keep the child away from others.

Diphtheria, a serious disease, can be avoided. A child who has received 3 injections in infancy, and booster shots on schedule has practically no chance of catching it. It begins with sore throat and fever; hoarseness and sharp cough may develop. The throat and tonsils may become whitish in appearance. If a child who has not been immunized is exposed to diphtheria, the doctor will give him antitoxin immediately in an effort to prevent the disease.

A sore throat caused by a streptococcus is called a *"strep throat"* or, if a rash is present, *scarlet fever.* Be sure to continue the medicine the doctor advises for the full period he prescribes even though the symptoms clear up quickly. To avoid later complications it should be continued for the full course of treatment.

A sore throat that gets out-of-bounds may lead to infection elsewhere in the body. *Rheumatic fever* is one such complication, and a serious disease because it can affect the heart. School-age children are more apt to be affected, but it occasionally occurs in preschool children.

Rheumatic fever takes on different forms, and may be deceptively mild—simply a low recurrent fever—or acute with pain and swelling in the joints. It tends to recur again and again, so take seriously the first attack, however mild. Furthermore, the mildness of the symptoms bears no relation to the damage it can cause. The doctor can guide you in ways to ward off further attacks, and may prescribe regular preventive doses of medicine.

A doctor needs to check any child who complains of aching legs or mild joint pains, who is pale and tired, or who has slight fever for more than a few days without obvious cause.

Chorea, or *St. Vitus Dance,* may be a symptom of rheumatic fever. The child has jerky movements of face, arms, trunk, or legs which may vary each time. Don't confuse chorea with the restlessness of a child who's tired of sitting, or with nervous twitches such as eye blinks, head jerks, or other mannerisms which the child repeats. A child with chorea should be under a doctor's care. He needs sympathetic handling at home, too, for he's apt to cry easily and be frustrated by the jerkiness that appears when he wishes to dress or feed himself, pick up small objects, or use a pencil.

Infection following a sore throat may center in the kidney, causing *nephritis.* With nephritis, the urine is scanty, dark-colored or bloody. Tell your doctor at once of any change in the amount or color of a child's urine.

Pneumonia is a general name for infection of the lungs and can be caused by a virus, bacteria, or foreign object. Each type has a different treatment. As a rule there is fever, cough and difficult, rapid breathing. Modern drugs bring about prompt recovery in most cases when the treatment is started early. A child with pneumonia may not seem to be very sick, but the disease may last a long time and needs medical supervision throughout.

Tonsils and *adenoids* are small, spongy masses of tissue at the back of the throat which are similar in their function to other glands in the body, particularly those at the side of the neck, in the armpit and groin. Like these other glands, tonsils and adenoids combat germs; they become involved whenever the child has a cold or throat infection. After repeated respiratory troubles, they may remain so swollen they can interfere with breathing or swallowing. If the situation becomes urgent, the doctor may feel that obstructive tonsils or adenoids should be removed. Nowadays, the operation is never done routinely, in a general attempt to improve the child's health in some vague way. Don't urge your doctor to remove tonsils or adenoids; he'll do it if he's convinced it is necessary.

Skin and Eye Infections

Itches and bites and sores on the skin are common with children. Some can spread to other members of the family. Treat any break in the skin with care, since it offers an easy entry for germs. Therefore, try to keep any sore place clean, and discourage a child from scratching even a mosquito bite. If you trim his nails short it may help to prevent damage if he scratches while asleep.

You'll need the doctor to treat all of the following conditions. Using patent medicines may waste time, or further irritate. If anyone has a skin disease, be careful to keep his towels, washcloths, linen and clothing separate from others. Launder them with very hot water and press with a hot iron.

Athlete's foot is a fungus infection that usually occurs between the toes where the skin is warm and moist. The medicine you use should be prescribed by a doctor. Keep the child's feet clean and dry. Dust them with talcum powder. Athlete's foot is most stubborn and prevalent in the summer. Change socks daily, and air the shoes. Open shoes and sandals may cut down on foot perspiration.

Cold sores are uncomfortable blisters on the lip, in the mouth, or on the tongue which generally heal by themselves and respond to simple cleanliness. They do seem to appear in some children when they have colds or other illness. Rinsing with warm water, containing ½ teaspoon of salt or bicarbonate of soda per glass, may provide relief for sores inside the mouth. If the child has fever, complains of a very sore mouth, or has bleeding of the gums, call the physician or dentist. These may be symptoms of "trench mouth" or other infections.

Conjunctivitis, often called pinkeye, is an infection caused by a variety of bacteria, and is extremely contagious. You may be first aware of conjunctivitis when the child wakens with his eyelids glued shut by pus. It readily spreads from one member of the family to another unless extreme care is taken to keep towels, washcloths and other toilet articles separate.

You can soothe the inflamed eyes with warm compresses, but check with the doctor about treatment. Neglect may damage the child's vision.

A child's eyes and eyelids may become reddened for a variety of reasons. Allergy sometimes causes red or inflamed eyes. Consider the possibility of eyestrain if a child blinks, squints or is generally irritable. Even very young children can be fitted with glasses.

Eczema and hives are discussed under allergy.

Impetigo is a very contagious skin infection. It usually starts on the face with an itchy blister which oozes pus and crusts over. The child can readily infect others, or other areas of his own body, by carrying germs from the first sore.

Prompt treatment can clear up the infection. See your doctor. If neglected, impetigo spreads rapidly and paves the way for other infections.

Lice are tiny animals which attach themselves to the hair or skin and cause irritation. If the child scratches, which he's sure to do, the excretion of the lice causes further irritation. Usually lice or their eggs, called nits, can be seen. The doctor can prescribe a treatment. Keep all clothing, bedclothes, and the child himself clean to avoid spread and reinfection of lice.

Ringworm is a fungus which may attack the scalp. It heals in the center and spreads outwards, resembling a ring. Frequently the hair will break off. It is stubborn and quite contagious. A doctor must treat ringworm.

Sometimes a child wears a tight-fitting skull cap (a stocking is often used) which can be changed frequently and boiled to kill the germs. This prevents the spread of ringworm to others. It has nothing to do with treatment of the infection.

Another form of ringworm causes round, scaly patches on the skin. It is more readily treated. Athlete's foot is another form of ringworm.

Scabies, sometimes known as "the itch," is caused by a tiny animal which burrows under the skin to live and lay its eggs. The intense itching is apt to be worst at night, and the child may cause sores as he scratches himself in his sleep.

Your doctor will prescribe a suitable ointment. Apply it after the child is bathed, while the skin is still moist. Bedclothes should be sterilized if scabies is present.

Styes on the eye and boils are caused by bacteria. Pimples are related infections. Warm moist dressing or soaks will relieve the pain and help to localize the infection. Do not open a boil or sty. When it erupts, wipe the pus away with a sterile pad. For a boil, apply a sterile cover.

If a child has a series of boils or styes, get advice from the doctor.

Stomach, Intestinal and Urinary Disorders

Nausea, vomiting, diarrhea, constipation and abdominal pain are all symptoms of a great number of ails which range widely in degree of severity. Eating too much, or of the wrong foods, may cause vomiting. On the other hand, it may be the first sign of a common childhood disease or an internal disorder. Stomach ache, loose or hard bowel movements may mean anything from emotional upset to having worms.

Check with the doctor when anything unusual appears. Treatment will vary according to the cause, not the symptoms.

There is seldom any rush about relieving a child who is *constipated*, and routine use of laxatives or enemas is unwise. In fact, they may gravely complicate the situation if the child's appendix is inflamed. Plenty of fluids, and fresh fruits and vegetables do no harm. Check with the doctor before giving any medicines.

Diarrhea in a small child is of greater concern. A child with frequent, loose stools should be carefully watched. Diarrhea may occur when a child eats some irritating or spoiled food, when he is cutting teeth, or has a head cold, sore throat, or other infection. It may be an infection known as *enteritis* or *dysentery*. This is very serious. If the child is vomiting as well, his body can become dehydrated which may threaten his very life. Until you can check with the doctor, keep the child quiet and try liquids frequently.

Worms can cause either constipation or diarrhea. Neither may be present, however.

Actually seeing worms in the child's bowel movement, or noticing that he seems itchy and irritated around the rectum may be the first sign of their presence. The common worms of childhood are pinworms, which appear to be active, white threads about half an inch long; and round worms, which are pale and smooth and about the size of an earthworm. Tapeworms are less common, and hookworms are confined to some regions of the South.

A child may pick up the eggs of worms anywhere. Try to keep his hands and nails clean.

The doctor will want to see a portion of bowel movement if he suspects worms. He needs to know exactly which type he is treating. In order to kill worms, the medicine must be strong. Therefore, it must be given in exact dosage and under certain conditions in order that the child himself not be injured.

An unusual appearance of bowel movements is one of the signs of *cystic fibrosis*. Large and foul stools may be passed because of poor absorption of fats from the foods the child eats. This disease is inherited from parents who carry the trait but usually have no symptoms themselves. Eventually, it disturbs many of the functions of the body. A child with cystic fibrosis is apt to have repeated or chronic lung infections. He usually has a large appetite, but may nevertheless gain weight slowly. Careful and continued supervision by a doctor is necessary.

Unusual appearance of the bowel movements can also be a sign of *celiac disease*. This is a chronic intestinal indigestion resulting from intolerance to certain food substances, most often to a protein found in wheat and rye. Frequent bouts of diarrhea during the first year of life may be the first sign of the disease; later the bowel movements are likely to be bulky, pale, frothy and foul smelling. If the disease is not treated, growth may be slowed. Treatment consists of a diet planned by the doctor to meet the child's nutritional needs while avoiding the foods which he cannot tolerate.

Any change in the child's urinating habits may indicate illness. In wet or chilly weather, he may naturally urinate more often. A persistent increase in voiding, however, may mean *diabetes* (diabetes mellitus), inability of the body to use sugar and starches. Untreated, the diabetic loses weight, no matter how much he eats, and eventually dies. A special diet and use of medicine now make it possible for a child with diabetes to live a full, normal life.

Cloudy or smoky urine may contain pus, the result of kidney infection. *Pyelitis* is more common in little girls than boys. The child may seem perfectly well except for the cloudy urine. In other cases, the child may seem sick, but without fever or pain, or there may be a headache and low fever. In any case, get a doctor's diagnosis. Take a sample of urine along with you in a clean, small bottle.

Vaginitis, a discharge from the vagina (the opening into the female reproductive system) may vary from mild and brief, to mild yet persistent, or to thick and profuse. The urine may appear clouded or bloody if it becomes merged with the discharge. The doctor should be consulted to clear up what may be a mild or more serious infection. Occasionally, a little girl has pushed some object into her vagina.

Common Communicable Diseases

Disease	First signs	Incubation period*	Prevention	How long contagious	What you can do
Chickenpox.	Mild fever followed in 36 hours by small raised pimples which become filled with clear fluid. Scabs form later. Successive crops of pox appear.	2–3 weeks usually 13–17 days.	None. Immune after one attack.	6 days after appearance of rash.	Not a serious disease; trim fingernails to prevent scratching; a paste of baking soda and water, or alcohol, may ease itching.
German measles (3-day measles).	Mild fever, sore throat or cold symptoms may precede tiny, rose-colored rash. Enlarged glands at back of neck and behind ears.	2–3 weeks usually 18 days.	Vaccine usually given at 15 months of age.	Until rash fades. About 5 days.	Generally not a serious disease in childhood, complications rare; give general good care and rest.
Measles.	Mounting fever; hard, dry cough; running nose and red eyes for 3 or 4 days before rash which starts at hair line and spreads down in blotches. Small red spots with white centers in mouth (Koplik's spots) appear before the rash.	1–2 weeks usually 10 or 11 days.	All children should receive measles vaccine at 15 months of age. If an unvaccinated child is exposed to measles, gamma globulin given shortly after exposure may lighten or prevent the disease.	Usually 5 to 9 days, from 4 days before to 5 days after rash appears.	May be mild or severe with complications of a serious nature; follow doctor's advice in caring for a child with measles, as it is a most treacherous disease.
Mumps.	Fever, headache, vomiting, glands near ear and toward chin at jaw line ache and these develop painful swelling. Other parts of body may be affected also.	11–26 days usually around 18 days.	Vaccine usually given at 15 months of age.	Until all swelling disappears.	Keep child in bed until fever subsides: indoors unless weather is warm.
Roseola.	High fever which drops before rash or large pink blotches covering whole body appear. Child may not seem very ill despite the high fever (103°–105°) but he may convulse.	About 2 weeks.	None. Usually affects children from 6 months to 3 years of age.	Until seems well.	No special measures except rest and quiet.

145

Disease	First signs	Incubation period*	Prevention	How long contagious	What you can do
Strep throat (septic sore throat) and scarlet fever (scarlatina).	Sometimes vomiting and fever before sudden and severe sore throat. If followed by fine rash on body and limbs, it is called scarlet fever.	1–7 days usually 2–5.	Antibiotics may prevent or lighten an attack if doctor feels it wise.	7–10 days. When all abnormal discharge from nose, eyes, throat has ceased.	Frequently less severe than formerly; responds to antibiotics which should be continued for full course to prevent serious complications.
Whooping cough.	At first seems like a cold with low fever and cough which changes at end of second week to spells of coughing accompanied by a noisy gasp for air which creates the "whoop".	5–21 days, usually around 10 days.	Give injections of vaccine to all children in infancy; if an unvaccinated child has been exposed, the doctor may want to give a protective serum promptly.	Usually no longer after 4th week.	Child needs careful supervision of doctor throughout this taxing illness.

Less Common Infectious Diseases

Disease	First signs	Incubation period*	Prevention	How long contagious	What you can do
Infectious hepatitis (catarrhal jaundice).	May be mild with few symptoms or accompanied by fever, headache, abdominal pain, nausea, diarrhea, general weariness. Later, yellow skin and white of eyes (jaundice), urine dark and bowel movements chalk-like.	2–6 weeks commonly 25 days.	Injection of gamma globulin gives temporary immunity if child is exposed.	May last 2 months or more.	May be mild or may require hospital care.
Infectious mononucleosis (glandular fever).	Sore throat, swollen glands of neck and elsewhere, sometimes a rash over whole body and jaundiced appearance, low persistent fever.	Probably 4–14 days or longer.	None.	Probably 2–4 weeks but mode of transmission is not clear.	Keep in bed while feverish, restrict activity thereafter.
Meningitis.	May be preceded by a cold; headache, stiff neck, vomiting, high temperature with convulsions or drowsy stupor; fine rash with tiny hemorrhages into the skin.	2–10 days.	None.	Until recovery.	Immediate treatment is necessary. Take child to hospital if doctor unavailable. Continue treatment with antibiotics as long as doctor advises.

Disease	First signs	Incubation period*	Prevention	How long contagious	What you can do
Polio (infantile paralysis or poliomyelitis).	Slight fever, general discomfort, headache, stiff neck, stiff back.	1–4 weeks commonly 1–2 weeks.	Be sure to complete the series of oral polio vaccine.	1 week from onset or as long as fever persists.	Hospital care is usually advised.
Rocky Mountain spotted fever.	Muscle pains, nosebleed occasionally, headache, rash on 3d or 4th day.	About a week after bite of infected tick.	Injections can be given to a child who lives in heavily infested area.	Spread only by infected ticks.	New drugs have improved treatment.

* Incubation period is the usual amount of time which elapses between exposure to the disease and onset of the first symptoms. For example, if a child is exposed to chickenpox, he can safely play with other children until 12 or 13 days afterwards. The following week, he should be kept away from other children since he may be in the early stages of the disease and it will be contagious before you note any symptoms.

—From *Your Child From 1 to 6*. Washington: U.S. Department of Health, Education and Welfare, 1969.

FOR FURTHER READING:

Holmes, Arnold W. *The Family Problem Handbook*. New York: Frederick Fell Publishers.

Olson, Lydia M. *Prevention, First Aid and Emergencies*. Philadelphia: W. B. Saunders Co.

DIVORCE

DIVORCE HAS BECOME increasingly more common, even among evangelicals, in the last few decades. In 1980 there were a record 2,343,000 marriages and a record 1,184,000 divorces. There are seven and one-half times as many divorces today as there were in 1900, and three times as many as there were in 1959. In California in 1979 there were 159,172 marriages and no less than 137,714 divorces.

Basic biblical teaching seems to be fairly clear. Most Bible scholars believe that Jesus placed divorce and adultery on an equal plane as an expression of the sinful behavior of human beings and not part of the ideal (*see* Matthew 5:32; 19:3–12; Mark 10:2–12; Luke 16:18; Romans 7:1–3; 1 Corinthians 7:10–16). Matthew's phrase "except for unchastity" (Matthew 19:9) has been much debated. The fact that he uses the Greek word for unchastity, not adultery explicitly, suggests that he is referring to all forms of unlawful sexual intercourse—incest, premarital sex, homosexual acts, prostitution, and adultery.

With secular pressure in the second half of the twentieth century to make divorce easier, however, many Christian families have come apart through divorce. The concern of Christian leadership has, therefore, shifted from the question of the morality of divorce to ways to minister to each member of the family involved in a divorce. This shift does not mean that evangelicals have abandoned their belief that divorce is basically evil and harmful, however.

Divorce or a Bad Marriage?

Many troubled marriages stumble on "for the sake of the children." Increasingly, however, Christians agree that certain kinds of emotional relationships in the home may be worse than divorce. If parents are openly hostile to each other or if they are cold and indifferent, children sense that something is wrong. Such a relationship between parents can be psychologically destructive to the children. Such parents are, in the words of one author "legally married, but emotionally divorced." One wonders how many young people who decide to cohabit (live together) come from homes in which bickering or hostility between parents was the only kind of marriage the young people knew.

Separation may be an alternative to a bad marriage. Though painful, by removing the tension between the husband and wife it might make the children happier. But it is seldom a long-term solution.

If, after talking to their pastor or Christian marriage counselor, Christian parents decide to get a divorce, they should determine to do everything they can not to hurt their children any more than necessary. They need to let their children know well beforehand that they are having problems and are thinking about getting a divorce. They should let their children know they are not to blame. And they need to assure their children that Mommy and Daddy both still love them.

When the decision to get a divorce has been made, let your children know. Do not, however, attempt to turn your children against their other parent. In the midst of such a traumatic experience, they need the love and attention of both parents. Both parents should endeavor, as unemotionally as possible, to work out carefully all the details of visiting privileges, vacations, financial arrangements, the time of future discussions relating to the children, and so forth.

After the divorce has been completed, make sure, even if custody of the children is shared, that each child knows where his home is. He needs that security.

The Effects of a Divorce on Children

The young child has often been called the "innocent victim of divorce." Since his whole life revolves around his mother and father, his whole world falls apart when his parents separate. He may think he's to blame, so assure him that he has not done anything wrong and that you still love him.

Older children are more able to cope with the divorce of their parents, though they too may feel responsible to some extent. Divided loyalties may tear them apart emotionally, as well as geographically. They may be angry at their parents for their failure to get along. And they may be ashamed to let their friends know their parents have gotten a divorce.

In the light of these effects, and in the light of the Bible's teaching on divorce, it cannot be too strongly emphasized that Christian parents ought to see either a pastor or a Christian marriage counselor before any such drastic step as a divorce is taken.

—LESLIE R. KEYLOCK

FOR FURTHER READING:

Bontrager, G. Edwin. *Divorce and the Faithful Church.* Scottdale, Pa.: Herald Press, 1978.

Bustanoby, Andre. *But I Didn't Want a Divorce.* Grand Rapids: Zondervan Publishing House, 1978.

Hunter, Brenda. *Beyond Divorce: A Personal Journey.* Old Tappan, N.J.: Fleming H. Revell Co., 1978.

Peppler, Alice S. *Divorced and Christian.* St. Louis: Concordia Publishing House, 1974.

DOCTOR'S VISIT

A BABY NEEDS to be under the supervision of a capable doctor right from birth. The doctor may be either a general practitioner or a pediatrician (a specialist in the medical care of children), so long as he has had good training, likes children, and knows how to handle them. Preferably, too, the baby's doctor should be one who is aware of the interplay of emotions and physical health. It is best to have the doctor chosen and all arrangements settled before the baby comes.

In many instances the family doctor either takes on the medical care of the new baby himself or recommends a pediatrician. If an obstetrician has delivered the baby, he usually helps the new parents choose a doctor. Other reliable sources for finding one, especially in a strange city, are the local health department, local medical societies, or the medical director of a hospital.

Most parents who can't afford a private doctor for their children can make arrangements to visit a well-baby clinic, child health station, or family nursing service instead. Information about such important community health services is available from city, county, or state health departments.

The child should be taken to doctor or clinic every month for a checkup during the first year, every three months during the second year, and twice a year thereafter until school age. At these regular visits the doctor makes sure whether the baby is growing and gaining weight satisfactorily, gives advice on feeding, inoculates the baby against certain diseases, and answers the mother's questions about the care of her child. These visits also help the doctor to get to know the child so that he can treat him with more understanding when he is ill.

The mother of a new baby may want to be in touch with the doctor more often than once a month, but it is important to remember that the doctor is a busy man. Questions that can wait may be jotted down as they occur and the list referred to at the next routine visit. Some doctors set aside special hours for answering questions by telephone.

Of course the mother who has a pressing question or who thinks the baby is ill should feel free to call her baby's doctor at any time, as in any emergency.

Routine medical checkups begun in early infancy not only protect the child's health but help him to build up a feeling of confidence in the doctor. By seeing the physician when he is well, the child learns to think of his doctor as a friend. He also learns to accept the sight of nurses in their white uniforms and the office equipment—all part of an atmosphere that can be frightening to youngsters if they see it only when they are ill.

Parents' attitudes also influence a child's feelings toward the doctor. Parents can either teach a child to fear the physician or help him to accept health checkups in a matter-of-fact way. Here are some rules that help make visits to the doctor pleasant.

1. Never use the doctor as a threat. Don't say things like "If you don't stop playing on the stairs you'll get hurt and I'll have to send for the doctor."
2. When children are present, don't discuss painful operations or personal ordeals undergone at the doctor's office. Discourage such comments from visitors.
3. Be truthful if an injection or a specific treatment is going to hurt the child. Say something like "Yes, it will hurt, but it will be over quickly and it will help to keep (or make) you well." If a child is told the treatment won't hurt and it does, he feels deceived and can easily come to mistrust the doctor. It is important to keep the parent-child-doctor relationship as trusting and friendly as possible.

—From *The New Encyclopedia of Child Care and Guidance*. Garden City, N.Y.: Doubleday & Co., 1968.

FOR FURTHER READING:

Cobb, Vicki. *How the Doctor Knows You're Fine.* New York: J. B. Lippincott Co., 1973.

Weber, Alfons. *Elizabeth Gets Well.* New York: T. Y. Crowell Co., 1970.

DRIVING

PARENTS OF ADOLESCENTS old enough to have a driver's license are apt to look back wistfully to the days when their children were too young to know the starter from the brake. Polls of teen-agers show that problems growing out of the use of the family car rank high on their list of headaches too.

Statistics on the accident rates of drivers under 25 are especially disturbing to parents. But in communities where most youngsters drive, nothing will be gained by trying to prevent an adolescent's taking the wheel. The desire to drive should not be looked upon as a mere whim; to the adolescent driving is a tangible token of his approaching adulthood—it means power in his hands and the freedom to move around.

As the automobile is so much a part of living in most American communities outside of large cities, there is much pressure for children to drive before the legal age. But though the temptation to let an underage child drive is great, parents must set standards in this matter. Even after the state's requirements for a license have been fulfilled and insurance qualifications met, most families still need to set their own standards and limits that the youngsters may reasonably be expected to honor. Letting them drive their elders provides an opportunity for parents to check unobtrusively on the young people's skill and judgment and courtesy or consideration. And such points as when and where they may drive alone, at what speed, what time they should be

home, and who is to pay for the oil and gas are best settled in friendly family discussion. Father might choose that occasion to explain clearly the serious legal and financial responsibilities that go along with the pleasures and convenience of driving a car.

Questions about when different members of the family may use the car are frequent causes of argument, especially in homes where several young people drive. Keeping a "car calendar" where parents and children record special occasions coming up can help prevent last minute arguments. When such conflicts do arise, decisions might best be made on the relative importance of the occasions. Driving the gang to a beach party is as important to the teen-age boy as comfortable transportation to a committee meeting is to his father. An awareness of this on the part of the parent will eliminate much of the bickering and lead to fairer arrangements.

The way parents drive exerts a powerful influence on their children. Fathers who try to beat the light or pass on a hill, mothers who conveniently fail to see "No Parking" signs when space is scarce need not be surprised when their boys and girls bring home traffic tickets for similar offenses. Parents who observe all traffic regulations, rules of safety and of courtesy, who handle their car with respect, have it checked regularly and repairs made promptly, are likely to find that their children do the same.

It is wise, however, to reinforce parents' good example with specific and preferably professional instruction in proficient, safe driving. Often the young people appear simply to absorb driving technique and take to driving so naturally that there seems to be little they need to learn. But learning correct techniques of driving, traffic regulations, driving manners, and how to handle emergency situations should not be left to chance. Parents often take too casual an attitude toward their youngsters' learning to drive. A few lessons can go far to instill a wholesome respect for sensible driving.

More and more high schools offer courses in driving that include basic information about motors, facts about speed and safety, and, in many cases, actual practice in driving. Parents interested in getting such courses started in their own communities can obtain information from casualty insurance companies, state highway departments, safety councils, and the American Automobile Association.

—From *The New Encyclopedia of Child Care and Guidance*. Garden City, N.Y.: Doubleday & Co., 1968.

DRUGS

DURING THE 1960's an old but relatively minor problem became a new problem of major proportions for the Western world: the problem of drug abuse. Parents everywhere have become frightened over the potential destruction that such abuse could bring to their children. Christians are no exception, although drug abuse among members of the Christian community seems to occur less frequently than elsewhere. Because of the potential dangers, it is important for every Christian parent to study the question, to know the facts and signs, and to learn what to do about the problem.

The use of opium, heroin and marijuana is not new. But the indiscriminate and illegal use of these drugs by vast numbers in Western society is a wholly new phenomenon. Eastern countries have had the problem for centuries. India and Nigeria, for example, after long experience with the unrestricted use of products manufactured from the cannabis sativa (hemp) plant, from which marijuana and hashish are produced, have banned their sale and use. The opium trade of the Orient has been well known for centuries.

Isolated individuals in the Western world have been known for drug dependence (Sigmund Freud, for instance, was dependent upon the use of cocaine in periods of depression). But drug use never became a matter of general concern until during the last decade. The use of these older "natural" drugs, together with the addition of a wide spectrum of new synthetic drugs that have recently become available, has quickly spread, so that the illegal production, sale, possession and use of drugs has grown almost overnight into a problem that has national and even international implications.

The natural curiosity of youth, coupled with the search of many young people for an experience and dimension in life that transcends the crass materialism of their culture, and the affluence, rebellion, distrust and basic disorientation of modern students, has given the various elements of organized crime a strong incentive to exploit this rapidly expanding portion of the population by the organization of an amazingly effective world-wide operation for the manufacture and marketing of illegal drugs at huge profits. Psychedelic experiences in which the perceptions are distorted, have been touted among youth as mind-expanding and offering the most exciting "trip" in our modern culture.

Modern advertising, and particularly TV commercials, with which the youth culture of today has grown up, has pictured the use of drugs and medications as the sovereign solution to all of life's problems. Parents, too, with over-encouragement by some physicians and (especially) psychiatrists, have set a forceful example for their children by their widespread acceptance of and dependence upon tranquilizers (they outsell aspirin) and other mood-enhancing drugs as the prime means of coping with the complex problems of society and the ever deteriorating inter-personal relations in families that are falling apart from the lack of a biblical foundation. Thus drugs have come to be used by our culture, either to give "kicks" to the user or to reduce his guilt and anxiety.

The influence of some early experimenters like Timothy Leary, who themselves have become dependent upon drugs, the widely publicized drug dependence of the Beatles and other rock musician idols, and the general distrust for an establishment that says "no," have also been potent factors that have combined to "turn on" English speaking youth. In Viet Nam and Korea the use of pot [marijuana] by American soldiers [was] widespread. Liberal theology, with its hollow promises and amateurish mimicking of political and social movements, has been found out. It does not challenge or speak relevantly to the under-30 generation because it is an echo. Like that generation from whose parents it took away the Scriptures and the gospel, and that it spawned without standard or principle, it has no program or eschatological telos. From such a sterile husk of Christianity young people are turning in droves to the oriental religions that offer a psychedelic religious experience beyond the coldly rational or insipidly irrational approach of liberal theologians. In increasing numbers they can be encountered on the streets of San Francisco, Dallas, or Philadelphia evangelizing the public by urging them to try a simple chant that will enable them to obtain their heart's desire. Oriental mysticism and the transcendent experience go hand in hand with the effects obtained through the "trips" arranged by the use of hallucinogenic drugs, the "highs" of the amphetamines (or pep pills), and the dream-like Nirvana of the opiates (heroin) and marijuana. All these, and doubtless many other factors, enter into the explosive situation that is currently spiraling beyond control.

Only a virile, biblical Christianity with truth spoken in sincerity and love can stem the tide. Only a powerful godliness that transcends mere form as the true vital experience in life can stand over against the psychedelic experience as superior.

Drug abuse involves the use of two classes of drugs: (1) those that are addictive, and (2) those that are habituating. Addictive drugs are those upon which a user may become "hooked" by becoming both physiologically and psychologically dependent upon them. The body builds up a tolerance for such drugs and demands even larger doses in order to obtain the same effects. When one "kicks" (withdraws from) the use of the drug, withdrawal reactions occur. These reactions in some instances may be quite severe.

Habituating drugs are those drugs that (according to the present state of research are said to) cause psychological dependence only and do not cause physiological dependence in the user. There is no withdrawal period upon the cessation of the use of a habituating drug, although as a result the user may become tense, uneasy, depressed and irritable.

Within these two larger classes are several sorts of drugs:

1. The Addictive Class
   A. Opiates: Heroin, Morphine, Codein, Paregoric, Demerol (Meperidene), Methadone (the last two are synthetically produced) are the principal drugs in this category. All opiates are narcotics. A narcotic is a drug that relieves pain (produces analgesia), causes sedation and depresses. The analgesic properties of the opiates distinguish them from other sedatives, depressants and tranquilizers. Of these, heroin ("horse") has become the most popular because of its strong effects.

Heroin wipes out fears and anxieties, brings on drowsiness and causes sexual responses (even to the point of orgasm). Heroin is sometimes sniffed, but more often "shot" (taken by injection). Thus opiate users often may be identified by the needle marks on their legs or arms. Heroin is illegally marketed and, therefore, may be sold on the black market at an enormous profit. . . . Theft and other associated crimes have increased markedly with the rise of drug abuse, since drug addicts who soon exhaust their own resources turn in desperation to robbery in order to obtain needed funds. Many themselves become "pushers" (salesmen) for the drug in order to obtain funds, and in this way the number of new users grows arithmetically. Female addicts often turn to prostitution in order to raise money for drugs.

B. Amphetamines: Benzedrine, Dexamyl, Dexedrine, and Methedrine are the principal "ups" or "pep" pills used by drug addicts. They are stimulants that cause excitement, euphoria, happiness and keep one awake. Amphetamines may be taken orally or by injection. Amphetamines impair judgment, make one reckless—heedless of himself and others, and if the user remains awake for two or more days, he may become subject through significant sleep loss to the same perceptual distortions that are caused by hallucinogens. Amphetamines may produce high blood pressure, accelerated or irregular heartbeat and even heart attack. Users of speed (methamphetamine or methedrine) may also suffer from liver infec-

tions, abscesses, abdominal cramps and respiratory disorders. They tend to become hostile, violent and even destructive toward others. Whereas opiates tend to relax, the amphetamines stimulate the user.

C. Barbiturates: Amytal, Barbital, Luminal, Nembutal, Phenobarbital, Seconal and Tuinal are the chief barbiturates on the market today. Barbiturates are sedatives that are taken in order to relieve anxiety, and may cause sleep. Sometimes they are taken by amphetamine users in order to counteract the effects of pep pills. By depressing the central nervous system barbiturates induce sleep; unlike opiates they do not relieve pain. Overdoses, particularly when used together with alcohol, can cause death. Barbiturates cause impatience and irritability, loss of balance, and slurred speech. Seventy-five percent of all suicides by drugs involve the use of barbiturates. Withdrawal symptoms are severe.

D. Tranquilizers: Equanil, Librium, Miltown, Placidyl, Valium are used to help one cope with life by reducing anxiety and bringing on euphoria and a who-cares attitude. Tranquilizers cause the mind to filter out and reduce sensory information, keeping the user from being agitated by his environment. Thus, judgment is impaired. Inappropriate attitudes may result. Under some conditions tranquilizers may damage white blood cells. Dangerous severe convulsions may occur upon withdrawal. Tranquilizers have been prescribed with abandon by psychiatrists and physicians as if happiness and the solution to life's problems were contained in a pill. But dependence upon tranquilizers in order to cope with life is merely the substitution of one inadequate pattern of problem solving for another.

2. The Habituating Class

A. LSD (lysergic acid diethylamide), and other hallucinogens (including mescaline, peyote, psilocybin, DMT, MDA, belladonna, and morning glory seeds). Hallucinogenic drugs are taken in order to "turn on" or "tune in" a whole new world of sensory experience. Because of their ability to distort sensory data by impairing perception, users become entranced by the distorted world and think (erroneously) that they are having a deep, transcendent or even religious experience. Time and space and one's body and mind may seem to float; one may seem to be outside of himself; hallucinations and delusions occur. Depth perception is impaired; and there is a 10 percent chance of suicidal or homicidal attempts. Hallucinogens are deceptive: rather than opening up a new world by "expanding the mind" they dangerously close the mind to the true world around and distort much of the data that reaches the mind. Wrong decisions are made based upon faulty perceptual information that may lead to dangerous and foolish courses and action. The same perceptual distortions are experienced by users of hallucinogens as in those reported by persons who suffer from acute sleep loss (two or more days) and those who have been labeled "psychotic" or "schizophrenic." LSD "trips" may

last as long as eight hours. "Bad trips" can occur to any user of LSD at any time, and are unpredictable. During a bad trip the user becomes confused, anxious, depressed, and may panic. LSD is a very dangerous drug that does not improve, but rather distorts perception, lowers intelligence, may damage the gene makeup, may bring about malformations in babies, and may possibly lead to leukemia, suicide or violence.

B. Marijuana. "Grass" users claim that since marijuana is physically non-addictive and does not ordinarily cause such violent reactions as LSD and other hallucinogens, its sale and use should not be prohibited. What are the effects of "pot"? Usually one becomes "drunk." Three or four "joints" (marijuana cigarettes) bring about . . . unawareness of time and space and may make colors seem brighter and the hearing keener; ten will lead to hallucinations. Reactions may differ from person to person. Reports include among the effects of "tea": depression, euphoria, confusion, hallucination, drunkenness, panic and fear, overconfidence, lack of self-criticism and judgment, loss of concentration, acute sensitivity to sound, dryness of mouth, enlargement of the pupils, and a floating sensation. Most of these reactions are also associated with LSD and the other hallucinogens. In current medical literature there are few defenses of marijuana. Instead, one reads about progression from marijuana to other stronger drugs, failures in school, loss of memory, inability to learn, listlessness and lack of initiative, and other undesirable results.

What should be the Christian's position toward the abuse of these several sorts of drugs? I should like to suggest at least six fundamental responses that may be given to that question.

1. A Christian may not buy, sell, condone, use or possess any drug illegally. The principles of Romans 13:1–5 and 1 Peter 2:13–17 are explicit: in such matters a Christian must submit to the laws of the land. Simply as law-abiding citizens Christians may escape many of the problems that plague others who skirt the law. Christian parents, then, by both precept and example must stress the importance of obedience to God's authority granted to the state.

2. A Christian may not use any drug that is harmful to the body (or is likely to be so—cf. Romans 14:23) in proportions that may be harmful. His body is the "temple of the Holy Spirit" (1 Corinthians 6:19) and should be used in order to "glorify the Lord" (vss. 13, 20; cf. also Romans 12:1). God has not given Christians an option about how they may use their bodies; their bodies, like the rest of themselves, belong to God (vs. 19), and must be used as He commands.

3. A Christian may not become addicted to or dependent upon a drug (1 Corinthians 6:12). While controlled use of drugs for medical purposes under some circumstances may be legitimate, habituation and addiction necessarily involve a "mastery" of the drugs (vs. 12) over the individual. When addiction is likely to occur as the result of medical treatment, the use of other nonaddicting medication ought always to be sought if available.

4. A Christian may not make use of drugs that distort his perception and thus mislead him to make wrong sinful responses. Erroneous data growing out of disperception may plainly lead to false judgments and actions. In 1 Corinthians 12:23, Paul observes that all things do not edify.

5. A Christian may not use drugs as a substitute for responsible action in the solving of life's problems. Drugs may not be used to relieve guilt and anxiety stemming from one's failure to handle problems God's way. Paul speaks disparagingly of those who "sear" (i.e., make insensible to pain) the conscience (1 Timothy 4:2) and characterizes the attitude of those who are "past feeling" as antithetical to Jesus Christ (Ephesians 4:19, 20).

6. A Christian may not rely upon distorted perceptual experiences and mastery by a chemical as a means of discovering truth or entering into a religious experience. Such an attitude shows rebellion against God, since it substitutes drugs for the study of Scriptures and the true worship of the triune God. God seeks true worshippers, who "worship in Spirit and in truth" (John 4:23, 24). Truth and true worship are incompatible with the disperception experience. The principle behind the verse "be not drunk with wine, but be filled with the Spirit" also seems to apply (Ephesians 5:18).

Pastors and other Christian leaders need to discover that they have more to offer in helping drug dependent persons to withdraw and find independence from drugs than they might think. The six reasons stated above are not merely reasons for drug abusers to abandon drug living. They also are good reasons for not beginning the use of drugs in the first place. The power of Christ to strengthen (Philippians 4:13) and the ability of the

Scriptures to give us all of the information that is necessary to meet every life situation (2 Timothy 3:17) are profound factors in helping drug abusers to withdraw. Christians themselves should undertake the task of helping drug dependent persons (if necessary, in conjunction with a physician) rather than refer to a psychiatrist or someone else.

There are some things that you as a Christian parent can do to prevent your children from becoming involved in the illicit use of drugs:

1. You should prayerfully instruct him in the six principles stated above. Do not begin such instruction too late. Studies have shown that drug experimentation usually begins during the Junior High School age.
2. You should instill strongly in your child respect for the legitimate authority of the state.
3. You should instruct him in the harmful results of drug abuse and warn him about the subtle ways in which such drug usage may begin.
4. You should take to heart earlier comments pertaining to the example of parents in dependence upon drugs, and reevaluate your own practices.
5. You should know where your child is at all times.
6. You should know all of your child's friends and help him to acquire the proper friendships.
7. You should take time to establish good avenues of Christian communication with your child. Perhaps no other factor is as vital as this.

Parents also may take various positive steps to help their child break away from the use of drugs (assuming that he has repented of his sin and wants to do so):

1. Speak to a trusted physician about the effects of the particular drug that your child has been using and the side effects and withdrawal symptoms that he is likely to experience.
2. Speak to your pastor and obtain his help. He will probably want to set up a weekly counseling program with you and your child extending over the next eight to ten weeks.
3. Insist that your child break off all associations with others whom he has known to use or sell drugs. He may need to write letters (don't suggest that he speak to them) to such persons, breaking off his relationship. Remember, "Evil companions corrupt good morals" (1 Corinthians 15:33).
4. Obtain and report the names of any known pushers (illegal drug sellers) to the authorities.
5. Be ready and available at all times to help your child over periods in which he may be tempted to return to drug use. Let him know specifically of your loving concern and availability.
6. Help him to schedule (he will need some rigid structure at first) a full and productive life in the service of Jesus Christ.
7. Help him to acquire new Christian friends. If he tells them frankly about his past problem and his present determination to remain off drugs and asks their help, possibly they can be of great help to him. Obviously, he should participate fully in the activities of a sound Christian church, particularly taking an interest in the youth meetings.
8. Help him to see the biblical answers to the problems that may have been disturbing him. Good counseling from the pastor in conjunction with your own help should be of value.
9. Remember that talk that does not result in positive biblical action leading to so-

lutions to problems is counter-productive. Always direct discussions toward God's solutions and agree upon as many as possible at each conference. Then, schedule the first step in taking the agreed-upon action. In structuring such discussions, the following agenda may be found helpful. Proceed by writing the answers to these questions:

(1) What is the problem?
(2) What does God want me to do about it?
(3) When, where and how should I begin?

Popular Names for Drugs
acid—LSD
barbs—barbiturates
bennies—amphetamines (Benzedrine)
blues—barbiturates
candy—barbiturates
cocktail—methadone substituted for an opiate
coke—cocaine
copilots—amphetamines
dope—a depressant
drivers—amphetamines
eye openers—amphetamines
footballs—amphetamines
goofballs—barbiturates
grass—marijuana
hard stuff—an addicting drug (usually heroin)
harry—heroin
hash—hashish, marijuana
horse—heroin
joint—marijuana cigarette

jolly beans—amphetamines
junk—any drug causing psychological or physical dependence
Mary Jane—marijuana
monkey—morphine
nimbies—barbiturates (Nembutal)
peanuts—barbiturates
pep pills—amphetamines
pink ladies—barbiturates
pot—marijuana
reefer—marijuana cigarette
seggies—barbiturates (Seconal)
sleeping pills—barbiturates
snow—cocaine
speed—Methedrine
stick—marijuana cigarette
stuff—drugs
sugar—cube of LSD
tea—marijuana
truck drivers—amphetamines
weed—marijuana
yellow jackets—barbiturates

—From Jay E. Adams, *The Big Umbrella*. Grand Rapids: Baker Book House, 1972.

FOR FURTHER READING:

Goodman, William. *Only Dopes Use Drugs*. Grand Rapids: Baker Book House, 1979.

Krusich, Walter. *Drugs: It Can't Happen to Me!* Denver: Accent Books, 1979.

McReynolds, James E. *America's No. 1 Drug Problem*. Nashville: Broadman Press, 1977.

Strack, Jay. *Drugs and Drinking: The All-American Cop-Out*. Nashville: Thomas Nelson, Inc., 1979.

E

EDUCATION

ALMOST ANY PARENT wants his child to have a good education. Many declare, "I want him to have a better education than I had." But few stop to spell out what they mean by a good education.

If pressed for a definition, some will speak in terms of time spent in school: "I want him to finish high school." Or: "I want him to go to college." These are definitions of quantity: How much education?

What we are really concerned about is the child and the adult he will become. Consequently we must consider what kind of education is best for him, not just how much.

It is easy to ask a teacher, "How is Richard doing in reading?" and reassuring to hear that his test score is 4.2, just right for his age and grade. That focuses on the skill as he uses it today. But if we are thinking of him as a person, not just of his skill, we will wonder, "What is reading doing to Richard? Is he happier, healthier and stronger because of reading? Does his fourth-grade reading inspire him to think more critically, to become more sensitive to his world and the people in it? Will his adult life be more satisfying because of what he has read and the way he learned to read?"

No test score tells us these things. And when you ask Richard about his school day, he won't talk in these terms. Some teachers find it difficult to report beyond the here and now because, in many cases, they work with a child for just one year.

As a parent, you have a long-range view of your child's growth. You want him to be able to read and write and spell. But you know, too, that these are steps toward bigger goals in education. For example, you know people who can read, but don't. And others who believe everything that's in print. For these people, reading is an underdeveloped area. That's not what you want for your youngster.

Four Long-range Goals. What aspirations do you have for your child?

Look beyond the demands of the moment at school—beyond long division and phonics and spelling. You will see a number of long-range goals for a lifetime of education.

First, you want the child to have a healthy personality. This means an inner happiness that grows out of self-assurance and trust in others. It means self-respect and respect for others, a feeling of importance as a person and a feeling of responsibility in the group. It includes a sense of purpose with ideas and plans to achieve that purpose.

There is no blood count that measures the healthy personality. But it shows in the way a child responds to people and the way he handles the decisions and tasks of daily living. It is what he is reading for all the time, whether he knows it or not. When he has the inner happiness and strength, his contentment shines. Without it, there is a restlessness, a dissatisfaction that may drag him down.

Second, you want him to live effectively with others in his group. In his early years, home and family are his world. Soon he is with neighborhood children whom he must learn to play with and consider. At school his world and his responsibilities are enlarged.

We say he needs "to get along" with people, yet we mean something much bigger. For a child must learn to share with others, to understand the needs of others and even to assume responsibility for the well-being of his fellow citizens.

If his education is effective, he will become so sensitive to the needs of individuals that he will take a stand for justice, even against a majority. He will speak out because he is sure of himself. He will be strong enough to assume leadership, tender enough to direct this leadership to the greatest good of all.

Third, you want him to think critically so that he can evaluate what he sees and hears and reads. He needs to explore science and history and arithmetic. But it is not enough to acquire information as a sponge takes up water. The living, growing person must go beyond the printed page or the science experiment or the politician's speech to think for himself.

As a first- or second-grader, he learns to read a simple story. Gradually he learns to read between the lines and thus get deeper implications and go beyond. He may recall some previous experience that throws light on what he is reading, or some idea that contradicts what he has read. He is thinking critically and coming to conclusions on his own. This is one mark of the mature person.

Fourth, you want him to work creatively, for only then does he express himself as a unique individual. At first a child will imitate what he sees and hears. If his education is effective, he will go on to make up his own stories and games. The young child will skip and dance to the rhythm of music he hears over radio and television. He will experiment with paints, using color to express the way he feels, not simply to fill in an outline someone else has made.

How Parents Can Help. Probably the most effective way to help a child achieve these goals is by setting an example. Children are prone to imitate. When adults follow good health rules, children accept them as a matter of course. If parents develop that inner happiness that is the mark of a healthy personality, children benefit.

If you are sensitive to the needs of others, regardless of race or social standing, you are helping children grow up unscarred by prejudice. If you dig to the root of things and come up with new ideas and raise new questions, you are encouraging them to do likewise. And if you work creatively, making a project your own and using it to express your ideas and talents, you are showing them the way to great satisfaction.

Education is more than the textbooks and lessons of formal schooling. It begins long before the child goes to school and continues long after.

In our eagerness to prepare children for adult living, we often think of education as preparation for life. But it is much more, for education is continuous unless we lapse into the disinterest and apathy of the numb and the dumb.

There was little chance that apathy and disinterest could overtake the settlers who moved westward in covered wagons more than one hundred years ago. Each day brought new scenes and new challenges. Men and women had to think critically and act creatively. Risks were weighed; consequences were evaluated; action was taken. These people were doers, and their journals resound with tales of their expanding education.

Few covered-wagon children had regular

lessons or school books. But as they crossed the plains, they got acquainted with coyotes and jack rabbits and tumbleweed. They learned to watch for clouds that warned of an approaching storm. They had to assume responsibilities and make good on the journey. They saw decisions made democratically. They learned to act for the common good.

Today children do not have these same opportunities. Instead of doing, they are viewing television and movies, comic books and coloring books. They are driven to school by family car or school bus. Dressing up at Halloween may mean buying ready-made costumes nowadays, not improvising from old sheets and hand-me-downs. In one school the possibility of making puppets brought mixed response because so many children owned store-bought puppets with professionally made costumes.

Too many children are learning to accept and not to create, to sit and view instead of do. This is secondhand education, terminating with formal lessons. It is hardly worth the name of education.

—From Nancy Larrick, *A Parent's Guide to Children's Education*. New York: Trident Press, 1963.

EMOTIONS

ALL EMOTIONS are expressed one way or another through our physical body. Bad feelings produce bad chemistry and sooner or later, these feelings manifest themselves in physical problems. The bad chemistry of anger, bitterness, and hatred tend to create negative tension and dis—ease. These emotions raise blood pressure and cause circulatory disturbances, ulcers, colitis, skin rashes, headaches, heart attacks, and a host of other dis—eases. The constant effect of this nega-

tive chemistry also depletes the adrenal glands—the shock absorbers of the body.

On the positive side, feelings of self-confidence, joy, happiness, and peace of mind, all tend to create a sense of ease within the body. These emotions allow the body to function at optimum capacity without any restriction. These good chemistry feelings tend to help our neurological and endocrine systems to function at their optimum levels. When you are happy and relaxed, you are free of negative muscular tension. When you are at peace with yourself, you can play and work in a much more efficient manner than a person who is compulsively uptight.

It's been said we live in the Age of Anxiety. Many say our century is more anxiety ridden than any other era since the Middle Ages. Anxiety is characterized by feelings of overconcern, worry, apprehension, dread, and uneasiness. The chemistry of these feelings is negative and self-destructive. If intense enough, they will lead to overt physical problems.

If you dread the future and are always apprehensive about what's around the next corner, you are living an unhappy, unsettled, and unfulfilled life. God does not want us to live in fear. "For God hath not given us the spirit of fear; but of power, and of love, and of a sound mind" (2 Timothy 1:7 KJV). He wants us to be able to face the future—and the eventuality of death—with confidence and faith.

Unexpected Emotional Problems

Many of our emotional irritations come neither out of the past nor the future. They attack us in the present—when we least expect it. None of us *plans on problems;* we live as if they are never going to come our way. But when they do, how we react is of extreme importance.

I'm convinced God is more interested in

our response to life's stress situations than He is in the problems themselves. He sees problems as stepping-stones for building our character. We often see problems as fearful, unbearable obstacles to happiness and peace of mind.

What do you think of when you see someone who is angry? You think of glaring eyes, a red face, tightened fists, tension, and stress. All of that is chemistry. Have you ever changed lanes on the freeway, only to discover that the person behind you did not want you to move into "his space"? He blasts on his horn, stomps on his accelerator, and passes you in a huff, leaving you wondering why he flew into such a rage.

The apostle Paul said, "Be angry, and yet do not sin; do not let the sun go down on your anger" (Ephesians 4:26). Anger is an emotion. Emotions are not, in and of themselves, sinful. We cannot always control all of our reactions to a problem, but we certainly do not have to let an irritation grow into a major sin on our part. And we can also learn, with God's help, not to react adversely to life's situations.

Being Able to Express Emotions

As children, we are often not allowed to express our hostilities, the hurts, and disappointments, particularly those that came from parents or others in authority over us. If your parents were insecure, they had so many hurts in their lives that they were not able to allow you to respond in an angry or hostile way. Thus, you did not learn to deal with the anger, the bitterness, and the disappointments that developed deep within you.

We should be able to express and work out these hurt feelings and experiences. It is as we are able to let go of them that love can flow into our hearts in such a way that enables us to become whole people. It is important for parents to allow children to be hurt and angry, and to express their negative feelings. A child should be able to express these feelings, without having them suppressed as being bad and wrong.

Remember, a parent can suppress the emotions of his children. He can force them to brood silently and angrily inside. Anger that is suppressed is transformed into depression, then bitterness, hostility, and so on. It is a major cause of youthful rebellion. It could even cause you to lose your children.

There is no logic or reason to "feelings." Emotions cannot be logically rationalized. When we say "I hate you because . . ." our statement of cause is irrelevant. Feelings have no "becauses." They just are. It's a mentally dishonest gymnastic we go through to justify our prejudices and biases. Ultimately we are only trying to deny the human weaknesses and inadequacies within ourselves. That causes us to get angry and hate and resent and be hostile. It's a reaction to our sense of having been wronged or sinned against.

I believe we can divide all emotional responses into positive and negative chemistry. Ultimately, all negative chemistry begins first in doubt and denial, then in disobedience. There is a carnal nature within each of us—a "little god," the self-god or ego—that chooses not to believe and to disobey. Out of disobedience comes guilt. Out of guilt comes fear. Out of fear comes bitterness, anger, resentment, hatred, and hostility. All these feelings produce negative chemistry.

Our brain is like a computer. It functions by logic and reason—without feelings. The heart or emotional side of our being is solely feelings. The sense of being loved, wanted, and needed doesn't have any explanation. Likewise, the senses of rejection, bitterness, and hatred are feeling responses that don't have any logical or reasonable explanation either. Life experiences which you respond to negatively may be things which other people tend to respond to positively. It's not what happens to us that counts as much as how we react to what happens to us.

—From David L. Messenger, M.D., *Dr. Messenger's Guide to Better Health*. Old Tappan, N.J.: Fleming H. Revell Co., 1981.

FOR FURTHER READING:

Bailey, Barry. *Living With Your Feelings.* Nashville: Abingdon Press, 1980.

Smith, Joyce M. *Understanding Your Emotions.* Wheaton, Ill.: Tyndale House Publishers, 1977.

Swihart, Phillip J. *How to Live with Your Feelings.* Downers Grove, Ill.: Inter-Varsity Press, 1976.

Wright, H. Norman. *The Christian Use of Emotional Power.* Old Tappan, N.J.: Fleming H. Revell Co., 1974.

EVOLUTION

MORE PEOPLE TODAY than ever are objecting to the exclusive teaching of evolution in the public schools. Strong pressures are developing aimed at opening the schools to the teaching of special creation as a viable alternative to evolution.

Resistance to teaching creationism is still very strong, however. Opposition usually centers around two related arguments. First, evolution is widely claimed to be the only acceptable scientific theory of origins. Second, creation is assumed to be strictly a religious concept, which on that account has no place in a public school curriculum.

Both of these arguments are wrong and invalid. Creation can be shown to be a more effective scientific model of origins than evolution, and evolution can be shown to require a higher degree of credulous faith than creation. It is the purpose of this paper, however, to encourage a careful and objective study of both concepts of origins, on a scientific level only, in the public schools.

Creationists Need to Become Informed. If this effort is to succeed, creationists must first of all be able to support their claim that creation is as scientific as evolution and that evolution is as religious as creation. Political or legislative efforts to require creationist teaching will be futile otherwise. Even if a favorable statute or court decision is obtained, it will probably be declared unconstitutional, especially if the legislation or injunction refers to the Bible account of creation. Furthermore, a teacher forced to teach creationism with no knowledge of how to do it and with a built-in prejudice against it is not very likely to give the students a fair exposure to it, probably doing more damage than if it were ignored altogether.

The only effective way to get creationism taught properly is to have it taught by teachers who are both willing to do it and adequately prepared to do it. Since most teachers now are neither willing nor able, they must first be both persuaded and instructed themselves.

This means that someone must do the persuading and someone do the instructing. This burden must ultimately fall on the concerned creationists of each particular community. However, although a community-wide census would almost certainly show a large majority favoring the teaching of both creation and evolution, only a remnant will be found willing to work to accomplish that end.

In any case, the concerned creationist minority, whether large or small, will need first of all to become informed on the issue and its various implications. Each individual needs to be aware of the significance of evolutionary teaching and of the scientific evidence favoring creation. He does not have to be a scientist to understand the latter, but he does need to take the time for a careful reading of some of the modern treatments of the subject by creationist scientists.

For example, he should read the two books, *The Troubled Waters of Evolution* and *Scientific Creationism,* or other books of comparable scope and treatment. The former shows the historical background and modern influence of evolutionary thought, and the latter shows the scientific superiority of creationism in every phase of the problem of origins.

He should then do his best to help others become informed. There are many ways to do this—Sunday School classes, letters-to-the-editor, gifts of books to libraries and key individuals, promoting creation seminars, etc. Perhaps the best way is by personal, friendly discussions with school officials and other people of influence.

In the following sections appear additional specific suggestions for creationists (or open-minded evolutionists) who are in various positions of key responsibility.

School Administrators. Members of state and local school boards, school superintendents, curriculum specialists and school principals are, of course, in the most important positions of all with regard to this problem. Some of these officials are creationists themselves and many others are sufficiently dedicated to true education and service to the community as to be willing to provide the young people in their schools an opportunity to hear both sides of this all-important question.

There are many ways in which this can be done. First, each teacher should be provided with a good reference handbook on scientific creationism and asked to study it. The Public School Edition of *Scientific Creationism,* prepared by the Institute for Creation Research, is designed specifically for this purpose, providing conveniently organized and well-documented scientific evidence for special creation on all aspects of the subject of origins.

The teacher should then be encouraged (not required) to use this information in his or her classes. As long as no religious instruction is given (for example, an exposition of the creation chapters in Genesis), there is no legal problem involved. For example, when treating such a subject as human origins, the teacher can balance the usual evolutionary discussion of Ramapithecus, Australopithecus, Neanderthal, etc., by citing the creationists' evidence that such fossils are invariably either of apes or of men, with no true and unquestioned intermediates between men and apes. Such a discussion need not deal with such theological topics as the divine purpose for man, but only with the factual evidence concerning the unique physical and mental characteristics of men.

If possible, arrangements should also be made to conduct Workshops on Scientific Creationism for the teachers of the district. These can be offered on a graduate credit basis, so that the teachers can apply the time spent on the Workshop toward a graduate degree. There are not many creationist scientists and teachers who are qualified to instruct in such Workshops, the purpose of which is to provide basic scientific orientation in the creation model of origins and in the deficiencies of the evolution model.

For those teachers who, for personal reasons, are unwilling to teach creation along with evolution, substitutes can be provided who would come in, say, for a special three-week unit on scientific creationism. It might be feasible to have one or more specialists available for rotating assignments of this kind.

Creationist literature can also be provided for school and classroom libraries. This is especially needed as source material for student papers and special projects. If only evolutionary books are available, as is true now in most libraries, it is obviously impossible for any student to carry out a meaningful research study on any topic related to origins. There is a great deal of sound scientific creationist literature now available. . . .

School administrators may have two serious reservations about taking any of the above steps, one political in nature and one financial. As long as the teaching of creationism is done strictly in a scientific context, however, without reference to the Bible or other religious literature, such teaching is perfectly constitutional, legal and proper. In fact, the exclusive teaching of evolution is not constitutional, legal or proper, since belief in evolution requires at least as much faith as belief in creation and is therefore a religious belief. Evolutionary philosophy is the foundation of atheism and humanism, which are nothing less than non-theistic religions. Exclusive teaching of evolution has the effect of establishing religious systems of this sort as state-endorsed and state-supported religions. The political reservation is, therefore, not only invalid but actually applies in reverse. This is the very reason why there is so much concern about this question around the country.

The financial reservation is understandable, as most schools supposedly do not have enough funds to adequately finance existing programs, let alone a new program such as this. However, it is a simple matter of priorities. New programs of other sorts are continually being introduced, and nothing can be more important than giving the students a fair opportunity to choose between two philosophies that will have profound influence on them, one way or another, all the rest of their lives. Furthermore, the cost is not really very much. Providing one book per teacher, plus perhaps a dozen books for library use, plus an annual workshop would altogether comprise only a miniscule per-

centage of the district's annual budget, and there are bound to be certain marginal items in other programs that could be postponed if necessary. In fact, most school districts actually have funds already budgeted for supplemental materials.

Teachers. Creationist teachers are in a unique position to play a critical role in this strategic conflict. First of all, they are better able than anyone else to win their fellow teachers over either to creationism or at least to acceptance of an equal time approach. If they have first become adequately informed themselves, they are then able, over coffee in the faculty lounge, in the faculty lunchroom, or in the homes of their colleagues, to discuss the subject on a friendly, scientific basis, and hopefully to convince them of the viability and importance of the creation model. Books and other literature can be given or loaned, invitations to hear creationist speakers can be shared, and other opportunities for personal help utilized.

As far as the teacher's own classes are concerned, by all means creationism should be included, no matter what the course subject or grade level may be. This is perfectly legal as long as the teaching is factual and scientific, and in fact, such teaching is necessary to balance the evolutionist bias that is almost certain to be present in the textbook and supplementary material for the course.

In some courses—for example, biology, ancient history, etc.—it may well be feasible to incorporate a formal unit on scientific creationism into the course content. The topics in the book *Scientific Creationism* would provide an excellent outline for such a unit, adapted by the teacher to the particular grade level.

More commonly, perhaps, the teacher should merely introduce creation as an alternative whenever the textbook or course plan contains evolutionary teachings or implications. For example, when an earth science textbook discusses the geologic age system and the great age of the earth, the teacher should also discuss the geologic evidence for the catastrophic interpretation of the fossil record and some of the scientific evidences for a young earth.

Other possibilities include the use of creationist films and slides, assignment of student projects which incorporate both evolutionist and creationist interpretations, and invitations to local creationist scientists as guest lecturers. In the latter case, the teacher may also be able to arrange for such speakers to address a school assembly.

Pastors. Because of their wide influence, not only with their own congregations but in the community as a whole, creationist pastors can often play a vital part in getting creationism back into the schools of the community. They have knowledge of the Biblical teachings on creation and are already aware of the problem and concerned about it. Once they realize the importance of promoting scientific creationism in the public schools, leaving Biblical and theological aspects to be taught in their churches and in the homes, they can often serve as leaders of community-wide creationist emphases, especially if they will work in cooperation with pastors of other churches and denominations.

Pastors are especially capable at the arts of persuasion and instruction, and this is exactly what is needed. They should be able to arrange opportunities to talk with school administrators at such length as necessary to present the case for creation adequately to them on a personal basis.

In his own church, the pastor should see that his own communicants are well instructed in the scientific, as well as Biblical, aspects of creationism. It is especially important that the children and young people

in his church be well equipped with factual evidence for creation.

He can accomplish such instruction through a series of special messages, through using creationist Sunday School literature, through having special speakers, by providing creationist literature in the church library and for his members, and by various other means.

Scientists. Scientists and other professionally trained people (engineers, lawyers, medical doctors, etc.) are often capable of special leadership in creationist efforts. Young people are often led to believe that all scientists and other educated specialists are evolutionists, and the best argument against this fallacious claim is the personal testimony of scientists who are not evolutionists. The fact is, of course, that today there are thousands of scientists who are creationists, and usually there are at least several in every community.

Scientists and other professionals who are Christians have a peculiar trust from the Lord. At the same time, the atmosphere of their professions, emphasizing intellect and prestige as they do, poses a real temptation and danger. People in these positions are especially sensitive to academic ridicule and ostracism and therefore especially vulnerable to intellectual compromise. Furthermore, Christian scientists who have themselves taken a compromising position toward evolution seem particularly antagonistic toward those Christian scientists who will not compromise. Somehow an attitude of sweet tolerance toward the unbelieving philosophies of anti-christian scientists is often accompanied by a bitter intolerance toward creationist scientists, whose very existence is a condemnation of such unnecessary compromise.

Nevertheless, creationist scientists must not be swayed by the objections of their evolutionist Christian colleagues. The facts of science, as well as the teachings of Scripture, are squarely against the evolutionary system and there is no reason whatever (except the fear of men) for yielding to such compromise.

Informed creationist scientists are perhaps the best qualified people in the community to deal publicly with evolutionists' objections to creation in the school, to serve as special speakers and consultants on scientific creationism where needed, and to engage in other similar activities. They should be conversant with all the literature on creationism, be active members in the Creation Research Society and generally serve as the scientific spokesmen for the creationist movement in their own communities. They can also help other creationists in the community who are not scientists avoid making unscientific statements which could react negatively against their cause.

Parents and Other People. The majority of concerned Christians and other creationists do not come directly under any of the above categories. Nevertheless each person is very important. The larger the group of vocal creationists in the community, the more probable it is that they can get a sympathetic hearing from school officials.

Parents are especially important, if they have children in the public schools of the district. Through personal conversations with teachers, principals, and school board members, in an atmosphere of friendly helpfulness, but also one of well-informed confidence in the soundness of their arguments, parents often can exert a very significant influence on classroom teachings and attitudes.

If feasible under the particular local circumstances, such citizens should establish a formal community organization, with some appropriate name (Citizens for Scientific Creationism, Parents Concerned for Educa-

tional Integrity, Civil Rights for Creationists, Committee for the Improvement of Education, etc.). Someone can be placed in charge of promotion and publicity, with a view to arousing community concern over the problem. Sympathetic news and television reports can be very valuable; on the other hand, a sarcastic news story on creationism can do a great deal of harm, so the search for publicity should proceed cautiously, and the Committee should be as certain as possible that the reporter really has an understanding of the whole issue.

One very worthwhile project which the organization might undertake would be a community census or poll, in which the feelings of the people in the school district on the subject at hand could be determined. Those that have been taken so far confirm that the large majority of citizens do want to see both creation and evolution (rather than either one exclusively) taught on a scientific level in their public schools.

Another project might well be to raise funds to provide creationist books for the classroom libraries in their schools. Another would be to underwrite and promote a Creationism Workshop for teachers, as well as a Creation Seminar for people in general. Debates between evolutionists and knowledgeable creationists might be arranged. Advertisements for creationism can be placed in campus and community newspapers. Many other such projects might well suggest themselves in the particular area.

Students. Finally, we come to those who are the most affected by this controversy, the students themselves. What can creationist students do to counteract the evolutionary teaching in their own classes and schools?

There are many things such students can do, but one thing they should not do is to react belligerently or sarcastically against the teacher. As students, their purpose is primarily that of learning rather than of teaching or witnessing. They are both legally and morally under the authority of the school and the teacher, and whatever witness they may be able to give will carry far more weight if done in the proper way and through the established chain of command.

Also, there is no doubt that a teacher will pay more attention to the suggestions and criticisms of a good conscientious student than to those of a lazy and indifferent student. In any kind of effective Christian witnessing, the witness must know what he is talking about, be winsome and tactful, kind and patient, and especially where someone of higher authority is involved, respectful and courteous. Cleanliness and neatness don't hurt, either.

Assuming the above conditions as prerequisites, then the opportunities available to such students might include: raising questions, or offering alternative suggestions, in class discussions; using a creationist approach in speeches and special papers and projects; talking to the teacher privately about available creationist literature and speakers; inviting the teacher and classmates to attend creation seminars or similar meetings; suggesting a classroom debate on the creation-evolution question; giving sound creationist periodical literature or tracts to the teacher, and other similar actions.

Even if the teacher does not respond favorably, the student can still consider it a profitable learning experience. If there is a problem relative to passing tests in the course, the student can usually handle it adequately by prefacing his answers by some such assertion as "Evolutionists believe that—."

In those few cases where the teacher seems intolerably and rigidly bigoted, insisting that the student not only know the arguments for evolution but also believe them himself, it may be necessary for the student to ask his parents or pastor for help in the situation. If this likewise fails, there may finally be no recourse except to withdraw from the course, giving a courteous written explanation as to reasons. Such a last resort, however, should seldom be necessary or desirable. Reports of student experiences around the country indicate, on the other hand, that one or two creationist students have often been able to make a tremendous impact on the class, and even on the teacher, through their careful, courteous, consistent Christian testimony.

—From Henry M. Morris and Duane T. Gish, *The Battle for Creation.* San Diego, Calif.: Creation-Life Publishers, 1976.

FOR FURTHER READING:

Custance, Arthur C. *Evolution or Creation.* Grand Rapids: Zondervan Publishing House, 1976.

Kunkel, Fritz. *Creation Continues.* Waco, Tex.: Word Books, 1973.

Ward, Rita R. *In the Beginning: Creation Vs. Evolution for Young People.* Grand Rapids: Baker Book House, 1967.

EXERCISE

ANY PLANS to attack the fortress of "Madame Sedentary" must take into account the fact that she is surrounded by a moat of misunderstanding and, possibly even more resistant to attack, a wall of indifference. Misunderstanding and indifference will be difficult to penetrate in the adult population—perhaps even difficult to push aside in the present school-age youngsters and college students. Community leaders and parents should be aware of the problems, needs, and possible solutions. The following suggested approaches are advanced in full knowledge that, although each is important, probably the critical and most helpful approaches involve the preschool program and a new and revitalized program of integrated health and physical education in the schools.

For School-Age Children and Youth. It is our firm belief that the most promising, long-range solution to this total problem lies in an integrated school health and physical education program for grades K–12. It is the purpose of this kind of program, some form of which is practiced at a few colleges and high schools, to supplement the traditional skills approach with opportunities to experience and evaluate objectively the need for and the values of being healthy and fit. These opportunities come through personal experiences in life—meeting personal needs based on capacities. In addition—and these are the missing ingredients in traditional health and physical education curriculums—our schools must teach the research-substantiated benefits and limitations of exercise and fitness programs; and they must emphasize the importance of a body of scientific knowledge for making intelligent decisions relative to exercise, health, and fitness. In such programs students can truly become "health- and fitness-educated."

It is our contention that misconceptions, frustrations, and fears often result from physical education programs limited to skills instruction and participation in games. We often forget that some youngsters do not enjoy these games, especially when skill level is poor and there is little or no success. Indifference often results over a period of years from the misconception that skills, health, and fitness are all one and the same. This indifference and frustration can best be prevented by a well-planned, early, and dynamic exposure to a sound personal health and fitness program. There is evidence that early learning is superior to late learning. Does it not seem logical that health and fit-

ness education should capitalize on this "law of nature"? It is possible that the much discussed lack of creativity and vitality in our people can be at least partially minimized through such an effective and creative approach to health and fitness. This entire text is aimed in this direction—making decisions relative to health and fitness certainly involves creativity and, hopefully, will also lead to improved "vitality" and fitness.

For Preschool Children. The importance of early training in the home has obvious application to the development of the total health and fitness concept. If health and fitness, including all controllable factors, is established firmly as a "way of life" in the home, we will have the best start possible in the push to develop for the future some semblance of a respectable health and fitness level in our population. If a baby sees from his crib a vigorous way of life going on about him, will he not be likely to join in that way of life on his own level at his own time and accept this as his way of life? Steinhaus may have been very close to the truth of the matter when he maintained that mothers are our first physical education teachers! (A recent study presents evidence that high school students who are active are given significantly better examples to follow concerning physical activity than are inactive students. Their fathers are physically more active and their parents give them more encouragement to participate in vigorous activities than is true of inactive students.) The quality of the early parental "instruction" and the example of planned, regular, and vigorous activity by mother and father may well be the key that opens the door to a creative and healthful life.

—From Perry B. Johnson et al., *Physical Education.* New York: Holt, Rinehart and Winston, Inc., 1966.

F

FAITH

The fruits of faith for children and youth. A way of looking at what faith does for children and youth has been suggested by David Elkind. He proposes that four distinct lifelong needs appear during infancy, early childhood, and adolescence. Faith provides answers to these needs or "searches" as he terms them.

The first search is for permanence. Knowing that the world does not go away when we shut our eyes is a foregone conclusion for most of us. We do not stop to realize that the infant had to acquire this sense of people and things. It is a developmental accomplishment. The major problem which all persons must face, however, is that people are not permanent. Their loved ones die. Faith offers a solution to this dilemma. By trusting God, the individual resolves the problem of permanence. God transcends time, space, and physical matter. He comes to us as the One who will not pass away, and he promises to conserve us and our loved ones in his eternal care. The first fruit of faith is a sense of trust in God to preserve us.

The second search is for the right words. In early childhood, the child learns his or her language. The excitement of a young child learning the names of things about him/her is awesome! This search for names continues throughout life. As experience becomes more complex, the task often includes the use of symbols or signs. When people realize there is more to life than everyday appear-

ances, the job becomes even more difficult. Being able to name something reduces anxiety and makes relationships possible. Remember the words of Moses at the burning bush: "(If) they ask me 'What is his name? what shall I say to them?' " And the reply of God was "Say this to the people of Israel, 'The Lord, the God of your fathers, the God of Abraham, the God of Isaac, and the God of Jacob, has sent me to you: this is my name for ever' " (Exodus 3:13–15). When we have a faith experience then God has a name. God becomes friendly and identifiable. The unknown is made known. The lifelong search for a name for the mysterious and the transcendent is over.

Third, the search for relations is the typical problem of childhood. In this part of life, school is the dominant force. And the prime message of school is to put things in proper relationship to each other. The child is intrigued with learning how things work, what they are made of, and to what use they can be put. Integral to this is the search for how one relates to this world of objects and persons. Even more puzzling is "Who am I in relation to the cosmos, to the transcendent, or to God?" Faith offers an answer to this question. In coming to accept the truths which we have always heard, we come to know who we really are. The Christian truth that people are deeply loved children of God becomes a personal reality that settles our search for relations. We have an identity

171

that cannot be taken away from us.

Last, there is the search for order during the adolescent years. Here, for the first time, persons are able to look for underlying principles which hold diverse facts and different historical periods together. Here, for the first time, persons realize they, too, are in history and that they need to feel a part of ideals and movements that transcend the moment. Faith, once again, provides the ultimate answer to this search. We feel attached to that which underlies the change of every day. Through worship and trust, we witness to an acceptance of meaning in spite of confusion and fluctuation. Thus, the search for trustful order and purpose is ended through faith.

These are the four fruits of faith from Elkind's point of view. They are developmental searches which appear at certain times in life but continue throughout life. The infant, child, and youth who have faith experiences settle these searches in ways that will continue to benefit them throughout their lives. The need to find permanence, identity, words for the mysterious, and underlying truths in life—all these continue. But these needs can be met over and over again through faith. Thus the fruits of faith, from this point of view, are knowing that God will not leave us, that he is who he said he was in Christ, that we can rest peacefully in our identities as his children, and that he has an underlying purpose which governs the world.

Let us turn to another model of fruits.

The fruits of faith for adults. William James has suggested several fruits of faith for adults. However, these effects are probably just as true for adolescents as well. They are characteristic of most faith experiences which date from the traditional age of accountability, i.e., about twelve years old.

The rewards of religious experience can come to us at three stages of development. . . . James calls them the Conversion state, the Assurance state, and the Transformation state. Faith does different things for us at each different point.

In the conversion state or decision period, there results a joyous feeling that a struggle has been resolved and that peace has been achieved. It is a joyous, warm sense of contentment and aliveness. Many of us can attest to such emotions. Most often they are more feelings than thoughts. We can recall and reexperience them in memory. Like Tolstoy we can agree, "The light has never wholly died away."

In the assurance state or incorporation period, several things happen to us as a result of our faith experiences. Initially, we find ourselves free from worry and willing to be ourselves even though the environment remains the same. Worry and striving are gone. We feel content with God's grace and presence. There is a sense of certainty that pervades our daily lives. Jonathan Edwards called it an inner sweetness down deep within us. Many of us would agree with this description of the feeling.

The second fruit of faith during this assurance state is a sense that we have a new knowledge which we did not have before. Here we put thoughts to our feelings. We use the words of faith in a different sense than ever before. We feel enlightened. It is like reaching a point of awareness. We exclaim "Ah ha! Now I see it." At this time we know the answers we have are true. We have a sense of knowing something we never knew before.

Third, the world around us looks different during this assurance state of faith. Things attract us which seemed mundane or repulsive before. There is a beauty to the world and our circumstances which had not been there before. Things have changed in a surprising way. We see through new eyes in an intriguing and amazing manner. As one man said, "Oh, how I was changed . . . everything became new. My horses and my hogs and everybody seemed changed." Many could agree with this description.

The state of transformation is called by Tippett the Period of Maturity during which faith experiences result in a deepening of life and a change of character. James suggests four fruits of faith during this time. The first effect is that we become aware of God's purpose for the world over and beyond our own self-interests.

We have another sense of knowing something new for the first time. We become exhilarated with the awareness that God is at work all about us in many ways and that this is as important as the personal work he has accomplished in our own salvation.

The second effect is a sense of friendliness of this powerful God of the universe. We experience his desire that we become part of his plan and purpose. Thus, we willingly surrender ourselves to him. It is this feeling of self-surrender and of a willingness to be used by God that permeates faith experiences during this time. The admonition of Paul to "present your bodies as living sacrifices" (Romans 12:1) becomes a live possibility for us. Many of us know this effect to be a reality.

Third, this self-surrender brings with it newer feelings of elation and freedom than we have ever known before. These are more sublime emotions than the peace and contentment of our conversion. They are feelings which tell us we are stronger and more dedicated than we were. They are emotions similar to the invigoration we feel when we tackle a job with enthusiasm. Many of us can attest to this excitement in our faith experience.

Last, this state of transformation results in a shifting of our concern from self to others. We freely say yes to the needs of those near and far. There is a definite increase in charity toward, tenderness about, and sympathy for the less fortunate. This is the culmination of the awareness of God's purpose and our sense of self-surrender to his work. Other people become important to us, and their welfare becomes our concern. Charity and brotherly love become dominant in our thoughts and feelings. Many of us could report experiencing these new unselfish attitudes.

So, these are the fruits of faith for adolescents and adults as conceived by William James. They describe the effects that occur during conversion, assurance, and transformation states. They begin with a sense of peace and end with a commitment to helping others. To sum up what faith can do for us, this article has suggested:

1. All faith is grounded in or results from our efforts to meet basic needs. These are roots of our faith.
2. Faith has certain results, rewards, or effects that are tied to our basic needs. These are the fruits of faith.
3. For some of us, the fruits of faith seem clearly related to anxieties or problems we are facing. For others of us, faith's fruits come as a surprise.
4. Whether we realize it or not, all the fruits of faith are connected to our needs, anxieties, or problems. In some of us the process can go on at a subconscious level. Thus, we are not aware of it.
5. Faith can have the following results for us as children and adolescents: End our search for permanance, for a name for God, for identity, and for purpose.
6. As adults, faith can give us joyous peace,

freedom from worry, contentment with circumstances, new knowledge about the meaning of life, new perception of the world about us, awareness of God's purpose in the world, a willingness to surrender ourselves to him, freedom, enthusiasm, and a feeling of unselfishness.

—From H. Newton Malony, *Understanding Your Faith.* Nashville: Abingdon Press, 1978.

FOR FURTHER READING:

Davis, Cos H., Jr. *Children and the Christian Faith.* Nashville: Broadman Press, 1979.

Guinness, Os. *In Two Minds.* Downers Grove, Ill.: Inter-Varsity Press, 1976.

Harbuck, Don B. *Dynamics of Belief.* Nashville: Broadman Press, 1969.

Hendrick, John R. *Opening the Door of Faith.* Atlanta: John Knox Press, 1977.

Marshall, Catherine. *Beyond Our Selves.* Old Tappan, N.J.: Fleming H. Revell Co., 1968.

FAMILY LIFE

JANET AND I were sitting in the university student union making a pretense at drinking the strong bitter coffee which must have come from the bottom of the pot. She had asked if we could meet to talk, and I found her direct, intelligent, eager to communicate how she felt inside. I wanted to listen and understand what was happening in her life with God. She spoke with intense feeling, and what she said teaches us something about the Christian home.

"When I was home I just fit into the pattern, never questioning what I had been taught. I believed all about God and Christ and the Bible. But since I've been here I've tried to evaluate what the essence of Christian faith is as I've experienced it. Frankly,

when I look back on my home and my church I don't think of a loving group of people, full of concern for each other. I don't think of reality in knowing God. I just think of people going through the ritual, all wearing masks.

"It has come to me with alarming clarity that the Christians I know not only don't love each other, they don't even know each other. Nobody in our family ever talked about how they felt inside about anything. We went to church and talked about God and truth, but I knew enough of what was going on in some families to know that there were brokenhearted people, disappointed with life, lonely people in those pews. But nobody ever talked about that level of life.

"Within our own family I knew my mother didn't tell my father how lonely she often felt, how she didn't feel needed, how she wished he would talk to her. She just kept busy with committees, pretending these other things didn't matter. Yet I know she hurt inside about this. But we never talked or prayed about how we felt inside— nothing was ever on the level of the real you. We were always acting out some kind of unreal, victorious superexistence.

"I've watched this—this phony kind of role playing—and I've about come to the conclusion that if this is what it means to be a Christian, if this is Truth—then you may be right, but I don't think I'm interested. I want warmth and openness and honesty in my relationships."

I had heard it all before, sometimes with different details, but the heart of the issue is the same. This generation wants honesty in relationships as never before! Perhaps it's the impersonal world in which we live, where people are numbers, IBM cards, often nameless and faceless. Maybe it is a sharpened perception about the world. The young are exposed to a wider, rawer world than their parents ever knew. Seeing it "like it is" disillusions people and makes them hungry for honesty, suspicious of people who have told them half-truths and won't admit to the other half.

When I listen to collegians spell out their disillusionment, I want to paint huge signs and put them on the front lawn of every church: WANTED: THOROUGHLY CHRISTIAN HOMES. We don't need better church programs, additional youth pastors, more catechism, more conferences on youth needs. We need better Christian homes.

Acceptance Within the Family. What should characterize a Christian home? What should it offer its members? Acceptance. The kind of acceptance that allows you to be the real you. It includes love, which always desires the other's highest good but which can be misunderstood, a smothering concept in some people's minds. Acceptance means you are valuable in that home just because you are you. It reflects God's kind of love. .

It means that the child who likes folk-rock has a hearing, an acceptance equal to the child who likes Bach and sings only hymns. It means you talk about how a person feels inside, about what he likes, and why he feels that way. Father doesn't snort off his prejudice without listening or ignore you because he doesn't care.

A Christian home is a safe place to try out your ideas, to verbalize what you believe is valuable, without being shot down. You are taken seriously. Here you can express even your heretical thoughts. Instead of being told that nice people don't think that way, there is an opportunity for intelligent discussion and questioning. Thoughtful leadership is given in discovering what is true and valuable and good. A Christian home is a safe place: not safe in the sense that you are never corrected, never made to make amends for wrongdoing—but safe in the

sense that your person is taken seriously. You get the idea that you are valuable there.

I have seen more conflict in families over the length of a boy's hair than almost any other single behavior item. Father doesn't think any decent, respectable boy would wear his hair like that; and besides, what will others think if he lets his boy look like that? The son, on the other hand, looks at his greatgrandfather's picture hanging in the hall and wonders when the length of hair became a moral issue. All communication stops—on every subject. Hair has clouded even the ability to discuss openly the reality of trusting Jesus Christ. An amoral thing— the length of hair—creates a chasm neither father nor son can leap across.

Hair length is only one example. It could be a disagreement on any contemporary fad or personal habit which flares up between family members, paralyzing and fencing off individuals who need to talk together about the real things of life. Like a red flag in a bullring, the response can be so irrational that we no longer hear what the other person is trying to say. We give up intelligent reasoning to the pressure of emotional tension.

That's a travesty on a Christian home. If Jesus Christ is the center of the home, the source of all reality, that makes the home Christian. Somehow I can't imagine Him and His pervading presence letting us get so sidetracked. He said Himself that men who judge only from the outward appearance judge amiss. I can't believe that He, whose knowledge spans the cultures of all time, always agrees with our value structure. It often needs evaluation. He may not care about the length of hair. He does care about rebellion in the heart. He cares about the inner person, not the exterior trimmings. If our home adequately represents Jesus Christ, if He controls our family conduct, then we get across the idea that He looks at the heart, that He cares about honesty and about principles. By our emphasis we show what we think is morally important and what the unchanging principles really are.

Honesty and Love. Jesus Christ unites families who pray together; not droning prayers which are so much alike that the children can guess what words come next, but prayers about the real stuff of life—loss of temper, poor attitudes, laziness, thoughtlessness, an understanding heart, rapport with a teacher—anything that touches that day and the people in it. He honors parents who confess, in the presence of children who already know it, that they are sinners. He blesses children who can say they are sorry and show spontaneous love. He forgives people. He heals the wounds and restores family joy.

Jesus Christ loves sinners, not sin. We ought to be like Him in our homes, distinguishing one from the other. Pretending, covering up sin, has kept people living as strangers in the same house. What strange unchristian pride keeps us from putting our finger on the wrong and saying, "I'm sorry," or, "I need help"? What silly self-consciousness keeps us from expressing love—not a cloying, sentimental kind of envelopment that suffocates a person—but the wholesome kind of expression that frees a person to be his best?

Love ought to flow out of the doors of our homes because we are daily experiencing authentic Christian fellowship within our families—fellowship which includes honesty, self-exposure, and forgiveness because home is such a safe place.

I don't know what it was like to see a Christian home in the first century, but I suspect such a home shone like a bright light. I can imagine the Roman world commenting on the husband's love for the wife, the wife's attitude toward her husband and children, the open fellowship of the family, their communication with God, a God so real He invaded every part of their lives.

Contemporary homes ought to be beacons of such reality. I'm not talking about the neighbors observing that we go to church and don't wash our car on Sunday. I mean that Jesus Christ would be so real in family life that no one would have to hide, to pretend, to wear a mask. Daily forgiveness would be a genuine experience. Interfamily communication would be the hallmark of our family life because we are so honest and open before each other and the Lord. Having His perspective, we would major on major themes, and put minor ones in their place of importance. And above all, our love for Jesus Christ would be more conspicuous than our religious observances.

We read in the Acts of the Apostles how unbelievers were attracted to Jesus Christ and joined in the fellowship and sharing of God's Word within the early Christian homes. That's how they got their name. Others referred to them as the Christ-ones, Christians. Our homes, by displaying this quality in our family fellowship, this integrity in our lives, and this outreach in our love, must be this same kind of witness.

Where to Begin. Nice, you say. But how do you go about having that kind of Christian home?

The key is your life with God. If your relationship with Jesus Christ is vital, your family will know it. They will know it, not by your professional utterances, but by your love, your willingness to listen to an idea different from your own, your patience, your personal honesty, your obedience. It's contagious when it is authentic. If you're a parent, it should begin with you and God. If you're a child, it could begin with you.

One of the most creative exercises in the world is taking the Word of God and letting its truth cut into your personal life. Our children ought to observe the Scriptures changing us. They need to talk with us about the practical, piercing application of its message to daily life. Do your children believe that the Bible is an alive, relevant, life-changing book, or have they classified it with the dull, religious volumes of the past? We ought to get quite excited about the fact that we have a message from God!

A second creative exercise is remembering that children are people from the minute they are born. Some people make the mistake of admitting children into full-fledged peoplehood only after they are out of school. People need to begin speaking about what is inside when they are little so they can continue communicating as they grow up—so they get used to having their thinking listened to, challenged, and believed. Talk together about the day, about God, about disappointments, about love.

There is a wise saying: Give your children experiences, not things. Experiences mean doing things together, sharing intimate moments that bind you together. It sometimes means putting these moments into words to increase their meaningfulness. A world of creative thinking and doing is involved here. It involves God and His world and you and all the little people God puts in your home. It means knowing Him together and being so glad about it that communication is just the natural overflow of hearts filled with His love. Then the world looks on and says, "That is a Christian home."

—From Gladys M. Hunt, *Focus on Family Life.* Grand Rapids: Baker Book House, 1970.

FOR FURTHER READING:

Christenson, Larry. *Which Way the Family?* Minneapolis: Bethany Fellowship, 1973.

Hubbard, David A. *Is the Family Here to Stay?* Waco, Tex.: Word Books, 1971.

Hyder, O. Quentin, M.D. *The People You Live With.* Old Tappan, N.J.: Fleming H. Revell Co., 1975.

LaHaye, Tim and Beverly. *Spirit-Controlled Family Living.* Old Tappan, N.J.: Fleming H. Revell Co., 1978.

Sandford, John, and Paula. *Restoring the Christian Family.* Plainfield, N.J.: Logos International, 1979.

FAMILY TRADITIONS

AS A FAMILY we have always enjoyed doing things together but now that the older children are into their teens we are struggling and trying to be creative in approaching family activities.

This is the period of our family life when the schedule becomes a dominant factor as we try to plan activities together. Each family member is so heavily committed to his or her own activities that group activities become more and more difficult to arrange.

Last summer we had an interesting experience. Our family had planned a camping trip to begin the 2nd week of June, just after school was out. There was an unusually heavy snowfall during the winter so I telephoned in early June to see if the campground would be opening on schedule. The report was "The snow is melting. It looks good." Another phone call the week before our trip was scheduled brought the report, "The snow is melted, but we won't be opening for another month. It will take that long to repair the damage done by the heavy snow." What now, I thought. How will I ever tell the family?

Our fourteen year old was planning to be on a ten-day walk for a charity and was going to have to leave the walk three days before the end. She said, "Great, now I'll get to finish the walk."

Due to the schedule change our thirteen year old would not get to go camping at all because of other summer traveling plans. I knew she would be heartbroken. On hearing the news, she said, "Oh good, now I'll be able to go to Angela's birthday party!"

Dealing with the schedule is a formidable job. But what can we do? Should we just throw up our arms in hopeless frustration? Can we ever do anything as a family?

For several years we had a banner displayed in our home with the saying, HOW IMPORTANT IS IT REALLY? This compelling line forced many prioritizations and re-prioritizations on us. Sure, families can do things together, but you have to want to and sometimes have to use all the resources at your command to make it happen. We found we needed to be flexible, yet firm.

With all of our children at home we are still able to plan Thanksgiving and Christmas together. Soon our children will begin to be scattered to the four winds and we'll have to be more imaginative. We may celebrate Thanksgiving the day after the "real" holiday. We may have to celebrate Christmas on Christmas Eve, Christmas morning, or the afternoon.

The importance of establishing and keeping up family traditions cannot be underestimated. Being together New Year's Eve is a small but sacred tradition in our home. We live in Los Angeles but when the children were small we stumbled across the idea of celebrating New Year's Eve on New York time, which is at 9 P.M. in Los Angeles. This way, everyone still got to be together to see in the New Year. Now that the older children are babysitting and will soon be dating, we are deriving a bonus from the original plan. They can make their own plans, but are requested not to plan to leave home until 9:30. The tradition has grown to be a point where the children want to be together and will adjust their schedules accordingly. The first time a party or babysitting job is allowed to interfere with our togetherness, the tradition will be dealt a serious blow.

As the children grow into young adults keeping traditions becomes very difficult. Conflicts in schedules, jobs, the cost of travel, all become factors. We fully expect in the future to have to spend some money to keep family activities alive, which we feel are important. If a daughter is on a tight budget and claims to need the money she could earn by working instead of being involved in a family activity, we might need to make a donation of half of her take home pay so she can be with us. If a son lives 500 miles away and claims poverty, it might be necessary to send him an airplane ticket.

We as parents might get to show how important a planned family activity is to us. If after a family activity has been scheduled, what would we do if we were to receive a prestigious social invitation?

We have a tradition of spending Easter as a family with several other families. Often this involves taking a short trip. To keep the whole family interested, we do our best to make sure everyone has a good time. Once in a while a child gets something new for the trip. Treats are dispersed semi-liberally as we drive to our destination. We usually bring along the "good kind" of pop, enough for whole cans apiece. We stop for a round of ice cream cones or granola bars to break the trip and indulge in other special things.

How can we start family traditions? This could be the subject of a terrific routine by Bill Cosby. "Children I've called you all together to begin a tradition." This cannot be done. We can only plan events and activities, and live the experience, making every effort to see that everyone involved has a favorable experience and a good time.

It's natural to want to repeat an activity which was enjoyed by all family members. But how soon should a repeat be scheduled? What is the optimum frequency for doing a particular project? A family might thoroughly enjoy an occasional outing to the beach or spending a day sailing at the lake.

However, the same family might quickly become bored if the activity is repeated every week. In our experience, we have found that some activities are best done just once a year. It's the fact that they're *not* done all the time which makes some family activities especially enjoyable.

In order to help our children to grow to be mature, "well-rounded" Christian adults we found that it is necessary to provide more than social and recreational experiences. Having meaningful religious and social justice experiences is at least equally important, though probably much less easy to plan and conduct.

In these areas it is more difficult to involve the whole family particularly where there is a wide spread among the children's ages. We do try to have family experiences but we complement these with experiences involving only one or two of the children. In this way we can give our growing offspring experiences that recognize their individual maturity. We try to provide family religious experiences by attending weekly liturgy. This means sometimes we have to "shop around" for liturgies that are meaningful to the whole family. For the past four years our entire family has had regular religious experiences as we come together with other families each month using the Paulist Family program as a framework for study and celebration.

During Advent each person draws the name of another family member and becomes the Kris Kringle to this person. This means we do at least one nice thing each day for the person whose name we drew. We celebrate Epiphany by exchanging one present held from Christmas, as well as a letter from their Kris Kringle revealing his or her identity and listing the kindnesses performed.

During Lent each person chooses a commitment (mortification, promise, etc.) to be done daily. Each day the person does the ac-

tion, they can take a jelly bean of "their color" from the bag and put it into the bowl or jar containing all the promises kept. On Easter everyone gets to devour all the jelly beans of their color.

Last Good Friday the family followed our own re-creation of the way of the cross along a trail with three other families with whom we were camping in the desert.

We have built other religious experiences around the administration of a sacrament. Many of our "recreational" activities are also religious experiences. While traveling, we discuss God's creations around us. While camping, we marvel at the wonders of God's creation from bugs and grubs to flowers and majestic mountains. When we are together we remember to thank the Lord for all we have received and ask His blessing and protection for all family members especially those who are not at the gathering.

In the area of social injustice we try to inculcate in our children a high level of social awareness and concern and motivate them to be active in some social justice activities. Finding opportunities for family social justice is difficult. They will almost never present themselves. However, once we took the time and effort to look around us, we were surprised at the number of opportunities that we found. Here are activities we try to be conscious of on a full time basis:

1. We model social justice concerns by being involved ourselves and by making sure our children understand what activities we are involved in, and, more importantly, *why* we are involved.

2. We keep informed about current social justice issues in our home, in our neighborhood, city, state, country, and in the world. Our children will be at least partly informed from the media and school about these issues. Once informed we share both facts and opinions with

our family while hearing out their facts and opinions.

3. We arrange for our family to come in contact with people involved in social justice whom we respect.

4. We constantly look out for social justice kinds of activities in which our young people can become involved. We do not force or coerce our young people to involve themselves, but we certainly encourage them to participate.

5. We have organized and participated as a family in parish supper held on Wednesdays during Lent. The supper consists of soup, bread, and water. We donated an amount equivalent to the cost of a normal family dinner. The monies were contributed to organizations aiding world hunger. Our family members of all ages participated by doing what they could whether it was shopping, cooking, serving, or cleaning up. In doing this, our family got to meet many people we otherwise wouldn't know. We shared community with the others in a Christian context. We experienced some small mortification at a time when this concept had become quite foreign to us and we felt in a very small way (perhaps only symbolically) a solidarity with the hungry people of the world.

The single most important ingredient we found to get started doing things as a family was to plan activities as a family where everyone's input counts. We try to schedule for the maximum possible convenience of all members of the family. Lastly and very importantly we relax and enjoy each other.

Reflection   What were the family traditions in my family as I was growing up?

What are the traditions in our family now?

What one new practice would we like to begin, which may become a tradition?

What are my personal feelings toward involvement in social justice concerns?

What attitudes would I like our children to have in regard to social justice?

As primary educators of our children what religious attitudes are we giving to our children? Are we reinforcing and supporting the formal religious education program our children are in? What more could or should we be doing?

—From Kevin and Rita Cronin, "Can We Ever Do Anything As a Family?" in *Christian Parenting: The Adolescent.* Ramsey, N.J. Paulist Press, 1979.

FATHERHOOD

FATHERS TODAY are on the way to regaining a lost world, the world of family living. They are giving more of themselves to fatherhood and drawing richer emotional rewards from it. And besides the deep satisfactions of their new or rediscovered role, they are finding that being a father is also fun.

Today's fathers—in the United States, at any rate—are actually giving more of themselves to their children and their home life than ever before. They are doing so in a different way than ever before, in a way that has more meaning and is more gratifying both to themselves and to their children. They have found out that sharing in the day-to-day care of their children has many valuable by-products of family togetherness, mutual understanding, pure enjoyment. Father is no longer set apart as the wage earner, the one who will attend to punishment when he comes home, the court of last resort on important decisions. Life with Father today is generally full and rounded.

Much has been said about Mother leaving home to go into the working world, but it was Father who left home first. The father of earlier days worked and lived closely with his children. It was from him as well as their mother they learned the values of growing up together. His personality, his attitudes, his ideals and standards, together with their mother's were their constant guide. But as industry developed, people moved to the cities, and by 1900 most fathers were traveling to work. Too tired to do more than eat dinner and retire behind a newspaper for the evening, they became virtual strangers to their children.

At first neither Father nor anyone else seemed to realize how much he was missed—or how much he was missing. When people first became anxious about family life in an industrial society, it was Mother they worried about. Father was merely reminded to keep her happy, because she was bringing up the children.

What is Father's place? More and more young parents are turning back to the home. Economic forces like the scarcity of domestic help and the shorter work week have spurred them on their way. But they also seem to be looking for something they missed in their own childhood, a closeness between parents and children and a more satisfying family life.

Father has also come to the attention of many people who decry the dangers of a mother-dominated home. Magazine articles, books, educators, and parent groups point out the importance of his place in his children's lives. Like any human being, child or adult, Father enjoys all this attention. But he is also somewhat confused. Is he merely a second mother to his children? Or is there something special a father has to offer, something fatherly and masculine as differentiated from the motherly and feminine?

What does Father, as a father, stand for in the family?

A child needs both Father and Mother, and he needs them to be different. To a boy and girl a father represents a man's strength and wisdom, his knowledge of the world and its workings, his judgment based on experience outside the home. They need to hear his voice in family decisions as well as their mother's. They need to see in him the protector and provider for Mother and children. From him they take their model of manhood, and from him they learn an attitude toward women. If mothers do all the managing while fathers sit by, both girls and boys may suffer a confusion about their own status which will handicap them in their relationships as they grow up.

Fathering a baby is not very different from mothering him. The baby sucking at his bottle feels comfortable also when Father's arms are holding him. Warmly and snugly held, he gets the same feeling of trust in the world; and Father enjoys the same glow of protective tenderness, the same pride that Mother feels in giving the baby comfort. Except for the mother-function of breast feeding, there is nothing specifically masculine or feminine about caring for an infant. A man may feel doubtful at first; his baby looks so fragile. But the newborn infant is hardier than he seems. A woman is just as uneasy in the beginning. If she gains confidence sooner, it is not because she is a woman but because she generally gets more practice. Nor is Father very different from Mother to the toddler learning the disciplines of family living from both parents. The child at this stage especially needs his parents to be consistent, to set the same standards and limits for him.

But most fathers are still away a good part of the day. A father who is close to his child from infancy finds it much easier to pick up each night where he left off. The joyous cry, "Daddy's home!" and the catapulting of small bodies into his arms as he opens the door give him a justified feeling of being important to the family and increase his own pleasure at being home.

The Early Days.   From the first weeks a father's closeness to his wife sets the stage for happy growth. Sometimes the doctor called to attend a colicky baby finds the baby's stomachache related to his mother's uneasiness. With almost his first breath an infant becomes sensitive to the feelings and attitudes of the persons who care for him. Tensions, anxieties, antagonisms in his parents are quickly conveyed to him, and he responds in that body language which is the first language he knows and which may persist or recur throughout life in psychosomatic illnesses.

A man may understandably feel displaced when the new baby first comes home. And he may well encounter perplexing new emotions within himself. As soon as his wife is pregnant a man may feel painful intimations of adjustment to fatherhood. The obstetrician's familiar comment, "We've never lost a father yet," is not just facetiousness, for the tensions of approaching fatherhood can cause real physical discomfort. Fatherhood is a test of a man's maturity. His wife can help him by wholeheartedly inviting his participation and accepting his help. If he shies away at first, she might remember that he was probably brought up on a definition of manliness which did not include baby care.

Many a father has thought he could never look after a baby—until an emergency arose and he not only did it but liked it. Then he felt really needed in a practical way. Mother can be understanding about Father's hesitations and accept with grace whatever contribution he can comfortably make. Father, for his part, can realize that it's a mistake to

force himself to bathe and diaper his baby when he gets no real satisfaction from doing so.

Most fathers, however, are both willing and able to take care of their babies. They quite naturally become part of their children's lives from the beginning. Even before a baby arrives, a man no longer says, "My wife's going to have a baby," but rather, "We're going to have a baby." Being fathers is part of what these young men want out of life, and they both give and take rich satisfactions in the living and growing together of the family. These are the new fathers. Children and mothers too are living more fully because fathers are happily taking their place again in the family.

At the same time, when Father is so unstinting in giving of himself, it is important to avoid overburdening him. It is a temptation to ask him to prepare the baby's formula, even though he has had such a hard day at the office. He has his own pressures and responsibilities. He is often tired at night and is entitled to relax in whatever way he pleases. He should be able to say to the children clamoring for a game, "Not now—I'm going to read the paper," and not feel guilty about it.

Of one thing any father can be sure: Whether he actually feeds and changes his baby or only looks on appreciatively while his wife does it, his warm interest will encourage the baby's well-being and growth, even the baby's progress in learning. Giving the 2 A.M. feeding is not necessarily an unalloyed delight, but many a young father finds it brings a closer feeling between him and his baby. Some fatherly tasks are trying, some acutely worrisome, like tactfully handling a balky child in public or watching a child through an illness. Some, like an afternoon of Parcheesi or double-feature Westerns, may take a lot of patience. But painful or happy, all make fatherhood a more intensely personal and profoundly enriching experience.

. . . . .

What Boy and Girl Learn From Father.
Father is the male to whom his son looks for a model. Without a strong "father image" a boy does not know what it is to be a man. Seeing how his father behaves toward his mother, his sister, and other women, he learns how a man behaves toward a woman. He learns how a man and woman in marriage work together to make a good life for themselves and their children. He learns from his father about the world's work and how he himself will someday make his contribution to it. His attitudes toward working for a living are largely shaped by the pride, the satisfaction, the responsibility Father displays toward his own work. Lucky is the boy whose father has the courage to share honestly with him his disappointments as well as his triumphs, for nowhere else will he learn to take hardship in his stride along with joy.

A girl learns all this about men from her father, too, but to her the lesson has a somewhat different meaning. Father is the man upon whom she will pattern her ideal of a husband. From her father's regard for her mother she learns how a man regards women; she also learns to value her own femininity according to the value he places on it. He shows her that she is not "just as good as a boy" but someone in her own right, with individual characteristics and with special contributions to make to the family. With his regard for her from little-girlhood on, she comes to expect such acceptance and consideration from boys and later from the men among whom she will choose her partner for life. This is the basis for her own good marriage in the future.

. . . . .

The Outgoing Years. The middle years of childhood are generally outgoing and active.

The school child is learning about the world and looks to Father, the man of the world, to help him understand it. He brings observations of people and events to the family dinner table for discussion, and Father has a golden opportunity to express his ideas about anything from electronics to naughty words. Instead of handing down opinions ready-made, Father can use this opportunity for encouraging his children to think for themselves.

. . . . .

The teen-ager has an abundance of energy to invest in relationships with other teen-agers, both boys and girls. He wants to know how he is doing but often is unable to ask advice or take suggestions. Father still stands as the symbol of strength and dependability in the adolescent's world of changing values and conflicting emotions. Despite open resistance, his boy and girl desperately need his approval, although not necessarily his blanket agreement to everything they want to have or to do.

. . . . .

The richer the family life, the more mellowness and maturity it brings to its adult participants. The father and mother who together have shared in their children's growing have built a relationship with each other which will not fail them now. They have also achieved a relationship with their children which will continue in love and friendship, though perhaps at a distance. And Father can begin to think of grandfatherhood, which, free of the daily demands and anxieties of child care, is for many fathers the crowning joy of all.

—From Richard E. Wolf, "Being a Father Today," in *The New Encyclopedia of Child Care and Guidance.* Garden City, N.Y.: Doubleday & Co., 1968.

FOR FURTHER READING:

Heidebrecht, Paul, and Jerry Rohrbach. *Fathering a Son*. Evanston, Ill.: Moody Press, 1979.

MacDonald, Gordon. *The Effective Father*. Wheaton, Ill.: Tyndale House Publishers, 1977.

Preston, William H., ed. *Fathers Are Special*. Nashville: Broadman Press, 1977.

Stanley, Charles F. *A Man's Touch*. Wheaton, Ill.: Victor Books, 1977.

Stein, Edward V., ed. *Fathering: Fact or Fable*. Nashville: Abingdon Press, 1977.

FEAR

HAVE YOU EVER been afraid? I'm sure you have—we all have. There's nothing disgraceful about being afraid. It's inevitable and natural for human beings—frail creatures that we are—to be afraid. Jesus wouldn't have said, "Fear not," so many times if he hadn't known how prone we are to fear. . . .

Of all people, Christians have the right to be confident and sanguine. After all, the phrase, "Fear not," was not a meaningless attempt to make us feel better, but was meant to be taken literally. For us, there is good reason to fear not.

Yet, as I listen to the talk of the average Christian and observe some of our behavior I discover that we are all too often as fearful and timid as those who have no faith at all. I believe we are failing to use the resources we've been given if we are always preoccupied by possible threats to our well-being.

A Realistic Basis for Coping. Becoming less fearful of life in general and learning to cope with specific fears began when I gave myself—along with all my anxieties—to Christ. That was the starting point and the basis upon which every step toward a more confident life was taken. The confidence, of course, had to be in Christ and not in myself.

It was not a matter of saying, "Come, now, there's nothing to be afraid of. All I've got to do is to have courage!" The courage just wasn't there.

Instead, and far more realistically, I was learning to trust Christ, who is everything I am not, and who has promised to be—in me—all that I can never be on my own. I use the word *realistic* because I am convinced that any other grounds for confidence are illusory. It *is* a terrifying world—without him. With him we have reason to be encouraged, and all the help we need to deal with whatever our fears may be.

When Fear Is Necessary. Before we begin we think about the fears which depress, immobilize, and take the color out of life, it must be said that there is a fear from which we ought *not* to be delivered, which is positively beneficial. It is that fear which sends adrenaline boiling into our bodies and impels us into action when sudden danger confronts us. As I am crossing the street and see a car roaring down upon me, my eyes and brain do an instant calculation which tells me it's not going to stop. Fear moves me into action. It's the fuel that propels me out of the way.

When the crisis is over, the fear is gone. It was *about* something immediate and it was necessary. After such experiences we release our heightened emotions by describing what happened and what our feelings were to others, ". . . and when I saw that monster coming right for me and he wasn't braking at all, I made it to the curb in one jump. I was so frightened I could hardly stand up. . . ."

When my daughter Carole Ann was a toddler I looked up from weeding the front lawn to see her starting into the street just as a taxi turned the corner. I will always remember that instant. I remember standing a few seconds later with her in my arms on the sidewalk, but I have no memory of the moments in between, only of terror which dictated my action, the sound of tires squealing and the taxi driver swearing. Fear got me into the street to get Carole Ann and out again in a hurry, and fear slammed the driver's foot on the brakes.

"Seein' Things at Night." There is a kind of fear, however, which rather than getting us into action, simply gnaws away at our serenity. It is the fear of possible eventualities which seem to be threatening. We may push these worries far back into our mind, even down into the subconscious mind, but an ominous headline in the morning paper or an unexpected pain is enough to bring them surging to the surface.

It doesn't matter whether you are afraid of nuclear war, a worldwide depression, a stock market collapse—or some purely personal disaster—if it's the sort of thing we can do nothing about. Fear of events out of our control is deadly just because there is no action we can take. When we are able to do something we use up the energy that otherwise, having to go someplace, turns back on itself and, like cancer, proliferates horribly. Boilers explode when the steam gets to a certain point, and some of us are so swollen with fear we are at the exploding point.

When I stop to think of all the demonstrations of that anxiety at hand, my mind goes back to a poem my mother used to recite— she used it as a half-sympathetic, half-derisory, counter to my constant fearfulness. It's by Eugene Field, and the person speaking is a little boy in the country:

I ain't afeard uv snakes, or toads, or bugs,
    or worms, or mice,
An' things 'at girls are skeered uv I think
    are awful nice!
I'm pretty brave, I guess; an' yet I hate to
    go to bed
For when I'm tucked up warm an' snug
    an' when my prayers are said,

Mother tells me "Happy dreams!" and
    takes away the light,
An' leaves me lyin' all alone *an' seein'*
    things at night!

"Seein' things at night," is an experience we all know firsthand, not to mention the gray wisps of worry that haunt us even in the brightest sunlight.

For some, the spooks rise out of the financial page of the morning paper; the possibility of financial disaster is omnipresent and all plans and decisions are taken with a view of its prevention. One man I knew tithed with a kind of grim calculation, convinced that in doing so he was meeting all of God's demands for righteousness, and it was therefore obligatory on God's part to keep him from any financial loss. There are many, many Christians who believe this and if you are one of them your blood pressure is already rising. Before you slam the book shut, stop a moment and think: Do you give because you love to, because having a part in what God is doing in the world is exciting and joyous, or because you are afraid if you don't you'll be punished? Giving *ought* to be out of a full heart, not out of fear—and if fear is part of your giving then you need this book.

On the other hand, there are those whose constant worrying about money prevents them from ever using it with joy at all. Spending has become a grim business; every dollar is laid out with anguish, and only after much trauma on the part of everyone involved. When money becomes so important in the scheme of things that what we do with it—whether we spend it, save it, or invest it—becomes the occasion for tension and quarrels, there is obviously a problem and it is usually fear.

We are also concerned to a high degree with our physical comfort—not just our safety, but our comfort—and that obsessive interest in keeping our bodies in just the right temperature and away from anything hard or wearing or abrasive is related to the money worry. They are first cousins, they both have to do with safety and with the absence of any kind of hardship.

The Last Enemy. Concern with one's bodily well-being leads inevitably to apprehension about illness, or accident, and the final threat—death. I don't mean a normal shrinking from that experience which is the ultimate mystery, but a dread so overwhelming that it dominates life. A young woman I knew always said she never wanted children, and she said it long before concern about overpopulation made her view widely held. When she married it was with the understanding that there would be no children; she said the world was getting rapidly worse and this was no time to bring more children into such a perilous place. When some years later she discovered that she must have a hysterectomy she said bitterly, "I might as well have gone ahead and had a baby. The chances of dying on the operating table are as bad as the chance of dying in childbirth." Her real fear was that of death.

We can reassure ourselves on other matters by consulting a doctor, an accountant, or possibly a lawyer, but the fear of death is something no man can banish. The Bible is our only word on that. I believe that when we see what it has to say, and all that Jesus said and did, we will be surprised at the magnitude of the deliverance from fear that is available to us. Not only freedom from the fear of death but freedom from fear of life, which is the other side of the dark coin.

Too Scared to Live. If that sounds paradoxical, it is nonetheless true. Those I have known who were inordinately afraid of death ended up by being afraid of living as well. Most of our activities in life involve a certain element of risk. It's a very small step from being afraid of death to being afraid of anything which exposes us to possible harm, which could lead to death.

My children used to play with a little boy in the neighborhood whose mother was so afraid that he would pick up a germ or have an accident that the poor child was never allowed to do anything. He couldn't have a bicycle because he might fall and hurt himself; he couldn't go outdoors if the temperature was a few degrees under normal because he might catch cold. If it was a warm day, he was told anxiously not to run about too much, he might get sunstroke. He was never allowed to eat away from home because his diet was carefully planned and, obviously, his mother didn't think the rest of us fed our children the right way. At the slightest sign of a sniffle, or a lagging appetite, out came the thermometer and an impressive array of medicine bottles.

When there was a gathering of the mothers in the neighborhood, this woman tried to educate the rest of us as to the proper way to raise our children, feed our families, and keep ourselves healthy.

"No thank you," she'd say when offered a cup of coffee, "coffee is very bad for you—it washes the vitamins right out of your body." She and her husband didn't socialize with anyone at all because their early bedtime was about the time most parties started. She read every book on health there was and quoted extensively from all of them.

Unless she derived some enjoyment from all she did in the name of good health, the regimen that dominated every day, there was very little return for all her preoccupation with being safe from all possible threat to life and limb. She was one of the dullest women I've ever met. I can't see that there was any other reward, for she and her family were not particularly heathly. There wasn't anything really wrong—they just all looked a little wan and pasty, and were prone to catch cold easily.

I admit she was an extremist, but not all that unusual. Life, for too many people, seems to consist mostly of trying to make sure that there are no risks. Of course, no one wants to get hurt or be ill, but to live every moment with that kind of fear makes life very bleak.

There is also the fear of being hurt emotionally. Whenever witnesses to a crime explain why they made no attempt to help the victim they usually say, "I just didn't want to get involved." That's the philosophy of a great many people today about life itself, which consists of relationships. They don't want to get involved because they don't want to get hurt. They are possibly the most to be pitied because their fear isolates them more surely than stone walls. It's a very contagious fear, too, at least these people seem to want to infect others. When I began dating after five years of widowhood, a friend called to warn me that I shouldn't allow myself to care for anyone. "I just don't want to see you get hurt, Eileen," she said earnestly. That's the way far too many people feel about relationships—don't get into them if there's the slightest chance of being hurt. That seems to be inconsistent with the Christian life, and certainly with any kind of enjoyment of life.

The Fear That Isolates. There is still another kind of fear which is prevalent in our Western culture—the fear of failure. It has its opposite side, too—idolatrous worship of success. I stated earlier that fear often immobilizes, and the fear of failure certainly does. The moment you begin any project you run the risk of possible failure, and one way to make sure that never happens is simply not to do anything.

We're all acquainted with this fear in one of its most uncomplicated forms—the anxiety with which we used to approach a final examination at school. Most of us were able to function pretty well in spite of our nervousness, but a friend of mine always broke out in fever blisters just before an examination. No matter how well prepared she was, no matter how thoroughly she had studied, two or three days before the examination the blisters began to break out. There was a very good reason for her tenseness—her father and mother demanded a perfect performance, and she was never sure she was up to it.

Perhaps that's the case with many of us. Someone—ourself or others whose good opinion we feel we must have—demands a perfect performance and we know we're not capable of it. . . .

Fear of failure can keep a man from leaving a job he dislikes in order to do what he really wants to do, because risk is involved. I knew someone like that and he remained at a job he really loathed because he was afraid that if he got into business for himself he wouldn't make it financially. His wife used to encourage him to make the break but he usually said, "Sure, that's easy for you to say—you don't have to bring in the money to pay all the bills and feed these kids." She told him she'd be willing to get a job. Since the children were all in school she would rather like to work again. At that he always became very huffy and told her he was still capable of supporting his family, and a little more encouragement from her would be better than telling him he wasn't taking care of them. This was so illogical that she tried a few times to convince her husband that it wasn't dissatisfaction with his provision for the family that was her motivation, but rather a desire to help him be free to do what he really wanted. These discussions always ended in an ugly quarrel and a strained relationship which lasted for days, so she finally gave up.

187

Her husband continued the work he found dull. When he got to talking with other men about work he frequently said, "Well, of course, I've always wanted to get into something for myself. I like fixing things, maybe a small appliance repair business or something, but the wife and kids kind of like money coming in regular." By implication, he handed the responsibility for his reluctance to go into business on to his own wife and children. She knew the real reason of course. "He's afraid he'll fail, Eileen," she told me once in a moment of rare bitterness, "and he's got to have someone to blame. He's told himself that I'm the one who wants security for so long that by now I guess he really believes it."

That man's fear of failure did something to his whole family. It left a disillusioned wife who regarded her husband with tolerant contempt, two children who went their own way as soon as they were old enough, sure that there must be more enjoyment and excitement to life than they had found at home. Fear does something to everyone it touches. Either it spreads like a disease or, as in this man's family, alienates and isolates its victims from those around them.

The Fear That Distorts. . . . The fear of failure and worship of success are inevitable when we become afraid of the world and seek to withdraw from it. Since it isn't possible to get completely out of the world (we do have to go to work, get an education, shop, and cannot escape the consequences of political and economic events), we often do the next best thing. We keep our relationships with people and organizations outside the church as nominal as possible and live our real lives totally within the society of Christians.

This is demonstrated by a sentence I've heard from women on so many occasions that when they utter the first words I know

what the rest will be. "Yes, we have to belong to the Rotary Club (or the Kiwanis or the Lions Club or the Chamber of Commerce) because of Jack's business. But *of course* we never go to any of their parties. We have nothing in common with them." My conviction is that the attitude of mind that brings forth such a sentence is profoundly unchristian. I believe we were meant to live our lives out in the world where the action is.

Fear Spawns Other Evils. . . . Just as we are of no use to Christ at all when we're afraid to get out in the world, we subvert and corrupt all we are meant to be as a church when we live as a segregated group of people determined to be safe from contamination by the world.

The church that is dominated by a fear of involvement in the world, and has turned in upon itself, shows four major characteristics which are the result of that fear: snobbery, the ghetto attitude (Christian subculture), social climbing within the church social structure, and an inordinate suspicion and fear of other Christian groups whose culture is slightly different. This last characteristic, the suspicion of other Christian groups, is exemplified by two statements that were made to me. One woman, speaking of her college-age daughter, said worriedly, "Of course, she's dating a fellow right now rather steadily, but we hope she won't get too serious. He's a *Lutheran.*" Another woman said to some of us in a Bible study group, "When you join a church, be sure it's a Bible believing church, not some liberal Presbyterian bunch." I asked her why and she replied, "Well, you all know what Presbyterians are." Managing to keep my temper, I said, "You'd better tell me. I've been a Presbyterian for years and didn't know there was anything to distinguish us from any other Christians."

The Threatening Face of Change. There is also another fear which is deadly to any real vitality in one's life—or the life of any church—the fear of change. We can be afraid of change for so many reasons. Often the known is less threatening than the unknown. We are more comfortable with what is familiar. We know what to expect, how to react. As we grow older, change of any kind is symbolic of changes in ourselves which we find hard to accept—all the signs of growing old. Though we can't stave them off indefinitely we can avoid facing them if we are able to surround ourselves with the comforting reassurance of an unchanged *milieu.* That is why, when the social structures, including the church, begin to change it is very difficult for us to accept these reminders of our own mortality.

The current wave of nostalgia which is evident in television, motion pictures, music, folk art, and literature, as well as in women's clothing, is an illustration that everyone is uneasy in a world which is changing too rapidly for comfortable adjustment. We long for simpler less complicated times. They weren't, of course. It's just that in retrospect, frozen in their period of time, we can remember them in tranquillity.

The fear of change which we all experience to some degree as individuals exists in the church because we bring it in with ourselves. Most of us view the transformations that are taking place around us with emotions varying from enthusiasm on the part of younger people to acceptance from most of us to hostility and resistance from a few. But hardly anyone contemplates changes in every segment of society around us with complacency; for many of us these changes appear likely to put an end to a life-style with which we are comfortable.

There is no way to eliminate the consequences of change in our lives, and some of them will be sad; but there is a way to accept, and cope with change gracefully, if not with enthusiasm. . . . It may look a little less ominous to us as we think about change to consider some of the inescapable results of trying to keep any part of life safe from its touch. There are some problems inherent in every condition of life, and we may discover that what results when we strive to keep "our group" untouched by change is worse than anything the change itself could bring.

The Fear of Witnessing. Witnessing is a vital part of the Christian life. Indeed, it is not just a part, it is inherent in the life itself. We can't help demonstrating to the world around us what we are, what makes us tick. As fundamental as witnessing is, however, it is also a problem to many of us. We may agree on its necessity, but we disagree on just how it is accomplished.

I believe this disagreement arises primarily out of a misunderstanding of witnessing, or an overemphasis on one of its facets. In my own life I've gone from one to the other of the two major views of witnessing, until it seemed that there must be a truer, more biblical way. One point of view is that it is chiefly a matter of telling others about Christ, and therefore how one goes about that is all that matters. Method becomes everything, a kind of salesmanship. The other way of thinking about witnessing, often arrived at in reaction to the obvious flaws in the first view is that the way one lives is all there is to it. We are what we do. We show, not tell, our faith.

In my own life I followed an almost classic pattern; adopting the first point of view with all the enthusiasm of a new Christian. Taking all the courses, learning the Bible verses, and then talking to everyone who came within my orbit. I *was* a kind of salesman—not very good. Eventually there was a reaction on my part; I swung widely the other way. The phrases and clichés often used in witnessing became abhorrent to me. I do not believe that was a balanced point of view, nor a healthy way to live the Christian life.

Facing and Conquering Fear. Life can be truly exciting when we are really free of crippling fears. Most of us have hardly begun to grasp the magnitude of the freedom that can be ours. We think being free of fear means being safe and protected, that there is no need for anxiety; but that's really not freedom at all. To live like that is to be in bondage to whatever set of circumstances we need to have in order to feel quite safe.

Real freedom from fear is present even when we are in the midst of very dangerous situations, or confronted with sudden disaster or bad news. It's the only kind of freedom from fear that God offers to us, not because he's unwilling to give but because this is the best there is. There are two things it does for us. It frees us from the slow, wearing poison of constant anxiety and apprehension; and it enables us to do and be what we were really intended.

We were meant to be God's agents in the world, not as spectators, observers, or advisers, but as participants. When we haven't been it has usually been out of fear—the fear of getting hurt or being laughed at or simply of being uncomfortable in a strange milieu. But nothing good ever happens in the world unless someone makes it happen, and we are the ones God intends to use. Delivered from the inhibitions and restrictions of fear, we *can* fulfill that task.

First, however, we must call our fears by name, describe them and what they do to us, and then put the remedy to work. It's a little like getting over an illness; first the diagnosis, then the treatment, and finally, freedom!

I was reminded of that recently when my three-year-old granddaughter, Megan, was here for a visit. She was terrified of all animals, and especially of our large black and silver German shepherd, Mike. No one knew why. I could sympathize with her; she was afraid of even small animals, and Mike was as tall as she was. He has long teeth and what must look to a child like a cavern for a mouth. For a long time she screamed whenever he was in the room, so he spent a great deal of time on the back porch. Then she advanced to the point where she no longer screamed but made a convulsive leap into my arms on his approach, locked her arms around my neck and whimpered, "He scares me."

Just admitting her fear seemed to quiet it somewhat. Eventually Megan grew bold enough to pet Mike—timidly, and ready to fly if he turned toward her too quickly, but she'd come a long way. I don't think she would ever have gotten over her first frantic fear if she'd simply kept screaming and hiding her head every time she saw him. She had to look at him, to see that though the teeth were large and the mouth wide that he wasn't going to swallow her, he was merely panting with enthusiasm. She saw that his exuberant bounds through the house and his waving plume of a tail were signals of good will.

We must do what Megan did—look at our fears in the face. Some of them will turn out to be exactly like a big black dog: menacing in appearance, but on closer examination we will find that the danger was in our own minds. There are other fears far more real. When Christ said, "Fear not," he meant those fears as well as the imaginary ones. Once we face them we will find there is a way to be rid of them, and then we will be really free.

—From Eileen Guder, *Deliver Us From Fear* (pp. 9–24, 47–52). Waco, Tex.: Word Books, 1976.

FOR FURTHER READING:

Coles, Robert. *Children of Crisis: A Study of Courage and Fear.* Boston: Little Brown & Co., 1967.

Hubbard, David Allen. *How to Face Your Fears.* Nashville: A. J. Holman Co., 1972.

Living Beyond Worry and Anger. Eugene, Ore.: Harvest House Publishers, 1979.

FEEDING THE TODDLER

SINCE HOW AND WHAT toddlers eat is tied in closely with their independent, crotchety stage, a few suggestions about this age follow.

By the end of the first year, a child usually has been having semisolid food for several months and has learned to chew. He has three meals a day, perhaps with planned snacks to supplement. He's probably taking milk from a cup, even though he may still want to nurse from breast or bottle. You plan to increase the amount of solid food you give him, as you cut down on nursing. But this isn't what he has in mind, at all.

It is a surprise to find that he loses interest in his food, and may actually eat less. What he does eat, he wants on his own terms, with his own method of getting it from dish to mouth. He may take a sudden dislike to foods which he has liked before, perhaps his cereal or vegetables. His behavior fluctuates from meal to meal. You had enjoyed feeding the baby, but now this satisfying time of the day for both you and the child has vanished.

It helps to know that these ups and downs are normal. The baby's rapid growth is slowing down, and he actually needs less food in proportion to his body size than he did a few months before.

You can't depend on the old system of feeding your baby with a spoonful of cereal first, a bite of fruit, and tucking in the less-cherished vegetable. He may snatch the spoon, as if simply possessing it is all there is to eating. When he finds this isn't the case, he may throw the spoon away and begin to eat with his fingers. Soon as you get another spoon, he may grab it and the struggle begins all over again.

Your child's desire to feed himself is, in the long run, exactly what you want. Therefore, let him do as much as he can, even if he is awkward. By 2 years of age, many children can do a pretty complete feeding job, if not a neat one. If you place a toy in his hands to keep them out of his food, you miss a good chance to let him begin. It also confuses him by making it a playtime. He's willing enough to play with his food already.

What seems like deliberate messiness may have a purpose all its own. A child feels his food and pours his milk on the tray and onto the floor because he is so interested in how things behave. What will pour? Is this cold or hot? What will happen if I bite the cup? A child does not see the difference between pouring his milk and pouring water in his bath. He does not yet know about the proper place for his experiments.

There is a big difference between the awkwardness of a child who is trying hard to manage food, and one who plays with his food because he is being forced to eat more than he wants, is getting tired, or has found this gets his mother upset.

You will want to help a child who has stopped eating because he is tired of feeding himself, although he is still hungry. And you'll try to give him food which is easy to handle; spacing his meals and time of rest so that he is not overtired before he starts. Cut down on distractions which pull him away from his food before he has had enough to eat. Such wise planning helps to make mealtimes smoother for the toddler.

When a child has had all he wants to eat, he knows it. You may deftly squeeze in another bite or two, but you run the risk of losing his natural appetite as the best incentive to enjoyment of meals. Remove the food when he refuses the next bite or begins to play. If he is too hungry before the next meal, give him a nourishing snack.

If He Won't Chew. A few children have trouble chewing solid foods. The longer you let them stay on strained or mashed food, the harder it is to get them to accept lumps. Frequently, these children will accept cookies or toast, but they refuse chewy or chopped items such as meats and vegetables.

Such a child may chew if you give him larger pieces of food and let him bite off what he wants. A leaf of lettuce, crisp bacon, a wedge of apple, or a whole cooked green bean may get him started. Permitting him to finger-feed himself seems to work better than shoving food into his mouth on a spoon. Start the meal with something he must chew. A lazy chewer needs a lot of encouragement. It rarely works to wait for him to change by himself. Peas, beans, and other foods with tough skins are frequently not popular with children and are especially unpleasant to a child who still prefers to have his food mashed.

Within limits, it is generally more important what your child eats than how much. Many youngsters overplay fats and sugars and underplay the other essential foods.

So long as your child is healthy and not seriously under- or overweight, it is a good idea not to push him to eat more or less than he naturally wants. Since each child has his own natural rate and style of growth, each will require varying amounts of food. However, if he suddenly loses his appetite, you will want to check on his physical and emotional health. When a normally enthusiastic eater turns down food, it can be a sign that something ails him.

Fortunately for you and your youngster, his daily food needs and yours can be met by many kinds of foods. You can pay attention to the special likes and dislikes of your family and still give them healthy meals. Remembering that people naturally have different tastes, you can be sympathetic to your child who, for instance, may heartily dislike cauliflower. As you study your family, your food guide, and your budget you will be able to work out meals that satisfy your family's health, happiness, and pocketbook all at once.

—From *Infant Care* and *Your Child From 1 to 6*. Washington: U.S. Department of Health, Education and Welfare, 1970.

FIRST AID

EMERGENCY TELEPHONE NUMBERS		Ambulance/
Doctor	Pharmacist	Rescue Squad
Hospital	Police	Poison Control Center
Dentist	Fire Dept.	Neighbor

IN CASE OF SERIOUS INJURY OR ILLNESS

- Call a doctor, a hospital, the police or other emergency service immediately.
- Keep calm, briefly explain what has happened and ask what to do until help arrives.

FIRST AID TREATMENT

- If you cannot get immediate help, the following safe measures may provide emergency relief.

Bleeding (Severe)

- Call for emergency help and transport to a medical facility.
- Do not use any antiseptics or other materials.
- Place a thick pad of clean cloth or bandage directly over wound and press firmly to control blood flow.
- Hold in place with strong bandage, neckties, cloth strips etc.
- Do not make tie so tight as to prevent circulation to the rest of the limb.
- In case of injuries to the groin, armpit or neck, where ties cannot be used, control blood flow with finger or hand pressure.
- Raise the bleeding part higher than the rest of the body, unless bones are broken.
- If injury is extensive, treat for shock (*see* page 195).

Nosebleeds

- Have patient in sitting position blow out from the nose all clot and blood.
- Insert into the bleeding nostril a wedge of cotton moistened with any of the common nose drops.
- With the finger against the outside of that nostril apply firm pressure for five minutes.
- If bleeding stops remove packing (no rush, here).
- Check with your doctor if bleeding persists.

Broken Bones

- If a fracture of any part of the body or any injury to the head, neck or back is suspected, the patient should not be moved without medical supervision unless absolutely necessary.
- If a patient with a back or neck injury must be moved, keep the back, head and neck in a straight line, preventing them from being twisted or bent during movement. Use a board to help keep back, neck and head rigid.
- For other fractures, until you get medical help, place the injured part in as natural a position as possible without causing discomfort to the patient. Protect from further injury by applying splints long enough to extend well beyond the joints above and below the fracture. Any firm material can be used (board, pole, metal rod, or even a thick magazine or thick folded newspaper). Pad splints with clothing or other soft material to prevent skin injury. Fasten splints with bandage or cloth at the break and beyond joints above and below it. Use pressure bandage to control bleeding (*see* Bleeding).

Burns and Scalds

- Get patient to doctor or hospital as soon as possible.
- If he is conscious and can swallow, give plenty of water or other non-alcoholic liquids to drink.

- Do not use ointments, greases, powder, etc.
- Until you get medical help, immerse burned area immediately in cold water or apply clean, cold moist towels.
- Chill water with ice, if possible, *but never add salt.*
- Maintain treatment as long as pain or burning exists. In case of chemical burns, flush skin with plenty of running water.
- Cover burned area with clean cloth to exclude air.
- Avoid breaking any blisters that may appear.
- If burns are extensive keep patient quiet and treat for shock (*see* page 195).

Choking

- Use Heimlich maneuver. (Learn this technique as soon as possible.)
- If you cannot hold the child, have him lie on his back.
- Kneel over the child.
- Press crossed hands firmly against stomach above navel.
- Have someone ready to reach in mouth and remove food or other object.
- If the child cannot breathe at all, turn him head and face down over your knees and hit sharply between shoulder blades.

Convulsions

- If caused by fever, sponge body with cool water.
- Apply cold cloths to head.
- Lay on side with hips elevated.
- Prevent biting of tongue.
- Be sure tongue is not blocking passage of air to the lung.
- Call physician.

Eye Contamination

- Remove contact lenses if worn; *never* permit the eye to be rubbed.
- Gently wash eye out immediately, using plenty of water (or milk in an emergency), for five minutes with eyelids held open.
- Call for emergency help and transport to a medical facility promptly.

Fainting

- Keep in flat position.
- Elevate legs and feet.
- Loosen clothing around neck.
- Keep patient warm.
- Keep mouth clear.
- Give nothing to swallow.
- If breathing has stopped, start artificial respiration.
- Have someone call for emergency help and transport to a medical facility.

Shock

Shock usually accompanies severe injury or emotional upset. The signs are cold and clammy skin, pale face, chills, frequently nausea or vomiting, shallow breathing.
- Call for emergency help and treatment.
- Until you get medical help, have patient lie down with legs elevated.
- Keep patient covered to prevent chilling or loss of body heat.
- Give non-alcoholic fluids if he is able to swallow unless abdominal injury is suspected.

Artificial Respiration

There is need for help in breathing when breathing movements stop or lips, tongue or fingernails become blue. When in doubt, apply artificial respiration until you get medical help. No harm can result from its use and delay may cost the patient his life. Start immediately. Seconds count.
- Clear mouth and throat of obstructions with your fingers.
- Place patient on back with face up.
- Lift the neck, tilt head back.
- If air passage is still closed, pull chin up by placing fingers behind the angles of the lower jaw and pushing forward.
- Take deep breath.
- Place your mouth over patient's nose or mouth, making leak-proof seal.
- If breathing into mouth, pinch patient's nostrils closed.
- If breathing into nose, seal patient's mouth with your hand.
- Blow into patient's nose or mouth until chest rises.
- Remove your mouth and let patient exhale.
- Repeat about 15 times a minute, or about every four seconds.
- If the patient's stomach rises markedly, exert moderate hand pressure on the stomach just below the rib cage to keep it from inflating.

For Infants:
- Place your mouth over patient's mouth *and* nose.
- Babies require only small puffs of air from your cheeks.
- Repeat 20 to 30 times per minute.
- Don't exaggerate the tilted position of an infant's head.

FIRST AID FOR POISONING

In all cases, except poisonous bites, the principle is GET THE POISON OUT or OFF or DILUTE it. . . .
CALL PROMPTLY FOR EMERGENCY HELP.

Swallowed Poison
- Dilute poison by giving water, one or two glassfuls.
- Make patient vomit if so directed, BUT NOT IF . . .

BUT NOT IF:

—patient is unconscious or having seizures.

—swallowed poison was a strong corrosive (lye, strong acid, drain cleaner, etc.)

—swallowed poison contains kerosene, gasoline or other petroleum distillates (unless containing a dangerous pesticide as well, which must be removed).

Induce Vomiting

- Give one tablespoonful (½ ounce) of syrup of ipecac for a child one year of age or older, plus at least one cup of water.
- If no ipecac syrup is available, try to induce vomiting by tickling back of throat with a spoon handle or other blunt object, after giving water. If no vomiting occurs in 20 minutes, this dose may be repeated *once only*. After vomiting has ceased, offer a slurry of activated charcoal (1–2 tablespoonsful) in a glass of water.
- Do not give salt or mustard to children.
- Do not waste time waiting for vomiting, but transport patient promptly to a medical facility. *Bring package or container with intact label.*

Inhalation Poisoning (Gas, Fumes, Smoke)

- Get into fresh clean air.
- Loosen clothing.
- If not breathing, start artificial respiration promptly. *Do not stop* until breathing or help arrives.
- Have someone else call for emergency help and transport to a medical facility promptly.

Poisonous Bites

Snakes

- Don't let victim walk; keep as quiet as possible.
- Do not give alcohol.
- Call for emergency help and transport to a medical facility.

Enroute, or while awaiting transportation

- Apply suction to bite wound with mouth or suction cup.
- If victim stops breathing use artificial respiration.

Insects

- Do not let victim walk, keep as quiet as possible.
- Place any available cold substance on bite area to relieve pain.
- A paste of Adolph's Meat Tenderizer or Baking Soda and water applied to the bite will often reduce the swelling and itching by its enzymatic action.
- If victim stops breathing, use artificial respiration.
- Call for emergency help and transport to a medical facility.

(Persons with known unusual reactions to insect stings should carry emergency treatment kits and an emergency identity card.)

—From Jay M. Arena and Miriam Bachar, *Child Safety Is No Accident: A Parents' Handbook of Emergencies.* Durham, N.C.: Duke University Press, 1978.

Home First Aid Kit

1. Syrup of ipecac (*not* the fluid extract) 1 ounce for each member of family
2. Epsom salts
3. Roll of 1 inch adhesive tape (1)
4. Sterile bandages 4 inch by 4 inch (12)
   3 inch by 3 inch (12)
   2 inch by 2 inch (12)
5. Sterile vaseline gauze
6. Elastic bandages 2½ inch
   4 inch
7. Hydrogen peroxide
8. Scissors
9. Tweezers
10. Insect sting kit (if someone in house is allergic)
11. Aspirin (child-proof cap if children in house)
12. Children's aspirin (child-proof cap)
13. Thermometer
14. Cotton-tipped swabs
15. Triangle bandage (1)
16. Anesthetic ointment
17. Antibiotic ointment
18. Gauze bandage rolls 1 inch wide
    4 inches wide
19. Adhesive bandages, assorted

—From *Emergency First Aid.* Skokie, Ill.: Publications International, Ltd., 1978.

FIRST BABY

ONLY PARENTS can know fully the new light and vitality that spreads through a home the day their newborn is tenderly placed in his own special place there. At the same time, however, they know, too, that caring for a new baby is a job. Viewing those early weeks as a period of learning about the job—of adding more to what they already sense and know about it—is a good attitude for a new mother and father. The job and the learn-ing are among the most thrilling and enriching in the world.

As precisely as they have planned, many a new father and mother have moments of bewilderment—even helplessness—during the first few weeks of living with a new baby. The sounds that are uniquely an infant's—the snuffles, grunts, snorts, and whimpers—can be disturbing to uninitiated adults. If an infant is not hungry and is generally comfortable, the queer noises are nothing to worry about. All babies make them.

Perhaps the most important step in these first weeks is for the new mother to trust in herself. An attempt to define maternal instinct would certainly include willingess and, out of that willingness, judgment. After all, it's mothers who invented ways of diapering and ways of burping. Parents can sense, for instance, that an infant is happier when he is handled slowly and easily. They can see that he wants a lot of uninterrupted rest. Visitors can have their "peek" noiselessly when he's asleep. Tender cuddling by relatives is an extra portion of love for him—but he can't take too large a portion. He has just come from the calm of a protecting womb, and he has to get used to his new world. Trusting their own feelings and common sense, and trusting their baby, the new mother and father relax sooner. In this they give an important first gift to the child—an atmosphere free of jumpiness and anxiety.

A most practical measure for new parents is having help in the house. The mother who sets out industriously to perform her usual household routine can render herself, her baby, and her husband a great disservice. She too has some adjusting to do, and fatigue comes easily. A father who has worked all day is tired when he comes home. When there are constant effort and toil to get things done, that easygoing atmosphere is lost. If there is no help to be had—not even that of a friend or relative—necessary tasks should be done the easiest way. In most cases, for instance, laundry can be sent out and heavy groceries sent in.

Another practical step is working out a daily schedule. Generally the baby is dressed, has his bath, nap, airing, and is put to bed at about the same time every day. Some infants establish a feeding schedule very early. Sooner or later that too can be counted on at about the same time every day. There are practical advantages for parents in self-demand feeding too. Even when he has established his own schedule, if the infant isn't asking for his meal there's no reason why his mother can't take another half hour to finish some chore before feeding him. It isn't going to harm him if his airing or bath is skipped a few times for her convenience. Routine and efficiency are helpful, but to aim for perfection in them is not. Getting the maximum comfort for everyone is a wiser goal.

—From *The New Encyclopedia of Child Care and Guidance.* Garden City, N.Y.: Doubleday & Co., 1968.

FLUORIDES

IN ABOUT 1908 a dentist in Colorado Springs noticed that many of the children he saw had mottled teeth but far fewer cavities than the average child. His curiosity piqued, he finally concluded that the anomaly had something to do with a substance in the community's drinking water.

But not until 1931 was that substance identified as a fluoride. The U.S. government then carried out studies that confirmed the connection between good teeth and fluorides. In 1946 fluoride was added for the first time to water that lacked adequate amounts

(one part fluoride per million of water). Today most of the nation's water is fluoridated.

Opposition to fluoridation came in three forms. A number of scientists objected that more tests were needed to determine the long-term effects of fluoridation. Some parents objected to what they saw as compulsory medication (advocates see it as a preventive, like chlorine, rather than a medication and insist that optional fluoridation would be more costly and less effective). Other parents argued that compulsory fluoridation was an abridgement of their religious freedom.

Because fluoride makes teeth harder by increasing their crystal content, doctors and dentists recommend that it be given to children either in drinking water, or in toothpaste, or by direct application every two or three years. It is much less effective in preventing cavities in adults who did not have fluoridated water as children.

—LESLIE R. KEYLOCK

FOR FURTHER READING:

Gotzsche, Anne-Lise. *The Fluoride Question: Panacea or Poison.* Briarcliff Manor, N.Y.: Stein and Day, 1975.

FORGIVENESS

HUNDREDS OF STORIES can be told of teenagers who pull against family values, or of parents who fail to make the right decisions in raising children. The sad part of family life is that we can and do hurt one another. These hurting times can come from big and small mistakes, from our own insensitivity and from poor communication. Forgiveness and reconciliation cement the bonds of family relationships and support members in both their strengths and weaknesses. Forgiveness is one of the main tenets of Christian life.

Forgiving another person in the family can be very difficult. We can't always forgive because it's expected of us, or because it's the loving thing to do. When we've been deeply hurt by another, especially by someone we love, we must eventually realize our ability to forgive.

Hearing or saying the words, "I'm sorry" will not always take care of things. They sound nice and they are a beginning, but feelings of alienation, of guilt, may still be present. Forgiveness takes time. When a family member makes a serious mistake, the shock is enough to handle for the moment. Sometimes it takes days or weeks or months to come to a point of understanding. Even when forgiveness is asked of other family members, they can't always respond. They may feel guilty about not being able to respond immediately. Reconciliation can be a complicated process, because it involves trust, honest communication, sharing of oneself and accepting the other.

A Negative Foundation

There is a subtle conditioning that happens in our culture. This conditioning has much to do with forgiveness in the home. It affects the ability to trust one another.

Parents are almost trained to suspect the teen years are going to be a time of trouble. In fact, from the time the children are small, well-meaning parents of teenagers begin to promote fear. "Just you wait," they warn, "your day is coming. They're little now, but when they're in high school, hang on." This implies that, no matter what we do or how we parent, there is no way to trust a teenager. We begin to brace ourselves for the unknown horrors of parenting adolescents. We wonder if there is really any way to survive the ordeal.

This conditioning can put us in a state of mind that is harmful to an open relationship with our children. The teen years in themselves are exciting, stimulating, and interesting, depending on what we bring to them. If we have been told to fear them, our ability to trust will weaken; we'll be looking for trouble instead of trust.

We can learn (or recall) much about the fullness of life from our adolescents. They bring with them a zest for life. Ironically, at times this approach to life can be the very thing that makes us suspect their motives. Their energy and enthusiasm can be misunderstood by parents as a personal act of rebellion. Just because they would rather go out than "sit at home," doesn't mean we have failed to make our home an interesting place. It simply means they are in the searching time of their lives, and part of that search is to be with their peers. They are restless by nature, which is probably to their advantage. If they were too satisfied, we'd worry about their health.

But somehow through fear and mistrust, we sometimes shut the door on a person-to-person relationship with our teenagers. Instead, we put them into a role, and we search for what a good parent should be, hoping that if we do everything just right, follow all the rules, we will avoid the problems and worries of raising adolescents.

As parents, we are challenged to see our teenagers as persons to love rather than problems to be solved. If, out of fear, we gather a list of do's and don'ts for them to obey, the only communication between them and us will be one of rule-keeping or rule-breaking. Somehow, love and faith and hope get lost in the bookkeeping. Rules are no guarantee that all trouble will be avoided. This is not to say that some reasonable rules are not needed. Every home needs some common-sense level of order. The security of the adolescent can be threatened if nobody cares enough to expect some accountability for actions. It's when rules are the only line of communication that things become difficult.

Learning to Forgive

Even though the years of adolescence are not as bad as some would have us believe, mistakes will be made. Some will be little mistakes, others may break our hearts. The real test in parent-teen relationships will come, not over the mistake that was made but in the ability to face the mistake together, to come to some kind of understanding so that we can renew our trust in one another. Renewing trust is part of being able to forgive. Without trust, forgiveness just isn't real.

How do we learn to trust our children? Prevention of mistakes by rules isn't the whole story. We must go through the painful process of letting go. During the baby and pre-school years, our children needed us every minute. As time went on, they needed us several times a day, instead of all the time. Now as adolescents, we see them go farther and farther away from us, but the need for us is still there. It just isn't the same kind or the same amount. We are called on to change right along with them, and yet maintain a stable force in their lives.

In gradually letting go of adolescents, our ability to trust them and to adjust to the possibility that they will make mistakes will be tested. We can't follow them to school; we can't ride around in the car with them; we can't stay home with them every minute. Somewhere along the line we must sit back and simply watch.

On their part, they may rebel, or they may act responsibly. This is the risk involved. Maybe their lack of good judgment will result in a serious mistake. Dropping out of school, developing a dependency on alcohol or drugs, getting involved in an unwanted pregnancy. Where do we begin to deal with such devastating problems? How do we struggle with guilt, forgiveness, trust, with beginning again?

Accepting Our Teens

We must deal with the practical side to every problem. First we look at the immediate needs. If, for example, our teen-ager drops out of school, and refuses to talk with us about the reasons why, we might have to look for someone other than ourselves to deal with the situation. It takes many people to parent a child, and in stressful times, the parent may be the last one who is able to communicate with the adolescent. Sometimes there is a need to just wait, to control the urge to "talk" too much, to wish for an immediate solution to the problem. Whatever the case, it's good to get a foot on the ground through practical efforts.

But the feelings of disappointment and hurt are still there. All the practical accomplishments in the world won't resolve deep feelings of hurt. Perhaps a daughter finds herself in an unwanted pregnancy. Even after some practical decisions are made together, there are still haunting questions to be faced: Why did she do it? What have I done wrong? Feelings in words can sound harsh: "I almost hate her for putting our family through all this." How do we deal with a teen-ager who has failed to live up to our expectations, our values, our hopes? We talked with her; we've informed her; we've checked her comings and goings; we thought we knew who she was with, where she went; but now we find she's not only pregnant, but she's been lying to us also. She lied about where she went, who she was with. Even after the pregnancy is finished, will we ever be able to trust again?

Forgiving Ourselves

Through all this pain, we begin to see that to forgive our child, we must forgive ourselves first. In facing our own guilt and perhaps a false sense of shame, we will clear the path to forgiveness of our adolescent. It will help to find someone we trust; someone we know will cherish not only our words, but our feelings. If we know of a parent who has experienced what we're now going through and we feel we can talk to that parent, this is a good place to begin. Also, we might turn to professional helpers, those who are trained to listen and to help. Sometimes a combination of good friends and trained professionals are the best help and support for we may need both the warmth and love of friends, and the objective help of a professional viewpoint. When we can begin to say to ourselves, "I've done the best I could," and know that we would never deliberately lead our children into trouble, we will get a better perspective on where we are as people, not just role-players caught in a parent-adolescent struggle.

Forgiveness of ourselves, and ultimately of our teen-ager is possible. After we know that we can forgive and begin to trust again, we must express our forgiveness in some believable way. It will do no good to say, "I forgive you," if we give no outward signs of that forgiveness. We will be challenged to show forgiveness and know that sometimes it is without reward. Adolescents may not give us much to go on. We are not always given the privilege of seeing our teen-ager's innermost feelings.

Realizing Their Pain

The quiet hours of the night bear heavily on a teenager who is frightened of losing the love of a parent. Doubts, loneliness, confusion set in. She or he doesn't know quite what to expect. A first reaction is, "I can handle this myself without any help from anybody!" It's the automatic reaction of any teen. Independence is something adolescents cherish and fear at the same time. They want our forgiveness, but not our pity. They need our help, but not our interference. They need our advice, but not our "sermons." In short, they haven't made the complete jump from childhood to adulthood. They are in a continual time of stress. Making a mistake, for which they need forgiveness from us and from themselves, must not be the end of the world for them. They learn one of the most valuable lessons of life from our forgiveness: that they are now, and always have been, worthwhile and lovable.

This is the example Jesus gave us as he forgave Peter, as he forgave Mary Magdalen, as he told the story of the prodigal son, and as he gave Zacchaeus a sense of his identity and worth by forgiving him.

—From Clarice Flagel, "Forgiveness ... A Painful Truth" in *Christian Parenting: The Adolescent.* Ramsey, N.J.: Paulist Press, 1979.

FOR FURTHER READING:

Cornwall, Judson. *Let Us Enjoy Forgiveness.* Old Tappan, N.J.: Fleming H. Revell Co., 1978.

Donnelly, Doris. *Learning to Forgive.* New York: Macmillan Publishing Co., 1979.

Evans, Colleen Townsend. *Start Loving: The Miracle of Forgiving.* Garden City, N.Y.: Doubleday & Co., 1978.

Mains, Karen. *The Key to a Loving Heart.* Elgin, Ill.: David C. Cook Publishing Co., 1979.

Ogilvie, Lloyd J. *Loved and Forgiven.* Ventura, Calif.: Regal Books, 1977.

FRIENDS

ALL PARENTS know that friends are important to their boys and girls, but some do not recognize just how important. When it becomes a nuisance to find friends the same age for a child or to accept the ones he does have, it's a temptation to take the easiest way out and not bother about it. If a two- or three- or four-year-old plays happily at home, his mother may feel there's no point in pushing the stroller to a neighbor's house or taking a bus to the playground. Time enough for friends, she feels, when he goes to school. But preschool children do need practice in getting along with other boys and girls. They don't exactly make friends—they do not even seem to play together much of the time, even if they have sisters and brothers. But children adjust to school life more easily if, from an early age, they've been used to having other boys and girls around—sharing toys, copying each other, or simply playing side by side.

Most children begin to make friends when they go to school. Often a classmate or someone next door becomes a child's "best" friend; often he likes several children equally well. They may quarrel daily, but they still remain friends. Intense friendships may continue for a long time or children may change "best" friends frequently, but while they last these friendships mean a lot. As boys and girls grow older it's sometimes hard when they seem to value their contemporaries more than their hitherto all-important parents. Friendships, however, are increasingly important to a child's happiness and emotional development, besides being a way of learning to get along with others.

Whether their child has one friend or many, almost all parents can find something wrong with their son's or daughter's choice of companions. Sometimes parents' objections are unfair or unrealistic, but sometimes they are well founded. A particular boy or girl may act in a way that is wild and destructive, or sneaky and unreliable. Those who have worked with parents and children agree, however, that only very rarely does a

child exert so bad an influence that other children must be denied his companionship. A little gentle guidance can often do a great deal. The children involved may be led toward more wholesome creative activities than those they would choose for themselves. Instead of forbidding Henry to play with John because John is so destructive, the parents of both boys might get together to set up a carpentry bench, for instance, and to take turns supervising until the boys show that they can use it constructively by themselves.

It broadens one's outlook to remember that other people's children are also in the process of growing up; they aren't permanently "a bad influence" any more than one's own children are. "Influencing" works two ways: sometimes one's own child is influenced, for good or bad; but sometimes it's he who has an influence, good or bad, on another child. We cannot always know what it is that one child sees in another, nor what he gets from the friendship. But we can be pretty certain that he is getting something that satisfies some emotional need. Whatever his parents' private opinion may be, he needs the chance to develop and express loyalty to his chosen friend, to entertain and to visit him.

If parents criticize certain friends or forbid friendships, this is likely to establish them even more firmly. Instead of trying to steer a child away from these friendships (except in most unusual cases), parents might find ways of supplementing them. If they think he's not getting enough intellectual stimulation or enough outdoor play with his friends, parents can use their ingenuity to provide these in other ways, while still respecting the child's own choices of companions.

When a child has a hard time making friends, whether he's 6 or 16, he needs help—occasionally the help of a trained

202

counselor. However, there's much that parents themselves can do. At first it may be up to them to make all the suggestions for getting together with other children. If the family lives in an isolated spot or far away from other children, the parents may have to find ways of providing companionship. When a child is unable to make friends for himself in the rough-and-tumble world of school and playground, his parents can make it easier by inviting one or two classmates to the house for a marshmallow roast or to a movie or ball game and then step into the background as soon as possible. Parents don't, of course, want to buy popularity for their children. But when a child is shy or in a new neighborhood or going through a particularly trying phase, then it does no harm to get things going by "priming the pump."

Whether a child makes friends easily or with difficulty, he will be helped if his parents remember that it is the friendship itself that counts more than the actual virtues of his friend. The closeness and the sharing and the feeling of belonging with one's own contemporaries are what matter.

—From *The New Encyclopedia of Child Care and Guidance.* Garden City, N.Y.: Doubleday & Co., 1968.

FOR FURTHER READING:

Anderson, Colena M. *Friendship's Bright Shinings.* Grand Rapids: Zondervan Publishing House, 1976.
McGinnis, Alan Loy. *The Friendship Factor.* Minneapolis: Augsburg Publishing House, 1979.

FRUSTRATION

TO BE THWARTED or disappointed at times is an inevitable part of human living. Everyone knows the experience of striving toward some goal and of being blocked in attaining it. Feelings of defeat, impotence, discouragement, possibly of rage and resentment, are likely to be involved in the pain of a frustrating experience. One of the many aspects of growing up is the increasing ability to deal with frustration, to tolerate disappointment, and to draw from a thwarting experience some positive result.

To the child, frustration is one of the important factors in learning, and he begins his experience of it early in life. He is frustrated both from outside and from within himself. The tiny infant is frustrated by his own helplessness when he is cold and wet and unable to make himself comfortable. He is also frustrated when he is hungry and the bottle his mother brings him is too hot or the hole in the nipple too small. The toddler's balloon bursts, or an adult snatches a packet of matches from his hand before he can investigate them. He is unable to open the cupboard door to get out the pots and pans he wants to play with. Or he may want to play in the sandbox with his sister and also to go to the store with his mother, and be frustrated by the conflict between two of his own desires.

Gradually the child learns to deal with his frustrations. The infant can only kick and scream in rage until someone comes to help him. The toddler may scream, but he also tugs at his mother to get him the toy he cannot reach, or he looks around for something else to play with.

The capacity to deal with frustration in realistic and constructive ways develops slowly. The child needs experiences of success as well as failure to grow on. He needs to know the satisfaction of achievement in order to have courage and inventiveness in the face of frustration.

The young child is not able to take too much frustration. He is so often balked by his own limitations that he can scarcely be expected to deal with more disappointments than are really necessary. Mothers and fathers generally recognize this and try to limit the frustrating situations in the young child's daily living. They remove the tempting but fragile ornament not only from the reach of the exploring toddler but also out of his sight. They try to give him safe play space and scope for his investigations.

At the same time parents realize that in life the child cannot always have what he wants and that disappointments will increase as he grows older and his activities broaden. The parents themselves must frustrate him in the course of teaching him necessary safety lessons and teaching him also that he needs to learn in order to become a social human being. His weaning, his toilet training, his steps in learning cleanliness, considerateness, carefulness, and many other aspects of civilized living all involve frustration.

While parents try not to add unnecessary frustrations to the young child's experience, they need not be afraid to expose him to the healthy and fruitful frustrations by which he learns. It has been observed that when a baby is successfully weaned, his learning takes a forward spurt in other ways. When a

youngster is ready physically and psychologically for toilet training, or to leave home for nursery school, he thrives on the challenge of this next step in his maturing.

Learning is largely a process of frustration followed by achievement. By their sensitiveness to the youngster's stage of growth and their care in measuring their demands according to his ability to meet them, parents make wholesome use of the frustrating experiences the child must go through in the course of growing up. In the life of a generally happy youngster, the realistic frustrations he encounters on his own are likely to be positive learning experiences.

Boys and girls need the strengthening encouragement of their parents and teachers to face and deal with frustration, right through adolescence and often into young adulthood. By the example of their elders and by their confidence gained from overcoming frustration in the past, they learn the difficult and maturing lesson of working out a way around an obstacle or of accepting an unavoidable disappointment and turning to other, more realistic goals.

—From *The New Encyclopedia of Child Care and Guidance.* Garden City, N.Y.: Doubleday & Co., 1968.

G

GENERATION GAP

FIRST OF ALL, I heard our young people saying: *"Love us for ourselves: not as your status symbol."* They are tired of their grades being your status symbols. They are tired of making an A and your bragging about it at the Bridge Club, for they suspect down underneath that getting an A and your prodding them to get an A is so that you can have your status in the community heightened. Now you may not feel that way, but they do. Many of us vicariously live through our children and they see this as not loving them for themselves. They get put in the category of a Cadillac, a job promotion, a new suit. All of this is our status system. They see our prodding them to excell as prodding them for our status. "Love us for ourselves. Do not love us the same way you love your Cadillacs or fur coats. Do not use us to tell everyone that 'I've made it.' "

They are tired of hearing you say, when they do something that doesn't please you: "What will my friends think?" I think that is a clue they have picked up from you. I heard it at both the high school and college level. They are tired of your seeing your friends as the ultimate authority. "What will my friends think if you bring that boy home? What will my friends think if you dress that way? What will my friends think if you act this way or go to that place?" Or, "I'm glad you've done that. My friends will like it." They have heard this until they can't stand it. You may be concerned about the gallery,

but you are really saying to them: "You don't love me for me; you love me for the praise I bring to you."

The second thing they are saying: *"You give us love only when we earn it."* In an effort to create in them the desire to excel, we have used love as a reward. Implicitly, and sometimes explicitly, we have used love as a carrot on a stick, hoping to motivate our children to achieve in order to gain the carrot. Sometimes we imply: the more you excel, the more love we will give you. Our young people understand that love is not something you earn. Love is not something you give if a person excels. They feel that when they move up two rungs on the ladder, you will give them two rungs of love. The higher on the ladder, whatever the ladder may be—grades, achievement, success, offices at school—the higher they go, the more love we give them. This actually says: "You have no worth apart from the status you earn for me."

It's all caught up in our sense of competition. The father competes in business to sell or to excel, and so he expects his child to compete with these other things for his love. And the successful child, he tells his family, is the one who competes the best for his love. Our whole educational system was built on this structure. The student who excels receives the most praise. I remember being sent to the blackboard when I was in the fifth grade to work a math problem. As was the custom in most of our schools, the children at the desks were working the same problem privately. Naturally, under the pressure of being at the board and in full view of the class, I panicked. Whereupon the teacher asked the students if any of them knew the answer. They all did, for they had no pressure on them at their desks. Another boy, who had worked the problem in the safety of his desk, was selected to go to the board and correct my work. He became the instant hero—I was the instant dunce. The system pitted us against each other. Our self-worth was determined by our performance. Our value to our society is determined much the same way.

When a child is required to earn love at home in this fashion, he may refuse to do so. All of us have the right to be loved by our family regardless of the value our society places upon us. Our children are incapable of competing with all else in the world for our love.

Another thing I have felt them saying: *They hunger for deep, personal relationships.* I have never seen people more hungry for deep, personal relationships than this current generation of young people. Watch their films or listen to [their] music. There is a deep hunger for personal relationships with people. In all of their movies I have seen, there have been two people who had had a deep personal relationship, and I am not talking about deep sexual relationships. I am talking about deep personal relationships where you love each other at gut level; where you can share yourself; where you can pour out your heart and soul to somebody who won't betray you and who will understand what you are inside. This is what they are crying for.

Being the children of the Electronic Age has produced this. They are taught in school by teaching machines, entertained at home by TV, and lulled to sleep by the transistor radio. Father travels for his company from Monday to Friday, plays golf on Saturday, and watches football on Sunday. They hunger to have someone treat them as people, not machines. They long to know the man behind the veneer who calls himself the "head of the house." One of the young people said to me, "I've never had an adult male listen to me." I had another one say to me, "I didn't think you would do it." Many said to me in these words (and others said it in different words): "I've never heard an adult say he hurts on the inside." And they know we do, but they have never heard us say it. They hunger for these deep, personal relationships.

Now I cannot begin in this short sermon to tell you how to establish these, but I want you to know that hunger is there. It is deeply imbedded in them. They are deeply afraid as they get older that they won't be capable of having deep personal relationships because they do not think you are capable of it. This is not an accusation against Mother and Father; they think it's an explanation. They are afraid that they are going to be as plastic as the parents are.

Also, they do not want to be as artificial as your world is or as artificial as the boss Daddy has. None of this has come through in any perfect expression. It is all mixed with a little hypocrisy on your side and on theirs. We have lost our sensitivity. They see Father going from winter to spring and not even knowing that the flowers are up, except that the Super Bowl is over and baseball has started. Mother gets caught in such important things as another club meeting. She's concerned about whether or not the car is as pretty as the neighbor's. They just don't want to be that way. I don't blame them. They have made me do some rethinking of our values too. They really are afraid they are going to be like the worst they see in us.

The fourth thing they are saying to us is

that the *surface matters very little:* the substance matters very much. Beards, clothing, hair, dress, style are really not the mark of a man. All of these things that we use to superficially categorize people just do not matter to them. Some young people say: "They judge my friends before they know them." However this comes across at your home, ask yourself the question, "Have I become too concerned on surface matters and not enough on substance?"

Many families have let a quarter inch of hair separate them from their children. I was visiting in another community during a series of speaking engagements in that area. While talking to a dear friend and his wife, their college son returned home for his visit of the fall term. He was sporting the most beautiful mustache I had ever seen. The family was aghast and for the next few days they did all in their power to get him to shave it off. They schemed, begged, threatened—all to no avail. Several days later I was driving to a speaking engagement with them, and they continued to plot against their son, hoping to get his upper lip clean again. Finally, I had had all I could take, I leaned over the front seat of the car and said: "I don't want to push into your life but . . . (now when anyone begins a statement like this, you can be sure he is going to push into your life) would you let a quarter inch of hair separate you from your son?" I extolled the virtues of the boy, for he was a good boy, and reminded them of his warm and gentle spirit. They paused, acknowledged my point of view, responded affirmatively to my suggestion that they had placed the quarter inch of hair out of proportion—but continued their plotting. Long hair may be the only way our boys can get our attention. The substance of a life is more important than the style of the surface.

Also, I think after listening to them that we violate their personal and sacred areas.

For instance, I have heard too many parents try to ridicule their children out of clothing, movies, life-style, and music. We cannot ridicule them out of anything, for you see these are sacred areas. When you begin to ridicule, you hurt them at the point where they are most vulnerable. To this they say: "All right, if I get exposed there, I just won't expose myself there again and I'll just get harder and more and more tough until you can't get into me." Then one day you find you just can't win any battles with them because sometimes they are bigger than you are and they know exactly how to get around you.

I think we violate their personal areas when we ridicule their music. I have been listening to it and have read some things about it—including an analysis. It is almost calculated to turn us off so they can listen to it privately. It is full of their own catch words. They know what they are saying. It is a subculture of its own. They have been watching us all of the years and they have put what they have seen down in their music. They purposely make it so we cannot stand it so they can listen to it and enjoy it without us.

The next thing they are saying to us is that *their hurts are real.* It may be "puppy love" to us, but it is real love to them. They have had a little "crush" on somebody, we think, and have gotten hurt. That's a real "crush," and that's a real hurt. There is nothing worse than your first heartbreak. And a "cheer up, you'll get over it" is not going to make any difference because they really hurt. Their struggle is real. Their struggle for identity and their struggle for faith is real. They want the privilege of struggling. Didn't you have the privilege of struggling? But when they tell us they hurt, we betray them. We say: "It doesn't really hurt."

Haim Ginott in his book, *Between Parent and Teenager,* recognizes this and he says in the book, "We have to understand that they have legitimate hurts." He suggests that we tell the child that we know he hurts and we recognize his feelings as being real. It does a lot to take away the pain.

Not long ago I saw one of our teen-age girls crying in the hall of the church. I stopped to talk to her and asked: "What's wrong?" She told me how she had just been jilted by her "steady" in all of its awesome details. My first reaction was to say: "Cheer up; you'll get over it; it's just puppy love." But better judgment prevailed, and I touched her on the arm instead and said: "I know that must have really hurt you deeply." She jerked her head up, looked at me straight in the eyes, and exclaimed: "You really know how I feel, don't you?" Later I saw her in the church service participating vigorously and after the service she stopped by the door where I was greeting people and said warmly and simply, "Thanks."

Here are some miscellaneous things I heard:

They feel we do not *trust* them. We don't trust them to taste life, make decisions, or to stand alone. They think we don't trust them to pick friends or companions.

They are tired of being compared to other children. "Johnny made all A's and you got a C minus last month!" "Why can't you be like Susie" or any other name of some girl or boy. "Why can't you be like them? You know they're always better than you are." That does not inspire them to do better. It just says if you don't like me like I am and love me where I am and love me out of this situation, I'm just going to be what you think I am.

They think our punishment is inconsistent. They do not mind being punished. They just do not like punishment overkilled. "You were out five minutes past your limit; so you can't use the car for a year!"

And if you want them to date a certain

boy or girl, don't tell them. That is the kiss of death!

And lose a battle occasionally with them. Pick the battle you are going to lose, but lose it. It won't hurt you to be wrong once. They know you are wrong, but there are two of you and one of them. Do not be right all the time because if you have to be right all the time, you must suspect underneath that you are wrong.

Here are some things I heard over and over again.

"If they don't pay attention to us, we'll get their attention." One girl said: "They won't pay any attention to me; so I'll just mess up that trip to grandmother's. I'll fuss all the way in the car—all the way there and all the way home—and make Mother mad and embarrass the whole family. Then they will notice me." Now it may not be anything that dramatic, but they will get your attention. Give them your attention now because they really want you.

I have never in my life heard people wanting parents, wanting to be loved by responsible, honest adults so much as I have in the past week. I have listened and wept until I can't do it any more. I think some of you ought to go home and just take them in your arms and hold each other hard. Don't argue about all the little nitpicking stuff; just love each other. They are going to get your attention. If you do not give it to them this way, they are going to get it another way. They are going to steal a car or get high on marijuana or something. And I am not telling you that this is going to solve all of your problems, but by the grace of God, it may get your foot in the door!

They will become exactly what you tell them they are. You tell them that they are no good and lazy, and they are going to be no good and lazy. You tell a child this all day long: "You're lazy, good for nothing; when I was your age, I had to get up and go to work." And you know what—he's going to be a lazy, good for nothing. They will be what you tell them they are.

In that story *So Big*, Edna Ferber's book, the poor but great woman, Salena, had a son. She was determined he would not be a cabbage farmer like her husband, and so she placed the only beautiful thing she had, a hand-carved chest, at the foot of the bed so that the last thing he saw every night and the first thing he saw every morning was something beautiful, for she wanted her son to grow up and be a beautiful man inside. And he grew up and had a choice to make between being crassly aggressive and successful or being beautiful, and it was this image that his mother had put in his mind that carried him through. She told him what she wanted him to be and that is what he became.

The government is having to sell off some buffalo from their protected herd, and they are not having any trouble selling the baby buffalo. It's the big 1,200-pound buffalo they are having trouble selling. The cowboys out West who are taking care of these buffalo say that "you can make a 1,200-pound buffalo do anything he wants to do." I think you can make a typical teen-ager do about anything he wants to do.

Now, one final word. I think many parents have done as good a job as they could do in these circumstances. We become so concerned. We think we are taking a piece of clay and molding it into something, but we are not. The clay won't be molded. What we are doing is watering a plant, and we are going to let it grow and be what God wants it to be.

I hope I have done a little to take the blindfold off your eyes and to cause you to touch each other. I have not heard anybody who was not in love. They just could not express it. I want you to love each other. And that word is not empty to me any more. You

are afraid of each other now. You are afraid he's going to "blow it" or that you're going to "blow it." And they are afraid they're going to "blow it" because they have caught this attitude from you like a virus. So just all of you love each other. This is no sentimental way out, but I believe that this is the beginning of a responsible relationship of trust, affirmation, and love.

—From William L. Self, *Bridging the Generation Gap*. Nashville: Broadman Press, 1970.

FOR FURTHER READING:

Dollar, Truman E., and Ketterman, Grace H. *Teenage Rebellion*. Old Tappan, N.J.: Fleming H. Revell Co., 1980.

Sayers, Stanley E. *Bridging the Generation Gap*. Nashville: Gospel Advocate Co., 1979.

Wagemaker, Herbert. *How Can I Understand My Kids?* Grand Rapids: Zondervan Publishing House, 1978.

GIFTED CHILD

IN 1921 a psychologist named Lewis Terman began a study of over one thousand . . . gifted children all of whom had IQ scores of 135 or above. It was planned that these people would be studied for their whole lives, and at present the project is still continuing even though Terman is no longer living.

In 1970, the "gifted children" reached an average age of sixty. Far from being sickly and poorly adjusted, these people are above average in terms of physical health, mental stability, marriage adjustment, and professional accomplishments. In addition to being highly creative themselves, they have produced offspring who are also intellectually superior and very successful. Apparently there is no support for the theory that the children of capable people are inferior.

Although Terman and his colleagues have focused greatest attention on the male members of the gifted group, others have shown that intellectually superior women are also superior to the less gifted. One recent study of highly competent women psychologists showed, for example, that these women as a group "tend to be more intelligent, socially aloof, dominant, serious, adventuresome, sensitive, flexible, imaginative, insightful, unconventional, secure, and self-sufficient than adult women in the general population . . . and less anxiety prone." It should be added (male readers please forgive me) that these women were also more intelligent and more radical than a comparable group of gifted men.

Problems of the Intellectually Gifted. It should not be assumed that gifted people sail through life without any problems. On the contrary, superior intelligence creates unique challenges for the individual who must grow up and live in a world where almost everyone else is intellectually inferior.

Consider, for example, the problems of being a gifted student. The school curriculum is often too easy and this leads to boredom. The child's superior ability along with the knowledge that may have come from his reading can lead to conflicts with teachers who are less knowledgeable. Because they feel threatened, teachers (and later professors) sometimes ignore or try to stifle the gifted student and to pass him off as a "smart little brat." Because school is of no challenge, superior students sometimes give up. They read a lot on their own but they refuse to do the assignments and soon there are poor grades. In high school they may be "underachievers" and in college they sometimes become "student radicals." Of course not all gifted children react in this way to their boredom. Because they are so capable, most

rise above the school situation and succeed in spite of their education.

Non-academic problems also beset the gifted, however. Sometimes parents who recognize the child's abilities set high standards and then exert considerable pressure for the child to succeed. This can lead to rebellion on the part of the young person while at other times it produces "driven people" who are so intent on getting ahead that they never develop smooth relationships with others. Perhaps it is not surprising that in one study over half of the gifted children thought of themselves as being failures.

None of this is meant to contradict the positive picture of the gifted that was [previously] presented. . . . It appears, however, that for many capable people their success comes "in spite of" as well as "because of" their superior abilities.

The Church and the Mentally Gifted. While educators and psychologists have shown an increasing concern over education of the gifted, church leaders have by and large ignored these people. If the intellectually superior child is bored in school, might he have a similar reaction to church programs that are planned for more average people? Attendance at school is required by law but if the gifted person is bored at church he simply stays away.

While there may be agreement on the importance of meeting the needs of the gifted, it is difficult to know how this is to be done. Research into the problem is continuing and some practical guidelines are already available. According to one report, the teacher of the gifted must teach more, teach rapidly, and teach differently. While there must be emphasis on content, the students should also be taught how to teach themselves. In church, for example, instead of giving pat answers, teachers should show students how to search the Scriptures on their own in pursuit of answers. Young children will appreciate a lot of variety and opportunity for creativity while the older students will want to see how the Bible touches their lives and how Christianity speaks to the practical problems of the day. Obviously, teachers of such groups must take their responsibilities very seriously and prepare fully.

There may have been a time when followers of Christ could remain in a theological ivory tower, ignoring the world around, and dutifully saying "amen" to the pronouncements of the preacher. If such an era ever existed it is now past. Our churches today are filled with thinking people and we must make special efforts to reach their needs. This means that sermons, while firmly based on the Scriptures, must also be intellectually respectable. Special Sunday school classes for the intellectually superior may be advisable but if begun they should be taught by the most capable people in the church. Perhaps the recent trend toward simultaneous "adult electives" in many adult Christian education programs is a more realistic and practical way to meet the needs of the gifted and non-gifted alike. When there are two or more adult Sunday school classes being offered at the same time, one of these can be geared to a more superior intellectual level. The members of the congregation are then free to attend the class which is most challenging to them.

—From Gary Collins, *Man in Motion.* Carol Stream, Ill.: Creation House, 1973.

Sample Checklist for Gifted Children (ages 10 and over)

Child's name _____

Age _____ Birthdate _____ Sex _____

Nationality and Race _____

Parent _____

School _____

Grade _____ Date _____

Evaluations made by _____

CHARACTERISTICS

I.   Mental Traits, Intellectual Qualities

1.   Is considered old for his years, "long-headed"; regarded as gifted by family and friends.

2.   Enjoys the challenge of intellectual tasks, excels in performance of difficult mental tasks; displays capacity for organized thinking, reasoning, and judgment beyond his years.

3.   Shows intellectual curiosity, desire for knowledge; questioning attitude regarding sources and causes; seeks reasons and explanations.

4.   Has keen powers of observation, excellent memory for items and topics of interest to him.

5.   Possesses a large fund of general knowledge and information.

6.   Is inventive, creative; shows imagination, originality in working on plans and projects.

7.   Shows maturity in comprehending and carrying out instructions.

8. Shows preference for games requiring concentrated thinking, involving rules and system; introduces more complexity into games.

II. Command of Language

9. Shows maturity beyond his age-mates in use of oral language, fluency in speaking, giving oral reports, etc.

10. Has effective choice of words in speaking, command of vocabulary typical of older children or adults; enjoys using long words.

11. Shows maturity and facility in grasping meanings in oral communication.

12. Shows maturity in written expression; fluency, accuracy, originality in stating ideas; effective use of words.

13. Shows talent in composing original stories, essays, poems, plays, material for school projects, etc.

14. Speaks, reads, and writes a second language with considerable fluency.

III. Academic Skills and Attainments

15. Learns easily and quickly at school; needs less explanation and repetition than his age-mates.

16. Has progressed through school more rapidly than other pupils his age; placed in rapid-advancement sections or honors classes.

17. Likes to study, considered a studious child; capable of independent study; has received academic honors.

18. Is advanced in independent use of library facilities; wide acquaintance with library resources.

19. Has reading skills above average for age level; enjoys reading books for older children or adult literature; uses advanced or adult reference materials.

20. Handles mathematics processes easily; long division, fractions, decimals, percentage, measurement, algebra, geometry, according to opportunity to learn; uses computation devices, slide rule, mathematical tables, etc.; handles written problems in mathematics with quick understanding, shows ingenuity in mathematical problem solving.

21. Has wide fund of information in the sciences; understands the processes of scientific thinking; uses science tools—magnifying glass, telescope, magnets, dissecting instruments—with ability beyond his years.

22. Has wide fund of information in social studies: history, geography, civics; grasps principles in social science; does reading beyond his years in these areas. Uses maps, globe, atlas; works with charts, graphic and tabular material.

23. Takes an interest in current events and political situations, government and world affairs; does critical thinking on issues of the day; reflective attitude toward ideas of a social and philosophical nature.

IV. Special Interests, Aptitudes, Talents

24. Shows many-sided interests and aptitudes; versatile.

25. Spends a considerable part of his spare time working alone at his hobbies and self-devised projects.

26. Shows initiative, enthusiasm, originality, persistence, sustained attention in working on favorite projects; strong drive to attain goals; good planning and execution of self-devised projects; has received recognition, prizes resulting from hobby interests.

212

27. Shows marked interest in science topics; enjoys discussion of science, mathematics, astronomy, etc.; shows preference for reading on these subjects; has a considerable fund of information in one or more of these subjects.

28. Is interested in working with mechanical devices and apparatus; shows mechanical ingenuity and inventiveness in mechanical construction; enjoys discussing and reading about mechanical devices and inventions; has a considerable fund of information in this area.

29. Has shown special talent for music; well advanced in musical studies; has given recitals, received special recognition for exceptional performance, prizes, scholarships, etc.; has a considerable fund of information about music.

30. Has shown special talent in graphic arts: painting, drawing, sculpture, handicrafts; work has been exhibited, recognized by prizes, scholarships, etc.; has a considerable fund of information in this area.

31. Has shown special talent in expressive and performing arts: dramatics, dancing; has given recitals, received recognition, prizes, scholarships, etc.; has a considerable fund of information in this area.

32. Has made unusual achievement in athletics, sports, games, physical contests; has won recognition, medals, prizes, etc.

33. Sets high standards of workmanship, has high degree of self-criticism, not easily satisfied with his achievement; strives for accuracy and precision.

34. Reads and uses books—a favorite activity.

35. Enjoys looking up facts, seeking out items of information, using classified sources of information, dictionary, encyclopedia, almanac, etc.; enters contests requiring a fund of information.

36. Makes collections of a systematic, orderly type, reflecting special interests.

37. Keeps a diary or journal; keeps systematic or periodic records related to his studies and interests.

38. Has indicated intention of entering a high-level profession requiring college education or professional training beyond high school.

V. Personal and Social Traits, Character Qualities

39. Prefers companionship of older children, or association with adults.

40. Is socially adaptable; adept at dealing with others in personal relationships.

41. Seems naturally to assume leadership; chosen by associates as leader in class activities, school and club affairs; is looked up to as an authority by other children; is asked to take charge or to organize activities; his decisions are respected.

42. Is considered "different" or "a brain" by other children; expresses impatience with those who respond more slowly than himself; shows aggressive or dominating attitude toward age-mates.

43. Shows rebellious attitude when situation offers no challenge or requests made of him seem unreasonable.

44. Makes mature response to authority, respects and observes rules and regulations.

45. Shows concern for the welfare of others; thoughtful, unselfish; shows desire to be of service, interested in social service programs.

46. Has mature ethical sense; understands and exemplifies justice and fair play in his conduct; resents injustice.

47. Is trustworthy, dependable; has high sense of responsibility.
48. Shows modesty in rating his abilities and accomplishments; respects the achievements of others; disclaims having abilities higher than others.
49. Enjoys humor with an intellectual flavor; shows cleverness in originating jokes.
50. Has mature physique for his age; good physical stamina, endurance, strength, agility, motor coordination.

VI. Background and Early Development
51. Was known as precocious child before school age; showed accelerated mental development at an early age.
52. Was advanced in the use of language by age 2 or 3; used sentences, original expressions, invented words.
53. Showed manipulative ability ahead of his years before school age, shown in handwork, building, using tools and mechanical toys, cutting, pasting, sewing, weaving, clay modeling, etc.
54. Showed early evidence of artistic or musical talent.
55. Showed early interest in picture books and reading aloud; retentive memory for characters, stories, rhymes, etc.; learned to read informally at home before entering school.
56. Learned to read at school easily; attained level of functional reading skill (grade level 4.5) well before typical age of 9 or 10 years.
57. Learned to write name, numbers, simple words before school age; early mastery of the alphabet.
58. Showed early interest in numbers, counting, computation; advanced in arithmetic, knowledge of money, stamps; interest and knowledge ahead of his years in time, distances, clocks, calendar, etc.
59. Was advanced in knowledge of common objects, their names and uses, operation.
60. Was ahead of age-mates in written expression by age 9; showed interest in composing stories, drafting letters.
61. Showed early interest in table games involving rules, system, scorekeeping.
62. Enjoyed solitary play of his own invention in early childhood years; tended to invent imaginary companions or an imaginary world.
63. Entered first grade before 5 years, 9 months of age; second grade before 7; made rapid progress on entrance to grade 1; skipped one or more terms in the primary grades.
64. Comes from home of relatively high literacy level and intellectually stimulating environment.
65. Parents encourage child's interests and activities, without coercion or overstimulation; parents encourage freedom of expression, independence, self-responsibility.

—From Gertrude H. Hildreth, *Introduction to the Gifted.* New York: McGraw-Hill Book Co., 1966.

GOD

Who can say how the young child thinks of God? He cannot quite tell you, and his questions merely reveal bits and pieces of his thinking. Childhood impressions are embedded deep in memory, and an adult, looking back, can seldom lift them to the surface and say accurately, "This is how I remember thinking of God."

It is rare to find a written description of what God means to a young child. But Carlos Romulo, widely known Philippine statesman, has captured a few of his earliest memories. He writes, "I was conscious of the security of the family circle . . . and that watching over us always was the familiar, mysterious, frightening but trustworthy presence of God. God knew everybody, saw all we did, and my infantile mind held Him in awe. I knew exactly the way He looked, and He bore a distinct resemblance to my grandfather."

Perhaps the child's ideas of God do begin with the security of the family circle. He links his family with God. The security that stems from God's love and that permeates the family has little to do with its economic, cultural, or social standing. It has everything to do with love, trust, forgiveness, and acceptance.

All of the young child's life revolves around father and mother. Through them he feels and learns about God's love. In fact he can know the love of God at first only through the love that he feels in his own family. As his parents show him love, he begins to comprehend what it means that God loves him. One child said, "You can't see God, but He's there." Another child, knowing God's care, exclaimed, "God's a real good guy." A third put it this way, "God can plan lots of nice things."

Romulo recalls that to him God was "familiar, mysterious, frightening, but trustwor-thy." Many a young child wants to see God. "Why can't I see Him?" he asks. He has heard about God, participated in family activities related to Him, sensed His nearness. Yet, like an adult, he is restless and uneasy. He wants to clear up the mystery, to know firsthand and for himself just what God is like. He wants to explain God in ways he knows. Knowing Him better might chase away some of the mystery.

Every child has concrete ideas about God and what He has done. The child's picture of God and His attributes springs directly from his world. Some children picture God with a beard and in a white robe, looking like someone near and dear to them. Even an idea like the fact that God hears when you pray turns to the specific and the literal. "Why doesn't He answer when I talk to Him?" "Let's whisper. God can't hear us then." "God heard you say that bad word." "How does God tell us things? I can't hear Him."

Facing the Problems

Once you begin to trace the young child's ideas about God, you begin to see the problems he encounters.

If a child learns about God's love through the way his parents love him, what about the child who does not know family love? How can he picture the love of a heavenly Father when he doesn't know the love of an earthly father? What about the child shifted from pillar to post? Does knowledge of God elude him because he has no family circle, no affectionate father, no understanding of love?

God is surely within reach of every child. Every child, disadvantaged or advantaged, knows what he would like God to be, just as he knows what he would like his earthly father to be or what he would like his family to be. He accepts his earthly father for better or worse. He accepts the earthly experiences that come his way, turning willingly to the idea that God is more than, better than anything he has known. Almost every child accepts the fact that God exists. You need not convince him or prove God's existence. It's true that he has questions about what God is like and where He is. But the child seldom doubts that there is a God once he has been made aware of Him.

Almost every child has confidence that God loves him. If adults have been careful to help him understand and feel God's love, it may not occur to him that God would not love him. For a few children, however, God is not love but a sort of policeman, an all-seeing censor who sits in judgment on their smallest act. Their fear of God looms so great that it has displaced their love of Him. This attitude stems from a variety of sources. One of them is the child's interpretation of the idea that "God is everywhere." Perhaps someone has said to him, "God sees everything you do. He hears everything you say." The wheels of a child's mind turn in a literal fashion. He pictures God looking down on him, ready to pounce at his slightest wrong. And then some parents use God as a threat of punishment to come. This is a terrible thing to do. A child consumed with fear of God needs to learn that God loves him all of the time, no matter what he does. God is pleased when he does the right thing and sorry when he commits a wrong. But even when he does a bad thing, God loves him even more than his father and mother.

To help the child associate a good feeling with God's omniscience and omnipresence, help him know that the love of God is everywhere. Use "God loves you" and "God cares about you." Then show the child by your actions toward him what these phrases mean.

Part of the child's understanding of God is the idea that some things he does displease God. The problem is for an adult to preserve the child's feeling that God cares about him without glossing over the wrong. Be truthful.

God does not like some of man's actions, be he child or adult. Be sure, however, that the condemned action truly is displeasing to God. Sometimes a parent attributes his own standards to God.

At about three or four years of age, the child begins to develop a conscience. He associates feelings of guilt with a wrong act and begins to take responsibility for his bad actions. Then he can understand that God is not pleased. He can feel sorry for his misdeed and be assured that God cares about him and what he does. In fact the child needs the assurance more than ever.

Although the child cannot recognize God as the Triune God, he does meet the threefold Person of God. When he discovers that God made and planned things, he is learning about God the creator. When he finds out how God loves and forgives him, he is growing toward the realization that God is the redeemer. As he feels close to God, he is learning to know God as the Holy Spirit.

Where the Child Learns

Long before the child is faced with a planned introduction to concepts of God in the church school, he encounters many things through which he constructs his ideas of God. He hears prayers said at his bedside. He listens to mealtime grace. He watches the special activities connected with adults going to church. He hears the name of God spoken in many moods—reverently, kindly, awesomely, casually, perhaps violently. He learns about God through the natural world. He asks questions that reveal his problems as he searches for God. What does God do all day? Who made God? Does God have a mother and father? Who will love God?

The adult who answers—or does not answer—his questions shapes the child's concept of God. This is as it should be because those who love the child are best suited to tell him about God and to draw him into the circle of God's care. When someone outside the family steps in to tell the child about God, the relationship is always a little less intimate. Leaders in the church are outsiders to the child. Your contact as a teacher is casual and intermittent. Your opinions count a little less than those of persons in his everyday circle. How many times have you heard a kindergartner say, "You're not my mother"? Of course. You are not in his primary circle of authority and love. Your love for him and your desire to share your love of God with him are consecrated, yet he weighs your words against those of his family. However, as your teaching reinforces what he hears at home, his knowing of God can be strengthened. For that reason the preschool teacher works closely with parents. The child also picks up ideas about God in situations beyond your control. He gleans them from the world apart from his church school, and the child lives in this world more than he lives in the church school.

The festivals of the church are high holidays for the young child. He forms impressions as he celebrates Christmas and Easter. Is God part of these festivals? What impressions do weddings in church, baptisms, the church service make?

Think about the visual images related to God that the child is likely to encounter. He may see a picture of God in his Bible storybook. What does he see in the church itself? Does the building do honor to God? Is it a worthy place in which to worship? All of these things are part of the child's world. You will want to relate it to God. Explain it in words that mean something to the child.

Questions of the Child

The preschooler is a veritable question mark, and his queries about God are legion. Does God call up the weatherman to find out what kind of day to make it? Do boy angels

take care of God? How can God see me? If God made everything, who made God?

The answers the child wants must be truthful and to the point. He loses interest when he hears a lengthy description of how God plans for this and that to happen in such and such a way. He is not yet concerned about the how, nor with the ultimate idea. Rather he wants to know what and who in clear short answers.

Many times a child asks questions just to be talking. In that case he is satisfied when you just listen. His asking a question is the big deal. He is thinking aloud.

On the other hand, his question remains a question until it is answered. What approach should you take? Too many words, too many explanations, too many picturesque phrases smother his thoughts. But you must be truthful, otherwise the child will build on misconceptions and untruths. Your manner is the key when you share ideas. What count are common sense, confidence, and actions matching your words.

Questions and their answers are important at this age because foundations are laid and inner resources developed in early childhood. Questions reflect the child's search in knowing God. Your answers help him associate God with the deep issues of life. Very early he comes face to face with the power, the mystery, the depth of God. Very early he can associate the basics of life with God: birth, love, praise, thanks, sadness, death.

Your answers sow many seeds. They
—assure the child that God cares
—explain puzzling ideas
—acknowledge the wonders of God
—reveal your faith
—express your joy in knowing God
—reflect your reverence.

The Pattern of Growth

Once more comes the question, who can say how the young child thinks of God?

What conclusions can be drawn? What pattern traced? Such a pattern will help you recognize highlights in the spiritual life of the child.

Here are some of the child's thoughts of God.

God is. He is in my world. I know Him.

God loves me. All of the time. In every way.

God takes care of me. He does things for me that show His love. He has plans for me.

God knows me. He is fair. He forgives me. He will not let me down.

I want to do things for God. I want to please Him.

God likes others, too. He cares about everyone.

—From Eleanor Zimmerman, *Bible and Doctrine for 3's to 5's.* Philadelphia: Fortress Press, 1963.

FOR FURTHER READING:

Battle, Edith K. *Our Children Ask About God.* Nashville: Abingdon Press.

Colquhoun, Frank. *Hard Questions.* Downers Grove, Ill.: Inter-Varsity Press, 1979.

Howard, David M. *How Come, God? Reflections from Job About God and Puzzled Man.* Nashville: A. J. Holman Co., 1977.

Kerr, William F. *God: What Is He Like?* Wheaton, Ill.: Tyndale House Publishers.

Schoolland, Marian M. *Leading Little Ones to God.* Grand Rapids: Wm. B. Eerdmans, 1962.

GRANDPARENTS

IN MOST CASES, becoming a grandparent is hardly a crisis. It is probably the most welcome sign of aging there is. "Grandchildren are the crown of old men" (Proverbs 17:6). Ruth Shonle Cavan says, "Women especially

visualize themselves as grandparents before a child is born and eagerly await the birth of a grandchild so they may express the grandmother self-image in an appropriate role" (Ruth Shonle Cavan, "Self and Role Adjustment During Old Age," *Family Roles and Interaction: An Anthology,* p. 461).

There are many people today who become grandparents in their early or middle forties, and some are great-grandparents in their sixties. It is not so unusual to see pictures of five generations together. This is due to the fact that there are many early marriages and also that people live longer than in previous times. It brings together a wider span of generations living at the same time.

The value of grandparents should not be underestimated. Grandparents frequently have more influence per time invested than do parents because of their unique relationship to their grandchildren. Grandparents are usually more relaxed than parents. This makes them approachable. They concentrate on giving love (sometimes called spoiling) without the necessity of meting out discipline. Their time with their grandchildren is usually better planned and more intentional than parents' time. All of this adds up to what some social scientists have called the "grandfather phenomenon." Children catch more of their grandparents' perspective on life than that of their parents. This can be a comfort if you are wondering about the effects of how your children are raising your grandchildren, and you may consider it a call to action to make the most of your time when you are with them.

Since becoming a grandfather, I have become aware of two things—that I can give and what I missed. Having seen my mistakes in fathering and having learned a bit since then, I want to pass on to my grandson a richer experience than I was able to give my sons.

I did not enjoy my children as I wish I

could have because of time absorption in earning a living. I missed some of the emotional satisfaction that I'm finding with my grandson.

—From J. Allan Petersen, *Conquering Family Stress.* Wheaton Ill.: Victor Books, 1978.

FOR FURTHER READING:

Brandt, Catherine. *God Bless Grandparents.* Minneapolis: Augsburg Publishing House, 1978.

Shedd, Charlie W. *Grandparents: Then God Created Grandparents and It Was Very Good.* Garden City, N.Y.: Doubleday & Co., 1978.

GROWING PAINS

MANY PARENTS are confused about what is involved in the term "growing pains." When a child complains of pain in the arms or legs, they may shrug it off as growing pains or go to the other extreme and assume immediately that the child has rheumatic fever. Actually, there is no pain that can be ascribed simply to rapid growth. Pain in any part of the body is usually a sign of some disorder, whether it is serious or superficial, purely physical or partly emotional.

Because it has been discovered in recent years that pain caused by rheumatic fever can be relatively mild, doctors are now alerted to make a thorough investigation whenever a child complains of even slight pain in the knees, ankles, elbows, or wrists. Most such pain, however, is not due to rheumatic conditions. Muscle fatigue, flat feet, ill-fitting shoes, or a twisted ankle unnoticed during an active play period—these are but a few of the many possible causes for pains in the joints or limbs.

To be on the safe side, when a child has pain in the arms or legs, it is usually best to consult a doctor to determine the cause and prescribe treatment. It is important to remember that children, like adults, differ in their sensitivity to pain and even in their awareness of it. Thus one child may be much more aware of aching muscles after a day of unusual activity than another.

—From *The New Encyclopedia of Child Care and Guidance.* Garden City, N.Y.: Doubleday & Co., 1968.

GUILT

EARLY IN LIFE children begin to learn—through imitation of and control by adults, through the consequences of their own acts—what people may and may not do. The "yes-and-no, right-and-wrong" standards of those around them gradually become part of their own thinking and feelings. At times, however, along with the slowly developing self-control, a youngster does something that is contrary to what he has learned—and then feels guilty about it. Often he feels guilty about some of the things he wants to do, even though he doesn't carry them out. To the young boy or girl the wish is equivalent to the deed. A three-year-old, for example, knows it is wrong to hit his baby brother, but he can't help thinking about what he'd like to do, and these "bad" thoughts can bring on guilt feelings. Although the seven-year-old realizes it is wrong to take someone else's property, he cannot resist pocketing a friend's toy—but he feels like a villain.

The development of conscience is necessary in living happily with others, and some guilt feelings are an inevitable, natural reaction to misdeeds. An overwhelming sense of guilt, however, can warp a child's outlook toward life and people. Persisting into adulthood, it can keep him from fully realizing many of his capabilities. The growth of knowledge of human personality has shown this. People know today what unfortunate results can come about, for example, if a youngster has persistently been made to feel that he is a thankless child for not following his parents' every wish, or that his sexual curiosity is evil, or that anger is shameful, or that bringing home poor grades shows lack of appreciation for his opportunities.

A child is not likely to grow up with a burden of guilt if he has been allowed to see and helped to understand, that it is normal not to be perfect. He can see that adults, too, make mistakes and admit them readily; that they, too, lose their tempers occasionally—and feel sorry for it, but not fearfully ashamed of it. He can see the difference between actually harming someone and just thinking about it—which occurs to everyone at some time or other. Living his childhood in an atmosphere of tolerant guidance, a youngster can grow up realizing that all human beings have their failings. To the degree that he understands and accepts his own without shame, he is very likely in the long run to have fewer general failings as an adult and to live comfortably with those he has.

—From *The New Encyclopedia of Child Care and Guidance.* Garden City, N.Y.: Doubleday & Co., 1968.

FOR FURTHER READING:

Becker, Arthur H. *Guilt: Curse or Blessing.* Minneapolis: Augsburg Publishing House, 1977.

Caldwell, Louis O. *You Can Stop Feeling Guilty.* Grand Rapids: Baker Book House, 1978.

Narramore, Bruce, and Counts, Bill. *Freedom From Guilt.* Eugene, Ore.: Harvest House Publishers, 1976.

Tournier, Paul. *Guilt and Grace.* New York: Harper and Row Publishers, 1962.

Warner, Paul L. *Feeling Good About Feeling Bad.* Waco, Tex.: Word Books, 1979.

H

HANDICAPPED CHILD

THE ACTUAL WAY parents' disturbed feelings will manifest themselves in everyday behavior differs from one person to another. It depends on the particular parent's personality structure and the nature of the child's handicap. But in general, research in this field suggests that there are four dominant kinds of reactions that mothers and fathers commonly exhibit. It is true that in a given parent these reactions may not always appear in a pure form. Instead, they may be seen as a mixture of two or more varieties. However, it is also true that one of these reactions or attitudes often dominates a given parent's reaction. . . .

1. *Acceptance of the Child and His Handicap.* This is the attitude we would hope for, because it typically leads to the healthiest personality development for the child. The parents have accepted the handicap in an objective way. They neither reject nor overprotect the child. They say, "He's our child; he has this defect, and together we'll make the best of it." They plan realistically for his education and his future. They do not express guilt or anger at the handicap.

Somewhere in their lives, these parents have developed a philosophy to care for this situation. In a study of parents of blind children it was concluded that "in most cases religion gives [the parents] mental and spiritual support."

2. *Overprotection of the Child.* Mothers, more often than fathers, exhibit this re-action. They are overcome with feelings of pity for the child or guilt for having produced an offspring so poorly equipped to face the world. Thus they protect the child too carefully, do too much for him, and prevent him from making decisions or carrying responsibility for himself. In response to such treatment he may remain infantile and overdependent. He avoids trying many tasks of which he is quite capable. In some cases the child becomes domineering. His parents (usually the mother) become his slaves. Mothers who adopt this role may actually be assuaging their own guilt feelings through their penitent dedication; or perhaps they fulfill their need for a person in whom to invest their love.

Sometimes the parents' oversolicitous attitude is really a disguised rejection of the child. They consider the handicap a disgrace. But because society takes a pitying attitude toward such children and because the parents have punitive consciences, they cannot outwardly reject their child. So they play the overprotective role. In doing so, they may harm the child's personality as much as if they expressed undisguised dislike for him. For instance, some parents of this type make it obvious to the child that they are denying themselves a normal life by their dedication to him. This causes the child to heap destructive guilt and shame on himself for being faulty.

3. *Overt Rejection of the Child.* This

type of parent openly resents his handicapped child. The parent is aware of his own resentment and dislike but assuages his own guilt feelings by projecting the blame onto the environment: onto society for its negative attitude toward the handicap, onto the doctors who have not seriously tried to help the child, onto the teachers who are prejudiced toward him, and onto the child himself for his resisting normality—"He does not half try to succeed as other children do."

4. *Denial of the Handicap.* Some parents will not accept the fact that the youngster is handicapped and that different aims and different treatment are needed for him than for other children. Typically they set overambitious goals for the child, insist on high achievement, and fail to accept guidance in planning a realistic future for him. Therefore, the pupil suffers because too much is expected of him and he is not given the special aid that could often improve his adjustment. But at least when parents have this attitude the child is permitted to try participating in the activities of normal children. He is not overprotected.

—From R. Murray Thomas and Shirley M. Thomas, *Individual Differences in the Classroom.* New York: David McKay Co., 1965.

FOR FURTHER READING:

Paterson, George W. *Helping Your Handicapped Child.* Minneapolis: Augsburg Publishing House, 1975.

Swindoll, Charles. *You and Your Child.* Nashville: Thomas Nelson, Inc., 1977.

HELPING WITH HOUSEHOLD CHORES

LONG GONE is the idea that the mother's main role is to pick up after the children.

From the age of two, children can be taught to pick up their toys. Progressively after that they can learn other "tidiness" skills: tidying up their rooms; making their beds; putting clean clothes into drawers and dirty ones into hampers; scrubbing out the bathtub after a bath.

By the time they are five, children are often eager to help with routine cleaning tasks. This satisfies their need for meaningful accomplishment, for making a real contribution to family life. They can run a vacuum cleaner—although you may have to finish up edges and corners. They can whisk down a set of stairs, or even damp-sponge an area of the floor. They can dust furniture and dry dishes. And these are tasks that children of four and five really delight in, because they can participate in "real grown-up work."

The wise parent will cash in on the child's time of interest, for when the child says, "Can I help you?" training is most efficient. Of course it takes time to show a child how to do the task. But it is time well spent. It is an investment in your child's development of confidence.

And, of course, with helping skills there are lots of educational side effects that are beneficial. Drying cutlery and sorting it by pattern, then putting away knives and forks and spoons in their places, teaches a child rather sophisticated matching skills. Counting and arithmetic games are a natural when working with dishes. "How many plates are there in the pan? Let's count." Or, "How many forks have you dried? Count them while you put them away." Setting a table can be taught by the time the child is five— and with this task, the child can learn to tell left hand from right hand. Perhaps the most important educational by-product is that the child learns to follow directions and to carry out operations that consist of several steps in a fixed sequence: all foundational to further educational experience.

I found it useful to train my children to answer the telephone. "I can always tell when we've gotten through to your place," an American publisher told me. "We get your kids with their cute little Canadian accents." After the age of four, children can be taught to answer the phone, speaking clearly and courteously. Later, they can learn how to take and record messages as well.

Survival skills. This is a group of skills which are essential to a child's survival in the event of an emergency. Telephone skills are important here, too. From the age of three or four, the child should be taught how to dial "O" for emergency help. By the time he is four, the child should know his own telephone number, family name, and address. These can be taught by simple rote memorization. By the time he is five, the child should know by heart, or at least know exactly how to find, the telephone numbers of several adults living nearby who could be contacted if help were needed.

Teaching a child how to make a simple meal: a peanut-butter sandwich and a glass of milk, or—when he is five or so—how to open and heat a can of soup, gives him another basic survival skill. Training children on routes for swift and safe evacuation of the house is also important—and a proven life-saver.

In our industrialized society, our children have been cut off from meaningful participation in the adult world. In more primitive societies, children were taught basic adult skills from an early age, largely by just being with adults who were engaged in growing or hunting food, preparing food, or making garments. Now, most adult activities are too technologically sophisticated for children to engage in, and take place far from the child's world. The home, however, can be a workshop in which children can participate in a wide range of activities which are not only interesting but real as well. This meets a child's need to be a functioning part of his society; it satisfies his *"sense of industry."*

Domestic skills are helpful to the parent and easily accessible to the child. However, perceptive parents can teach many other competencies as well. Simple carpentry, sewing, basic mechanical skills, gardening: these and numerous other skills can be taught to children, at least in rudimentary form, from a very early age.

Competence does bring about confidence, and it is in that confidence that children can become contributing members of society. Parents who are hard on their kids, expecting a good level of performance from them and offering the training necessary to meet those expectations, will have kids who make a contribution to family life, and kids who feel confident that, with experience and training, they *can do*—whatever needs to be done.

—From Maxine Hancock, *People in Process*. Old Tappan, N.J.: Fleming H. Revell Co., 1978.

HOBBIES

BY THE TIME your child is seven he may show an interest in hobbies. Although even earlier than that he may gather rocks or seashells, they would not normally constitute a hobby unless he is able to classify them and attempt to add kinds he doesn't have.

A hobby may be very broadly defined as any leisure-time activity that is pursued somewhat systematically. There are, therefore, thousands of different hobbies.

Among the most popular hobbies are stamp and coin collecting and genealogy. Most hobbies involve some kind of collecting. What is collected can be as diverse as antiques, dolls, figurines, comic books—and even beer cans! Of special value educationally are collections of flowers, minerals, fossils, butterflies and other insects, and historical memorabilia.

Not all hobbies involve collecting, however. Wilbert D. Newgold, an authority on hobbies and crafts, has developed a four-fold list of hobbies: (1) hobbies relating to the arts, such as painting, pottery and sculpture, music, theater, photography, and writing; (2) hobbies relating to the past, such as antiques, coins, stamps, and transportation, sports, and military memorabilia; (3) hobbies relating to nature, such as gardening, bird watching, nature walks, and collecting rocks, minerals, shells, artifacts, and fossils; (4) hobbies relating to handicrafts, such as models and hobby kits (chemistry, and so forth), needlecraft, ceramics, and woodworking. Others add such sports as cross-country skiing and such leisure-time activities as the care and study of animals such as gerbils and horses.

Some parents wonder if hobbies are a waste of a child's time. While hobbies absorb a child's interest so completely because they are pleasurable fun, they also perform many other useful functions. Most hobbies involve a great deal of learning. A hobbyist who gets a coin or stamp from Kiribati, Tuvalu, or Tannu Tuva frequently learns where these places are and something about their history and life. As children find others who share their hobbies and trade, they develop valuable social skills. As they try to add new items to their collection or new pieces of equipment, they learn to manage money. If they produce something for sale, they may earn money and even develop a career out of their hobby. If they develop expertise in the field, they may win prizes and gain valuable recognition. But the most valuable part of a hobby is the pleasure it gives the child.

Parents need to do their best to encourage a child to develop an interest in one or more hobbies. They should not be upset if children, especially younger children, switch from one hobby to another as they learn more about God's wonderful world.

If a child becomes interested in a hobby, parents should not demand that he show them what educational value it has.

Sometimes a child's collection will make demands on your house's living space; efforts should be made to find room for it, if at all possible.

Expensive hobbies such as photography need to be discussed, with the child understanding that he has to earn part of the money or team up with a friend to purchase more costly items. If a child has to work, plan, and save for a particular item, it will mean a lot more to him than if a parent provides it for him.

Parents should encourage a child by letting him know about a number of different hobbies until one strikes his fancy and he pursues it.

On rare occasions the Christian parent may be disturbed by his child's choice of a hobby. If your child develops an interest in TV star magazines or rock records, you may want to encourage a Christian orientation by giving *Campus Life* or Larry Norman, Randy Stonehill, or Barry McGuire records as gifts.

—LESLIE R. KEYLOCK

FOR FURTHER READING:

MacDonald, Craig. *At Your Leisure.* San Diego, Calif.: Beta Book Co., 1979.

HOMEWORK

NOT ALL ELEMENTARY SCHOOLS give homework assignments. Proof is lacking that youngsters of this age necessarily learn more if they have extra lessons to do at home. Some educators believe children should have such lessons only when their work shows they need special practice. Children of this age need considerable time for play and exercise as well as for school work.

However, if your child does have homework, the best way you can help him is to give him a good, quiet place to study and to guide him in planning his time. Be sure he has the tools he needs, such as paper, pencil, ruler, and so on. You may be called on to help him find reference books and other materials. If you find that your child is not understanding his assignments, it is a good idea to ask his teacher how you can help him.

Sometimes homework can trigger a crisis. There's a problem that just can't get solved, the story that isn't written, the test that hasn't been studied for. Your child is in tears or tantrums and you are tempted to rush in to save him. Ideally, you should guide him in getting his work done without doing it yourself. In practical terms, you might have to lend a hand to get him out of a "bad spot."

Teachers say, however, that when parents make a practice of being partners in a child's homework, he is likely to get lazy, irresponsible, or confused.

Most schools have "go-to-school" night. At this time, teachers explain something about how and what they teach. Your school also is likely to have a parent-teachers organization. Find out more about your child's school by visiting it and taking part in activities for parents.

Schools vary so throughout the country that it is impossible to give an exact picture of what goes on in your school.

—From *Your Child From 6 to 12*. Washington: U.S. Department of Health, Education and Welfare, 1966.

HOMOSEXUALITY

SINCE THE ADVENT of "Gay Rights" and the resistance there has been to this movement, homosexuality has become a common household term. Teachers of kindergartners have told me that five-year-olds talk to each other about "queers" in terms that show they understand what being "queer" is. Most parents have a horror of their child's becoming homosexual, and yet they do not know what causes it or how to prevent it. Everything from genes and chromosomes to demons has been blamed for this condition, and there is actually very little that we know about it.

Much of my early psychiatric teaching was done by Doctors Karl and Will Menninger from the well-known Menninger Clinic. Few people in the psychiatric specialty have enjoyed the enduring and universal respect that these men so deserve. They believe that it is approximately between two and five years of age that a child develops the sense of sexuality. The qualities of maleness or femaleness, as they are defined by the parents' way of life, are learned and imitated in miniature. The early mannerisms and habits become fixed as the child grows. To have this happen in a normal fashion, a child needs to have some enjoyable time with the parent of the same sex, with the approval of the parent of the opposite sex.

No one really knows how many homosexual people there are in this country. A thoughtful article in *U.S. News & World Report* in April 1980, estimates there are 20 million lesbians and gay men in the United States. The article quotes Dr. John Money, from Johns Hopkins Medical School, as saying that some 13 percent of males and 7 percent of females in America are gay.

Homosexuality is certainly not a new way of life. In Old Testament times, it was practiced as early as the days of Abraham and Lot. God's condemnation of Sodom and Gomorrah, as told in Genesis 19, was clearly related to the practice of homosexuality and violence. The word *sodomy*, in fact, is named after that ancient city. In the New Testa-

225

ment, homosexuality is specifically condemned as sinful by Paul in his writings.

A friend of mine is chief of the Department of Child Psychiatry in a state-university medical school. In a recent lecture, he suggested that an infant's parents, especially the mother, assign to him what he called the "core gender." That is to say, by their unconscious preferences, they will treat a child, despite its anatomy and physiology, as though it were the sex they wanted it to be. According to this theory, a boy whose parents wanted a girl will be treated as a girl is treated. He will be petted and handled gently like a girl instead of tossed and rough-housed as most parents treat a boy. As he grows, he will be dressed in feminine style and will learn to talk like a girl, play, and in general, act like a girl. Even his toys will tend to be those girls are taught to play with. It is easy to see how such a boy will tend to prefer playing with girls, and at puberty, will intuitively want to date another boy. With a girl, of course, the reverse will be true. This theory is evident in many families with whom I have worked.

When a parent teaches a young child that all people of the opposite sex are bad, stupid, or undesirable, the child will tend to believe this is true. This is especially so when that parent is powerful and threatening. And this belief is totally convincing to the child when the other parent's way of life seems to prove the first one right.

Yet another influence in the causing of homosexuality is divorce. Until very recently, children of a divorce were routinely given into the custody of their mothers. The very fact of the divorce meant that the parents had anger toward each other. To a child's simple way of thinking, "If mother's anger could get rid of Dad, I'd better be careful or she'll get rid of me." This fear of a controlling, angry parent is a common factor in homosexuals. Add to such fear the loss of a male role model and the loss of the opportunity to work through the normal conflicts of growing up with both parents, and it is likely that some divorces, at least, may produce children with borderline sexual identities. A common experience in the lives of many homosexuals is an early encounter with an older homosexual.

Many homosexuals state that they are perfectly happy in their life-style. Homosexual patients with whom I have worked, however, tell me that this is not always true. They describe lives haunted with the fear of rejection, jealousy, and endless anger. They say it is a superficial life-style, in which a person pretends to please a partner for his immediate gratification. He may even yearn for a lasting and meaningful relationship. It is common, however, to suffer repeated losses of partners as each person becomes involved in a desperate search for happiness that requires more and more effort, but gains less and less satisfaction.

Homosexuality is one of the most difficult of all psychological conditions to cure. In fact, many psychiatrists will only attempt to help the gay person to live more comfortably with the problem. Because of this fact, it becomes of paramount importance that parents prevent the development of homosexuality in the first place.

When a young person reaches puberty and finds himself truly homosexual, prevention is no longer possible. At that time or at any time, a cure can be considered if the person honestly wants help. In my experience, it is rarely that an older practicing homosexual sincerely wants to change. Even if he does, the very nature of the causative influences creates serious barriers to getting help. Due to the dominating, frightening parent, the ability to trust and work with the therapist is very hard to develop. Since the influences on the person's self-concept began so early, it may be impossible to remember enough to understand and work through the old problems and to make new decisions. Often, unconsciously, the person has used the homosexuality as a means of getting even with a parent who is seen as cruel. And commonly there is a deep, unswerving belief that in the next homosexual partner one may find the elusive ingredient that was missing with the father or mother.

—From Grace H. Ketterman, M.D., *How to Teach Your Child About Sex*. Old Tappan, N.J.: Fleming H. Revell Co., 1981.

FOR FURTHER READING:

Bahnsen, Greg L. *Homosexuality: A Biblical View*. Grand Rapids: Baker Book House, 1978.

Davidson, Alex. *The Returns of Love: A Christian View of Homosexuality*. Downers Grove, Ill.: Inter-Varsity Press, 1977.

Drakeford, John W. *A Christian View of Homosexuality*. Nashville: Broadman Press, 1977.

French, Joel and Jane. *Straight Is the Way*. Minneapolis: Bethany Fellowship, 1979.

Lovelace, Richard F. *Homosexuality and the Church*. Old Tappan, N.J.: Fleming H. Revell Co., 1978.

HONESTY

Confronting and Handling Dishonesty

In spite of teaching and training, children are at times dishonest. How we respond to their dishonesty is crucial. Handled properly, the situation can foster confidence and effective training. Handled wrongly, it can make our children bitter and distrustful. A wise parent plans his strategy before a problem occurs. Here are a few ideas on what to do.

1. *Know the facts.* Unjust accusations and punishment damage our credibility with our children. Let's think through a possible example. Stan drove into his driveway after a day of hard work and extra pressure on the job. He breathed a sigh of relief as he switched off the motor. Now he could relax. Just as he closed the car door behind him, the front door of the house flew open ahead of his ten-year-old daughter, Marcia. She ran into his arms sobbing, "Rick kicked me and scratched me!" He saw some long scratches on her arms, and she screamed as he touched her leg. Anger welled up inside him, and he ran up two steps at a time to his twelve-year-old son's room.

"All right, Rick, what's the idea of treating your sister that way?"

"Dad, I didn't . . ."

"What do you mean you didn't?" Stan interrupted. "I saw those scratches and the bruise. Did you do that?"

"Yes, but . . ."

"But nothing! I'm going to spank you. We don't do that sort of thing at our house."

Stan spanked him soundly and left Rick crying in his room.

As he went back downstairs his wife asked what was happening. He told her the situation and saw a puzzled look in her eyes. She said she had overheard part of the altercation and wondered if he had all the facts. He got both of the children together and found that the scratches were not deliberate but accidental, and that Marcia had grabbed a handful of Rick's hair. He felt sick as he realized he had jumped to a conclusion and could not take back the spanking. He asked Rick to forgive him and apologized for not listening. Then he had to punish Marcia.

Frequently we act without knowing all the facts. Whenever you suspect dishonesty, be certain you really know what happened. If your child is generally honest with you, it may be possible to simply ask for the facts and share your concern. Above all, do not jump to conclusions on skimpy information.

Hear the child with patience and understanding.

2. *Pray.* Before you take any specific action, pray. This is particularly essential when facts are incomplete and you cannot determine if the child was dishonest in some way. When you are trying to determine appropriate punishment or training, you must rely on God for insight. God is more interested in a child's personal and spiritual development than any parent. We desperately need insight from Him and His Word. "If any of you lacks wisdom, let him ask of God, who gives to all men generously and without reproach, and it will be given to him" (James 1:5). And when are we more dependent on God's wisdom than in training our children? Pray in every circumstance and for each child, because each circumstance and each child is unique and deserves special consideration.

3. *Give them opportunity to confess and explain.* Correction frequently consists of simply punishing an act rather than preventing further wrongdoing. We must focus our correction on building into the child's inner person the will and desire to do the right thing, and punishment may not contribute to that goal.

For more enduring correction, confession and repentance are two of the most important concepts for a child to learn when he has sinned. Confession should be to God and to the parent. Children need to learn that sin breaks relationships with both God and man, and confession restores the relationship. "If we confess our sins, He is faithful and righteous to forgive us our sins and to cleanse us from all unrighteousness" (1 John 1:9).

Learn to ask gentle questions that do not assume guilt. "How do you feel about what you told Dad this afternoon?" "Did some other things happen this afternoon that you thought of after we talked?" "You look a little unhappy. Is anything bothering you?" When children admit guilt, especially in cheating or stealing, stimulate them to express how they feel inside: "I know you feel bad about that. Would you like to talk about it?" "I know you were upset and scared when we talked earlier. How do you feel now?"

At times, forcefulness and direct pressure may be needed, but such occasions should be rare. In encounters with my children, I sometimes approached them like a prosecuting attorney. But that was unfair. Children need the love of a parent, not the accusations of a lawyer.

The Word of God, the Holy Spirit, and their conscience are the instruments God uses to convict children of wrongdoing. But the development of these aspects of life takes time. We must be patient, pray, and wait for God to work in our child's heart. In this delicate and sensitive area of honesty, true character cannot be developed in a brief incident of punishment. We must allow God to work in His time, and to use us in the process.

In addition to confession, many children need the opportunity to explain why they acted as they did. We are usually too quick to blurt out, "I don't want excuses. Just tell me the truth." But we may learn far more about the inner thoughts of our son or daughter by carefully hearing them out. And we must hear them out—without impolite interruptions. In line with their sense of justice and fairness, they feel deeply that they deserve an honest hearing. With older children, it is often best to listen first, and not respond fully until an hour or two later—or even the next day. Even as I write this I feel a pang in my heart, and wish I had more carefully followed this advice.

"A brother offended is harder to be won than a strong city" (Proverbs 18:19). Spiritually, our children are our brothers and sisters, and they do get offended. It may take a lifetime to win them back.

4. *Confront the issue, not just the act.* Since our purpose is not to accuse but to change, we need to discern motives as well

as actions. Actions are seen, but motives are discerned. *Why* a child or teenager lied or cheated or stole is more important than the act. Was it from fear, peer pressure, greed, laziness, or rebellion? It may take several instances to give you insight on motives. When you punish or confront only the act, remember that you have not yet dealt with the real issue.

5. *Punish when punishment is due.* In a stealing incident . . . the mother returned to the store and sought out the manager. She explained to him what had happened. He saw the tears on the girl's face as she handed back some candy to him and he said, "Oh, that's all right. Don't worry about it." As the mother began to protest, he insisted that it was no problem. Finally she said to the manager, "Please don't say that it is all right. It is not. She stole it and I am trying to teach her that it is wrong."

Punishment and restitution must be part of the training process for all ages. Occasionally punishment may consist of a strong discussion and verbal chastisement. But frequently for younger children the punishment must be physical. Older children may be helped most by a deprivation of their privileges. Making restitution is often one of the most effective punishments for cheating or stealing. Restitution can be embarrassing and humiliating, but it makes a memorable impression.

But whatever form is used, parents must realize the necessity of punishment. "Because the sentence against an evil deed is not executed quickly, therefore the hearts of the sons of men among them are given fully to do evil" (Ecclesiastes 8:11). Here are a few guidelines for applying punishment:

• Make the punishment fit the crime. Don't overpunish for small misdeeds.

• Be as consistent as you can in dealing with each issue. Punishment one time and not the next confuses a child.

• In corporal punishment (spanking) be careful not to hurt the child, or to spank for every little thing. As a child grows older, you must rely more and more on persuasion and influence.

• Never punish when you are angry.

• Be consistent with all the children in the family.

• Punishment, both physical and verbal, should be in private. Public correction humiliates and angers a child.

• Assure the child of your love in the process.

• Be certain the child understands why he is being punished.

6. *Forgive and reassure them.* Children (and adults) need to know they have been forgiven. We cannot live under the burden of unforgiven offenses. Both younger children and teenagers need reassurance of love and confidence from parents. They also need to know that parents do not bear a grudge against them.

When our son, Steve, was in the sixth grade I received a note from his school principal saying Steve had been reported as speaking certain swear words to another child. I talked to Steve and, as he always did, he honestly admitted what he had said. After some serious discussion about it, I let him know that it was over and forgotten. Yet the note was a very condemning thing to have. I thought of how he could imagine me keeping it and holding it over his head later. So Steve and I went to the kitchen sink, and I took a match and set the note on fire. The ashes in the sink provided a visual emphasis that the incident was done, forgiven, and forgotten. It never occurred again.

Use every opportunity to teach and train. Certainly, confronting and handling dishonesty provides a unique opportunity for teaching by a godly, concerned parent. Do not abandon one of the most significant opportunities God has given you as a parent.

"And, fathers, do not provoke your children to anger; but bring them up in the discipline and instruction of the Lord" (Ephesians 6:4).

—From Jerry White, *Honesty, Morality and Conscience.* Colorado Springs: NavPress, 1978.

FOR FURTHER READING:

Hart, Archibald D. *Feeling Free.* Old Tappan, N.J.: Fleming H. Revell Co., 1979.

HYPERACTIVITY

THIS HAS COME TO be a household diagnosis. Most children, however, who are *called* hyperactive are not truly that. The genuinely hyperactive child is best described as "driven." He is a wall climber, never still for even five minutes, constantly moving, making noises, and into everything. Even sleep may be interrupted and brief. It is difficult to believe the energy such a child consumes— and puts out. It is hard or impossible to cuddle, play games, watch television, or read with a truly hyperactive child.

Such a driven child needs to be seen by a pediatrician, a neurologist, and a child psychiatrist. Sometimes this is a sign of *severe allergies, slight brain damage, or infantile autism.* If none of those is diagnosed, you may be quite sure your child will outgrow this, but you will not be as sure that you will live through it!

Causes of Hyperactivity

Brain Damage. If there is brain damage in a hyperactive child, it is of a type that is very difficult to diagnose and probably brain damage as a cause is quite rare.

Allergic Factors. These are also hard to diagnose (or to rule out, for that matter). A special diet that eliminates the coloring matter and additives that prevent spoiling, most carbohydrates, and certain fruits has been widely recommended. This is called the *Feingold Diet.* Some people believe it is a miracle worker, and others have had no improvement. That may be due to the fact that some hyperactivity is due to biochemical factors in food and some is not. If you believe your child has an allergy, have your doctor check that out, and follow any recommendations he makes.

Sensitive Nervous Systems. Some children are born with extrasensitive nervous systems. They see, hear, taste, smell, and feel much more sharply than other children do. It is possible that these children also react more intensively and are more active.

Lack of Communicative Ability. We know that children who cannot hear or speak are frustrated by their inability to communicate. Helen Keller is a classic example of a child whose wild behavior changed rapidly when she began to learn language. Perhaps some bright, young children are frustrated by their lack of words to say what they want to say. And certainly they must be checked for hearing problems.

Form of Manic-Depressiveness. There are some significant studies going on that suggest hyperactive children may have a mild form of manic-depressive illness or its equivalent. Some of them improve on lithium, a very successful medication for such a problem. A doctor especially trained in child psychiatry can help you find out whether this may be your child's problem.

Depressed Child. Sometimes a grief-stricken or depressed child may cover his tender feelings with wild activity. We have seen children act this way after a death or a divorce.

Need for Firmer Guidance. Evidence is building that strongly implies the need for firmer and more consistent guidance from parents. In an effort to show respect and consideration for so-called children's rights, parents give them illogical choices, and then may disapprove of a child's decision. An example of this is the experience we shared in which a young mother gently asked her two-year-old, "Susan, wouldn't it be nice if you put away your toys and took a nap now?" Susan, not thinking it at all nice, angrily threw the toys all over the room, and then ran about the house to avoid the nap!

Varied Treatment of Hyperactivity

Complete Medical Evaluation. This is absolutely necessary. Many doctors recommend a trial on certain medications. If your child's problem is severe, we recommend you try it at least long enough to see if it helps. If so, use it long enough to help your child form new habits. Then try him without it if your doctor is willing. We do not like children to become dependent on medicines, but there are cases in which such medication works.

Allergy Tests. Have any possible allergies tested by your child's doctor or an allergy specialist. The results of those tests will tell you whether you need to put your child on a special diet or have other allergy treatments.

Handling All Hyperactive Children

Be firm, gentle, and very certain in your training and discipline. If you are indecisive or inconsistent in your rules and consequences, your child is bound to feel anxious and act out that anxiety in hyperactive behavior.

Tell your child exactly what you want him to do and make him do it, if it is important. The soft approach, "Mark, don't you want to go to bed now? Mother wants you to," just

won't work with a hyper child. Mark usually doesn't want to stop playing, even though he wants to please Mother. How can he decide that? Don't give him such choices. "Mark, in five minutes the timer will go off. That's your bedtime signal, so be ready for your snack and story" (or whatever your bedtime ritual is). He can feel safe and secure in your better judgment and healthy authority. If there are realistic choices, limit them and help him learn to choose.

Keep the environment calmer for a hyperactive child. Rock him slowly, sing and speak softly, have lower lights, and softer music. Even colors in his room should be subdued, if you have a choice.

Limit and carefully supervise television for the hyperactive child. Violence, loud noises, and the sudden scene changes can add to his nervousness.

If you have a truly hyperactive or "driven" child, get professional help. In addition, line up a collection of relatives and friends who will give you an hour's relief now and then. It will save your sanity and won't hurt the child.

Be sure to have a trade-off of Dad's and Mom's time. Sometimes one will be able to quiet a child more than the other. The more quiet moments such a child finds, the sooner he will settle down.

—From Grace H. Ketterman, M.D., and Herbert L. Ketterman, M.D., *The Complete Book of Baby and Child Care for Christian Parents.* Old Tappan, N.J.: Fleming H. Revell Co., 1982.

FOR FURTHER READING:

Feinbloom, Richard I., M.D. *Child Health Encyclopedia.* The Boston Children's Medical Center. New York: Dell Publishing Co., Inc., 1978.

Wender, Paul, and Wender, Estelle. *The Hyperactive Child and the Learning Disabled Child.* New York: Crown Pubs., Inc., 1978.

I

INDEPENDENCE

THE WORD "independence" has meaning mainly in relation to a child's age; it isn't always a sign of wholesome maturing. Sometimes it may be forced on a child too early; it may be achieved at the price of loneliness or in other ways that do violence to a child's basic needs. The young infant is normally almost completely dependent, and dependence at this time should be fully accepted and enjoyed by his parents. He will at first need almost constant care from his mother or from other people close to him; the trust and mutual joy between them in this dependent relationship is of the profoundest importance in building future strength.

Gradually wise parents will begin to help a child toward greater self-direction, encouraging him to do more and more "on his own." But gradually, too, they will help him discover that although they approve of his wish to act, think, feel, and express himself according to his inner promptings he will need his parents' judgment and experience for many years as a guide and check. They will furnish him with daily experiences to make it clear why his personal wishes must always be limited to some extent by the rights and feelings of others.

Ideally, parents hope to give a child all the independence he can use safely and constructively; but it is best to keep in mind the fact that even older children need the security of some dependence, some wise restraints, at the same time that they have more and more opportunities to act on their own judgments and to "go it alone." This is a long road; the balancing of freedom and restraint in the life of a child is the essence of discipline and the crux of successful parenthood.

For human beings, independence is never an absolute goal. Interdependence—the ties of love, friendship, loyalty, devotion to ideals and principles—is fundamental in the character of a mature person. By the values they acknowledge and by their own way of life, parents hand on this belief to their children.

—From *The New Encyclopedia of Child Care and Guidance.* Garden City, N.Y.: Doubleday & Co., 1968.

INFANCY

INFANCY is the most important period in an individual's life. It is then that a baby develops the foundations of faith—in himself, in others, in life itself. His earliest experiences give him the feeling that he can trust his body to function well. His first handling by his parents provides a baby with confidence in other people. A baby's introduction to his world sets the tone for his future feelings about it. What happens during the first few weeks and months of a person's life lays the basis for the years that lie ahead.

Your faith in yourself as a parent develops early in your baby's life. It is then that you gain confidence in yourself and in your ability to be good parents. If you have a struggle in meeting your baby's needs, you may end up with a feeling of inadequacy that is hard to shake off.

Your feelings about becoming parents begin long before the baby's birth. As soon as you learn that a baby is on the way, you either are delighted or you feel less enthusiastic about becoming parents. If you have longed for a baby beforehand, learning that at last you are to become parents can be a cause for rejoicing. But, if you already feel swamped with more responsibilities than you can handle easily, the anticipation of still further calls upon your time and attention can seem like just too much.

One family expert has suggested that a couple have four possible combinations of reactions to the news that they are to become parents; (1) They are both delighted. (2) She is pleased, and he is upset by the news of a baby's coming. (3) He is thrilled, and she is less enthusiastic about becoming a parent just now. (4) Neither husband nor wife really want to have a baby at this time. Still other couples accept their pregnancies without question and do the best they can in caring for their children whenever they arrive. Now that reliable birth control is so readily available to married couples, unwanted babies are less numerous than they once were.

Preparing for Parenthood

Long before the baby's actual arrival, most couples prepare for his coming. The expectant mother goes regularly to her doctor or nearby clinic for prenatal checkups. She follows the regimen that is suggested to her as best she can, and her husband encour-

ages her diet, exercise, and other procedures in his own way.

Classes for expectant mothers and fathers are offered in many communities by various health agencies and services. These help a couple know what to expect of themselves and their baby-to-be. Prenatal instruction usually includes enough about the development of the embryo and the fetus to give expectant parents some insight as to what is happening as their baby grows within the mother. This adds a great deal to the interest of many a couple and impresses them with the miracle of human growth and development, even before they can see their baby.

Getting ready for the baby can be simple and inexpensive, or it can be elaborate and costly. One pair of married students we knew simply dumped the contents of a dresser drawer into a pillow case, and lined the empty drawer with washable padding for their new baby's bed. They bathed the baby in the bathroom wash basin, carried him slung on their backs, and accepted his care casually and easily. Other couples remodel an entire room as a nursery and buy expensive equipment and layettes in anticipation of their baby's coming. Interestingly, the baby himself thrives as well with either kind of physical setting. It is the way he is cared for rather than the things in his home that the baby cares about.

Preparing the older children for the new baby happens whether you do it or not. If you say nothing about your expected baby, the older children probably will learn about what is happening and that you don't want to talk about it. If you speak openly about your plans for the new baby and about what having a brother or sister will mean (both a nuisance at times, and a blessing at others), the children are more likely to feel "in" on what is happening in the family.

Questions about where babies come from

arise naturally when a new baby is on the way. It is then that a youngster old enough to talk will want to know where he came from, how boys and girls differ from the beginning, and how a baby gets started. Some of these questions are difficult for many a parent to answer comfortably. Fortunately there are excellent books available that answer his questions in a child's language. It is a good idea to read such a book to or with a child, look at and explain the pictures, and discuss his questions openly with him. If you need help in finding just the right book, or in answering your child's questions, do not hesitate to get it from a source you trust—your doctor, pastor, librarian, or other competent confidante.

Help the first week or two should be arranged in advance. When the new mother returns from the hospital with the new baby, she needs time to get her strength back, and to gain confidence in caring for the new baby. Perhaps her mother, or her husband's mother, comes to help care for the family while the mother and baby are in the hospital and after they return home. Sometimes, a household helper can be employed for this period. There are some men whose temperament and work schedule allow them to care for their growing family themselves.

Father—Insider or Outsider?

There was a time when a father felt like a fifth wheel during his wife's pregnancy, and the baby's infancy. Such a man took the position that having a baby is a woman's job and caring for infants is the mother's role. So, he kept out of the picture as much as possible and began to relate to his son when he was big enough to take fishing, or at least was housebroken. Such a man missed most of the thrill of fatherhood and all of the miracle of growth in a baby's early weeks and months.

Some mothers unwittingly keep their husbands out of the baby's life by insisting upon taking complete care of the baby themselves, and acting as though their husband is incapable of doing anything for the new baby. Wiser by far is the wife who encourages her husband to feel in on the process of baby-making and baby-care from the beginning. She is careful not to bore her husband with unpleasant or unnecessary details but shares with him all the facts and feelings that he wants to be a part of as much as she can. When he holds his baby in his arms, she lets him get the feel of it himself without unnecessary admonitions and advice. When he wants to help bathe the baby, she lets him do just as much as he wants to without interference. As he begins to feel confident as a father, she lets him know how pleased she is with him, and the baby. In such a family, both mother and father share the joys and responsibilities of parenthood as a team.

Naming the baby can be a joint undertaking. It may be that both know well in advance of the baby's coming what name will be best for a girl or a boy. They may have decided that the baby will be named for some favorite relative. They may feel strongly that the first girl should be named for her mother, or that the first boy should become Junior. Or, as likely as not, the couple begin to look for a new name for the baby that will be uniquely his. This involves name-searching with an ear for how the first name fits phonetically with the middle and last name. The couple should be aware of how the initials will look on luggage some day (Frederick Allen Tucker is a fine name, but how about the initials?). They should make sure that the probable nickname will be acceptable and that close relatives like the name they are choosing. Keeping in mind how the individual may feel about his or her name as a grown-up is a good idea in choosing the new baby's name.

Feeding Your Baby

Feed your baby when he is hungry. Sounds so simple, doesn't it? Only the baby knows when he needs nourishment; his tummy tells him so in no uncertain terms. The newborn's stomach is small, and holds little at a single feeding. Some babies need to be fed more often than others, for a number of reasons that we need not go into now. Your baby tells you when he is hungry in the only way he can—by crying. It starts with a restless mewing when he is very little, and then builds up to a lusty howl, if the feeding is delayed. Making him wait when he is very hungry makes him angry, and it can make him feel that he has to fight for what he needs and that he is not living in a very loving, considerate world.

Schedules are for nurses, not for babies. In a busy hospital, it is easier for the nurses to feed all the babies at about the same time. Visit any hospital nursery and peek in through the glass, and you'll be able to see whether feeding time is but recently over. Then most of the babies are sleeping peacefully. But as the time goes on more and more of the newborns become restless, and start to cry, many because they get hungry before it is time for their next feeding.

Some parents attempt to carry out the schedule the hospital had tried to establish. And, with some babies it works just fine. But others are miserable with that particular timing. The mother may have to waken the baby when it's time for his feeding. Or, worse yet, baby wakens hungry, cries for food, and because the time has not yet arrived for his feeding, he must wait; while his mother anxiously bides her time until the clock says it's all right to feed her baby. Nonsense! The simple principle to follow is feed your baby when he tells you he is hungry. In time he will set his own schedule, as most happy babies do. Then you'll be able to

predict fairly well when he'll be ready for his next feeding and plan your time accordingly.

Breast or bottle is for you to decide. This must be done by the second day of the baby's life. This is a critical time for such an important decision, because mother and baby are often not free to work things out for themselves. The doctor feels strongly one way or the other, and the nurses are too busy, oftentimes, to give the new mother the patient attention and encouragement she needs to get her baby started at the breast. Then, it is almost too simple to suggest that the baby get a bottle instead.

A bottle is easier in some ways than breast-feeding. You can tell how much the baby gets at each feeding, as is never quite so simple in breast-feeding. The bottles can be prepared ahead of time and given the baby by any convenient person. A baby may seem to prefer the bottle to the breast because the nipple can be adjusted to his sucking, and fits farther back into his mouth than does the human nipple, usually.

Many a mother chooses bottle-feeding because she knows that she is to be too much away from her baby through the first few months to be able to nurse him. An occasional husband would rather his wife not nurse their baby, because her breasts are so important in the couple's lovemaking, or because the wife will be more available to go out with him without having to get back for the baby's next feeding. These are all valid reasons for choosing bottle-feeding, all other things considered.

Breast-feeding is preferable to bottle-feeding for a number of important reasons. It brings the baby the food nature has prepared for him with all its good nutrients, immunization, and taste. Nursing at the breast gives the young infant more sucking time than most bottle feeding, which is important for a baby who needs to suck as well as to get food. Nursing her baby is supremely satisfying to many a young mother. She thinks of it as a culmination of the whole process of conceiving, delivering, and nurturing her baby. She feels close to her baby in a very special way that is satisfying both to the infant and to mother. As the baby nuzzles and snuggles close to her body, his hands fondle her skin, and she cuddles him close with the very special relationship that only babe and mother can share. Nursing the new baby at the breast may be threatening to the next older child of the family, who may need some special reassurance that he too is loved by his mother, as "her big boy, now."

Bottle or breast is not a life or death matter. Babies thrive on both methods. The important thing is that the parents feel good about whichever way they decide is right for them and then relax and feed the baby when he is hungry.

Weaning should be at the child's pace and time. As soon as he can hold a spoon and cup, they can be given him as playthings. As he watches others drink from a cup, he will try to when he is ready. That is the signal to put a little water or milk in the cup and let him have his first experience in drinking rather than sucking. The doctor in whom you have your child's care will advise solid foods when he feels your baby is ready for them. Some of them the baby will enjoy, and others he will not like at all. So don't make an issue of the one he pushes away. Remove it for the time being and offer it again a few weeks later when he may like it. Most babies continue to want a bottle long after they have begun to eat solid foods. Especially at bedtime a bottle is soothing, and there is no reason why your baby should be deprived of it. When he is ready to get along without a bottle, he'll let you know. Don't let some other child's earlier weaning upset you. You are caring for *your* baby, and he is like none other that is or ever was!

Diapers—a Big Deal?

For baby's sake and yours, don't let diapers become a big deal. Much of what goes into the baby, is going to come out in baby's own time, and way. He is not ready for toilet training for at least a couple of years, usually, and it doesn't do any good to rush him. When he is ready, and his muscles are mature enough, he will happily take to the potty chair (unless you have made an issue of it). Until that time comes you are stuck with dirty diapers, and the daily laundry.

Change the baby when he needs it. Unless it is cold, a baby is not uncomfortable in a wet diaper; he doesn't even mind a soiled one most of the time. When he does, he will fuss and let you know that a change is needed. Of course, you'll clean him up before letting Grandma hold him. You'll want him sweet-smelling yourself. And, you'll watch out for the telltale diaper rash that lets you know that his skin is sensitive and requires clean, dry, soothing attention.

You make changing the baby's diaper a fun time as soon as you feel comfortable about it yourself. Talk to him as you take the old diaper off, tell him what a fine body he has to be functioning so well. Pat him affectionately as you clean him up, and smile at him as you lift his legs to position the clean diaper. Then cuddle him and tell him how sweet he smells and what a good baby he is. He'll like it, and so will you.

Bathtime can be fun for the whole family. The baby will enjoy it as soon as you find that you can hold a slippery, wriggling baby without letting him fall. You will enjoy it when you let yourself see it as relaxing, rather than as a chore to get done. The older children in the family, and in the neighborhood, enjoy being in on the act, handing you the baby oil or powder, and helping get the tiny arms into shirt and gown. Father may ask for his turn at bathing the baby, when he gets home from work. If so, why not? Routines are made to be broken, and the father-baby tie should be encouraged for both their sakes. Talking, laughing, splashing, and water play continue to be fun for baby and the rest of the family well into the second and third year. Just be sure that baby is not left alone in the water even for a few minutes. If the phone rings, let it or bundle him up and take him with you.

Your Baby Is Unique

From the moment conception took place, your baby has been uniquely himself, unlike any other child. His experience prenatally and since he was born has been peculiar to him alone, and different from that of all other children—even brothers and sisters of the same family.

Where the child comes in a family makes a difference. The oldest child arrives at a time when both his father and mother are new parents and inexperienced in caring for a baby. The first child grows up close to his parents in a way no other children do because he is the oldest and is expected to be the responsible one. The youngest child of the family is "the baby" as long as he lives, never quite catching up to the older brothers and sisters who arrived before he did. The in-between children being neither the oldest nor the youngest find their own roles in the family, each in his or her own way.

One child may be the social one, making friends easily all up and down the street. Another may be musical, or mechanically inclined, or athletic, or with intellectual interests. The simple fact is that each child in the family is and must be different from all the others!

Babies differ greatly from others of the same age. Girls and boys respond differently from the first. Some babies are alert and vigorous, others are quiet and sleep most of the time. One baby may be sensitive to all sorts of stimuli that other babies seem to ignore. There are tense babies and others that seem from birth on to be placid and unflappable. Some infants are inquisitive, alert, and enthusiastic, while others are much more matter-of-fact. Each baby is as unique as his fingerprints, and you'd best remember it. The cardinal rule is: Accept the child you have and learn to enjoy him for the very special person that he is.

Parents' Time Off

Taking care of a baby twenty-four hours a day, seven days a week can be a terrific strain on even the most mature father and mother. Especially if they have little help in the home (as most families used to when grandparents and assorted other relatives were readily available), a modern pair of parents occasionally need some relief from full-time baby care.

Spelling each other is a simple inexpensive way to relieve parental burdens. Nowadays it is not at all unusual to see father taking his baby with him on a shopping trip or to the neighborhood launderette, while his wife catches her breath or mops the kitchen floor! Husband and wife can alternate evenings out, for a movie or a class, or some other relaxation. This gives the baby-caring father a chance to be on his own with his baby without his wife's well-meant interference. The trouble is it keeps the parents apart.

Parents in some neighborhoods form cooperative systems in which they sign up as sitters for other couples, who in turn are available for them when they want an evening out. This is convenient, inexpensive, and assures you of a competent sitter when you need one. Taking care of another baby or two along with your own is not too much of a hardship, and often gives you a new pride in how nice a child you have.

Finding, training, and instructing other

sitters who can spell you is well worth the effort. You learn to take advantage of time off to recharge your batteries and feel that you are a person too. Nearby relatives can be enlisted as mothers' helpers sometimes. In most communities, the local home economics teacher can recommend responsible high school girls (and boys) who have shown promise in child development units or baby-sitting preparation. Older women in the church are often hungry for little ones in their lives and can be of help as they make their time and talents available to young families nearby.

Keeping up your personal interests while your children are small need not make you feel guilty. You will be a better mother for keeping your sense of personal identity intact, even while you are being a full-time mother. Being available to go with your husband on a trip as soon as your baby is weaned from the breast is important—to you, to him, and probably to the baby too. Taking the baby with you is possible in a good many circumstances. It provides a change of scene for you all, and unless there is sickness to be wary of, it is a healthy thing to do. The older children in the family can help out, without making an issue of it. Baby will enjoy them, and they him, in time.

Baby Development Is Fascinating

Your baby's development is a wondrous process, and you can see it all. A newborn has a big head, a small body, and tiny bowed legs. He usually is red, wrinkled, blue-eyed, and lumpy-headed. He isn't much to look at, except by his adoring parents and grandparents, but he is a bundle of tremendous potentials. He develops more in the first few months and years than he ever will again. His growth is phenomenal. If his body continued to grow at the rate he started at, he'd be a giant before he reached his teens.

By the end of your baby's first four years, he has already achieved 50 percent of his intelligence. Another 30 percent is reached by the time he is eight, and the remaining 20 percent by his seventeenth birthday. By intelligence is meant the ability to mentally handle the information he acquires. His knowledge will continue to increase as long as he keeps on learning, but the capacity to learn is established early in his life, fully half of it before he ever goes to school. His genetic potential was laid down at the moment of conception. What happens to him the first few years of his life determines how much of his innate capacity he is likely to develop.

Your baby learns through his senses: taste, sight, hearing, smell, touch, and the way he feels about what he experiences. When he mouths the nipple and sucks his thumb or a corner of his blanket, he is learning through his mouth. From the first week or two, he watches faces and follows them with his eyes. He early discovers his hands and what he can do with them. You can watch him turn his head this way and that, as he discovers that he controls hand movements. A little later, he can grab a small block with his fist, then with thumb and forefinger opposite one another on the cube. He finds that he can shake and hit and drop small objects from his crib or high chair, which delights him, so he repeats the motion over and over. Your patience may wear thin unless you can sense what is happening from his point of view and rejoice with him in his newfound ability.

Playthings encourage your baby's learning. While he is still flat on his back in his crib, an unbreakable mirror where he can see it will interest him. You can rig a mobile above his head that he can watch and hang a crib gym that he can manipulate as soon as he can grasp it. By this time he is ready for an infant seat, that plastic padded slant into which he can be strapped. This will change his position and let him watch what is going on around him.

Bathtime can be fun for all of you when you give him something to hold: a little cup, a solid rubber toy, a small swatch of terrycloth. When you bathe him in the bathroom sink, he probably can catch glimpses of you and him in the mirror that adds still another dimension to his enjoyment, and yours.

Anything that can be looked at, handled, banged, felt, seen, or heard is a plaything for an infant. You need very few special toys, save those doting grandparents bring. Your baby is perfectly happy with anything that gives him a new sensation and that he can manipulate himself. Let your ingenuity be your guide as soon as he can sit up and hold onto things. As long as the object is larger than a plum so that he cannot swallow it and washable so that you can keep it clean, he will find a use for it. Present him with something new to feel: a piece of washable corduroy, a clean strip of soft wool, a piece of satin, a terrycloth animal, a set of plastic spoons or measuring cups, a rubber jar ring, smooth baby blocks, and in time a large plastic jug with the top cut off into which he can drop his treasures.

Infancy is the time for a rocking chair in your home. Baby will like it, especially when he is restless and in need of a little cuddling. Mother may find it just the thing to nurse him in with the satisfaction both of them get in gentle rhythmic motion during and following his feeding. A little soft music from radio or record player turned low is soothing to him and his family. Little songs and lullabies have their place in his life. Sturdy cloth picture books are good from the first few months on, especially when he can "read" them as you name the objects one by one.

Baby's own body is a source of pleasure to him and can be to you as soon as you get over any residual hang-ups about certain body parts being "not nice." It is natural for him to explore his body. As soon as he can get his hands to his mouth, he will taste them and maybe suck his fingers or thumb if you don't make too much of a fuss about it. He'll probably be able to get his toes to his mouth in time, too. His hands will touch his genitals and the feeling will be pleasurable, until someone makes a scene about what he is doing. You can teach him that he is all right by your acceptance and encouragement of his learning about himself. Or, you can just as easily teach him by your attitude, voice, and words that he is dirty, bad, nasty, and naughty. Long before he can speak he already has learned to feel as you feel about his body, its parts, and functions, and feelings. Fortunately most parents today marvel at the wonder of life and give their babies good feelings about themselves.

Faith Begins in Confidence

You gain confidence in your ability as a parent, in time. When you learn your strengths and weaknesses as a person, you will be a more relaxed mother or father. Then you can exercise your competence and get help for the gaps in your knowledge and skill.

Find a doctor or neighborhood clinic you have faith in, as soon as you can. There are bound to be unexpected illnesses, accidents, and anxieties that can be greatly relieved with professional competence. Many childhood diseases and difficulties can be avoided entirely with preventive medical attention. A bad night of croup or digestive upset can be alleviated with prompt and reassuring attention.

Learn what to expect of children, in general. There is a great deal of knowledge about child development that you may find helpful as parents. This does not mean that you will have a textbook baby, who is exactly as described in anyone's book. But there are certain stages of a child's development that can be anticipated, understood, and prepared for in advance. Knowing what to expect of a child of any given age is a great help in deciding your priorities as parents.

Knowledge of critical states of child development are of immense help in having a happy baby, and being a confident parent. This book emphasizes the most important development taking place stage by stage in a child's life. Chapter by chapter throughout this volume you will be glimpsing what is critical in your child's development at his stage of life.

Children go through a reliable process of development that can be understood. Each child develops at his own pace and in his own unique way, but all share the same general sequence of development. All children must learn to eat before they are ready for instruction in table manners. All children must learn to talk before they are ready to reason or to take responsibility for their conduct. All children have to be messy before they can be clean. All children have to feel good about themselves before they are self-confident.

Your baby's basic trust in himself lays the foundation for his faith in life. He cannot be spoiled, except by neglect and abuse, at least during his first two years. So, this is the time to do what comes naturally to you in ways that make him feel good, too. Being together can be fun if you don't work too hard at it. Your growing faith in yourself as a capable parent is important for your baby's development as well as your own, now and later.

—From Evelyn Millis Duvall, *Evelyn Duvall's Handbook for Parents.* Nashville: Broadman Press, 1974.

FOR FURTHER READING:

Palmer, Marjorie, and Bowman, Ethel. *The Young Mother's Book of Ideas.* Wheaton, Ill.: Tyndale House Publishers, 1973.

Youngren, Frances, ed. *Our Baby, God's Gift.* Evanston, Ill.: Moody Press, 1966.

INFATUATION

ONE OF THE FOUR questions most frequently asked by young people in discussions having to do with dating or marriage, according to Dr. Oliver Butterfield and others, is: "How can I know when I am really in love?" . . . For simplicity we will identify infatuation with romantic love, although some would prefer to find some distinction. Admittedly, we can only speak of tendencies and general characteristics, for it is not possible arbitrarily to draw lines and say: "Love is always like this, while infatuation is always like that." The distinctions are not perfectly distinct!

Romantic love has a very real place in the development of true married love, but infatuation does not. Romantic love is first romantic infatuation, but it has a place as it becomes less and less a part of infatuation, and more and more a true and abiding quality in the couple's relationship. What we are saying is that infatuation may be the start of a real love when the first spell of excitement transfers over into something genuine. So we cannot be too rigid in drawing contrasts, recognizing that infatuation can evolve into love, and that it is a mighty difficult task to say just when it becomes no longer infatuation but is now love. There are no simple rules or neat little formulas that can take the place of emotional maturity and sound judgment when an individual must evaluate his own experience of involvement with a person of the opposite sex. Each situation is as unique and distinct as the lives of the two persons who make a part of it.

It must be noted that young people confront the need for making the distinction between romantic infatuation and love when they are emotionally least able to do so. The decision comes when they are caught up in a highly charged emotional atmosphere, and are acting more on the basis of emotional compulsion than on rational judgment. How much this fact ought to call forth the sympathetic understanding of their seniors who have long since forgotten their own problems along this line!

If only one word could be said about how to recognize true love as opposed to romantic infatuation, it would have to be the common-sense word: "Wait!" Time clarifies most of life's issues and enigmas, and certainly the important issues can afford the test of time. Every romantic relationship requires the test of time, as well as the test of an occasional separation. This is a fundamental law in determining the will of God. The passing of time affords opportunity for change, growth, and experience. Surely young people for whom the choice shall determine the whole course of future years and happiness can afford these tests. As someone remarked: "It's pretty serious business choosing the ancestors of your children!" The one who chooses a wife or husband truly marries the whole family, for an entire family strain is taken on, and out of the marriage shall come a totally new strain. In distinguishing between romantic infatuation and love, one makes the greatest of decisions in life as to whether he shall limit or expand his own possibilities for personal enrichment in the years that lie ahead.

Romantic infatuation is the ground upon which is erected America's greatest cult, the cult of romance. Its adherents number in the millions. The entertainment and advertising worlds promote the great American worship of romance. Real love has become identified with reel love. It makes up the colossal fairy story at the heart of our culture. . . .

1. Romantic infatuation may happen suddenly and without warning, whereas love grows, and all growth takes time.

2. Romantic infatuation may arise from an acquaintance with only one, or at best a few, characteristics of the other person. Love grows out of an appraisal of the total personality of the other, and through exploration of all the known characteristics of the other.

3. Romantic infatuation is self-centered and looks at the other as a means to an end. Love is other-centered, outgoing, releasing and investing the energies of life in joyous and spontaneous concern for the security and well-being and growth of the other person.

4. An infatuated person tends to think of the other person as strangely separate from himself despite their strong emotional unity, whereas a person in love feels a true identification with the other one.

5. An infatuated person may be "in love" with two or more persons simultaneously, whereas genuine love centers in one person only.

6. An infatuated person tends to have a false sense of security about his love affair, which is based on wishful thinking, or sometimes upon a compulsive need for reassurance. A person in love tends to have a true sense of security in his relationship, based on a growing range of trust and affection and mutual concerns.

7. An individual who is infatuated sustains a mental picture of the object of his attentions. This mental image is largely an idealization. Persons in love also idealize to a certain extent, and to that extent it is proper and to be expected.

8. Lastly, we come to the place physical attraction plays in infatuation and love. In infatuation it plays a relatively more important role in the total relationship of the two persons, whereas in love it plays a relatively

less important role in the total relationship.

—From Dwight Hervey Small, *Design for Christian Marriage.* Old Tappan, N.J.: Fleming H. Revell Co., 1969.

FOR FURTHER READING:

Dobson, James C. *What Wives Wish Their Husbands Knew About Women.* Wheaton, Ill.: Tyndale House Publishers, 1975.

INFERIORITY COMPLEX

ONE OF THE MOST OBVIOUS characteristics of a person who feels inferior is that he talks about his deficiencies to anyone who will listen. A fat person feels compelled to apologize to his companions for ordering a hot-fudge sundae. He echoes what he imagines they're thinking: "I'm already fat enough without eating this," he says, scooping up the cherry and syrup with his spoon. Likewise, a woman who thinks she's dumb will admit freely, "I am really bad at math; I can hardly add two and two." This kind of self-denigration is not as uncommon as one might think. Listen to yourself in the weeks that come. You might be surprised by how often you emphasize your faults to your friends.

While there is no virtue in becoming an image-conscious phoney, trying to be something we're not, I believe it is also a mistake to go to the other extreme. While you are blabbing about all of your ridiculous inadequacies, the listener is formulating his impression of you. He will later "see" you and treat you according to the evidence you've provided. After all, you're the expert on that subject. Furthermore, having put your feelings into words, they become solidified as fact in your own mind.

Therefore, we should teach a "no-knock" policy to our children. They should learn that constant self-criticism can become a bad habit, and it accomplishes nothing. There is a big difference between accepting blame when it is valid and in simply chattering about one's inferiority. This might be a difficult distinction for your children to grasp, although you can get excellent help from the "Peanuts" comic strip. Charlie Brown is so perceptive of his own inferiority that he worries about it out loud to all his friends. Lucy, the sweetheart, then smashes him over the head with the information he provided.

What a wonderful memory of childhood Charles Schulz, the "Peanuts" creator, has shown. The phenomenal success of his cartoon is based on his recollection of humiliation in school, unbearable blunders, and feelings of failure. We laugh because he hits so close to home. You have stood in Charlie Brown's lonesome shoes, and so have I. When I was in the third grade, I was playing left field in a hotly contested baseball game. How clearly I remember that black day. Willie Mays was up to bat and he hit a routine fly ball—a simple little pop fly—and all I had to do was catch it. But there in front of five million fans, mostly girls, I let the ball drop right through my outstretched fingers. In fact, it jammed my thumb on its way to the ground. I can still hear the pounding feet of four base runners heading for home plate. In desperation, I grabbed the ball and threw it to the umpire, who stepped aside and let it roll at least a city block. *Booo!* yelled half of the five million hostile fans. *Yeaaa!* yelled the other half. I bled and died right out there in left field that afternoon. It was a lonely funeral; I was the only mourner. After careful deliberation in the days that followed, I gave up baseball and have seldom played since. I've enjoyed basketball, tennis, track, and other assorted sports activities, but baseball

243

and I parted company on that afternoon. Charlie Brown, who also takes himself too seriously, might well consider the same course of action. And by all means, he should keep his "failures" to himself. If he'd close his big mouth, people might not even notice—they are, as you know, thinking about themselves anyway.

—From Dr. James Dobson, *Hide or Seek*. Old Tappan, N.J.: Fleming H. Revell Co., 1979.

INFERTILITY

SEX IS INTENDED for pleasure, and one of the sweetest pleasures comes as children are born. Young couples yearning for a family and failing to produce a child should find out why. There may be an infertility problem, and in at least a third of the cases this problem can be overcome.

Doctors define infertility as failure to conceive after one year of regular intercourse without the use of contraceptives. Infertility should not be confused with sterility, which is an absolute inability to reproduce. Infertility simply means the failure to achieve pregnancy within a specified period of time.

Studies have shown that 66 percent of pregnancies occur within three months of the initiation of unprotected intercourse. Within six months of such continued exposure, 75 percent of the women have become pregnant, and by the end of one year about 80 percent of the women have conceived. The remaining couples may want to seek help. Examination and counsel by their own physician might be all that is necessary.

The essentials of fertility are normal ovulation, unobstructed fallopian tubes, and normal semen. These factors must be present for pregnancy to occur:

1. The husband must be able to produce a normal number of healthy, motile (or mobile) sperm cells.
2. The sperm cells must be able to be discharged through the urethra during ejaculation.
3. These sperm cells must be deposited in the female, so that they reach the cervix, penetrate the cervical mucus, and ascend through the uterus to the fallopian tube. This must occur at the proper time in the menstrual cycle for the ovum to become fertilized.
4. The wife must produce a normal, fertilizable ovum which must leave the ovary, enter the fallopian tube, and become fertilized.
5. Once conception has taken place, the fertilized ovum must begin to divide. After four days this tiny cluster of cells should drift down the fallopian tube and move into the uterus, where it becomes implanted in a properly developed lining membrane, and there undergoes normal development.

If a couple are unable to achieve pregnancy, it is because a breakdown has occurred in one or more of these essential factors. Infertility is usually not the result of defects in only one partner, but the result of several factors, often minor, in both partners. In seeking help, both husband and wife should begin by having a complete physical examination, asking their doctor to search for any condition that might keep them from having a baby.

The physical examination of the wife includes a routine pelvic examination, with special attention to possible fibroids, polycystic (enlarged) ovaries, and vaginal and cervical infection. The hymen may even be intact, indicating that semen has never been deposited at the cervix.

It is possible for infectious organisms to

produce substances that injure the husband's sperm as soon as the semen enters the vagina. The cervix of the uterus may be obstructed by thick or heavy mucus. Tumors in the uterus (fibroids) or an inflamed lining membrane could be the problem. An improper tilt or position of the uterus can be a barrier to the path of the sperm. The tube where ovum and sperm meet can be blocked by mucus or obstructed by scar tissue from an earlier infection. The ovum itself may not mature properly because of an endocrine disturbance.

During a physical examination of the husband, any of these problems may be easily detected: undescended testicle, very small or atrophic testicle, varicocele, or prostatitis.

Fertility is often influenced by one's general health, so the physician will look for any kind of chronic infection, malnutrition, anemia, or a metabolic problem. We know that endocrine disturbances, particularly hypothyroidism and deficiencies in the hormones from the pituitary, adrenal, and reproductive glands can definitely affect fertility. Vitamin A is needed to maintain the production of the sperm. B complex vitamins are essential to pituitary function. Vitamin C (ascorbic acid) is thought to be involved in preventing sperm destruction. So both husband and wife will be encouraged to follow the basic rules of good health, with a balanced diet, as well as adequate exercise and rest.

The physical examinations of husband and wife may be only the beginning of the physician's search to help the couple. Obviously, it is no simple matter to pinpoint the cause or causes of infertility.

Although infertility has traditionally been regarded as a female problem, it is traceable to the male in 30 percent of childless couples. In an additional 20 percent, the male is a contributing factor. (The Bible long ago recognized the possibility of the barren male: "Thou shalt be blessed above all people; there shall not be male or female barren among you . . ." [Deuteronomy 7:14].) If the couple must be referred to a specialist, the husband will be studied first, since his evaluation is less time-consuming and less expensive.

However, infertility is always viewed as a couple problem, and each couple is thought of as a "reproductive unit." The family doctor will attempt to rule out other obstacles to conception before the husband is referred for a full fertility workup.

For instance, has the couple tried for *one full year* to have a child? The length of time is important in diagnosing infertility. How frequent has their intercourse been? Once every two weeks sometimes is not often enough to determine infertility. Have they been using any kind of artificial lubricant during intercourse? Some lubricating jellies are spermicidal. So is petroleum jelly (Vaseline). And any cream or jelly, even K-Y Jelly, will interfere with the mobility of the sperm. The use of artificial lubricants, particularly those that kill the sperm, will cause temporary infertility, but the situation can be easily remedied.

Has the wife been douching before intercourse for the purpose of cleanliness? This will have an undesirable effect upon the male sperm, changing the normal acidity of the vagina, so that normal sperm function and mobility are altered. Was the wife using oral contraceptives prior to the start of unprotected intercourse? (There is now strong evidence that after long-term use of the pill, the return to normal ovulation may be quite slow.)

The doctor will turn his attention to sexual dysfunction as a possible cause of infertility. Is there in reality an impotence problem? Or retrograde ejaculation, where the man feels that he is ejaculating, but the semen goes into the bladder, rather than through the penis?

The husband's occupational history must be considered, as well as his recent emotional and psychological history. Diminished fertility often results from strong physical or emotional stress, or from a buildup of psychological tensions. Fortunately, fertility seems to often be restored when the stress is reduced.

Certain environmental agents, such as heat and radiation, may contribute to male infertility. One important function of the scrotum is to keep the testes about 2.2 degrees cooler than the abdominal cavity. But the husband may be inadvertently heating the scrotum to body temperature level by wearing tight bikini or jockey-type underwear, or by the taking of long, hot tub baths. In primitive tribal rites, the men sit in a cold stream before having intercourse! Heat can reduce the sperm count enough to cause temporary infertility, but by wearing loose-fitting clothing for a few weeks, a normal sperm count will be restored.

Radiation exposure, either medical or occupational, may be the source of infertility. The germinal cells of the testes are extremely sensitive to this. However, depending upon the dosage of radiation, fertility may be restored.

A particular medication may be at fault. Most of the anticancer drugs inhibit the production of sperm, as do certain cortisone drugs, antimalarial compounds, diuretics, nitrofurantoins (used to treat urinary infections), and some drugs used in treating depression. Taking testosterone will tend to shut off production of the hormone which, in the male, stimulates cell function and development. It has even been considered as a male contraceptive!

The difficulties pressuring the infertile couple actually have the potential of drawing them closer as they begin to understand each other, reach out to comfort each other, and experience a deepening fellowship together in prayer. They can strengthen each other with the shared assurance of God's perfect plan for their life together, and they can develop the patience and faith to wait on Him and to see Him bring it about.

What counts in any traumatic situation of life is how you choose to respond to it over a period of time. Some couples who have responded to the problem of infertility with faith and the determination to express their love in other positive ways, find that there *are* alternatives which bring them great joy as they give of themselves. The love that might have been centered on one child is poured out to many individuals.

The Bible expresses this principle with words that have comforted through the centuries: "Sing, O barren, thou who didst not bear; break forth into singing, and cry aloud, thou who didst not travail with child; for more are the children of the desolate than the children of the married wife, saith the Lord" (Isaiah 54:1).

—From Ed Wheat, M.D., and Gaye Wheat, *Intended for Pleasure*. Old Tappan, N.J.: Fleming H. Revell, 1981.

IN-LAWS

MANY PEOPLE find healthy problem solving to be a major area of dissatisfaction in their in-law relationships. Here are a few techniques which will help you avoid an angry explosion.

1. Recognize conflict issues early. No one has to look for conflicts, but if a disagreement arises, accept it as an opportunity to gain understanding of yourself and the other

person. Consider it a time of growth. Your attitude toward the problem will determine the outcome. Your pessimism or optimism will influence conflict resolution.

2. As soon as you can, verbalize the problem or complaint. The longer you let a problem fester, the greater the possibility of resentment and bitterness eroding the relationship.

3. Share your problem or concern in private so you don't embarrass the other person or cause him to feel that he must save face.

4. Select the most appropriate time. (See Proverbs 15:23.) It is very important to select a time that will allow for the greatest understanding and cooperative effort.

5. Let the person know that you are pleased with several aspects of the relationship before sharing what it is that bothers you.

6. Use "I statements" such as "I feel" and "I don't like to be" rather than "you are" and "you did this." "You statements" sound like accusations and quickly lead to self-defense and nonlistening, and perhaps even to counter-complaining.

7. Pinpoint the actions that concern you. Don't try to be a mind reader by focusing on what you think the other person's motives are. Perhaps he was rude or didn't listen, but you don't really know that he definitely planned to do that.

It is often very helpful to put your feelings down in writing. This will produce a much better understanding of the entire situation, especially how the problem relates to unfulfilled needs. As you describe the problem in writing, be sure you consider both your own and the other person's behavior, along with the circumstances that surround these behaviors. Carefully define how you understand the problem. Then attempt to look at the situation from the point of view of the other person. How might they define the

problem? As you write, you may discover some of the real issues involved that you may have overlooked before. The more narrowly you define the conflict, the easier it will be to resolve the problem.

8. Identify your own contribution to the problem. In resolving a conflict, your approach must be "We have a problem." Even though you believe you have not contributed to the conflict, the way you approach the other person and the words you use will affect the potential resolution. When you are willing to accept some responsibility for a problem, the other person perceives a willingness on your part to cooperate and will be much more open to working together towards a solution.

As you consider what you are going to say to the other person, keep in mind these practical steps:

Choose one word that best indicates what you want to talk about.

State the word or subject you want to talk about in one complete sentence. Be precise and specific. Try not to blame, ridicule, or attack the other person. Do not overload him with too much information all at once.

Take responsibility for the problem. Tell the other person why you are bringing this matter up for discussion. For example, "I have a problem. I have something that is a little difficult for me to talk about, but our relationship is very important to me, and by talking about it I feel that we will have a better relationship. I feel that_____is the problem, and this is what I am contributing to it:_____. I need to hear what you think and how you feel about it." This is an example of a very healthy way to express yourself in what otherwise might be an explosive confrontation.

If your partner approaches you in this manner, respond by saying, "Thank you for telling me. If I understand what you feel, the problem is_____. I can agree that you feel this way." Restate the problem to make sure you have correctly understood your partner.

9. Comparing this person's actions and behavior with the failings of others does little to help solve the problem you are concerned about.

10. Forget the past. Talk about the present issue without making reference to past difficulties.

11. Deal with only one complaint. It is too easy for the other person to feel dumped upon if he receives a barrage of problems all at the same time.

12. Suggest in a nonangry, nondemanding, nonjudgmental way some of the realistic solutions that could be implemented.

13. Allow the other person to share his feelings and ideas about the problem. If he responds in anger to what you have said, his response is no reason for you to become angry.

Remember, a valid complaint always has two characteristics. It should be specific and positive. Statements like, "You're always complaining about something," "You always make comments about my housecleaning," or "You always seem to interfere when we are disciplining the children," are negative and nonspecific. Here are some examples of positive and specific complaints which will elicit a more constructive response.

"I would really appreciate your sharing some positive things about what's going on with you."

"When you have a complaint, I would really appreciate it if you would also suggest a positive alternative or solution."

"When we are disciplining the children, I would appreciate your not saying anything about what we are doing in front of them. I am always open to positive suggestions, but please share them with me later when they are not around."

You really don't have to be caught in the middle. You can eliminate much of the pain of a push-pull conflict by honestly asserting to the other person your feelings and reactions. If done in a spirit of love and concern, the results can be constructive.

—From H. Norman Wright, *In-Laws Outlaws*. Eugene, Ore.: Harvest House Publishers, 1977.

J

JESUS CHRIST

IN HELPING a young child learn about, love, and respond to Jesus, you face several problems.

The first lies in the nature and purpose of Jesus. The Savior was no ordinary man, and anyone who acknowledges him as Christ becomes immersed in a profound mystery. The unity of God-man in his person is incomprehensible. Yet he is the same Jesus whom the child is to know and love. The first problem is how can you help the child grow to know this Jesus.

The second problem lies in the nature of the child you teach. He can tell you so little of what he feels and the reason for his feeling. He is ready for such tiny pieces of knowledge about Jesus, yet these become foundation blocks. So your second problem is to teach the child only what he can absorb now, but making sure that it builds a firm base on which he can grow in knowledge, attitude, and service toward his Lord.

Growing to Know Jesus. Long before the child understands many facts about Jesus, his feelings toward Jesus can begin to develop. A preschool child can love Jesus. His love grows not only from the knowledge that Jesus loves him, but also from the way adults around him feel about Jesus. Love is a feeling, not an idea. Your feeling colors your tone of voice, your gestures, your facial expression. When you talk to the child about Jesus, everything about you combines to re-veal to him your true feeling. You can cultivate the child's love of Jesus very early just by letting your love come through when you tell him about Jesus. Somehow he will understand and absorb your feelings.

The preschool child will sense that the relationship between Jesus and God is very special. This simple idea marks his first step toward the concept that Jesus is both human and divine. To the basic understanding, he will add more complex ideas in his elementary years. At three, four, and five years of age he can recognize that Jesus loved God, that he told others about him, that he prayed to God, that Jesus is like God. All of these ideas help him discover that there's something special between Jesus and God.

The five-year-old is ready to know that Jesus is God's Son. . . . He begins by becoming familiar with the words, "Son of God." Then he will study Jesus' ministry on earth to help him explore the concept further. . . . He will hear stories of how Jesus helped and healed people. . . . He will learn that Jesus' love and guidance is one of God's ways of caring for him and for all of God's children. All of these things will help him sense the close relationship between God and Jesus. Finally . . . the child will be helped to realize that Jesus is God's Son.

Even if you try to present this relationship as simply as possible, the preschool child still faces problems. One four-year-old asked, "Is Jesus really God's little boy?" The child poses this kind of question because relationships trouble him. If he has difficulty knowing what mother-daughter, father-son, uncle-niece, brother-sister mean, think of his problem in sorting out just who is Jesus and who is God. Many a child confuses them. Many a child points to a picture of Jesus and says, "That's God." Your best course is first to keep a clear picture of what the child is ready to understand about the relationship between God and Jesus. Second, listen to his questions. Answer them clearly and simply. Third, if he doesn't make a point of it, you need not attempt to clarify the relationship for him. Answer his questions when he asks them. He is more likely to be ready to learn at that point. You will find that each child has his own particular questions, too. They stem from his own unique background, the experience he has had at home and in his neighborhood and in church school, the ideas he has picked up. If you try to straighten out the relationship by talking it out with the whole class, you might miss the mark with the individual child.

Another quality of Jesus that the child can grasp is that Jesus himself is special. This understanding represents the cornerstone of the far more complex learning of Jesus as Savior. Many things will teach him directly that Jesus is special: stories such as the Christmas story, the episodes of Jesus' healing, songs, and Bible verses that the child learns are sayings of Jesus. Indirect means also teach him of Jesus' special quality: the emphasis of festivals such as Christmas and Easter, your own approach, the manner in which he hears Jesus' words read to him from the Bible.

The preschool child is not ready yet for an understanding of the mission of Jesus. To talk about him as Savior, Redeemer, Lord means using terms beyond his comprehension. Words such as salvation, sin, and cross are steeped in adult experiences. When questions about this aspect of Jesus arise, accept them, offering common sense interpretations. In following that kind of approach, you are not ignoring the purpose of Jesus on earth. You yourself know why Jesus lived, died, and rose again. This concept lies at the base of your teaching and colors your relationship with the child.

Those then are the three general objectives for the three-, four-, and five-year-old child: (1) to grow in his love for Jesus; (2) to know that a special relationship exists between God and Jesus; (3) to know that Jesus himself is special.

Getting Specific. The young child can learn some specific things about Jesus. As you study the concepts, you will see the relationship between these specific learnings and the general objectives above. They say something about Jesus' love for the child. They help him to increase his love for Jesus. They contribute to his idea of Jesus as a special person or to his idea of the unique relationship of God and Jesus.

The first of the specific learnings is that Jesus lived and grew up, just as the child does. The story of the birth of Jesus brings joy and wonder to the hearts of everyone. The young child especially finds warmth and joy in the presence of the baby Jesus. What a marvelous way to learn to know Jesus. How easily he can love and adore the Wonder of wonders!

The family life of Jesus helps the child to establish friendly feelings toward Jesus. Mary and Joseph did for Jesus what all mothers and fathers do or should do! They loved him and cared for his needs. They taught him as he grew up. Those experiences, common to the child, make him feel comfortable about Jesus.

It is interesting that children feel free to

call Mary and Joseph by their given names. After all they never hear a last name for the Holy family! Children seem to understand the parents' roles without too much explaining.

Incidents in the adult life of Jesus also draw the child to him. Jesus ate with friends. He watched children at play in the market place. He talked about the out-of-doors. He lived near the water and knew the ways of fishermen. He lived close to the countryside and knew the ways of farmers. There is a warmth about Jesus, a universal appeal that attracts the young as well as the mature. There is a simplicity about Jesus that makes even the youngest child feel a personal attachment, as though Jesus were meant for him alone.

Telling about Jesus the baby and then Jesus the man in rapid succession snarls the young child's thinking. One Sunday the child sees a picture of the infant in the manger, the next a picture of the man. "Just which is Jesus, anyway? Were there two Jesus'?" asked a four-year-old. "Was one a baby and another a big man?" Such a confusion seems absurd to an adult who knows time and the cycle of life. But to a child the process of growth and concepts of history are mysterious. How can Jesus be little and big at the same time?

This troublesome situation furnishes you with some clues for proceeding. If the child has been hearing about Jesus the baby and you want to tell him about the grown-up Jesus, carefully bridge the gap. Using the child's own idea pattern, tell how Jesus grew from a baby to a big boy and then into a big man. Draw parallels to the child's own experience. He knows he was a little baby. But now he is bigger. He can run, jump, dress, and feed himself. Soon he will go to school and be big enough to read. Then he will

grow to be a big man. You might show pictures of Jesus the baby, boy, and man as you describe this process.

Listen for questions that come casually, at any moment in the session, that indicate the child's confusion between Jesus the baby and Jesus the man. Answer the individual child, drawing on his knowledge of his own babyhood and early childhood to help him grasp the point.

The second of the specific learnings is that Jesus loved people. The child longs to hear it. Jesus loved all kinds of people. He loved happy and gay people. He enjoyed sharing holidays and festivals with them. He liked to eat with them.

Jesus loved sad people. He knew how mothers and fathers felt when their children were ill or when their children were disobedient. He knew how families felt when they were poor. Jesus loved people when they were frightened and when they were hungry. He loved even those who were mean, spiteful, and full of hate.

Jesus loves. Jesus loves. The child finds security in knowing that. He finds relief and understanding of his own behavior. He feels assured that Jesus knows all of his problems and still loves him.

Providing the child with a background of many experiences that say, "Jesus loves you," "He loves all people," helps him see Jesus' personality. The child needs such guidance in knowing what Jesus was like.

Sometimes a teacher is so eager to tell what happened to Jesus or what he did and said that she neglects the person of Jesus. Often the life of Jesus is emphasized to the detriment of his personality. The child need not be deluged with facts to help him appreciate what Jesus was like. Think of your own friendship with the young child. What about you matters most to him? It's probably that you take time to be with him. You listen. You are friendly. You share good days and bad. You understand. You help and encourage. You show your love for him. The child doesn't care about your life history or your accomplishments or your goals for the future. He just loves you. That is what he needs to see in Jesus, too.

The third specific concept that the child can learn is that Jesus loved God. Whatever Jesus did reflected it. His love for people expressed his love for God. He searched the Hebrew scriptures to know more about God's love. His love for the Temple and Synagogue gave him an opportunity to worship and honor God in the presence of others. It led him to seek God in prayer.

The times when Jesus prayed are meaningful to the young child. He blessed the loaves and fish. He prayed in church. He prayed when he needed guidance in selecting his disciples. The child learns many things from Jesus' prayers. He recognizes the need to pray, the desire to pray, the confidence that God will listen, the willingness to listen to God.

The fourth concept the child can learn is that Jesus wants helpers. Even a young child can feel the urgency to be a helper of Jesus. The Christian life must be lived, and the child can do that. He can be kind and loving, too.

Be careful how you interpret the concept of helping Jesus. It does not mean that tidy-ing up a cluttered room or setting the table is done for Jesus—although it could be. Those things help parents. They want them done, even order them done. Such actions reflect neatness, obedience, and a willingness of the child to do his part, but you want to arouse the child's desire to live in the loving spirit of Jesus, to give of himself by taking the initiative in being friendly, by showing cheerfulness and cooperation. It is the child's attitude that is important, more than his deeds.

Being Jesus' "follower" is a difficult idea for the young child to grasp. "Follower" to him means someone who comes next in line. To follow Jesus means for the child literally to go where Jesus went. Because of that connotation, it's best not to use the word follower, but to say "helper."

—From Eleanor Zimmerman, *Bible and Doctrine for 3's to 5's*. Philadelphia: Fortress Press, 1963.

FOR FURTHER READING:

Adams, Jay E. *Christ and Your Problems*. Grand Rapids: Baker Book House, 1976.

McKenna, David L. *The Jesus Model*. Waco, Tex.: Word Books, 1977.

Muggeridge, Malcolm. *Jesus*. New York: Harper and Row Publishers, 1976.

Smith, Joyce Marie. *The Significance of Jesus*. Wheaton, Ill.: Tyndale House Publishers, 1976.

Stewart, Ed. *Here Comes Jesus*. Ventura, Calif.: Regal Books, 1977.

L

LEARNING DISABILITIES

Dyslexia

There are many children in schools today who have handicaps in specific areas of learning. For many, this problem is limited to reading and is called *dyslexia.* In others, it is related to mathematics, and for many, it is spelling that seemingly defeats them. In some cases, the reading and spelling problem is associated with a reversal of letter shapes. When *b* means *d* to a child, *bad* becomes *dab* or vice versa. We can all agree that such confusion would make it difficult to master spelling and writing as well as reading.

The Mechanism of Learning

Not only is there a problem with mastering the sounds and shapes of letters, but there also are neurological factors that enter into the learning process. As the eye sees a letter or word, it sends a message to the visual center of the brain, which then connects with the cortex (or outer layer) of the brain. Apparently it is there that the original object or word seen by the eye is decoded into something we have seen or heard before, or that seems new. People who study learning problems believe that perhaps some short-circuit takes place in these complex nerve tracts that interferes with the recognition of words or, in similar ways, with sounds through the hearing devices.

Overcoming Learning Disabilities

While authorities are still studying the reasons for learning disabilities, educators are working hard to find ways to overcome them. Many schools have teachers who are especially trained and gifted in teaching such children to read, write, spell, and master arithmetic. If you believe your child has a special problem with learning, ask for him to be tested and placed with someone who can help him learn.

Even with a minimum amount of specialized help, many people seem to "outgrow" their learning disabilities. Usually by the seventh or eighth grade, these young people begin to develop enough successes to believe in themselves, and once they begin to do well, they can't be stopped.

Practical Considerations of Learning Disabilities

Lack of Concentration. Whatever obscure neurological or biochemical factors there may be, there are some practical issues involved in learning difficulties. When a child worries too much, when he has only partial information about family concerns, and when he has too few successes on which to build, he will have trouble concentrating. It's difficult to deal with multiplication tables when you're worried about your parent's reaction to your grade card, or you know your grandpa has had a heart attack.

253

We see many children who are so preoccu-pied with television or even exciting plans for special coming events, that they are un-able to focus on mundane topics like the Civil War or the people in Latin America.

How Parents Can Help. While it takes spe-cially trained teachers to help a child learn proper letter and word formations, you, as parents, can help with the emotional blocks to learning. Let us suggest these steps for your consideration:

1. Consider and write down all the things about which your child could be worry-ing. Do this with your spouse or a person who knows your child well. Then ask your child about any worries he may have, and add them to your list.
2. Take one or two of these issues each day, and discuss them with your child. As much as possible, get the child to talk about them and about his feelings re-garding these problems.
3. Give him whatever information you can that will clear up those worries and really put them to rest.
4. Do not exaggerate or minimize your child's concern or feelings. Regardless of what they seem to you, they are real to him.
5. Help your child know that he may come to you with any worry he has at any time. Let him borrow your wisdom and strength.
6. Both you and your child may talk with the heavenly Father about any and all concerns and leave them with Him.
7. Be available to each child every day for the purpose of keeping that child's mind free of stored-up worries. If he doesn't come to you, go to him and ask if he needs to talk. Please avoid nagging, but simply be open.

Stop Worrying. Try to leave the teaching of your child to his teacher. If she asks you to help him with some exercises or homework, do so. Avoid worrying, because unfortu-nately, rather than helping him, that will only convince him that he is a terrible prob-lem. He already suspects that. There is a big difference between *having* a problem, for which you will eventually find the answer, and *being* a problem, for which there are no solutions. Help your child discover the areas in which he is successful, and let him know your honest pride in him. Don't overdo that, or he will think you are covering up your own worry or pity.

Relaxed Evenings. With the best intentions in the world, some parents keep a child plugging away at homework so much that he simply rebels. Dr. Grace's sister, who taught elementary school for over forty years, found that children did better in school when most of their evenings were times of fun and warmth within the family.

God's Plan for Your Child. Occasionally, tutors may help a child with a specific learn-ing disability, and prevent the tension be-tween you and your child that ends up de-feating all of you. But again, *keep enough free time for your child to relax and be a child.* Almost always, children outgrow learning problems. If you don't allow those to be compounded by personality disorders or rebelling, he will compensate for them and forge ahead when he is ready. *Remem-ber that God has a special plan for every child's life.* He will make that plan work, if you all work with Him.

—From Grace H. Ketterman, M.D., and Her-bert L. Ketterman, M.D., *The Complete Book of Baby and Child Care for Christian Parents.* Old Tappan, N.J.: Fleming H. Revell Co., 1982.

FOR FURTHER READING:

Feinbloom, Richard I., M.D. *Child Health Encyclopedia.* The Boston Children's Medical Center. New York: Dell Publishing Co., Inc., 1978.

Wender, Paul, and Wender, Estelle. *The Hyperactive Child and the Learning Disabled Child.* New York: Crown Pubs., Inc., 1978.

LEFT-HANDEDNESS

BY 5, most children prefer one hand or the other. While some children have a strong preference from the beginning, many continue to use either, until they are 3 or more. The preferred hand may change more than once during formative years.

No one is really sure what determines handedness, as well as which foot or eye is preferred, but experts agree that the preference is a basic part of the individual's physical makeup, possibly even inherited. Since it is so deepseated, forcing a child to go against his natural tendency is extremely upsetting to him.

About 90 percent of our children turn out to be righthanded. The number of left-handed people has increased in the last generation as we stopped making an effort to change those who naturally used their left. Some, of course, seem to use either hand equally well.

If a child seems unable to settle on either hand, and is markedly awkward with both, you may wish to have a test made to determine which is better. Ask your doctor about this. Once it is settled, you'll want to encourage him to use his best one by placing his drinking glass nearest it, by handing things to him correctly, and in other ways. As far as school work or athletic ability is concerned,

you don't need to worry if your child is left-handed.

—From *Your Child From 1 to 6.* Washington: U.S. Department of Health, Education and Welfare, 1969.

LOVE

SCIENTIFIC STUDIES support the biblical emphasis on the importance of love (*see* 1 Corinthians 13:13).

The New Testament suggests that we do not know how to love members of our families properly until we understand and experience the kind of love God had for us in sending His own Son to die for our sins. That, at least, seems to be the best interpretation of Jesus' statement that "Whoever comes to me cannot be my disciple unless he loves me more than he loves his father and his mother, his wife and his children, his brothers and his sisters, and himself as well" (Luke 14:26 TEV).

The New Testament uses a Greek word for love that was not the one most commonly used in the first century. It emphasizes the unconditional quality of Christian love. Whereas most forms of love are based on attractive qualities we find in another person, God's love is not based on any such attractiveness. The Christian parent's love for his children is to reflect in some small way that same kind of unconditional love.

Careful studies have shown that children who grow up with love and affection are healthier not only emotionally but also physically than children who lack that love. Difficult children become even more difficult until they are loved. Fortunately, most parents have love and affection for their children, though they may not always express it as openly as they should. Dr. D. Ross Campbell, a Christian psychologist, stresses the importance of such actions as touching and eye contact as ways of letting your child know you really do love him.

Sometimes, of course, parents who feel they have loved their children are puzzled and upset when their children seem to act in the same way as children who aren't loved. Given the infinite variety of personalities God has created, it is not surprising that some children react in unusual ways. These parents need to be more patient with such children and pray for them—and themselves—more than they might otherwise.

Love does not require that you approve of everything your child does. Just as God hates sin but loves the sinner, so you too must make it clear to your child that the things he does or fails to do are sometimes wrong, even though you love him very much. At times, the child's behavior may make it very difficult for you to *feel* very loving toward him. At such times especially you will need to ask God to give you His perspective and attitude of unconditional love. Temporary feelings of anger and even hatred need not be seen as a basic contradiction of the underlying love you have for your child, any more than they are in God Himself.

When a second child is born, parents need to be especially careful to let the older child know they love him. From being the center of his parents' world, he can so easily feel rejected by all the attention the new baby receives. From time to time each parent needs to devote his full attention to the older child and to assure him that he loves him just as much as ever.

During adolescence, as a child becomes increasingly independent and appears to resent any and all restraints on his independence and freedom, parents can easily spend most of their time arguing and resenting their offspring's inability to see beyond his own needs and interests. If Christian fathers take time to pray and talk with their sons and Christian mothers with their daughters at bedtime, some of the negative feelings can be eliminated and strong, positive, loving ties developed.

Christian parents need to remember that, just as God's love for the sinner, no matter what he has done, is often the main factor in his ultimate conversion, so too the Christian parent's love for a wayward child is often what one day brings him back to his senses and his spiritual home (*see* Luke 15:11–24).

—LESLIE R. KEYLOCK

FOR FURTHER READING:

Campbell, D. Ross. *How to Really Love Your Child.* Wheaton, Ill.: Victor Books, 1977.

Chervin, Ronda. *Love and Your Everyday Life.* Liquori, Mo.: Liquori Pbns., 1977.

Elliot, Elisabeth. *Love Has a Price Tag.* Chappaqua, N.Y.: Christian Herald, 1979.

McNair, Jim. *Love and Gifts.* Minneapolis: Bethany Fellowship, 1976.

Ogilvie, Lloyd J. *The Beauty of Love.* Eugene, Ore.: Harvest House Publishers, 1980.

LYING

ONE OF THE MOST important character traits is integrity: honesty in word and honesty in action. It is the mark of an "integrated" person—one who is not putting up false fronts, not pretending to be something he is not, not telling lies to cover up or distort; one whose word is his bond. The person of integrity is the kind of person who can let his yea be yea and his nay, nay (James 5:12), and who doesn't need to say anything more to bind himself. He is, as the Psalmist put it, the man who "... swears to his own hurt, and does not change" (Psalms 15:4 NAS). He is the kind of person who fills in credit-card applications accurately and income-tax forms truthfully. He is the kind of person who is *real*. This kind of person can be depended upon, for having accepted a job, he accomplishes it. If he says he'll be there at ten o'clock, that's when he'll arrive!

All of this sounds great, but how do we set the stage for this development?

(a) By telling our children the truth, always. We must avoid half answers to children's honest questions or untruthfulness in our own talk with others. How quickly the children catch on to our little "social lies" and discover that truth is not strictly necessary if it is embarrassing. This kind of parental honesty includes drawing a clear line between make-believe, imaginative pretending, and honesty. Parents should not lead their children to believe untruths, even as a form of teasing—or, as with Santa Claus, of play. Children are wonderful at entering the world of "Let's pretend" and are able to imagine endlessly. But they should know where imagining starts and reality stops. And they should have that line clearly drawn by parental example.

(b) By insistence on truthfulness in the child. Every child will attempt to lie, usually in self-defense to "cover up"—particularly if he thinks he is about to get into trouble. Parents need to make a clear line between truth and lying in their children's communications. Punishment for a lie should be more severe than punishment for any other offense.

I used to question my children, looking straight into their eyes. "Are you telling me true words? It is most important that you tell me true words *always*, otherwise I can't trust what you tell me *ever*." Usually a child betrays his guilt or attempt to cover up. There is nothing wrong with saying, "I don't blame you for being afraid to tell me, because this is a mess and I'm pretty mad. But you must tell me the truth even when you are afraid." You may have to reassure a child. "If you tell me exactly what happened, I won't spank you this time. But if I find out that you have not told me true words, I will certainly have to spank."

(c) Insisting on truth in action. A child who helps himself to a neighbor child's toy must be taught that taking what is someone else's is stealing. A child must learn to "just look" in stores. If a child does take something that belongs to someone else—even if it is as little as an apple from your neighbor's apple tree—deal with the matter seriously. Apology must be offered by the child. Restoration or restitution must be made where possible. The parent who explains away a child's petty theft leaves the field of property ownership without the moral demarcation laid down in Scripture.

—From Maxine Hancock, *People in Process*. Old Tappan, N.J.: Fleming H. Revell Co., 1978.

FOR FURTHER READING:

Dugan, LeRoy. *Help Yourself to a Healthier Mind*. Minneapolis: Bethany Fellowship, 1980.

M

MANNERS

THE WORD *polite* never appears in the King James Version of the Bible—or most other translations. The word *manners* in the sense of observance of polite customs also appears nowhere in the Bible, though in the King James Version it does appear in a different sense in Acts 13:18 and 1 Corinthians 15:33.

The idea of observing certain traditional practices does occur in the word *custom*, however. When Jesus was twelve, His parents went to Jerusalem "after the custom of the feast" (Luke 2:42). As He began His ministry, He attended the synagogue services on the Sabbath "as his custom was" (Luke 4:16). After the Last Supper, Jesus went to the Mount of Olives "as he was wont" (Luke 22:39). Jewish Christians are somewhat later criticized for failing to attend the services in their house churches: "Not forsaking the assembling of ourselves together, as the *manner* of some is . . ." (Hebrews 10:25).

But in all of these cases we have only a blending of the religious and the habitual. Nowhere is the idea of the polite associated with the word.

Should we, therefore, conclude that "good manners," in the modern sense, do not form part of the Christian parents' task? Hardly. The New Testament is full of references to the importance of conforming to the customs of the day that do not contradict biblical teaching in the way some of the customs of the Pharisees did. When Paul exhorted the Romans, "If possible, so far as it lies with you, live at peace with all men" (Romans 12:18 NEB), he implied that Christians will not needlessly violate the customs of their neighbors. The dress and behavior of Christians is not to conflict too dramatically with the customs of the people among whom they live (*see* 1 Corinthians 11:2–16; 1 Timothy 2:8–12).

The idea of what constitutes good manners changes. We no longer believe that a child is well mannered simply because he is "seen and not heard." The strict conformity to adult standards implied by the use of the cane, ruler, and strap is no longer seen as a guarantee against the "spoiling" of a child. Women no longer sit on one side of our church buildings or see religious value in wearing hats to church.

But at the same time, we are no longer so sure that "permissiveness" is as psychologically healthy as some exponents a few years ago believed. We do not feel the rude, inconsiderate, obnoxious child is the freest child. Manners may change, but they do not disappear as long as people care about each other. The strict formality of manners in the past has been relaxed, and most of us feel grateful. But sincere expressions of gratitude will never go out of style. Customs may change but not consideration for others.

Christian parents need to encourage their children to develop good manners, without being excessively rigid, especially when the children are young. Even many adolescents are notoriously poor about saying, "Thank you," or, "I'm sorry." Fortunately, however, they almost always grow out of their indifference or neglect because they come to realize the importance of "proper" behavior in getting along with others.

What constitutes good manners is usually determined by parents. Children tend to copy their parents' behavior—especially in public, much to the pleasure of some and dismay of others!

During preadolescent years some children, especially boys, think it smart to be impolite or rude. During this phase the Christian parent may have to overlook some inconsiderate behavior, confident that it will not last long. Loud corrections by parents in public are as offensive to good taste as the rude remarks of children.

Although their standards may not duplicate ours, most adolescents develop a very strong sense of what is proper and what isn't—and woe betide the unfortunate teenager who doesn't conform! When they are dating today, the boy may not consider it quite as important to walk on the curb side of a sidewalk (when they do happen to walk on a sidewalk!) as his parents did. But the more sophisticated adolescent boy will still open car and building doors and let the girl go first down the aisle in church.

The best approach to manners, however, is a fairly relaxed one. The reflective Christian parent knows that other things are far more important than the customs we have developed to regulate social behavior.

—LESLIE R. KEYLOCK

FOR FURTHER READING:

Post, Elizabeth, ed. *Emily Post Book of Etiquette for Young People.* New York: Thomas W. Crowell Co., 1967.

MARRIAGE

IF WE READ the first three chapters of Genesis, where it is recorded that God created *male* and *female*, we find that "God saw everything that He had made, and, behold, it was *very* good." Interestingly, the creation of light was "good," the creation of land and sea was "good," and, likewise, the creation of vegetation, of fish and birds and animals was also "good." But not until He had created man and woman did God call for our attention with "Behold, it was *very* good."

With so many "good" things in the Garden and on earth, only one thing was *not good:* "And the Lord God said, "It is not good that the man should be alone; I will make an helpmate for him" (Genesis 2:18). In those few words God taught us that for man there is no substitute, no alternative plan, no better companion than his wife. The void which originally was caused by taking "bone of my bone, flesh of my flesh" can be filled only by the presence of woman. Since a part of Adam went to make Eve, a man remains incomplete without his Eve.

God placed almost top priority on sexual union in marriage. We can see in the Genesis account that after God told man not to learn evil by experience (Genesis 2:17), His *second* teaching told man and woman how to relate in marriage: "Therefore shall a man leave his father and his mother, and shall cleave unto his wife; and they shall be one flesh" (Genesis 2:24). God had first divided the woman from the man when He made Eve. But now He commands them to be joined together again as one flesh. In this brief counseling session, even before any sin and its resulting selfishness had entered the human race, we find three basic commands:

First, when we marry, we should stop being dependent on our parents or our in-laws. We are to become completely dependent on our mates to satisfy *all* our needs.

Second, the man is the one who is responsible for holding the marriage together by "cleaving" to his wife. *Cleaving* in this sense means to be welded inseparably, so that each becomes a part of the other. Therefore, the man is to be totally committed to his one wife.

Third, we are commanded to be joined together in sexual union, to be *one flesh.*

The ideal situation God intended for us is shown by the blissful words "they were both naked, the man and his wife, and were not ashamed" (Genesis 2:25). Adam and Eve could see each other as they really were, without shame, disappointment, or frustration. The sex relationship God had designed for them brought the blessings of companionship, unity, and delight—and note that this was some time *before* the command to bear children was given (Genesis 3:16).

God's plan for our pleasure has never changed, and we realize this even more as we consider how we are "fearfully and wonderfully made" (Psalms 139:14). When we discover the many intricate details of our bodies which provide so many intense, wonderful physical sensations for husbands and wives to enjoy together, we can be sure that He intended for us to experience full satisfaction in the marriage relationship.

Some have assumed that the sex act became an unholy practice when sin entered into the world. However, this is ruled out when we see that God's basic counsel on sex in the first chapters of Genesis was repeated by Jesus Christ to the religious leaders of His day: "But from the beginning of the creation God made them male and female. For this cause shall a man leave his father and mother, and cleave to his wife; and they two shall be one flesh. What therefore God hath

joined together, let not man put asunder" (Matthew 19:5; Mark 10:6–9). Jesus reemphasized this to His disciples in the next two verses in Mark 10, and again we find these commands reinforced in Ephesians 5:31.

As a matter of fact, the sex relationship in marriage receives such emphasis in the Scriptures, that we begin to see it was meant not only to be a wonderful, continuing experience for the husband and wife, but it also was intended to show us something even more wonderful about God and His relationship with us. Ephesians 5:31, 32 spells it out: "For this cause shall a man leave his father and mother, and shall be joined unto his wife, and they two shall be one flesh. This is a great mystery, but I speak concerning Christ and the church." *Thus, the properly and lovingly executed and mutually satisfying sexual union is God's way of demonstrating to us a great spiritual truth.* It speaks to us of the greatest love story ever told—of how Jesus Christ gave Himself for us and is intimately involved with and loves the Church (those who believe in Him). In this framework of understanding between two growing Christians, the sexual relationship can become a time of intimate fellowship as well as delight.

This, of course, explains why the marriage union is the only way man and woman can truly enjoy the riches God has planned for them. Because the relationship is specifically designed to illustrate God's unending love for His people, sexual intercourse must be experienced in the context of a permanent, giving commitment. Anything less shortchanges those involved.

Some people have felt uncomfortable about sex because they somehow equate the sexual desire of men with the sexual drive of animals. They should remember that animals breed according to instinct with biological motivation. But man has intercourse as a whole person. He of all creatures is the only one to use reason in choosing to have sexual relations. Husband and wife are the only creatures capable of gaining spiritual unity and a deeper knowledge of each other through the sexual relationship. Let us realize how the bodies of men and women are designed. Even in the sex act itself we are reminded that this is a relationship of persons, not just bodies, for it is no coincidence that man is the *only* creature of God's creation who relates sexually face-to-face.

Scripture suggests that just as we can know God, so we can know our husband or wife in a deeper, higher, more intimate way through the physical act of marriage. *Know* is the term used in the Bible to define our relationship to God; it also is the term used to designate the intimate union of husband and wife. "Adam *knew* Eve" (Genesis 4:1). Mary, speaking of her virginity, said, "How shall this be, seeing I *know* not a man?" (Luke 1:34). Matthew 1:25 says that Joseph *"knew* her not" until after the birth of Christ. The sex relationship offers no more cherished pleasure than this *knowing* of the one you love. With the understanding that our marriage relationship portrays the truths of our relationship with God, we can become free as never before to express our love for our husband or wife fully through the dynamic opportunity of the sex act.

God's viewpoint comes forth vigorously in 1 Corinthians 7:3–5 where the husband and wife are told they actually *defraud* one another when they refuse to give physical pleasure and satisfaction to their mate. The only activity which is to break regular sexual relations is prayer and fasting for some specific cause, and this is to be only by mutual consent for a very limited time.

I cannot begin to describe the dimensions of the marriage relationship as experienced by the Christian couple who have a total commitment to Jesus Christ, and flowing from that a realization of their own security

in spiritual and physical oneness; who have an excitement found only in each other, knowing this is for as long as they live. This genuine, total oneness and completeness somehow cannot be explained to the one who has not yet experienced it. When this kind of relationship exists, many times you will both want to praise our Lord and have communion with Him in prayer, each thanking Him for the other and the complete love you share.

Because all phases of the biblical plan for marriage must be in operation before we can fully enjoy the sexual union as God designed it, we need to have a clear understanding of His plan. Unfortunately, most of us were not counseled in these matters before we married and so we stumbled through the first few years, at least, trying to find our way to happiness. As a family physician for twenty-five years, I have observed that marriage with its tremendous significance often turns out to be the least-prepared-for event of life. Even as divorce takes on epidemic proportions, young couples continue to venture into marriage remarkably unprepared. Sometimes a brief meeting with the minister before the wedding, then an often elaborate ceremony, and the newlyweds are on their own, to hit or miss in their quest for happiness, while family and friends hope for the best.

I consider premarriage counseling an essential part of my responsibility as a family doctor. It is not only a preventive measure, protecting against family breakups, but it also can trigger a positive course of action which will bring pleasure and joy as the young couple learn to love in an enduring relationship.

For the premarriage counseling session I have prepared a sheet the couple may keep, which lists in brief outline eleven biblical principles that help to ensure a happy marriage. Applying these vital principles will improve anyone's marriage, whether that person is a believer in Christ or not. God has set up certain principles by which men are to operate, and these are effective in anyone's life. The only problem is that the non-Christian is unable to implement these principles consistently on a lifelong basis. Only the Christian has within him the person of the Lord Jesus Christ and the Holy Spirit to empower him to carry out what is so clearly specified in the Bible.

Here is the way I discuss these principles point by point with the engaged couple:

1. Reserve funds to allow for a few weeks of uninterrupted time for a honeymoon. "When a man hath taken a new wife, he shall not go to war, neither shall he be charged with any business, but he shall be free at home one year, and shall cheer up his wife whom he hath taken" (Deuteronomy 24:5).

Now in our day we could hardly expect a man to take off for one year. However, there is a definite scriptural principle here. It is that the first few weeks of marriage are a crucial time for the young couple. To "cheer up" the wife means literally in the Hebrew "to know sexually and understand what is exquisitely pleasing to her" in the physical relationship.

If, like other young people, you are considering spending several thousand dollars for the wedding and a few leftover dollars for an overnight honeymoon, I certainly advise balancing your funds so that you can be free of responsibility for a few weeks, while you have time to get to know each other. During that period you will have clearer communication lines than you may ever have again, and if each of you does not come to know the other at the first of your marriage, you will find those communication lines becoming progressively blocked, as time goes on.

Never plan on getting married just before

entering college or graduate school, when the demand on your time and efforts will be so great. Seminary or medical school, for instance, will require intense concentrated study. So schedule your marriage at the beginning of a vacation time or during a break in employment. Concentrate on each other to establish the right pattern of caring in your marriage.

2. Borrow no money. "Owe no man anything but to love one another" (Romans 13:8). Borrowing money before marriage or soon after is like adding another phrase to the marriage vows: "Till debt do us part." In other words, let not money put asunder what God has put together. A psychology textbook's listing of the most common problems in marriage puts the handling of money at the head of the list. The key factor which creates problems is not how much money but the attitude toward money or the use of money. In fact, in my counseling experience, I have found much more conflict among people with money than those with limited funds.

This advice could be rephrased "Borrow no money to buy depreciating items." Many young couples go deeply into debt to purchase an expensive automobile, or a house full of fine furniture. You will be much happier if you buy only what you can afford, and then spend your weekends together, fixing up your car or building furniture or searching for "treasures" at used-furniture sales.

I know one young couple who make a car payment to their savings account each month. When they have enough cash, they buy a car, and go on making payments to themselves for the next car. They collect interest instead of paying it out to someone else, and enjoy freedom from debt at the same time. Financial freedom gives you power to utilize your money as you choose, not as the moneylenders choose for you. If you want to enjoy each other and find pleasure in your marriage, do not commit your funds to such an extent that you do not have available cash for the little things that are so much fun to do together.

3. Be independent of in-laws. Leave father and mother. "For this cause shall a man leave his father and mother, and shall be joined unto his wife, and they two shall be one flesh" (Ephesians 5:31). However, *you should not marry without their approval.* "Children, obey your parents in the Lord: for this is right" (Ephesians 6:1).

Before sin entered into the human race, two commands were given to Adam. One was not to eat of the tree of knowledge of good and evil (in other words, not to learn evil by experience). The other command was to get in-laws out of marriage! Looking down the corridors of time at future causes of marriage problems, God said in-laws should not be involved in your marriage. Separating from parents physically, emotionally, and financially is the best possible way to begin a new social unit.

The *man,* by the way, is told to leave his father and mother and to cleave (to be united totally and inseparably) to his wife— a welding together so that there can be no taking apart. He is commanded to cleave to his wife, even before he is told to love her. The Bible does not specify the best age for marriage, but it does establish the principle that the man must be able to be totally independent of his parents and to establish his own home. Statistically, age twenty-six is the best time for a woman to get married and age twenty-seven to thirty-one for a man. That is, fewer divorces result when people marry at these ages. Three out of five teenage marriages now end in divorce.

I encourage you to listen to your parents if they do not want you to marry, or if they disapprove of your choice of mate. Not only is this biblical, but remember that your parents know you better than anyone else does.

They have the knowledge to discern the qualities you need in a marriage partner, far better perhaps than you do. I suspect that nine out of ten marital problems could be avoided if children would listen to their parents' careful evaluation before they married.

4. Do not get a TV set for at least one year. "Ye husbands, dwell with them according to knowledge, giving honor unto the wife. . . . Be ye all of one mind . . ." (1 Peter 3:7, 8). This is one of the most surprising things that young people hear from me. It may sound absurd. But did you know that television can be the greatest, most subtle thief of your time? It will steal away those moments that you should be devoting to your mate and, later, to your family. It will take away the most wonderful hours of your day—hours which could be spent in personal communication and sharing, moments when you can best learn to relate to one another. There is no giving, no receiving, when you spend your time watching television.

Husband, you are urged to do two things in Scripture: First, study the Scripture; then study your wife. Dwell with her. Be totally at ease together, with full knowledge of each other. This is what marriage is all about.

5. Never go to bed with unresolved conflict. "Let not the sun go down upon your wrath" (Ephesians 4:26). "Forgive as Christ forgave" (Colossians 3:13).

The Bible warns us not to harbor anger so that it corrodes into resentment or bitterness. Some people simmer and fume under the surface for days or weeks at a time, but this is not God's way, and it will damage any marriage. Resolve negative attitudes toward each other by the end of the day, or do not go to bed until you do. In every marriage, conflicts arise because two people have come together from different backgrounds, with different educational levels, emotional makeups, desires, and objectives. Conflicts are inevitable. But a conflict becomes a problem only when it is not quickly resolved.

6. Seek outside spiritual counsel if unable to resolve a conflict within one week. "Brethren, if a man be overtaken in a fault, ye who are spiritual, restore such an one in the spirit of meekness . . ." (Galatians 6:1). "Follow peace with all men, and holiness, without which no man shall see the Lord . . . looking diligently lest any man fail of the grace of God, lest any root of bitterness springing up trouble you, and by it many be defiled" (Hebrews 12:14, 15). ". . . forgetting those things which are behind . . ." (Philippians 3:13).

The "one week" is a time limit I have suggested. The Bible does not say how soon spiritual counsel is to be sought. But it is important not to let a seed of bitterness take root and grow up to smother your marriage.

7. Seek counsel if the wife is consistently unable to attain good sexual release. "Let the husband render unto the wife her due; and likewise also, the wife unto the husband. The wife hath not power of her own body, but the husband; and likewise also the husband hath not power of his own body, but the wife. Defraud ye not one the other . . ." (1 Corinthians 7:3–5).

We are told in this passage that the husband and wife are actually robbing one another if there is not mutual pleasure in the sexual relationship. The Bible implies that husbands and wives are entitled to certain rights. However, sexual fulfillment is the only one specifically spelled out. God says husband and wife have the right to be sexually satisfied.

If, early in your marriage, each of you comes to realize how great your responsibility is to fulfill your mate sexually, most problems will be eliminated even before they begin. In almost every case sexual satisfaction can be reached with good counsel, proper information, and an application and practice of the right techniques.

8. Have some Bible study together every day. "Man shall not live by bread alone" (Matthew 4:4). "Let the Word of Christ dwell in you richly" (Colossians 3:15–17). "Cleanse with the washing of water by the Word" (Ephesians 5:26, 27). *Accompany this with prayer:* "If any of you lack wisdom, let him ask of God" (James 1:5).

In Ephesians 5:25–28 we read something which is highly applicable to this principle of marriage: "Husbands, love your wives even as Christ also loved the church and gave himself for it, that he might sanctify and cleanse it with the washing of water by the word; that he might present it to himself a glorious church, not having spot or wrinkle, or any such thing; but that it should be holy and without blemish. So ought men to love their wives as their own bodies. . . ."

Christ meets the needs of the Church by washing it and cleansing it with the water of the Word. So ought we to love our wives. It is our responsibility to place before our wives and our families the Word of God.

Husband, as the Word of God is allowed to course through your wife's mind, personality, and very being, she will become the beautiful person God designed her to be. All that would make her less than pure, all that would limit her from becoming a wonderful wife, will gradually be removed as the two of you share in daily Bible study. It is the responsibility of the husband to initiate this. If you don't know how to begin, one way is to listen together to Bible teaching on cassette. Bible Believers Cassettes, Inc., a free-loan library, offers more than a thousand different messages on the subjects of dating, marriage, and the Christian home. (Send two dollars for catalog: 130 North Spring St., Spring-dale, Ark. 72764.) Do have Bible study that is applicable to your personal situation. Build your home life around Bible study and prayer; this will lead to more happiness and harmony in your home than you could ever imagine.

9. *Husband must be 100 percent committed to loving his wife. Wife must be 100 percent committed to being submissive (Ephesians 5).* As the husband loves his wife, she is going to be more submissive to him. As the wife submits to her husband, his love for her will surely grow. Do not marry someone who is not a Christian (2 Corinthians 6:14). Only when there is a certainty of one's trust in our Lord Jesus Christ alone for salvation can that person be considered a Christian (Acts 4:12). Only when submitting to Christ can anyone live the life-style of submission (Ephesians 5:21; 1 Corinthians 11:3).

What kind of love is a husband to bring to his wife? It is a strong, stable, mental attitude, always seeking nothing but the highest good for the one he loves. It is a love expressed in word and action which motivates the one being loved to give of herself in return.

What does it mean for a wife to be in submission to her husband? The word *submit* comes from a military term which actually means to move in an organized manner, to do an assigned job in an assigned way. Submission is the most important gift a wife can give her husband. A responsive and receptive wife willingly demonstrates that she surrenders her freedom for his love, adoration, protection, and provision.

Marriage must be a giving relationship. While the husband is giving love, giving every bit of energy, every bit of knowledge that he possesses to do that which is best for his wife and family, the wife is to respond to that love, adoration, and provision. This response will lead to an eagerness to meet her husband's needs, even before he asks. It is an

attitude of willing adaptation to that which God is leading her husband to do. We know submission has to be a gift from her to him, because it is contrary to all natural tendencies. As it is given, it releases a supernatural flow of love between the husband and the wife.

If these two attitudes of love and submission are ignored, difficulty, possibly disaster, looms ahead. If love and submission are put into action, a wonderful marriage will result, because God says very simply that this is the way He designed it.

10. *The husband is to be the head of his home.* "But I would have you know that the head of every man is Christ; and the head of the woman is the man; and the head of Christ is God" (1 Corinthians 11:3). "For the husband is the head of the wife, even as Christ is the head of the church . . ." (Ephesians 5:23). "One that ruleth well his own house . . ." (1 Timothy 3:4).

The husband's authority over the wife is rooted in Christ's authority over the Church. In fact, all authority we have is delegated authority, and the husband who keeps this in mind will never abuse that authority. On the other hand, the man who relinquishes his leadership position is sowing seeds which will yield trouble in due season.

The husband *is* the head of the house, whether he functions in that capacity or not. Any break in the marriage relationship is the man's responsibility. Now, I did not say it was his fault. I said that God holds the man accountable for any break in the marriage, because he is the one commanded to cleave inseparably to his wife. This principle of responsibility applies in every area of the relationship, whether spiritual, emotional, or physical.

The bride-to-be should realize before the wedding how important it is to marry a man she can gladly respond to and submit to as the head of her house. I have told many young women, "If you cannot look up to a man, do not look at him."

11. "And the wife see that she reverence her husband" *(Ephesians 5:33)*. What does it mean *to reverence* the husband? It means *to give him respect.* Fellows, it is difficult for your wife to respect you, if you are not respectable. It is impossible for a woman to revere her husband, if he is not worthy of reverence. The husband needs to live his life before his wife so that she can see that he is worthy of the respect God asks her to have. In the full meaning of the language of the Greek New Testament, the wife is told to respect, admire, enjoy, fear or be in awe of, defer to, revere, adore, be devoted to, esteem, praise, and deeply love her husband. This is her full-time job, and the original language of the Bible infers that she will be personally benefited as she does it.

If the wife does not trust and respect her husband, it is devastating to him and finally to the marriage. The greatest grief of love is not to be believed. But if she is able to look at her husband with eyes of reverence, he becomes a king among men!

In turn, he should give his wife the place of honor, a place of special privilege and preciousness. Many men have second-rate wives because they treat them in a second-rate manner. They never gain the real princess they would like to be married to; they just do not realize that the wife in many ways is a reflection of her husband. The wife is elevated to the position of princess by the wise and loving husband, as the great principles of the God-planned marriage are put into operation.

Some of you reading this have children who will be entering marriage in a few years. And you want to do all you can to prepare them for a good marriage. Let me make these suggestions:

The most important thing a father can do for his children is to love their mother. The home should be the most attractive place in the world to the children, and the mother should be the greatest attraction.

Without a warm atmosphere in your home and marriage—an atmosphere of love, of generosity, of forgiveness—your children will not know how to love. The only person who knows how to love is the person who has been loved, who has seen love, who has experienced love. The Christian home is a laboratory in which the love of God is demonstrated.

If you do not have this kind of love in your home, your children are likely to grow up with a feeling of inferiority, emptiness, and lack of worth. But it is not too late for you to develop this. It is never too late for two people who want a transformed marriage. Remember that the only course on marriage most children will ever take is the one at home! As fathers and mothers in a Christian home, we can provide the best in marriage preparation for our children by having a genuine love for one another, and by learning all we can about how to express that love, so our children will have a visible ongoing demonstration of real love.

I have had the opportunity as a family doctor to see results in the marriages of the couples who received this kind of premarriage counseling, based upon the absolutes of the Word of God. Over a period of years I have watched the couples who have applied these principles develop stable, loving, satisfying relationships. *These basic instructions from the Bible, if followed, will ensure happy marriages.*

Applying heavenly principles to a marriage can produce a heaven on earth. This is my desire for every young couple and for every home.

—From Ed Wheat, M.D., and Gaye Wheat, *Intended for Pleasure.* Old Tappan, N.J.: Fleming H. Revell Co., 1981.

FOR FURTHER READING:

Hardisty, Margaret and George. *How to Enrich Your Marriage*. Eugene, Ore.: Harvest House Publishers, 1978.

Landorf, Joyce. *Tough and Tender*. Old Tappan, N.J.: Fleming H. Revell Co., 1981.

Scanzoni, John. *Love and Negotiate: Creative Conflict in Marriage*. Waco, Tex.: Word Books, 1979.

Swindoll, Charles R. *Strike the Original Match*. Portland: Multnomah Press, 1980.

Wiese, Bennard R., and Steinmetz, Urban G. *Everything You Need to Know to Stay Married and Like It*. Grand Rapids: Zondervan Publishing House, 1975.

MASTURBATION

MASTURBATION is a conscious act which gives relief from the craving desire for the satisfaction of sexual appetite. This appetite is essentially healthy and natural, but in the Christian should be yielded to the controlling power of the Spirit of God. Masturbation is now known to be so common a practice that it is difficult to justify the former arguments that it is abnormal or unnatural. It is not, in itself, a sign of mental, emotional, or personality disorder. Physicians are now agreed that it is not physically harmful in any way, but it can cause shame and guilt in those who have been brought up to believe it is a sin.

In the male, nocturnal emissions at regular intervals provide the physiological release of the spermatic fluid stored in the seminal vesicles. Without masturbation, these would normally occur about every two or three weeks in a young man. However, they in no way reduce the emotional or psychological tensions associated with pent-up sexual urges.

Women and girls also have sexual urges which can be relieved by self-stimulation to the point of orgasm. According to reputable medical surveys, however, the percentage of single women who masturbate is considerably less than the 99 percent ascribed to males.

According to the strictest interpretation of the church's teaching, the good Christian would be expected to have no sexual activity of any sort from puberty until his wedding night. I submit that this is an unrealistic expectation for a healthy young person, unless he has achieved a degree of spiritual maturity considerably in advance of his years. Indeed, only a deeply devout person using all the spiritual resources available to him can successfully combat so powerful a drive as the need for sexual release. Complete abstinence *can* be achieved by a young person but such a saint is indeed very rare.

For the Christian, the problem is that it usually causes guilt feelings which adversely affect his inner peace and fellowship with Christ. He feels guilty because he believes that masturbation is a sin. The guilt comes not so much because of the act itself but rather because of the accompanying fantasy of performing sexual intercourse. The fantasied object is usually someone of the opposite sex to whom one is not married, and the sin consists of enjoying the thoughts and feelings of imagined fornication or adultery. To masturbate, therefore, is to indulge the ego with thoughts primarily focused on self-gratification rather than on the unselfish giving of pleasure to another. Fantasy is almost always a stronger stimulus to the mind than reality and, since the fantasied object is usually unattainable, achievement of satisfaction in reality becomes more difficult. Masturbation thus reduces the ability to enjoy to the very fullest that highest form of human communication, the reality of sexual intercourse within marriage.

Masturbation *per se* is not mentioned in the Bible, though Paul indicts those who "dishonour their own bodies" and who are "abusers of themselves" (*see* Romans 1:24; 1 Corinthians 6:9). The "sin of Onan" (*see* Genesis 38:8–10), regarded by nineteenth-century preachers as this form of self-abuse, was actually not masturbation but coitus interruptus. In defiance of his duty to his deceased brother's wife to give her a child as required by levirate law (*see* Deuteronomy 25:5) Onan refused to obey by withdrawing during intercourse to prevent conception. His sin, which brought the penalty of death, was not the fruitless ejaculation, but the disobeying of the law.

In the Sermon on the Mount, Jesus said: ". . . whosoever looketh on a woman to lust after her hath committed adultery with her already in his heart" (Matthew 5:28). This further emphasizes that it is primarily the fantasied thought which is the real sin.

The young person who desires God's will in his life knows that, when he has sinned, a sincere repentance leads to total forgiveness and full restoration of fellowship with Christ. True repentance involves the sincere desire not to repeat the repented sin, and this desire to avoid the sin in the future leads to the feeling of restored peace within. This is almost impossible, however, with masturbation because the Christian knows that he is extremely unlikely never to do it again. He doubts if God can really forgive him when he knows he will probably repeat the sin a few days later. For this reason he is prevented from receiving the emotional freedom that comes with assurance of forgiveness.

In counseling a young person, my approach essentially is to point out that even though masturbation is a sin, God understands, because He made us all the way we are. From time to time the young person needs some emotional and sexual release from tension. It can be regarded as a sort of safety valve. Certainly it represents the lesser of two evils if the alternatives to masturbation were either fornication or the development of acute internal tension or neurotic anxiety. Some therapists try to tell their patients that it is normal, healthy legitimate fun—even a gift of God. The problem is that if the patient believes it is a sin, he will still feel guilty.

The Christian who wants to avoid the spiritually growth-stifling guilt to which masturbation often leads should remember two things: First, if he believes it is a sin, he should repent of it as sincerely as he can but not allow the possibility of future sin to come between him and his Lord. He should live one step at a time. Forgiveness means cleansing, which leads to fresh power in his life. Once confessed, he should fully accept the promised forgiveness in Christ and then forget the sin and move on.

Second, he should so organize his life that he is physically or intellectually occupied most of his waking day. There is nothing like boredom to stimulate wandering erotic thoughts. He should get rid of pornographic pictures and literature, and avoid movies which are made with the intention of stimulating his sexual urges. Needed rest and relaxation can be enjoyed without having an empty mind which is vulnerable to thoughts and desires unworthy of his own highest moral aspirations. It is a well-established psychological fact that when imagination and will are in conflict, imagination always wins. If imagination or fantasizing can be controlled, the will can then more easily control the actions. Positive activities and positive thinking are the greatest cornerstones of healthy living. "Casting down imaginations . . . and bringing into captivity every thought to the obedience of Christ" (2 Corinthians 10:5).

A more positive approach is to encourage the young person to reduce the craving as well as the act itself. One can almost never succeed in stopping masturbation by gritting the teeth and determining to exercise supreme acts of self-control. This usually only lasts a short while and almost inevitably ends in failure, with yet another round of remorse. The psychological term used to describe the positive reduction of craving is *sublimation.* Sublimation, in psychoanalytic terms, means the deflection of the energies of instinctual drives to aims that are more acceptable to the ego and superego. Sexual craving can be reduced by directing energy into more socially acceptable activities.

It is well known that the track athlete, football star, or competitive swimmer generally has little difficulty controlling himself the night before the big event. There are more important things on his mind, and in any case he often believes (erroneously) that continence during the previous day or two will enhance his athletic performance later. The essential point is that substitution of athletic activities for masturbation has provided an alternative focus for emotional energies.

We are not all competitive athletes, but the same principle can be applied to any healthy activity which sufficiently engrosses the individual's interest and enthusiasm. Intellectual or social pursuits which absorb his time and energies help to take his mind off his sexual urges. Paradoxically, even dating can actually reduce the frequency of masturbation in spite of the associated physical closeness to the opposite sex. If the relationship is a reasonably platonic one, even with warm affections expressed verbally, the natural wholesome activity of spending time with the opposite sex without being sexually stimulated to the point of genital contact can itself provide healthy sublimation of the sex drive.

All that has been said so far has been with respect to the healthy normal young person,

male or female, whose personal Christian life has been affected by guilt over masturbation. There are, however, cases where the practice becomes, not merely a natural physiological release mechanism, but definitely excessive and therefore pathological. To masturbate several times daily, for example, indicates serious underlying emotional problems in need of psychiatric treatment or at least personal counseling. Social maladjustment, insecurity, fear of inadequacy, feelings of frustration or rejection, fear of close interpersonal relationships, an abnormally overdeveloped sex drive, or any sexual perversion are all neurotic or personality problems which can lead to excessively frequent masturbation. This is merely a symptom, however, and the basic causes are urgently in need of professional help without which the sufferer is unlikely to improve.

—From O. Quentin Hyder, M.D., *The People You Live With.* Old Tappan, N.J.: Fleming H. Revell Co., 1975.

FOR FURTHER READING:

Adams, Jay E. *The Big Umbrella.* Grand Rapids: Baker Book House, 1976.

Miles, Herbert J. *Sexual Understanding Before Marriage.* Grand Rapids: Zondervan Publishing House, 1972.

Trobisch, Walter and Ingrid. *My Beautiful Feeling: Letters to Ilona.* Downers Grove, Ill.: Inter-Varsity Press, 1976.

MENSTRUATION

IN THE OVARIES and the uterus, estrogen interacts with several other hormones to cause ovulation and menstruation. Ovulation is the process in which a microscopic egg (ovum) which has lain sleeping in the ovary begins to grow and is pushed out of its tiny pocket into the body cavity in the pelvis. Normally it is sucked up at once by the soft, waving motions of the fimbria into one of the Fallopian tubes, then moved gently into the womb.

While the ovary has been busy producing the ovum, the womb has been at work building up a velvety lining, rich with little blood vessels and nourishing fluid. If the egg is united with a sperm while it is in the Fallopian tube or the womb, it will rest on this soft uterine lining and then nestle in to begin the long process of becoming a baby. If it is not fertilized by the male sperm, it will die in a day or two and later will pass out of the womb along with some blood, serum, and tissue that were waiting for it. This is called menstruation. Many years ago, I was told, a medical student described this process as "the weeping of a disappointed womb." While this is picturesque language for the womb, it doesn't always describe the feeling of the woman!

The process of ovulation takes place about once every four weeks. Usually this happens midway between menstrual periods, though it may be as early as one week after or as late as a week before the period. While the average menstrual cycle is twenty-eight days, many women have shorter or longer ones. The period of menstruation may last from three days or less to a week or more. Not only do these facts vary from woman to woman but occasionally within a person, as well. This does not necessarily mean there is anything wrong.

A change in schedule, moving, emotional upsets, physical illnesses, and many other factors may influence the delicate and intricate processes that are responsible for women's menstrual periods. Furthermore, it may take many months, or even years, for a young woman to settle into her individual cycle. It is important to know this to avoid worry and to realize the importance of being

sexually responsible. Many girls believe that ovulation does not take place in the early months of their menstrual periods. While ovulation is irregular at first, it does frequently occur from the very first period, and as soon as ovulation begins, pregnancy can take place. I have seen several pregnant young girls who did not know this significant fact!

The signs of trouble with a girl's menstruation need to be noted. For these, a physician should be consulted. 1. A total irregularity of periods continuing two years after menarche (the first period). 2. Excessive bleeding—using more than one regular box of pads or tampons (and soaking them) per period. 3. Bleeding between regular periods. 4. Severe pain, cramping, and especially a tendency to faint during a period. Usually these symptoms do not indicate serious trouble, but a physical evaluation by a competent doctor can reassure both the girl and her parents.

Every girl needs to understand menstruation and be prepared for it before it takes place. You need to watch your daughter for signs of her sexual development. The growth of hair in the pubic area (groin) and under the arms usually begins about one year before menstruation will take place. The growth of breast tissue also precedes this process by one or two years. While it may be difficult to see these changes in girls, who prefer a great deal of privacy, your awareness will help. Don't be afraid to ask your daughter, and by all means, as soon as you even suspect that she is approaching puberty, discuss it with her and tell her what to expect.

Because you, the mother, or an older daughter began menstruation at age fourteen is no reason to believe any other girls in your family will start at that age. Each woman has her own special alarm clock. So observe, think, and talk. Tell your daughter

271

what is beginning to happen to her, what it means, and how to take care of herself physically as well as socially. The possibility of pregnancy needs to be explained, and at this time, I believe it is urgently important that each girl learn about sexual intercourse and pregnancy.

As a young adolescent, I did not know how a girl became pregnant. I knew only that a missed menstrual period might mean pregnancy. So when I was late (and I was one of those irregular people) I would worry. Perhaps, I feared, I had become pregnant from a toilet seat or the abhorred kisses of my girl friend's overly affectionate father. In my reserved family, I did not know that I could have asked and found reassurance. Unnecessary worry could so easily have been prevented had I been taught the simple facts about sexual relations and conception.

Debbie, at twelve, was pregnant and in a home for unwed mothers. The social worker, in taking a history, asked her when she had started to date. Debbie looked at her in utter amazement. "Why, Mrs. Jones," she said, "I'm too young to date!" Debbie tragically taught me that sex education needs to be a constant process and that rules are not enough. She had become pregnant while on a walk during halftime at a basketball game.

An almost universal problem related to menstrual periods is the physical pain that accompanies them. In Genesis, we are told that as a result of Eve's disobedience to God's orders against eating the fruit of the tree of knowledge of good and evil, she would have to bear her young in sorrow and pain. Today, a slang expression for menstruation is "the curse." Many girls exaggerate this discomfort and some even take advantage of it to gain an extra day in bed, but there is no doubt that it is an uncomfortable and even miserable time for some.

As part of the hormone cycle that is responsible for menstrual periods, for a week

or more before their periods women store up fluid in their bodies' tissues. This may amount to several pounds and will, in most women, produce a feeling of physical heaviness and emotional tension. They cry easily, feel gloomy, have headaches and a tendency to be explosively angry. Unfortunately, many women today deny this process because they feel it means they are in some way inferior to men. Instead of denying them, women need to be aware of these physical differences in order to take good care of their bodies.

Besides the fluid accumulation, there are other factors that cause menstrual cramps or discomfort. One of these is the increased size of blood vessels in the pelvic area. Sometimes constipation may add to the sense of pelvic pressure. General fatigue or mild infections such as colds or flu are likely to affect the degree of discomfort.

There is a remarkable influence on menstrual discomfort by one's attitude. Carol began her menstruation at the age of eleven. She resented the inconvenience of those monthly periods and felt especially put upon since none of her friends as yet shared in this experience. She was irritable and moody and struggled against the discomfort, needing a heating pad, several hours in bed, and constant sympathy. After some months of such general misery, she said to her mother, "Well, I guess there's not a thing in the world I can do about it, so I'll just have to make the best of it." She put away the heating pad, initiated daily exercises, ate a balanced diet, and tried to get extra rest during the more difficult days. Carol's attitude didn't eliminate all the discomfort, but it enabled her to cope successfully with the realities of life and helped her develop maturity and wisdom.

A relatively new discovery shows that severe menstrual cramps are associated with the level of still another hormonelike substance called "prostaglandin." While this discovery is new and the treatment is experimental, there is great promise of real relief from the few truly severe cases of menstrual misery caused by this.

The use of pads and tampons to absorb the menstrual flow is historic. For several decades, schools have shown films and led discussions for preadolescent girls and their mothers. These are wonderful opportunities for parents to teach, guide, and share in this important event in their daughter's lives. A mother's sharing of the memories and feelings of her own puberty can draw her daughter close in a bond of understanding. This is the time for a mother to invite her child into the world of womanhood and begin teaching her how to become a beautiful woman. By accepting the fact of her daughter's new, though incomplete, adulthood many of the troublesome mother-daughter conflicts of the teen years can be avoided.

Finally, the use of tampons needs to be discussed. The widespread mass-media advertising campaigns leave little privacy to today's woman, so various sanitary supplies are well known. Tampons are specially made devices that fit into the vagina and absorb the menstrual flow directly from the womb. They are convenient, comfortable, and allow more freedom than do pads in activities such as swimming. Some people believe, however, that they cannot be used by a young woman who is a virgin.

Let me explain that in girls there is a protective membrane that partially covers the opening to the vagina. It is called the "hymen" and protects a child from getting dirt or germs into the genital area. Normally, there is an opening in this that adequately allows for the flow of the menstrual discharge and is usually big enough to easily insert a tampon. Some mothers have found their daughters using these without their knowledge and panic, thinking the girl has

had sexual intercourse and broken the hymen. This is not necessarily true. It is possible for the hymen to tear through strenuous activities or minor injuries. On the other hand, in less than 10 percent of women, the hymen is so tough and the opening so small that tampons cannot be used. Such young women may need to consult a physician regarding possible treatment for this condition.

Newspapers have widely publicized a rare but occasionally fatal disease called "toxic shock syndrome," which may occur during menstruation. Gynecologists believe the evidence relating this syndrome to the use of tampons is as yet inconclusive. It would be wise for each woman to consult her doctor on this subject.

Boys also need to understand the process of menstruation in girls. The proper time to discuss it is not as crucial as with girls, but they may avoid or better handle some embarrassing situations by knowing about this process before they start dating. Occasionally a girl will have an accident while menstruating, resulting in blood stains on her clothing. If boys understand this, they need not stare or laugh out of their uneasiness. When a boy starts dating, there will be some times when his special girl simply doesn't feel like taking part in a tennis game or going swimming. If the boy understands why, he can help her choose a quieter event or simply postpone the date without embarrassment.

Many young people today discuss sexual issues of all sorts very openly, and much of this seems wholesome. When a girl's period, however, is called "the curse" or she is described as being "on the rag," I feel the negative implication is far from wholesome! A simple explanation by a girl that she is having her period seems quite acceptable. If a girl is not comfortable even with this, however, the boy who knows can value her privacy and not press her for explanations.

I see no reason that a boy should not be told the entire story about ovulation and menstruation, just as a girl is told. He needs, however, to hear it in the framework of respect and dignity, not uneasiness, ridicule, or put-downs. The use of proper words rather than slang is a part of both good attitudes and right information.

—From Grace Ketterman, M.D., *How to Teach Your Child About Sex.* Old Tappan, N.J.: Fleming H. Revell Co., 1981.

FOR FURTHER READING:

Dalton, Katherina. *Once a Month.* Pomona, Calif.: Hunter House, 1979.

Dobson, James C. *What Wives Wish Their Husbands Knew About Women.* Wheaton, Ill.: Tyndale House Publishers, 1975.

MID-LIFE CRISIS

THE EXPRESSION, "mid-life crisis" has been popularized, more than any one thing, by *Passages.* The mid-life crisis . . . has the greatest opportunity for bringing constructive change to your life or destruction and hopelessness. It will become the old age of youth or the youth of old age. When secular people act responsibly, they find that life moves more constructively. I believe, however, that Christians have unique resources for facing the mid-life crises that are unknown outside the family of God.

Though talking about having a mid-life crisis is now fashionable, the experience of it is certainly not new. Author Joe Bayly observes, "The mid-life crisis is not some new discovery by our super-brilliant American psychologists. Saul went through it. So did

David. And Solomon. They make good case studies" (Joseph Bayly, "The Me Generation," *Eternity,* October 1977, p. 81).

The "destruction that wasteth at noonday" is a phrase from Psalm 91 that effectively describes (though that is not its biblical intention) the feelings that plague people at this time of their lives. This psalm is a powerful promise of God's care and protection that the believer can claim:

He that dwelleth in the secret place of the most High shall abide under the shadow of the Almighty. I will say of the Lord, He is my refuge and my fortress: my God; in him will I trust. Surely he shall deliver thee from the snare of the fowler, and from the noisome pestilence. He shall cover thee with his feathers, and under his wings shalt thou trust: his truth shall be thy shield and buckler. Thou shalt not be afraid for the terror by night: nor for the arrow that flieth by day; Nor for the pestilence that walketh in darkness; nor for the destruction that wasteth at noonday (Psalms 91:1–6 KJV).

Mid-life and Middle Age. Our language can be confusing when we talk about mid-life and middle age, for they are not the same. Mid-life is a time of upheaval, uncertainty, and questioning. Middle age, on the other hand, is marked by growth, stability, serenity, and satisfaction. For many, the questions of adolescence that they thought were settled, rear their confusing heads again. Interestingly, this frequently coincides with the adolescence of their children. So perhaps one reason many parents have difficulty helping their teenage children with their questions, is that they are unable to answer the same questions for themselves. But by middle age, they have found a more relaxed life-stance and can enjoy their grandchildren.

Though the term "mid-life" appears to be mathematically derived (35 is half of the life expectancy of 70), its onset is not mathematically predictable. The internal life-clock is paced by a variety of outward elements: age at marriage and age of spouse, age and number of children, career history. "Working-class men describe themselves as middle-aged at 40 and old by 60. Business executives and professionals, by contrast, do not see themselves as reaching middle age until 50, and old age means 70 to them" (Gail Sheehy, *Passages*).

The passing of time and an awareness of aging are at the core of the mid-life crisis. The youthful sense of limitless, infinite time vanishes. The central question is, What am I going to do with the rest of my life?

Men and women seem to respond in almost opposite ways to that question. For men and career women, the time is compressed to an urgency to do something significant before it is too late. Sheehy characterized the attitude of the mid-life men and career women this way: " 'Time is running out. Time must be beaten. Can I accomplish all that I'd hoped before it's too late?' To women who have been at home, time is suddenly seen as long: 'Look at all the time ahead! After the children are gone, what will I do with it?' " (Sheehy, *Passages*, p. 353).

Like many other predictable crises of life, this one passes. The questions and doubts of mid-life may seem trivial or even juvenile from the perspective of middle age, but at the time they are being experienced, they are real and intense. It hardly seems possible that what is so distressing and perplexing today will be a chuckle of private embarrassment in a few years. For this reason, you need to prepare to act when these difficult

days come, and not be swept away in their confusing eddies and crosscurrents.

The Brevity of Life.   The Psalms again offer a perspective on the passage of life and the priorities of its brevity. Moses spoke from the security of the Lord's "dwelling place in all generations" when he wrote of life's frustrating briefness (Psalms 90:9–12 KJV):

For all our days are passed away in thy wrath: we spend our years as a tale that is told. The days of our years are threescore years and ten; and if by reason of strength they be fourscore years, yet is their strength labour and sorrow; for it is soon cut off, and we fly away. Who knoweth the power of thine anger? even according to thy fear, so is thy wrath. So teach us to number our days, that we may apply our hearts to wisdom.

Death is the inexorable, inescapable limit to human dreams. Most people have half of their lives ahead of them at the mid-life crossing, but are aware of the final deadline creeping closer. Their own death becomes a reality for the first time and more of life seems behind them than ahead of them.

A specific death may bring this realization. Perhaps the first of their parents or their spouse's parents dies. The grief of that is enough, but if they subtract their age from that of the deceased, they recognize the limited time that is left. When the last of these parents is gone, the blow can be even greater. They have fully "come-of-age" and become the senior generation.

If the deaths of parents is the frontal attack, the deaths of friends is the sneak attack from the flank. People are unprepared for facing the mortality of those their same age. When my friend, Paul Little, of Inter-Varsity died in an accident, I was stunned. He was younger than I and I began to feel my days were numbered. Even a close call can leave someone gasping, "That could have been me!" . . .

A *Turning Point.* More than any other crisis, mid-life fulfills the definition of a crisis, drawn from Erik Erikson, . . . "Not a catastrophe, but a turning point, a crucial period of increasing vulnerability and heightened potential." It is a time of reevaluating dreams and goals. Whether or not the first half of your life has seen your dreams come true, you are vulnerable at mid-life. How well I know the struggle!

On the surface, those who have succeeded early in their careers may not seem susceptible to the disillusionment that comes at mid-life. However, without a new goal and a new reason to expend energy, the rest of life becomes hollow. Especially dangerous are careers built on youth, accompanied by a great deal of public recognition. Many professional athletes, entertainers, and entrepreneurs have had difficulty finding a suitable goal to follow early success, and their later lives have been wasted. Alexander the Great is reported to have wept as a young man that there were no more worlds to conquer.

Some who have seemingly done it all before 30 have launched into new endeavors to find even greater fulfillment. Charles Percy had become president of Bell and Howell before he was 30. He is credited with turning a sagging company into a profitable success. Where could he go when he was already on top of the corporate heap? He turned to public service and has been an active and renowned U.S. Senator.

More common, though, is the person whose dreams have not been fulfilled by age 35. Few people are able to reach their secret goals. If this is your situation, as is quite likely, you may feel that your life has been wasted. You may doubt your competence

and question whether you have found your place in the world. You may give up believing that your dream was ever possible, valid, or worthy.

If these feelings take their natural course, you will dig yourself into despair. You will lose your sense of self-respect and ask how you could have been so foolish as to think you could realize your dream. You may even feel guilty that you committed yourself to such an illusory goal. And, perhaps worst of all, you may feel guilty that you sold out your dream, your ideals, your very self to get ahead when getting ahead turned out to be an empty prize.

As these emotions sweep down on you, you may discover a whole emotional dimension of your inner self. This can be an emotion-laden time of life which may catch you by surprise. Men, particularly, are alarmed at the emotions that emerge. If you let these emotions determine the course of the crisis, you will find only disappointment. You can, however, discover a new meaning and fulfillment in life if you act to guide your journey through the transition.

I remember the trauma and confusion of my mid-life experience. I had traveled for years in a God-blessed ministry and had had more opportunities than I could say grace over. Outwardly, there was no reason to feel restless, but I could not go on, even though many new avenues of ministry were open to me. Early every morning I drove to a park to meditate and pray. I had an empty feeling that I was on the sidelines and the whole work of God would go by me. I longed to be in the harvest field and made a new commitment to God and whatever He wanted. God graciously helped me. The new vision, positive emotions, and clear guidance that emerged from this crisis thrust me into the greatest opportunity of my life.

The potential for disaster, however, is real and significant. When you begin to feel you have the experience and maturity to give others guidance, particularly your teenage children, you lose your own sense of direction. But the opportunity for a renewed and more realistic vision, a more focused and genuine contribution is also great. A serious self-evaluation is necessary, with possible alterations in your course of action.

If your priorities have put family and church ahead of your job, you will find that getting satisfaction through serving will be much easier than if career success has been your consuming life goal.

Self-evaluation. To undergo a systematic self-evaluation at mid-life may be threatening. It may seem like a return to your high school or college career guidance counselor. Yet it is the most wholesome act of faith you can take at this time. It affirms you still believe God has something for you. He does, and you can find it. You might try reading up on some great people who have achieved some of their most significant accomplishments in the second half of their lives: C. S. Lewis, Corrie ten Boom, T. S. Eliot, Albert Einstein, Paul Tournier, Igor Stravinsky, Ethel Waters, Margaret Mead, Norman Rockwell, Malcolm Muggeridge, Katherine Hepburn, Pablo Picasso, and Thomas Edison.

To do the evaluation requires commitment, but the commitment that really counts is to change your life pattern in response to what you learn. As frustrating as the career you have now may be, it is a security. The risk of starting over is frightening. However, it is a risk you can take if you trust God with the outcome of your life.

Changing Relationships. Relationships change with time even more than careers, for they are dynamic and constantly readjusted. Several primary relationships shift noticeably at mid-life and need to be rene-

gotiated. Your relationship with your spouse is of first importance, followed by your relationship with your children. Your parents alter their relationship to you at this time; there is a shift in your friendships.

You will encounter a great deal of tension and stress if you allow your relationships to drift through this period. Social pressures will pull against your intentions.

Consider marriage: even among Christians, divorce seems to be considered an avenue for making this adjustment in the marriage relationship. But to take that approach is to treat the marriage commitment too lightly. The commitment is permanent and within this permanence you can affirm that God has drawn you together and can guide you through the remainder of your lives. You can trust Him to make each of you a support to the other, rather than an unbearable burden.

For example, contrast two husbands Joe Bayly describes: "I heard of a man whose wife was diagnosed as having cancer. His first reaction? 'I'll divorce her.' . . . I knew another man whose wife was totally incapacitated by a stroke. For nine years, until he himself was struck down, he took care of her total needs. After that long period, she had no bedsore. Two weeks after she was put in a nursing home, she developed them; another two weeks, and she died" (Bayly, "The Me Generation," *Eternity*, p. 81).

If you are committed to each other, you can face the prospect of changing together. The alternative is drifting apart. You can trust God to give you a common ground of marital fellowship even when you discover differences you never knew you had. Then you can courageously embark on an open evaluation of your marriage which is the only way to bring new vitality into your mid-life relationship. The alternative is deadly boredom.

This evaluation process can easily degenerate into a struggle between you if there is not a positive attitude. The natural human tendency is to fix blame on the other. Rather than seeing a shared responsibility to work on the relationship, each tries to blame the other for not only the marriage troubles but all of the problems of this mid-life muddle— the restlessness, heightened emotional needs, and changing roles.

Seeking Professional Help.   Often, "the two people go round and round the accusation tree until one of them says, 'You really need some help. I think you should see a psychiatrist or a marriage counselor.' The trouble with this suggestion is the motive. What the mate usually wants is a judgment that the other is the guilty party. Sensing this, the partner who has been told to go to a psychiatrist often digs in his or her heels and refuses because to set foot inside this arbiter's office would be an admission that 'I'm the sick one' " (Sheehy, *Passages*).

I know I've said it before, but it is so important I must say it again. Seek help if you get to the place where you are not making progress on your own. This is much wiser than fighting your way through and permanently damaging your relationship. Your pastor is probably the best person to start with. A responsible pastor will soon detect if your problem is beyond his ability to help and will send you to another professional. This move can usually only be made as a joint effort: share the problem together and seek help together.

If you feel that outside help is needed, but your partner refuses to go, swallow your pride and go by yourself. You will thus assume responsibility for your share of the problem and your share of the solution. I've often seen a stalemate broken when a partner steps out of the accusing role and puts himself in the help-seeking role. The con-

ventional defenses of an uncooperative partner are turned around. Whatever you do, don't use this as a new weapon on your spouse or seek for vindication of your position. Honestly ask God to enable the counselor to give you the understanding you need. In this way, you can commit yourself to positive action as a start toward improving the relationship. You are the key in this situation.

The mid-life crisis could be described as the "death-throes" of adolescence. It is a necessary upheaval and rethinking before the maturity of middle age. You may look to your parents, as you did when you were an adolescent, but may be shocked at how little they can help. One or both of your parents may have died, or may be weakening physically and lacking the wisdom you need for coping with your world. They may even be looking to you to be their caretaker, reversing the parent-child role.

Career Changes.   Constructive action on the career front can help you resolve other mid-life issues. It can give you a stable base from which to reestablish relationships with your spouse, your children, and your parents. A diligent reevaluation of your life priorities, giving success a proper place behind spiritual and family relationships, will make a career change less distressing. Your new career direction may even bring growth to these relationships rather than additional frustration and discord.

Working through career uncertainty can give you a whole new lease on life and does not necessarily mean you must change jobs.

One couple lived their whole lives in the upper Midwest. The husband had grown restless and when their last child was married they both felt free to move. Financial responsibilities were minimal, with only two of them, and the risks of moving manageable. They sold their home and with great expectations moved to the Southwest. But what had been a winter escape from snow became an oven in the summer. They found it difficult to establish strong relationships in a new church and the new job was not as ideal as had been expected. They decided to return to their old hometown and lived in an apartment till they could find a suitable home to purchase. The experiment was costly and unpleasant, but they learned. They could never have been satisfied with the old town, the old job, and the old church, had they not made the pilgrimage. The risk of action was necessary to know the direction for the future.

Another couple made a similar move when the last child was married, which precipitated several years of disorientation before finding a new niche. They had lived in the same house for 20 years, the husband had always worked for the same company, and they attended the same church for 30 years.

He quit that job and took another in an entirely different field, though they stayed in the same area. That proved unsatisfactory, so they explored other possibilities. The direction of their church began to change and they felt rootless and disappointed. Finally, they moved to another city and struggled through several other disappointments. It was a tough time of change and adjustment, but they are now both settled in satisfying jobs in two Christian organizations with a sense of ministry they never had before.

A transition may be forced on us rather than voluntarily chosen. This may be God's way of directing us to the future. Two friends of mine—a married couple—experienced this. They both lost their good jobs at about the same time. What could have caused panic became an opportunity. They took over a gas and grocery operation in a booming suburb, and are running the business together. They have a closer relationship than ever before because they feel the pressure of the business drawing them together. In spite of the expected difficulties, both marriage and business are now thriving.

These three couples took different paths through the mid-life crisis. Yet they shared in common the commitment to take action that implied risk. In each case they faced difficulty. The first couple found the difficulty to be an affirmation of their previous life-style. The second persevered through the difficulty to find a new fulfillment in ministry jobs for both husband and wife. The third couple discovered that the difficulties of starting a new business drew them together and helped develop their marriage relationship more fully. In every case, they had to do something to know if they were on the right track. They had to trust God with the risk of their futures. They did not give up when the emotions and disruptions of mid-life surprised them and derailed what they had assumed would always be stable.

The crises brought them to the youth of old age and they started over with new vision, vigor and victory.

—From J. Allan Petersen, *Conquering Family Stress*. Wheaton, Ill.: Victor Books, 1978.

FOR FURTHER READING:

Barks, Herb. *Prime Time: Moving Into Middle Age with Style*. Nashville: Thomas Nelson Inc., 1978.

Conway, Jim. *Men in Mid-Life Crisis*. Elgin, Ill.: David C. Cook Publishing Co., 1978.

Conway, Sally. *You and Your Husband's Mid-Life Crisis*. Elgin, Ill.: David C. Cook Publishing Co., 1981.

Morley, David C. *Halfway Up the Mountain*. Old Tappan, N.J.: Fleming H. Revell Co., 1979.

Ray, David. *The Forty-Plus Handbook*. Waco, Tex.: Word Books, 1979.

MODERN MOTHER

WOMEN IN THE PAST 50 years have not merely exchanged old occupations for new ones. They have managed to become voters, property owners, educated people, and job holders in addition to the formerly full-time role of wife and mother. The young girl today can reasonably expect to have an education as good as her brother's, to find work she enjoys in business or a profession until she marries and has children, and to go back to the same or some other work of her choice when her children are older.

A modern bride can look forward to managing her household without dictation from family elders. She will share equally with her husband in planning their way of living, their finances, their children's education, even in making decisions about his job or business advancement. She will be sought after as a member of P.T.A. and other organizations and can have a voice in school policy, in local affairs, and in national issues if she chooses. She takes it for granted that she will be her husband's companion on all levels and will be listened to on any subject in which she is interested and about which she is informed. All this, unheard of in her great-grandmother's day, is now part of a woman's normal living, besides the running of her household and the rearing of her children. Most women enjoy some part of these new freedoms and broadened horizons. With all their active, busy lives, they are young and vigorous at 40 and even 50, with years of living still ahead.

Such achievements are not painlessly absorbed. Many women meet every day, with courage and ingenuity, problems their great-grandmothers would scarcely understand. Many a modern mother feels that each new advantage brings its own crop of difficulties. Her valued education and job experience have opened windows on the world which seem to shut tight again when she turns to full-time housekeeping and child rearing. Her independence of relatives, in a home of her own, is sometimes a lonely business; she would be grateful for an aunt to hold the baby, a nephew to run to the store, or just anyone more than six years old to talk to during the day.

Her very labor-saving devices make more labor: she does all the washing in her home laundry instead of sending some to a commercial laundry; she freezes fresh fruits and vegetables in season to make economic use of her freezer. If she has the family car by day, she is likely to be chauffeuring her children to Scout meetings, to lessons and parties long after they are old enough to walk or take the bus, and she does not only the marketing but all the family errands besides.

Even the better health and youthfulness of her middle years become a problem. With her energies and interests still unspent, with her small family grown, what is she to do with the added life expectancy presented to her?

Meanwhile standards of child care and family living have risen. The modern mother thinks about and decides for herself many questions that traditionally were decided by rule of thumb and applied to every child whether suitable or not. This, too, makes new demands on her.

Wanting the best for her husband and children, for her home, and for herself, the modern mother sets her standards of performance high. She expects a great deal of herself, and a great deal is expected of her. To be a wise mother, sensitive to each child's needs; to be an attractive, companionable wife; to be a competent housekeeper and budget manager, a useful member of the community, and perhaps a wage earner as well sometimes seems too much to ask of one human being.

There are signs that young mothers today

are beginning to feel more comfortable in their many-sided role. Fathers are taking a hand with the children and the housework whether or not the mothers are also contributing to the family income.

Many young mothers are finding ways to overcome their isolation. They get an afternoon of refreshing leisure by taking each other's children, turn and turn about; in some communities of young families this custom has led to cooperative nursery schools. The growth of community activities has opened up, to many women in the home, opportunities of meeting and working with others. The volunteer organizations are more realistic in their demands on young mothers today than in the past. With the expansion of adult education, study groups and courses in the arts and skills, both for home and for business, are giving many women the chance to follow an interest of their own for personal satisfaction, sometimes to develop or revive a business skill for a paid job when their children are older.

The question whether to combine home-making with a job is bluntly settled for many by economic necessity, and with young children this brings complicated problems. It is beginning to be recognized, however, that mothers who work need help from the community. Day-care centers, low-fee nursery schools, foster day-care plans, and afternoon recreation centers for school-age children offer some relief.

Often today a wife seeks a job, not to help with bare necessities, but because it takes two incomes to maintain the desired standards of living. Her situation will improve as more employers in more areas of business and industry recognize the real economy of part-time employment. So far only a few islands offer a foothold to the woman with only part of her day free for paid employment; in the department stores, for instance, employees who come late and leave early

solve the problem of peak hours during the day. Women have exerted much imagination in finding ways to earn money through small businesses or services carried on at home.

Solving one problem often leads to the solution of another. The mother of school-age children who takes on outside work, whether paid or volunteer, relieves her own isolation and begins to lay up interests and skills for the time when her children are grown. Her children, at the same time, have the valued experience of taking more responsibility for themselves and in the home.

Part of the solution, too, lies in the way girls manage their education and preparation for womanhood. Instead of planning only for a job or profession in place of marriage, a young woman today can prepare herself for work combined with marriage and motherhood, or work that can be carried on with modifications or interruptions if she marries.

Her preparation for the other side of her future life, the wife-and-mother role, may or may not include homemaking courses, but she can surely absorb the household arts as she grows up. Her mother, of course, will need to recognize that it is no service to a daughter to protect her from home responsibilities. Even though in her family there may be no babies or little children for a young girl to help care for, she can begin early to cook and clean with her mother, help to shop for herself and other members of the family, and learn some of the wisdom that mothers have always passed on to their daughters. Nor is this home teaching necessarily limited to girls. Like their fathers, many boys today learn to shop at the supermarket, to run the vacuum cleaner and washing machine, often to cook, and certainly to set the table and wash the dishes. The growing tendency today to let children share in family work and planning is valuable preparation for their future role as mothers and fathers—and incidentally lightens the modern mother's burden.

In a century of unprecedented technical and scientific progress, each day continues to bring new knowledge and new ways, and each change brings its own problems. Not only the modern mother, but her husband and children, too, must absorb these changes. It is important to recognize the problems, but it is also important to assess the gains. Frozen foods and canned baby foods, detergents and running water and a gas or electric range certainly make life easier, to say nothing of the telephone to save a trip or bring help in time of need. The open doors to education are confusing, but they give each woman a measure of freedom to make her own choices, set her own goals, and develop a way of being a modern mother to her own satisfaction.

—From *The New Encyclopedia of Child Care and Guidance.* Garden City, N.Y.: Doubleday & Co., 1968.

FOR FURTHER READING:

Bush, Barbara. *Successful Motherhood.* Grand Rapids: Zondervan Publishing House, 1981.

Doan, Eleanor. *A Mother's Sourcebook of Inspiration.* Grand Rapids: Zondervan Publishing House, 1969.

Garrison, Jayne. *The ABCs of Christian Mothering.* Wheaton, Ill.: Tyndale House Publishers.

Howard, Linda. *Mothers Are People Too.* Plainfield, N.J.: Logos International, 1976.

Rockness, Muriel Huffman. *Keep These Things, Ponder Them in Your Heart.* Garden City, N.Y.: Doubleday & Co., 1979.

MONEY

LEARNING ABOUT MONEY matters begins in the home and serves as a strong preventive measure for later problems. Imparting knowledge to their children about money and material things is one of the most critical functions parents have. Children are educated along these lines in ways that can either be positive or negative and the parents' messages do get through in a variety of ways.

Parents who have always given in to the requests of their children may set them up for spending problems at a later age. When an "I want the ice cream cone now" request is immediately gratified at all times, the child may always expect things done right now. The parent in this case may do it because of his own hang-up—maybe for fear of disappointing the child or out of a fear of rejection. By constantly being given in to, the child does not learn the ability to wait at certain times for need gratification.

Parents should also be extremely careful about showing love with money. Another mistake is to always pay for good behavior and affection. The child who is unable to work it out in his mind will draw a strict relationship between the two. So, overgiving can present problems.

Giving too little to children also has its drawbacks. Deprivation of material things may carry over into feelings of psychological emptiness. When they become adults, this may be transferred by relieving those feelings by overspending or compulsive stealing.

A balance is needed. This may be attained by giving the children an allowance out of which some of his expenses should come, like snacks, milk money, and so forth. This way the child learns to spread out his money to meet several needs. The allowance should go, most of the time, for fun things. As with so many things in life, above all, when a child is made to feel worthy by those around him, he will probably not grow up with an unusual financial hang-up.

Would you believe that parents frequently

are guilty of actually teaching their children overindulgence. Because of affluence or guilt they will have a tendency to give their children too much. Such behavior may also be prompted by a great fear of rejection or the belief that if they buy the kids everything, they can control them. This is bribing with dollars.

The guilt often comes from some failure like a divorce, or because they don't have much time to devote to the children. By giving them an overabundance of things, they hope to make up for the lack of time shared with the children.

One of the most important things we need to give our children is a value system. Money is a much-needed concept to be taught when they are small, because self-reliance is developed by such learning. It is more important than giving them cars or even college educations.

—From David Juroe, *Money*. Old Tappan, N.J.: Fleming H. Revell Co., 1981.

FOR FURTHER READING:

Burkett, Larry. *What Husbands Wish Their Wives Knew About Money*. Wheaton, Ill.: Victor Books, 1977.

Dayton. *Your Money: Frustration or Freedom?* Wheaton, Ill.: Tyndale House Publishers, 1979.

Mace, David R. *Success in Marriage*. Nashville: Abingdon Press, 1980.

Otis, George. *God, Money and You*. Van Nuys, Calif.: Bible Voice.

MOTIVATION

MOTIVATION is the study of why people act as they do. Why does one man attend church regularly and another come only occasionally? Why does one child rebel against his Christian background and another accept it enthusiastically? Why does one pastor like to study while another prefers visitation?

. . . The causes of behavior are often very complex. Even when two people show similar behavior—as when two members attend church regularly—they may do so for very different reasons.

How People Are Motivated. In their experimental investigation, psychologists over the years have arrived at several broad explanations to describe how people are motivated.

Instinct. Studies of animals have shown that certain behavior seems to be inborn. Hens always sit on eggs, orioles always build deep, U-shaped nests, the mating behavior in male rats always occurs in the same way, even when the animal has had no chance to observe the behavior of others.

In the early part of this century, many psychologists concluded that much of man's behavior was also instinctive. Great lists of "human instincts"—including such things as liking people, wanting money, boldness, aggressiveness, and hundreds of others—were compiled, reported in psychology books, and memorized by students. The use of instincts to explain human actions did not last long, however. Students of animal behavior began to conclude that instincts were not nearly so common as had been previously assumed. Some psychologists began to doubt whether instincts really existed in people, and it was pointed out that use of the term "instinct" explained nothing. To say that a man takes a wife because he has a "marriage instinct" doesn't really help us to understand much about the man's behavior. The term "instinct" has, therefore, largely dropped out of human psychology, although animal researchers still make use of the term occasionally.

Need reduction. It is common knowledge that hunger, thirst, pain, fatigue, or other physical needs influence our actions. If an animal is in need of food, it seeks about until it can find something to eat so that the need is eliminated. Biological organisms are always responding to physical needs which drive them to action. This observation has led psychologists to conclude that the satisfaction of biological needs is an important determinant of behavior.

Such an explanation is far too simple to account for complex human behavior, however. . . . It must be recognized, therefore, that men have needs other than those that are biological. In addition to innate needs there are acquired (learned) needs such as the need for success, acceptance, and love.

Several years ago a psychologist named Abraham Maslow identified and arranged men's needs in a pyramid. . . . At the base are physical needs. Without their satisfaction we would not survive as a biological organism. Once these needs are being satisfied, we can then be concerned about our safety needs. Then there emerge the needs for belonging and love, for esteem and for self-actualization—the desire in man to become in actual fact what he has the potential to become. Self-actualization, in Maslow's words, is "to become everything that one is capable of becoming." The needs at the base of Maslow's hierarchy are innate, but as we go up the pyramid, we see needs that are acquired. Notice that there is no place here for spiritual influences on behavior and the theory has difficulty accounting for the behavior of people who are more concerned about higher needs (self-esteem, for example) than they are about lower needs (getting enough to eat). It is also possible to criticize Maslow's choice of needs. Other psychologists have different lists and although men undoubtedly have needs that they act to satisfy, it may be that the need-reduction explana-

tion is only a little better than the long-rejected instinct theory of motivation.

Desire for Stimulation. At the basis of the need-reduction theory is the idea that people want to have their needs met and their tensions reduced. At times, however, people seem to want an increase in tension and stimulation. If we simply have to reduce our hunger need periodically, why do some people spend $6.50 on a carefully cooked steak, in preference to a 45¢ hamburger? If we want to satisfy safety needs, why do people go on roller coasters, engage in scuba diving, swallow LSD, or take chances that could easily be avoided?

Apparently in order to survive everybody must experience changing stimulation. There are, however, individual differences in the complexity of stimulation to which we are attracted. What is too simple for an adult may be just right for a child. What is too complex for a beginner may seem simple to an expert. What is a "normal" level of noise for a teenage musician may be too much for his grandmother.

Several years ago some interesting experiments were done at McGill University in Montreal. Student volunteers were paid $20.00 a day to lie on a bed with ears, eyes, and hands covered and with instructions to do nothing. The subjects soon got bored. They sang, whistled, and talked to themselves in an effort to provide stimulation. Before long they became angry, discouraged, and unable to think clearly. These people were not getting enough changing stimulation to keep them happy and thinking clearly. At the other extreme, people sometimes get perplexed and inefficient when there is too much stimulation.

To use a more familiar example, let us assume that someone is listening to a sermon which is very boring. As the preacher drones on, the listener is not being stimulated very much so he fidgets, daydreams, and tries to create stimulation in his own mind. On the other hand, if the sermon is exceptionally good—a progression of meaningful ideas—the listener may be overwhelmed as he tries to assimilate all that is being said. Ideally the message should hit some hard-to-define middle point. But this is not easy. What is ideal for a college student might not be ideal for the high schooler or businessman. What is good for one listener may be too complex for some and too simple for others.

When people are in situations which are not very stimulating they look for extra experiences. Although there are various reasons for taking drugs, it is probable that many people want to be "turned on" so that they can experience vivid sensations in place of the dull routine of their ordinary lives. Other people may engage in dangerous sports or daring activities for similar reasons—to find excitement. At the other extreme, when the stimulation is too intense we try to ignore it or avoid it. For some people the stimulation is so intense that their only alternative is to withdraw into a state of schizophrenia.

Unconscious Motivation. The satisfaction of needs and the seeking of an ideal amount of complex stimulation do not account for all of our behavior. Sometimes we act in accordance with habits which have been learned or future goals which we are trying to attain. It is also very likely that much of our behavior is caused by unconscious influences. Freud first proposed this idea as a major part of his theory of motivation.

According to Freud, all behavior is motivated, including slips of the tongue, dreams, forgetting, and even accidents. One of the tasks of counseling, according to Freudian theory, is to uncover and help the counselee to become aware of the underlying influences on his behavior. Unconscious motives

are difficult to observe and measure, but undoubtedly they do have some influence on our actions.

An alternative explanation. . . . If we want to understand behavior at any point in time, we must be aware of the stimulation which is influencing a person at that moment and we must know something about the person who is behaving. Notice that this explanation makes room for a variety of causes for human behavior; it recognizes that needs, the desire for stimulation, habits, past learning, and unconscious influences might all be significant; it acknowledges that the Holy Spirit and satanic "principalities and powers" can influence men; and it recognizes that the causes of behavior change constantly. . . .

Motivation and the Church. The topic of motivation has been studied intensively by psychologists, but most of this work has been done with animals and relatively little has dealt with the practical issues of how people are motivated. The following conclusions are consistent with the conclusions of psychological research that has been done.

People are motivated to engage in activities which satisfy needs. The same students who are bored in class sometimes have an avid desire to read or to work on car engines. Presumably they have needs which are not being met in class, but which are being met in other activities. In one survey of church drop-outs. . . , it was found that many people left the church because it did not satisfy their needs. If their needs are being met in church, people will come. This is another way of making the oft-repeated statement that we have got to be relevant. It should also be remembered that what is relevant and need-satisfying for one person or age group may be irrelevant for another. Once again the issue of individual differences raises its head.

Incentives are important. An incentive is a desired goal. Sunday schools sometimes give pencils or books to students who learn Bible verses. The pencils and books are incentives for some people, although—as every teacher knows—what is desirable to one person is not an incentive at all to another.

. . . An incentive need not always be something tangible. College students often work for a grade or a degree and most of us are willing to work for acclaim. Sometimes the incentive is internal—a feeling of success or achievement, for example—but it takes time and training to instill these values. The Scriptures talk about rewards in heaven, abundant life on earth, the experience of joy and peace—all of which are incentives for the Christian. Every church leader would do well to periodically think about the issue of incentives and to consider how these might be used to motivate people in the church.

The level of changing stimulation is important. It has become a widely held joke in our society that sermons are dull and that the height of boredom is a Sunday school picnic. In many situations this is undoubtedly an accurate picture. We must remember that young people need more varied stimulation than older people, and that most people in the church need more than they are getting. A college student who is encouraged to think all week won't have much time for a church where he listens to dogmatic assertions and is told not to ask questions. Happily a church which seems to teach the principles of Scripture need not be afraid of stimulating thought and discussion about the Word of God, since truth has nothing to fear from questioning. Many church leaders need to rethink their form of worship and to update and add variety to their church programs in order to make them more stimulating.

People are better motivated when they have a clear goal, when they are given some guidelines in reaching the goal and when they have some expectation of success. In any organization—including the various departments of a church, it is well to ask periodically, "What are we trying to accomplish?" When our goals are unclear, or when we have no idea how to reach the goals that we do have, then we aren't likely to be highly motivated. Even with clear goals and clear strategy, we get discouraged if we can see no chance of success. Sometimes it is best to reach a major goal by setting intermediate but more easily attainable goals. For a college freshman, a Ph.D. is a long way into the future but there are other, more accessible goals—like passing freshman English—that can help a person to reach his ultimate ends.

High stress and anxiety can hinder our motivation. As with learning, so in motivation a little anxiety can help in our behavior, but too much anxiety and stress interfere with motivation.

The Holy Spirit can and does motivate. Every church leader has seen situations where behavior changes noticeably following a conversion experience or the committing of one's life to the Holy Spirit's complete control. The third person of the Trinity moves men (2 Peter 1:21) and guides them (John 16:13). In this theology, A. H. Strong notes that "we perceive the presence of the Holy Spirit, not by visions or voices, but by the effect he produces within us in the shape of new knowledge, new love . . . new energy." (And we might add, new motivation.)

Summary. When we study motivation we are considering the question of why people act as they do. The reasons for a person's behavior are highly complex and involve the reduction of needs, the seeking after stimulation, and the satisfaction of unconscious influences. To understand why people behave involves some understanding both of the stimulation that influences a person and of the behaver's current state and characteristics. In the church we must be aware of how people are motivated and attempt to use this knowledge in motivating Christians to be more diligent in their service for Christ.

—From Gary Collins, *Man in Motion.* Carol Stream, Ill.: Creation House, 1973.

FOR FURTHER READING:

McDonough, Reginald J. *Keys to Effective Motivation.* Nashville: Broadman Press, 1979.

MOVIES

IT IS SAID that 12,000,000 children in the United States go to the movies each week. While the figures may fluctuate, there can be no doubt that large numbers of children of all ages, most of them without adults, attend motion picture theaters in cities, towns, and villages across the land. None of the feature-length pictures produced for commercial showing is expressly made for or addressed to this young audience. Yet a good number of these films do offer excellent entertainment as well as educational and cultural values for children, along with much that is unsuitable. The problem for parents is to help their children learn to choose among the many films that are offered. Motion pictures are an important part of today's culture, and children and young people can be helped to find the best they have to offer.

The question is often asked: At what age can a child be taken to the movies? The answer, of course, depends somewhat on the individual child and his readiness for paying concentrated attention. Most children under six find it hard to sit still for the duration of an ordinary commercial film showing. As a matter of fact, except for short features and cartoons, there are few films that have meaning for children under eight or thereabouts. Since most of the films shown in the regular motion picture programs are addressed to the adult audience, young children should be taken seldom, and then only to carefully selected films. It is wise, too, to keep their visits short, timing attendance to eliminate a possibly unsuitable "second feature."

While children are young, this matter of selection comes well within the parents' control. As boys and girls grow older, however, movie-going becomes a social matter: they go with their friends and want to see "what everybody's seeing." Parental selection now becomes more difficult and gives place rather to parental supervision. Parents may at times find it necessary to rule out some film that they consider definitely undesirable; but such prohibitions should be used rarely, and only with good cause. They often have the effect of whetting the appetite and arousing curiosity about the "forbidden" film. It is important to invite children to ask questions about the films they see or want to see—to ask with confidence that they will get straightforward answers. They need adult guidance and interpretation of the many confusing standards and ways of life they see portrayed on the screen. And they need adult help, too, in learning to discriminate in their own choice of films, so that their taste and appreciation may grow.

What to do about the "movie habit"? Should a child be allowed to go to the movies every Saturday afternoon, rain or shine? Again this depends on each child and his particular reasons for going to the movies. For many children the movies are simply a way out of a boring Saturday afternoon. Parents can often break this routine of movie-going by offering something more exciting—a picnic or a trip to some place of interest, or perhaps a home party—and inviting the child's friends to come along. For older children some activities of their own may be more alluring than the movies—they can be helped to put on their own show, with puppets perhaps, or their own play-acting. Parents may need to provide suggestions as well as the makings for such activities—and be prepared for an upset living room or kitchen.

In many communities groups of parents, teachers, and others organize to secure special Saturday programs for children. They enlist the cooperation of a local theater in planning carefully selected programs. The Motion Picture Association of America, with the cooperation of a committee representing interested national organizations, selects suitable films for the eight-to-twelve age range; and the entertainment value of these pictures is also tested on a young audience. These films are maintained in a National Children's Film Library, which can be drawn upon for special children's programs.

The production of 16-mm films for special educational purposes has been increasing tremendously. A great number of excellent films on a wide variety of subjects are available for use in schools and elsewhere. A catalogue of these films is maintained by the Library of Congress Film Library, and lending libraries are available in a number of large universities and state departments of education. As the value of motion pictures in teaching becomes more and more clear, school systems are becoming aware of the importance of budget provisions for acquiring and maintaining projection equipment and for the purchase or rental of films.

—From *The New Encyclopedia of Child Care and Guidance.* Garden City, N.Y.: Doubleday & Co., 1968.

FOR FURTHER READING:

Drew, Donald J. *Images of Man.* Downers Grove, Ill.: Inter-Varsity Press, 1974.

White, John Wesley. *Man From Krypton: The Gospel According to Superman.* Minneapolis: Bethany Fellowship, 1978.

MOVING

EACH YEAR, one out of every five families packs up its possessions and moves. Sometimes this is only a few blocks, sometimes many miles away, leaving behind the familiar world.

For a young child, moving may not be as upsetting as it is to somewhat older youngsters who do mind terribly saying goodby to beloved teachers and friends. As long as the young child stays with his family, things right themselves rather quickly as a rule, especially when he sees his familiar bed and toys and chair again. For this reason, it is worthwhile to haul along shabby or outgrown objects important to him. Through these possessions, the child re-creates the familiar in his new setting. Seeing the objects he treasures thrown into the trash pile is not an easy thing to take at any time, but it is more upsetting when grownups are busy and preoccupied, or upset themselves in the process of upheaval.

Moving does threaten some children. Occasionally a child takes it in stride at first but shows balkiness or irritability some weeks later. Others are upset from the beginning, and may show it in nightmares, bedwetting, timidness, or unusual clinging.

These signs of upset are particularly annoying at just the moment you have your hands full getting settled. You're eager to get out to buy new curtain rods, shelf paper and the million and one things the new house needs. Nevertheless, you'll be rewarded if you try to devote as much time as possible to the reluctant transplant. In the long run, you are apt to save both time and emotional energy. The child whose needs are ignored may take up even more time later on.

—From *Your Child From 1 to 6*. Washington: U.S. Department of Health, Education and Welfare, 1969.

FOR FURTHER READING:

Booher, Dianna D. *Help, We're Moving*. Nashville: Broadman Press, 1978.

MUSIC

"YOU PICKED a fine time to leave me, Lucille, with four hungry children and crops in the field" was a country song my sister, Jan, heard when she first turned on the radio one morning. She said, "It entwined itself around my mind and had me tied up all day long."

Her statement reminded me of the tremendous power of communication that music has. A catchy song can literally dominate our thinking at times. Barry Manilow points this out in his song "I Write the Songs." He says a songwriter's words have a way of making a home within us, and this songwriter is aware of the truth that music can reach right into our souls and wrap itself around our hearts.

The power of music has been known by many for years. Peter, Paul, and Mary frankly admitted, "We could mobilize the youth of America today in a way that nobody else could. We could conceivably travel with a presidential candidate, and maybe even sway an election . . . not that we're going to use this power. It's enough to know that we have it."

Our enemy, Satan, will do anything to draw us away from the fabulous way of life God has planned for us. First Peter 5:8 warns us to be on guard against his clever and subtle traps: ". . . keep a clear head and watch!

Your enemy, the devil, is prowling around like a roaring lion, looking for someone to devour" (BECK). Satan knows the key to influencing us is through thoughts placed in our minds. "For as he thinks in his heart, so is he . . ." (Proverbs 23:7 AMP). That's the reason God tells us to "Keep your heart with all vigilance . . . for out of it flow the springs of life" (Proverbs 4:23 AMP).

The Trap of Lyrics

Satan knows the power and influence of music, and he uses it. He begins to trap us into his way of thinking by taking a catchy tune and placing words in the song that suggest very subtly the wrong way of thinking about ourselves and our relationships with others. A good example would be the song, "Afternoon Delight." The music is good but listen to the words. Although not actually stated, the lyrics hint at the attitude that sex is permissible, just because one feels like it. While we might not fall for the flagrant references to premarital sex in the song "Tonight's the Night," sung by Rod Stewart, it's easier to let the subtle message of "Afternoon Delight" settle down in our minds.

Some six years ago only one out of fifteen songs was about illicit sex. Now, approximately 50 percent are about sex. In 1971 the FCC drew up guidelines on the airing of dope lyrics because of so many complaints about songs like "White Rabbit" and "One Toke Over The Line." However, the agency is powerless about sex. Jason Shrinsky, the lawyer who represents two hundred radio stations before the FCC explains: "Sex is so subjective. The FCC doesn't know what standard to use." *Time* magazine said, "Just a twist of the AM dial demonstrates how far things have gone. On the average 15 percent of air time is devoted to songs like 'Do It Any Way You Wanna,' 'Let's Do It Again,'

'That's the Way I Like It' and 'I Want'a Do Something Freaky to You.' "

"Love Machine" is another enticing song. This catchy little tune says, "I'm just a love machine, a huggin', kissing thing." Do we believe we're nothing more than sex objects? That's what this song advocates!

Whether we realize it or not, every song we hear is permanently recorded in our minds. One teenager said, "That's not true for me because I don't listen to the words." With our active, conscious minds we might not listen to the words, but nevertheless, the subconscious mind functions automatically to record everything we hear. This information is stored in the subconscious and influences our actions and decisions. Psychologists tell us that approximately 90 percent of our reactions to environmental stimuli are the result of habitual or conditioned responses.

How will you react when you and your steady break up? Will your response be conditioned by the thoughts in songs like Chicago's "If You Leave Me Now" or the song "Without You"? The music is nice, but the words convey the wrong message. "If you leave me now, you'll take away the biggest part of me. . . . take away the very heart of me." The other song says, "I can't live if living is without you."

The underlying message is that another person can fulfill you, and if you lose him your life goes down the tubes. That's Satan's lie. God says He can fulfill you and make you a total person and that another person isn't necessary. Of course, your mate will richly add to your life, but he is not your life. If you've been conditioned by such songs, once your love life falls apart, you are likely to fall apart, too, because that's the way you have been programmed.

Rock music is not the only music that contains unscriptural songs. Country and West-

ern songs are filled with divorce, affairs, and the like. "Strawberry Curls" recorded by Freddy Weller or Lou Rawls's "Natural Man" are examples. Glen Campbell's song "Gentle on My Mind" says romantic love can survive only in the absence of permanent commitment. "San Quentin" sung by Johnny Cash puts down authority. Even Frank Sinatra's "My Way" cleverly says, "I did it *my* way." "The Force," a country song, written by Tom T. Hall is a strong occult song pointing its listeners to another power other than the true God for Guidance.

Of course, it is possible to get too picky or go to extremes about the words of a song as well as any other issue in life. Perhaps, the most important question to consider is, "What do the songs I listen to mean to me?" The condition and attitude of one's heart is the most important issue. The expression, "beauty is in the eye of the beholder," reminds us that beauty is a result of our perspective. The same is true with music. Our attitudes or the condition of our hearts determines the effect a beautiful scene or the words of a song has on us. This very point was made by a teenager the other day. As we had the car radio playing, she said, "Often when I am listening to a song, I imagine it's talking about my relationship with Christ even though the song itself was not written about God."

Nevertheless, it's only smart to start examining the lyrics of the songs to which we listen. For instance, does the song encourage the listener to be antipatriotic? "Back in the U.S.S.R." was a hit of the Beatles a few years ago and it still gets a lot of air play. Although written as a satire, it could be misconstrued as advocating a better way of life in Russia and putting down the U.S.A.

Be on guard against songs which approve sexual promiscuity, crime, revolution, peace at any price, disarmament, fear of death, atheism or anti-Christianity, international-ism, committing suicide, occultic practices, defeatism, or a pessimistic outlook on life. The first time we hear a flagrant, vulgar song, we are shocked. The next time it doesn't seem quite so bad. Finally, our defenses are broken down, and we accept the idea as a normal way of life. God gives us a measuring stick with which to evaluate the type of lyrics we should listen to in Philippians 4:8: ". . . whatever is pure, whatever is lovely, whatever is admirable—if anything is excellent or praiseworthy—think about such things" (NIV).

Know the Singer

Once we know the beliefs of a singer, we can know what kind of philosophies his songs will advocate. Robert Schumann wrote: "Music to me is the perfect expression of the soul." Jesus said in Matthew 12:34 ". . . out of the abundance of the heart the mouth speaketh" (KJV). In other words, what is in a person's heart is going to show up in what he says. In the language of music, which in a very real sense is amplified speech, is the clear evidence of what is in the heart of the performer and will be communicated to the listener.

The following insights into some singers' beliefs can help you determine if you want to be influenced by their thinking.

The Eagles are five musicians in their twenties and their songs are a product of the writings of a young intellectual Carlos Castaneda. Castaneda is a Mexican mystic who apprenticed himself to a Yaqui Indian sorcerer named Don Juan. His book *The Teachings of Don Juan* contains accounts of the occult and the demonic. These young musicians spent long, sleepless nights in the desert, indulging in raw tequila peyote and studying the sorcery of Don Juan. Their songs are a product of drug inspiration and the occult.

The Beatles' own press agent, Derek Taylor, said they are anti-Christ. "They're rude, they're profane, they're vulgar, and they're taking over the world. They're completely anti-Christ. I mean, I'm anti-Christ, as well, but they're so anti-Christ they shock me, which isn't easy." John Lennon's song "Instant Karma" is a reflection of the fact that he is a Krishna follower. Listen closely to George Harrison's "My Sweet Lord" and you'll know he isn't talking about Jesus Christ. The line, "It takes so long," is a reference to the meditative processes of Hinduism and oriental mysticism in which union and communion with God are never achieved.

The Rolling Stones openly and admittedly claim to be Satan worshipers, according to *Time* magazine. Just looking at the titles of some of their songs, "Their Satanic Majesty's Request," "Sympathy for the Devil," and "Prodigal Son," tells whose side they represent.

According to *Time* magazine, Frank Zappa, of the Mothers of Invention, sees himself as an advocate of the devil. Beach Boys's star, Brian Wilson, attributes his recovery from a nervous breakdown to TM. Elton John admitted in *Time* magazine that he's bisexual and says making love with boys is as good as girls. A musician's life-style is sure to come through in his music, because it's natural to communicate in song what is in his heart. When Peter Frampton sings "Show Me the Way" and "Wine Glass," is he saying "I'm lost, and this is the life-style I lead"?

Anyone listening to hard-rock groups or singers such as Kiss, Santana, Black Sabbath, Eagles, Rolling Stones, or Alice Cooper, is, in my opinion, placing himself in very dangerous company.

Control—Good or Bad?

For centuries it has been known that music can soothe or incite. Doctor Howard Hanson in the *American Journal of Psychiatry* once commented, "Music is a curiously subtle art with innumerable, varying emotional connotations. It is made up of many ingredients, and, according to the proportions of those components, it can be soothing or invigorating, ennobling or vulgarizing, philosophical or orgiastic. It has powers for evil as well as for good."

God created music and makes more than five hundred specific references to music in the Bible. Ephesians 5:18, 19 tells us that one of the natural results of being filled with the Spirit of God is singing. First Samuel 16:23 shows the power of healthy music to refresh a person and actually drive away an evil spirit. King Saul was troubled by demonic powers as a result of his disobedience to God. Yet when young David played his harp, we are told that ". . . Saul would be refreshed and be well, and the evil spirit would depart from him" (1 Samuel 16:23 NAS).

Healthy music has a proper ratio between melody, harmony, and rhythm, just as a healthy person has the proper balance between the spirit, soul, and body. The melody should be the dominant factor in a song just as our spirit should be the controlling factor in our lives. The harmony is to be controlled by the melody just as our minds should be controlled by the Spirit. The rhythm in music corresponds to the body. The healthiest rhythmic beat is one that is nearest the heartbeat. Our bodies can handle an increased heartbeat at times, so rhythm can be faster at times. But a body whose pulse is continually too slow or overworked will be sick. The same is true for music.

Satan distorts and abuses every beautiful creation of God's and music is no exception. How does he do it? He destroys the balance of healthy music and capitalizes on any other abuses he can maneuver. For instance the volume of rock music is consistently loud. Just how loud is loud? Sound is measured in decibels. Seventy decibels is a comfortable level, equivalent to the sound of traffic on a relatively quiet city street. Note that the volume of rock music has been measured in nightclubs and discotheques between 100 and 116 decibels, which is extremely high, and some hard rock has been measured as high as 138 decibels. This is only two points under the threshold of pain where a person is unable to control his nervous system and hence loses control of his body.

Not only does such a high volume in rock music cause drastic reactions within the body's autonomic nervous system, but it can cause a person to lose his ability to hear. Studies show that many teenagers have the hearing of the average sixty- to sixty-five-year-old. Robin Adams Sloan's column recently reported that Roger Daltrey, the great singer from The Who, is going deaf. When asked what caused his problem, Daltrey said it's probably due to working with a noisy group like The Who. The next edition of the *Guinness Book of World Records* will list the Rolling Stones as the loudest rock band in the world. The group was measured at an ear-splitting 120 decibels at a recent concert.

Couple a high volume with continual repetition of words and a heavy throbbing, pile-driving beat and somehow it "nerve jams" a person so that he will not feel pain. This explains to some degree some of the weird things that have been reported at many heathen rituals. For instance, a man in India can lie down on a bed of nails for hours and not appear to feel pain as long as the sensual music with its pulsating rhythms is being played. Men have been known to push darts through their hands or cut themselves with hunting knives and not bleed under the same conditions.

The continual repetition of words or chord patterns can produce a hypnotic effect on a person. The dangers in this hypnotic effect become alarming when one considers the words that are being fed into the minds of the listeners. When the mind is hypnotized, it is under the control of whatever has the person hypnotized. In some cases demon possession has been known to occur while a person is hypnotized by hard-rock music.

Bob Larson, a former rock-music player, tells of an experience in his book, *Rock and the Church*, which occurred while he was in Singapore observing the Thaipusam, a penance and self-mutilation rite of Hinduism. While some of the Hindus participated in a self-mutilation rite, others gyrated to the incessant, pulsating, syncopated rhythms heard in America's hard rock. Suddenly one teenager screamed, his body became stiff, and he fell to the ground, writhing and kicking. A man explained that they dance to this music until the spirit of their god enters into them. It seems that the natives remain under the control of the incessant, pulsating rhythms until they enter a state of hypnotic monotony and lose active control over their conscious minds. The throb of the beat from the drums brings the mind to a state where a false god, or demon, can enter it. This power then takes control of the dancer often resulting in sexual atrocities.

There is evidence connecting demonic activity and rock music.

Bob Larson tells another uncanny story in *Rock and the Church*. One of his close friends explained that for several weeks he dealt with a sixteen-year-old boy who, by his own admission, said he communed with demon spirits. One day he asked his friend to turn on the radio to a rock station. As they listened, this teenager related, just prior to the time the singer on the recording would sing them, the words to songs he had never heard before. When asked how he could do this, the sixteen-year-old replied that the same demon spirits that he was acquainted with had inspired the songs. Also, he explained, that while on acid trips, he could hear demons sing some of the very songs he would later hear recorded by acid-rock groups.

You may be thinking, *I do not intend to be spaced out on an acid trip or participate in a heathenish self-mutilation rite, therefore this doesn't apply to me.* The fact is that our enemy, Satan, uses unhealthy music to weaken Christians. Much like drugs, rock music's pulsating, hard-driving beat can, over a period of time, affect one's will, making him vulnerable to satanic influence.

Many teenagers are coming to grips with these facts today and are concluding that they want nothing to do with anything that has the appearance of evil. "Abstain from every form of evil" (1 Thessalonians 5:22 NAS).

Inventory Time

Take stock of your music life. Does the music you listen to have a healthy balance between melody, harmony, and rhythm? Does it reflect the ideals and standards that God requires of a Christian? Do you turn to music to forget your disappointments or to get yourself in the mood you desire? We are to enjoy music but never are we to try to make it fill the needs in our lives that only Christ can meet, "God is our refuge and strength, A very present help in trouble" (Psalms 46:1 NAS).

Can you move easily from listening to your favorite music to reading your Bible or talking to God in prayer? If not, you should evaluate your musical tastes. If it's not drawing you closer to God, it's drawing you away from Him (*see* Romans 12:1, 2). Our musical life should simply be an overflow of the life we have with Christ (*see* Colossians 3:16). All good songs do not have to quote Scripture, but they should jibe with biblical truths.

The best way to get a catchy little song with the wrong message or the wrong kind of music out of your mind is to replace it with a new song. "He put a new song in my mouth, a praise to our God . . ." (Psalms 40:3 MLB). Turn the dial of your radio to a healthy station, and as you listen, trust Christ to de-

velop in your soul a thirst for good music that honors Him. He will as you cooperate!

—From Darien B. Cooper, *How to Be Happy Though Young.* Old Tappan, N.J.: Fleming H. Revell Co., 1979.

FOR FURTHER READING:

Benson, Dennis C. *The Rock Generation.* Nashville: Abingdon Press, 1976.

Larson, Bob. *Rock and the Church.* Wheaton, Ill.: Tyndale House Publishers, 1981.

Topp, Dale. *Music in the Christian Community.* Grand Rapids: Wm. B. Eerdmans Publishing Co., 1976.

N

NAGGING

MOST PARENTS have occasional periods when they nag, and most youngsters don't suffer from it. To a tired mother a display of normal high spirits in her children seems like inconsiderate boisterousness, or a worried father may treat a toddler's dawdling as a "bad habit to be broken." The spells of nagging that arise temporarily from inevitable situations like these leave no prolonged impression.

Constant reminders and fault-finding, however, are different. They may appear to have no effect whatsoever on some children, who seem to develop an immunity to them (although, underneath, this is unlikely). But persistent nagging has unhappy effects on most youngsters. It can make them feel that they are generally disapproved of, not trusted to do things on their own, that nothing they do is "right." Many parents are surprised to discover that when they manage to stop their constant proddings and reminders their boys and girls become quite reliable. This is true except when a child has become so dependent on nagging that he can hardly mobilize himself without it, or when he feels that this is his mother's way of showing that she cares for him and will therefore miss it when she stops.

"How many times do I have to tell you not to leave those skates in the hall!" Apparently, hundreds of times. As a matter of discipline, nagging is ineffective for most children. More likely to bring results would

be a clear explanation of the dangers involved or, if necessary, withholding the privilege of skating for a day or two.

Anxiety is often at the root of chronic nagging. Mother, for instance, nags about eating because she is too much concerned about proper nutrition. Or a five-year-old who has been capably putting on his own shoes for some time nags to have it done for him because he is anxious for a little extra proof of love. A teacher may nag for higher marks if she is worried about meeting the standards of scholarship set up to gauge her teaching ability. The five-year-old doesn't know why he nags. But an adult who suddenly realizes he is becoming a constant nagger can at least say to himself, "Relax." Often just the simple act of consciously trying to relax, and of taking the time to think about what in one's daily life has become an irritant, will in itself accomplish what nagging could not do.

—From *The New Encyclopedia of Child Care and Guidance.* Garden City, N.Y.: Doubleday & Co., 1968.

NAIL-BITING

WHEN BOYS OR GIRLS take to biting their nails, it is because they are tense. A child will put his fingers to his mouth unconsciously while waiting to be called on in class, doing lessons, watching an exciting television program or movie, even while reading or standing around in apparent calm when there's no immediate cause for excitement or anxiety. Excitable boys and girls are more given to nail-biting than calm ones, but even a relatively successful and happy child may do it for a while.

To nag or punish a child or to put bitter-tasting medicine on his nails does not help him to stop biting them but does increase the tension. More can be accomplished by trying to find and relieve some of the causes of the child's tenseness. Perhaps he is being held to too rigid a schedule, being expected to do too many things or to do them too well, either in his behavior at home or in his schoolwork. Nail-biting may be his reaction to too many reminders to keep himself clean, to pick up his things, to mind his manners, or to too much scolding, punishment, or other expression of Mother's or Father's disapproval. At some stages of a child's growth the inner changes he is wrestling with make the ordinary pressures of his life too much for him to handle for a while. At such times parents do well to let up on little omissions in his behavior and create a cheerful and tolerant atmosphere at home. A talk with his teacher may reveal how he can be helped in his schoolwork or in getting along with classmates.

Along with relieving the pressures, a gift of a manicure set or some nail polish, together with her mother's friendly encouragement in taking care of her nails, often gives a girl the needed incentive to stop nail-biting. A pair of shiny nail clippers he can safely use himself, or a pocketknife with nail-clipper attachment, may do the same for a boy.

—From *The New Encyclopedia of Child Care and Guidance*. Garden City, N.Y.: Doubleday & Co., 1968.

NEW BABY

PARENTS CANNOT easily imagine just how world-shaking an event the coming of a new baby can be to other children in a family, especially when it is the arrival of the second child in the life of the first. Preparing children for the new brother or sister is, of course, necessary, and many parents have learned to do this casually and effectively. This does not, however, settle matters. There will be grief and hurt and some resentment mixed with pleasure in the newcomer and a wish to love him as their parents do. Situations will have to be met day by day until the baby's place in the family is comfortably established.

Some measures can be taken ahead of time to help children accept the new baby. If a child is to be moved from his crib or entered in nursery school, the change is best made in advance—not because of the new baby but as proof that the child himself is getting bigger. Whoever will take over while Mother is away can begin helping to care for the younger children beforehand.

Children like to share in the preparations, and even a young child can help sort baby clothes. But it is wise not to announce the news too far ahead nor to draw an unrealistic picture of the new baby as a playmate. A child who has never seen a newborn infant had better be told that it will be quite a while before the baby will walk and talk and do other things he can, but that it is fun to watch and help the baby learn. A visit to a new baby is better yet. If Mother is going to a hospital nearby, a casual stroll past it some afternoon helps to allay anxious imaginings.

Bringing the baby home can be more comfortable if the child is not at home when the baby is installed. If he is at home, someone else can carry the baby so Mother's arms are free for a welcoming hug. The child can be invited to help care for the baby, fetching and handing things, and to hold the baby for a few minutes if he likes, sitting in a big safe chair with a grownup nearby. It is misleading, however, to try to tell him this is "his baby," for he will have plenty of evidence to the contrary.

The first few days, especially, call for tact. Father helps by not asking about the baby first when he comes home. Some parents frankly forewarn visitors to "speak to Janie first" and let Janie show them the baby.

Adjusting to the new baby is hard, and the younger the child, the harder it is. More "grown-up" privileges, more time with Daddy, some excursions without the baby help to lessen jealousy.

Some of the ways a young child shows his unhappiness are annoying and inconvenient. Scolding, telling him he is "bad" or "acting like a baby" only drive him deeper into his troubles. He needs to be restrained from hurting the baby or anyone else, but he also needs extra love and attention. There is no harm in letting him behave like a baby, making it a good-humored game while giving him the cuddling he longs for.

If he goes back to wetting, Mother can encouragingly tell him she knows he will be ready to use the toilet again pretty soon. He will not cling to baby ways long if he feels sure of his parents' love. He may be less likely to demand attention at inconvenient times, either by playfulness or mischief, if Mother can manage to give him her whole attention when he does not demand it, as well as when he is being difficult.

Resentment may be concealed under behavior that looks just the opposite. "Janie just loves the baby" may mean that Janie is hovering anxiously over him, boasting or talking too much or being too sweet about him, covering up angry feelings of which she thinks her parents will not approve. It is nat-ural for young children to resent as well as love the new baby, and these feelings are better expressed than buried. Talking about them helps. Play materials like clay and paints, mallet and pegs offer outlets. The child will play more readily if his play space is close to Mother and the baby. Little boys as well as little girls find great relief in letting out their feelings on a doll family.

Children of school age have less urgent claims on their parents, but they too need attention for themselves and a share in the new baby's life. Parents can honestly admit that the baby makes additional work, but it is wiser not to agree with the child in resenting it. Stories about the time when he was little will remind him that he had the same care and will give him a feeling of kinship with the baby.

Parents sometimes concentrate on sparing the older child, only to find later that the younger one has felt neglected. Too much protection for either only postpones the time when both come to accept each other. Parents can best lay the groundwork for future affection among their children by welcoming the new baby while they continue to cherish and enjoy the older children as warmly as before.

—From *The New Encyclopedia of Child Care and Guidance.* Garden City, N.Y.: Doubleday & Co., 1968.

NIGHTMARES

ALL CHILDREN experience fearfulness: lions spring out of dream TV sets to tear and devour; villainous faces from television cartoons and books return to haunt and harry; monsters lurk in the corners of darkened rooms. And, however absurd the fears may seem to the adult, they are very real and terrifying to the child. Learning to cope with fearfulness is important if the child is to develop confidence.

Where do all the monsters and all the nighttime terrors that haunt children come from? Some can be directly traced, such as images replayed from television. Yet that still leaves unanswered the question of why little children are so morbidly fascinated by the horrible. There is something in the monstrous that answers to the child's unconscious awareness of evil within himself. The pain and bondage of these fears can be seen as a direct result of the Fall. I have been impressed by the prevalence of the snake image in terror-inducing dreams my children have wakened from. It seems to me that children somehow inherit mankind's troubled memory of Paradise Lost.

Many of the monsters are fears with faces. As adults, we name our fears and thus identify them. We say, "I have claustrophobia," or "I can't stand heights." But children do not have the words or the concepts with which to handle the great, dark world of human fearfulness. And so they have monsters instead—monsters that seldom materialize except at night. And the more vivid the child's imagination, the greater the input into his mind of bizarre or malicious faces of TV and comic books, the more acute will be his dread as nighttime reactivates memories and inflates them into full-sized terrors. It is partly because children do cope with monstrous fantasies, with frightening nightmares and terrifying imaginations, that those really horrible fairy tales are so popular with children. In those stories, the monsters or villains are clearly identifiable and they get what they deserve: they get chopped up, decapitated, utterly destroyed. This is entirely different from the television serials in which the villains linger to return week after week—and are only punished, never destroyed. In the vengeance wreaked upon the

evil giants and trolls of fairy stories, children find some of their fears exorcised.

Fearfulness in children is unavoidable— and it is not all negative. When it leads to proper reassurance, it can lead the child on toward confidence. But some measures can be taken to reduce the amount of fearfulness that troubles children. It is wise to limit the amount of "fearful intake." Much of what is called "children's programing" on television is in the form of cartoons that play up fear or cruelty as an element. Use the "off" button firmly to reduce the number of ugly or horrible faces that get implanted in your child's mind. Avoid having comic books—"Christian" or otherwise—for little tots to see. They tend to be ugly in their exaggeration of facial expressions and are potentially troubling to very young children.

Another preventive step for nighttime fearfulness is a reassuring sequence of bedtime rituals. A fun-filled bath-and-story time is sometimes more than a tired mother can muster, but it surely is ideal. Perhaps husband and wife can work out a system for sharing the duties of this highly important time of the day. Perhaps Dad can wrestle and roll with the children and then bathe and get them into pajamas while Mother tidies up the kitchen and gets the dishes done—or at least in soaking. Then the family can sit down together for a quieter phase: story time, a song, a good-night prayer together.

Wrapped in his parents' love, clean and tired, a little one can be tucked into bed and expected to go to sleep. It is well not to darken the child's room entirely: leave a door a bit ajar so that the hall light glows in; or have a tiny night-light to plug into the wall. Now, with the little one in bed, you can stand by the bedside for a few moments and talk softly and reassuringly. "Jesus has promised to be with us always, in the nighttime as well as in the daytime." Speak positively of the dark, quiet night. "God sends us night-time so we can sleep and get ready for another day. What a good plan. I'm so thankful for bedtime." (And *that* is sure to be a true statement from a mother tucking preschoolers into bed!)

I'm no soloist, but the children used to love to have me sing for them as they snuggled into their beds. We had a favorite good-night song which assured them, "My God is watching o'er you, His presence goes before you." Apart from the time that one of the children called me back to ask when he could open "God's presents," that song seemed to be a good, reassuring closer.

A favorite doll or toy to tuck in alongside the child is another kind of reassurance. One particularly pleasant good-night toy we were given was a Raggedy Ann doll with a built-in music box that played "Brahms' Lullaby" when the cord was pulled. An occasional after-lights-out visit from Mother or Dad helps children to feel positive and happy about bedtime, too.

Preschoolers, even after having settled peacefully for the night, are often awakened by nightmares. It can save you from getting up several times a night if you have an open-door policy on your own room after you have settled for the night. A little one can feel free to come to your bedside, talk to you, or climb in for a short time of hugging and reassuring. Remember that vivid dream images may linger in technicolor for several minutes after a dream has been broken off. During that time, let the child talk about the dream, then gradually divert his attention to happier things. "Let's list five of our favorite things. . . ." "Let's talk about how Jesus stilled the storm. . . ." Gradually center your child's attention on the power and presence of Jesus Christ, helping him to develop positive patterns of thought. A prayer together can go a long way toward emptying a child's mind of difficult images and reassuring him of God's presence.

Children are, of course, incredibly knowing. A child who finds that his parents respond to his fearfulness may come down night after night whispering, "I'm afraid." And your thoughtful reassurance may serve to reinforce a behavior pattern which is disruptive both to you and to the child. You will have to be prayerful and careful in discerning when this game is being played. Firmly but briefly reassure the child and send him back to his own room with the words, "I don't want you to get up again tonight."

—From Maxine Hancock, *People in Process.* Old Tappan, N.J.: Fleming H. Revell Co., 1978.

O

OBEDIENCE

TODAY'S CHRISTIAN parent is not comfortable with either the absolute obedience demanded of children in Victorian times or the absolute permissiveness of some extreme child psychologists following World War II.

A child growing up in our culture needs to learn how to do what he is told so he can learn how to do things correctly. As he matures and learns, he will need to obey less and less—though even most adolescents have not learned the sense of responsibility expected of adults and still need to be taught to obey and listen to parental guidance. Most adolescents will often ask for reasons. Christian parents should encourage this practice, since in a democracy their children are expected to become reasoning adults, not robots who automatically carry out everything they are told and never ask questions. Unfortunately, many teenagers are still not able to see the cogency of parental requests and may ask for reasons only to cloak their objections.

It is easy for parents to fall into the habit of making loud, imperious demands. Such a habit tends to foster a rebellious attitude in the child. The parent who can control the tendency to issue autocratic orders and make requests in a pleasant, reasonable voice will find that when he does raise his voice his requests will be taken more seriously. Every parent, no matter how controlled, has times when he will be exasperated and annoyed. The one who is always loud will find it more difficult to get a child to obey him without resorting to violence.

At the other extreme are parents who make tentative suggestions instead of clear requests. If your child does not understand your suggestion as a request, you may end up carrying out the request yourself. Some parents, in fact, become so tired of disciplining their children that they do things themselves when their children fail to respond to their uncertain propositions. They need to ask, however, if they are depriving the child of experiences he needs to learn. If he does not carry out your requests now, he may have a harder time implementing them for an employer later. Other parents, however, feel that such responsibility normally comes with maturity.

Try to avoid giving your child orders from another room. You have no way of knowing if your child has heard your request unless you have eye contact with him. Some parents become very upset with their child's "disobedience" when in fact the child was concentrating on something else and didn't hear the parent at all. A quieter, more orderly house will result if you take the time to go to the child and quietly tell him what you want him to do.

Punishment for disobedience is ideally less often physical today, though the number of cases of child abuse is startling. Instead of spanking a disobedient child or slapping his hand, most parents prefer to send a child to his room or some other place of isolation, or to deprive him of certain privileges, especially when they are related to the act of disobedience in some way.

The Bible provides the Christian parent with a balance on the question of disobedience. Children are exhorted to obey their parents (Ephesians 6:13), but parents are also cautioned not to overcorrect their children: "Don't keep on scolding and nagging your children, making them angry and resentful. Rather, bring them up with the loving discipline the Lord himself approves, with suggestions and godly advice" (Ephesians 6:4 TLB). No child obeys all the time. If you are always scolding your children, you need to assess what you are doing and depend more on "suggestions and godly advice." In the past children often obeyed out of fear. Today, hopefully, the children of Christian parents obey more because they love and trust them.

—LESLIE R. KEYLOCK

ONLY CHILD

EVEN IN THE DAYS of large families there were some "only" children, and nowadays there are even more one-child families. Most couples who plan their families usually want to have two or more children, feeling that a child should have brothers and sisters if possible. But when there is no choice, when a couple can have just one child, it need not be thought of as a near tragedy. There are some advantages to being an only child, and parents can try to make the most of these. At the same time, of course, they will look for ways to make up for what their child misses through having no brothers and sisters.

Every child needs to learn to share his toys and even his home. He must learn to work with other children, play with other children, give and take in the ordinary fights and squabbles. He needs the feeling of being close to another child or a group of children—the kind of feeling most children get from their brothers and sisters. How can parents of an only child provide these experiences?

If they want to avoid having him a lonely child, parents must first of all be generous with their home—inviting other children into their back yard, their kitchen and living room—and forget about the mess. They can invite their child's friends to meals and to stay overnight more often than in larger families. It doesn't matter if the meals are simple and the house is small; it is the sharing and the closeness that are important. Sometimes a friend can be invited to go along on a trip or for an entire vacation.

For the only child, cousins and other relatives are especially important. His parents can help to keep this family feeling strong by encouraging visits and, if the others don't live nearby, by exchanging letters, snapshots, and little gifts. If an only child lives far away from his cousins, his parents can try to arrange for him to visit large families where, in time, he will get to feel at home. Holidays such as Thanksgiving or Christmas are good occasions for planning joint celebrations with other families, relatives or friends.

An only child will sometimes feel sorry for himself (as every child does occasionally) and he will sometimes feel especially lucky, but parents should neither treat him as a "poor little thing" nor tell him how lucky he is. If they can be casual about their three-member family and enjoy it, their child will follow the lead.

Jealousy of an older or a younger child is one painful feeling which the only child is spared. He can grow up with the cozy, secure feeling that his parents love him best, that there is no doubt about it.

Then, too, the couple with but one son or daughter has the chance to establish a kind of companionship that is difficult to maintain when there are two or more children. It is easier to take one young child along on trips or visits or to have an enjoyable meal with him in restaurants. More important, however, is the kind of relationship parents can sometimes have with their only child. When there is no bickering and no necessity for continually settling disputes, there is less need for imposing discipline and the relationship can be on a more relaxed and equal basis. Parents then have more of a chance to build up mutual interests with their child, to share experiences, ideas, and fun.

Pleasant as this may be, every child needs as well the experience of sharing his parents' attention with others. Mothers and fathers have to avoid smothering their son or daughter with constant and undivided attention, with intense and undiluted concern. Fathers usually have jobs that claim their interest; the mothers of only children should probably be even more alert than other women about finding outside interests of some sort, such as an absorbing hobby or useful work in the community.

It was once taken for granted that only children were almost always spoiled, unsociable, given to temper tantrums, and "problem" children generally. But over a period of many years psychologists have made careful studies on only children as compared with those who have brothers and sisters, investigating such things as their initiative, self-confidence, self-control, industriousness, school achievement, independence, sociability, cooperativeness, and reliability. The chief thing these studies show is that there is no need to be especially concerned about only children; in their general problems and adjustment, they turn out to be very much the same as other children.

—From *The New Encyclopedia of Child Care and Guidance*. Garden City, N.Y.: Doubleday & Co., 1968.

OVERPROTECTION

NOW LET'S LOOK at the threats to self-esteem that must come as your child matures. From about three years of age, your little pride and joy begins making his way into the world of other people. He plays near his home with neighborhood children; he is often enrolled in nursery school, and a year or two later, he will toddle off to kindergarten. Whereas his self-concept could be carefully guarded during the first few years, it now becomes very difficult for Mom to control his environment. Other children may mock him and laugh at his deficiencies; he may be incapable of competing in their games; or he might even be crippled or killed in an accident of some kind. This initial "turning loose" period is often extremely threatening to his compulsive mother. Her natural reaction is to hold her baby close to her breast, smothering him in "protection." By watching, guarding, defending, and shielding him night and day, perhaps she can spare him some of the pain she experienced in her own younger days. However, her intense desire to help may actually interfere with his growth and development. Certain risks must be tolerated if a child is to learn and progress; he will never learn to walk if he is not allowed to fall down in the process.

It is probably easier to foster an unhealthy dependency relationship between parent and child than it is to avoid one. It often begins during the early days of infancy. At the moment of birth, a little child is completely and totally helpless. One forgets just how dependent a newborn is—in fact, I want to forget it, just as soon as possible! That little creature lying there can do nothing for himself: he doesn't roll over, he can't scratch his head, he is unable to verbalize his thoughts, and he won't lift a finger in his own behalf. Consequently, his parents are responsible for meeting his every need. They

303

are his servants, and if they're too slow in meeting his demands, he is equipped with a spine-chilling scream to urge them into action. He bears no obligations whatsoever. He doesn't even have to appreciate their efforts. He won't say "please" or "thank you"; he doesn't apologize for getting them up six times in one night; he even offers no sympathy when at 3:01 A.M. his exhausted mom drives the point of a safety pin through the fleshy part of her thumb (without doubt, the greatest agony in human experience!). In other words, a child begins his life in a state of complete and total dependency on those whose name he bears.

About twenty years later, however, at the other end of childhood, we expect some radical changes to have occurred in that individual. He should then be able to assume the full responsibilities of young adulthood. He is expected to spend his money wisely, hold down a job, be loyal to one woman, support the needs of his family, obey the laws of the land, and be a good citizen. In other words, during the course of childhood, an individual should progress from a position of *no* responsibility to a position of full responsibility. Now, friends and neighbors, how does little John-John get from position A to position B? How does this magical transformation of self-discipline take place? There are many self-appointed experts on child raising who seem to feel it all should happen toward the latter end of adolescence, about fifteen minutes before Big John leaves home permanently. Prior to that time, he should be allowed to do whatever he wishes at the moment.

I reject that notion categorically. The best preparation for responsible adulthood is derived from training in responsibility during childhood. This is not to say that the child is horsewhipped into acting like an adult. It does mean that the child be encouraged to progress on an orderly timetable of events, carrying the level of responsibility that is appropriate for his age. Shortly after birth, for example, the mother begins transferring responsibilities from her shoulders to those of her infant. Little by little he learns to sleep through the night, hold his own bottle, and reach for what he wants. Later he is potty-trained (hopefully), and he learns to walk and talk. Gradually, as each new skill is mastered, his mother "frees" herself that much more from his servitude.

The transfer of responsibility ordinarily runs along smoothly until the child reaches about eighteen months of age. At that point, he suddenly realizes two things: (1) Work is definitely an evil to be avoided at all costs! He hates the very thought of it! (2) With every new task he is forced to accept, he loses his momma a little more. Whereas she was his full-time servant before, now she is slipping away. He must pick up his blocks— she isn't going to do it for him anymore. He must wash behind his ears—she won't be there to wield the washcloth next time. And at this age, he craves adult attention. Therefore, if he is going to retain his playmate, he'd better keep her on the job. His thoughts are not this conscious or rational, of course, but anyone who has ever raised a toddler knows it happens! Consequently, a great tug-of-war ensues. Mom is trying to get Junior to grow up, and he's trying to maintain his infancy.

Enter again the emotional and physical threats of which I've spoken. They can easily cause an anxious mother to turn loose of the rope in the tug-of-war described above. Her idea is: "If I keep him dependent upon me for as long as possible, I can better protect him from the cruel world." Therefore, she won't let him cross the street for several years after he could make it safely. She does *everything* for him, requiring nothing in return. She enters into each neighborhood argument that occurs among his friends, taking his side regardless of who was right. Later she walks him to school, holding his hand with the proud assurance that she is being a good mother. And heaven help the teacher who tries to discipline her little tiger! You see, all through childhood she fosters a continuation of the infancy relationship, retaining all the responsibility on her back.

Does Junior prosper under this setup? Of course not. Mother is giving of herself totally, which seems like a loving thing to do. However, at the same time, she is allowing her overprotected child to fall behind his normal timetable in preparation for ultimate release as a young adult. As a ten-year-old, he can't make himself do anything unpleasant, since he has never had any experience in handling the difficult. He does not know how to "give" to anyone else, for he has only thought of himself. He finds it hard to make decisions or exercise any kind of self-discipline. A few years later, he will steamroll into adolescence completely unprepared for the freedom and responsibility he will find there. And finally, his future wife is in for some swell surprises which I shudder to contemplate.

Have you allowed your child to enjoy the freedom and responsibility that are appropriate for his age? Does your fear of emotional and physical hardships keep him locked in your arms? Are you afraid to make him work because he protests so loudly?

The biblical story of the Prodigal Son in the Book of Luke is a brilliant guide to follow at this point. The father knew that his boy was going to squander his money and live with prostitutes. He knew he would make many mistakes, and possibly destroy himself in the process. Yet he permitted the young man to leave home! He did not chain him to a tree, or even condemn him verbally. Nor did he bail him out when he ran aground in the distant land. The love with which the father said good-bye made it possible for his son to return after making a mess of his life. We would do well to follow the father's loving example.

In summary, our final task in building self-esteem for our children is in transferring responsibility from our shoulders to theirs, beginning with the rudimentary skills of infancy, and terminating with their emancipation during the late teens or early twenties. Letting go is not an easy task, but good parenthood demands it.

—From Dr. James Dobson, *Hide or Seek*. Old Tappan, N.J.: Fleming H. Revell Co., 1979.

OVERWEIGHT

CHILDREN SHARE with adults the tendency to be merciless to those who differ in any way from them. The child with thick glasses, the child of a foreign background, the child who dresses "funny"—these and others are often the target of jokes and teasing.

The fat child is especially prone to such ridicule. He may also in rare cases have some form of glandular abnormality.

Most children who are fat, however, have either inherited a stocky build from their parents or simply eat too much.

What should parents do about such a child? If he has simply inherited a sturdy build from his predecessors, all that can be done is to make sure he wears clothes that do not emphasize his size. Muted colors, vertical lines, and plain styles usually help a child look less large. Parents need to point out that the Lord is more interested in the child's personality than He is in his weight.

If a child is fat because he is eating too many starchy foods and candy, parents can make an effort to change the kinds of food that are available at snack time. If the child complains that "we never have any good food around any more," explain that the wrong foods are bad for people. You may also want to point out that our bodies are God's temple (*see* 1 Corinthians 3:16, 17; 6:19; Ephesians 2:21; Revelation 3:12) and that we do not honor God's temple by filling it with improper foods. Be alert for causes of overeating—lack of friends, problems in school, and so forth—and seek to solve the difficulties.

If the overeating continues despite your best efforts, you need to seek outside help. Your doctor may be able to help by giving your child a special diet.

—LESLIE R. KEYLOCK

FOR FURTHER READING:

God's Answer to Overeating. Lynwood, Wash.: Women's Aglow Fellowship, 1975.

Maynard, Leslie-Jane. *When Your Child Is Overweight.* St. Meinrad, Ind.: Abbey Press, 1980.

Wolff, Jurgen M., and Lipe, Dewey. *Help for the Overweight Child: A Parent's Guide to Helping Children Lose Weight.* New York: Penguin Books, Inc., 1980.

P

PACIFIER

THE PACIFIER, much in favor with past generations for keeping babies quiet and happy, has again enjoyed some vogue. If it is made of solid rubber, the child doesn't swallow air, and if washed often and kept clean, it is not unhygienic. For children a year or two old it may be a preferable alternative to continual thumb-sucking or useful as an intermediate device while they are growing out of the need for the thumb. But certainly a pacifier should not be offered to a child who shows no need for it.

Ordinarily, as a child grows more active and develops wider interests, he tends gradually to lose the intense need for sucking natural to many children in the early months. But often his parents have to help him to achieve this by encouraging and appreciating his efforts. If a child clings to the use of a pacifier for too long a time, it probably means—like persistent thumb-sucking—that he is using it for solace, and it would be wise to find out why he needs this.

—From *The New Encyclopedia of Child Care and Guidance.* Garden City, N.Y.: Doubleday & Co., 1968.

PARENTING

A HEALTHY CHRISTIAN home atmosphere is one in which biblical teaching is applied and lived. Many people today know what the Word of God says, but do not demonstrate it in their daily life. For example, you are probably familiar with Ephesians 4:32, in which Paul says, "And be kind to one another, tender-hearted, forgiving each other just as God in Christ also has forgiven you" (NASB). Are these attitudes seen in your behavior within your home? What does it mean to "be kind to one another"? How can we show kindness toward one another in our family?

I remember an evening service in our church several years ago. This was a special two-hour service for all members of the family with a focus on family relationships. For over an hour we worked on the passage that I have just mentioned. I asked everyone there to write down how they saw themselves putting this passage into practice in their own home during the next week. They were given five minutes to write down what they would do during the week, and then I asked several of them to share what they had written.

Instant conviction took place when one lady stood and shared her intentions. In fact, most of the group recoiled as though they had been hit, for her application was one that almost every family needed. She said, "Well, this week in showing kindness to my family *I am going to speak to my own children as I speak to the neighbors' children."* She hit the nail on the head. That *would* be an act of kindness. Most parents speak with more courtesy, tact, and patience to those outside of the home than they do to their own children. This is one way that a person can apply the teaching of Scripture as well as have it serve as a model for others in the family.

Love and Discipline. The healthy home atmosphere should be characterized by an abundance of love. The love of the husband and wife will set the pattern. The Apostle Paul instructed husbands to love their wives "just as Christ who loved the church and gave Himself up for her. . . . So husbands ought also to love their own wives as their own bodies. He who loves his own wife loves himself" (Ephesians 5:25, 28 NASB). Love also involves discipline. "If you refuse to discipline your son, it proves you don't love him; for if you love him you will be prompt to punish him" (Proverbs 13:24 TLB). A home without discipline provides little direction for the children. What does discipline mean?

Let's start out with the assumption that *discipline* and *punishment* are not the same. *Punishment* implies hurting someone in retribution or paying someone back for an offense. It is similar to "an eye for an eye." You punish to hurt another, to appease anger, or to satisfy the requirements of our society's legal system. Punishment can be a part of discipline when it imposes a penalty for undesirable behavior. But usually one punishes a child for one's own sake and not for the sake of the child; that is where punishment differs radically from discipline.

Discipline refers to acts or actions taken by someone in authority to restrain or rectify the behavior of someone under him. Discipline may include remedial measures, harsh or mild, that are taken to cause an improvement in conduct. These measures may be imposed in the form of precise rules or regulations to govern behavior. The words *correct* or *correction* are used in discipline; they

refer to the pointing out of error in order to help the child as well as to change his behavior.

Dr. Bruce Narramore, in his excellent book *Help! I'm A Parent,* gave a helpful description of the difference between discipline and punishment.

	Punishment	Discipline
Purpose	To inflict penalty for an offense	To train for correction and maturity
Focus	Past misdeeds	Future correct acts
Attitude	Hostility and frustration on the part of the parent	Love and concern on the part of the parent
Resulting Emotion in Child	Fear and Guilt	Security

You discipline with the intention of helping a person improve himself to learn a lesson that will make him a better person. You hope that your child will learn through the experience so that he will not repeat the act that brought about the discipline. In many cases the learning process with take some time. You also hope that your child will accept your rules and make them a part of his own value system.

Authority. Teaching must be a part of discipline. A person, in order to be receptive to learning, must see the teacher as having authority. Do your children see you as an authority? I'm not talking about an authoritarian person. That is different from an authority. You might ask your children or teens what they feel is the difference between the two words. An authoritarian person instills fear in others, does not listen to others or take into account others' wishes, and rules with an iron hand in a dominating, harsh, rigid manner. An authority knows what he or she is talking about, is a consistent source of information, and is a specialist.

One of the first and kindest acts in disciplining any child is to teach him that there is authority in this world. At times this authority has to rule without explanation. A young child should learn to accept the authority of his parents. His safety and his welfare depend on being obedient to them. There are occasions when time does not permit an explanation, or when the child could not really grasp an explanation if it were given. When a mother cries out, "Stop!" to a boy about to run into the path of a car, she wants him to stop immediately, without waiting for reasons. When a father counsels his daughter not to get into a car with strangers, he cannot burden her young mind with all the things those strangers might do. As the child grows older he will begin to ask questions, and as his reasoning develops so that he can handle explanations, more and more information will be given to him. But in the beginning he needs to see his parents as authorities, as teachers.

Trust. Children need good teachers. A good teacher is one whose teaching can be trusted. *A child needs to learn that he can trust the teaching of his parents. Parents must establish early in a child's life the dependability of their word.* Then the child will have a greater sense of security and will be on the way toward developing a healthy self-concept. In addition, a reliable trust relationship between parent and child makes it easier for the child to enter into a trust relationship with the Lord. Your child needs to be able to say, "My parents always mean what they say; I can rely on that!" This trust on the human level helps the child learn that he can rely upon what God says is His Word.

Necessity of Discipline. The Word of God tells us that we should discipline our children. Bruce Narramore illustrated it in this way:

Since children are born without knowledge and with a bent to evil, it was necessary for God to provide a way of training each new member of society. A child's old sinful nature doesn't magically pass away. It must be controlled, disciplined, and eventually yielded to the new influence of the Holy Spirit. To accomplish this task, God gave kids parents! There are a few biblical passages on the necessity and responsibility for parental discipline!

"And now a word to you parents. Don't keep on scolding and nagging your children, making them angry and resentful. Rather, bring them up with the loving discipline the Lord Himself approves, with suggestions and godly advice" (Ephesians 6:4 TLB).

"Withhold not correction from the child; for if thou beatest him with the rod, he shall die. Thou shalt beat him with the rod, and shalt deliver his soul from hell" (Proverbs 23:13, 14 KJV). In other words, discipline is for our children's good. It is essential if our children are to live happy lives on earth and also be prepared for heaven.

Encouragement and Openness. A spirit of encouragement and helpfulness to one another is essential. Children thrive on encouragement. It is a part of our response to one another as Christians. "Therefore, encourage one another, and build up one another . . ." (1 Thessalonians 5:11 NASB).

In a healthy family atmosphere emotions are displayed freely, accepted, and encouraged. Children should be taught at an early age that emotions are a gift from God and they should be taught also about the origin of emotions, their purpose, and their proper expression.

Another mark of this atmosphere is open and honest communication. Ephesians 4:15 commands us to speak the truth in love. We are admonished in Proverbs 28:23 to speak to the point: "He who rebukes a man will afterward find more favor than he who flatters with the tongue" (NASB).

This is a home in which there is guidance and direction, but not an authoritarian atmosphere. Dr. David Augsburger described this feature in terms of autocratic and Christocratic personalities.

The Autocratic Personality gives orders without asking questions, without permitting questions;	The Christocratic Personality asks questions, seeks to truly hear, suggests alternatives;
makes demands, dishes out directives, lays down the law, defensive if challenged;	respects freedom and dignity of others, can affirm the truth clearly and concretely, but nondefensively;
requires compliance regardless of consent or agreement;	values willing cooperation, works for open agreement and understanding;
pushes and manipulates one-man rule in over-under position;	leads, attracts, persuades personal relationships in side-by-side identification;
says "you do, you must do, you ought to have done, you'd better do";	says "come, let's do, we might have done, we can try"
depends on his own external authority to motivate others;	depends on his internal integrity to motivate others;
generates friction, resistance, and resentment;	generates acceptance, cooperation, and reconciliation;
separates and isolates people.	unites and helps persons relate to one another.

Freedom for Growth. Family members need freedom to grow and become independent persons through discovering their own potential and spiritual giftedness. Paul, in Ephesians 4:2, describes some of the behaviors that encourage freedom for growth: "Living as becomes you—with complete lowliness of mind (humility) and meekness (unselfishness, gentleness, mildness), with patience, bearing with one another and making allowances because you love one another" (AMP).

The Scriptures also speak to parents of nurturing their children. The word *nurture* or *nourish* means giving the object the best possible care. It does not mean that you give enough barely to sustain, but that you go out of your way to give the best possible care so that the child can develop to his fullest potential. You ought to provide your children with resources and experiences so they can develop to their maximum possibilities.

Unfortunately there are some homes in which the parents are insecure and become threatened when their children begin the normal process of expressing their independence. Often they try to convince their children that they cannot survive without the parents' support or knowledge in making decisions for them. One of the basic principles for healthy child adjustment is for parents to "let go and let grow"!

You see, parents are the ones to set the tone of the family life. You parents have more resources available because of your age, maturity, experience and skill. Children and even teenagers should not be the ones who control the atmosphere. "If only my child weren't the way he is, we would have a peaceful and happy home," is often said, but it is not accurate. A family member may not be contributing to the happiness or peacefulness, but are you as parents allowing him to control you and everyone else too? Do you allow a negative person to sour the entire atmosphere? It does not have to happen. It is possible for you, as parents, to set the tone in the midst of upsetting experiences.

Respect. Respect for the rights of other family members is important. Parents have rights and expectations; so do children. A child has the right to expect:

1. A father and mother who love each other and show it daily in small ways and big ways.
2. Two persons who place on their list of priorities God first, then each other, and their children next.
3. Two interested, kind, and loving guides. Two examples, not perfect, but good.
4. Parents who put relationships first, always (before rules, what others may think, etc.).
5. Enough time in the average week with parents (actually there, in person) to build a relationship. Regular times to talk (one-to-one).
6. To be allowed to be a child. The right to feel and think as an individual.
7. Expressed affection, appreciation, and respect.
8. The feeling of being understood. It is often difficult for parents to accept and understand why what is serious to parents cannot be as serious to children.
9. Consistent, reinforcing acceptance. To be treated as a valuable, capable human being. Never being torn down, never being attacked personally.
10. To be listened to always (not unhearing anger or patient endurance until you can "tell them a thing or two").
11. Parents who never treat lightly what is important to a child.
12. An attractive home—one of order and tranquility (that is, most of the time).
13. The right to privacy.
14. Guidance in forming good health habits. (Being overweight is more than just a physical burden to bear.)
15. Information about God, the Bible, a relationship with Christ, life, worthy goals, values, standards, sex, morals, alcohol, and drugs.
16. A single standard for both parents and the children regarding alcohol, drugs, honesty, church attendance, etc.

Attention-getting Mechanism. If a child is raised in a home in which these characteristics are lacking, he does not have as great an opportunity to develop a healthy self-image. In fact, a lack of these factors can help to create a poor self-concept. A child in such a home may become discouraged. Often he will have a *desire for undue attention.* He begins to believe that he has meaning or value only when he is the center of attention. He begins to develop a repertoire of attention-getting mechanisms, including becoming witty, cute, or obnoxious. Some children find that attention derived through negative means is better than no attention at all. Many disturbing methods such as whining, teasing, dawdling, and spilling food can come about. Many parents fall into the trap of responding. When a parent gives in to these excessive demands for attention, he just reinforces the child's mistaken self-concept. Other children may respond with a *power struggle.* If a child cannot get the attention he wants, he may decide to defeat his parents by using power. His satisfaction comes from refusing to do what the parents want him to do. If he were to give in to his parents, then he would be giving in to a stronger power and thus lose his sense of personal value.

A third approach, which is the result of intensifying the power contest, is *retaliation and revenge.* Some children choose this approach as their only means of feeling significant and important. They feel that they count only when they can get back at others.

The totally discouraged child chooses another approach. He demonstrates his *com-

plete inadequacy. He gives up completely. Why try when he has no chance to succeed? He begins to act helpless and uses this tactic to avoid any activity or task where he might show his failure and increase his embarrassment.

It is important to notice what your child is doing. Then if these behaviors are evident, action can be taken.

—From H. Norman Wright, *The Family That Listens*. Wheaton, Ill.: Victor Books, 1978.

FOR FURTHER READING:

Bettelheim, Bruno, Ph.D. *Love Is Not Enough*. New York: Avon Books, 1950.

Brandt, Henry and Landrum, Phil. *I Want to Enjoy My Children*. Grand Rapids: Zondervan Publishing House, 1975.

Caplan, Frank, ed. *The Parenting Advisor*. The Princeton Center for Infancy. Garden City, N.Y.: Doubleday & Co, 1977.

Cook, Barbara. *How to Raise Good Kids*. Minneapolis: Bethany Fellowship, 1978.

Feinbloom, Richard I., M.D. *Child Health Encyclopedia*. The Boston Children's Medical Center. New York: Dell Publishing Co., 1978.

Ketterman, Grace H., M.D., and Ketterman, Herbert L., M.D. *The Complete Book of Baby and Child Care for Christian Parents*. Old Tappan, N.J.: Fleming H. Revell Co., 1982.

Narramore, Bruce. *Parenting With Love and Limits*. Grand Rapids: Zondervan Publishing House, 1979.

Pedrick, Bob. *The Confident Parent*. Elgin, Ill.: David C. Cook Publishing Co., 1979.

Swindoll, Charles. *You and Your Child*. Nashville: Thomas Nelson, Inc., 1977.

PATIENCE

IN THE REARING of children, parents are aware and are repeatedly cautioned that they must be patient. Having patience means the ability to wait calmly, to persevere quietly, to endure annoyance or pain with self-possession. It implies stability, self-control, and courage. All these qualities, summed up in the counsel of patience, are basic in the relation of parents to their children.

Being patient with children has a short-term and a long-term significance. In the day-to-day management of routine, mothers and fathers need to remind themselves often that a young child moves at a much slower pace than an adult in every way. Dressing, eating, bathing, picking up toys, ending one occupation and beginning another, getting ready to go out or to go to bed—all take longer with a young child. However much he wishes to please his mother, he is incapable of moving quickly or thinking ahead. He does not have the coordination to dress himself, for example, with the speed of an older child. To put on a sock requires concentration and painstaking effort. If he is hurried, it takes him longer, or he is discouraged from learning to dress himself at all.

A quick mother finds that she must school herself to wait, to walk slowly, to stop often, to listen calmly while her little boy or girl gropes for the words to tell her something. She must try especially to avoid a feeling of annoyance by remembering that this is the best a young child can do, the fastest he can go. It helps a mother to be patient in the daily management of her young child if she can so arrange matters that she is not constantly under pressure to get too many tasks done. Occasionally there is a need to make haste, and then she finds a way to distract him and carry him along kindly but firmly.

Quiet persistence is another meaning of the word "patience," and this is essential in helping the child to learn. It is not enough merely to wait while he learns. It is necessary also to hold firmly to the few rules that are made and to guide him in learning to keep them. The child needs the stable, steady guidance of his parents on which to depend while he learns.

In the long-term view, parents are called upon to exercise patience with the child's rate of growth. Much is now known about individual differences in the way children develop and the unevenness that marks their growth through various stages. Some babies are slower than others to accept new foods; some youngsters find toilet training or some other step hard to accomplish. A little boy or girl may be quick in developing muscular co-ordination and slow in learning to speak, or slow in walking and quick to respond in other ways. Parents need patience to avoid annoyance or anxiety when their own youngster is not as advanced as the neighbor's child at one skill or another, or as the boys and girls in school. They also need patience through the adolescent years while their boy or girl reaches out for independence and stumbles in managing his new freedoms.

Patience can be overdone. While parents need to be patient with the impulsive, often irrational demands of their children, boys and girls must also learn that there are limits. Patience is no longer a parental virtue when it permits children to be uncontrolled, for example, in inconsiderate or destructive behavior, or in demanding satisfaction of unreasonable wishes. Being patient with children means being positive as well as tolerant in meeting the many and varied situations of family living day by day.

—From *The New Encyclopedia of Child Care and Guidance*. Garden City, N.Y.: Doubleday & Co., 1968.

PERMISSIVENESS

Dr. Benjamin Spock has been blamed at one time or another for almost all of America's problems, from the student revolution of the sixties to the fall of Vietnam. Now it is true that a generation ago he counseled young parents not to be so restrictive with their children; to respond more naturally to the child's needs. His famous book which sold over twenty-two million copies, *Baby and Child Care*, was published during an era of rigid rules of child care. Mothers were being told to wake their new babies every four hours for feeding whether they wanted to be fed or not. Spock, however, is not the chief culprit who led to today's permissiveness. It is a part of a much wider social problem related to the home.

It is true that there are some parents who spoil, pamper, and overprotect their children with the belief they are showing love, but instead raise incorrigible and irresponsible children. Some of them may have carried Spock's advice to extremes he never intended. In this generation, however, they are most certainly in the minority. Our problem today is far more serious and widespread than the doting parent of the past.

Permissiveness Is Neglect. Permissiveness among modern parents, in general, is not in response to the advice of Dr. Spock, but rather springs from neglect or indifference. Many modern parents, caught up in their own vocations and life goals, have found the care of children to be inconvenient. There is an observable trend to have fewer children, and many couples have decided to have no children because of the intrusion into their private lives. A recent survey of parents in their fifties indicated that a substantial number would not have children if they could do it over. Sociologists have called the new young-adult society of the seventies the "Me-centered generation."

Permissiveness today is often the failure to get involved in the life of the child—to take the easy way out. The child perceives this lack of discipline as lack of concern and love, and the result is predictable. Solomon wrote,

"The rod and reproof give wisdom; but a child left to himself bringeth his mother to shame" (Proverbs 29:15).

Often parents say, "I only want peace and harmony in my home. I want peace at any price." Generally what their actions show is that they are unwilling to set limits and enforce them if these go against the wishes of their child. They cannot tolerate the anger or disappointment this generates. They pay a high price for the questionable peace so attained. That price is the loss of that child through rebellion.

A child, in order to develop healthy emotional strength of identity, requires love and recognition of his self-worth. William Glasser maintains that identity is one of the single basic needs of every person: "[It is] the belief that we are someone in distinction to others, and that the someone is important and worthwhile. Then love and self-worth may be considered and the two pathways that mankind has discovered lead to a successful identity. If, however, a child fails to develop identity through love and self-worth, he attempts to do so through two other pathways, delinquency and withdrawal."

Permissiveness by the parent is not an act of love, but neglect. It does not produce strong, creative, and emotionally healthy children. Children need limits, and they are a requirement for emotional growth. Limits imply concern for the child's well-being. When parents fail to set limits, children will continue to test until they meet with resistance. An observer of the Kent State riots noted the young people continued to surge toward the National Guard troops, testing how far they could go. "It was almost as though they were searching for the limits."

—From Truman E. Dollar and Grace H. Ketterman, *Teenage Rebellion*. Old Tappan, N.J.: Fleming H. Revell Co., 1980.

314

PERSONALITY

JESUS SHOULD BE SET before the child as the ideal personality and the Son of God. As parents, we are often painfully aware that we fall far short of the perfections of Jesus. We always face a tendency to pretense of greater perfection than we really have. Our constant admonition of our child may well be "Follow me as I follow Christ." If we have genuine affection for Jesus and if we sincerely and practically in everyday living make Him our pattern and our perfection, our child, in identifying himself with us, will come to have the same kind of affection and faith.

The child needs to be trained in worship. Through the exercise of true worship, a human being derives inspiration for becoming more worthy. "Whatever we are, we are not what we ought to be," said St. Augustine. Worship is most helpful to the correction of wrong attitudes and to the stimulation of new and better ones. He who truly worships gets away from the imaginative unrealities of daily living and faces himself as he is in the sight of God. Confessing his wrongs, adoring and honoring his Creator, coming into the presence of higher ideals and rededicating himself to their attainment make for the reorientation of life and the reorganization of energies for the realization of higher aspirations.

The child should have impressed upon his consciousness a sense of the worth of every person. In these pages much emphasis has been placed upon the fact that the child should be treated as a person. If he is so treated, he develops a sense of personal worth—something that is a protection against inferiority feelings and an essential to normality. Every person feels unworthy at times, but a constant sense of unworthiness is not normal. The realization that every individual has worth as a person helps one take the right attitude toward both himself and other persons. Recognition that other persons have worth equal to one's own protects against the dangers of feeling superior to others and taking wrong attitudes toward them.

Christian faith must find expression in action; without works it is dead. By works alone can it be perfected. It has within itself an urge to growth. Feeling, knowing and willing, or doing, are the three aspects of mental life. Every feeling carries with it an impulse to action. Every such impulse that is given expression in action contributes to normality of personality and life. The child should be trained to live outwardly in terms of unselfish devotion to human needs, carried out as unto God.

Finally, it is important to train the child in the discipline of the Christian way of life. Observance of rules is essential to healthy living. Nothing so harms personality as want of discipline; softness is dangerous. Submitting one's will to honored authority is uplifting and strengthening. No life can be strong apart from discipline. Restraints on expression of native drives and primitive urges are healthful. One who lives in pleasure is dead while he lives. A prevalent cause of unhappiness is unrestrained desire—wanting what is not necessary or wanting what is harmful to the life. Christians are followers who submit themselves to discipline. They deny themselves present gratifications and keep the things of the spirit and the things of eternity in the first place. Thus, they have a goal for life and a purpose to fulfill. Living so, they are not subject to aimless uncertainty. Living so, they have a center for the integration of personality on constantly higher and higher levels.

By way of gathering up into a short summary the essence of what normal Christian personality is, one may say that it is a personality that has God and the doing of His will for a center. This gives it an inner harmony and singleness of purpose about which to integrate all of life. Sin is accepted as a reality, with the consciousness that it deserves penalty, but Christ is seen by faith as the Saviour who bears that penalty. Life is lived in complete surrender to and with unfaltering trust in God whose omnipotent power makes possible victory over sin, weakness and failure. Confidence, courage, hope and joy take the place of fear, discouragement, despair and sorrow, for the outlook is upward and outward instead of downward and inward. Unselfishness, desire for the welfare of others and sense of mission give point to living. Life, far from being vain and empty, is under helpful discipline that eliminates self-indulgence and inactivity. Being free in spirit, the person feels the exhilaration that comes from unlimited opportunity for and constant challenge to growth and expansion of the powers of his being.

—From C. B. Eavey, *Principles of Personality Building for Christian Parents.* Grand Rapids: Zondervan Publishing House, 1952.

FOR FURTHER READING:

Barrett, Ethel. *Don't Look Now.* Ventura, Calif.: Regal Books, 1968.

Bustanoby, Andre. *You Can Change Your Personality.* Grand Rapids: Zondervan Publishing House, 1977.

Cranor, Phoebe. *How Am I Supposed to Love Myself.* Minneapolis: Bethany Fellowship, 1979.

Osborne, Cecil. *The Art of Understanding Yourself.* Grand Rapids: Zondervan Publishing House, 1968.

Tournier, Paul. *The Meaning of Persons.* New York: Harper and Row Publishers, 1973.

PETS

WHEN YOU GIVE your child a pet, you don't just add a dog or cat or gerbil to your household; you change the emotional dynamics and psychological undercurrents of your family. You may do your youngster great emotional good—but you also must be wary of several possible pitfalls.

So says Dr. Boris Levinson, professor emeritus of psychology at Yeshiva University and an expert on people-pet relationships.

"A pet is too important and plays too great a role in the child's personality development for its choice to be left to mere chance," Dr. Levinson emphasizes. His answers to common parental questions may save you hours of cleaning up after a problem pet or fretting about what to do with an unwanted animal.

What kind of pet is best for a child?

Whatever the youngster has been asking for—provided it doesn't cause more inconvenience than you can tolerate, says Dr. Levinson. Before you get any pet, work through your own feelings about animals, decide how much time you can spare for pet care and discuss the choice thoroughly in a family conference, he advises.

If you can't manage the kind of pet your youngster wants, sit down and reason out with him what kind of animal would fit into your family.

A pet a child can take outdoors and play with around other youngsters has the most value, explains Dr. Levinson. An animal that is soft and cuddly, responds to a youngster's actions and shows its love and loyalty gives its owner more satisfaction than one that doesn't. Dogs are the first choice of both boys and girls, but girls rank cats higher than do boys as second choice.

What should you do if your youngster fails to care for his pet as he promised? Remind him constantly? Get rid of the pet? Do the work yourself?

It's best to sidestep this dilemma completely, according to Dr. Levinson. A parent should realize that caring for an animal is a learned skill acquired gradually by children, with considerable backsliding. If you praise your youngster enthusiastically when he does help care for his pet but don't rush turning over total responsibility to him until you are sure he will do it, you avoid this problem.

What is the best way to handle the death of a pet?

Realize that your youngster will have to go through the work of mourning and learn the agony of losing something he loves.

"If you don't work through a bereavement, you can't love anyone else again," Dr. Levinson points out. Like a vaccination, the loss of a pet can immunize a child against overwhelming emotional shock at the death of a family member.

Permitting a child to hold a burial service for a dead pet helps in the work of mourning. "Let him mourn for a week or two and then replace the pet," Dr. Levinson advises. "If you give him a new pet right away he may get the idea that life has little value and that he could also be replaced just as quickly."

What if a child feels he has contributed to the death of his pet by carelessness?

Discuss it with him, saying, for example, "You didn't know your dog would run into the street just when the car was coming." Talk about other families in which pets have had accidents. And if your child continues to have guilt feelings, get psychological help, for such emotions can be repressed for years, only to cause depression later in life, Dr. Levinson notes.

Will it be harmful to a child to have an old pet put to sleep?

Parents should avoid this move, cautions Dr. Levinson. Instead, they should use the pet's old age to teach their youngster how valuable life itself really is.

When a youngster brings home a stray animal you can't keep, what should you do?

First, praise the youngster for his goodness

in caring about the animal, advises Dr. Levinson. Then discuss with him what kind of plan you can make together to find a home for the animal. "This helps the child learn that his parents aren't arbitrary and that his own innate feelings of caring are good."

—From Joan Beck, *Effective Parenting.* New York: Simon & Schuster Inc., 1976.

FOR FURTHER READING:

Stevens, Carla. *Your First Pet and How to Care for It.* New York: Macmillan Publishing Co., 1978.

PETTING

THE VERY ESSENCE of the petting question is whether one's association with a person of the other sex shall be based chiefly on the physical or the social plane, and whether it is purely a pleasurable pastime, or the symbol of a permanent oneness in love. This very question reveals at once how intricate the problem really is, and why it is apparently difficult for a majority of young people to understand and evaluate the implications for themselves. Some frankly put their association chiefly on the physical plane, others on the social. But for many the distinction is not clear enough, and the relationship becomes something of both. When one's values are confused it is easy to fall into inferior ways of conduct.

Petting has an indefinable quality about it, since an individual reacts as a whole, not as a series of disconnected anatomical parts. Nor can the physical be separated from the psychological. Petting has physiological, psychological and social effects and implications. It has also spiritual implications which make it sacramental. One's behavior, then, can only be evaluated in terms of what happens to him as a person, not merely in terms of what part of his anatomy is involved in what particular process. So "necking" and "petting" belong to the over-all process of personal interaction.

The considerable freedom of physical contact between the sexes in our day creates a problem for young people in knowing how to discriminate between the degree of contact that is wise and beneficial, and that which is unwise, full of risk, and emotionally destructive. In this connection a girl has the delicate problem of where to draw the line in sex appeal. This is something she can govern to a certain extent. Undeniably, the desire of a person to make himself or herself attractive to members of the opposite sex is a legitimate part of mate selection, and sex appeal is one of a number of legitimate and necessary elements of attractiveness. The real question is what form the appeal should take and to what lengths it should go.

Petting is a process of physical and emotional involvement between two persons of opposite sex. It consists of kissing and fondling of a nature that tends to be sexually exciting and stimulating. It is physical contact for pleasure which is an end in itself, and involves fondling the erogenous zones, even to the point of bringing about an orgasm, but does not include sexual intercourse. In petting there is necessarily a deliberate attempt to effect sexual arousal. In marriage the same thing is called foreplay because it comes before and prepares the couple for intercourse. When petting is merely two persons enjoying themselves through each other, it is mutual lust. It is not calculated on their part to help them meet as persons at all, and something less than personality is fulfilled.

It is important to understand the difference between stimulation and satisfaction. Petting is sexual stimulation, not satisfaction. Even petting to climax is classified as stimulation, for while it brings physiological release, it falls short of the personal dimension of true satisfaction. It ends in tension. And as one can see, failure to understand this will lead to false expectations.

Most dates are relatively brief in time, so necessitate centering attention upon relatively few activities. If attention is focused upon petting, a false center is created which excludes the other possible experiences open to those who are seeking to know each other better. It excludes activities which afford greater rewards and satisfactions over a longer period of time. So petting tends to put the whole relationship on a restricted basis. It may exploit the one fact they are already agreed upon and nothing more.

Jesus said: ". . . whosoever looketh on a woman to lust after her hath committed adultery with her already in his heart" (Matthew 5:28). Lusting begins with looking. Or one might say that lusting can begin with imagining, for one can look through the eyes of imagination. It is this feature of moral evil that is not fully recognized by those who pet to a climax and then suggest that the moral quality of that act is not as bad as intercourse because it leaves the woman still a virgin! In such a case a man is actually "looking" through his hands and imagination, in fantasy violating the body of another person in a more thoroughgoing way than the man whom Jesus condemned as committing adultery in his heart because he merely looked on a woman to lust.

Persons can touch in many ways; they touch with hands, arms, lips. They can touch by kissing, hugging, carressing. They can also touch with thoughts and imaginations, with letters or photographs. We say commonly "Let's keep in touch."

Now any act is what it is because of its meaning to the persons involved. Thus two persons engaged in petting can hardly say with honesty that there is less meaning than

in actual intercourse, for mentally they have touched with the most intimate meaning. By touch and imagination they have invaded the inmost precincts of each other's personal and sexual being. The bodily secret of both has been revealed. Actual intercourse would add little beside the possibility of pregnancy. So one must conclude that the Christian view of petting is to put it on the same moral level as intercourse itself.

Petting makes common and vulgar what God intends to be noble and pure. The greatest value of kisses and caresses is that they are unique and precious gifts reserved for the beloved alone. They are given when they can lead fully to satisfaction and well-being. So really petting is playing at love in such a way as tends to make the more genuine expressions of love seem dull, stereotyped, and unsatisfying. The finer sensitivities of true love are dulled. Many a young woman has failed to recognize true love in a properly restrained lover because her experience of intense petting prompted the false expectation that a true lover would always be sexually aggressive and free to initiate familiarities.

One of the greatest self-deceits is to think one is strong enough to be careless and not be harmed. But beyond self-consideration, the one who indulges in petting must answer not only for the stimulation of lust in one's own life, but for the unknown degree of lust, self-contempt, and spiritual defeat brought about in the partner.

For every Christian young person this is a decision in the realm of self-discipline with the help of the Holy Spirit. The Scriptures say: ". . . know ye not that your body is the temple of the Holy Ghost which is in you, which ye have of God, and ye are not your own? For ye are bought with a price: therefore glorify God in your body . . ." (1 Corinthians 6:19, 20).

Whatever the standard of the non-Christian, the standard for the Christian is clear.

His body is a sacred trust from God, its functions meant to be restricted to and preserved for the ends designed by God. Since petting is an unnatural function which substitutes for intercourse when intercourse is not appropriate, it is certainly not within God's will for a child of His.

Petting outside of marriage is sexual immorality, and Paul said distinctly: "... The body is not meant for immorality, but for the Lord ..." (1 Corinthians 6:13 RSV). Again, he said that a Christian must "... possess himself of his own vessel in sanctification and honor, not in the passion of lust ..." (1 Thessalonians 4:4, 5 ASV). To this is added the word of Peter: "... abstain from fleshly lusts, which war against the soul" (1 Peter 2:11). And again, Paul's word to Timothy was: "Flee ... youthful lusts ..." (2 Timothy 2:22). So the issues are clear and the decision is plain enough for those who are honest with themselves and with God.

—From Dwight Hervey Small, *Design for Christian Marriage*. Old Tappan, N.J.: Fleming H. Revell Co., 1959.

PLAY

"THE FAMILY that plays together stays together," said many mental-health posters a few years ago. That philosophy still holds true. Yet many families do not know *how* to play—at least they rarely do so.

At various ages, children are capable of playing with different toys and in different ways.

The New Baby

A baby at birth experiences pleasure when held, when nursing, and probably when being touched and talked to. By three months of age (and often sooner), a baby enjoys looking at and banging on a mobile or a sturdy toy that he may grasp (only reflexly at first) in his own hand. His greatest pleasure continues to be the close attention of loving family members. Get close to a baby's face (if you don't have a cold!), blow on his neck, or tummy, and tickle his feet. Pull on his hands and feet to exercise those muscles, and enjoy his happy laughter as he responds to you.

At Six Months

By six months, a child is highly responsive, laughs and coos readily, and will make you think you'd like another baby just like him any day. Don't listen to that thought, because in a few months he will be teething and crawling and wearing you out! The six-monther will hold onto toys for a while, but he will learn to love dropping them to see you bend over and retrieve them. Be inventive! Fasten toys that are bright, that make noises, and that move a lot, onto his bed or high chair, so he can't throw them away. Continue to play with him physically as much as *you* both enjoy.

At Eight Months

Around eight or nine months your baby will be crawling. Help motivate him to do that by putting toys around his play area. As he crawls to them, he will be developing those important arm and leg movements that help decide his right- or left-handedness. He will play happily near you for longer times without your direct attention, but he still needs and wants plenty of that, too. Singing or talking to your child while you are busy will keep the baby happily aware of your presence and more content. This is the time to reorganize your schedule so you can begin to catch up with a lot of household chores you dropped a while ago.

319

At One Year

At a year, many children are walking and can get into things at higher levels, than a crawler, so re-child proof your house! At this age, babies love to poke their fingers into holes and they enjoy putting items into and out of a container. Be certain that all electrical outlets are covered so the baby won't get hurt. Large beads or small blocks and a box or pail will intrigue him for many minutes. Think constructively now! If you interrupt that in and out process on the "in" cycle, you can actually teach your year-old child to begin putting away his toys! It's so much easier to develop that habit now, than to battle a child of two about it. Learn by watching your child's interest and readiness and think about using that information to your advantage—and his good training.

Twixt One and Two

Between one and two years of age, babies begin to build. They stack two or three blocks—but mostly they knock down the ones you stack! That's not because you did a bad job, or because baby is a destructive monster. It's because he likes to see things move and bounce, and because maybe you will build another one. The play process is important now—not the height of that block tower! Pull or push toys are great at this age. Babies love to cuddle stuffed toys and still like holding, tickling, and romping.

Now Comes Two

As you approach that second birthday, you will become aware of behaviors in your child that seem aggressive and stubborn. They are! That's how your child learns to be a real person, and finds out what he can do or can't do. He wants to explore, and when he is stopped for any reason, he is frustrated.

We believe a two-year-old should be taken out-of-doors a lot. Help him find a safe place to climb, and supervise him so he won't fall! Help him swing, run, and walk on a wall—holding your hand. He will love wild flowers and will tear them up. Caterpillars are a thrill, as are wild animals and birds. As you guide this time of exploration, you will find fewer areas to fight about and can direct his energies into wonderful, constructive activities.

Toys for Twos. Toys for a two-year-old need to include a pounding board. Let him hit it when he is angry, or just when he needs to pound. He loves to take things apart, so blocks that stack inside of each other will interest him, as will things you may build out of interlocking blocks. He will do some building of his own with big wooden or plastic blocks. Usually by two, children are ready for books with one big picture to a page. Their vocabulary will grow by seeing the A for *apple* and B for *ball* pictures, though you will be weary of them. By two, some children can sit still for short stories.

TV for Twos. "Sesame Street" and other excellent children's TV programs will interest a two-year-old for a while. Spend some time watching with him and help him learn by talking with him about the program. Children may see life in bits and pieces, unless an adult helps those pieces of information to fit into the whole of life. And two-year-olds can understand those bits of knowledge. Our grandson and Grace were making a cake when he was only two and a half. As he "helped" her measure and stir, he said, "Grandma, that's cooperation!" His mother told me he had learned that big word on "Sesame Street," but it obviously made sense in the kitchen!

Importance of Praise. Be sure to praise your children from the first day you have them at home. Many parents are, by nature, critical, and there are times when you need to be so. You will find, however, that children respond far more to praise than to scolding. So begin early to develop your own habits of finding your child's good points, and tell both the child and another person about them. Honest praise to a child and to another adult about him, begins to reflect a positive self-image that will help him for a lifetime!

Between Three and Six

These children blossom in their own imaginations and creativity. They need play items that give them the opportunity to explore and develop these qualities. More nature hikes are great. Large crayons and blank paper, clay, or similar substances can lead to great artistic feats. Post these on the refrigerator or a bulletin board or send them to relatives. Children learn to believe they are worth something because the things they create are important to others! Tea parties and playing house are a source of great fun and a caricature of yourselves, Mom and Dad.

Stories. After three, stories become increasingly fun for children. Reading a library book or telling a story you've made up are equally delightful at this age. From three to seven, children are capable of vivid imaginations. Pretend friends, pets, and games are wonderful adventures to share. Just be sure the child and you both know you are pretending.

Building and Taking Apart. Both are possible in the late preschool years. Any old appliance can be a storehouse of fun. Be careful to teach your child how to dismantle the object, and do be careful of its safety. Any glass or sharp areas make it off limits. Be certain that your child understands which appliances are *old* and which are *new!*

Games Children Play at Four and Five

At Four and Five. These children often enjoy some of the board games with spinners and pegs. These can help them learn to recognize colors and numbers. They catch on early, however, to the thrill of winning. We believe in cheering when they win, and helping them learn to lose, as well. That obviously means that once in a while, you need to win (honestly), and then help the child to accept that—even grudgingly. It is wise to play one more game after you win, so the child has another chance to win. Don't be too tough a competitor until the child's skills grow to a point where he can handle it.

Starting School. Once your child starts school, he will enter the era of physical sports and school games. Usually he will prefer playing with friends to spending time with parents. You may be really useful if you will teach him how to do well in those sports his interest and physical skills are best suited for. But also teach skating, swimming (which may best be started in the preschool years), tennis, golf, or other games which offer social advantages.

At About Eight or Nine

Now you may want to explore "little league" sports for your child. For some athletically gifted children, these offer a chance to develop real skills and a team spirit. Our frank opinion, however, is against such sports for an average or unskilled child. We have watched the sad faces of the chronic bench warmers and have seen their growing embarrassment and depression. Maybe you can find teams whose coaches care about giving every child a chance to play rather than having to win every game. This happens in less-organized competition, so choose a team that is good for your child.

Backyard Fun and Games

These still seem the most democratic and best suited to the healthy fun of childhood. Help your child learn how to give, take, and share in playing together. When children are under seven or eight, they enjoy adult participation in playing, if it isn't too controlling. This enables you to help your child (and even his friends) to develop good sportsmanship.

Family Night

We strongly urge every family to keep at least one evening every week as a family-fun night. As soon as children are able to do so, they may take turns choosing one of the games or activities that you, the parents, can offer. Everyone must be a good sport and enter into the fun. As you set the mood, your children will irresistibly be drawn into the fun. Sometimes you won't feel like doing this, but do it anyway!

Skipping only one time can spoil the ritual, and you will have a hard time recapturing it. It was our experience that we had to fight the school, church, and entire community to do this, but it was worth it.

—From Grace H. Ketterman, M.D., and Herbert L. Ketterman, M.D. *The Complete Book of Baby and Child Care for Christian Parents*. Old Tappan, N.J.: Fleming H. Revell Co., 1982.

FOR FURTHER READING:

Hancock, Maxine. *People in Process: The Preschool Years*. Old Tappan, N.J.: Fleming H. Revell Co., 1978.

Madaras, Lynda. *Child's Play: A Manual for Parents and Teachers*. Culver City, Calif.: Peace Press, 1977.

Singer, Dorothy G., and Singer, Jerome L. *Partners in Play: A Step-By-Step Guide to Imaginative Play in Children*. New York: Harper and Row Publishers, 1977.

PORNOGRAPHY

SCIENTISTS tell us that the brain is our most important organ because it determines the function of our other organs, such as the pituitary, hypothalamus, heart, nervous system, and so forth. We have little control over the involuntary function of the brain, except to provide it good nutrition (both physically and mentally) upon which to operate. The voluntary part of the brain we do control, however, and that largely consists of the three areas we have discussed:

WHAT WE SEE / WHAT WE HEAR / HOW WE THINK

Ever since God first spoke to Adam and Eve, explaining to them how to think, so they would know how to live successful and happy lives, there has been a consistent battle over who will control the thought processes of man's mind—man or God. Sooner or later, every human being makes that decision, and the result is his philosophy of life. Until this generation, parents were the most influential force in helping a child formulate his philosophy. That is no longer true. Modern technology has found ingenious ways to assault the mind of man and child with incredibly beautiful sounds, colors, and visual imagery. Millions of parents have already lost their children's minds to rock stars, atheistic-humanistic educators, sensual entertainers, and a host of other anti-God, amoral, antiman influences.

Since you are what you think, your thought processes today are largely the result of the input that has come to your mind via your eyes and ears. If you are not careful, you will lose the battle for control of your mind and the minds of your children.

One of the great myths of our times is that feelings are spontaneous. Actually, they are created by what you put into your mind. Computer people repeatedly warn, "You get out of a computer only what you program into it," or, more crudely stated, "Garbage in—garbage out." The same can be said for the mind. Whatever the eyes and ears communicate, the mind in turn dispenses. The other senses—smell, taste, and touch—influence our thinking but do not have as significant an impact on our mind.

Consider the unmarried, twenty-one-year-old college student who acknowledged a serious problem with sexual thoughts. Realizing that he was at the zenith of his sex drive, I was not surprised by his confession. In an attempt to help him learn to control his emotional passions, I asked, "What have you been reading and seeing lately?" After skirmishing a bit with vague references to newspapers and magazines, he finally acknowledged a more-than-passing acquaintance with *Playboy* and certain pornographic books. When pressed about movies, he admitted that he had been watching X-rated movies on cable TV. I pointed out to him that such a large intake of pornography was like pouring gasoline on a fire.

The old truism, "You are what you read," could be enlarged to, "You are what you see." What the eyes feast upon forms an impression on the mind, which in turn feeds the emotions. Just as drugs or alcohol influence thoughts and feelings physically, what we see and hear affect our thoughts and emotions.

There is growing evidence today that our warnings to civil leaders a few years ago— that overturning the moral laws upon which this country was built would increase crimes of sex and violence—were fully warranted. In the name of free speech and freedom of the press, we have polluted the minds of our young with pornography, until crime and sexual assaults are now commonplace. The problem will not diminish until we elect public officials with sufficient moral sanity to pass laws prohibiting the distribution of corrupting materials.

Not only are just our morally minded citizens concerned. A recent demonstration of feminists in New York highlighted their concern that the widespread use of "porno" is a threat to them, for they become the victims of rape and assaults.

Sociologist Marvin Wolfgang has stated, "The weight of evidence now suggests that the portrayal of violence tends to encourage the use of physical aggression among people who are exposed to it." Of course it does. Whatever you see or hear influences your mind, which in turn affects your feelings and your emotional center. Feelings, then, are aroused as much by what you see and hear as by who and what you are. If you want the right feelings, see and hear the right things, so you can generate the right thoughts.

Thousands of minors have been taken into custody for crimes that never would have been committed, had it not been for the abuse of porno. I visited a sixteen-year-old in juvenile hall, after he had committed a sex crime that startled everyone who knew him. In checking his room, we found two-thirds of a drawer filled with pornographic filth. It was easy to understand how this lad brought disgrace upon his family and shame to himself. At a time when he was beginning to experience new sexual passions, he *artificially* fanned them by the misuse of his eyes, until his emotions were ignited beyond control. He will probably be haunted by that evil action the rest of his life.

However, that boy was not abnormal. He simply underwent a natural reaction to an abnormal stimulus. Pornography is abnormal! Our youth seem obsessed with sex because depraved adults are providing them the pornographic fuel with which they are burning up their lives.

Admittedly, all visual filth, whether in TV, movies, or books, does not result in crimes of violence. But my counseling experience indicates that it frequently occasions an equally negative effect: reducing the beautiful expression of love in marriage to a sexual expression of passion. In fact, pornography is one of the leading causes of our skyrocketing divorce rate.

Pornography, of course, is not the only phenomenon that influences the emotions. I use it as a graphic illustration pointing up that what you see and hear largely influence how you think, and how you think influences your feelings.

Here is a healthy rule of thumb to follow, when you recognize wrong or harmful feelings: Examine what you have been seeing and hearing lately and how your mind has been thinking. Feelings are not spontaneous; to control them, you must first control your mind.

—From Tim LaHaye, *The Battle for the Mind.* Old Tappan, N.J.: Fleming H. Revell Co., 1980.

FOR FURTHER READING:

Court, John H. *Pornography.* Downers Grove, Ill.: Inter-Varsity Press, 1980.

Gallagher, Neil. *How to Stop the Porno Plague.* Minneapolis: Bethany Fellowship, 1977.

PRAYER

PRAYER . . . is the outcome of knowledge and of love. Such a knowledge of God and a love for God are not slow in coming to birth in the child's heart, if, in his life, he has known somewhat of the happy experiences upon which alone such knowledge rests. For where love is, God is; and the child is ever ready to give love in return for love; ever quick to understand the thought of a Living Source of all Love behind its visible manifestation.

When he knows and loves he is ready to pray, but not before. Then if he is one of the more fortunate children brought up in a happy home, one night his mother suggests to him that he himself should pray, first reminding him of all his gladness—gladness which brings him nearer to God. Would he himself not like, now that he is bigger, to tell God how happy he is? she asks him. Till now, his mother has spoken to God for him, as, with bowed head and folded hands, he has knelt at her knee. She was always grave and quiet when she spoke to this Unseen Father, and, child though he is, he has caught somewhat of this gravity, this quiet reverence, from her, and linked it up in his mind with his thought about God. At first, because of this, he may be a little awed at the thought of speaking to God. But God has been so good to him—he remembers all that—and even though he cannot see God, God can hear him when he speaks; about that he has no doubt. Shyly and quietly, and in a glow of conscious gratitude, which it is good to be able to express, come the child's first words: "Dear Father, thank you for making me happy. Please make everybody happy. Amen." Gradually, this first shyness passes away, and for a while, at any rate until he is a good bit older, speech comes to him more and more easily. Naturally and spontaneously he begins to tell God of his joys, to confide in Him his troubles, to ask Him for His help. "Please take care of me to-night, dear Father, and don't let me be frightened in the dark." "Please help me to be a better mother to my dolly, 'cos I'm not a bit the right sort of mother now." "Please help me not to grumble to-morrow, but it's the first day of the holidays, and you know, dear Father, it's always hardest on the first day. Thank you for all the lovely things you send us—thank you for mothers and fathers. Thank you for books, for toys, for babies, for flowers, for houses, for—heaps of things!"

When God is first known and loved, the child's thoughts about God are wondrously simple. Geoffrey was nine when he prayed: "Thank you for trying to make us all happy, and please make yourself happy too, if you can; and if you can't, don't worry"; and Mary was the same age when she hoped God would have "a good night" as well as herself. "It didn't matter my saying that, Mother, did it?" she whispered. "I love God, that's why I hoped He'd have a good night."

Responsive children, brought up under happy circumstances, are ready to express themselves in prayer by the time they are between two and three years old, but there is no uniform period at which every child is ready. Some respond to their spiritual environment rapidly, others slowly. Consequently we need have no anxiety if prayer is delayed, and all forcing should be avoided. A capacity for religious life is innate in all, though the period when response is complete varies according to the fineness and depth of the child's moral nature and the fullness of his power to imagine the Unseen. Some children, lacking in the power of imagination, find the very realization of an Unseen Father difficult. In others, unusually independent or self-centered, the realization of a Father does not awaken a responsive love. Others, though "knowing" God as well as loving Him, though conscious of their need for Him, are "shy" at the thought of themselves speaking to Him, as the result of an imagination which is morbid. Only gradually, as such children gain confidence, can they find comfort for themselves in prayer.

The age at which the child himself is ready to pray can only be determined by the stage of his development. Feeling is essential to all prayer, and care must be taken that prayers are never "said" as a mere outward form only.

For this reason, it may be better at first not even to teach the child to repeat regularly Our Lord's Prayer. Later, when he has grown accustomed to speaking to God in his own words; when too he has learnt to know and to love our Lord and has begun to understand that it is only through Him that we know God in the way we do, as a Father who cares for us, His children—then, what can be more natural than to add at the end of his own prayer the words which our Lord Himself has taught? "All this, dear Father," the child can now add in conclusion, "I ask because Jesus taught me to ask, Jesus who taught us how to pray, saying 'Our Father which art in Heaven,' etc." Never as a mere form of words only, but always slowly, reverently and thoughtfully, the child can be taught to say these words. As the reverent attitude of the body has power to engender in the soul a corresponding feeling, so through the whole-hearted saying of such words as these, somewhat of the spiritual attitude which they embody becomes for the time the child's own attitude. Charged with emotion, expressing—in a few simple words—love, trust, reverence, gratitude, dependence, aspiration and consecration, this prayer—the most selfless prayer ever breathed—interprets for us all our inmost feelings, inspires our highest efforts, and can never be outgrown.

I am sure that the dawn of religion is brightest when the child comes to a knowledge of God in the very beginning of his life, as easily and as naturally as he comes to a knowledge of his own mother. Yet sometimes all teaching is omitted, either through neglect or through ignorance on the mother's part; or it is deliberately postponed until the child is older.

If the mother and the father in the home

are unable for any reason to enter into this side of their children's lives, then the school must take the place of the home, and the child win there his first intimate and conscious understanding of God. But, whether at home or in school, the general process of spiritual growth follows the same lines.

Knowledge of God and love for God can only be acquired by the slow, and for the most part unconscious, sifting-out of repeated experiences of God.

All that it is in the mother's or the teacher's power to do is to provide those experiences and choose wisely times and seasons for their spiritual interpretation.

Until love is awakened, as well as knowledge gained, the child is not ready, as we have seen, to pray by himself.

"We have asked God to retire into the back parlour nowadays," someone once said, referring to the religious reticence of the more leisured classes, "and we feel as if we ought to apologize whenever He comes into the front room." Is there not some truth in the expression? Does not this reticence of ours make it more difficult for some of us to give to our children the natural religion which they need?

Where religion is expressed simply and naturally in life, the seeds of understanding, whether sown at home or in school, are sown in a fertile soil.

—From E. E. Read Mumford, *How We Can Help Children to Pray.* Longmans, Green, 1933.

FOR FURTHER READING:

Allen, Charles L. *All Things Are Possible Through Prayer.* Old Tappan, N.J.: Fleming H. Revell Co., 1975.

Marshall, Catherine. *Adventures in Prayer.* Lincoln, Va.: Chosen Books, 1975.

Shoemaker, Helen S. *The Secret of Effective Prayer.* Waco, Tex.: Word, 1976.

Smith, Joyce Marie. *Learning to Talk with God.* Wheaton, Ill.: Tyndale House Publishers, 1976.

White, John. *Daring to Draw Near: People in Prayer.* Downers Grove, Ill.: Inter-Varsity Press, 1977.

PREGNANCY

Understanding the Experience

Creating a brand-new life is no laughing matter, but it certainly is one of the most exciting experiences one can ever know—perhaps *the* most exciting. I have always felt a bit sorry for men in general, and my husband in particular, because they can never know all the feelings—good and painful—that are involved in those nine months and their climax in that ancient miracle of childbirth.

Since this is such a profound experience, I want you husbands to understand as much about it as you can. You wives may read this, too, but you will be experiencing it anyway, so let your husband read it first.

Somehow your lovemaking becomes even more meaningful when you have decided to have a child. There is a special purpose in it that will reach completely into eternity, and that is awesomely wonderful. Once that one little sperm has found the ovum, fertilized it, and the new life has started, you, the father, are pretty much outside of things, but here are some events your wife will go through.

The Growth of the Baby

The two half-cells that have become one in the Fallopian tube (usually) move into the womb. There, the egg settles into the soft uterine lining that is full of tiny blood vessels and nurturing fluids. Around this potential baby a protective and nourishing cover called the *placenta* is formed. Through this the developing baby is fed and its waste products are carried away. The mother's body has to work overtime to provide these processes.

Morning Sickness

At first the womb and its tiny occupant lies in the mother's pelvis, protected and confined by the pelvic bone. During this time (about three months), the pressure of the enlarging uterus creates a sense of discomfort. Your wife will need to urinate more frequently and will find her sleep disturbed. In some women this pressure, or some other factors, causes a feeling of nausea. This is especially common when getting up in the morning and is called *morning sickness.* A mother may have to vomit and, in some cases, this may take place repeatedly throughout the day. Your wife may feel really miserable during these weeks, and she will need all the encouragement and support you can give her.

Be careful, however, not to pity her or feel so sorry for her that she feels even worse. Your doctor will tell her what to do to relieve this discomfort to some extent, so just reassure her that you care, and remember that it will pass. Helping her with food preparation is especially beneficial, because the odors of certain foods may make her feel even worse. Ask her what she needs from you without hovering over her or babying her too much.

Second Trimester

In the second three months (called a trimester), the uterus rises out of the pelvis, and usually the nausea and vomiting stop as abruptly as they began. During these months the uterus enlarges quite rapidly, and this makes necessary an entirely new wardrobe.

Now let me tell you something very important. Women in today's society are considered beautiful only if they are tiny-waisted and slender. Your wife will be anything but slender for the last five or six months of her pregnancy. She may feel fat and ugly. It is extremely important, therefore, that you help her select an attractive wardrobe. It need not be large or expensive, but a few new items from time to time, over these often tedious weeks, will encourage her and can help her feel pretty and valued by you. Your interest in her body's changes will help her to feel special and it will also help you to feel more a part of this process.

Movements of the Baby

Some time during the fourth or fifth month, a mother first feels her baby move! She may not even recognize this at first. It feels a bit like a gas bubble. But as the baby grows and its very tiny arms and legs move, she will recognize the feeling for what it is. This is usually an experience of profound joy. The fact of the presence of a life within her becomes a reality. For most mothers this is intensely moving, and helps to compensate for the earlier discomforts.

It will be late in the fifth or early in the sixth month before you, the waiting dad, can feel the movements of the baby. But that, too, will come in due time, and most fathers find excitement similar to the mother's in the early acquaintance with their awaited baby. The more you involve yourself in the early growth of your baby, the more you will feel a part of this process of becoming a parent. Do be sensitive, however, to your wife's moods and her need for some privacy. If you are honest and kind in your interest—not idly curious or demanding—you may expect your wife to enjoy sharing this developing baby with you.

Let me urge you, as an expectant father,

to visit the doctor who will deliver your baby. Getting to know each other will be another step in your really becoming a father.

Lamaze Method

The wonderful practice of including dads in the actual birth of the baby is relatively new and I strongly encourage your doing so. This procedure, called the Lamaze Method, involves a series of classes during the last three months (or last trimester) of pregnancy. The process of labor and delivery is explained, and fathers are taught how to "coach" the mother through this somewhat difficult experience. The dad helps the mother to relax and breathe properly with her contractions and thus hasten delivery. Mothers seem to feel safer, do not resist the muscular contractions, and avoid some of the difficulties of delivery. Many young fathers have personally expressed to us the deeply emotional—almost spiritual—experience this has been for them.

Last Trimester Discomforts

Back to the last trimester of pregnancy. Fathers, let me prepare you for a somewhat trying period. In shorter mothers especially, the enlarged uterus climbs relentlessly to the mother's rib cage. The active baby's motions kick her stomach and ribs and cause real discomfort. At night the baby may be so active, he disturbs her sleep. Her urinary bladder, more comfortable during the second trimester, is crowded again, and the regular nightly trips to the bathroom resume. Often the pressure of the uterus against her stomach causes some of the bitter contents of the stomach to be regurgitated into her esophagus and mouth. This is called heartburn, and is especially likely to happen at night. It is miserable for her, and she is likely to disturb

your sleep. Try to be patient and sympathetic with her. A gentle touch and encouraging word, or a small drink of milk, will help her to endure these traumatic nights. I know you have to work the next day, but so do many pregnant wives. At least you don't have to feel the discomfort!

During this trimester, your wife's enlarging abdomen will create pressure on the large blood vessels in her pelvis. This will cause swelling of her feet and legs. Her doctor will watch this and will probably require her to elevate her feet and lie down more. He will also restrict her salt and will want her to watch her diet. Gaining too much weight at this time is very risky for her and the baby. Again, your understanding and support will help. Please believe she is not getting lazy or spoiled, but do go out for walks with her and encourage her to do whatever exercises her doctor recommends.

By the sixth month, most mothers develop purple lines over their hips, lower abdomen, and often the breasts. These are called *striae* and are permanent. Their color will fade, but they are lasting marks, and most women hate them. They don't look good in a bikini! Your consolation and love will help. Let your wife know that it is her inner beauty that is most important to you. Remind her that the baby will bring more joy to her than these marks bring disfigurement. You may even get her a one-piece swimsuit that is especially attractive, but be sure it can be returned!

With all of these painful or uneasy feelings, you must be wondering why I described becoming a parent as such a marvelous event, but you will understand that, as soon as your baby is born.

Getting Ready

You and your wife will need to be prepared for that momentous occasion. She will have her bag packed and ready for her hospital stay. You need to help her prepare everything for the baby's arrival before leaving the house for the hospital. A special surprise for her (such as a bottle of her special perfume or a single flower) during labor, or as soon as she is in her room, would be especially appreciated.

Before the birth of our first baby, my husband and I thought we had everything possible ready for her. She was a tiny baby—only five pounds when we took her home—and I'll never forget how excited and nervous we were. Of course, she began to cry as soon as we reached the house, and I was sure she was hungry. Feeling tired and weak, I asked my husband to bring her bottle—only to discover that we had totally forgotten that life-sustaining item! I managed to quiet and comfort the baby while my husband went in search of the prescribed formula. All three of us survived and have laughed together over that historic oversight. You will have them, too, and you also will work creatively through or around them. I hope you will learn to laugh together over them and not accuse or blame yourselves or each other.

The television caricature of the calm expectant mother, in labor, driving herself to the hospital, while her nervous husband is frantically hunting the left shoe he holds in his hand, is unfortunate. I, for one, believe you fathers have been the brunt of bad jokes long enough. Your image has faltered and failed at the hands of media people searching for a laugh.

"The Dry Run"

You will, of course, feel worried and nervous when your wife goes into labor. There are too many cases of taxicab deliveries for you to feel perfectly calm, but you will make it. In her last prenatal visits, your doctor will have prepared your wife (and hopefully you)

for the procedure of getting admitted to the hospital. If you have been taking the Lamaze classes, the other people there will be discussing such matters. Nevertheless, I strongly suggest that you both do a "dry run." Find the best route to the hospital, and an alternative one, in case you must drive in rush-hour traffic. Ask for the way to the admitting office of your hospital, and be sure you carry your health-insurance identification with you. Hospitals are costly to run, and they really do need prompt payment for their services if they are to maintain the quality of care you want for your family.

Some hospitals conduct tours through the labor rooms and delivery area, and explain what to expect there. Most doctors and hospitals now encourage the presence of the father and his help all the way through delivery. The old fears that fathers will faint, fall, and suffer a cerebral concussion are found to be groundless, although it does happen occasionally. You men are much tougher than we thought. Your involvement in the birth process, as well as that of holding and giving bottles to your own infant and learning to change diapers, is now part of all good hospital routines.

Alternatives for the Squeamish

There are people, men and women alike, who are squeamish about medical situations. Having a finger pricked for a blood count can cause our daughter to faint. If you are one of those people, you may find that you simply cannot go through with all this labor and delivery coaching, but perhaps you can do parts of it. Be assured that this does not mean you are a coward, or that you don't love your wife, and emphatically explain that to her. It has, in fact, happened that a waiting father has fainted and fallen, taking away medical staff who were needed to assist at the baby's birth, in order to help him. So know yourself and have an alternative plan.

One young couple borrowed a woman friend of the mother to coach her through labor. They all shared in the birth of a beautiful boy, and this helpful friend has continued to give both parents support and love as their baby grows. Such a person is especially wonderful if you are far away from relatives.

—From Grace H. Ketterman, M.D., and Herbert L. Ketterman, M.D., *The Complete Book of Baby and Child Care for Christian Parents.* Old Tappan, N.J.: Fleming H. Revell Co., 1982.

FOR FURTHER READING:

Hambrick-Stowe, Elisabeth A. *Expecting.* Valley Forge, Pa.: Judson Press, 1979.

Patterson, Janet, and Patterson, Robert C. *How to Live with a Pregnant Wife.* Nashville: Thomas Nelson, Inc., 1976.

PRESCHOOL CHILD

Introduction. The preschool child's ideas of right and wrong depend upon his experiences, his socialization, and his intellectual abilities. The first two years of his life are spent mainly in learning through sensorimotor (combining the five senses with action) activities, and the child has no true concepts at all. He continues activities that are reinforcing (that are encouraged or rewarded by others) and forgets those that are discouraged or punished. So even though a child's behavior is somewhat predictable, the child has no general sense of right and wrong. The preschool child is actually in a premoral stage of development.

Because your child attaches personal significance to important people in his life, he wants to please them—especially you, his parents. When you're happy, your child is happy, too. He often doesn't understand why

he is permitted to do some things but not others. Getting clues from your reactions to his behavior, your child notes that when you say good or big, you often smile. He will try to remember to do things that make you say these words.

Lying. The preschooler knows that you don't accept lying, but he doesn't view it quite as adults do; his thinking capacity is not that well developed. Suppose you see your daughter hit a vase with a ball that you had told her not to throw in the house. But she knows that balls are for throwing, and she doesn't think about balls breaking things, as you do. Your child knows that saying "I'm sorry" seems to make you feel better, but it doesn't really change the situation for her. She still doesn't see why you are so upset; she told you she didn't break the vase. She was just throwing—the ball did the breaking.

It takes time for your child to develop the mental ability to think things through, and you need to develop patience with these immaturities. Having lived a long time in society, you have developed desirable moral qualities, but your child's experiences have been very limited.

You can make your child promise to never lie again, but he won't understand that, either. It's going to take him until he is an adolescent to develop "a truly systematic and internally integrated morality." Until then your child will repeat what you have said about right and wrong, but he will not take it seriously or question it; he simply doesn't have the needed intellectual abilities. Trying to instill insight and responsibility in your child when he cannot comprehend them will be as useless as treating him like a baby when he is sixteen years old.

Behavioral Changes. In general, at age three a child obeys only when he is being watched. At four he begins to internalize your demands, judging other people by the results of their acts and not by their intentions, but realizing the difference between intentional and unintentional rule-breaking for himself. According to Piaget (an expert on childhood who is read by most education students and many parents), moral realism is strict adherence and obedience to a rule—with results that are evaluated by the motives. The preschooler can judge what a person does only by the results of the action (not by a person's motives or intentions), and he can judge only from his limited point of view. When asked which was worse, a child who accidentally broke five cups or a child who deliberately broke one cup, the preschooler will say the first child is worse, because more cups were broken! It will be a while before he can be classed as having developed "moral realism."

The child also has some early feelings of guilt and may even express them verbally—"That wasn't nice." By age six the conscience is fairly well internalized, there are definite feelings of guilt, and the child uses language in evaluating his actions. Before school age, the conscience will develop slowly, but two things will help it progress: (1) a good, supportive, affectionate relationship between you and your child, and (2) his ability to reason.

You may be displeased with your child's tattling, but you might as well get used to it, because it is a natural stage in his conscience development, especially during the fourth year of life. Unless someone's safety or health is endangered, send your child back to his playmates to resolve the situation. If you must get involved, do so in a nonjudgmental manner. Chances are that you don't know the circumstances, although everyone will be willing to tell them to you. If you do take sides, somebody will be sure to yell, "Unfair!"

Between the third and sixth years, your child begins to take some of the expectations of society onto himself; when he has your loving support, this process will be easier. Your child will accept your role in acknowledging acceptable behavior and in disapproving unacceptable behavior. If your child can adapt his behavior and can evaluate it, he will also be able to accept your disappointment. Your child knows that you are showing him that you think he can live up to your expectations. Your child believes in his ability, too—even though it hurts when you disapprove.

Developing Values. During the preschool period your child doesn't have any values of his own. You will probably try to impose yours—a good idea only up to a point. As soon as your preschooler begins to have the ability to make his own decisions, you can help him carefully evaluate things. Your child needs to develop his own value system based on reason and good judgment; the many values you want to pass on because of your family or cultural heritage must also be understood by your child. Help your child do things for the right reasons rather than because he is told to do them.

Work is one of those assets valued by our society. A child as young as three or four years of age can accept the fact that work brings benefits. If he helps you now with household tasks, you can have fun together later, after the beds are made—or he can even earn some coins for his bank. It feels good to help someone—your child feels bigger, more important, and independent.

The two of you may disagree on what work really is. You may think all your child does is play, but actually everything is work to him—although not in the negative sense. Play—the child's work—is how he learns about the world. Doing things for himself and for others returns a sense of accomplishment and strength as the child assumes adult roles.

Here are seven Cs to practice that will help your child like and appreciate work:

Cooperation—let your child help you with jobs you like to do, and you help him with jobs that are big or unpleasant for him.

Completion—let your child see the end of the job in sight.

Competition—give your child jobs he can do successfully.

Criticism—expect your child to do a good job within his capabilities, and approve of the results (perfection will come later).

Conditions—give your child guidelines as to how and when to work and provide good tools for him to work with, but leave some room for individual variation.

Congeniality—have a good attitude toward things that have to be done; maybe offer the choice of trading jobs with your child.

Complexity—give your child some easy and some harder jobs, but always give him a variety. (Something you always do may look more appealing, or your child may think he always gets the undesirable jobs.)

Since you will be very influential in which values your child adopts or rejects, be honest in your interaction. For example, try to value things that are a part of your child (such as a creative drawing, a block structure, or an original idea), and play down those things that are stereotyped (such as behavior that is copied from someone else or an answer that you expect as "right"). Because the things you value now or in the past may not be in vogue with the current generation, look at your own values with a critical eye and an open mind, but do help your child to understand and value some of the things you hold sacred: religion, honesty, morality, character, cultural and subcultural traditions, family unity, and service to others, for example.

Sometimes the earning and spending of money provides a source of conflict between parent and child. With the young preschooler, you could have an understanding and an arrangement to resolve this conflict early for both of you. Because your child doesn't yet know the value of money or even how to spend it, he needs your help. Perhaps your child could get a small allowance or earn some money, and then be allowed to spend it however he wishes. Don't be too harsh if your child buys something impractical or if he wastes his money. Early experiences like this can help later when your child has more money, more desires, and more ability to make decisions. How did you learn about money—through lectures or "the hard way"?

Also teach your child some honest concepts about sex. Use the proper names for the parts of his body or for his bodily functions so that he doesn't have to try to interpret the meanings of all those different expressions ("potty," "tinkle," and "wet," for example). When your child asks questions about sex, just give an honest, short answer to his question. When he is ready for more, he will ask.

It's important for you to encourage your child to have a positive attitude about his body. When a preschooler stares at another person's unclothed body, he is just trying to get concepts of femaleness and maleness in mind; he is not really being "bad" or immoral. Actually it's healthy for him to see another person's body and to have his curiosity satisfied before he gets much older. Bathing with a brother or sister or a parent can answer many of the preschooler's questions before they are asked. A calm, reassuring attitude on your part will really help. Your attitudes about sex will probably become your child's.

Don't get caught in the "where did I come from?" trap. Find out what it is that your child is asking, and then give him a simple answer. He may not want as much information as you think he does. Your casual acceptance of his questions and your honest answers will cause your child to return to you for more information later; your anxious, lengthy, inaccurate answers will send him elsewhere.

Language, experience, and personal development will help your child establish a moral code. Assist him by providing him with the opportunities he will need, but also be understanding of his questioning and reasoning.

Guidelines for Parents. You can help your young child achieve moral maturity in several ways:

Let your child participate in democratic discussions to organize ideas and actions. Through verbalization your child can evaluate his actions—such evaluation is the foundation for developing guilt, which is evident at four or five years of age.

Reward the behavior you want your child to continue, and ignore the behavior you want discontinued. If your child repeats undesired behavior, stop and evaluate what caused it, and then change the situation.

Interact with your child in a positive rather than a negative way, tell him what he can do rather than what he can't do.

Give your child a choice when there really is a choice.

Establish important limits and enforce them.

Show respect for your child as an individual by doing these things:

—warning him about the need to stop or change an activity

—valuing your child's ideas and letting him try them out

—listening attentively when he is talking

—providing opportunities and activities

appropriate for his developmental abilities

—explaining logical reasons for your expectations (first find out the characteristics, the abilities, and the expectations for a child of that age)

—From Barbara J. Taylor, *Dear Mom and Dad Parents and the Preschooler* (pp. 136–140). Provo, Utah: Brigham Young University Press, 1978.

FOR FURTHER READING:

Hancock, Maxine. *People in Process: The Preschool Years.* Old Tappan, N.J.: Fleming H. Revell Co., 1978.

PUNISHMENT

"A FATHER who spares the rod hates his son, but one who loves him keeps him in order" (Proverbs 13:24 NEB). Notice in these words of wisdom that love and discipline are brought together. The word *rod* does not necessarily imply spanking, though this is sometimes needed. Some important points about discipline should be made.

A child must always be disciplined in love. This means that punishment for wrongdoing must be meted out in such a way that the child understands that his transgression in no way affects his parents' love for him. Indeed, discipline itself is an act of love imposed so that the child might benefit and become a better person.

The goal of punishment is correction— teaching improved conduct. Self-will needs to be tamed and brought into subjection. With careful leadership, parents can help the child achieve this without damaging a healthy self-image. Every child is entitled to understand clearly why he is being punished. Explanation, at his level of understanding, as to why he is being spanked, must accompany the act. Point out that rules have reasons. Explain that self-control and self-discipline are cardinal qualities of the future mature adult. Even a young child is entitled to opinions. Take these seriously, even if you believe them to be wrong. Help him to understand the reasoning behind your point of view. In this way, he will comprehend better and be less likely to make the same mistake again.

*Punishment should be for disobedience—*not for ignorance or accidents. Parents must teach their children the expected standards of behavior, and maintain those standards by discipline. Do not punish a transgression perpetrated because the child did not know that it was wrong. Do not punish for the genuine accident, even if partially blameworthy. Remember that young children are relatively uncoordinated and accidents will happen. Forgive, explain, and clearly warn of punishment the next time. Teach him to respect other people's property rights and to be unselfish and thoughtful of others.

Never strike a child through your own impatience or exasperation or as a reaction to your own worrisome problems. A spanking should be done with emotional control and within the principles of "due process of law"—never as an impulsive frustrated retaliation to vent explosive feelings or to achieve a satisfied feeling of revenge. On the other hand, mothers should deal with disobedience quickly and not say, "Wait till your father comes home." Parents should act consistently and agree on discipline principles. Never let a child play one parent against the other. If successful, he may feel insecure.

Standards must be clearly set and maintained. Reasonable degrees of flexibility are of course necessary but the child must know where he stands, and the limits set. He becomes insecure if he finds that overstepping the known limits is not immediately and appropriately dealt with, in the manner in which he has previously been warned. There is the additional danger that this insecurity will be compounded later with a lack of respect for his parents when he becomes old enough to realize the inconsistencies in their standards.

Mode and severity of punishment should not be unreasonable. Excessive punishment can lead to lying, through fear, and can cause serious inhibition of the healthy self-expression which is such an essential part of personality development. Avoid saying, "You are a bad boy"; or "You make me unhappy when you do this." This may develop either a poor self-image or sense of guilt. Deprivation of some pleasure or privilege is sometimes more severe than a spanking because it lasts longer, and it might be more appropriate to a particular "crime." Deprivation is usually more appropriate in older children. Spanking should be administered on the rear end and nowhere else, to avoid injury. In a small child use a slipper, rolled-up magazine, or similar harmless object for spanking, rather than the hand. The young child will then tend to equate the slipper with punishment. He should learn to equate his parents' hands not with pain, but with giving and holding and loving.

After each punishment forgive and forget. Never bring up the subject once it has been dealt with. Reassure the child of your continued love. This and your forgiveness will be nonverbal examples to your children of God's grace towards us.

In disobedience situations be calm but firm. Let reprimands, whenever possible, be in private, not in front of houseguests. Try not to blame one child rather than another, even if only one seems to be to blame: young children usually get into trouble *together.* Avoid comparing one child adversely with another in an individual situation; but especially do not let one child feel that he is always the one in the wrong. Be strictly fair and equal to all the children in discipline or punishment problems.

Remember you are a parent not a pal. A child needs pals, but he usually has plenty of them in school, church, or youth activities. He only has two parents to admire, respect, and emulate. Parents dilute or even destroy their roles as leaders, teachers, and inspirers if they do not maintain a balanced authority gap. A parent is authority with forgiveness, flexibility, and understanding; conscience with reason, discipline, and love.

—From O. Quentin Hyder, M.D., *The People You Live With.* Old Tappan, N.J.: Fleming H. Revell Co., 1975.

Q

QUARRELING

THE SQUABBLING that crops up between children is one of the most exasperating problems parents face. Children's quarrels are often over such trivial things that it is hard to understand how they become so violent. Many a mother wonders what this fighting means. Mothers and fathers ask how to handle their children's quarrels. When a particularly difficult situation has been dealt with, the question arises, "How can we prevent such a hassle from happening again?"

Are Children's Quarrels Inevitable?

The evidence is that all children fight at some time in their growing years. Some are more aggressive than others and seem bent upon quarrelling at the slightest provocation. Others, docile and sweet-tempered most of the time, become embroiled in struggles with their brothers and sisters upon occasion. Intensive interviews with several hundred mothers by a reliable research team found every mother at some time or other forced to cope with angry outbursts on the part of her children.

Fighting phrases children use are familiar to every parent. In almost any family with more than one child, there is heard from time to time the belligerent, "Mine's better than yours." This represents a struggle for supremacy between children. It arises from each child's need to excel. In a competitive society like ours, the race to be first among siblings is bound to occur from time to time.

"He started it," is a frequent phrase of youngsters trying to place the blame for a fight. Parents may unwittingly bring on such a stance by attempting to "get to the bottom of the quarrel" by finding out who began it. This is usually a fruitless endeavor. Oftentimes the children do not know who, or what, started the fuss. The first overt act of hostility usually is provoked by some covert act of aggression by another angry child.

Tattletales are a problem for parents. A self-righteous child brings a tale of woe to his mother. "Just look at what he did," is the complaint. The mother is torn between rewarding her child for immediate reporting of trouble and discouraging the youngster from becoming a tattletale. One wise mother we knew would ask her child, "What did you do to make him so mean?" She did not always get a straight answer, but at least she helped her child see that it takes two to fight and that one child's attack may have been provoked by the other youngster.

Should Your Child Turn the Other Cheek?

Christian parents are puzzled about whether to teach their children to turn the other cheek and risk being browbeaten by some bully or to fight for their rights as individuals against aggression. Parents find it hard to agree upon the policy they will follow. Fathers often feel it best to teach their sons to fight in order to defend themselves. Mothers are more apt to want their children to avoid open aggression by quietly taking it, or walking away from it.

Worldwide dimensions of the fight-or-flee question impress parents with the need to prepare their children for the reality of conflict as best they can. They realize that mankind has not yet resolved the question as to how to handle overt hostility. Men of all nations talk peace, while wars rage around the globe. Billions of dollars go for national defense when the people want freedom to live in peace. Parents are caught upon the horns of the dilemma in trying to bring up their children to live in harmony with one another. What you do depends upon how you feel deep down inside about the whole question of war and peace.

Why Children Quarrel

It helps to understand the reasons for children's quarrels. There are a number of universal forces that provoke children to fight with one another. Let us discuss a few of these causal factors, and then you may enlarge on the list out of your own experience as parents.

They are frustrated and angry. Children are easily frustrated. They are small in stature, strength, skills, and power. They are pushed around by adults who are bigger and stronger than they are. They are challenged by other children in every aspect of their lives. They cannot get their way much of the time. So, they respond to frustration as humans do, by getting mad and lashing out in anger.

They feel jealous. Brothers and sisters share the same house, its equipment and facilities. Even more important, they share the same parents whose love they need urgently. So, at times when a child does not feel that he is getting his share of his parents' atten-

tion, he becomes jealous of the child he feels is the more favored. Jealousy is not a pleasant state for the child or for his parents. But it is very real, and very urgent, and cannot be denied. When a youngster feels jealous, he lashes out in anger. He accuses his parents of not being fair. He is aggressive toward the threatening sibling in ways that provoke many a fuss between the children.

They want to be first. Children compete to be first in line, first in favors, first in any activity where scores are kept. Like their parents and other adults, they like to win. It is hard to lose repeatedly. When a child does not get enough chances to win, he cheats, or quarrels, or refuses to play. None of these responses is encouraged by his parents. So, the child is left with unhappy options unless his parents guide him into situations in which he can succeed at least part of the time.

They are tired, hungry, or out of sorts. Quarrels are more frequent when one or more of the children is tired, hungry, or under pressure. One survey conducted by mothers themselves found that their children quarrelled most often in the late afternoon when they were tired from the day's work and play. Just before mealtime, children as well as adults are more edgy and ill at ease. One way of avoiding some of children's quarrels is to maintain a healthful schedule of food and rest in comfortable family routine.

They release tensions built up at school and play. A school child builds up a lot of tension in both schoolroom and playground. He rarely is as bright, or as successful, or as favored as some other child in his class. He may be taunted, harassed, and bullied by some disturbed classmate. He and his teacher do not always see eye to eye on classroom behavior. His own conduct gets him into trouble from time to time. When his frustrations pile up, he releases them in the safest place he knows—at home. So, he takes out on his brothers and sisters the tensions he has experienced that day.

When Children Quarrel

Perceptive parents find out when their children are most apt to quarrel, so as to be able to prevent hassles from developing. You can keep track of your children's quarrels for one week and plot the frequency of their fusses as a basis for your own strategy.

Between the time they get home from school and their evening meal, school children tend to quarrel. When they are full of the day's frustrations and low in levels of blood sugar, they are prone to scrap with one another. This may be met by an afternoon snack—a glass of juice, a piece of fruit, or whatever is appropriate in your household. When you sit down with your children and hear about their day at school, this snack time has a double value. It gives you a chance to relax with the children. And, it gives the youngsters an opportunity to vent their feelings by telling you what happened and how they felt about the events of the day.

When injustice has been done, children quarrel. This is a familiar, "He took the biggest piece," complaint. A simple way around this particular problem is to let one child cut the cake, and the other child choose the first piece. It is not always that simple, of course. Sometimes there is a grossly unfair situation that any normal child should protest. Parents, teachers, and other caretakers find that most children have a well-developed sense of fair play. Adults are wise to be as fair as they can in their distribution of favors and privileges among children just alike. It does call for giving each child his fair share of your attention.

When something unfair happens to your child, he can be helped to see that such things happen to each of us from time to time. It only complicates the problem to make a big issue of it. The child who learns to lose with poise has mastered an important social skill for which he can be congratulated. When he knows how to handle injustices without losing his cool, he has learned an important lesson that will serve him well all his life.

Children quarrel when things are uneasy at home. Children get upset when the family undergoes drastic change. Moving may be necessary for your family, but it probably will not be easy for the children for a while. Then you can expect more fusses, unless you are successful in helping each child feel secure and a part of the activity going on in the family.

Children sense dissension in the family and often respond by quarreling. When parents argue or complain, the children in the family react in kind by squabbling with one another. A new member of the family can be especially threatening to a child. When the new member is another child who competes for your time and attention, you can expect some evidence of sibling rivalry on the part of the older children.

Why the Eldest Is So Mean

Your firstborn probably is not as thoughtful of his or her younger siblings as you would like. When you see things from his point of view, you can do a great deal to make it easier for your oldest child to be good to the younger one(s).

He was once the only child, and now has been displaced. When he was a baby he had you all to himself. Then along came his younger brother or sister who took all your time and attention as the baby in the family. You help to prepare your eldest child for the new baby by letting him feel that the baby is his as well as yours. But do not expect that this will completely eliminate sibling rivalry. It is not that easy!

You expect your oldest to be responsible. You impress upon your firstborn that he or she is now a big boy, a big girl. You make him or her your first lieutenant and place more responsibility upon your firstborn than he or she may find comfortable. So, the oldest child in the family may revert to baby ways when a new baby arrives. He may be rough with the younger children. You must keep him from becoming cruel, of course. But you are wise to let him tell you how he feels and to let him know that you understand. You can help him express his feelings in ways that protect the younger children, at the same time that you make him feel loved and appreciated.

Younger children in the family usually have more privileges than were given the oldest when he was their age. Parents generally are more strict in disciplining their firstborn than they are with their later children. Then they relax and allow more leeway than they did with their first. The oldest child may well resent this leniency that he did not have and vent his feelings on his favored siblings. When he complains of your unfairness in giving his younger brothers and sisters privileges he did not have at their age, you can admit that this may be true. But also remind him that he had advantages as your oldest child that no other shares. Let him know that he is special to you. Tell him you understand how he feels. Assure him that he is loved and he will be a happier, more considerate oldest child.

Younger children are a nuisance. They get into your oldest child's most cherished possessions. They disturb his collections. They disrupt his projects. They tag along after him and require more patience than many a child can muster. You compound the problem by insisting that he always include his younger siblings in his play. You help by giving him

privacy and a chance to protect his treasures from the intrusion of his younger brothers and sisters. You do well to listen to your children's complaints. Not in an effort to argue them out of their feelings. But in an attempt to feel with them as much as you can.

Reducing Jealousy in Children

Jealousy is the anger that comes from feeling that someone else is better loved. Every child needs to feel that his parents love him. He needs to be loved for himself, and he needs that kind of love every day. It is not enough to have been loved once upon a time when he was a baby, although that was crucially important as a foundation for his later security. He needs to be sure that you love him now, and that you love him enough.

Do you love all your children equally? You may want to answer "Yes, of course." But wait! Does anyone love any two people alike? Actually, you probably love each of your children in quite different ways. This is all right. It is what your children need of you. So, you err when you try to tell your children that you love them all just the same. You know you don't; they sense that you should not. It is far better to let each of your children know without question that you love him for himself.

Each must be loved in his own special way. One of your children is a cuddler; another is more circumspect in his expression of affection. Children differ in the way they love and in the ways they like to be loved. As a parent, you learn to respect each child's preferences, and to give and receive affection as he prefers. This is not always easy. If you are a demonstrative person, it may be hard for you to hold back from your more aloof youngster, and to shower your love on the child who responds as you do. Fortunately most children have two parents and a number of other relatives, some of whom will click with their types, amounts, and rhythms of expressing affection for one another.

Recognize each child's special talents. Every child has certain lovable characteristics that you can applaud. It will not make him egotistical if your praise comes spontaneously and genuinely from time to time. This is one reason why it is a good idea to spend some time alone with each of your children every day that you can. Take one child with you when you shop or go on an errand. Enroute there will be time for a tête-à-tête in which the two of you can achieve a level of intimacy impossible with others in the situation. In these intimate moments, your child can confide his plans. You can talk over his problems. Most importantly, you can point out those potentials and possibilities of his that impress you especially. You let him know that you love him for what he is, and for what he is becoming. This is what your child needs from you. It is the heart of the parent-child relationship.

Curbing Competitiveness in Your Children

Competition cannot be eliminated entirely from a society like ours. It can be minimized by parents who care enough to rear their children without too much pressure to excel. This in itself reduces some of the stress between children in the family, and makes for a more relaxed atmosphere.

Don't expect your child to be first all the time. There are some parents who are so eager for their children to succeed that they put undue pressure on them to be first in everything they do. This puts a strain on the children, and on their relationship with one another.

Making issues about grades is self-defeating. There are some parents who are never satisfied with their children's report cards.

When a youngster has mostly C's and B's his parents ask why he did not get A's. He gets an A one month and they expect him to do at least that well ever after. Keeping an interest in a child's progress in school is all right. But putting too much pressure on school children to work for higher and higher grades can be damaging—to the youngster, to his relationship with his peers, and with his parents. In time he may rebel and lose interest in school work. Or he may try so hard to measure up to his parents' expectations that he develops a nervous stomach, a facial tic, or some other indication that he is under too much pressure to excel.

Avoid comparing one child with another. It is all too easy for a dissatisfied parent to ask a child, "Why can't you do as well as your older sister (or brother) does?" Teachers sometimes compare a younger with an older sibling who got higher grades when in the same class. This accentuates the rivalrous feeling between the children in the family. It rarely motivates the younger child to improve. It only makes him feel that he is not as loved, or as well understood, or as acceptable as the older child with whom he is compared.

Rivalry arises from wanting to do better than someone else. Some sibling rivalry is to be expected in any family. When brothers and sisters compete constantly and with intensity, their relationship becomes explosive and quarrels erupt over trivia. This is the "Mine's better than yours!" taunt that so unpleasantly initiates many a children's squabble.

Helpful parents expect only that each of their children will develop his own talents in his own way. They are not impressed overmuch with grades, and comparisons with other children's accomplishments. They are concerned that each of their children has the opportunities he, or she, needs to grow straight and strong and satisfied with his life.

This takes some doing, as any parent can testify. But it is worth the struggle. At stake is not only the children's concord now, but their future as persons.

Reducing Violence

Many a parent suspects that too much violence in what a child sees can encourage him to be aggressive himself. This is being borne out in studies of the effects of violence in television programs, movies, and other media on the aggressiveness of children.

There are some who argue that a child vicariously gets rid of his own hostilities by watching angry people hitting one another on television screens. Actually, studies now find that after watching a particularly brutal scene, children tend to act out what they have seen and to be more aggressive than they had been before.

Monitoring children's television programs is a good idea. There are programs with too much sadism, too much aggression, too much rough talk and conduct to be good for children's viewing. Some parents find that their children cannot sleep after seeing a particularly frightening program. They report that their children's quarrels are more hostile after having witnessed overt hostility on TV or movie screen. They feel responsible for regulating their children's viewing intake, much as they supervise what they eat and drink. Parents would not think of feeding their children garbage. Should they not be quite as careful about what goes into their minds and spirits?

Accompany the children to the movies sometimes. One way of reducing aggression in the family is for parents to go with their children to a movie that has not been specifically recommended as suitable for children. This may not be as easy as letting the youngsters go alone. But it has the advantage of letting the parents see for themselves what their children are witnessing. This prepares the parents for questions arising, or for untoward behavior rooting back to one or more scenes in the film.

Parents in some communities are banding together to request managers of theaters catering to children to be selective in their matinee fare. When enough families refuse to let their children attend the trashy, pornographic, or violently aggressive movies, it eventually affects the producers as well as the local theater managers. This is too idealistic? Perhaps, but how else can people clean up the visual and audial pollution that fouls their children's lives?

Physical punishment sets a bad example. You may have been brought up according to the "spare the rod and spoil the child" principle. You may regard whippings as "necessary." This no-nonsense philosophy of child-rearing prevailed in earlier centuries, when life itself was hard. A child's survival in a dog-eat-dog wilderness may have depended upon his harsh treatment. It may not have been as necessary as people used to think. It may possibly account for much of the warfare that has gone on in families and between peoples throughout the history of man.

The evidence is that physical punishment teaches children that hurting others is sanctioned by adults. They tend to copy their parents as they attack those who displease them. They even practice venting their anger on their toys. It is not unusual to hear a tiny tot spanking his stuffed animal with the identical tone of voice he has experienced at the hand of an irate parent. Later he treats his brothers and sisters in much the same way he has learned from his parents' discipline.

Children at Peace With Themselves

Every child needs three things—food and love and room to grow. When he receives these basic ingredients of security, he feels at peace within himself. When he is deprived of one or more of these essentials for healthy growth, he is at war with himself, and with others around him. A hungry, tired, unloved child is a quarrelsome child, "hurting for a fight."

Quarreling is kept to minimum by sensible routines of eating, sleeping, exercising, and growing within an atmosphere of loving care. You parents set the example for your children in getting along with one another. You can try to keep their squabbles within bounds by following these guidelines.

(1) Feed your children before they get too hungry

(2) Establish healthy rhythms of rest and exercise

(3) Provide opportunities for each child's achievement at his own pace

(4) Help your children when they need it, not before

(5) Set clear limits that your children understand, at every age

(6) Disapprove violence in any form, anywhere, in ways your children understand

(7) Do not physically punish your children as a regular practice

(8) Discourage violence in movies, television programs, and other media

(9) Let each child know that you love him in his own special way

(10) Express your affection for one another openly, often, fully

(11) Keep yourself from getting too uptight or out of sorts

(12) Let God guide your daily life

—From Evelyn Millis Duvall, *Evelyn Duvall's Handbook for Parents*. Nashville: Broadman Press, 1974.

R

READING

"DAD SOMETIMES wore cardboard in his shoes," writer Charles Paul Conn reminisces, "but he always seemed to have a dollar or two for books. Each child got a dime for reading and reporting to Dad on a book. For something off the classic shelf such as *Pilgrim's Progress*, he'd pay a bonus. We'd save the money and go buy more books." The heritage of books is one we should share generously. Our children have teethed on books, sat on books, and, at an early age, read books. I'd like to share with you some of the books we have found helpful, and some of the approaches to books that parents can use to help their children into the world of good books.

We are experiencing a publication explosion. This means that there is a wider selection of children's literature now available on the market than at any prior time. The result is that good books are available for our children at reasonable cost, but they are competing on the marketplace with much mediocre material. We want our children to have access not only to books but to *good* books as well. By what criteria, then, shall we determine which books are good? The very best books are books which combine several of the values listed below. But many good books will be good because of their contribution to the child in one of the value areas.

1. Aesthetic value. A beautiful book is one which is attractive because of its form, its art content, or because of its balance of beautiful art and graceful language. The most obvious attraction to children will be visual. Watch the delight with which children greet a book illustrated by Brian Wildsmith. Preschoolers love color, yet they are equally fascinated by pen-and-ink drawings such as the famous Shepherd drawings for *Winnie the Pooh.* Good books should introduce children to a wide range of beauty: from fine pencil sketches such as those by Dorothy Lathrop through to the richly simple art of Eliza Jack Keats, with collage textures that are almost palpable.

2. Interest value. A good book is an interesting book. It may be interesting because it is teaching the child something new, as with the fine *National Geographic* publications for children, or because the experiences parallel those of the child. *Let's Be Enemies* and *I Hate Dogs* are of this type. A book may be interesting because of its detail. In this field the Richard Scarry books lead the day.

3. Humor value. A book may be good because it is funny. Most funny books have other kinds of significance as well, but of course there are books such as the Dr. Seuss "Bright and Early"—designed simply to introduce children to the world of words in a way that is fun. Laughing together over a funny book is one of the joys of the parent who spends time with his little ones.

4. Truth value. When we come to Christian books, we need to bring these same criteria. To think that a book is a good book just because it contains a "good message" is really to underestimate our children's needs and their ability to appreciate aesthetic values, interest values, and humor values. The best books in the Christian field for children will combine at least some of these values with the message of the Bible, or with the message of the reality of Jesus Christ in the individual's life. For parents who would like to investigate further ways in which to judge books, I recommend Gladys Hunt's excellent little handbook *Honey for a Child's Heart* (Zondervan, 1969). It should be a standard reference work for Christian parents, with its excellent text and bibliography.

The single clearest thing that should emerge from any review of children's literature is that if you are going to invite your children into the world of good books, you will give them a wide variety of books. Some you will choose because they are funny. Some will be bought because they are easy to read. Some we will make available because they have a beautiful story to which the child can respond.

The ultimate criterion of whatever books or reading material we bring into our home should be that of Philippians 4:8 (NAS): "Whatever is true, whatever is honorable, whatever is right, whatever is pure, whatever is lovely, whatever is of good repute, if there is any excellence and if anything worthy of praise, let your mind dwell on these things."

For the youngest child, the ideal book is one with very large illustrations and a few words. For the book which he is going to be allowed to handle and manipulate himself, the plasticized books such as the C. R. Gibson "Little Plastic Books," or washable cloth books are ideal. These books are virtually indestructible. We have one which survived the teething years of all four children, somewhat chewed and dog-eared, but still intact. Children should learn to hold books, to feel

books, to turn pages, just as early as they show any interest. These tough little books can take it.

From the book which is designed mostly to introduce the child to the act of turning pages, we move toward books which combine artwork and story—the "Read to me" storybooks of which there are now many on the market. The Concordia Arch Book series led the way in bringing a whole new look to the Bible-story idea—giving the children vivid contemporary illustrations, catchy rhymes, and occasionally very beautiful prose-poetry as in *The Little Sleeping Beauty* and *The Little Boat That Almost Sank*.

Another entry in the field of contemporizing the Bible storybook is the Muffin Family series by V. Gilbert Beers (Moody Press). This series couples Bible stories with contemporary application stories. An outstanding feature of these books is the art: beautiful and delightful and funny.

We have always made use of library resources as well as buying books. We have in our home the World Book Childcraft series with its rich resources of stories and poetry, as well as Marguerite DeAngeli's *Book of Nursery and Mother Goose Rhymes* (Doubleday), which is the delight of bouncing English rhymes and lovely pencil sketches. A set of books which are neither beautiful to look at nor great literature but which still command the loyalty of children are the Thornton Burgess Bedtime Stories. The children enjoy the humor and pathos of the talking animals.

My own personal delight in Winnie the Pooh has been translated into several readings with the children. The special joy of *Winnie the Pooh* and *The House at Pooh Corner* is that you read them once and chuckle; read them the second time and laugh; and by the third or fourth time you laugh in anticipation of the humor. Mitchell and I in particular have laughed together over Winnie the Pooh. And A. A. Milne's little rhymes, *When We Were Very Young* and *Now We Are Six*, vie with Robert Louis Stevenson's *A Child's Garden of Verses* for first place in children's poetry.

In the wide field of children's periodicals, two are worth the attention of Christian parents. The *National Geographic* children's magazine *World* is full of beautiful photography and fascinating nature lore. For literature and art, *Cricket* stands out above all similar magazines.

Very early reading materials need to be carefully selected. The story needs to be simply told, of course. But extreme limitation of vocabulary may not be as important as intrinsic interest or funniness in the story. *Go, Dog, Go* in the Dr. Seuss reading series ("Bright and Early Books for Beginning Beginners") is excellent. So is Else Holmelund Minarik's near-perfect *Little Bear* (in the Harper and Row "I CAN READ" series). Perhaps one of the biggest deterrents to reading is that many primer stories are not worth the intense effort reading requires of a little child.

When actually teaching your child to read, find out what reader series your school uses and scrupulously avoid using that. You are probably safe with Christian-reader series (unless, of course, your children will be attending a Christian day school). Our children learned to read through *Basic Bible Readers* (Standard Publishing). We now also have a set of the new *Learning to Read From the Bible Series* by V. Gilbert Beers (Zondervan). Because they were learning to read about the Lord Jesus or learning to read Bible stories, our children were excited with what they were reading. The effort that sometimes brought perspiration to their foreheads seemed to them worthwhile.

As our children reached a basic proficiency level in their readers, we gave them their first Bibles. We chose from the *Lollipop*

Series (Zondervan) for our children's first Bibles. The King James Version was still used most generally in our church and it seemed important to us to have the children have a Bible that would coincide with what the minister was reading from. Each child chose his own color, and so we have a green Bible, a brown Bible, a black Bible, and a blue one—reminders of milestones in reading for each child. Since then, the children have also been given copies of some other translations.

There are many lovely children's Bibles available today. I like the children's edition of the New International Version. This edition features large type and key verses set out in clear print in the "memory margin"—an open invitation to memory work. Now both the Old and New Testaments are available in this version. The children's edition of the Living Bible is less attractive, despite some lovely Richard and Francis Hook illustrations. The very small print is difficult for children's eyes to follow. The Bible Society's Good News Bible (Today's English Version) has imaginative and fluid line drawings—several on every page. It is probably the best-illustrated Bible available.

In choosing a Bible for a child, you must first determine which translation you wish. You should take into consideration what translation is in most common usage in your church. You should also choose a translation suitable to family Bible reading. We are in the somewhat confusing situation of being a transition generation as far as Bible translation is concerned. By the next generation there will, I hope, be more general consensus. Perhaps by that time either the New American Standard or the New International Version will have gained the hearts of a large enough sector of Christian public that there will be more standardization. Meanwhile, we must evaluate translations carefully and make our personal choice.

Having decided upon translation, I would

give attention to additional features: size of print, size of illustrations, and explanatory notes could be considered. Children do not need cross-references, India-thin paper, or expensive leather covers in order to have the thrill of "a Bible of my own."

Children move from early reading experiences to reading the Word of God themselves: a natural and rewarding progression in the Christian home. Then, with a sure base in the Word of God, our children can reach out to all the world of good books and great authors: from Beverly Cleary and Carolyn Haywood to Laura Ingalls Wilder and Louisa May Alcott; from A. A. Milne to C. S. Lewis, Madeleine l'Engle, and Tolkien. The golden chain will lead on and on. We will encourage them to read, read, read, evaluating all by the plumb line of Scripture. And we will encourage them to respond to good books with gratitude to God, the Giver of everything, everywhere, that is truly good.

—From Maxine Hancock, *People in Process.* Old Tappan, N.J.: Fleming H. Revell Co., 1978.

FOR FURTHER READING:

Hunt, Gladys. *Honey for a Child's Heart.* Grand Rapids: Zondervan Publishing House, 1969.

Lindskoog, John and Kathryn. *How to Grow a Young Reader: A Parent's Guide to Kids and Books.* Elgin, Ill.: David C. Cook Publishing Co., 1978.

REBELLION

IT MAY WELL BE that the most painful human experience is for one member of a family to reject another, especially if one is a parent or a child! A range of emotions and questions runs painfully through the heart of a concerned parent who has a rebellious child—

just as they have run through the life of a child to produce such rebellion. Every time a book or article comes out on such a topic, the troubled parents who read it suffer from anxiety, self-blame, guilt, self-analysis, and remorse. Chief among the plaguing questions is, "What can I do to bring back my child?"

. . . . .

It would, however, be criminal to catalog a long list of failures by parents and children without some assurance that there is a way back. Children can be brought home. Relationships can be stronger than ever if proper steps are taken. It is only helplessness and despair that are to be feared. When parents are willing to throw away the mask of false pride and risk reaching out with new tools of understanding, patience, and love, a plan can be made that will work. It takes time, commitment, sacrifice, and tenacity. But it is worth it!

The biblical story of the prodigal son is as instructive as it is beautiful. At first glance, it seems merely a happy episode of a reunion between a wayward son and a concerned, waiting father. A more careful study, however, will show that, although the emphasis is on the joyous reunion, the broader backdrop of rebellion, patient parental concern, the long waiting and forever watching in vain are all resolved. There is the eventual return and reconciliation. The son is restored. The story, like life, is a process, not an isolated incident. The threads which run through the account and tie together the waiting for the wayward son are patience, faith, and time.

This chapter is devoted to practical, constructive steps that may be taken to restore family unity. They are built upon the foundation of biblical principles and common sense. After choosing the particular suggestions that fit your problems, you as parents of a rebellious child, are urged to decide to take action. The sooner you begin, the sooner your goal of the restoration of a loving relationship will be realized. Here are the steps:

Acknowledge Parental Responsibility

Like it or not, you are primarily responsible for your child's behavior—good or bad. Mental or physiological abnormalities complicate your job as parents; so do cultural and social influences, peer pressure, and certain negative educational factors. But your influence is and always has been the greatest. To blame anyone else is only to deny or belittle your positive influence.

The first step you must be willing to take, if you would restore your relationship with your child, is to know and accept that his behavior and beliefs are fundamentally of your doing. Little can be accomplished until you reach that point. Many families focus the blame on the child, and by his resentment he becomes still more rebellious. By frankly and honestly sharing this blame, the *culprit* is joined by the *judge.* He no longer stands alone, condemned; they stand together. This acknowledgement, though it may appear insignificant and even simplistic, is profoundly important to changes.

Make Full Restitution for the Wrongs of the Past

It may be painful to admit and correct the wrongs of the past. Many of these wrongs can never be undone. To confess them as your offenses to your own child will begin a remarkable work of healing. It takes a strong, mature person to admit mistakes, and your child will experience a new respect for you as you express this to him. He has been more aware of your faults than you ever guessed—more even than you yourself were aware.

. . . . .

The child as well as the parents needs to make right his wrongs. After the child has time to experience healing through the new attitudes of his parents, he may be helped to make right his own misdeeds. It may take months or years of maturing before he has the strength of character to admit and correct his wrongdoings.

Restoring your child means loving and accepting him as he is. It is easy to love a child who acknowledges his rebellion, repents, cuts his hair and dresses to please you, and returns to church and family prayers; but, rebellious children need love before any of this takes place. There is no technique, no science, or advice that is a substitute for genuine, unconditional love. It is urgently important to accept and love them just as they are—with greasy, stringy hair; reddened, vacant eyes; and dirty, smelly bodies.

. . . . .

Contracts and Commitment to Change

Out of the admission of mistakes, the acceptance of responsibility, and making right the wrongs, hopefully, parents will spell out some specific changes that need to be made. Perhaps you have worried too much and have overreacted. You may have lectured or nagged. You may have controlled or dominated your child's life rather than guiding and teaching him a sense of responsibility and wisdom of his own. Perhaps you were too busy and unwillingly neglected his emotional and personal needs. Maybe you abdicated as a parent almost entirely and allowed your child to grow up alone or literally with only one parent.

. . . . .

Demonstrate Genuine and Lasting Personal Changes

Children are far more perceptive than we give them credit for. It is not infrequent that parents have made a series of well-meaning but false starts in reshaping the relationship between parent and child. A wary child may need time to test the parents' honesty in admitting mistakes. He may suspect them of playing psychological games to trap him when rebellion has reached a deep level of intensity. Parents must decide if there is time to live out the changes of their admitted mistakes. The risk of overdosing or aggression that could result in suicide or a serious accident is a very real danger in the youth culture of today.

A child needs to sense that there have been real changes in the personal spiritual life of the parent. Spiritual continuity and integrity must be evident. Real spiritual changes are internal, but their reality is easily seen. "But the fruit of the Spirit is love, joy, peace, longsuffering, gentleness, goodness, faith, meekness, temperance . . ." (Galatians 5:22, 23). Any child will recognize those qualities, given sufficient time to observe.

A child, during the time of healing, needs to see consistency in the parent. Erratic shifts of attitude toward a child, alternating between promises of a new beginning and sudden outbursts of anger, are unconvincing. A parent who will allow himself to be controlled by God's spirit can provide the emotional support of predictable and concerned behavior.

Communications Corrections

Every parent of a rebellious child must believe that it is never too late for a reconciliation. Though personalities are formed early and temperaments may be largely hereditary, changes in behavior and attitudes can be brought about at any time. These changes, however, do not just happen. They take place because someone cares enough to work for them. The major tool that affects this change between parents and children is good communication.

Communication is the giving and receiving of information. This requires the careful translation of one's thoughts into words that can be understood by the other. It demands checking out by questions what the other one has heard. Words must be accompanied by a tone of voice, facial expression, and other physical mannerisms that convey the same meaning if real communication is taking place.

Discipline

It is necessary to define the word *discipline* to have a foundation on which to build one's understanding. It comes from a Latin word *discipulus* meaning, in its various forms, "to become acquainted with" or "to learn." *Disciples* are learners. Discipline may be well intentioned, but it turns into punishment unless some learning is involved. And the latter often results in rebellion rather than maturing.

Effective discipline involves three components: (1) clearly defined expectations or policies; (2) enforcement of these policies through an agreed upon process; (3) consistency and follow-through. In earlier childhood this entire process is up to the parents. By adolescence, however, it is important for the child to be included in such planning. This gives parents a prime opportunity to know their child's ways of thinking and show him respect for his ideas and feelings. Input from the child enables parents to be fair and considerate.

What Kind of Help Is Needed to Cure Rebellion?

A child who has been deeply hurt, is angry, or drug addicted, may be incapable of making wise choices or cooperating in any way with his parents. Help from sources other than the family may be the only answer for these young people. When spiritual needs or issues are involved, a pastor is invaluable. But sometimes there are physical, mental, or emotional issues at stake that demand the aid of a skilled mental health professional. In many cases, especially involving drug addiction or suicidal risks, hospital care may be necessary to save life and begin the long road back to mental health.

Parents commonly dread this separation and reject the only logical means of help because of an unnecessary sense of shame or guilt. First you need a clinical therapist whom you can trust for spiritual, as well as mental, health. The advice of a trusted family physician, minister, or friend can help in this first step. Heartbreaking as it is, you must marshal your courage, decide to trust this person and essentially turn over to him the care of your child. In working with a great many institutionalized youths, it was discovered that those who made the most complete and rapid recoveries, were those whose parents found the strength to do this.

. . . . .

Spiritual Help for Rebellion

This aspect of the cure for rebellion was placed last because it is so vitally important. Man is the only one of God's creatures who has a spiritual nature. Since it is unique to mankind, we must maintain its foundational significance if personal, as well as family, wholeness is to be achieved.

Thousands of years ago, God inspired Moses to write in Deuteronomy 6:7, "And thou shalt teach them [God's commandments] diligently unto thy children, and shalt talk to them when thou sittest in thine house, and when thou walkest by the way, and when thou liest down, and when thou risest up." God obviously planned for par-

ents to communicate Him and His way of life to their own children. The abdication of parental responsibility for this teaching to any other resource is offering children the second best.

. . . . .

When everything possible is done, wait! There comes a time in dealing with a rebellious child, when nothing more can be done. If you have reached this place, with all the help you can get, let your child know you love him and accept him as he is. Tell him that you will wait for him to return—either physically or emotionally to you. Threats or pursuit beyond this will have diminishing returns and will even create a wider gap.

Sometimes, when we have obeyed, trusted, and searched ever so diligently, all we can do is wait. Waiting with God will certainly bring results.

—From Truman E. Dollar and Grace H. Ketterman, *Teenage Rebellion.* Old Tappan, N.J.: Fleming H. Revell Co., 1980.

RELIGION

WHENEVER THE BIBLE refers to *religion*, it refers more to the outward expression of belief than to its content or doctrines. This appears most clearly in James 1:26, 27, which says in part, "The kind of religion which is without stain or fault in the sight of God our Father is this: to go to the help of orphans and widows in their distress and keep oneself untarnished by the world" (NEB).

Some Christians are reluctant to group Christianity among the world religions because they hold it to be given by God whereas the other faiths are held to be human creations. If, however, the word *religion* is understood as James uses it, as faith in Christ that expresses itself in action, Christian parents are concerned about it.

The last quarter of the twentieth century has seen an enormous growth and maturity in evangelical Christianity as many men and women have accepted Christ as their personal Savior and moved to deeper levels of Christian commitment than mere church membership evoked. These men and women, now parents, want to transmit to their children the insights and beliefs that mean so much to them.

The Sunday school and the home together have given the evangelical church the ability to transmit faith in Christ to the children of Christian parents, especially where dedicated, Bible-believing Sunday school teachers have been sufficiently concerned to discuss salvation with their youngsters. Dynamic programs of evangelism have enabled many evangelical churches to reach out into the community and win unchurched youngsters to Christ and His church.

Sociology has pointed out that the father has the strongest influence on the religious commitments of his children. A godly father who attends both Sunday school and church and is actively involved in their programs with his family is providing the kind of spiritual leadership that is God's ideal.

Parents who drop their children off at Sunday school are often doing little more than getting free baby-sitting. Children very quickly see that their parents do not think Sunday school and church have any value for them. In early adolescence, unless a teacher has been able to lead them to a strong personal commitment to Christ, most of these children drift away from the church and its programs. Some of them will repeat the pattern with *their* children; others will remember so little from the hour a week of Christian education they received that they do not even pass this minimal religious training on to their children.

In homes in which there is a Christian mother or father whose spouse is not actively involved in church, the effectiveness of Christian education is less than it usually is in the case of homes with two active Christian parents. Sometimes mothers dutifully take their children to church from birth on, only to be heartbroken by children who in their adolescent years follow the inactive father's example. But the effort is nevertheless worthwhile. Not only do such children have the influence of Christian teaching lodged in their minds, where it may later bear fruit, but also many children with faithful Christian mothers make solid commitments to Christ.

Unlike some "mainline" churches that baptize people "into" the church only to confirm them "out" in their adolescent years, evangelicals have emphasized the importance of Bible study for all age levels. Many active Christians can recall the godly influence of classes for junior and senior high school students and "college and career" and "singles" classes, and they continue as members of adult Bible classes. Some relatively small churches have a number of different adult classes to meet the varied needs of their membership.

Without further teaching in the home, however, Sunday school training will not have its maximum effect. Families that encourage all members to take their turn in thanking God for their food, that pray with their children at bedtime, and that have family devotions after the evening meal are providing everyone with Christian training that enhances the church's efforts. Some Christian fathers know the happiness of seeing their children talk intelligently about the Bible and pray sincerely to God about their lives. Today good Christian books relating to the family are available. Some families have been successful in reading and discussing brief sections from them after Bible reading.

—LESLIE R. KEYLOCK

FOR FURTHER READING:

Inchley, John. *Kids and the Kingdom: How They Come to God.* Wheaton, Ill.: Tyndale House Publishers, 1977.

Iversen, Rachel. *Talking Together with Young Children.* Ventura, Calif.: Regal Books, 1978.

Klink, Johanna. *Your Child and Religion.* Atlanta: John Knox Press, 1972.

Meier, Paul D. *Christian Child Rearing and Personality Development.* Grand Rapids: Baker Book House, 1977.

Popham, J. K. *Spiritual Counsel to the Young.* Grand Rapids: Baker Book House, 1977.

RETARDED CHILD

BOTH THE HEALTH of your marriage and your family life will depend upon your acceptance of this "different" child.

"Sorrow can make you better or make you bitter," and those of us who are parents hope we are becoming better. But our lesson in learning sometimes seems too expensive when we feel it is at the cost of full opportunity for our child. What is your definition of full opportunity? Would it not vary for every individual? Can it be that your pride has been hurt since your child will never become a doctor or lawyer or teacher? More humble occupations may still be useful and satisfying. You yourself will probably never become a world-famous scientist. Does this mean that you have been denied full opportunity or a chance to contribute to the lives of others? The question is relative, of course, and it is best left to God. Your child may contribute more to the understanding of others than you or I ever will.

It is not unusual for parents to think that God has punished them for some wrongdoing. If you are agonizing about this, remember that God as He reveals Himself in Christ is a merciful and gracious God. In the ninth chapter of John the similar question: "Teacher, whose sin was it that caused him to be born blind? His own or his parents' sin?" received this divine reply: "It was not that this man sinned, or his parents, but that the works of God might be manifest in him."

The mystery of tragedy cannot be answered glibly. In all of God's dealing with us, we must keep in a central position His forgiving love for us in Christ. That will take care of our guilt and feelings of guilt. Beyond that the mystery is impenetrable—until He makes His ways plain to us one day when we are able to understand. Right now, at this very moment, forgive yourself and your marriage partner if you are still trying to place blame. Your child's condition results from a metabolic disorder, chromosome abnormality, or some cause beyond your control. This cause is a medical problem and not a religious one. When you sincerely accept it as such, you will have taken the first step toward accepting your child and building the foundation for a happy, healthy family life.

You must also realize that having one retarded child does not necessarily mean that other children you may have will suffer the same condition. You may wish to have some chromosome tests made at a hospital where you can obtain counseling in this matter. It will reassure you if you plan to have more children.

In our day and time we know that the birth of a retarded child is no reflection upon the parents' intellectual level. The Kennedy family is certainly an example of this, and when you join your local association of parents with retarded children you will meet many wonderful, intelligent men and women. Join your nearest NARC chapter and share your concerns frankly with other parents; then if you find that you are still unable to resolve your own problems about the birth of your child and that they are affecting your acceptance of the child or your marriage relationship, don't hesitate to talk with your minister, a psychiatrist, a marriage counselor, or all three!

When you bring your baby home from the hospital it will soon be apparent to the other children in the family if Mother and Dad are unhappy. The best act in the world seldom deceives children for long, and they will sense that something is wrong. Even if the homecoming is a relatively cheerful one, some periods of depression will follow. It is my own opinion that it is best to tell the other children as much as you feel they can understand. Certainly they must not think that when you are going through a low period it is due to something they have done.

The simpler the explanation to young children the better. It may be sufficient just to tell them this baby will not develop as quickly mentally and physically as most babies, and Mother and Dad are very sad about it. Your own spirits will improve after the first few weeks, but in the meantime your children will understand why you are not as cheerful and happy as you would ordinarily be. It is the unknown that creates apprehension in all of us, and it is important that the situation not be cloaked in mystery. If your normal children understand that your distress has no connection with them, they may not be as likely to demand undue attention as reassurance of your love.

After all, the attitude of your normal children will tend to mirror your own reactions toward the baby. If you regard this as a challenge, they will do the same. If you regard it as an affliction, so will they. This is a real opportunity for your normal children to learn understanding and acceptance of those who are different from themselves.

At the same time it is important to overcome your preoccupation with the problem by being as loving and attentive to the other children as possible. Nor should you neglect your own needs as an individual; if you have

a club or hobby that takes you out of yourself, participate in it. Go off and play golf or bridge, dig for rocks, work in your garden— do whatever you enjoy most. It is excellent therapy.

Don't waste time worrying about what your neighbors will think of the baby. Most of them will be uncertain as to what to say when you return from the hospital, so they may say or do nothing for a while. In any event they have problems and troubles of their own, although you may not be aware of them, and they will be too busy to think about your situation for long.

You may find that parents and in-laws who have arrived to bring comfort or help with the new baby sometimes prove more upsetting than helpful. This is especially true if they know very little about retardation or are unaware of these children's potential and the improved opportunities for them. The advice of a distraught though well-meaning parent, with opinions formed in the light of conditions 20 or even 10 years ago, may not be the most helpful for you to hear right now. A visit a few months later might be better for everyone, for by then parents and relatives will have a more balanced perspective. You will be able to accept this new situation more quickly than you realize, and you will be surprised as moments of happiness begin to return. . . .

Families with a retarded youngster who have adjusted happily are those in which the parents have a strong commitment to their own relationship, accept the different child lovingly, and try to treat him as much like the other children as possible. You will have to make a real effort not to go overboard in sacrificing the needs of the other members of the family or overprotecting your slower boy or girl. You will want to be realistic in evaluating what they are capable of doing. Your child should feel needed and useful and will benefit from opportunities to help in the house or yard. The more independent your child becomes in taking care of his physical needs, performing simple tasks, and learning good social behavior, the easier it will be for him in school and in your neighborhood.

You will probably see some parents who have given up all hobbies and outside activities, never leaving their youngster with a sitter but carrying their child everywhere they go. It is my own feeling that this is harmful to the relationship between the parents and can also cause resentment on the part of the normal children. Your boy or girl will enjoy going to the playground, shopping center, restaurants, movies, Disneyland, and all the things normal children like. You will be amazed at how much he remembers and talks about afterward, but it just isn't any fun for most of us to take a retarded child *everywhere*—or any child for that matter! There are times parents need to be alone together for a week or a weekend or just an overnight pleasure trip. There are also family activities such as waterskiing, boating, or mountain climbing that could present real hazards for a poorly coordinated youngster (although skiing is now being taught to retarded boys and girls in the North Carolina mountains!). Don't feel guilty about doing some of these things at times.

Many fine, responsible older women supplement their income by taking care of children when their parents are out of town, or you may be fortunate enough to have a relative who will do so. If this is begun while your child is still a baby, you will not be reluctant to take occasional trips later, although you may want to leave special instructions with the sitter. Perhaps you can plan a family vacation while your child is in a residential camp. Staying at home constantly when you really need a break indicates no great virtue but rather that you may wish to play the martyr.

Parents who enjoy life and each other are happy, loving parents, and are able to communicate a healthier emotional outlook to their boy or girl because they are not "uptight" themselves.

—From Nancy Roberts, *You and Your Retarded Child*. St. Louis: Concordia Publishing House, 1974.

FOR FURTHER READING:

Allen, David F., and Victoria S. *Ethical Issues in Mental Retardation: Tragic Choices, Living Hope*. Nashville: Abingdon Press, 1979.

Hawley, Gloria Hope. *Laura's Psalm*. Nashville: Impact Books, 1981.

Koch, Richard A., and Dobson, James C., eds. *The Mentally Retarded Child and His Family*. New York: Brunner/Mazel Inc., 1976.

Perske, Robert. *New Directions for Parents of Persons Who Are Retarded*. Nashville: Abingdon Press, 1973.

Swindoll, Charles. *You and Your Child*. Nashville: Thomas Nelson, Inc., 1977.

ROOM, CHILD'S

JERRY'S OWN ROOM can play a very important role in his development as a child. Therefore its furnishing and decorating deserves all the careful attention you would lavish on, say, your living room. Your interest in its planning and your general attitude toward it can do much to foster his feeling of belonging, of being an important person whose needs and likes and dislikes receive equal consideration with those of other family members.

Bear in mind as you plan that this is *his* room. Remember, too, that he's much more concerned about what he *can do* in it than he is about *how it looks*. Take care, then, not to make it a room that's arranged and decorated solely from an adult point of view. Make it as cheerful and attractive as you can, but design it primarily to satisfy his young needs and interests.

With some thought, Jerry's room can be made to serve him, with few alterations, from the time he's a baby until he's well into his school years. Of course, you'll eventually have to replace the crib with a junior- or full-size bed. And his changing interests and ever growing supply of toys and other play equipment will call for additional storage units. But, in general, wise planning today will reduce the number of changes that may have to be made tomorrow.

Whether you're planning a new room or rearranging Jerry's present one, you may find material among the following suggestions that will stimulate your own ideas.

Space for Free Play. All young children need plenty of space for free play, indoors as well as out, space in which they can move about unhampered as they build with blocks, develop creative ideas, experiment with new things. How to provide the indoor facilities that children need often presents a problem in today's small or moderate-size homes. However, there are a number of ways by which advantage can be taken of every available inch of space.

Built-in chests, shelves, and cabinets can be located in corners and under the eaves, and they'll make Jerry's room seem larger. They'll also enable you to reduce the amount of free-standing furniture and save on playable floor space. You'll economize on time and money, too, if you plan these built-ins (and all furnishings, for that matter) to grow with Jerry so that he'll always be able to reach them easily. Shelves and clothing rods, for example, can be designed to be moved upward.

One good way of keeping the maximum amount of floor free for play is to slide or roll the bed into a compact recess during the day when it's not needed. Another way, if two children share the one room, is to arrange their beds against the walls at right angles to one another or to place them lengthwise along one wall instead of extending into the room. Bunk beds are space savers. They can be placed lengthwise against a wall, and the space beneath the bottom bunk can be converted into storage drawers for toys, games, or some extra blankets.

Drop-leaf tables attached to the wall will reduce free-standing furniture; they're quickly put out of the way when not in use. Their corners should be rounded to minimize accidents. When hooked up against the wall at the end of a busy day, an extra-large drop leaf—one that provides ample space for even the most ambitious play projects— takes up surprisingly little room.

Wooden blocks, measuring about 12 by 15 inches or larger and left open on one side, might double for child-size tables and chairs. When Jerry isn't using them, they can be stacked against the wall, where they'll serve as storage shelves for play equipment.

If you have two children and are buying a new house or remodeling your present one, you might consider the possibility of their sharing one large room rather than having two smaller ones—providing, of course, that you and the children feel this would be a happy arrangement. Even though he has a roommate, it's possible for a youngster to get off by himself when he wants to if there's a folding-type door or screen that can divide the room in two. Without any loss of space, the children can then have a large, free area for play, and when the folding door or screen is extended across the room, each one will have his very own private domain to enjoy in any way he pleases.

Furniture and Furnishings Scaled to Size. For his comfort and to best aid him in doing for himself, the furniture and furnishings in Jerry's room should be suited to his small size. You'll find it most economical if you start out with a few pieces of good, simple lines that can be matched and added to as he grows older.

Furniture can "grow up," too. The hanging space for dresses or rompers in an infant's three-piece bedroom suite becomes excellent for storage room for blouses, skirts, shirts or jackets in later years. Shelves used for toy storage become bookshelves or the home of special collections.

When Jerry decides he's too big for his crib, you may want to look at juvenile beds, which are somewhat smaller than the adult size and have protective side rails. Bunk beds also come with these rails, and demountable ones can be attached to most full-size beds. Jerry's bed should have a good, firm mattress on which he can relax completely; its level support will help him to develop a straight and sturdy spine.

In order for you or Jerry to move his furniture about easily, use smooth-rolling casters. Also, Jerry may find it easier to open the drawers of his furniture if they're equipped with finger holes or cut-out grips rather than hardware.

Floor and Wall Coverings. Both you and your youngster will better enjoy a room that's easy to clean and keep clean, a room where an accidental spill or smudge won't be a catastrophe or a source of worry. Knowing this, you'll want to install floor and wall coverings that can "take it" and will wipe clean with a sponge or damp cloth.

There's a great variety of easy-to-clean, long-lasting floor or wall materials from which you can choose. The most suitable type of floor covering is a smooth one on which Jerry and his friends can easily play with pull toys, cars or trains and that makes a good foundation for block building. Linoleum can be bought in patterned, room-size rugs. Special effects or designs can be devel-

oped by using inlay or linoleum tiles. Varying patterns are also obtainable in asphalt, cork, rubber and plastic tiles. You'd do well to select a tile or linoleum whose color goes all the way through and therefore won't wear off. Simplified methods of installing these modern floor coverings make it possible for you to do the job yourself and at a considerable saving.

A soft rug or two will add a cozy touch; these can easily and quickly be rolled up or moved aside when Jerry needs more smooth floor space.

There will be little need for you or your child to be concerned about nicks and fingermarks on the walls if you choose appropriate wall coverings—and the choice is almost limitless.

Several materials are available that won't show nicks, even when nails are pulled out, and their texture will add interest to any wall. Burlap, for example, is easily applied, like wallpaper, and comes in many colors. Youngsters enjoy pinning pictures or other objects to it. Felt, too, comes in an array of exciting colors and can be used on a pin-up wall. A canvas wall covering, colorful and patterned, serves the same purpose and stands up well under hard use. Another idea is to install composition board between molding and baseboard. There you have a bulletin board on which Jerry can pin all sorts of things of interest to himself or the whole family. Large sheets of paper can be thumbtacked to this material, and Jerry can paint or draw to his heart's content. When the paper is used up, merely rip it off and replace it with a clean sheet.

And while we're on the subject of drawing, don't overlook the fun a youngster can have with a chalkboard that's installed in or painted on one wall at a convenient height. A commercial chalkboard can be used (for eye ease, they're often green instead of black), or you can paint your own chalkboard with a green paint especially prepared for the purpose.

If you plan to paper the walls of Jerry's room, investigate the many washable papers, especially those papers having a plastic coating; these wipe clean with very little effort. When you've narrowed your selection down to three or four designs, why not let Jerry choose from these the paper he's going to have to live with?

You'd do well to avoid all-over wallpapers that have an overwhelming amount of action, although one wall of such paper may be quite satisfying. There's nothing restful or soothing about a room whose walls are completely covered with racing horses or capering clowns jumping up and down. There will be times—when he's sick in bed, for instance—when Jerry will welcome less lively surroundings. On the other hand, a paper with too little life in it can become monotonous to a youngster. Plain walls can be given a touch of life by decorating them here and there with appealing decalcomanias or wooden cutouts of favorite storybook characters, chosen by Jerry himself. Arrange these decorations, as well as any pictures that are to be hung, fairly low on the walls. If they're placed at or very close to his eye level, Jerry will be better able to enjoy them.

If the room is small, a paper or other wall covering in one of the lighter tints will tend to make it look larger. Dark colors, when used on large areas such as walls, make a room seem smaller; however, they help to counteract glare in a very sunny room. The room's exposure will probably influence color selection. Blue, violet, blue-green, and white that has been tinted with these colors create a cool atmosphere and are well suited to rooms that face south or west and so receive a great deal of sunlight. Warm colors—red, red and white, orange and white, and particularly the yellow tones— are good for rooms facing north or east. However, warm colors should never be given full rein in a decorating scheme; they need a balance of cool color. So if a warm color is used on the walls, paint accessories in the cool colors. Children's own color choices lean toward the warmer tones, so if it's at all possible, let Jerry exercise his choice in at least one part of his room. This could be the wall at one end, certain pieces of his own furniture or perhaps the window shades.

You'll want to provide hangings at the window that can control the light and air, simple ones that are easy to clean. Window shades, roll-type bamboo shades, venetian blinds or draw draperies will serve the purpose. All are available in colors and patterns that are attractive to children. There's no practical reason, however, to have curtains or draperies *and* another type of window covering; one will be suitable.

Good Lighting. Good light, and plenty of it, is very important for young eyes. An indirect ceiling fixture or an indirect standard lamp is satisfactory for general lighting. You'll also want to avoid eyestrain and fatigue by providing adequate local light for every visual task. Over a worktable, for instance, light coming from the left is best for the right-handed child and from the right for the left-handed child. Pin-up lamps are a good, inexpensive way to provide adequate localized lighting. Make sure that there are plenty of lamp outlets in Jerry's room so that an ample light source can be moved to wherever he decides to work or play. When not in use, extra outlets can be sealed off with little plastic plugs sold for that purpose.

Closets With a Purpose. One of the great advantages of closets, built-in or otherwise, is that they can be tailored to serve a child's particular needs or to solve specific storage problems. As you plan them, apply the same space-saving principles you'd use in planning a convenient and efficient workshop, with the items your child uses most frequently located within his easy reach.

Give some thought to the outside of the closet as well as to its interior. You'll save free floor area for other and more important purposes if you equip Jerry's closet with a sliding door, which takes up less space than a swinging-type door. However, if you decide to retain the swinging door, make good use of its outer surface by attaching to it a low book rack or rack for small toys. Its inner surface, too, can be made to support one or more racks for shoes or other articles and some low hooks on which Jerry can be encouraged to hang his own play clothes.

A closet from 22 to 24 inches deep gives sufficient room for hanging coats and suits or dresses and blouses. It would be a good idea to equip any small child's closet with an adjustable rod that can be raised as he grows. Also, provide a reachable, adjustable shelf for storing caps, mittens and so forth.

Often the bottoms and tops of closets are wasted space that could be put to good use. You'll be able to take full advantage of this space—and at the same time eliminate the need for a free-standing chest of drawers—if you build several drawers into the bottom of Jerry's closet and a shelf or cupboardlike arrangement into the top. The height and depth of the drawers can be tailored to Jerry's particular needs; they'll take care of most of his everyday clothing. The shelf or cupboard in the top of the closet may be used for storing items that are less frequently worn and that Jerry won't be called upon to reach. He may like having a favorite storybook or cartoon friend painted across the closet drawers. Such a picture would become complete only when all the drawers

are tightly shut, and it might encourage him to keep his closet neater than he otherwise would.

A Place for Toys. Since play is a child's work, he needs and deserves adequate tools and a place to store them. And if you can arrange to have his playthings, like his clothes, within easy reach, he'll be more apt to take care of them and to put them away after play.

The problem of where to store toys, games and other play equipment can be ideally solved if you're fortunate enough to have one closet in Jerry's room that can be devoted entirely to this sort of thing. Racks, shelves and bins built into it will not only help you and Jerry to keep the closet orderly, but they'll also keep the equipment in good condition since there will be less reason to pile one piece on top of the other. Vary the height and depth of the shelves and racks to accommodate the items to be stored on and in them. Jerry will like to have his step stool handy here so he'll be able to safely reach things kept on the higher shelves.

Low shelves along the walls of the room are generally more satisfactory than hinged-top chests or benches into which toys are usually thrown and often broken. You can make them at home or buy them unpainted and finish them to match other furnishings. Installed on adjustable standards and supports, they'll serve Jerry indefinitely. In later years they can be used for books and collections. If possible, locate a few shelves near the head of his bed so he'll be able to have his playthings close at hand during sick-abed times.

Make the shelves of different heights and widths—from 4 to 9½ inches in height to 6½ to 20 inches in width. Round their corners to prevent accidents. To determine the height of a unit of shelves, make the base of the uppermost shelf correspond to Jerry's eye level.

And because all children are squirrel-like hoarders at heart and like to have privacy for their most cherished possessions, close off at least one shelf with a door, preferably a sliding one that won't be bumped into if it's left open.

If Jerry has a special seat under the window where he sits to watch goings on in the outside world, make the seat serve a double purpose. Equip it with doors and use its interior for toy storage.

A bench along one wall of his room makes a fine place for Jerry to work out some of his creative ideas. The space beneath it needn't go to waste but can be used to house a good-sized toy-storage chest on casters and fitted with doors. If the chest is made with a pronounced overhang to three sides of its top, Jerry and his little friends can use it as a table which they can easily pull into the center of the room when it's wanted.

Low, traylike boxes on wheels or casters will hold quite a lot of Jerry's overflowing collection of smaller toys and they can be rolled under the bed to be out of the way.

—From Lorene K. Fox et al., *All Children Want to Learn.* Danbury, Conn.: Grolier Educational Corp., 1954.

RUNAWAYS

YOU HAVE PROBABLY HEARD the frightening statistic: Over 1 million children ran away from home last year. One of the tragedies of that statistic is that *many of them will never return!*

Adding to that tragedy is the realization that a million children will run away from home this year, a million next year, a million the year after that, a million the year after that. . . .

Young people of this nation are on the move, and they are bailing out of our homes like mad!

Parents are concerned about their children, and they want to prevent their offspring from becoming part of those ever-growing statistics. Probably because my wife, Elsie, and I operate the Walter Hoving Home in Garrison, New York—a home for girls, most of whom have run away, at some time, from their own homes—I'm frequently asked what makes children run away.

The answers to that question are complicated and varied. But one big reason is you and I. Parents!

Look at it this way. We've never raised children before, so we're novices at one of the most complicated jobs in the world. Trying to do something we don't know much about always has the potential of ending in failure. What started off as a soft, cuddly bundle of joy in your arms can end up as a frustrating headache! One of those 1-million runaways could be your child! Perhaps one of your children is already part of that statistic.

Or maybe your children are still small, and you wonder if that dark night will ever come when you look into a bedroom and discover to your utter horror that your child is gone. You need help to avoid that moment.

If your children have already run away, you obviously need some encouragement. Maybe, even reassurance.

But what I really want to stress to all parents at this time is that somewhere, sometime, you could face the problem of a runaway.

After visiting many homes, I have concluded that some parents are raising potential runaways and don't know it. Other concerned parents have asked my help because they knew something was wrong.

How about you? Are you raising a potential runaway? Here are four danger signals to look for.

First, Your Children Are No Longer Talking to You

I know that "communications gap" is a worn-out term. But it isn't a worn-out concept. It's very real in many homes. Some children feel that communication with their parents is next to impossible. And some parents have all but given up trying to get anything across to their children. They are worlds apart.

Second, Your Children Are Associating With the Wrong Kind of People

Ever take a close look at whom your children pal around with? . . . But, at this point, you need to recognize the wrong kind of friends as a potential danger signal.

If your children's friends don't look right and don't act right, you've got a problem. Your children are probably just like their friends!

Third, Your Children Are Threatening to Quit School

Some parents think the public school system is all out of whack. There may be some problems in it. But there is one thing that has always remained the same: Many young people don't like to go to school.

Remember your school days? I sure remember mine. And I don't ever remember jumping out of bed early in the morning and yelling, "Yippee! I get to go to school today!"

If you're like me, you lived for Saturdays and vacations.

Schools do have their problems. And not too many children really enjoy applying themselves to their studies. But if your children are threatening to quit school, you have a problem on your hands.

Fourth, Your Children Evidence a Lack of Spiritual Values

I have never met a Christian runaway, a Christian drug addict, a Christian alcoholic, or a Christian shoplifter. The combinations are simply incompatible.

When young people have given their hearts and lives to Jesus and have learned to live for Him, they will stay home and ride out the storm. God teaches them that.

The best answer to the runaway problem is for young people to live for Jesus. If your children have grown cold toward God, or if they have never turned their lives over to Him, or if their Christian commitment is only in their heads, you have potential runaways on your hands.

But if your children are spiritually alive, on fire for God, you should be able to sleep well. They will still be home when you get up in the morning.

God has a very special purpose for children. They are not meant to be trouble; they are meant to be a blessing in our homes.

If you want to keep your children out of trouble, then try these suggestions:

1. Know where they are and what they're doing.
2. Never give up on them.
3. Minimize their problems by getting them into perspective.
4. Keep them active and involved in worthwhile projects.
5. Provide for their spiritual stimulation.

God loves children. God loves your children. He is going to help them because He is more interested in their welfare than you are.

The Bible talks about our being "workers together with God." That goes for raising children too. What a privilege it is for us to work with Him and with the children He has entrusted to our care.

With His help, everything in your family is going to work out for your good and for your Heavenly Father's praise and glory. Believe it—and see it happen in your home too!

—From John Benton, *Do You Know Where Your Children Are?* Old Tappan, N.J.: Fleming H. Revell, 1981.

FOR FURTHER READING:

Dollar, Truman E., and Ketterman, Grace H. *Teenage Rebellion.* Old Tappan, N.J.: Fleming H. Revell Co., 1980.

Williams, L. Weinberg. *Our Runaway.* Valley Forge, Pa.: Judson Press, 1979.

S

SCHOOLS

IN SPITE OF HOW GOOD or bad schools may be or can be or should be, the frightening truth is that you have as much responsibility in educating your child as anyone. I am assuming that you want your child to read, to write, to score well on standardized tests and to demonstrate other indications of having been educated. But I am also assuming that you are willing to make some sacrifices of your own time and talent to see that this happens.

With the rise in private and Christian schools in recent years, many parents have been given more choice in where their children attend school. It is good that parents should have this choice, and it is also good that public schools do not have a monopoly on children's education. But the very existence of this choice places an unusual responsibility on parents. They now must know enough about the whole, wonderful process of education to be able to make a wise decision. Don't be deceived. Make a careful and systematic assessment of your child's school—of its philosophy, the teaching techniques, the probability of success, the inducements of learning, and the lifelong possibilities it offers your child.

If, after that assessment, you decide the school is not right for your child (be careful, you are dealing with a young person's life— twenty, thirty, fifty years) find another school which will offer him what he needs. But make sure. Just because a school *claims* to be something doesn't mean that it is. Dif-

ferent is not necessarily better. Some schools which have originated in recent years are not sound in their educational approach, are staffed with poorly trained and poorly paid teachers, and greatly limit the future decisions of the graduates. Now that you have the choice, you must accept the responsibility to be able to make a wise decision.

But your responsibility does not end there. Even if you choose to send your child to a nonpublic school and make the financial sacrifices needed to keep him there, you are fulfilling only part of your duties as a parent. Although you may be paying double taxes for schooling, you are still the single most important educational agent in your child's life. If you reject this responsibility your child's growth will be retarded, and both of you will have to live with the consequences.

. . . . .

Your role as a parent is to coordinate all the child's experiences into one unified, consistent, teaching agent. The difficult work here is to coordinate, not control. Parenthood would be a less frustrating, if not easier, enterprise if we could just control what our children encounter, eliminating all the negative and harmful. Since we can't do that even if we want to, we must settle for the task of coordinating.

While your child is in school, he will be under the direct supervision and influence of more than forty different adult authorities. During that time, he will also be subjected to the power of scores of his peers. Obviously, some of these people are going to contradict your suggestions. Some will contradict each other. Some will contradict your child's own value and knowledge systems. But these contradictions won't do much damage as long as your child has a stable, consistent, understanding, sensitive touchstone to help him evaluate, integrate, and unify these diverse sources and experiences. That's what parents are for, to be that touchstone, to have a close enough relationship with their child to provide stability in his life.

Let me conclude on a positive note. After having studied the educational scene firsthand for all these years, I am convinced that your child can survive and even thrive in school. Thousands do. Although he may even make it by himself, it would be easier for him if he doesn't have to tackle the task alone. And who knows, helping your son or daughter through the mysteries of school and school relationships might become some of the most memorable and rewarding moments in parenthood. You may make some lifelong friends. You may discover some dedicated, loving people. You may find some professionals who need your sympathy and concern.

—From Cliff Schimmels, *How to Help Your Child Survive and Thrive in Public School.* Old Tappan, N.J.: Fleming H. Revell Co., 1982.

Failure

When a child fails in schoolwork it means that he has not met the standards of achievement set up by his school. Standards vary somewhat from school to school and even between one teacher and another, but on the whole the requirements are the same for all children.

All children, however, are not the same. Before their child starts school, parents are usually aware that he does better in some ac-

tivities than in others, that he is interested in and quick at learning some skills and not others. The same is true of all children. It is not reasonable, then, to expect every child to do equally well in all branches of schoolwork.

An educational system, however, must have standards to measure its effectiveness in preparing children for adult living and adult work. A certain minimum of competence in reading, writing, and arithmetic and a certain basic knowledge are essential for getting along in the modern world. Some subjects in which a child is having difficulty can be dropped without serious loss to his total education. But in required subjects it is necessary, sooner or later, to achieve a passing grade.

While children must learn to read and write, for example, and while they are surrounded from infancy by people who read and write, these are skills that do not come naturally. Most children want to learn the tool subjects, but this desire to learn is, with some children, not so direct and simple a wish as the desire to use their muscles in running and climbing, to dig or build or romp with the dog or play with other boys and girls. Parents and teachers need to realize that they are asking something extra when they ask a child to sit quietly and work at his reading or arithmetic.

A failure noted on a report card thus indicates where a particular boy or girl needs help in meeting a general standard. Even though the schools tend to take an increasingly individual approach, it is for the parents, who know their own child, to take the initiative in discovering where the trouble lies and what can be done to overcome it.

Their first step is to pool their knowledge of the child with what the school knows of him. Parents and teacher, with the help of special tests to discover the reason for his trouble in certain areas, can decide on measures to lift him over his particular obstacle. On the basis of talks with parents, a teacher can often give a child the extra attention or opportunity he needs. The teacher can also usually recommend an older student or an outside tutor when one is needed, and parents can act accordingly. Some schools have child psychologists and guidance counselors who can help to uncover an emotional factor contributing to the failure, if one exists. Sometimes it is only by a failure in school work that a child shows he is troubled about getting along with classmates, a new baby at home, the absence of his father, a move to a new neighborhood, or some other anxiety unrelated to the schoolwork itself.

In many cases a physical checkup reveals that a boy or girl is in a low state of general health or has vision or hearing a little below normal. Then eyeglasses, a hearing aid, or perhaps merely a seat at the front of the room may help.

Parents and teacher together can be of great help to a youngster in working out with him a schedule for getting his lessons done, with due regard for what the child likes to do outside of schoolwork. A boy or girl is better able to give up indiscriminate television viewing, for example, if time is left in the schedule for some favorite programs than if all television is banned.

If a child does not seem to be trying, the reason may be significant. A boy or girl who must struggle with work the other children seem to do with ease may be too discouraged to try. A child who feels that too much is expected of him often gives up in advance. The example of a more successful brother or sister or the implied criticism of a quick, impatient parent can convince a youngster that he is stupid and unable to learn. Such a child surely needs to have his self-confidence restored and to be assured that he can meet all reasonable demands made upon him.

A child or his parents may say that he is "failing everything," but this is hardly ever literally true. A boy who seems unable to learn spelling or grammar may be far ahead of his class in science and have his own laboratory although science is not part of his schoolwork at the time. Or he may be skilled in manual arts and know enough practical mathematics for complicated constructions and yet be unable to pass a mathematics examination. Many girls and boys excel in English, the social sciences, or languages, and have trouble with algebra. Often a child knows the subject but is unable to use what he knows in class or in a test. A boy or girl may be slow, or shy about speaking up in class, or thrown into a panic by having to pass a test or solve a problem on the blackboard. A child is often found to have missed an important step in learning during an illness or other unavoidable absence from school.

It is generally not advisable for a father and mother to tutor their own boy or girl, since the emotions of both child and parents are likely to become involved in the lessons. Parents can, however, talk with the child about what he is studying and help him to find the connection between his daily living and what he learns in school. His interest can be stimulated and his knowledge and understanding broadened in the course of ordinary family conversation.

Parents help their child most by their own attitude. Their sympathetic interest and desire to help him are sometimes enough to spur him to fresh efforts. He needs their help in seeing also that, while for practical reasons he must pass in mathematics or English, he need not be a mathematical genius or a literary scholar either to hold their respect or to get along in the world. Each child is different, and each individual has some area in which he finds his greatest satisfaction and success. By seeing in their child's school failure some clue to his needs, parents can help him achieve the best of which he is capable.

Many schools are doing away with the system of reporting on children's schoolwork only with respect to subject matter and that vague term, "deportment." Some write report letters to tell parents in what areas a child is doing well, where he has trouble, where he has improved, and where he seems to be falling down. Some hold individual conferences with parents. Many use formal printed report cards, but sometimes, instead of A, B, C, and D, the only marks given are S for satisfactory and U for unsatisfactory. To be more helpful, these marks are sometimes accompanied by a sentence or two to give parents an idea of the child's strong and weak points. In the upper school grades, however, where there are many subjects for boys and girls to master, the more formal systems or marking are still generally used— sometimes grading by letters and sometimes by percentage figures.

Whatever systems they use, most schools are tending to evaluate all aspects of a child's adjustment to school life. Parents usually welcome this, for they are concerned not only with their boys' and girls' learning but also with their attitudes, their school interests, how they get along with their classmates.

Individual parents cannot change the marking system used by their child's school. But if they understand the purpose of a particular marking system, they themselves can interpret any type of report card in a way that will be truly helpful. They can find out, for instance, whether the school gives marks on an absolute scale, on the basis of individual achievement, or on the basis of comparison with the brightest in the class. Knowing their own youngster and his previous school record, a mother and father can look behind the impersonal marks and give the real meaning to them. For example, an uninteresting C will have entirely different meanings on the report cards of two different children. For one who has been consistently failing in arithmetic, C is a triumph; for one who has always done excellent work in arithmetic, C is a warning signal. For the child to whom arithmetic comes hard, the first C means that the first hurdles have been overcome. From then on the chief goal is not to turn the C into a B or an A but to help the young student keep a grasp of the subject as it gets progressively harder.

To the child who has fallen from an A to a C, neither a severe scolding nor a long, disappointed face is helpful. Real aid lies in a sincere, unbiased effort to find out why the mark has gone down. A teacher approached in this spirit will be glad to help. Has the work itself taken a new and difficult turn, leaving the child behind? If so, it is constructive to go back to where the subject matter was clearly understood and to take the next steps slowly. Perhaps, if his teacher cannot give individual aid, one of the other teachers or an older student can work with the youngster on this under the teacher's guidance.

In some cases it may be not so much a question of the subject matter as some other difficulty in a child's school or personal life that is interfering with his work. Here again, with tact and understanding, parents want to find the source of trouble, whether in school, at home, outside, or within the child himself, and work toward getting rid of it. With their child they can decide whether or not to enlist the teacher's help. Sometimes— not to improve his school marks but to help a child to a full and satisfying life—the trouble calls for the help of someone trained to find the cause of children's emotional problems and to treat them. Such problems are often reflected in school difficulties.

Since parents are naturally pleased about good marks and disappointed about poor ones, they may want to know why they shouldn't be "natural" and show it—praising and rewarding a child for his A's, taking away certain treats or privileges for the D's and F's. Wide experience with school children has shown clearly that this does not really help a child. Nor is it helpful to treat the coming of each report card (good, bad, or indifferent) as a major family event. The very good student whose parents encourage him to work primarily for A's and B's can, because he is working mainly for outside rewards, fail to experience the inner reward and real growth that can come from intellectual pursuits and achievements.

The child who has a low intellectual capacity, on the other hand, will not be helped by being scolded and shamed for his poor school marks. The feeling of failure this treatment gives will probably make him do even worse at school. What helps him most is his parents' acceptance of the fact that schooling is hard work for him. If he is working to capacity, he needs their help in accepting the fact that he is doing what he can, and he needs their protection from a general sense of failure because he cannot meet certain standards. And he needs appreciation of his desirable qualities—praise for doing the things he is able to do well.

Most children, of course, fall between these two extremes of the very good student and the very poor student, but the same is true for them. The "average" student, too, needs to be encouraged to do his best, to get pleasure and a sense of achievement from intellectual pursuits, rather than encouraged to work for the C's and B's. He may need extra help with subjects in which he is weak and, like the very poor student, he needs to know that his parents like him fine the way he is. He also needs to be encouraged in the things he can do well, whether his talents lie in sports, in music, or in the valuable art of getting along well with other people.

This is not to belittle the importance of schoolwork. Of course becoming educated is important, but learning four or five "subjects" is not all there is to becoming educated. Parents must, for one thing, see the schoolwork in relation to other things in life; for another, they must genuinely accept the fact that there are enormous individual differences among children. Not every child can be a good student, and not every child can learn mainly through studying. But parents can help a child to do his best and, thinking of his life as a whole, help him to develop his other potentialities.

—From *The New Encyclopedia of Child Care and Guidance*. Garden City, N.Y.: Doubleday & Co., 1968.

FOR FURTHER READING:

Ginott, Haim G. *Teacher and Child: A Book for Parents and Teachers*. New York: Macmillan Publishing Co., 1972.

Kessler, Diane Cooksey. *Parents and the Experts*. Valley Forge, Pa.: Judson Press, 1974.

Lockerbie, D. Bruce. *Who Educates Your Child*. Grand Rapids: Zondervan Publishing House, 1980.

Stein, Sara B. *A Child Goes to School*. Garden City, N.Y.: Doubleday & Co., 1978.

SELF-CONSCIOUSNESS

EVERYONE IS FAMILIAR with times, whether fleeting or prolonged, when he has felt uncomfortably overaware of himself. Some inner uncertainty can leave a person confusedly conscious of his own thoughts or appearance, actions or words. When the lack of security is severe, there can be excessive thinking about how one appears to others. Adults can be self-conscious and not display it outwardly. But in children such feelings often show themselves in self-conscious behavior.

367

As a rule, however, people do not associate self-consciousness primarily with very young children. A youngster is not often self-conscious unless some awkward situation has been imposed on him. Johnny may well dig his toe in the ground when he is called on to recite for company, or squirm uncomfortably when rude grownups discuss him in his very presence. But, as a thing without immediate external cause, the term is usually linked more with older children, from about the time of puberty on through the teen years.

The classic example of self-consciousness that occurs to most adults is the blush of an adolescent boy whose voice cracks in the middle of an earnest speech. But parents of young people know that teen-agers' self-consciousness is not limited to embarrassment over individual incidents or blunders. There are periods when the most self-assured boy or girl seems to have lost all poise. Considering the maze of physical changes, emotional adjustments, social pressures, intellectual questioning, and new self-awareness that young people must find their own way through, the lack of self-possession is more than understandable. When it seems as though anything can be different tomorrow, inner sureness can be lost for a moment or for a month. The degree of the self-consciousness and how long it lasts vary, of course, with individual personalities, but they also develop a good deal on adult reactions.

When there are specific areas of self-conscious behavior, parents can sometimes come to the aid of their young people in equally specific, practical ways. . . . Rehearsing a few simple rules of etiquette at home can bolster the young girl who gets flustered in introducing people. But the over-all, permeating self-consciousness of some teen-agers is a thing over which parents can only bide their time. Although their continued affection, support, praise, and respect, by

building up the adolescent's feeling of being worthwhile, is a big contribution, it is very often what adults do *not* do at this time that is important. A sensitive person doesn't remark on the "fuzz" on a young man's chin or the unusual length of his legs; on a young girl's "development" or the fact that she's going on her first date. And of course saying, "Don't be so self-conscious"—however kindly—only makes matters worse.

Some young people seem to glide through their teen years without ever losing their self-assurance. But most of them do have to flounder through periods of sometimes painful self-consciousness. Gradually, as they begin to see how they fit into the world around them and where they are heading, they can begin to attain the much-sought poise of adulthood.

—From *The New Encyclopedia of Child Care and Guidance.* Garden City, N.Y.: Doubleday & Co., 1968.

SELF-ESTEEM

WE WANT OUR CHILDREN to be happy—to know joy in uniqueness and in putting their mark on life. We want them to realize the joy of being persons in the fullest sense of the word—knowing both freedom of their individual natures and responsibility to themselves and to others. Self-esteem is bedrock to it all.

Having self-esteem does not mean that it is forever indestructible. Trials and anguish of spirit can shake it to the core, but the way we deal with our children and with one another can give a solid reserve of strength in the face of shattering experiences that come along with life.

Self-esteem, a positive self-concept, is a powerful base of operations through all of life. How our children feel about themselves will affect every portion of their lives: their success in school, in interpersonal relations, in their choice of careers and life plans, and in their ability to face and to make change—or to stand firm against it. Self-esteem affects their ability to affirm others and themselves, to face reality, to value their own uniqueness and that of others. Self-esteem helps them know the joy that is basic to life, and that can help lighten the times of darkness and disruption.

How can we help our children develop a positive self-concept while we are also realizing our adult needs for self-esteem? How is the self-image formed? What are the effects of negative self-image? What is the relationship between building self-esteem and healthy sexuality? Answering these questions is the main concern of this essay.

Self-Esteem: A Need for Our Children and Ourselves

We can best examine the formation of self-esteem in our children in the context of our own parenting journey and our accompanying needs for self-esteem throughout life. Although as parents we have, it is hoped, come to a certain maturity and fairly consistent identity, we still need others to affirm us—to help us hope in ourselves. We can be going through life-cycle stages, and have very human needs for caring. We need to be made more whole and to be healed when hurting. When feeling uncomfortable with a self that is changing or suffering crisis we need to feel understood and loved. We have the universal basic needs present in us from birth to death to feel lovable and worthwhile.

We help form our children's self-concept at the same time life is shaping our own changing needs, while our own self-esteem is being firmed up, maintained, or destroyed. The way life affects us and the way we think of ourselves affects the way our children think of themselves.

Thinking of the developmental stages of life can help us in building the self-esteem needed in stages of growth of various family members. Knowing something of what to expect can keep us from demanding too much of ourselves or others. Considering that we as well as our children can be experiencing developmental changes or traumas, and trying to be aware of the accompanying needs, can more readily help us affirm one another.

Erik Erikson (in *Childhood and Society*) has given us a pattern of life-cycle development which can help us see accompanying needs for self-esteem throughout life. These are not, of course, absolutely fixed according to the age dimensions listed, but present a basic guideline of growth. Throughout all of the phases, we are engaged "in being, in doing, and in becoming." Some of the qualities of Erikson's developmental cycle include the following: first year, trust in oneself and others; second and third year, autonomy and self-mastery; fourth to fifth year, initiative; sixth to eleventh year, industry; 11th to 18th year, identity and identification of the past with the question of "Who am I?"; the young adult years, intimacy and commitment to others; adult years, generativity and productivity; years of maturity, ego integrity and acceptance of life.

Each of these stages is integrated with and built upon the earlier ones. If children arrive at adulthood, for example, without having realized the basic foundation of trust, they can withdraw from others, live in isolation, divert the energy needed for loving relations and use it as a force for self-hatred or hatred of others.

Even if these early stages of inner development have not been experienced, we can still help their formation in others by filling these needs as best we can. In the same light, as we grow in our life journey, we can periodically go back, as it were, to draw present strength by "reforming" early needs of trust, autonomy, mastery and so on. There is never a cut-off period of complete interior development. Basic to each of these stages is our need for feeling lovable and worthwhile.

How the Self-Image Is Formed

From the moment of birth—even before it—forces of life can give children security that is a basis for self-esteem. From their earliest moments, from the way the children are handled, loved, talked to, and tended to, they can come to know the world and its people as trustworthy or untrustworthy.

Even before birth, in the security of the womb, the child experiences continuity in hearing the rhythm of the mother's heartbeat as it flows soundly, strongly, and regularly through the aorta past the uterus. The child leaves this pre-natal continuity for a world of disparate sounds and needs. Providing as smooth a transition as possible helps the child to the needed basis of trust.

From this early security and trust, children, with their natural urge to grow, come to realize a separateness in themselves. With this comes a sense of "I must be able to cope," and also the initiative of wanting to achieve and have some control on their arena of life.

All along the way—from the basis of trust, self-concept is being formed or modified. It is as if the child is an absorbing mirror drawing in images from the environment. The first images, of course, come from the home. From parent expectations and plans and place in the family, from beliefs and faith and commitment to values and principles, from innumerable influences, children draw in the first picture of themselves. These images from the family join with the other impressions from outside the home—from church, relatives, peers, media, from everything children meet in life. Important as all these influences are, however, they do not alone determine self-concept. For self-concept comes from these impressions together with *how the child gathers, assesses, and internalizes* these influences into his or her self.

The Foundations of Self-Esteem

It is our acceptance which allows children to achieve more. Thus along with acceptance we must provide increasing opportunities for achievement. At the same time we must remember that self-esteem also comes from allowing for failure and avoiding undue expectation. True self-acceptance comes from unconditional love. In being loved, children come to know what it is like to give love.

Affection, acceptance, achievements, and allowance for failure—these are the foundations for self-esteem. We love and respect children as they are; we try to understand and respond to their individual natures—and children move on to find added accomplishments they can realize. Feeling the satisfaction with achievements helps them keep moving on to what they can become. Discipline and controls and encouragement consistent with the child's growth are part of parental love.

We communicate our values and acceptance, respect, understanding, and love both verbally and non-verbally. Listening, watching, and assessing how each family member is absorbing life experiences allow us to see in what way the family and social imprinting are shaping our children—and ourselves. It helps us see how we can help one another meet or cope with traumas or forces of society that shape self-esteem.

The picture children hold of themselves is, in turn, reflected back to society. Back and forth the reflection is sent—the picture they absorb *from* the world; the picture which they send *to* the world.

Similarly, the picture we as parents hold

of ourselves is reflected to the world and especially to the family atmosphere. And, as we have stressed, it is this atmosphere in which children first form the image of what they are like. If we as parents are not trusting; if we are fearful, dishonest, isolated, trapped in rigid conformity; if we do not like ourselves or feel perpetually embittered or outraged at life, we risk imprinting these same trembling messages on our children's self-concept—the core of personality which influences all of their behavior and all of their life.

Effects of Negative Self-Esteem

A sense of outrage with life and ourselves can be reflected in a negative or damaged self-esteem in behaviors of varying disruptiveness: the rapidly spiralling increase of teenage suicides; the vast numbers of runaway children; the sexual promiscuity in looking for nurturing and love; the rise in teenage alcoholism; the rise in female crimes, which some social scientists feel are causally related to a confused and poorly defined role of women. There are neuroses, anxiety, uncertainty in interpersonal relationships, placing impossible demands on oneself, wearing masks and pretending to be someone else, the increase of overall juvenile crime—all reflections of poor self-esteem. And there are the child-abusing parents whose low self-esteem results in physical and mental abuse of children who cannot meet the parents' unrealistic demands.

Earlier in this essay we have stressed the results of positive self-concept. It is good to know that even if it wavers under stress, conviction of worth can bring freedom to grow and to try new tasks with confidence as well as underlying happiness and a feeling of value.

And this includes happiness and value for one's sexual nature. It includes a sense of re-spect for who one is that begins in infancy to be a force for stability in adolescence. It includes a self-acceptance that enables one not to be devastated by failure.

Building Self-Esteem and Healthy Sexuality

Education in sexuality begins in infancy when children first learn love from others. It continues in the way we reflect our own attitudes of sexuality to them, how we respond to such things as early exploration of body parts and functions of elimination, to their first curious explorations and questioning in various ages.

As our children grow, we want them to know that wholesome sexuality is not just genital, but that it involves our whole scope of closeness with others, that it includes reaching out and sharing who we are—and thus growing in mutual enrichment. It involves trusting and welcoming one another, with reconciling after conflict, with healing and allowing others to be healed by us, with our listening, with our words that "touch" and transform, with our physical presence that translates into care, with a real communion of spirit.

Our language has much to do with the way children form wholesome sexuality. When a two-year-old takes off his clothes at the suggestion of older children; when a three-year-old son takes a bath in the garbage can with a three-year-old neighbor girl, do we say, "That's bad! Bad boy," or "This is inappropriate behavior," or something similar to this? When they ask, "Where do I come from?" do we cover over with fantasy or answer honestly with as much information as necessary for the time? Do we use proper language for body parts? Do we talk with pre-teenagers (before physical changes occur in them which can cause embarrassment in discussion) about changes they can expect in their bodies and emotions?

371

From the beginning do we communicate with them—listening to feelings as well as ideas, letting them know feelings are a part of being whole and that it is all right to have feelings, but that they do not have to be acted upon?

Do we provide outlets for releasing feelings? Do we provide skills that go along with various ages? Wholesome sexuality—it is part of our overall idea of ourselves—the esteem we hold about the person each of us is. It is formed in the very way intimacy and love are first shown to one another—and to our children. It is formed in providing opportunities for our children to love others.

Do we like our children and one another? Avoid demanding good feelings into existence? Not derogate or cause guilt about any physical characteristic or function? Do we allow for failure? Accept feelings? Accept the whole person? Do we accept ourselves?

How we answer these questions helps form the atmosphere from which our family draws the picture of life and of who they are. Our responses give fortitude, courage, and the spiritual force of will that can accompany feeling worthwhile.

These virtues can be refreshingly life-giving. And they are continually needed. They can be a reserve in times of trauma. They can give a base of security to our own lives, and from our lives can reflect to the security of society. Such is the power—and the possibility—of each of us as we reflect to others the value of being ourselves.

—From Maureen Miller, "Valuing Who We Are: Self-Esteem for Our Children," in *Christian Parenting*. Ramsey, N.J.: Paulist Press, 1979.

FOR FURTHER READING:

Briggs, Dorothy. *Your Child's Self-Esteem.* Garden City, N.Y.: Doubleday & Co., 1970.

Birkey, Verna. *You Are Very Special: A Biblical Guide to Self-Worth.* Old Tappan, N.J.: Fleming H. Revell Co., 1977.

Dobson, James C. *Hide or Seek.* Old Tappan, N.J.: Fleming H. Revell Co., 1979.

Miller, William A. *You Count, You Really Do!* Minneapolis: Augsburg Publishing House, 1976.

Osborne, Cecil. *The Art of Learning to Love Yourself.* Grand Rapids: Zondervan Publishing House, 1976.

SEX EDUCATION

FOR BETTER OR WORSE, parents are normally the first adults to introduce their children to snow, squirrels, daffodils, seatbelts, football, swings, airplanes, swimming—and sex. Facts fade, but impressions linger. If early, but innocent, inquiries about body parts or body functions are met with censure or evasion, ridicule or suppression, a pattern is slowly but resolutely woven which will subsequently choke communication in the adolescent years. On the other hand, one of the great joys of parenthood is in being the first to expose the wonders of the zoo or ice cream or sex to this inquisitive, awesome little miracle God has helped him create. Candor and control, confidence and conviction in the formative years will pave the way for dialogue during the teenage years.

Many sociological studies document the breakdown of communication about sex in the home. William Blaisdell, a public health specialist employed by the U.S. government, discovered in interviews with 25,000 teenagers from 1958 to 1963 that

—1 in 14 teenagers learns sex information from his parents before from other teenagers

—1 in 22 teenagers learns from his parents about venereal disease

Fortunately, it appears that the times are changing; more and more parents are becoming concerned that this generation of children be advised by them of their sexual responsibilities. The pressures of society together with an increased sophistication (in the best sense of the term) of parental skills argue for home instruction before vulnerable children are emotionally and physically exploited by manipulative peers and by Madison Avenue.

Scripture has always taken seriously the role parents are to play in bringing God's viewpoint into focus for their children. In the biblical view, Christian education begins in the home and always includes, as a worthy part of God's good creation, human sexuality. Both Deuteronomy 6 and Ephesians 6 instruct parents (actually fathers) to assume personal responsibility in bequeathing their faith to succeeding generations. The latter reference is familiar: "Fathers, do not provoke your children to anger, but bring them up in the discipline and instruction [nurture and admonition, KJV] of the Lord" (Ephesians 6:4). The Deuteronomy passage merits several comments. It follows, significantly, a recital of the Decalogue by Moses. The land "flowing with milk and honey" is reserved for those who love God and who keep his commandments. Following the Shema ("Hear, O Israel: The Lord our God is one Lord") comes the very practical—and sobering—command:

And these words which I command you this day shall be upon your heart; and you shall teach them diligently to your children, and shall talk of them when you sit in your house, and when you walk by the way, and when you lie down, and when you rise.

Deuteronomy 6:6, 7

In other words, the good life, in God's view, comes with a price tag: discipline and diligence. Masculine leadership instead of

religious momism is envisioned. It is the primary responsibility of the father, not the religious community, to teach these commandments to the children. "Let George do it" is not a biblical proverb.

Spontaneity rather than religious ritual is prescribed. Pastor Charles E. Cook of Denver, Colorado, passed along to the writer an apt summarization of this principle:

In the spiritual, be natural;
In the natural, be spiritual.

If, then, the ancient Deuteronomic prescription were to be transformed into our milieu by modern paraphrasing, it might read:

You, dad, are basically responsible to teach God's Word and ways to your children. You should talk of them naturally whenever the occasion arises: when you sit by a campfire, when you all are walking on the beach, when you are relaxing in the hammock, and at the breakfast table.

Everyday experiences and familiar landscapes become springboards for discussing both God's natural and special revelation.

One further comment is necessary; it is important to note also in the Deuteronomic record another sound pedagogical principle at work, namely, that lessons learned in childhood are retained well. Childhood is the optimal time for memorization and recitation. The seeds of moral behavior are best sown then. In a sense family dynamics have changed little over these many centuries; the biblical author relates that existential movement that parents of all teenagers know:

When your son asks you in time to come, "What is the meaning of the testimonies and the statutes and the ordinances which the Lord our God has commanded you?" then you shall say to your son, "We were Pharaoh's slaves in Egypt; and the Lord brought us out of Egypt with a mighty hand."

Deuteronomy 6:20, 21

The biblical record joins issue with answer. Information learned in childhood is now clarified by mature interpretation. A teenager's natural query is followed by dad's testimony. A father's personal experience and personal commitment reinforce a youth's catechism. Part of that catechism includes the Decalogue's prohibition of adultery and coveting (Deuteronomy 5).

Whenever parents fail to provide a home atmosphere in which there can be trust and respect, love and sympathy among family members, their children become ready targets for emotional and social catastrophe. Overly permissive or excessively rigid parents deter their children from a healthy psychosexual development wherein external value systems become personally internalized. The lack of a personally meaningful moral code is one of the major stumbling blocks of the Now Generation. Unfortunately, too few homes are Christocentric in their orientation. Instead, many are so culturally conditioned that all of their moods and mores, all of their values and virtues are derived from the rather bland criterion of "middle class respectability" (or hypocrisy). The ratio of adolescent respect for parental authority and belief is directly proportionate to parental integrity and consistency.

Consequently, the relative value of sex education done in the home will be contingent upon the wholesomeness of the home. Chronically discordant marriages will seriously cripple family life education. Christian parents, secure and mature in their own loving commitment, must bring guidance and encouragement to their children as these young persons seek to establish their own feelings of self-worth and self-realization. Love, affection, trust, honesty, protec-

tion, respect, and integrity rather than prejudice, contempt, hostility, fear, humiliation, and domination must be the prevailing mood in the home. Budding biological impulses need to be coordinated with spiritual values. Parents who have sought conscientiously to infuse both love and communication into their children's growth patterns merit hearty commendation.

The discussion of sex within the Christian home presupposes a Christian understanding of human sexuality. While in our pluralistic society other agencies will be assisting parents in family life education (the church, the school, boys' and girls' character organizations, literature, the communications media, etc.), the primary responsibility still rests with them. Through reading, special courses, and reflection, parents can gain skill in this vital area. Dr. John Rock, professor of gynecology at Harvard Medical School and a pioneer in the development of the pill, has stated that "sex education must be started by the parent with the three-year-old and carried along adequately during his development while in primary school years."

There are many compelling reasons for parents to be the ones to handle their children's inquiries about human sexuality. Most are aware of their responsibility; what is lacking is confidence. At least six basic reasons argue for parental involvement:

1. Parents are the first to meet the problem. By the time a youngster is in school, or the Sunday school is functioning significantly in his life, innumerable questions will already have been raised. In the family situation, it is possible to give individual rather than group attention to the problem.

2. Parents have the best interests of the child at heart. Their profound concern for the well-being of their own offspring argues for a depth of relationship not possible or likely in institutional situations.

3. Parents should be the most perceptive

as to their child's true mood and interest. Much of the time it is the question behind the question which needs answering.

4. Parents are in a position to know whether or not the information their children have (both from previous parental instruction and from peer influence) is understood. Often it is distorted, confused and forgotten by the child. Questions are asked and reasked.

5. Children spend more time during their formative years with their parents than with their teachers. Questions about sex are not programmed for scheduled times. Baby brother's bath, a neighbor's pregnancy, guppies reproducing, and all kinds of situations produce spontaneous inquiries.

6. Children should be reared in a relationship of trust, admiration, and love for their parents as these questions come along. These feelings are foundational to an open and healthy discussion of human sexuality, or any other issue for that matter. Fairy tale answers to life's deepest mysteries are excluded from this holy relationship.

Consequently, parents should be well equipped to provide sex education in the home environment. Parents who either freeze or giggle when human sexuality is discussed are probably not prepared to handle their children's natural questions. Evident in all of the conversation needs to be the Christian parent's love for God and his awe at God's creative workmanship.

Questions at Different Age Levels. Alert and loving parents of all generations have found that some of their fondest memories record those choice moments when a son or a daughter turned to them for information and guidance on what was, for them, a particularly delicate and difficult problem. On the other hand, those parents who are uncomfortable with the earliest questions of curious children will very likely be seriously

threatened by the inquiries of older adolescents—if they are still asking by then. Emil Brunner, in speaking of the "unparalleled and indissoluble relation" which father, mother, and child have entered into within the Christian family, calls this threefold relationship a "trinity of being." Irrevocably the three are cast on life's seas in the same boat; the equipment, the facilities, the provisions, the view is common to all three. Fortunately, the three may be under the hand of a wise Captain—the Lord Christ.

Preschool children ask many innocent questions about themselves and their world. The curiosity, spontaneity, and honesty of little children should be appreciated and encouraged. A basic rule of thumb for sex education here: little questions raised by little people deserve little answers.

Preadolescent youngsters, through contact with peers and pets, will find many occasions for displaying both their knowledge and their ignorance of human anatomy and reproduction. Parental counsel should clarify and orient information for these inquiring minds. In some cases, few questions may be forthcoming. A surgeon friend of ours, feeling that not enough questions were being raised by his children at this age, brought home some guppies and hamsters. Soon the conversations were rolling.

By the time a child reaches the junior high level, a moderately good grasp of body parts and body function should be his. Menstruation for the girls and both nocturnal emissions and voice changes for the boys will precipitate many further inquiries. Advantage should be taken of the personal changes which are taking place now within the youngster to orient these immediate bodily modifications to a worthy life-view. This is the age when Christian parents should discourage a flip attitude toward sexuality and encourage a sacred viewpoint.

The senior high student, confronted by the

sexual lure and leer of an adult world he is not yet prepared to enter, either emotionally or legally, soon discovers that moral ambiguity and ambivalence abound. In the midst of ethical chaos he is expected to find a firm footing, or else. Little wonder Christians of high school age are perplexed and perturbed. Any parent who is trying to help his child cope with this dilemma needs reinforcement from the church and from the Lord Christ. The importance to high school youth of a personal commitment to the Lord of life and love cannot be too strongly emphasized and encouraged. An absolute commitment at this time will be of immense assistance later in the face of relative propositions.

This period in a teenager's life when the normal identity crisis is conjoined with an ideals crisis is a crucial one. The wise parent will not "lose his cool." Reaction, within prescribed limits, may be just as necessary and healthy a way to establish personal values as conformity. The parent's role becomes one of providing stabilization, structure, and strength—with a touch of stoicism. In many situations the youth finds a parental surrogate with whom he readily identifies. This is not to be discouraged; the influence of either official or unofficial godparents is intended to be a part of the benefit of belonging to the community of Faith.

Dr. Mary Calderone views sex in the life of the adolescent as designed to accomplish four goals:

1. To separate yourself from your parents
2. To establish a male or female role
3. To determine value systems
4. To establish your vocational role

The Christian home, providing the nurture and discipline awakened hormones need, should stand as a fortress for youth. In Fairchild's perceptive words, "living in the 'sea of influence' around it, it is the problem and

the privilege of the Christian family to both filter and flavor that sea." Home then becomes a bastion within which to gather perspective and strength and from which to encounter and to influence the world, confident of God's presence.

The college student who is home only during vacations still needs the security and stability of parental love. Having been confronted now at the university with the Playboy mythology and often, an amoral atmosphere, there yet remains a place for dialogue between the generations, without napalming the undergraduate. The generation gap exists only for those who don't listen or read. Drugs, drink, and sex become for many students solely a matter of taste, not of morality. But many desire more responsible decision-making. A discerning spirit coupled with persistent love will nourish many a troubled sophomore. . . .

Principles for Student Sexual Behavior. The goal of family life education is to coordinate budding biological impulses and psychological feelings with personally meaningful spiritual and social values. For the Christian, those values must also be harmonious with God's Word, the final authority of faith and practice. Dale White, in an article entitled "How to Develop Healthy Sex Attitudes in Your Children," suggests five objectives:

1. We want our children to grow into adulthood with the inner freedom to live out of their own integrity.
2. We want our children to grow up reasonably free from inner compulsions or impulses.
3. We want our young people to rejoice in themselves as male and female.
4. We want our young people to be able to love warmly and spontaneously.
5. We hope our children will be able to feel

with and for people—to go out to meet others with an inner assurance born of wholeness.

His article elaborates further the key role parental example plays in the formulation of healthy attitudes children assimilate.

Some principles for sexual behavior at the junior high, senior high, and college levels are listed below as a suggested point of departure for dialogue between parent and child. Differences of opinion and individual modification are inevitable and desirable. But whatever course of action is advocated, for the Christian it should be emotionally sound and ethically certain.

Junior High Students:

1. Understand the bodily changes now taking place in one's self.
2. Understand the bodily changes taking place in members of the opposite sex.
3. Understand the elementary facts of human reproduction and correct misconceptions.
4. Relate the biblical view of human sexuality to one's own sexual development.
5. Give attention to personality development.
6. Discover the purposes and manners of dating.
7. Learn good grooming habits.
8. Learn personal discipline in handling sexual problems.

Senior High Students:

(Note that, for the most part, the principles at each level are cumulative, building on those introduced at the previous level and including them.)

1. Play the field; don't go steady.
2. Double date.
3. Develop your own personality, and help your date to do likewise.
4. Develop your own self-respect and respect for rights of others.
5. Develop your own value system, based

on a personal understanding of the Christian ethic.

6. Learn personal discipline in handling sexual problems; let males as well as females know when to draw the limits.
7. Balance physiological development with emotional maturity.
8. Note personality characteristics admirable in dates so that you begin to file a mental profile of the "ideal" mate.
9. Gain an appreciation for the dynamics of a healthy, happy Christian family.
10. Be an individual. Learn to be popular without always being influenced by what "everybody else" is doing.
11. Learn to desexualize our modern oversexed environment.
12. Plan participatory as well as spectator activities; excel in something.

College Students:

1. Looking for the "ideal" mate? Be the ideal mate!
2. Males: Treat girls as persons, not objects.
3. Females: Learn the difference between being alluring and being attractive—and when either is appropriate.
4. Act responsibly: explore the other person, not his body.
5. Be further ahead psychologically than physiologically in your relationship.
6. Courtship is not designed to be a contest of wills; learn what psychiatrist Erik Erikson has called "discipline and devoted delay."
7. Alcohol and sex do not mix; drugs and sex do not mix.
8. Adopt a moral code you would want your sister and daughter to follow.
9. Retain your virginity as a male or a female; for both virgins and non-virgins, there will be stresses and problems; instant sex is no utopia.
10. No petting before engagement; no coitus before marriage.

—From Lewis P. Bird and Christopher T. Reilly, *Learning to Love* (pp. 65–73). Waco, Tex.: Word Books, 1971.

FOR FURTHER READING:

Amstutz, H. Clair. *Growing Up to Love: A Guide to Sex Education for Parents.* Scottdale, Pa.: Herald Press, 1966.

Howell, John C. *Teaching Your Children About Sex.* Nashville: Broadman Press, 1973.

Ketterman, Grace. *How to Teach Your Child About Sex.* Old Tappan, N.J.: Fleming H. Revell Co., 1981.

Mace, David R. *The Christian Response to the Sexual Revolution.* Nashville: Abingdon Press, 1970.

SEX IN ADOLESCENCE

A NATIONAL SURVEY of adolescents between thirteen and nineteen years of age found that 52 percent had engaged in premarital intercourse at least once, as reported by Robert Sorensen in *Adolescent Sexuality in Contemporary America.* As the age increased, of course, the percentage became much higher. This statistic is frightening to many parents, and it should cause us serious concern. Many adolescents are in headlong gallop toward sexual experimentation that can leave them with deep hurts and serious scars.

There is a positive side to these figures, however. Note that 48 percent of this sample had not engaged in premarital intercourse! And the same researcher found that the majority of virgins were at least fairly regular church attenders, while only a third of the nonvirgins reported any kind of regular church attendance. These figures should give Christian parents encouragement. Sometimes we wonder if our spiritual training really makes a difference in nitty-gritty areas like this. Obviously it does!

Before leaving the topic of dating and sex, let's take a few minutes to think about the process of sexual education and guidance during adolescence. Ideally we will have come a long way in the process of helping our teenagers develop positive attitudes about their sexuality by the time they reach the beginning of adolescence. Our teenagers will have a positive attitude toward their masculinity or femininity, because of positive relationships with us. They will see sex as a normal part of life and feel comfortable using appropriate words for bodily parts and sexual activities. They will not feel guilty or ashamed about the topic of sex. They will know we are comfortable with the topic. They will know how babies are conceived, how they develop within their mother, and how they are born. And they will understand that sexual intercourse and childbearing are designed by God as a vital part of marriage.

If you think your teenagers or preteenagers have not moved a good way in this direction, you might benefit greatly by reading a good book or two on sex education. One that I have found helpful is *From Parent to Child about Sex* by Wilson Grant (Zondervan). Reading and discussing a book like this can help us with our own anxieties, as well as give some good possibilities for sharing naturally with our teenagers in this vital area of life.

No matter how successful we have been in our early years, however, adolescence does bring a few new challenges. Openness is probably the single most important ingredient of effective sexual education during adolescence, as well as in the earlier years. To the degree that we are comfortable talking about our bodies and sexual processes, our offspring will tend to adopt good attitudes toward their sexuality. And to the degree we are uncomfortable, embarrassed, or ashamed of our bodies and our sexuality, our teenagers are likely to develop similar attitudes.

From the earliest years of life, children need to recognize their bodies and their sexual functions are God-given and good. We should name bodily parts and functions by using terms like *penis, breast, vagina,* and *intercourse,* when appropriate. They are not forbidden or shameful words, though they are to be used discreetly. If we get embarrassed and hesitate to call a bodily part or process by its proper term, our children sense our own anxiety and begin to think that sex is somehow "bad," frightening, or something to keep quiet about. This, of course, increases children's curiosity and spurs them to seek more information from friends, books, magazines, and movies. These sources surround sexuality with an aura of secretiveness, or sensationalism, distorting the facts and producing negative emotions of fear and guilt.

During adolescence, the openness begun in childhood should continue. By this time, of course, discussion of topics are different, because our teenagers are already quite knowledgeable about some areas of sexuality. Discussions about contraceptives, petting, premarital sex and pregnancy can all be extremely helpful to our teenagers, if they occur in the normal course of conversation and are handled without undo anxiety.

Take the matter of "the pill" as an example. Some parents have real struggles over the advisability of talking about this issue with their teens. On the one hand, they would like to be sure that their teenage daughters do not get pregnant out of wedlock. On the other, they don't want to give them any ideas by bringing up the topic! Let me encourage you to feel free to discuss premarital contraception with them. The chances are your teens are already aware of the issues. If not, it is high time they learn. But *be careful.* Don't get real serious, sit them down and let them know you "want to have a talk"! Instead, look for natural opportunities to discuss the subject of pregnancy: the world's population, the size of your own family, or a local girl who has gotten pregnant out of wedlock.

All of these can give us a natural opportunity to make sure our teenagers know about contraceptives. Frankly, if we have been open about our own and our children's sexuality, they are probably well aware of at least the basics of contraception by the time they reach adolescence. If you have used any form of contraception, it is likely your kids have raised questions which you have answered with a forthright response, such as, "That's a pill Mother takes so her body won't produce eggs or ovum, because we have decided we already have just the right-size family."

Open talk about contraceptives with our teenagers has several advantages. The first is that it tells them contraception is no big deal. They don't have to sneak around to gain their information about sex. We can talk about it with them freely. Nearly all adults use contraceptives of one kind or another. We do because we do not want a larger family. We assume they will not need them before marriage because of their Christian standards, but they may as well know that some of their friends are probably using them and that others may wish they had!

The inclusion of sex-education programs in public and private schools is an area of concern for many parents. Ideally, sexual education should be carried out in the home and in the church. Realistically, however, the majority of parents are not adequately preparing their children to face the challenges of adult sexuality. Therefore, it is understandable that schoolteachers and administrators are stepping in to fill the gap.

Unfortunately, this puts Christian parents in a bind. We know all teenagers need constructive sex education, but we also know

379

that effective sex education cannot be taught apart from a set of moral and spiritual values. Probably the best solution is for us to get involved at the local-school level to see that the sex-education program being given is carried out by responsible, mature individuals with a respect for moral and spiritual values.

In addition to this, we must be willing to fulfill our own responsibility to our offspring, so that any negative influences communicated at school will not adversely affect our adolescents. They should have already been well taught about both the anatomical facts of sexuality, and the moral, spiritual, and emotional foundations of mature sexuality. Our own open and effective sex education will be more than enough to counteract any negative influences from less-than-ideal training at school.

Open discussion also eliminates some of the appeal of gutter language, sexual stories, and exploitive accounts that many teenagers engage in. In other words, our frankness is good prevention. A final obvious value is that in case our teenagers do become overly involved sexually, they will not have to suffer the additional problem of a pregnancy. I personally see no need to warn our teenagers to be sure to use contraceptives, if they decide to have intercourse. I assume that, if we have a good relationship with our teens and that if they are committed spiritually, they will be able to control themselves. To warn or threaten them about pregnancy is really saying, "I don't trust you." And this is one of the best ways to push a teenager toward premarital sexual experiences! If they know about contraceptives, they are old enough to make their own decisions, in case they do become involved in premarital sexual encounters.

The same principle of openness and naturalness applies to petting. Most of us had at least a little experience of our own in this area, and our knowledge should contribute to the guidance given without making our mistakes or practices a blueprint for our children's eyes. Some of us are afraid to hint we were ever tempted by attractions of the opposite sex. We just keep quiet about it and hope and pray our children will somehow reach their wedding day unscathed. Others are tempted to use their own experiences to frighten their teenagers away from close encounters of the sexual kind. A balanced position is much more helpful.

Our teenagers will be relieved and encouraged to know that we struggled with some of the same problems they face. Our frankness can help them form definite guidelines about conduct on a date, instead of ignoring the problem. They will respect us for being open and honest with them and they will be able to gain support and insight from our sharing. On the other hand, they don't want to know all the gory details of how far you went with everybody you dated before you met your spouse! They can hear those stories from their peers. What they want from you is an understanding parent, who is aware of some of the struggles they are facing, and who has made enough progress in resolving them that they can be supportive listeners and, when asked, can offer helpful suggestions.

If your teenager goes too far in physical involvement, your most critical time of parental influence has arrived. In such a moment we are tempted to respond with anger, fear, or confusion. What is needed is self-control first, then careful listening to your son or daughter, and only then our deliberate and prayerful counsel.

After you get a grip on your emotions, draw your adolescent out. Let him tell you what has happened and how he sees the situation now. This helps the young person to think through the problem and begin thoughtful reaction. The actual condition must be confirmed, the options available carefully explored, and adjustments planned for relationships with people and with God.

Pregnancy out of wedlock is very serious, no matter what consequential steps are taken. But parents' compassionate assistance may prevent the ruin or blighting of a whole life. Parental forgiveness will help teens understand that God is a forgiving and loving Father.

Our role in family-sex education grows through the years. Either wisdom or grievous experience will eventually convince us of its great importance. Next to spiritual training, healthy development of sexuality is one of our most far-reaching influences.

As parents of teenagers, we realize our teens have to make some of their own decisions and live with the results. If those decisions fall short of our standard, our teenagers need a listening ear and sympathetic understanding, not stinging criticism and rejection. If we are able to lovingly help them through a crisis or a failure, they will learn to avoid another one, and perhaps draw closer to the One who provides strength and wisdom for successful decisions.

—From Bruce Narramore, *Adolescence Is Not An Illness*. Old Tappan, N.J.: Fleming H. Revell Co., 1980.

FOR FURTHER READING:

Miles, Herbert J. *Sexual Understanding Before Marriage*. Grand Rapids: Zondervan Publishing House, 1972.

Smith, Jim. *Sex and the Single Teen*. Wheaton, Ill.: Victor Books, 1972.

SHYNESS

As a CAPSULE summary for parents or for those working with children and adolescents who have a problem with shyness, we have distilled the following suggestions from our knowledge of biblical and psychological principles:

1. Know yourself. Work out your own personal perspective of yourself and the world in a realistic fashion. See this self-perspective as a constantly changing panorama rather than a fixed photograph.

2. If you are living with your spouse, communicate honestly, openly, and continuously about yourself and your understanding of your spouse. The cardinal rule of communication between husband and wife is:

We listen to understand the other;

We talk to understand ourselves.

Too often our listening and talking to our spouse is for the purpose of altering him or her. Too often we think that our joy and contentedness depend on the other, and hence we try to manipulate and change the other for our own gratification. This inevitably is destructive to the marriage relationship and is destructive to the children.

Single parents or those whose spouses are not mature enough to handle discussion must find a safe friend to share with, someone mature enough to provide freedom and objectivity without threatening the relationship.

3. Pay attention to your child's wishes, feelings, and desires. Children need to feel that they are important. They need someone to notice their ideas and feelings and expressions. Children should not, of course, be indulged in all their wishes, choices, and fears, but they do need to be understood. If their parents listen when they talk about scraped knees and pollywogs and tricycles, children learn that they are valuable and they develop confidence in speaking with others.

4. Be free in giving compliments. Honest expression of approval is helpful to both children and adults. When we mention this to some parents, their first response is, "We don't want Jane to become conceited so we

381

don't tell her when she does well or looks good."

In fact, compliments have just the opposite effect. Conceit and self-centeredness develop in people who feel inadequate, inferior, and insecure. People who are not complimented or who are insulted develop fantasies about their greatness and form exalted opinions of themselves. Persons who are reasonably complimented are free to gain more realistic views of themselves.

It is impossible to compliment a person too much. Compliments create problems only when they are given for the purpose of motivating or manipulating the other person for selfish purposes. When we give compliments to get compliments or when we give compliments to make the other person feel obligated, then the compliments are damaging. But a genuine compliment can only be helpful to our children, to our spouses, or to other human beings.

5. Develop the perspective that feelings are neither good nor bad per se. Joy, pleasure, anger, grief, depression, and anxiety do not have any moral quality and will continue to be normal human responses. The Bible never condemns feelings. Destructive fantasies and behavior are condemned, but feelings are not.

Every feeling that can lead to destruction can also lead to good. Anger can kill, but it can also be channeled into highly productive service—study, writing, teaching. Fear, which can shackle, can also be turned into an invention to save lives or make the world more livable.

Parents who assure their children that feelings are OK help their children build self-confidence. On that foundation children can build respect and love for other people because they respect themselves.

6. Spend time on a regular basis in conversation with your children. It is not the quantity but the quality of time that is important. A half hour of pleasant conversation at dinner is much better than two hours of arguing or bickering. Parents must resist substituting entertainment for conversation. Families who do not converse together grow perverse together.

A father once brought his teenage daughter into our office, complaining that the girl was beyond his control, disrespectful, and a drug addict.

"She's out to destroy herself," he said, ending his tirade.

The 17-year-old girl sat calmly with grim face. When she could speak, she said in a strained but modulated voice, "Dad, I've been trying to tell you for a year that I've stopped using drugs. One of my best friends died from an overdose and I quit immediately."

The girl went on to relate how she had become part of an antidrug poster campaign at school and was known as one of the straights because of her antidrug position. This had been going on for months, but the father was so confirmed in his anger that he wouldn't sit down and talk with his somewhat reformed daughter.

Kids can handle current problems, too. If dad loses his job or feels depressed or angry, they can deal with that information. Children are usually more realistic and optimistic than adults.

7. Don't dwell on your child's shyness. Most parents want to know if they should bring up the subject. In all problems, the children should set the pace for discussion. Parents can bring up the issue occasionally just to let their youngster know they are aware of it, but they shouldn't push for detailed conversation until the child is ready and brings it up first.

8. See the child as a total person. Too often defects such as shyness begin to domi-

nate our view of who the child is. Many strong points are forgotten.

It's very comforting to children to know that things they say at a given moment do not represent the totality of their thinking and feeling and won't be held against them. Children can make some rather wild statements occasionally and parents should not see this either as a trend or something that is fixed in concrete. Very often children say things they don't really believe. They are merely sampling new ideas and testing their parents' love. Your child is far from what he or she is going to become. Children, especially teenagers, have radical thoughts and feelings, but the great majority of children revert to the standards and attitudes of the home in which they grew up.

9. Let children know that all their friends are welcome at your house. If you're home, accept these friends with good spirits. An open front door supports the shy teen, builds self-esteem, and encourages peer acceptance. Provide snacks and let the gang have privacy and music.

10. Share with your children your own shy experiences in the good ol' days. Young people have a somewhat mystical view of adulthood. To them it's a world of achievement and total control. When children understand that their parents have struggled and are struggling with feelings of inadequacy, passivity, and shyness, they take courage.

11. Present a healthy attitude toward sexuality. Relationships with the opposite sex are critical, especially during adolescent years. The views of sexuality they develop during childhood influence people greatly.

The more openly affectionate parents can be, the more mature will be the attitude of their children. If adolescents are free to talk about boyfriends or girl friends and dating, they will have a much healthier attitude to-

ward the opposite sex. Encourage moral behavior and discourage acting out of sexual behavior, but allow adolescents to verbalize feelings.

12. Don't look on shyness as "the plague." If parents try to identify with their "suffering child," and are bothered by suffering they imagine their child is enduring, they strengthen the grip of shyness.

Parents do not have total control over the development of shyness in their children. But interaction of parents and children from birth on is very important and does a great deal to determine the degree of shyness or freedom from shyness that children will experience throughout their adult lives.

Summary. For shy children there is no sure path through these troubled waters. Raging emotions wash out bridges, smash down communication lines, and erode peaceful valleys where they could have dwelled in reasonable tranquility. But communication between parents and children is essential. Aim to spend a half hour each day with each child. It is good for both boys and girls to have time alone with each parent individually. Girls like to have dates with their dad. Go to a coffee shop together and have fun listening and sharing. Sons find perspective from their mom concerning female feelings. Both sons and daughters are watching and learning.

—From Norman B. Rohrer and S. Philip Sutherland, *Why Am I Shy?* Minneapolis: Augsburg Publishing House, 1978.

SIBLING RIVALRY

IF AMERICAN WOMEN were asked to indicate *the* most irritating feature of child rearing, I'm convinced that sibling rivalry would get their unanimous vote. Little children (and older ones too) are not content just to hate each other in private. They attack one another like miniature warriors, mobilizing their troops and probing for a weakness in the defensive line. They argue, hit, kick, scream, grab toys, taunt, tattle, and sabotage the opposing forces. I knew one child who deeply resented being sick with a cold while his older sibling was healthy, so he secretly blew his nose on the mouthpiece of his brother's musical instrument! The big loser from such combat, of course, is the harassed mother who must listen to the noise of the battlefield and then try to patch up the wounded. If her emotional nature requires peace and tranquillity (and most women do) she may stagger under the barrage of cannonfire.

Columnist Ann Landers recently asked her readers to respond to the question, "If you had known then what you know now, would you have had children?" Among ten thousand women who answered, 70 percent said No! A subsequent survey by *Good Housekeeping* posed the same question and 95 percent of the respondents answered Yes. It is impossible to explain the contradictory results from these two inquiries, although the accompanying comments were enlightening. One unidentified woman wrote, "Would I have children again? A thousand times, NO! My children have completely destroyed my life, my marriage, and my identity as a person. There are no joys. Prayers don't help—nothing stops a 'screaming kid.'"

It is my contention that something *will* stop a screaming kid, or even a dozen of them. It is not necessary or healthy to allow children to destroy each other and make life miserable for the adults around them. Sibling rivalry is difficult to "cure" but it can certainly be treated. Toward that objective,

let me offer three suggestions which should be helpful in achieving a state of armistice at home.

Don't Inflame the Natural Jealousy of Children

Sibling rivalry is not new, of course. It was responsible for the first murder on record (when Cain killed Abel), and has been represented in virtually every two-child family from that time to this. The underlying source of this conflict is old-fashioned jealousy and competition between children. . . .

If jealousy is so common, then how can parents minimize the natural antagonism which children feel for their siblings? The first step is to avoid circumstances which compare them unfavorably with each other. Lecturer Bill Gothard has stated that the root of all feelings of inferiority is *comparison.* I agree. The question is not "How am I doing?" It is "How am I doing compared with John or Steven or Marion?" The issue is not how fast can I run, but who crosses the finish line first. A boy does not care how tall he is; he is vitally interested in "who is tallest." Each child systematically measures himself against his peers, and is tremendously sensitive to failure within his own family.

Accordingly, parents should guard against comparative statements which routinely favor one child over another. This is particularly true in three areas. First, children are extremely sensitive about the matter of physical attractiveness and body characteristics. It is highly inflammatory to commend one child at the expense of the other. Suppose, for example, that Sharon is permitted to hear the casual remark about her sister, "Betty is sure going to be a gorgeous girl." The very fact that Sharon was not mentioned will probably establish the two girls as rivals. If there is a significant difference in beauty between the two, you can be assured that Sharon has already concluded, "Yeah, I'm the ugly one." When her fears are then confirmed by her parents, resentment and jealousy are generated.

Beauty is *the* most significant factor in the self-esteem of Western children, as I attempted to express in *Hide or Seek*. Anything that a parent utters on this subject within the hearing of children should be screened carefully. It has the power to make brothers and sisters hate one another.

Second, the matter of intelligence is another sensitive nerve to be handled with care. It is not uncommon to hear parents say in front of their children, "I think the younger boy is actually brighter than his brother." Adults find it difficult to comprehend how powerful that kind of assessment can be in a child's mind. Even when the comments are unplanned and are spoken routinely, they convey how a child is "seen" within his family. We are all vulnerable to that bit of evidence.

Third, children (and especially boys) are extremely competitive with regard to athletic abilities. Those who are slower, weaker, and less coordinated than their brothers are rarely able to accept "second best" with grace and dignity. Consider, for example, the following note given to me by the mother of two boys. It was written by her nine-year-old son to his eight-year-old brother, the evening after the younger child had beaten him in a race.

Dear Jim:
I am the greatest and your the badest. And I can beat everybody in a race and you can't beat anybody in a race. I'm the smartest and your the dumbest. I'm the best sport player and your the badest sport player. And your also a hog. I can beat

anybody up. And that's the truth. And that's the end of this story.

Yours truly,
Richard

This note is humorous to me, because Richard's motive was so poorly disguised. He had been badly stung by his humiliation on the field of honor, so he came home and raised the battle flags. He will probably spend the next eight weeks looking for opportunities to fire torpedos into Jim's soft underbelly. Such is the nature of mankind.

Am I suggesting, then, that parents eliminate all aspects of individuality within family life or that healthy competition should be discouraged? Definitely not. I am saying that in matters relative to beauty, brains, and athletic ability, each child should know that in his parents' eyes, he is respected and has equal worth with his siblings. Praise and criticism *at home* should be distributed as evenly as possible, although some children will inevitably be more successful in the outside world. And finally, we should remember that children do not build fortresses around strengths—they construct them to protect weakness. Thus, when a child like Richard begins to brag and boast and attack his siblings, he is revealing the threats he feels at that point. Our sensitivity to those signals will help minimize the potential for jealousy within our children.

Establish a Workable System of Justice

Sibling rivalry is also at its worst when there is no reasonable system of justice in the home—where the "lawbreakers" do not get caught, or if apprehended are set free without standing trial. It is important to understand that laws in a society are established and enforced for the purpose of protecting people from each other. Likewise, a family is a mini-society with the same requirement for protection of human rights.

For purposes of illustration, suppose that I live in a community where there is no established law. Policemen do not exist and there are no courts to whom disagreements can be appealed. Under those circumstances, my neighbor and I can abuse each other with impunity. He can take my lawnmower and throw rocks through my windows, while I steal the peaches from his favorite tree and dump my leaves over his fence. This kind of mutual antagonism has a way of escalating day by day, becoming ever more violent with the passage of time. When permitted to run its natural course, as in early American history, the end result can be feudal hatred and murder.

As indicated, individual families are similar to societies in their need for law and order. In the absence of justice, "neighboring" siblings begin to assault one another. The older child is bigger and tougher, which allows him to oppress his younger brothers and sisters. But the junior member of the family is not without weapons of his own. He strikes back by breaking the toys and prized possessions of the older sibling and interferes when friends are visiting. Mutual hatred then erupts like an angry volcano, spewing its destructive contents on everyone in its path.

Nevertheless, when the children appeal to their parents for intervention, they are often left to fight it out among themselves. In many homes, the parents do not have sufficient disciplinary control to enforce their judgments. In others, they are so exasperated with constant bickering among siblings that they refuse to get involved. In still others, parents require an older child to live with an admitted injustice "because your brother is smaller than you." Thus, they tie his hands and render him utterly defenseless against the mischief of his bratty little brother or sister. Even more commonly today, mothers

and fathers are both working while their children are at home busily disassembling each other.

I will say it again to parents: one of your most important responsibilities is to establish an equitable system of justice and a balance of power at home. There should be reasonable "laws" which are enforced fairly for each member of the family. For purposes of illustration, let me list the boundaries and rules which have evolved through the years in my own home.

1. Neither child is *ever* allowed to make fun of the other in a destructive way. Period! This is an inflexible rule with no exceptions.

2. Each child's room is his private territory. There are locks on both doors, and permission to enter is a revokable privilege. (Families with more than one child in each bedroom can allocate available living space for each youngster.)

3. The older child is not permitted to tease the younger child.

4. The younger child is forbidden to harass the older child.

5. The children are not required to play with each other when they prefer to be alone or with other friends.

6. We mediate any genuine conflict as quickly as possible, being careful to show impartiality and extreme fairness.

As with any plan of justice, this plan requires (1) respect for leadership of the parent, (2) willingness by the parent to mediate, (3) occasional enforcement or punishment. When this approach is accomplished with love, the emotional tone of the home can be changed from one of hatred to (at least) tolerance.

Recognize That the Hidden "Target" of Sibling Rivalry Is You

It would be naive to miss the true meaning of sibling conflict: it often represents a form of manipulation of parents. Quarreling and fighting provide an opportunity for both children to "capture" adult attention. It has been written, "Some children had rather be wanted for murder than not wanted at all." Toward this end, a pair of obnoxious kids can tacitly agree to bug their parents until they get a response—even if it is an angry reaction.

One father told me recently that his son and his nephew began to argue and then beat each other with their fists. Both fathers were nearby and decided to let the fight run its natural course. During the first lull in the action one of the boys glanced sideways toward the passive men and said, "Isn't anybody going to stop us before we get hurt?!" The fight, you see, was something neither boy wanted. Their violent combat was directly related to the presence of the two adults and would have taken a different form if the boys had been alone. Children will often "hook" their parents' attention and intervention in this way.

Believe it or not, this form of sibling rivalry is easiest to control. The parent must simply render the behavior unprofitable to each participant. Instead of wringing their hands and crying and begging and screaming (which actually reinforces the disruptive behavior and makes it worse), a mother or father should approach the conflict with dignity and self-control.

I would recommend that a modified version of the following "speech" be given to quarreling children, depending on the age and circumstances: "Tommy and Chuck, I want you to sit in these chairs and give me your complete attention. Now you both know that you have been harassing and irritating each other all through the morning. Tommy, you knocked over the castle that Chuck was building, and Chuck, you messed up Tommy's hair. So every few minutes I've found myself telling you to quit quarreling. Well, I'm not angry at you, because all

brothers fight like that, but I am telling you that I'm tired of hearing it. I have important things to do, and I can't take the time to be separating a couple of scratching cats every few minutes.

"Now listen carefully. If the two of you want to pick on each other and make yourselves miserable, then be my guest [assuming there is a fairly equal balance of power between them]. Go outside and fight until you're exhausted. But it's not going to occur under my feet anymore. It's over! And you know that I mean business when I make that kind of statement. Do we understand each other?"

Would that implied warning end the conflict? Of course not—at least, not the first time. It would be necessary to deliver on the promise of "action." Having made the boundaries clear, I would act decisively the *instant* either boy returned to his bickering. If I had separate bedrooms, I would confine one child to each room for at least thirty minutes of complete boredom—without radio or television. Or I would assign one to clean the garage and the other to mow the lawn. Or I would make them take a nap. My avowed purpose would be to make them believe me the next time I offered a suggestion for peace and tranquillity.

It is simply not necessary to permit children to destroy the joy in living, as expressed by the frustrated mother to *Good Housekeeping*. And what is most surprising, children are the happiest when their parents enforce these reasonable limits with love and dignity.

—From Dr. James Dobson, *The Strong-Willed Child*. Wheaton, Ill.: Tyndale House Publishers, 1978.

FOR FURTHER READING:

Hancock, Maxine. *People in Process: The Preschool Years*. Old Tappan, N.J.: Fleming H. Revell Co., 1978.

McDermott, John F. *Raising Cain—And Abel Too: The Parents' Book of Sibling Rivalry.* New York: Wyden Books, 1980.

SICK CHILD

THERE HAVE BEEN many studies made in an effort to discover what effect illness and temporary or permanent separation of a young child from his/her parents has on later life and what effect the child's illness has on the parents. What seems most significant is to realize that there *will* be an effect of some sort and that what is important is to minimize the detrimental effect.

In his study of the reactions of children in a disaster, Stewart Perry drew several conclusions also confirmed by other researchers. A child tends to re-establish earlier types of relatedness with parent-figures—"to regress"—such as increased dependency needs and a desire to remain close to the parent and close to home. The parents' response to and way of handling the disaster (a tornado), is very influential in the child's response. In daily life, a child takes clues to behavior from his/her parents; this is true in times of stress, too. At such times, parents should be *present* and *supportive.* There are some parents, however, who demand help for themselves from those around them, including their children. Such a response creates disturbances later in the children, although they do respond as their parents demand at the time.

Communication and honesty are also extremely important. Initially, children tend to know what they need. The older they become, the more self-knowledge is trained out of them through discouragement and lack of affirmation for their self-expression (for example, the dictum that "a strong person does not cry"). In Perry's study, it was found that parents had much difficulty answering their children's questions about the tornado, especially when the questions involved the death of their playmates or other children. Consequently, they would lie to children, ignore their questions, or deny the reality of what had happened: hence, prohibiting the open discussion of issues very much within the awareness of the children. Since the parents thus communicated that one could not openly discuss the experience, the disaster came to seem even more frightening to the children.

It is important for a child not merely to have open communication with his/her parents, but also to be able to depend upon them for a consistent attitudinal framework in the family for the discussion of the tornado. Shifting attitudes and anxious vacillation was also upsetting. The ominous silence and unpredictable or untrustworthy responses from those adults on whom they depended for support and information concerning the experience of living were more harmful to the children than the actual experience of the tornado.

Children need security. They need to be included in times of crisis and to have their questions answered. Otherwise, their fears may simply grow out of all proportion. John Bowlby reports the results of an experiment of foster-parenting in which four infants were left, at different times, with one family while their mothers were hospitalized during the birth of their second child. Before the time of the hospitalization, the foster parents visited the child in his/her own home, and during the separation, the fathers of each child visited him/her in the foster home. The length of separation was 10, 10, 19, and 27 days, respectively, for children ages 28, 17, 21, and 29 months. Despite the precautions, all four children showed unmistakable signs of strain and from time to time they clearly were aware of the absence of their mothers.

These signs included yearning and searching for her, sadness, increasing protest at her absence and growing anger with her for staying away, increased ambivalence on return home, and evident fear of being separated again. Bowlby concluded:

> Their experience has served to reinforce the view . . . that separation is dangerous and whenever possible should be avoided . . . Whether a child or adult is in a state of security, anxiety, or distress is determined in large part by the accessibility and responsiveness of his principal attachment figure.

A very young child (all of those in this example were within the first two stages of Erikson's life cycle) is not aware of the passage of time and does not really understand why the principal attachment figure is absent. He/she does understand, however, that the person is missing. That this awareness is very much present, and disturbing, should be remembered by families and other involved persons in a time of illness. Although the separation may be unavoidable, special effort can be made to make it as innocuous as possible.

There are additional difficulties when the young child him/herself is hospitalized. The stress of a child's illness is such that, in Steven Kline's research, for example, about 70% of the families of children with leukemia divorced or separated within the first year after diagnosis. Effects on all the family are inevitable. In the White family,

> As a result, Parker and Shelly, then in fourth and first grades, had frequent "stomach aches" and were quick to tears. After a difficult session with Checkers, . . . sometimes I would be moody over supper or snap at minor things, and Marny (his wife) would be easily fatigued, joyless in

her work . . . the signs of strain were telling on us all.

Both younger children took a good bit of abuse from other children who knew Checkers but were afraid to pick on him. But "what tore us was the totality with which his presence consumed the family . . . there was the strident, continual, domination of us all." Illness of one affects the whole family; that is true in a special way when the sick member is a child.

Anna Freud (1952) discussed what occurs in the ill child him/herself. First, there is a change in the way the parents respond to the child, emotionally and physically, so that the child experiences increased and unexpected handling, such as forced feeding and forced bowel evacuation. The reaction will likely be a feeling of helplessness and bewilderment, because behaviors which formerly were strictly forbidden are now encouraged. His/her wishes may be unexpectedly indulged, which makes it difficult to return to old patterns after recovery. The experience of being cared for in these ways may be detrimental to a child's development because they have just been recently mastering various bodily functions and learning acceptable behavior when standards and expectations are changed dramatically. He/she experiences loss of control in many areas where control was only recently learned, which results in a pull toward regressions and greater passivity. Gilbert Kliman summarized her findings as follows:

> Two extremes of pathology may result. Children whose defenses against passive learning and regressive pulls are very strong tend to become very obstinate, intractable patients. Others may lapse into a state of helpless infancy from which they reluctantly or never fully emerge.

389

L. Jessner added documentation and confirmation to Freud's work, and concluded that since a child's parents are devalued through their helplessness to prevent the child's suffering and also are separated from the child, a kind of grief reaction occurs on both sides. Temporary regression—return to a simpler state of organization—is likely to occur in the adaption and response of a child to any emergency. The final outcome, however, through reincorporation of the loved person, may spur maturation and improve realistic relations between the child him/herself and the parents.

During the emergency situation within the family, the child has an important need to know and a need to share in what is going on around him/her. Children observe strange things going on. Family patterns and expectations are no longer predictable. If it is the child who is ill, many things are happening within and being done to his/her body which don't make sense in the world as he/she had come to understand it. Without explanation, the child begins to feel isolated, to believe that others are not aware of what is happening in his/her own world, to feel that what is happening is "too awful" to talk about—all of which work together to form a space not at all comfortable to be in. "The child quickly notices that people whom he had previously trusted are now keeping something frightening from him." Since this emergency is the most important thing occurring within the family during this time, being unable to discuss it effectively isolates the child from all that he/she had come to know, trust, and love—at the time when familiarity, honesty, contact, and caring are most crucial.

The National Cancer Institute has found that:

> Children wait for adults to show a readiness to anticipate and deal with their serious concerns. Only then will they reveal the pre-existing worry. Vernick and Karen also caution that the child who is gravely ill is "worrying about dying and is eager to have someone help him talk about it." If he is passive, it may only be a reflection of how little the environment helps him to express his concerns.

Discussing such situations is difficult for the adults who are significant to the child because of their own anxieties and fears and their involvement with the child. Because it is "untimely" it is especially hard to accept the terminal illness of a child. But with both children and adults, even just having the issue "in the open" for discussion makes it less frightening. The child should be encouraged to express his/her feelings and share what is causing anxiety. "Overcontrol of fear, suppression, denial, and avoidance of anxiety-related topics are measures which are liable to 'collapse with a bang.'"

It must be remembered through all of this, however, that the person experiencing all these emotions is a child. Children's understanding of illness and separation is incomplete. Their expressions of anxiety and sadness are brief and small in quantity compared to adult outpourings.

> Children are thus often thought to be lacking in feeling, although careful investigation reveals that their emotions are profound and often more fatefully long-lasting than those of more quickly mourning adults.

Kliman also cautions against giving a child more information than he/she can cope with. As with all powerful medicines, he wrote, the smallest doses should be reserved for the smallest children. But also as with medicine, the child, too, is a human being who experiences pain and distress, and needs to receive honest and appropriate response to that pain.

One final aspect of a child's need to share should be mentioned: that children feel the emotions of guilt even more intensely than other persons if they happen to be young enough to imagine they are magically responsible for the person's illness. (For example, if a child said in anger, "I wish you were dead" and the person becomes ill, that child may feel responsible for that illness.) Thus, it is very important that they be encouraged to verbalize this guilt and be reassured that it is unfounded or forgivable.

Crisis within a family is a time when there is both danger and opportunity. During such a time, family relationships may deepen and grow—or may become more and more superficial as communication channels are increasingly closed off. It can also be a time when children, especially, suffer from the disturbance in normal family life, of which they are very aware, if uncomprehending. It is, therefore, very important to be aware of their needs too when responding to a family experiencing the illness of one of its members.

—From Elizabeth Catharine Baker-Smith, *The Impact of Illness on the Family and the Ministry of the Christian Community.* Ann Arbor, Mich.: University Microfilms.

FOR FURTHER READING:

Bittner, Vernon J. *You Can Help with Your Healing.* Minneapolis: Augsburg Publishing House, 1979.

Hardgrove, Carol B., and Dawson, Rosemary B. *Parents and Children in the Hospital: The Family's Role in Pediatrics.* Boston: Little, Brown & Co. 1972.

Stine, Jovial B. and Jane. *The Sick of Being Sick Book.* New York: E. P. Dutton, 1980.

SINGLE-PARENT FAMILY

GOD CREATED US to have parents of both sexes—a mother and a father. Appropriate sex identities must be maintained by these parents. They should interact in complementary ways with one another and with their children.

This is the ideal! Unfortunately, we live and function in a less than ideal world. Life includes death, divorce, separation, and desertion of one or possibly both parents.

We have no control over death. Because of this lack of family structure, a child's emotional development may be impaired if a parent dies. But divorce is also shattering. It is the death of a relationship.

Living creatively with your children as a single parent is a double challenge as you must do the job alone. Living creatively will be defined here as finding active, meaningful, and diverse outlets for your children and yourself—outlets which will lead to the production of mature and well-rounded lives. Before we discuss living creatively with our children we need to understand how our children feel and react to death and divorce. Children respond in different ways according to their age, interests, and how they perceive death or divorce.

Small children have limited ideas about death. They accept it somewhat as a matter of course. Sometimes they feel responsible for the death of a loved one. Children may think that if they are good the loved one will not die. As they grow older they become more emotional about death. They are very concerned that their mother may die. Children in the seven-year-old to nine-year-old bracket may think of dead people as skeletons or ghosts. One of my nieces, when confronted with the question, "Have you ever seen a dead person before?" answered, "Well, only the ones at the museum with their skins off." But by nine or ten children are able to understand more about death and realize that when death occurs an individual does not breathe.

Each child will respond differently to death. Much depends on how his family responds to the experience, particularly his remaining parent.

Dr. J. Louise Despert, child psychiatrist and author of *Children of Divorce*, says, "It is not divorce, but the emotional situation in the home, with or without divorce, that is the determining factor in a child's adjustment. A child is very disturbed when the relationship between his parents is very disturbed."

Dr. Despert reviewed more than a thousand cases of disturbed children who came to her and found there were far fewer children of divorce in her group of disturbed children than in the general population; but there was trouble between nearly all of the parents of the disturbed children who were brought to her for help. The problem lies in the unhappiness of the parents, which exists even before the divorce takes place. Dr. Despert calls this "emotional divorce" and says it is more disturbing to a child than the actual divorce.

Dr. Despert gives four guiding principles in discussing divorce with a child of any age:

1. Acknowledge that there has been a decision to separate. He already knows there is trouble, and to talk with you calmly and simply about the impending separation will help relieve his anxiety.

2. Acknowledge that grownups can make mistakes, and that his parents have made them. He must one day accept the fact that his parents are human; it is part of his growing up. You may be hurrying him a little, but the truth is a more durable basis for his confidence in you than a fiction of your godlike perfection which in any case cannot be maintained.

3. Assure him that he is in no way to blame for what has happened between his parents. No matter what may have been said in anger or impatience, the trouble lies only between his parents and quite apart from him. In this way you help to relieve the guilt which most children take upon themselves when there is trouble between their parents. But be careful, in freeing him from blame, that you do not by implication lay the blame upon someone else, that is, upon each other. "Bad" and "good" are words which have no place in this discussion. His parents simply do not get along with each other. This period of your own emotional confusion is no time to make judgments, and certainly not to a child.

4. Finally and most important, assure him in every possible way that despite your differences with each other, you both still love him as you always have.

You may be asking yourself: Where do I go from here? How do I live in this less than ideal situation? Since statistics are stacked against my family and me, can I prove statistics wrong? Can my children live purposeful, fulfilled lives, or will they suffer emotionally, mentally, intellectually, spiritually, or physically?

The first and most important step in living creatively is to learn about God. This should be given top priority in the single parent's home and can best be accomplished in everyday situations—through normal conversation, mealtime prayers, nighttime stories, Christian friends, and church. A single parent's attitude toward God will be important to a child in forming his own concept of God.

J. B. Phillips in *Your God Is Too Small* says:

But what has this to do with an adequate conception of God? This, that the early conception of God is almost invariably founded upon the child's idea of his father.

If he is lucky enough to have a good father this is all to the good, provided of course that the conception of God grows with the rest of the personality. But if the child is afraid (or worse still, afraid and feeling guilty because he is afraid) of his own father, the chances are that his Father in Heaven will appear to him a fearful Being. Again, if he is lucky, he will outgrow this conception, and indeed differentiate between his early "fearful" idea and his later mature conception. But many are not able to outgrow the sense of guilt and fear, and in adult years are still obsessed with it, although it has actually nothing to do with their real relationship with the living God. It is nothing more than a parental hangover.

The child whose father leaves through death, divorce, or desertion has not had a lasting relationship with a father and finds it difficult to relate to a Heavenly Father. He cannot understand, let alone believe, that God is a God of love and will never fail him.

When a father is gone from the home a loving nurturing mother may help her children form a correct concept of God through the teaching of God's Word, by her own example, and by helping her children find and observe godly male models.

Sociologists have noted that families are more successful in riding out separation if it is prepared for well in advance. According to E. Reuben Hill ("Social Stresses on the Family"), they have also discovered: "Family adaptability, family integration, affectional relations among family members, good marital adjustment of husband and wife, companionable parent-child relationships, family council type of control in decision-making, social participation of wife, and previous successful experience with crisis were all confirmed as important factors in enabling families to adjust to crisis" (*Social Problems: Persistent Challenges.* Edited by E. C. McDonagh and J. E. Simpson).

Dr. Roger Crook in *An Open Book to the Christian Divorcée* says: "As you face the prospect of rearing your child without the help of his father or mother, you will do well to keep one fact in mind: Your child's needs are exactly the same as the needs of all other children. He needs food, clothing, and shelter. He needs to love and to be loved. He needs friends. He needs adult models from whom he can learn what it means to be a man or what it means to be a woman. He needs an education. He needs a right relationship with God. Your problem is to supply those needs without the help of your husband or wife."

God has not left you helpless in raising your children alone, but will give you strength, courage, finances, and all else required to parent your children successfully.

What are some of the aids we have for living creatively with our children? How do we actually go about it? The following is a list of ten major areas in which you may creatively participate with your children. Listed under each heading are specific activities; many of these I have personally found to be creative outlets for myself and my family.

Reading. From the earliest possible age, children should be exposed to a variety of good reading material. For example: the Bible, Bible stories, poetry, classics, fairy tales, stories rich with traditional warmth and humor, educational material, travel and adventure books, sports, biographies, and picture books. My oldest daughter, at twenty-nine, still cherishes an adventure book about Russia, *Old Peter's Russian Tales.* She read and reread the book in childhood and looks forward to sharing it with her own children.

No child should be without books in our society today. They may be purchased new or secondhand, or borrowed from the public library or bookmobile. Books may be handed down from child to child and should be treated with respect and care. Early reading to the child and continued reading by the child are most valuable assets. Teachers from elementary school through college stress the importance of reading to successful scholarship throughout life, and have found good reading habits to be basic to success in any endeavor.

Games. If a parent has actively engaged in playing games with his children from early childhood, he will continue to do so throughout adolescence and even into adulthood. As with books, there is a vast selection available for every age and every pocketbook. There are indoor and outdoor games, educational, fun, technical, mind-expanding, writing, and active games. They may provide entertainment on a rainy day, at a party, and for family fun-time during holiday vacation. Games may often be educational aids in teaching history, math, or spelling; they may also be valuable in teaching cooperation, good sportsmanship, decision making, and in developing a sense of humor. I often found personal delight in playing make-believe or homemade games with my children.

Music. One need not be a musician to share the delights of music with his children. Early exposure to good music will be beneficial throughout life. Children's television programs often use classical and semiclassical music, operas, and marches as backgrounds, and a child thus becomes familiar with a variety of selections in an entertaining way. Children should be encouraged to take music lessons, sing in school and church choral groups, and play in the band or or-

chestra. Music can be enjoyed individually or as a family. Music was not only a pleasant experience for me but became a means of adding to the family income, as I gave private piano lessons. Children who have a variety of interests have less chance of becoming bored. If more than one area is at least partially developed, there will be less trauma should one area of endeavor fail.

Arts and Crafts. The world is an exciting place in which to live today, with a variety of creative crafts everywhere. The youngest child to the oldest grandmother can find something to do with their hands and do well. My youngest son spent hours painting by number. He also enjoyed his workbench where he built birdcages and cars. My daughter, Sharon, delighted in sewing and today is able to produce anything from clothing to curtains to pocketbooks. A walk through the woods will provide leaves, flowers, weeds, and small fruit to make an elegant picture.

Arts and crafts can be a source of entertainment for the entire family as well as an added means of income. Mothers, fathers, and children alike can share in creating a variety of items which may be practical or beautiful.

Organizations. Society is providing more and better organizations to help the single parent and his child. Churches have Boys' Brigade, Pioneer Girls, Awana Clubs, mothers' clubs, singles groups, young people's organizations, and camps. The Y.W.C.A. and Y.M.C.A. offer swimming classes in which everyone can participate. Boy Scouts and Girl Scouts are organizations which are available in every community. Single parents may enjoy becoming leaders in one or more of these groups. The need for vital leaders is great; children love to have their parents become active in such groups. Belonging to social groups provides a variety of friends and activities for children and enlarges the single parent's circle of friends.

Physical activities. Boys have traditionally been spotlighted in the area of strenuous physical activity, and this activity should rightly continue. Good models for boys, such as coaches, can be a great help to the single parent. Fortunately, the traditional picture of sports being for boys only is changing in today's society, and girls can now enjoy almost every competitive sport—at least through high school. Whatever your views on what sports male and female children should participate in, athletics teach good sportsmanship, how to win and how to lose, cooperation, enthusiasm, skill, stick-to-itiveness and how to perform in public.

One of my sons became proficient in several sports. This was beneficial to him because it provided: a good outlet for pent-up energy, an opportunity to observe and work with adult male models, many hours of hard work, fun, and competition, and success experiences which helped him through difficult adolescent years.

An entire family may be participants or spectators in such sports as swimming, bowling, skiing, ice-skating, and tennis. Single parents should learn enough about several sports so that they can enjoy and discuss them with their children.

Travel. Children delight in trips, whether short or long, near or far. If well prepared for, a weekend camping trip will be exciting for the entire family. It's great fun to travel to Detroit or Chicago (or a large city near you) to see a professional ballgame, visit the art museum, or attend a concert. Children should be exposed to various modes of travel—car, bus, train, airplane, or boat—and sometimes be allowed to travel alone. Many families enjoy the beautiful world God created by biking to a lake, park, or forest preserve. Much in life is still free of charge—all it takes is a little effort, time, and energy.

Sharing Household Responsibilities. It can be fun! Every member of the household should be involved in cleaning the house, washing the clothes, cooking, yard work, shoveling snow, painting, papering, repairing, and carrying out the trash. Children should be taught at an early age to perform simple tasks. Greater responsibility should be added with age. Responsibility can be fun when everyone pitches in; the tasks are soon completed so everyone can relax and have fun. Boys can learn to bake cakes and cookies, make hamburgers, wash and dry clothes, vacuum, and dust the furniture. Girls, on the other hand, need to learn to repair a lamp cord, paint a window, or hammer a nail when necessary. After my husband died, our family ripped up the old carpet (saving thirty dollars), papered the living room, dining room, and one bedroom, painted the other rooms, repaired torn screens, made curtains and bedspreads, antiqued a bedroom set, and then proudly enjoyed our creativity.

Teaching and Learning Social Graces. Children need to learn how to keep themselves clean and neat, how to dress for various occasions, and how to carry on a conversation with others—being neither shy nor overbearing. Young children should be taken to a variety of places where they can learn how to behave properly in public. In church they need to be quiet and reverent—within reason. In a restaurant they will observe how to eat as ladies and gentlemen, how much to tip the waitress, how to pay the bill, how to seat a lady, and which fork to use. Going to McDonald's will not be particularly beneficial in learning social graces, so once in a while single parents need to save their nickels and dimes to take the family to a special restaurant.

Sharing Preparation for Life's Major Transitions. Important events such as entrance to high school, leaving for college, starting a career, and preparing for marriage and family life provide an opportunity for the family to share in the planning.

Preparation for one's entire life begins in the home. This is not only sensible and practical, it is also scriptural. In Deuteronomy 6:6–9 we read: "And these words, which I command thee this day, shall be in thine heart: And thou shalt teach them diligently unto thy children, and shalt talk of them when thou sittest in thine house, and when thou walkest by the way, and when thou liest down, and when thou risest up. And thou shalt bind them for a sign upon thine hand, and they shall be as frontlets between thine eyes. And thou shalt write them upon the posts of thy house, and on thy gates."

The creative activities of infancy, early childhood, and adolescence which were shared by parent and child should now make the big decisions (college, career, marriage, parenthood) easier for the child becoming an adult.

Dr. Bruce Narramore, in his book *An Ounce of Prevention,* gives us this word of advice: From birth onward, our goal should be to free our children from our control and prepare them to accept responsibility for their own decisions. As we are sensitive to their capabilities, our role gradually changes from protector and director to guide and friend. By late adolescence our role should have become largely that of example and friend. Hopefully, we will also be their welcome counselor or experienced guide."

Dr. Frank Cheavens in his book *Creative Parenthood* cites a study done in a midwestern town by two behavioral scientists at the University of Chicago, Peck and Havighurst. They were trying to discover why character developed as it did in children and youth in this community of 10,000 people. Five character types developed from the study, but Cheavens reports: "The most positive character development, perhaps the only truly positive character development, was found in the group designated 'rational-altruistic.' Parents were consistent, trustful, democratic, and loving. Punishments were not harsh." The authors write, "To be intelligently and effectively ethical it appears necessary to add to this pattern (of love) the element of democracy, the opportunity to experiment in making decisions, and to develop and trade ideas, unafraid, with parents and other family members."

Stanley Coopersmith, in his "Studies in Self-Esteem" (*Scientific American* magazine, February, 1968), found evidence to support what has already been said in this chapter. "Looking into the backgrounds of the boys who possess high self-esteem, we were struck first and foremost by the close relationships that existed between these boys and their parents. The parents' love was not necessarily expressed in overt shows of affection or the amount of time they spent with their children; it was manifested by interest in the boys' welfare, concern about their companions, availability for discussion of the boys' problems and participation in congenial joint activities. The mother knew all or most of her son's friends, and the mother and father gave many other signs that they regarded the boy as a significant person who was inherently worthy of their deep interest. The family life of the high self-esteem boys was marked not only by the existence of a well-defined constitution for behavior but also by a democratic spirit. . . . It seems safe to conclude that all these factors—deep interest in the children, the guidance provided by well-defined rules of expected behavior, nonpunitive treatment and respect for the children's views—contributed greatly to the development of the boys' high self-esteem."

Living creatively with our children as single parents is critical, not only for our own well-being, but for the development of stability and maturity in the lives of our children. The days ahead may bring experiences for them which are similar to the ones we have had—perhaps better ones, but perhaps worse. How creatively we have lived with them in their formative years will greatly affect their handling of similar crises which may arise in their own adult lives.

—From Virginia Watts, *The Single Parent*. Old Tappan, N.J.: Fleming H. Revell Co., 1976.

FOR FURTHER READING:

Atlas, Stephen L. *Single Parenting*. Englewood Cliffs, N.J.: Prentice-Hall, Inc., 1980.

Baruth, Leroy G. *A Single Parent's Survival Guide: How to Raise the Children*. Dubuque, Iowa: Kendall/Hunt Publishing Co., 1979.

Bosco, Antoinette. *A Parent Alone*. West Mystic, Conn.: Twenty-Third Publications, 1978.

Christoff, Nicholas B. *Saturday Night, Sunday Morning: Singles and the Church*. New York: Harper and Row Publishers, 1978.

Stewart, Suzanne. *Parent Alone*. Waco, Tex.: Word Books, 1978.

SLEEP

FORMERLY children's feeding problems were brought to doctors more often than any other management difficulty, but now sleeping problems have taken first place. In trying to meet feeding problems, parents learned that the child's body is a good self-regulator in regard to the food it needs; that the mother's anxiety and forcing only make the problem worse; that, above all, it is important to avoid "battles" over food and to keep mealtime pleasant and relaxed. While getting a child to sleep is a somewhat different matter, parents may have an easier time if they apply these same points to sleeping problems.

The chief difference between feeding and sleeping is that children of all ages naturally like to eat, but as boys and girls grow older they become more reluctant to go to sleep. An infant regulates the amount of sleep he needs; but the picture is different after one or two years, when life becomes more and more interesting. Bodily needs change enormously; newborn babies usually sleep as much as 22 hours, but this usually tapers down to eight or nine hours during the teens. It is also helpful to remember that children differ in their sleep needs. It is impossible to set up rules about how much sleep any individual child needs. For example, in a study of the sleep habits of 783 children, aged two to three, the average number of hours slept was 13—but some children slept only eight and others as much as 17 hours. A child who is healthy, happy, and rested is probably getting the right amount of sleep.

When a child is obviously tired, however, what keeps him awake? A baby may be wakeful because he is hungry, uncomfortably warm or cold, because his diaper needs changing, his gums hurt, he hears unaccustomed noises, or perhaps he needs to be burped. At times it may seem that he just "wants to be loved," and since he cannot express his need, it is sometimes wise to sit with the baby until he falls asleep. Even if this goes on for a while, it is in the end a short cut to helping him feel secure. It is not uncommon for young children up to five or six to pass through anxious periods or nights when they have nightmares and obviously need the reassurance and the physical closeness of their parents.

A preschool child's demand for continued attention at bedtime may also represent a real need. But when an obviously exhausted toddler insists that he's not tired, when he asked for a drink 10 or 20 times and keeps coming into the living room at 10 and 11 o'clock, then his parents have to help him get over this seeking for constant attention, for they cannot reasonably be expected to give it to him all night. If they can take a firm, consistent stand, if they themselves act as if they are convinced that this is the end of the day and time for sleep, their child will usually accept this attitude. As a rule, forcing and tenseness only stir up battles over sleep similar to the futile battles over food. Adjusting home conditions so that going to sleep is easier will accomplish much more than battles.

Perhaps the chief reason why going to sleep has become such a problem is that at six o'clock (once official bedtime for babies and small children) most households now become alive. Fathers come home from work and want to play with their children. Older children want to tune in a noisy television or radio program. Mother is trying to get the younger children to bed so she can prepare dinner. As in other aspects of enforcing discipline, what has to be remembered is that children's needs and wants are not always the same. It is because of this that a less rigid eating schedule generally presents fewer problems than getting a child to bed does. The child needs to eat and also (when the situation is pleasant) wants to eat. However, he needs sleep for his health but often wants to avoid sleep, to stay up as late as possible so that he doesn't miss the life going on for the rest of the family. Parents, of course, have to put themselves on the side of the child's needs.

Here are a few suggestions that may ease the situation:

Try changing the bedtime of small chil-

dren and even infants. They want to see Father at the end of the day, and he wants to see them. If a child goes to sleep at seven or seven-thirty or eight at night, he may sleep till seven or seven-thirty or eight the next morning. If not, his mother can see to it that he makes up the lost sleep during the day, either with an extra nap in the morning or with an especially long nap in the afternoon.

Go over television and radio programs with the older children and try, if at all possible, to arrange things so that they get to see their favorite programs. For their part, however, boys and girls will be expected to turn the programs off at suppertime, at bedtime, and (if necessary) while the baby is being put to sleep.

Children of all ages will go to sleep more readily when they are given advance notice that bedtime is approaching. Even year-old babies like a regular ritual of singing a little song, putting the teddy bear to bed, etc. The ritual itself and the time just before it should be calm, however, and not exciting. As the little boy or girl grows old enough to understand, it is a good idea to give a choice of things to do before going to bed—listening to records, hearing a story, or building with blocks. This gives a child the feeling that, even though his parents have decided the actual hour, he has some say about his bedtime. When he is old enough to read to himself and to draw, bedtime notice should be given in plenty of time to let him finish his chapter or his picture. For some youngsters, the same pattern of arranging the blankets, a hug and a kiss seem to be enough. Other school-age children enjoy a pre-bedtime chat with a parent—especially Father, since they see less of him—and fall asleep with the warm feeling of having talked things over with someone who loves them.

Whatever the routine, repeating it each night makes nestling under the blanket the natural conclusion. If parents are affec-.

tionate and easygoing at bedtime, yet firm and sure of themselves, children will generally accept bedtime without much fuss.

No matter how relaxed the evening ritual, however, there are some babies who usually cry a bit before falling asleep. This is nothing to worry about, and a baby will outgrow it of his own accord. When the crying lasts longer than about 15 minutes, however, or becomes hysterical and panicky, his mother will naturally go in to soothe him till he quiets down.

Boys and girls sometimes resist going to bed because they remember bad dreams they have had and are fearful of having them again. A small light or the door left open after the child goes to sleep will often be reassuring. Some children find it harder than others to leave the family group where so many interesting things seem to be happening. One four-year-old was helped to accept bedtime when her mother began to describe to her in detail everything that usually happened after she was asleep. The little girl then felt she wasn't being left out of the after-bedtime life.

When a child reaches school age he will often argue with his parents about bedtime, probably comparing his going-to-bed hour with his classmates'. What he doesn't know, of course, is that these classmates may sleep late in the morning, take naps, or need much less sleep than he does. In any case, while parents let children have their say and listen sympathetically, they have to make it clear that each family has to work out the ways that are best for the individuals in it.

As boys and girls go into their teens, however, their lives are more directly influenced by what their friends do, and each family can no longer go its own way. One youngster cannot be made to come home at 10 o'clock on Friday and Saturday nights if the curfew for the rest of his group is 11 or 12. The best a mother can do then is to see that her child gets the sleep he needs through late sleeping or rest periods over the weekend. In most communities parents agree that there are to be no parties or movies on school nights, but occasionally there is a group whose young people are allowed to stay out late on school nights as well as much too late on weekends. In such a case it would be a good idea for the parents who feel this is undesirable to get together with the other parents and come to some mutual agreement—rather than to make their own youngster observe a set of rules that most of the other young people in the neighborhood do not observe.

Most teen-agers can be relied on to get enough sleep, although a casual reminder may be necessary once in a while. In general, they are more likely to go to bed at a reasonable time on school nights if parents are reasonable about late hours on date nights.

Almost every boy and girl has restless nights at one time or another (though not as often as very young children do), and these are usually connected with some slight illness, temporary excitement, or a passing worry. But chronic sleeping difficulties, or nightly rebellion at going to bed, are a signal that the child needs help. If a physical checkup reveals nothing wrong, he probably needs help with emotional problems. Of course a child frequently just isn't tired when adults think he ought to be. On the other hand, parents are people, too, and need some time for themselves. This dilemma can usually be worked out amicably. Many mothers with three- and four-year-olds who take a late afternoon nap (and are consequently still full of vim late in the evening) eliminate the nap and, instead, arrange new activities for the late afternoon which are more appealing than the nap. Then the children usually go drowsily and happily to bed at seven o'clock.

The best rules for sleeping, as for everything else, are flexible—rules that can be broken under special circumstances.

399

Most children pass through some difficult periods in their sleeping. But if going to bed has been generally treated with an air of casual, calm expectancy (and never used as punishment), these difficulties will eventually iron out.

—From *The New Encyclopedia of Child Care and Guidance.* Garden City, N.Y.: Doubleday & Co., 1968.

SPANKING

ALTHOUGH SOME Christian parents feel children should be spanked more often than they are, most accept the conclusion that all other means of persuasion should be exhausted before they resort to spanking. They are supported in this view by the fact that the New Testament places little emphasis on chastisement and more on gentle instruction and correction. Spanking, like bullying, is sometimes a way of using physical superiority to hurt another individual. The Christian parent today who understands something about child psychology and learning patterns is less likely to use physical abuse to express his personal anger at behavior that is typical of youngsters. It is so easy for a parent to punish when no punishment is really merited.

Spanking is often inappropriate in several ways. Some parents use it to prevent a child from doing something they don't want him to do. They fail to realize that in many cases he is too young to connect his spanking to the undesirable act. Or he may be too immature to remember the next time.

Second, some parents use spanking to make a child do something they feel he should be doing. They fail to realize that in many cases the child does not have the ability or maturity to do what they want him to do.

In the light of the Bible's connection of discipline with instruction and correction, the Christian parent will try to control his temper and calmly explain to his child the behavior he desires. If the child is too young for such explanations, he is too young for a spanking to do anything other than release the parent's wrath. If a child is of school age, a spanking often produces bitterness and resentment. Some of us can remember spankings at this age; in many cases we harbored ill will against the parent who administered them until we were old enough to understand parental behavior.

Sometimes parents fail to see the irony in their spanking. If you spank a child for hitting his playmate, for example, you have done the very thing you have punished him for!

The Christian parent wants his children to do what is right because it is God's will, not because they are afraid of being punished for doing wrong.

Most parents, including Christian parents, have spanked their children. The sensitive Christian parent, however, will remember the connection between his anger and spanking, and between a child's behavior and his age. That will keep spanking to a minimum. He will, however, realize that biblical discipline involves instruction and correction, and not neglect these more effective forms of discipline. Occasional spanking may be justified if the child is old enough and the parent is not merely venting his own emotional outrage.

—LESLIE R. KEYLOCK

FOR FURTHER READING:

Kesler, Jay. *Too Big to Spank.* Ventura, Calif.: Regal Books, 1978.

Lessin, Roy. *Spanking: Why? When? How?* Minneapolis: Bethany Fellowship, 1979.

Robley, Wendel, and Grace. *Spank Me If You*

Love Me. Harrison, Ark.: New Leaf Press, 1976.

Spock, Benjamin. *Baby and Child Care.* New York: Pocket Books, Inc., 1980.

SPECIAL CHILD

Who Is Special?

While books on parenting and psychology can define the stages of growth and development for all children, each youngster has a set of unique characteristics, abilities, and qualities that make him/her special. Reading a book cannot begin to unfold the mystery and specialness of each child. So the question, "Who is special?" is unfair because *each* child is special in his/her own way.

The word special carries certain connotations depending on the circumstances. Most people think of special in a positive way, like a special delivery package or a special friend. But when special is used as an adjective before education, the meaning usually shifts to something set apart or even "less than." Being special isn't always such a positive thing.

The specialness of a child, then, can be either positive or negative. It can refer to assets or to limitations, to good things or bad, to talents or flaws. Those special aspects or needs of a person can be attributes or handicaps. Some are temporary and others permanent. Some have a far-reaching effect into adulthood while others fade away in maturity. Some can be changed with discipline or medicine or therapy, while others will always be present. Some can be lost through negligence or indifference or lack of care, while others can be found or nurtured by perseverance and discipline and reflection.

Most importantly, specialness is not only what one can or can't do but who one is. It has more to do with the inner person than the outward signs. The qualities that are extra-ordinary (plus the usual) are the ones to be recognized and nurtured; each person has several things that set him/her apart from the others.

There are different kinds of special needs, and many children will have more than one. Parents need to be sensitive to what makes each of their children unique. These needs can include: being sick, getting into trouble at school, being rebellious, having braces, being mentally retarded, being gifted, having a learning disability, being a perfectionist, being shy, excelling in sports, being tall for one's age, having cerebral palsy, being overly sensitive, having an artistic or musical gift, being deaf, stuttering . . . the list could go on and on. While several of these seem to have a negative connotation, some have a positive thrust. Each of these, and others that could be added, brings its own share of joys and sorrows, celebrations and difficulties to the family.

The Effect of the Special Child on Parents and Siblings

The special child—one with a handicap or an asset that goes beyond the uniqueness of each person—can help the family in a profound way. Without any intention of doing so, the child's needs affect both parents and siblings.

The effect will be different for each family depending on the age and status of each parent, the child's age, his/her place in the family, and the age, sex, and number of siblings. Economic and other restraints also come into play in family relationships with a special child. Any one of these factors can make a difference. So the terminally ill child in a family with four younger siblings and an unemployed parent has a far different effect than the terminally ill child who has no siblings and wealthy parents.

Having a child with special needs—whether temporary or permanent—is a crisis situation for most families. The crisis can be as small as what to do about the family outing because Jean is sick today or as important as a family decision about paying the bills for John to go away to a residential treatment center. Crisis doesn't necessarily mean disaster; it means a turning point or a time for decision. The turning point could be that the entire family talks about and resolves the tension and fighting that have arisen because of Mike who is mentally handicapped, or that a parent confronts the rest of the family for not supporting Beth who's being teased about her braces, and the siblings agree to do something about it.

While the major crises seem the most critical, it's often more difficult to deal with the everyday events like the wet bed or the rejected baseball player or the struggle over 2 + 2. It's at those times the parent needs to remember the specialness of each child and to say in some way, "You in your own way are best at what you can do. And I love you for who you are."

Parent and Sibling Stress

The presence of a child with a special handicap and its needs brings up several questions in parenting, highlights feelings, and can cause additional difficulties in a family. What are some of those areas?

Depending on the special need, the parent will have additional worries about the child's future. Parenting involves being concerned about not only the child's present well-being but also what lies ahead. The parent-child bond is one that's never completely broken, and that is probably felt more when a child has a permanent handicapping condition. "Will he/she find a job?" "Where will he/she live?" "What will happen when I'm

gone?" are all pressing questions for the parent of a mentally handicapped child, for example. A parent can see an end to direct responsibility for other siblings but not for the mentally handicapped one. The implications of this concern are far-reaching and can't be addressed here, but they should be recognized as real and valid and need to be discussed with qualified persons.

Uncertainty about the cause of a handicap or the diagnosis, not knowing where to go for help or what to do—these concerns are not dealt with once but many times as the child grows and changes. A parent can be confused, angry, or lost in the shuffle of services, paper work, the lack of educational help, the bureaucracy. If the child was handicapped at birth, anxiety about having another child is a normal reaction.

A parent might also feel guilty about having a handicapped child or a child who has some other special need. The parent may feel the fault belongs to him/her for a rebellious child or a Down's Syndrome youngster. This guilt needs to be acknowledged and then dispelled.

Some parents are embarrassed by a special child. Many times the burden of helping these parents falls on the rest of the community who can accept the child and the family without reservation rather than making it more difficult.

A parent may need to readjust priorities because of a child with special needs. The time or money needed to help a special child must come from somewhere, so activities or other needs must be re-examined and priorities made. Often this will be a painful process, a letting-go of things that are important. The parent needs to acknowledge any negative feelings he/she has. A parent needs to look at his/her needs as well as the children's and to somehow achieve a balance so that each person, child, or adult can continue to grow.

A child with special needs may bring about disagreement between parents. The conflict could be over discipline, privileges, priorities, or several other things. The child can also become a scapegoat for other more deep-seated problems between husband and wife. If disagreement occurs, the parents should get at the reasons for their differences and try to resolve the conflict with the best interests of all who are involved. They may need an outsider to help them see the problems more clearly.

Dealing with siblings may be one of the most difficult problems in parenting a special child. Siblings can become jealous of the child with special needs, whether justified or not. If the special child is a favorite and receives privileges and a lot of extra attention, the jealousy can be justified. But siblings also need to understand the additional care or help the special child needs, whether the youngster has the flu or is in a wheelchair.

Jealousy can turn into hatred of the special child if a parent isn't sensitive to the needs of *all* the children in a family. Good parenting means listening to what each child is saying verbally and nonverbally. It means looking at the needs of the whole family and doing as many "normal" things as possible. If the handicapped or gifted sibling is looked upon most of the time as just another one of the children, family life will probably flow more smoothly. *Each* child—and each *parent*—has special needs.

Siblings' interaction within the family is one thing to consider, but just as important is what happens outside the family. The embarrassment, shame, guilt, disgust, or aloneness that a parent feels is often shared by siblings as well. Sometimes youngsters won't bring friends home because of a handicapped sibling, or they "disown" their sibling with a special need because of peer pressure. While parents may not like such action, they should try to discuss it and come to some mutual resolution. There are many feelings and attitudes involved that are deep and complex; they should be treated with respect and patience.

Lastly, for many parents the overwhelming additional responsibilities, the anxiety and frustration, and the myriad other reactions toward having a child with special needs brings a feeling of aloneness. "Is there anyone else who has to cope with things like this?"

The solution to the last dilemma and to several of the other difficulties is contact with other persons who have similar problems. Most likely another parent felt the same way at one time, or is struggling with the same questions or has fought the same battle. Sharing the joy and the burden is healthy for anyone parenting a child with special needs.

Specialness as a Plus

The special child does not have to be divisive or cause problems. In many families that child is the inspiration or the nudge for siblings and parents to be more understanding and compassionate or to take on responsibility in the family and the larger community. The special child is often the cause for increased communication and sensitivity in the family. The family can be a more cohesive unit because it includes a child with special needs.

Most importantly, the child with special needs is a visible reminder to all family members that each person is unique, each has exceptional needs, and each needs to be and to be loved just for who he/she is.

—From Brigid O'Donnell, "Someone Special," in *Christian Parenting: The Young Child.* Ramsey, N.J.: Paulist Press, 1979.

SPEECH DIFFICULTIES

INDISTINCT or hesitant speech, lisping, lalling, and other difficulties occur frequently between the ages of two and five, when children are learning to talk and to express themselves in words. In most cases these disappear naturally if the child's life is generally healthy and happy and if parents are relaxed and do not call attention to his speech.

Between 5 and 7 percent of children do not outgrow their speech difficulty. In only a small number of these cases, however, is the trouble due to physical causes, such as poor hearing, cleft palate, or the effects of cerebral palsy or other serious illness in infancy. Many speech disorders result from unhappy experiences when learning to talk. Authorities feel that if parents and teachers understand how a child learns to talk and how he can best be helped, most of the speech irregularities that have no physical cause can be prevented.

It takes nearly a hundred muscles moving in coordination to say a single word. Most of this muscular activity is unconscious. When something goes wrong, the child cannot correct or control a particular error merely because he is told to do so. Calling attention to a fault, interrupting him to correct him or to make him repeat the word, punishing, shaming, ridiculing him only make him more anxious and increase his trouble. Even patient correction of a young child tends to make him conscious of efforts to produce effects that are best worked out unconsciously.

Children learn to speak by imitation. Many children grow up speaking indistinctly or with weak or nasal or breathy voices through being with adults who speak in such ways. Parents can help their children develop clear speech and pleasant voices by speaking clearly, pleasantly, and unhurriedly to them.

Lisping (difficulty with sounding s and z) and lalling (trouble with l or r) are generally baby speech carried on past babyhood. Some children take longer to master certain consonant sounds and continue substituting easier ones. A youngster also clings to baby talk for many of the same reasons that he clings to other baby ways: he has been babied too long or called "cute" and shown off, or a new baby or some other upsetting situation may have held him back. If a child's baby speech is marked and persists into the school years, other children are likely to tease and ridicule him. Before he starts school, then, is a good time to consult a clinic or speech teacher on whether he needs help and in what ways.

Hesitancy in speech, repeating or prolonging syllables or sounds—generally called stuttering or stammering—often occurs in the early years. All children between the ages of three and eight are repeaters, and some repetition is normal. Children have a strong urge to talk, but they need encouragement. Parents are usually unaware of how often they are inattentive to the child trying to tell them something, or they interrupt or finish the phrase for him. A quick-thinking, quick-speaking mother may need to curb not only her speed but also her impatience with a slow-talking child. A youngster who fears that he will not be listened to or that he might annoy a parent by talking is likely to become hesitant in his speech or to try to get the words out so fast that he stumbles. So with a child who fears that what he wants to say will be criticized or disapproved. A child may stutter simply because he cannot think of the right word or cannot pronounce it. At the age of three or four, ideas and questions often come faster than a little boy or girl can express them. The urge to talk is greater than the youngster's resources in ideas or words.

A child sometimes stutters if he is telling something that he fears will bring him punishment or will upset his mother, or if he is pressed to tell the details of an accident or unhappy experience while he is still shaken by it, perhaps sobbing. Showing a child off, making him recite, pressing him to talk before he is ready or when he is shy or afraid may make him stutter.

Children who develop a stutter are sometimes found to have had repeated unhappy experiences connected with the organs of speech: for example, anxiety about food or being forced to eat, being punished for or forcibly restrained from thumb-sucking, being slapped on the mouth or having the mouth washed out with soap.

Some emotional situations not directly connected with speech or its organs may contribute to stuttering. Tension, anxiety, a too strict or too protective attitude on the part of parents are often found in the background of a child who stutters. A youngster who is unsure of his parents' relationship to each other—who, for instance, has often heard them quarrelling or feels a coldness between them—may show his anxiety in a speech difficulty as well as in other ways.

Most children who stutter do so only in certain situations—for example, when called on in school or when speaking on the telephone or to strangers. A child may stutter only when talking to adults, or with one parent but not the other, or when he is angry; another may speak fluently only when he is angry. Observing the circumstances in which a child shows his difficulty can lead to clues for helping him.

Early stuttering without accompanying mannerisms can be outgrown as the child learns more words and gains ease in pronouncing them. Parents might try to reduce causes of tension, hurry, or excitement in the youngster's life and see that he gets more rest as well as healthy active outlets for his energies. It will help him also if they can spend time with him, talking and letting him talk about things that interest him, at his own pace, without hurry or correction. He needs to feel that he has his parents' friendly attention and that they have time enough to listen to what he wants to say, in whatever way he can say it.

If stuttering seems to persist or to grow more marked as the child approaches school age, parents would be wise to seek professional help. In early stuttering the youngster seems unaware that anything is amiss in his speech, and if this lack of awareness can continue, the so-called stuttering is likely to be outgrown. But if the stuttering persists, sooner or later others will make him conscious of it, and then he may begin to twist his face, stamp his foot, or develop other tense gestures to help get the words out. This stage, called secondary stuttering, is much harder to cure.

It is advisable to exercise great care in the choice of a speech teacher or therapist. The child's personality as a whole needs to be considered, as well as the background of his difficulty.

—From *The New Encyclopedia of Child Care and Guidance.* Garden City, N.Y.: Doubleday & Co., 1968.

The Speech Foundation of America encourages the following goals parents should attempt to accomplish in order to ensure speech fluency in the child:

(1) Become as sensitive as possible to the infant's many ways of communicating with us—verbally and nonverbally;

(2) Tune in more to the feelings being expressed, rather than to the fact or intellectual content spoken—how one speaks is very often much more crucial than what one speaks;

(3) Learn what it takes for normal speech to develop—learn the ways of giving a helping hand, and make definite efforts to guide your child's speech development;

(4) Provide good models of speaking for your child—you are his first and most important teacher;

(5) Learn how to listen, and how not to listen—yes, it takes some doing to know how to listen well;

(6) Make your expectations concerning your child's speech and other behavior reasonable—try not to expect too much too soon;

(7) Make certain there are plenty of opportunities for feelings to get out into the open—especially the distasteful feelings—not only your child's, but your own as well—then work at figuring out why they built up and what you can do to improve the situation;

(8) Encourage speech spontaneity in your child by strengthening his self-confidence and his desire to share his world with you—as you share yours with him;

(9) Be a good conversational partner for your child—too often our conversational traffic-patterns are one-way streets—or dead ends;

(10) Keep family relationships as harmonious as possible—especially those between husband and wife for they set the pace and provide the key to successful speech growth.

The very process of reaching, itself, for these goals will improve the possibility of your child's growing up to speak normally.

—From Dominick A. Barbara. *Questions and Answers on Stuttering*, Springfield, Ill.: Charles C Thomas Pub., 1965.

FOR FURTHER READING:

Ainsworth, Stanley. *Stuttering: What It Is and What to Do About It*. Lincoln, Nebr.: Cliff's Notes, Inc., 1975.

Ryan, Bruce P. *Programmed Therapy for Stuttering in Children and Adults*. Springfield, Ill.: Charles C Thomas Pub., 1974.

SPOILED CHILD

THE QUESTION of spoiling a child worries most parents—from a new mother who can't decide whether to pick up her baby every time he cries to an exasperated father who doesn't know what to do about a seventeen-year-old who's goofing off in high school. These guidelines may help:

1. It's spoiling a child to try to buy his love and immediate approval with material things or extra privileges, or to substitute toys for your time and care because it's quicker and easier. Once you start doing so, your child becomes more demanding because his real needs aren't being met, and the relationship can slip into an unhappy battle.

But you don't spoil a youngster by giving him a variety of playthings and seeing that he has all the sensory stimulation he needs for physical and mental growth. And you don't spoil him by bringing him an occasional surprise or gift just for the joy of it.

2. It's spoiling a youngster to let him change your mind by sulking, having a temper tantrum, threatening to run away, whining, crying or demanding. But you don't spoil him by listening to his opinions, considering his preferences and letting him make choices that affect him whenever it's possible.

3. It's spoiling a child to let him do whatever he wants for fear you will lose his love, even temporarily, or that he'll be angry with

you. You don't spoil him by encouraging him to be self-reliant and by trying to limit your "no's" as much as possible.

4. It's spoiling a child to encourage him to use minor injuries or illnesses to win concessions from you that you wouldn't otherwise grant. You don't spoil him by giving him comfort and extra attention when he really needs it because he is hurt, sick, tired, discouraged or trying something too difficult.

5. It's spoiling a child to let him interfere unnecessarily with your privacy, rest, meals and the entertainment of your friends. You don't spoil him by recognizing that sometimes his needs must take priority over your plans or giving him similar rights of privacy, freedom from unnecessary interruption and hospitality for his friends.

6. It's spoiling a child to give him your time and attention only when he misbehaves, whines, cries, fusses, sulks or acts inappropriately babyish. You don't spoil him by understanding that he does have great need for loving attention and for your interested sharing of your time with him.

7. It's spoiling a child to hand him increasing privileges without increasing responsibilities. But you don't spoil him by recognizing his growing abilities and granting him new privileges without forcing him to whine or fight for them.

8. It's spoiling a child to wait on him constantly and do things for him he can do for himself, on the grounds you can do them faster or better. You don't spoil him by taking the time to teach him, step by small step, the skills he wants to learn because they will make him more independent of you.

9. It's spoiling a child to let him wheedle or dawdle or complain his way out of jobs that are his responsibility. You don't spoil him by helping him out occasionally when he's overloaded with homework or isn't feeling well or is involved in a special activity at school.

10. It's spoiling a child to do his homework for him and to assume the responsibility of seeing that it's done. You don't spoil him by helping him learn points that he's confused about in school, suggesting sources for class projects or showing an interest in what he's learning.

If your child is usually happy, undemanding, relatively independent and self-regulating in reasonable relation to his age, you can feel quite sure you're not spoiling him. But if he's usually whining, demanding, unhappy and behaving in undesirable ways, it might help to take another look at his real needs and your ways of responding to them.

—From Joan Beck, *Effective Parenting.* New York: Simon & Schuster Inc., 1976.

STEALING

THE PROHIBITION against stealing, the sixth of the Ten Commandments, is closely related to the tenth commandment and its prohibition of coveting (Exodus 20:15, 17). The New Testament repeatedly confirms the validity of the prohibition (Matthew 19:18; Mark 10:19; Luke 18:20; Romans 13:9; Ephesians 4:28).

The young child does not, however, understand that certain things "belong" to others. He treats everything as if it belongs to him when he wants it. He has to learn that certain things belong to his brothers and sisters and that he has to ask for them if he wants to play with them.

This is not easy for the very young child. In fact, if parents take something away from a child because it belongs to someone else, he will usually have a temper tantrum and clutch the desired object as tightly as only a small child can. The wise parent knows, however, to attract his attention with a substitute object and thereby avoid the tantrum.

A young child is not really "stealing" because he still has not developed a sense of personal ownership. Understanding this fact, a parent will teach rather than punish the child who takes something from a playmate.

By the time a child begins school, however, he has developed some sense of personal ownership. Yet children at this age can pick flowers from a neighbor's tree with little or no sense that the flowers belong to someone else and should not be picked without the neighbor's prior approval.

Both the preschool and the school-age child occasionally find the urge to take attractive objects in a store. Older ones may hide them, knowing that their parents don't approve but apparently sometimes not yet able to understand that the objects "belong" to some invisible store owner and must be paid for. The Christian parent needs to see such occasions more as opportunities for teaching than justification for punishment. The best approach is to go with the child to return the object.

If, however, the child still steals when he is older, the Christian parent may need to take a different approach. If the child seems to be taking things other children have, you may need to ask him, perhaps at prayer time, if there is anything he'd very much like to have. Then you can plan to give it to him as a gift or work out a plan whereby he can earn it. You may also want to evaluate the adequacy of his allowance. If none of these steps ends the stealing, there may be emotional problems the parent will need to work out with the help of a Christian counselor. Your pastor should be able to provide you with the name of such a counselor in your area.

In adolescence a different motivation for stealing sometimes arises. To demonstrate his courage to his peers or to prove his ability to accept a dare, a teenager may go into a store with the deliberate intention of stealing. With good Sunday school teaching, such yielding to temptation may not occur often. Unfortunately, parents are usually unaware of such antics until or unless the child is apprehended. If parents can get their children involved in Boys' Brigade, Pioneer Girls, young people's groups, or similar church programs that satisfy the child's desire for adventure and even danger, such episodes can usually be kept to a minimum.

—LESLIE R. KEYLOCK

FOR FURTHER READING:

Belson, William A. *Juvenile Theft: The Causal Factors.* New York: Harper and Row Publishers, 1975.

STEPPARENTS

EVEN THOUGH they may not show it, children react profoundly to the loss of a parent by either death or separation. A stepparent thus faces not only the usual experiences of child rearing but also the child's problems and feelings resulting from a major upset in his life.

Essentially, a child who has lost a parent is frightened; even an infant shows in various ways that he feels a sense of loss and helplessness when the well-known touch and voice disappear. A young child does not understand separation from his parents. He may feel that his naughtiness made his father or mother go away, and this makes him feel guilty. Children also often cling to the hope that the lost parent will come back, and they see the new father or mother standing in the way of the original one's return.

At the same time, a child may need the comfort of someone who is a mother or father to him. In many ways that he cannot put into words he both wants and doesn't want his new parent.

For all these reasons it is wise for a stepfather or stepmother to go slowly in assuming the new role. A chance to make friends, if possible a good while before moving into the family, helps both the children and the prospective new parent. It is well not to overwhelm a child with affection and attentions or try to win his love with lavish presents. The child is more comfortable and the new parent less in danger of disappointment if the youngster is allowed to make the first advances. This means that the stepparent offers warmth and friendly interest but does not insist that the child accept or return affection until he is ready.

It is wise for the new parent taking up family duties and responsibilities to make changes gradually. A stepmother, for example, may justifiably feel that a routine can be improved or a household managed better than it has been. But she will make better progress if she is cautious about throwing out a child's old possessions or radically changing his ways.

Toys, collections, even junk, are a child's old, true friends; they stand for love and safety and give him hold on a world that he is trying to keep steady in the face of great upheavals. His affection for his own mother or the relative or housekeeper who has looked after him is important to him; to speak slightingly of these predecessors or change the family's ways too fast is likely to upset the child. Making too many or too strict new rules, even for the child's own good—such as more regular meals or an earlier bedtime—may frighten him into an uneasy obedience or arouse open resistance. Some rules, of course, need to be established for health, safety, and family peace; they can be made clear and enforced in a friendly way.

What to call a new parent sometimes troubles a child, especially when he is old enough to remember his own father or

mother and cherish the memory. Many children, especially young ones, quite naturally use the new parent's first name, since that is the one they hear, or they invent a pet name. In time the relationship establishes itself, no matter what name the child uses. Often a youngster who has been calling his stepmother by her first name at home is overheard on the street confidently telling a friend, "My mother says. . . ."

A baby is likely to respond more quickly to love and care from a new parent than is an older child—his needs are more urgent; to the parent, too, a baby's helplessness makes a more immediate appeal. The toddler is already striking out for independence and would resist his own parent, but loss of parent can have a particularly disturbing effect in the preschool years, and a youngster between the ages of two and six is probably more in need of love and warmth the more he seems to resist. School-age and adolescent boys and girls need less constant care and may also be less approachable. To these older children the new parent can in time become a valued and trusted friend.

A stepchild may reject food or resist bedtime, going to school, going to the doctor. Such behavior reflects worry. The child needs time to accept the new situation, and he needs to be assured by word and deed that his new mother or father will see that he is not hurt or forced to do things he doesn't want to do. Pilfering objects and telling tall tales are not unusual in most children at some time; but when excessive or prolonged, such behavior indicates that the child is anxious. Punishment or scolding only increases his fears. The parent can gently help the child to distinguish between the real and the imagined, between his own and others' possessions. Shopping trips together, during which the child has some choices in toys and clothes, can be helpful. Above all, the child needs to be shown that his new father or mother likes him, protects him, and is his friend. A welcoming attitude toward the youngster's own friends and interests also helps to set up a cheerful, healthy atmosphere around him.

When, as after a divorce, the child lives with his mother and visits his father, the stepmother does well to offer the youngster a friendship that does not compete with his love for his own mother. Other situations also may need thoughtful handling, as when the stepparent has children of his or her own, or children are born in the new family.

The stepparent cannot walk into a family a full-fledged mother or father, or solve all difficulties at the start, once and for all. As children grow, their needs and attitudes change. Old feelings of unhappiness and uncertainty rise again from time to time. A youngster needs new assurances of his firm place in the family. A paint job for his room, a small surprise gift, going out together, playing a favorite game, all are tokens of the love his new mother or father has for him.

The stepparent's task often seems more difficult than an ordinary parent's. Resentful and angry feelings, which are natural in ordinary family life, are likely to be intensified for a stepparent. The new father or mother also needs to gain confidence and may make good use of a sympathetic, trained outsider, such as a family or other professional counselor, to relieve bottled-up feelings and work out problems. On the other hand, free of the background of emotional conflict that is usual between parent and child, the stepparent can regard a new son or daughter as simply a young individual who needs love and understanding, and can become the child's well-loved friend.

—From *The New Encyclopedia of Child Care and Guidance*. Garden City, N.Y.: Doubleday & Co., 1968.

FOR FURTHER READING:

Emery, Anne. *Stepfamily.* Philadelphia: Westminster Press, 1980.

Reed, Bobby. *Stepfamilies: Living in Christian Harmony.* St. Louis: Concordia Publishing House, 1980.

STRANGERS

PARENTS FIRST BEGIN to be concerned about their child's reaction to strangers at about seven to nine months, when the baby who had previously been most friendly to everyone suddenly begins to be disturbed at the sight of strangers. This is a passing phase of the child's growing awareness of differences between his mother or others close to him and the people in the outside world.

Accepting strangers comes more easily as a child grows older, sometimes to the point where it may be necessary to discourage indiscriminate familiarity. The five- or six-year-old can be told firmly not to go off with people he doesn't know. His natural sociability needn't be frightened out of him with detailed accounts of possible dangers. He can be helped to understand, however, that though most people—millions and millions of them—can be trusted there are a few who are not reliable, and so he should not go off with anyone he doesn't know.

—From *The New Encyclopedia of Child Care and Guidance*. Garden City, N.Y.: Doubleday & Co., 1968.

SUICIDE

A BOILING POT of pressure and change exists inside thousands of young people, and occasionally it blows up. Many young people don't know how to reduce the steam, and sometimes they can't keep the lid on.

The number of youth suicides in America is increasing. In the past twenty years, suicides in the 16–24 age group have tripled. These are all types of youth: dropouts, drug users, and straight-A students who have never failed at anything.

A mother and father in an Ivy League town were shocked when they found their seventeen-year-old daughter unconscious in her bed. She had taken an overdose of sleeping pills and was only partly alive. Their girl had never given them a moment of trouble. She did everything right and was a popular student. Only now did they realize Ann had hostilities and frustrations that she had never expressed before.

Youth suicide is not limited to the high-school and college-age. Today and every day of the year two youths under sixteen will end their lives. These figures do not include those young people who are bored, depressed, and don't care if they live or die. They drive their cars as if there were no tomorrow or take drugs as if they are trying to see how close they can get to death. If they die, their death will not be listed as an official suicide. But they certainly exhibited destructive behavior and possibly even a death wish.

The specific causes of increased youth suicides are hard to determine. We are sure of a number of contributing factors. The large number of broken homes adds to the feelings of insecurity and doubts about love. Seventy-one percent of youths who commit suicide come from divorced homes. Many cannot work out their feelings about the change in their homes, and often they feel personally responsible for the split.

The enormous pressure from the educational process is crippling to some young people, and yet others thrive on it. Confusion over shifting standards leaves some youths completely torn. Some young people

commit suicide after having intercourse because of the tremendous guilt. Some are unsure about their role in life. In the process of growing up, they may have lost a healthy self-respect, and they consider themselves the dandruff of the world.

Drugs do play a role in the number of youth suicides, but the exact extent is difficult to determine. Some authorities believe drugs are involved in half of the adolescent suicides. But which came first, the chicken or the egg? Are some youth so depressed and suicidal that they turn to drug abuse? Or are they fairly stable until the drugs diminish their ability to think? Many young people see drugs as an opportunity to live and die at the same time. The drugs allow them to escape life and its pressures; consequently, they often take them. Yet drugs let them return to life for whatever it offers. In this game of escape, a number of youth venture too far too often. Sometimes they don't make it back. At other times, they never intended to come back. The difference between an overdose and suicide can be paper-thin.

Young people, despite their cries of independence, are, like all of us, vulnerable to suggestions and influences. When suicides are romanticized in our culture, a spark ignites that results in many self-inflicted deaths. The deaths of Marilyn Monroe, Ernest Hemingway, Judy Garland, Freddie Prinze, Janis Joplin, Sylvia Plath, or Japanese author Yukio Mishima all took their toll. People say to themselves, "If he can't make it with all he has, what chance do I have?" The publicity surrounding these suicides set off a chain of sudden deaths.

Sociologist David Phillips of the University of California in San Diego has gathered some facts. He studied five large California newspapers to check the publicity they gave to "famous" suicides. Then he checked the records of vehicle fatalities. Three days after the publicity of a notable suicide, the number of vehicle fatalities rose by 30 percent. The rest of the week, it remained 9 percent above normal.

Because of our effect on each other, there are those who are afraid to discuss suicide. Why bring up such a morbid subject? Talking about it will only cause more people to end their lives.

One man was scheduled to speak for a week on a college campus. His topic on the fourth day was announced as "Suicide." A school administrator came to him privately. "Speak on anything you want," he said, "sex, war, even communism. But leave suicide alone. It will only cause a rash of them on campus."

The educator's apprehension is understandable, but his energy may be misspent. The important factor is not whether suicide is discussed, but how.

The topic of suicide suffers from a communication problem. Most youths who commit suicide are trying to communicate. Possibly because of their own problems, they cannot express their desperate hurt. Killing themselves is the final message. "See, I really was hurting." At last they got it across.

Knowledge is better than ignorance. Sharing is better than seething. If the environment says suicide is something we do not discuss, what are the victim's options? He feels drawn toward it. He wonders about it. And he has to bottle up these feelings, because talking about suicide is taboo.

Larry was a Christian in his early twenties. A major concern in his life was to follow Jesus Christ as a committed disciple. He tried to examine every aspect of his thoughts, his motives, and his actions in a spiritual context.

He was single and found sex becoming an overriding factor in his mind. Yet he fought it and then felt doubly guilty for even thinking about it. But there was no one for Larry

to talk to. Sex was a subject that received a few sneers from the pulpit, but nice people didn't talk about it.

Larry became so overwrought with his "burden of sin" that he started to consider suicide. But since nice people also didn't discuss suicide, he was trapped again. One evening he was found standing on the edge of a high-rise roof. He threatened to jump but did not really want to. Larry was trying to find some way of letting people know he hurt.

Now people are willing to talk to him. They discuss anything he wants. He has spent the past fifteen years in and out of mental hospitals and clinics.

A pastor in the Midwest took seriously the rumors he heard about high-school students who were discussing the merits of suicides. He made it a point to befriend these youths individually, without mentioning suicide. Eventually, each brought up the subject. One day, to his complete surprise, all four showed up at his office. They had compared notes and wanted to discuss it together. After several sessions, the two who were not Christians invited Christ into their lives.

To discover how much people want to talk about suicide, tell everyone you are writing a book on the subject! Many have a relative who tried it or did it. They have always wondered about this or that. Perhaps during the last couple years they have considered it themselves. People are more curious about suicide than we may have thought.

The two hundred suicide prevention centers across the United States are vivid evidence. Their phones ring continuously. The center in Los Angeles gets twenty thousand calls a month. In a medium-sized city like Omaha, the number is two thousand. People want to talk about it.

But where can a young person go to discuss his problem? Some are boxed in and do not feel free to bring it up. Traditionally, local ministers have been a good source for counseling, but many youths have avoided them when it comes to suicide. Churches often speak of suicide only in terms of condemnation. Hopefully, ministers will do more to demonstrate a helpful spirit—to show they do understand and would like to help. For many young people, pastors and chaplains are more easily accessible than psychologists, psychiatrists, or even school counselors.

Parents are often embarrassed when their child seeks counseling. They take it personally. It seems to point up their failures. We need to be glad that, if our child needed someone to talk to, he had enough sense to find a listening ear.

—From William L. Coleman, *Understanding Suicide.* Elgin, Ill.: David C. Cook Publishing Co., 1979.

FOR FURTHER READING:

Collins, Gary. *How to Be a People Helper.* Santa Ana, Calif.: Vision House Publishers, 1976.

Hewett, John. *After Suicide.* Philadelphia: Westminster Press, 1980.

Parker, A. Morgan. *Suicide Among Young Adults.* Hicksville, N.Y.: Exposition Press, 1974.

Rabkin, Brenda. *Growing Up Dead: A Hard Look at Why Adolescents Commit Suicide.* Nashville: Abingdon Press, 1979.

SUNDAY SCHOOL

THE QUALITY of relationships that are built between teacher and student largely determines the effectiveness of instruction. While the content of the Bible is of critical importance in Sunday School teaching, the rela-

tionships that are developed often determine the long-term effectiveness of the lessons. In fact many people remember the relationships far more explicitly than the lesson content. Such is true in my experience.

A Personal Memory

My parents saw to it that I attended Sunday School regularly, and they attended with me. But as I look back upon those early Sunday School experiences, I remember persons more than facts.

I remember attending Sunday School when I was in the Primary Department. We probably participated in interesting learning activities. There must have been visual aids, and interesting stories, interest centers, and visualized songs. Bible facts were taught and application was made. And yet, I've forgotten those things.

But I do remember a teacher who loved me. She was interested in me and concerned about me. She communicated that love in such a way that almost 30 years later I still remember that she loved me. I don't remember what she taught, but I remember the relationship. I remember Mrs. Harvey Hiles.

I remember attending Sunday School when I was in the Junior Department. Actually, I remember more about my experiences in the Junior Department than in the Primary Department, partly because I was older, and partly because of how I was involved. I remember a teacher with incredible patience; when we acted like grade-school boys, or worse.

The class arrangement was not conducive to effective education to begin with. We all sat around a long table made of three wide boards with open cracks between them. And our teacher sat at the end. When we all leaned forward, with our shoulders against the table, no arm motion was visible. And all six boys would gaze with innocent expressions of wonder as pieces of paper would mysteriously emerge through the cracks in the table, only to disappear as the teacher grabbed for them and then reappear at another place on the table.

I remember what was underneath that table. The bottom was covered with so many wads of gum that it felt more like a gravel driveway than a table bottom. After all, we wouldn't think of chewing gum in Sunday School! And I remember the active trading that went on under the table. Trading of the wonderful and strange things that can be found in the pockets of sixth-grade boys.

But more than these things I remember a man—a quiet gentle man who would get frustrated at the antics of the boys he loved. It probably was not very evident that we were learning. But we were. The dedication and commitment of that teacher was apparent to us. And we learned, not so much from what he said, but from what he was. I remember a teacher who loved me. I remember J. Rollin Ewen.

I remember attending Sunday School when I was in the Junior High Department. That's when the statistics indicate we were supposed to drop out of Sunday School. And some of us may have considered doing just that. But our parents decided otherwise. I only remember one specific thing that was said in that class. And I remember that because I argued with it. But I learned as a junior high student. I learned that we had a pastor who, in spite of being busy, was concerned about us.

In addition to his preaching and pastoral duties, he accepted a teaching assignment. He accepted the class because he was concerned. And he communicated this concern. We knew he loved us. And because of that we loved him too. And so we respected him for what he was. We learned from him— from his Sunday School lessons and from his

sermons, but mainly from his life. I don't specifically remember the content of those lessons or sermons. But I do remember a relationship that was built. I remember Rev. James N. McCoy.

Provision for a Personal Touch

You see, Sunday School's value extends beyond the facts that are communicated. You cannot have an effective Bible teaching ministry without teaching those facts. But in order to gain maximum benefit, meaningful relationships must be cultivated in the process. The Rev. Sherm Williams affirmed this concept. "The genius of the Sunday School is the provision for the personal touch. There must be a 'rub-off' from teacher to pupil. His life must incarnate the truth he teaches. The 'shepherding' concept is basic to the success of the Sunday School" (*The Sunday School Today and Tomorrow*, p. 18).

In *The Pattern of God's Truth*, a book that has profound insights for Christian educators, Frank E. Gaebelein stressed the importance of the teacher. "In one way or another, every teacher expresses the convictions he lives by, whether they be spiritually positive or negative" (p. 37). He was applying this concept to formal education institutions, but it applies to all Christian education. The quality of the spiritual commitment of the teacher determines the quality of Christian education. For the teacher communicates by what he is far more than by what he says. He communicates by relationships.

Dr. Howard Hendricks, dean of Christian education, frequently relates the impact that a Sunday School teacher had upon his life. He describes how a man with little formal education took a personal interest in each of the boys in his class. He spent time with the boys, helped them with their homework when he could, shared with them what he was, and influenced their lives. Because of the relationships that were developed, he played a strategic role in his students' lives.

It wasn't fantastic teaching methods, and it wasn't the teacher's profound insights. But it was his genuine love, expressed through significant contacts. Dr. Hendrick's attributes much of the credit for his ministry today to the impact of the relationship with that Sunday School teacher.

What does it take to be an effective Sunday School teacher? It takes a knowledge of the Bible. For without that there is no true Christian education. But in order to deeply influence students, to help them become true disciples of Jesus Christ, a teacher must cultivate deeply personal relationships with his students. What a teacher is matters more than what he knows.

The relationship of a teacher with his students is portrayed in an account written by Michael J. Boyd, and published in *The United Methodist Reporter*, April 27, 1979.

He stood before me in the small classroom of the Franklin Street Evangelical United Brethren Church—now called the United Methodist Church—of Union City, Ohio. One by one, he called upon each boy assembled to read Bible verses and lesson elements. On my part, it was more of an act of courtesy than a sincere attempt to find a true meaning for Christian living that I read for him.

Yet, Harry Porter, my Sunday School teacher, exemplifies that true Christian person that we all should strive to be. In many ways, it was not what he said in those Sunday School classes that impressed me, but in his overall Christian manhood that helped guide me toward our heavenly Father. For all this strong Christian example, I thank God every day.

In the first place, I now realize that Harry is an honest person. In fact, his gentle, truthful manner frequently transcended from church to Wednesday evening baseball, which he organized for the boys of the church.

For example, if Umpire Porter called us out on strikes, we frequently argued. But his sincere nature usually calmed us with this reply: "That's the way I saw it!" Through many church activities, which he planned and organized himself, Harry maintained a warm, honest relationship with us.

Moreover, I now realize just how dedicated Harry is to the church and our loving Father. Recently, he told me that he wanted to be a school teacher, but the Great Depression altered his plans. Since I believe that Christ calls many teachers into His service, I am convinced that He called Harry to serve Him as a Sunday School teacher. I truly felt the dedicated concern that Harry must have felt for me long ago when he shared with me some of his trials and tribulations of teaching young people today.

Most of all, I admire Harry's quiet humility. Although his quiet manner could be misconstrued for shyness, I now realize that it is because of a close, humble relationship that he shares with our heavenly Father that extends itself toward those around him. In short, Harry Porter is a man with a sincere mind, dedicated heart, and humble spirit.

I shall always remember my Sunday School teacher!

—From Wesley R. Willis, *200 Years—and Still Counting*. Wheaton, Ill.: Victor Books, 1979.

FOR FURTHER READING:

Allen, Charles L., and Parker, Mildred. *How to Increase Your Sunday School Attendance*. Old Tappan, N.J.: Fleming H. Revell Co., 1980.

Schorr, Vernie. *Building Relationships with Children*. Ventura, Calif.: Regal Books, 1978.

SWEARING

THIS IS THE USE of crude or downright profane words as exclamations or in routine speech. It never occurs until the child hears and can repeat such language from another person.

Causes of Swearing

Hearing Others Swear. This may intrigue your child. Friends, especially older ones, may swear in a childish effort to prove their "toughness." This can be done with such a show of strength and energy that it invites duplicating.

Need for Peer Approval. This may prompt your child to adopt the coarse talk and other habits, too, of "tough" young people. If your child seems to need the approval of such friends, you need to explore his own self-concept. He may feel very weak and inadequate. Tough associates can seem to offer safety and power to such a child.

Need to Rebel. If you have been too strict and perfectionistic, your child may feel he has to do something drastic to break away from your hold over him.

Oftentimes, a child's swearing is a passing whim, started by fascination with the swagger of the one who teaches him. Give it some careful ignoring and a chance to die a natural death. If your child does not stop by himself, however, do pay attention.

Dealing With Swearing

Discuss the issue, person-to-person, with your child. Explain your values and your reasons for wanting him to stop using bad words.

See if your child, himself, can figure out why he is swearing, and recognize the reasons as being unworthy of his own values. If he can't explain the reasons, give him some ideas, and ask him to think them over. Allow your child time to think through the values that are at stake here. These concepts are usually involved and profound. The more he can really comprehend them, the more likely he will be to truly adopt them as his own.

If he is feeling weak or inferior, think out a plan to make him aware of his strength, so he can believe it. Be aware that telling this to a child never really convinces him. He has to see it for himself in his own behavior and successes. The best way we know to teach a child his capabilities is for you to indicate clearly to him the good qualities he demonstrates and the achievements he has made.

Help him set up a plan for breaking the swearing habit. Fining him a nickel or a dime, and having him work at a special job to pay that off, sometimes works. (Children often have very respectable ideas for discipline that work for them.)

Help your child find some acceptable word he can use to express strong feelings. Everyone needs some means of expression.

I know some of you will say, "Just whip him and make him stop." Perhaps that will work for you. We never argue with success. *But we can show you countless young people who have been driven by angry whippings into severe rebellion.* Spankings may work for smaller children, but in older ones, the loving, logical, but firm approach works far better and more often.

Help your child see for himself, then, the crudeness of bad language and how quickly its use becomes a habit. Remind him of God's special commands against taking His name in vain. Tell him clearly but kindly that you want him to stop, and then work out the plan for doing that.

—From Grace H. Ketterman, M.D., and Herbert L. Ketterman, M.D., *The Complete Book of Baby and Child Care for Christian Parents*. Old Tappan, N.J.: Fleming H. Revell Co., 1982.

T

TALKING

WHEN A MOTHER and father tell their friends in great excitement, "He's talking!" it usually means that their baby is about a year and a half old. He has probably been saying things like "muh-muh-muh." This sounds like "mama"—and pretty soon as he hears loving voices clearly repeat "ma-ma," he really is saying it.

Long before this, of course, the baby has begun to pay heed to the human voice; he has been making sounds of all sorts and having long, babbling conversations with himself and others. Mother babbles his own sounds back to him, and this not only gives him a feeling of affection and companionship but is the beginning of authentic and helpful "baby talk."

It also gradually gives him the idea of imitation, which he himself will use when he begins to speak words. Once his real words begin, however, the wise parent leaves imitation to the baby. Having an adult mimic his first "cute" pronunciations is the kind of baby talk that is not helpful. No matter how much it may seem to express the well of warmth his mother feels toward a baby, it makes his own understanding of ordinary adult speech come harder.

Friends and relatives become excited, too, over those first baby syllables that resemble language; but excitement that turns into eager urging doesn't really hasten the child's use of words. What it may do instead is to worry him and possibly slow up his progress.

He will say "father" as soon as he can master the difficult sound of f and the very difficult th. For now, he is more likely to make all the advance he is capable of if the adults around him use simple words and sentences and talk about things that have some immediate meaning to a child, especially the everyday experiences he remembers. Gestures, where they fit, help to convey the meanings of new words to young children.

More parents do these things naturally, just as they naturally lengthen their sentences as the child grows older and his vocabulary increases. "Go bye-bye?" was perhaps the best phrase for the one-year-old, but before long he understands and learns from "Let's go out now."

Some parents feel it their duty to correct the speech mistakes of a child; others believe that any suggestion of correcting will retard his fluency. A policy somewhere in the middle seems best—the most important thing being when and how the correcting is done. An interruption in the middle of an eager narrative can, of course, discourage and disappoint a child. But if he has demonstrated for some time, for instance, that he can pronounce r in other words but persists in saying "wabbit," it may simply be a hangover from the baby days when he did think of it as a "wabbit." Of course he can become anxious not only about r but about speech in general if he's corrected every time he mispronounces the word or if he's coaxed or punished. It would be more helpful to say something like this: "Do you know, dear, you just said 'wabbit.' But it's really 'r-r-rabbit'—the same sound as when you say 'ran' so perfectly." A game with mother and child both rolling r-r-r's can be enjoyable and instructive.

The so-called "slow" talker is not necessarily a "slow" child. Some of the most reticent toddlers are extremely bright and, just about the time their parents are growing concerned over their silence, turn out to be chatterboxes. If a youngster's speech is really seriously limited or clumsy by the time he is two or three years old, the first helpful step is having his hearing checked by a doctor. If it is normal, spending more time with other children—in a nursery school, for example—may be a spur to talking better. When a child is with other children, talking becomes imperative and somehow more attractive. Here he does not have parents or older brothers and sisters to anticipate his needs, to accept pointing and motioning as a substitute for words. In the event association with other children does not change the situation, a qualified speech teacher, with a sound understanding of children's needs, will probably be of great help.

To a child it must often appear that everyone is very careful and helpful with regard to his first efforts to speak—and then when he actually can talk, grownups seem to forget that talking is give-and-take. The school child says confidentially, "You know what happened, Dad?" and launches into his recital. He has an encouraging feeling of friendship and understanding when his father takes time out really to listen, doesn't interrupt, doesn't get impatient if he hesitates over a few words, doesn't anticipate his thoughts and put them into words for him. And when his father participates in the conversation, replies with grown-up observations, the boy adds new words to his own vo-

cabulary and unknowingly acquires ease in speaking with people. These will be invaluable assets to him throughout his life.

—From *The New Encyclopedia of Child Care and Guidance.* Garden City, N.Y.: Doubleday & Co., 1968.

TEASING

THOUGH THERE ARE no explicit references to teasing in the Bible, the phenomenon is all but universal, and it is hard to believe that, for example, Jacob and Esau did not tease each other.

Older children will sometimes tease their younger brothers or sisters. Since younger children are usually unable to understand teasing, they frequently get annoyed, which seems to amuse the older children. The parents' role at this stage is to teach older children that younger children do not understand teasing and to teach younger children that their brothers and sisters are only playing a game with them.

The younger adolescent sometimes uses teasing as a way of indicating interest in someone of the opposite sex. Other young adolescents will use teasing to indicate jealousy at another child's good grades in school or other kinds of success. These forms of teasing are cloaked expressions of self-consciousness and inferiority. They are usually temporary and harmless.

Sometimes teasing can become cruel, however. When gangs of boys make one boy the object of their teasing over a period of weeks, life for that boy can be miserable. Frequently he will mention his problem to his parents and the problem can be solved by a phone call to school authorities.

If your child engages in cruel teasing, it may be his way of indicating that he wants more attention and love. Authorities also point out that teasing seems to be more common in homes in which there is too much or too little discipline.

Sometimes teasing will lead the very sensitive child to cry. Teasing seems to make the child feel he is being laughed at. This makes him feel inadequate. Parents need to give the child extra love and affection at such times. They need to make the child understand that the best way to end teasing is to ignore it. This lesson is usually not an easy one for the child to learn, however.

Teenage children are often acutely sensitive to teasing. The adolescent girl who indicates interest in a particular boy at school or church may not appreciate her father's friendly teasing about her "wedding plans." A boy who is insecure about his physical development may not appreciate a parent's teasing about trying to locate a muscle in his biceps. Friendly teasing in such sensitive areas may even lead to a sudden and unexpected outburst of anger or deep, unrevealed resentment.

Most children, however, actually delight in a bit of friendly teasing.

Christian parents need to be sensitive as to when a child enjoys teasing and when teasing may evoke his insecurities.

—LESLIE R. KEYLOCK

FOR FURTHER READING:

Dobson, James C. *Hide or Seek.* Old Tappan, N.J.: Fleming H. Revell Co., 1979.

TEETHING

THAT FIRST TOOTH is a perfectly normal—even eagerly awaited—event.

There's an old saying, "One tooth at 6 months, 6 teeth at a year." This may be true on the average, but there are wide variations. Some babies are born with a tooth; just

as often, parents have to wait till the first birthday or later for that event. Brothers and sisters are apt to be like each other in the time their teeth appear. Usually, but by no means always, the first to come are two center teeth of the lower jaw, followed by four center upper teeth. They are called incisors because of their sharp cutting edges. You'll know, if you carelessly put your finger in the baby's mouth. He just naturally clamps down. There are the six teeth that the old saying refers to.

After a pause of several months, six more teeth will erupt: the two remaining lower incisors are followed by four molars with flat grinding surfaces, set back a little. Toward the second birthday, four pointed teeth, called canine or "dog" teeth, come through in the spaces between the incisors and the molars. Four more molars appear behind the first ones to complete the first set of 20 teeth. These are the baby or "milk" teeth which will be shed as the permanent teeth come in, starting around age 6. A baby's teeth may appear in a somewhat different order than the one listed. It won't matter.

Sometimes you don't know that your baby is busy getting a tooth until you get bit, or hear the click of the spoon against it. You may notice some drooling, but this happens anyhow while he learns to control his saliva better. Frequently, however, a baby is cross and fretful, may lose his appetite for a few days or waken at night, crying. He may suck his fingers or fist more than usual, or anything else he can get in his mouth. Many households more or less proudly display a ring of tiny toothmarks in the coffee table or the leg of a chair made by a teething baby who is also learning to pull up.

But teething rarely accounts for an illness. If the baby is feverish or coughing, has prolonged loss of appetite or other signs of illness, it is probably not related to teething, and you should check for other causes.

To ease the baby's discomfort while he is teething, probably the best thing is to be patient with him and soothe him every way you know how. Give him zwieback, hard toast, or a teething ring of hard rubber or plastic. Be sure he doesn't chew on things that would break or splinter in his mouth. Watch that he doesn't gnaw wood finished with paint containing lead. If he wakens at night, he may need a warm bottle to help him go back to sleep. When the discomfort of teething is over, he'll be eating better during the day and less fretful at night. When he's again ready, he will give up the night bottle.

The health of the gums and teeth is directly connected to the baby's diet. Even while he's cutting baby teeth, buds of his permanent teeth are being laid down in the jaw. For this reason, a diet which provides plenty of vitamins and minerals is important throughout infancy.

Fluorine is a mineral that is especially important for sound tooth development. Many communities add small amounts of fluorine to their water supply if it does not naturally contain enough of this mineral. Some doctors prescribe small doses of fluorine for babies who do not get as much as they need from the water they drink. Since too much fluorine can be harmful to tooth development, it is important to follow the doctor's directions carefully if he prescribes it for your baby.

—From *Infant Care*. Washington: U.S. Department of Health, Education and Welfare, 1970.

TELEPHONE

THE PRESCHOOL CHILD needs to be taught when and how to answer the telephone. A short simple phrase like, "Hello, this is Tammy Smith," or "Smith residence" is easy to teach. The child also needs to learn how to say, "One moment, please," or "Hold on, I'll get him/her," when the caller asks for another person in the house. A caller can be understandably annoyed by the child who picks up the phone but has never been properly trained to use it.

Otherwise the telephone is seldom a problem—until children become teenagers! Teenagers need to be taught that the telephone is for the convenience of every member of the family and should not be tied up for lengthy periods of time if important calls are expected. Frequent calls in the morning when everyone is getting ready to leave for work and school can be time-consuming and unnecessary. Parents may find that they have to stop such morning phone calls if they are going to leave for work on time. A reminder the night before to call friends and make arrangements for the next morning may solve the problem.

Parents react in various ways to the telephone marathons of their teenagers. Except when expecting important phone calls, some parents accept such marathons as a natural part of the growing-up process. Other parents get a separate phone number for their children and expect them to handle the bills with their own earnings. In some cases the parents agree to pay up to a certain amount and expect the child to pay for any excesses. Long-distance calls should not be made without prior parental approval.

Occasionally special problems emerge. If friends make excessive use of the child's phone, parents may have to make it clear that the phone is for the child's personal use only. If friends call up too early or too late, the child should be expected to tell his friends that they shouldn't call at those times. If a parent needs to use the family phone when a teenager has been on it for some time, a simple note on a pad of paper is an easy way to request an end to the call.

You should make clear in advance, however, that when such a note appears the person on the phone is expected to hang up in a very short period of time.

—LESLIE R. KEYLOCK

TELEVISION

MOST OF THE PROBLEMS parents face with television are not directly related to television itself, but to its control. In Marie Winn's, *The Plug-In Drug: Television, Children, and the Family* [we read]:

Interviewer: Many people say that TV takes away from the imagination, making kids dull—like zombies—and that they are no longer creative.

Seventh grader: When people say that it turns kids into zombies and everything, it's only about kids that watch TV eight hours a day—constantly and everything. But that's for the unaverage people that watch TV.

"UNAVERAGE PEOPLE" watch television eight hours a day, fifty-six hours a week, according to this seventh grader. Surveys prove him correct, but they also suggest that average people watch too much: up to thirty hours a week for preschoolers, over twenty hours for grade-schoolers, adolescents, and adults.

A more reasonable amount of TV viewing would be half of that. What studies we have on the effects of excessive viewing demonstrate, for example, that pre-schoolers begin their zombie transformation after one hour a day, or seven hours a week.

As is so often the case, children want guidance. A high-school boy, asked to make up his own question about television and then answer it, said, "Do you think that TV today is hurting the imaginations of young children, that when they're bored, they just watch television?"

His response: "Without proper parent control this could happen easily. But I believe that any kind of restriction will stop this from happening, whether it be in the type of program, or the amount of TV watched. This is up to the parent."

This high-schooler has given us part of the formula. If you want television to be a friend rather than a foe, exercise your parental control. Establish some limits on the amount of television your child may watch, on the time he or she may view (not after 9:00 P.M., or 8:00 P.M., central time, when programming is for adults), and on the type of program your child may watch.

Your only other answer is to remove the television set entirely. This only admits that the family—and particularly the parents—are unable to handle a significant feature of modern life. Besides, you deprive your child of a fantasy source that, if handled well, could be useful and meaningful to the child and the entire family.

Bruno Bettelheim said this way back in the 1960s when television was much less sophisticated—and therefore much less appealing. (Remember "Howdy Doody" and the "Lucy" shows?) "I am by no means suggesting," Bettelheim said, "that we do away with the TV sets in our homes. If we wish to enjoy their advantages without paying a price, we will have to take action."

But we must be wise in the type of control we exercise. Listen to one fourth grader's version of control in her home. "My dad usually comes down and shuts it off, because he has a lot of this inventory stuff to do . . . He's always reading and concentrating.

They got in a system of computers, and so he has all this stuff to do."

This parent is in a bind. But his attempt to control television is improper, because it lacks any appreciation of the TV experience and is ultimately self-serving.

Now consider a situation Marie Winn describes in her book. Alexander is a young boy who often came to the dinner table wanting to talk about the TV he had been watching. He'd want to sing a jingle or retell a story. But the parents had their own agenda. They neither watched with Alex, nor did they want dinner conversation "spoiled" by TV talk. This is an example of improper parental control.

Alexander eagerly repeated his TV fantasy because it had a lot to do with what he was really feeling—from his fears to his longings. Poor Alexander, maybe even impoverished Alexander. His parents mistakenly assumed that such storytelling or jingle-melodizing were just extensions of watching television, with nothing to do with what he thought or felt.

For weeks after finishing *The Plug-In Drug*, I was haunted by that dinnertime scene. Alexander comes fresh from some TV fantasy or other, and his excited response is met by, "No, we're sorry Alex, that's not GC." Crushed, Alexander tries to remember what GC stands for. Oh, yes, General Conversation. In this instance, the parents' failure to nourish this vital fantasy world led to the final failure, the removal of the storyteller, which Winn mistakenly applauds.

Proper parental control begins with watching TV with your youngster. Dr. Gerald Lesser has shown that those young viewers who profit most from TV have a parent who watches with them and talks about the show. His studies also demonstrate that watching and talking with youngsters about their favorite shows gains their respect, and the right, in their eyes, to help them control

and select. Slowly the child's own capacity to judge what is good viewing will grow naturally.

Listen to the response we got from one child whose parents were interested enough to watch television with her.

Question: Does your family ever watch TV together?

Answer: Usually we do watch it together, unless it's like in the afternoon or something. But usually it's in the evening, and then we all watch it together.

Question: Do you like watching TV with your whole family?

Answer: Uh-huh.

Question: Is there any show that your parents do not want you to watch?

Answer: My parents respect my feelings, and they let me be independent. They have raised us to believe that if you can't make your own decisions of this type by the time you are eleven or twelve, something has gone wrong. Usually if I feel that a show is not worth watching, I turn it off, or try to find something better.

Question: Are there shows that you have turned off?

Answer: Oh, yeah. I've turned off "Maude" quite a few times, "All in the Family," some movies.

Question: Why did you turn off "All in the Family"?

Answer: Because I felt that it was getting suggestive. I think a couple of times it was running down Christianity, which I don't approve of.

The question of control is really a question of how we can best teach our young charges to care, to control, and to discriminate. And that's a family affair, just like some TV viewing should be a family experience.

At least half of your child's TV viewing should be with you. That means timing. After-school shows may need to be cut back or eliminated, although there are some marvelous "for children only" offerings like ABC's award-winning "Afterschool Special." Most of the rest—reruns of older and often adult drama—are best eliminated.

So we have the evenings. Family viewing time, the one or two hours before 9:00 P.M.—or 8:00 central—can be used to good effect. At least two or three of the five school nights will offer worthwhile shows during this time.

Aside from our family's reduction of viewing amount to under ten hours a week, the most important and beneficial rule is "TV goes off at 8:00 P.M.—every night of the week." (We're in the central time zone.) At first this wasn't noticed by our children, since they were very young. Now, at eight and twelve, they assume that TV programming comes to a crashing and mysterious halt at eight o'clock. That's an exaggeration, but we rarely have trouble with that rule (and we do have trouble with rules, and our children, like most folks).

This matter of time is crucial, not only to avoid TV shows with a more questionable content but also to provide a free hour before the child's bedtime. This hour between TV and bedtime has given me the most memorable hours of my adult life. Much of the inevitable conversation that the children initiate just before lights out—partially a stalling technique, I'm sure—spins out of their television experience.

But too much TV blurs their focus. What is the right amount for your family, and how do you control that?

That all depends . . . which can be a most discouraging way to begin an answer. Even the best-established answers may not apply in your case. Take, for example, the reasonable guess by some child development experts that a preschooler should not watch more than one hour of TV a day, which, I think, is a good rule of thumb.

But there can be a difference, for example, between watching alone or with others. Preschoolers who watch TV with other children or even with a parent will talk along with the television and other viewers almost constantly. Alone, these same viewers talk less and tend more toward a private and probably passive experience if the amount of viewing exceeds about one hour. Only a wise and caring parent can evaluate those two different viewing experiences.

Researchers have discovered that "Sesame Street," viewed in groups, is a springboard for socializing: pointing things out, expressing delight, or murmuring disappointment. Though not necessarily less active in his response, the solitary viewer builds up a sense of a nonshared or private world. Going public is important for the preschool viewer. So one hour of TV a day might be too much for the child watching alone, while a little more than one hour might be fine for the group participant.

How much TV for those in grade school? Ten hours? Our family has settled on ten hours or less a week, but this is such a rough figure that it cannot cover the multitude of individual circumstances. The national average of over twenty hours a week seems immoderately high in almost all cases. Younger children especially can easily adapt to smaller amounts of television. Only a few of the children interviewed for this guide watched under ten hours, but those who were limited to that never complained about not being able to watch more.

Rigid control of any sort becomes more and more difficult and perhaps undesirable by the junior-high and high-school years. As comments from students reveal, viewing patterns established early become influential in later years, which we might expect. Children who receive loving care when young will return the favor on their own. Such children have had respect for the television experience as both a possible friend and a potential foe.

Go through your children's viewing time for an average week and mark everything down. You may be surprised.

Even the children we interviewed were surprised at how much television they actually watched. Parents will be, too.

Once you know how much television your child is watching, you may be able to come to an agreement about how much is too much. Together you may be able to establish some guidelines that will be more beneficial. As we all know, parental control is always wisest when exercised with discretion.

If you are unsuccessful, maybe you need to analyze how much time you spend together as a family. Or think of ways to divert your child's attention from television. Some planned family activities, a special effort on your part to play a game or read to a younger child, or a part-time job for a teenager may disrupt the long viewing hours. We all can think of ways to involve our children in other activities if we really try. It's taking the time to put these ideas into action that is difficult.

When our family cut back on the amount of TV, the children were permitted to select their favorites, with parental approval. Our son was then 6, our daughter 2½. For several years we didn't have to veto one show. If the amount is controlled, the selection process almost takes care of itself.

—From Paul Borgman, *TV: Friend or Foe?* Elgin, Ill.: David C. Cook Publishing Co., 1979.

FOR FURTHER READING:

Hancock, Maxine. *People in Process: The Preschool Years.* Old Tappan, N.J.: Fleming H. Revell Co., 1978.

McNulty, Edward N. *When TV Is a Member of the Family.* Nashville: Abingdon Press, 1976.

TESTS—INTELLIGENCE AND ACHIEVEMENT

SINCE EACH PERSON grows at his own individual rate, each child is a bit different from others in a classroom. Because abilities develop at different rates, at one age a child may struggle hopelessly to acquire a certain skill, such as writing. If he is given time to grow, he may acquire it easily when he is a little older.

If your youngster is a "slow developer," he may be 8 or 9 years old before he is ready to do well in school. A number of youngsters, especially boys, are not ready for such skills as reading until they are about 9. This doesn't mean that such children are less intelligent than others. It can mean that some have grown slowly and that, when their growth "catches up" with them, they may do much better work.

This matter of different rates of growth in children is so important that some experts are now urging that children not start the first grade until they are clearly ready for this experience. This depends on many things, such as physical size, ability to work with a group, capacity to speak fairly clearly, and interest in working with words and numbers.

Most schools study each child in a number of ways to find out how to guide him, his parents, and his teachers in making the most of his educational experience.

If your school gives intelligence tests, it is unlikely that you will be given your youngster's exact score. You may be told that he has below average, average, good, or excellent intellectual ability as measured by the test. One reason that schools hesitate to give exact scores is that they can be misleading. Intelligence tests, especially group ones, do not always give accurate results. Also, scores may change from time to time as a child is tested over the years. A good deal may depend on what test is used, how it is given and scored, a child's state of health, and how he feels about himself and school at the time he is tested.

When used carefully by trained persons, intelligence tests may be useful as one of many guides to your child's capacity to learn in school and to understand most school subjects, especially those which are based on reading and the use of words. These tests do not tell much about his special talents. Moreover, children who think in original and creative ways may not do as well on intelligence tests as might be expected.

The special aspects of a child's intelligence are least likely to be discovered when he is tested as part of a group. If you think your child is not getting all he might from his education and that more should be known about his mental ability, you might be able to arrange for him to have an individual test at school or elsewhere.

Parents often have strong feelings about intelligence and other tests. There is so much pressure today for success in school that it is common for everyone concerned to put too much emphasis on scores and grades. When parents get overly worried about these matters, children are likely to get upset, too. Upset children do not do as well on tests as their intelligence merits, and some do not enjoy or make the most of their education. It is more important for your child to be interested in what he is learning and to experience the joy of knowing than it is for him to get good test scores and honor grades.

Achievement Tests

Your child's measured intelligence is only one guide to his ability to learn in school. Other things, such as his interest in education, his health, and his self-confidence, play a big part in what he can and will do at school.

You can find out a good deal about what your child has learned so far through the scores that he gets on achievement tests. Many schools give these after a child has finished one or several grades. These tests are given in such fields as reading, use of words, number reasoning, and so on. Achievement test scores may be a useful guide as to what kind of individual help your child may need. However, the same warnings given about how intelligence tests are used apply to achievement tests, too.

Your child may need no help at all with his school progress. If he gets average or better scores in achievement tests, all may be well with his education. However, if his measured intelligence is high and his achievement scores are average or below, it's worth trying to find out why. Some very bright children coast along in school because they don't have enough to keep them interested or because standards are not set high enough for them. Some do poorly because their parents push them too hard.

On the other hand, some children get higher marks on their achievement tests than would seem likely in terms of their measured intelligence. There may be no reason to worry about differences of this sort unless your child seems to be working too hard and is anxiously pushing himself to be a school success.

—From *Your Child From 6 to 12*. Washington: U.S. Department of Health, Education and Welfare, 1966.

THUMB-SUCKING

NURSING FROM BREAST or bottle satisfies a deep need. A child who has not had a chance to suck sufficiently as he drinks milk may begin to suck his fingers, his thumb, or a blanket. Some children suck such objects practically from birth. Nursing is more than just getting milk, however. The feel of warm milk flowing into an empty stomach and the comfort of being cozily held bring emotional satisfactions as well. So what started out to be a physical response soon carries deeper meanings. Sucking re-creates the contentment of being held and fed.

In most cases, the child who is going to suck his thumb begins before he has been completely weaned. If he hasn't started by then, he probably won't except for brief trials during a time of particular stress, such as the discomfort of teething, or when he wants to test how it feels in imitation of a thumbsucker.

Many children will give it up of their own accord by the age of 3 or 3½. They outgrow the need for this type of comfort. Occasionally a child will suck his thumb when he is tired, or finds himself at loose ends, or feels temporarily unsure. At other times, he is his busy, sunny self.

A few children persist in sucking their thumbs long past the age of 4. They may suck so vigorously and for such a long period that they push the roof of the mouth up and may change the position of the upper teeth. Such children usually show in other ways that they are unhappy or feel discouraged. It works better to try to find out what the matter is than to interfere directly with the thumb-sucking. Splints, bad tasting medicine, and mittens do not work because they intensify the child's feelings of being unloved.

Parents who object to thumb-sucking may say that they are worried about germs, or that it looks babyish. They may feel uneasy about the pleasure the child gets from his body. Yet the germs a child will get from his thumb are no more numerous than those he gets in the natural course of his day. Remember, he's at the stage where he puts everything he can into his mouth. It's a way of learning. If you object to the appearance, remind yourself that the child is, after all, quite a young thing and has years ahead of himself to look grownup.

Some parents prefer to give the young baby a pacifier to give him all the sucking he needs. While it seems like the same thing, pacifiers and thumbs are different. Unlike a thumb, a pacifier can get lost, or become weakened by use and can cause choking if bits are swallowed the wrong way. If you decide to use a pacifier, keep two or three spares on hand in case one becomes mislaid or worn out.

One problem with a pacifier is that parents may get the habit themselves. It is so easy to reach for it automatically at the first whimper. They thus encourage the child to suck long past the time he might have stopped naturally. They need to be alert to little signs that the child is ready to give it up.

—From *Your Child From 1 to 6*. Washington: U.S. Department of Health, Education and Welfare, 1969.

TOILET TRAINING

THE TIME TO BEGIN to toilet train depends on the child. How can you tell if a child is ready? Physically he needs enough muscle control to stop a natural release. He has formerly let go whenever he felt pressure of urine or bowel material. Training involves teaching him to hold back, then. Just holding back isn't all, however. He needs to be able to tell you with a word or a sound, or a look on his face—or be able to get to the bathroom by himself. Even so, he'll probably need help with his clothing. After all this, he is to let go—promptly. Good toilet habits are a complicated business and require timing. To stop a natural release, to hold, and then to let go at a right time and place is what we are asking the child to do. You help, but it is up to him to manage it somehow.

Here is another clue to success in toilet training. Take advantage of his eagerness to be on his own and independent of you. This is quite different from "breaking" him of a bad habit, or punishing him for all his misdeeds by confining him to the toilet or other harsh methods. You know he is eager for your approval, and wants to cooperate. At the same time, however, he has ideas about being his own boss. A mother so often takes credit for training her child when actually the child should get the credit! He certainly gets the blame when things go wrong.

When the baby is 8 or 9 months old, some mothers begin to place him on a potty or toilet at a time when he usually has a bowel movement. If he is regular about his movements, they will be successful at catching him.

Success depends upon intimate knowledge of the child's pattern, and the fact that they began to place him on the toilet before he reached the stage where he wanted to be on the go every minute. They may proudly announce that they haven't had a messy diaper in weeks. As soon as their star pupil learns to crawl or walk, however, or if the rhythm changes, many find they are back where they started. The toddler acts as if he never heard of the idea.

Real bowel control can only be taught to most children after they learn to walk. If you're eager to get started, try it out to see if the child catches on. Supply a word for him to announce his wish to go to the toilet, or use his own sound. Place him for brief intervals on the toilet with the diaper on or off— so he learns how it feels.

Comfort and stability are important. A child should have good support for his back and feet. He may find a low seat less frightening than an adult fixture, with a child's toilet seat added. Bring him when you ex-

pect a bowel movement. Stay and talk with him. Take him off the toilet, success or no, after a while—seldom longer than 5 minutes.

If he struggles to be free, you gain nothing by forcing him to stay longer. He may be content to stand beside the toilet without removing his diaper. While this doesn't save a diaper, that isn't the goal here anyhow. The goal is to gradually get the idea of right place, at the right time, accepted.

Little children feel quite possessive about the products of their bodies, and don't view bowel movements with disgust. They are sure, at some point, to dabble in the toilet bowl or smear a bowel movement on the crib or walls. Try to temper your dismay as you clean up smearing with an understanding of the child's experimental frame of mind. In fact, you yourself are apt to act joyous about bowel movements when the child places them in the toilet. Some authorities observe that it must seem quite callous to a child when his mother noisily flushes them away. For this reason, or because the child may fear being flushed down himself, some mothers tactfully wait until the child has left the bathroom. Later on, of course, children enjoy working the handle themselves.

Fear of being flushed down the toilet occurs at a time when a child may also fear that he will slip down the drain in his bath. Such fears seem ridiculous to adults, but the child has a very poor notion of relative size. He experiments with the bulk of things in his play, fitting little things into big ones, and tries to shove big things into small spaces. It takes months of practice to get it all figured out. He hasn't much of an idea of his own size, either, in relation to doors, and drains, to chairs or doll carriages.

Regular, daily bowel movements have become a symbol of good health in the minds of many people, but such a pattern is not necessary at all. Many children have movements every other day or so. Unless the doctor pre-

429

scribes it during an illness, the use of suppositories or enemas is unwise. A diet which helps to keep the mass soft, plenty of exercise and fluids are better than medicines which lead to overconcern about a natural process.

Training the Bladder.   Training a child to stay dry is the next step. Without pressure, the child will gradually shift from wetness to dryness. This is better than an all-out push. "I'm training Bobby this week," implies that everything else is forgotten except concentration on trips to the bathroom. There may be tension about the state of the diaper at any time of day. Wet? A defeat. Dry? Run up the flag!

Around 1½ or 2, a child will tend to increase the space of time between voidings, as the bladder will fill up instead of emptying automatically. He understands more and has a few words he can use. He may be in a more cooperative frame of mind than he was at 1 year. He will be wanting to imitate others. He isn't so completely wrapped up in learning to walk and has a little extra time on his hands. Training will probably go faster if you wait until 18 months or so to start. Girls may be ready somewhat sooner than boys, as they are with other activities which require control and maturity.

Start by taking the child to the toilet when you find him dry. Very often this will be after a nap if you've gone to the child promptly when he awakens. Put a child in training pants. They are easier for him to manage and may give an incentive to stay dry. If you've been premature about making the change, though, don't threaten him about returning to "baby" diapers.

Some parents set up a regular schedule, such as before and midway between meals. The child's own rhythm is the best schedule to follow at the beginning, however.

Frequently, a child who has been doing well will have relapses. His learning is not fixed, and will be easily unsettled for months by such things as cooler weather, a slight cold, a visitor in the house, or excitement about a trip. Try to take these relapses without fuss or comment.

Sometimes even more serious troubles show up. A child may refuse to go to the bathroom at all, or will plainly show that he is so worried about having an accident he can scarcely do anything else. When this happens, relax your training, or give it up for a while. Disturbances may show up that seem not connected to training at all. He may be quite upset about getting his clothes dirty, for instance, or avoid touching soft or gooey things, or refuse to cooperate at mealtimes.

A child who has shown for a time that he understands what the toilet is for does not forget it easily. He probably catches on to things very quickly, much quicker than you want him to—such as where you keep the lemon drops. Therefore it is not necessary to scold or punish to fix the idea of toilet training in his head.

You may have started too soon. Or, he may feel he needs to boss this himself. A look at his life may give an answer. Does he have a chance to make decisions about how and what things are done to him? Is he getting any satisfactions from growing up, or has he decided that it is better to be a baby? Is he so afraid that he'll have an accident—he can't help having one?

Whatever the cause, you help him most by encouragement, not by punishment. Most children are 3 years old before they stay clean and dry in the daytime.

A child working on his toilet habits may be unable to perform in a strange bathroom or out of doors. The 2-year-old easily gets into a rut, and depends on familiar surroundings to respond. So, it is a good idea to vary the place and get him used to changes. On a trip, take along his toilet seat. You might tell him in advance that he will be using a new bathroom, or will have to urinate in the woods. Since his toilet seat may be a sign for release, parents may be able to hold the seat for him, over the grass or any suitable spot.

Little boys first urinate sitting down. The age when a boy learns to stand probably varies with the amount of male company he keeps (including father, of course) more than anything else. Male example will give the little girl ideas about a new way to urinate as well. While the results are discouraging to her, she will doubtless keep trying, on and off, until she accepts herself as she is.

Night Dryness. Staying dry at night comes later and hardly belongs in a chapter on toddlers. However, since parents want to be consistent, night dryness can be placed here. Before 4 years of age, occasional night wetting is to be expected, although some children are dry at nights even though wetting in the daytime. If you haven't struggled over daytime training you'll usually find that night dryness comes just as easily with your encouragement.

Some parents take their child to the toilet about the time they themselves are going to bed or very early in the morning. Some children are able to perform quickly, still asleep. If the child doesn't succeed so easily, is annoyed or upset, it is well to give it up. Some people feel that taking a sleeping child to the toilet may make him urinate in his sleep longer than if he were let alone.

Cutting down on liquids after 5 P.M. may help a child who understands the connection between drinks and an overfull bladder. However, if he regards this as a deprivation or a punishment, he may become rebellious

or fearful of an accident. When a child who has been dry at night feels unsure about the way things are going, when a new baby comes, for instance, wetting the bed may be a symptom of his doubts.

—From *Your Child From 1 to 6.* Washington: U.S. Department of Health, Education and Welfare, 1969.

FOR FURTHER READING:

Azrin, Nathan H., and Fox, Richard M. *Toilet Training in Less Than a Day.* New York: Pocket Books, Inc., 1980.

Mack, Alison. *Toilet Learning: The Picture Book Technique for Children and Parents.* Boston: Little, Brown & Co., 1978.

TOYS

BUYING TOYS for children is a lot like playing baseball. You strike out far more often than you get a hit. In fact, a good batting average is about the same: .300.

How can you avoid buying toys that your child plays with once and rarely again? Or that break so quickly you can scarcely remember them when you get the bill for them the following month? What toys will give your youngster the most play value per dollar of cost?

Here are some toy-buying suggestions compiled from interviews with mothers, children and preschool teachers and from material prepared for parents by the Illinois Montessori Society:

You should begin by shopping for toys with the interests, readiness and needs of your particular youngster in mind—not by basing your choices on an age group, a TV commercial or a memory of your own past childhood. In evaluating a toy purchase, you should think through exactly what your youngster will be doing with it. Wind-up-and-watch gadgets usually hold small-fry interest for only a short time, while toys that engage a child's active creativity—like blocks or a baby doll—may be enjoyed for years.

You should consider whether your youngster can successfully use the toy you are considering. Usually a child gets the most pleasure and use from a plaything that challenges him to some degree, but not so much that he is constantly frustrated.

Age levels suggested on many toy and game packages are often unrealistically high, particularly for children from mentally stimulating homes. Montessori teachers point out that if a youngster is shown how to handle delicate materials carefully, he usually can do so, even at a surprisingly young age.

You shouldn't buy a toy your child can't use without instructions from you—unless you are prepared to give him the patient, tactful kind of help he will need. Too many parents, for example, expect a five-year-old to play for hours with a dump truck, although he has never seen one in operation.

"Don't let the toy increase your child's dependence," advises the Illinois Montessori Society. "Avoid toys which require too many verbal directions (this does not rule out games which child and parent can play together).

"Choose toys that are self-correcting, that have a built-in control of error (such as an inlaid wooden puzzle). Remember, the child isn't embarrassed if the toy tells him he made a mistake, but he may be if the parent has to tell him so."

You should make sure the toy you are considering is fun to play with—and that it gives your youngster something new to learn. "The fun value increases the learning value and vice versa," notes the Illinois Montessori Society. "A child can't learn from a toy he doesn't use."

You should also check to see how durable and well made the plaything is. Will it last long enough with reasonable handling to serve the purpose for which it is intended? Is it aesthetic rather than over-gimmicked and garish? Is the design good or does it detract and distract from the purpose of the toy? Do the parts that are supposed to move really work? Are your youngster's fingers strong and skilled enough to do what the toy requires?

Do you have room for the toy now? Big road-racing sets, indoor croquet, electric-train layouts and large-size building blocks come with built-in problems if your home is small. Do you have storage space for the toy you're considering? Is the container adequate? Does it have lots of little pieces that will be easily lost? Can your youngster care for it and put it away himself?

In choosing toys, you should consider the overall balance of playthings your child possesses. He needs toys to encourage him to use both large and small muscles, to provide indoor and outdoor activity, to develop eye-hand coordination, to suggest restful activity, to stimulate creativity and to teach new skills. He should have toys that provide him with comfort and companionship, that help him develop new concepts, that give him opportunities to play with other youngsters and with adults.

"Don't let your child's toy collection overemphasize one type of activity, though the emphasis may change from one period to another," advises the Illinois Montessori Society. "For instance, the toddler is in an active stage and will need toys that require a lot of large muscle manipulation, whereas the pre-teen is ready for more quiet, intricate activities."

You should learn to know the manufacturers that produce good toys. There are several companies which are more interested in marketing low-key, aesthetic playthings children really use than in flashy gimmicks that can be oversold via TV commercials.

You can often find excellent "toys" in places other than toy stores and toy counters. One wise and understanding grandfather, for example, bought his grandson, six, an adult safe with a combination lock because he realized how often the boy was frustrated and upset when his small treasures were disturbed by three younger children. The six-year-old was delighted.

Most youngsters would rather have "real" objects than toy replicas and usually the real equipment is easier to manipulate than the toy copies. You can find excellent gifts for children in a hardware store, lumber yard, florist shop, art-supply store, stationery store, drug store, camera store, pet shop, biological supply house—and book store. When the Illinois Montessori Society surveyed parents to learn what toys their children used and enjoyed most, many of the items listed were not toys at all. Included on the list were kitchen tools such as a cheese grater with turning handle, a peeler and a cheese slicer.

Other top play-value-per-dollar toys included a child-sized sink and cupboard, an indoor slide, a rope swing, a jumbo inflatable ball, several varieties of blocks, wooden puzzles, wooden shape-sorting boxes, colored pencils, reading and phonics materials, dominoes and easy board games.

—From Joan Beck, *Effective Parenting*. New York: Simon and Schuster, Inc., 1976.

FOR FURTHER READING:

Kaban, Barbara. *Choosing Toys for Children: From Birth to Five*. New York: Schocken Books, Inc., 1979.

Spock, Benjamin. *Baby and Child Care*. New York: Pocket Books, Inc., 1980.

TRAVEL

THE MOST DIFFICULT time to travel with children is the early years, especially if cribs, playpens, toys, and similar requisites are not available en route or at your destination. Many families find when they are traveling in a car with small children that they have to invest in a cartop carrier or trailer to carry everything they need.

The child himself, however, especially under the age of one, is not much trouble on a trip. Fathers and mothers can share the driving and diapering. Mothers who breast feed can usually do so inconspicuously as they travel on the open highway. Mothers who bottle feed their babies have an enormously more complicated task; Benjamin Spock's *Baby and Child Care* has detailed recommendations.

Travel makes special demands on every member of the family. Most families today travel by car or plane. As children get old enough, involve them in the planning of the trip. If you sit down around the dining room or kitchen table and spread out maps, children can learn early how to read a map and locate interesting places to see.

When the day to leave is a day or so away, children can be encouraged to plan what they want to take on the trip—toys, teddy bears or dolls, and so forth. Many families find that children enjoy having their very own suitcase. Parents can help them pack the suitcase. In addition, pillows and blankets should be put inside the car, along with a box of foodstuffs, tissues, and selected storybooks, punch-outs, and games.

An early start for a long trip is usually advisable. Some families like to load up the car

433

the night before, except for such last-minute items as pajamas. Before you drive off, pause for a moment to pray together that the Lord will protect you as you travel and keep you alert and happy as a family.

As you travel do not forget that small children need frequent stops to stretch their legs and go to the bathroom. Service stations and roadside rest stops should punctuate your trip. Many parents find it a good idea to change their children's seats as they change drivers. Children will be happier too if parents try to keep reasonably close to the family's usual schedule for meal and bed times. Children will often come up with their own games and activities. When arguments and quarrels break out, however, parents should be ready with a game or other diversion, such as finding the letters of the alphabet or numbers in sequence on car license plates or billboards. If parents plan on hourly stops, the family should arrive at its destination in a reasonably comfortable state. They should, however, plan on stopping early enough to locate a motel and get older children fed and in bed at their usual times if they plan on more than a one-day journey.

—LESLIE R. KEYLOCK

FOR FURTHER READING:

Gieseking, Hal. *The Complete Handbook for Travelers.* New York: Pocket Books, Inc., 1981.

Kaye, Dena. *The Traveling Woman: An Indispensible Guide to the Pleasures and Perils of Traveling . . . with Kids.* Garden City, N.Y.: Doubleday & Co., 1980.

TRUANCY

MANY BOYS AND GIRLS complain about school, dislike to see vacation end and school begin, and occasionally build a real or fancied indisposition into an excuse to stay home from school. Perhaps they "play hooky" now and then. Despite their protests, however, such children, like most children, accept the fact that they must go to school, and probably any one of them would protest if he or she were individually kept from school while the other youngsters continued to go. When a child persistently stays away from school without his parents' knowledge or consent, his behavior is unusual and can be taken as a sign that he is struggling unsuccessfully with some difficulty.

A child may have compelling reasons, according to his own lights, for staying away from school. If he is a slow learner or through some other cause has fallen behind in his work, the frustration and discouragement of the school day may be more than he can face. His relationship with his classmates may not be happy; some physical or other difference may be making him feel an outsider. An older child may feel he needs to prove his daring to his friends.

Talking it over, especially with a child in the lower grades, sometimes reveals a relatively simple problem. He may be staying away from school because the teacher scolds, or his classmates play too roughly, or he is afraid of the tests. A school program is sometimes too far out of line with an individual youngster's interests and capabilities. Children are bored when they are ahead of the class and the work offers no challenge. In high school, academic subjects often seem useless and a waste of time to a boy or girl who wants vocational training. If there is no sympathetic teacher or school adviser with whom to talk over a difficulty, and if for some reason he does not feel free to discuss it with his parents, staying away from school may seem to an unhappy youngster the only way out.

Even when a specific school difficulty is discovered and dealt with, however, a boy or girl may continue to play truant. Serious truancy is usually a sign of deeper difficulties than appear on the surface, and many factors are likely to be involved. The reasons such a youngster offers for staying away from school are for the most part excuses, confused, inconsistent, and not really capable of being talked out. Emotional conflicts having to do with home or school or friends, or a combination of these, perhaps of long standing, may be the cause both of the child's trouble with schoolwork and lack of interest in it and his staying away from school.

Whatever the basis for an individual child's truancy, truancy itself brings problems. A youngster who is not in school when he should be is necessarily furtive about where and how he spends the time. Even if he does not become involved in activities or with companions harmful to his welfare, at best he is simply waiting out the school day unproductively and without genuine satisfactions. He is compelled to lie and deceive and in many ways to put himself farther and farther out of line with what he knows is right and what his parents and teachers expect of him. His truancy may momentarily relieve his resentments as a way of hurting his family or lashing out against the world for his unhappiness; but, far from solving his difficulties, it increases his guilt, anger, and fear and makes him feel still more isolated and alone. Truancy is not necessarily a forerunner of delinquency, but most delinquent boys and girls are found to have been truants.

Attempts to force a truant into regular school attendance, either by parental threats and punishments or by the police methods of the old-fashioned truant officer, are rarely effective. Today's attendance supervisor, as he is called, tries rather to understand the child and his emotional problems and to enlist the co-operation of parents and teachers toward helping the youngster work out his difficulty. Usually the attendance supervisor also makes use of community agencies and other resources to guide a boy or girl to a club or youth center for companionship, interesting activities, and sympathetic adult leadership; to help a teen-ager find an afternoon or Saturday job for the worth-while experience of earning money and doing useful, responsible work; to help a family improve a situation that may be part of the child's trouble.

Many general causes are offered to explain truancy, such as poor educational methods, unsympathetic teachers, overcrowded schools, prejudices against children of minority groups, low community standards, and parental neglect. The background of an individual child's truancy, however, needs to be individually explored and understood, and the child needs all the help that parents and school authorities can give him.

In cases of serious truancy the services of a child-guidance counselor are almost always necessary. If the situation is not corrected, the law eventually steps in. It is worth every effort to help the truant out of his trouble before he is involved with the juvenile courts.

—From *The New Encyclopedia of Child Care and Guidance.* Garden City, N.Y.: Doubleday & Co., 1968.

FOR FURTHER READING:

Lichter, Solomon O., et al. *The Drop-Outs.* New York: Free Press, 1962.

TWINS

LIKE ANY RARE and unusual occurrence, the arrival of twins is bound to arouse considerable excitement and curiosity. It also confronts the parents with many questions and situations requiring special answers and solutions.

Biology of: There are three types of twins: the identical, the non-identical of the same sex, and the non-identical of mixed sex. The three types occur in approximately equal numbers. Identical twins develop from one ovum which, at an early stage, splits into two equal parts; non-identical or fraternal twins result from the nearly simultaneous fertilization of two ova.

When twins of the same sex look very much alike, it is often difficult to determine whether or not they are identical. Examination of the placentas at birth furnishes no conclusive evidence for or against identity. It is difficult to establish really conclusive criteria; most authorities agree that twins can be presumed to be identical if they have the same blood type, the same coloring of eyes and hair, and similar fingerprints. The only positive proof of identity known so far is impractical for general application—the successful transplantation of skin from one twin to the other.

The scientific study of twins has contributed substantially to today's understanding of heredity. Since identical twins develop from the same egg, fertilized by the same sperm, they have exactly the same inheritance. Differences in their environment as they grow up may be taken to indicate how modifiable the human personality is. Significant results have come from the study of many pairs of twins who had been separated at an early age and could be compared as adults. Differences between being brought up in city or country, in a relatively poor or well-to-do home, differences in religion and schooling, in trade or occupation, and other environmental factors have displayed themselves as differences in interests, skills, practical or theoretical intelligence. On the other hand, details of appearance, body structure, physiological details such as graying of the hair and balding, voice, and the onset of communicable diseases have appeared with

striking similarity. Such studies suggest that the heredity is more fixed than was generally supposed, and that capacity for various kinds of learning and adjustment is more subject to external conditions than was generally assumed.

There is considerable evidence that the likelihood of having twins is in itself hereditary, in that it is more frequent in some families or races than in others. According to latest statistics, about one mother in 97 is likely to have twins. Women are more likely to have them between 30 and 38 than at other ages. The greater age of the father appears to be another factor, regardless of the mother's age.

Care and guidance of: Even though a baby may have been born at full term, he is considered premature if his birth weight is less than five and a half pounds. With most twins, one or the other, if not both, usually weighs less.

Depending on the degree of their prematurity, twins will need special care, particularly in connection with their feeding. Usually it is necessary for one or both babies to spend at least the first few days in an incubator. Thus it is impossible for the mother to nurse them, even if she has sufficient milk.

Only in rare instances is the mother able to nurse both infants. Exceptional cases have been reported of mothers who not only nursed both twins but managed to do so on a flexible schedule according to the needs of each child; when both were hungry at the same time, they were even nursed at the same time.

Feeding both infants by bottle is certainly less strenuous, even though time must be found to prepare the formula. Since all babies need warmth and cuddling almost as much as nourishment, bottle-fed babies should be held as though they were being nursed. The happiest situation for twins, therefore, occurs when two people are available at feeding time, or when one of the babies can wait a short time for his bottle without too much distress. When both twins are hungry at the same time, a compromise may be made by holding one and propping the bottle for the other, alternating the procedure at the next feeding.

It is of the greatest importance that twins should receive as much individual attention as possible. At best, each will receive only a portion of the attention that is normally given to a child born singly. This fact is frequently overlooked, especially since twins inevitably take much more of a mother's time than would a singleton. Many instances have been reported of twins who developed a language of their own, and in most cases this could be traced to lack of sufficient individual attention. This private language not only retards their learning to talk but also delays their communicating with others and thus handicaps their social development.

Twins usually learn to share and to wait their turn at an earlier age than other children. Contrary to popular opinion, however, their feelings of rivalry and jealousy are frequently stronger than those of brothers and sisters of different ages. As twins become aware of their own individualities, the competition usually diminishes.

There is often a tendency to forget that twins are individual persons and want to be themselves. Mothers and fathers can help a great deal by not emphasizing the twinship. Giving them names that are not too similar helps to establish the individuality of each twin; dressing them differently is another way. If similar types of clothes are bought while the twins are small, it is a good idea to select them at least in different colors. The children can enjoy their twin-ship in their own ways, without being hindered in the development of their respective personalities.

Again, when the twins reach school age, it is desirable to have them placed in different sections of the same grade; when this is not possible, perhaps the teacher can be impressed with the fact that they are individuals and that it is important to distinguish between the behavior, the personality traits, and the abilities of the two children.

One twin may always take the lead, appear more capable and quicker to learn. Usually this is only temporary; the roles reverse and continue to alternate. One twin may take longer in learning to read and then, once he has learned, prove to be the better reader; however, he may be prevented from reaching the peak of his ability if parents and teacher decide from the beginning that the other twin is the better reader. This danger can be avoided by letting each take his own pace, in different classrooms when possible.

Attending different sections of the same grade has another important advantage. It is then easier for each child to make his own friends and to feel that he is liked for himself, not because twins as such are popular.

The amount of attention that new twins in the family are bound to attract can cause the older children to feel more than the usual resentment against the babies. Since the twins necessarily take up most of the mother's time, the other children not only feel, but unavoidably are, somewhat neglected. The older child is apt to make a determined play for attention—by being naughty or becoming a showoff, to mention just two of the most frequent methods. His parents help him by treating this behavior leniently at the same time that they let him know they understand the reason for it and try to give him some of their time for himself.

The child who is younger than the twins will experience feelings similar to those of the younger child in any family. Unable to stand up against the two, he may try to "divide and conquer" or to play one twin against the other. When they gang up on him, as they often tend to do, he is likely to develop considerable belligerence in trying to hold his own.

The twins themselves gain a great deal of satisfaction and reassurance when they are able to act as a team. It becomes the difficult task of their parents to find a delicate balance between permitting the twins the pleasure and security they can derive from their satisfying but exclusive relationship without letting them grow so dependent on it that one feels lost without the other.

—From *The New Encyclopedia of Child Care and Guidance.* Garden City, N.Y.: Doubleday & Co., 1968.

FOR FURTHER READING:

Noble, Elizabeth. *Having Twins: A Parent's Guide to Pregnancy, Birth and Early Childhood.* Boston: Houghton Mifflin Co., 1980.

Theroux, Rosemary, and Tingley, Josephine. *The Care of Twin Children: A Common-Sense Guide for Parents.* Chicago: Center for Multiple Gestation, 1978.

V

VACATIONS

THE LENGTHS AND TYPES of vacations are almost numberless. With over half the families of the country containing mothers who work outside the home, most vacations today are two or three weeks in length. Many people today prefer to take several short vacations rather than one extensive trip, especially with the cost of gas having skyrocketed in the last decade. Where both parents work, vacations need to be planned in advance so both parents can arrange to take the same days off.

The type of vacation will depend on family interests. The majority of vacations involve relatives in some way. Most common are visits to grandparents. Some families travel by car to visit interesting tourist attractions in their own and surrounding states and provinces. The array of recreational vehicles now available provides an almost infinite spectrum of camping opportunities, from the pup tent to the luxurious "Class A" motor home. Most popular is the pop-up trailer that can be pulled by the family car and hooked up to outlets at campgrounds and national parks. Other families prefer to buy or rent a cottage near a lake rather than travel. Each family has to decide which of the alternatives most suits its interests.

Families need to remember that the purpose of a vacation is relaxation, rest, fun, and variation from the normal busy routine. Do not plan on doing so much you arrive back exhausted and needing to "rest up from your vacation" on the job. It is also usually not a good idea to allow too little time for the return trip so you arrive home tired and irritable.

A vacation in God's beautiful world can be one of the greatest gifts you can provide your family. Whenever possible, you should give your children the benefits of a vacation away from home, even if you can only afford to take a day or two at a not-too-distant beach or historical or tourist attraction.

—LESLIE R. KEYLOCK

FOR FURTHER READING:

Belgum, Harold J. *Family Vacation Idea Book*. St. Louis: Concordia Publishing House, 1966.

Calhoun. *Vacation Time, Leisure Time, Any Time You Choose*. Nashville: Abingdon Press.

VENEREAL DISEASE

THE LAST TOPIC we need to discuss that relates to the risks of sexual promiscuity is venereal disease. Since VD (the abbreviation for venereal disease) is reportedly at epidemic proportions in this country, let us briefly discuss the main types. Knowing about these will enable you to teach your teenager about the dangers of these diseases when they are unrecognized or untreated.

439

Gonorrhea

The most common form of VD is gonorrhea. It is caused by a germ that can be easily identified under an ordinary microscope. In the female cervix and vagina, this germ may live without causing much discomfort, though it often causes severe infection and great pain. During sexual intercourse with a woman who is infected with this germ, it is almost certain to infect the man's urethra and penis. This infection causes severe pain upon urination and a thick, yellowish discharge. The condition will, in time, tend to improve, but meanwhile he will infect anyone with whom he has sexual contact. Each, in turn, will infect other sexual contacts, and an epidemic is underway.

Though this germ is developing a resistance to the antibiotics that can kill it, gonorrhea is still quite easily cured by proper medical care. When untreated, however, it may cause such inflammation and scarring of the sensitive tissues in the reproductive tract, that sterility may result. A person so damaged may never be able to have children. A baby born to a mother who carries this germ in her vagina during its delivery is very likely to develop a serious eye infection. It is obvious that, when untreated, this disease has extremely serious complications that can be completely avoided by good medical care.

Venereal Warts

Another common form of VD is known as venereal warts. This disease causes the growth of wartlike tissue that is ugly and annoying, though not painful. The warts grow in a coarse, grayish brown cluster about the penis or on the labia. They are caused by a virus and must be treated by a physician, but they are entirely curable.

Syphilis

The most serious type of VD, because of its long-range complications, is syphilis. It is caused by a corkscrew shaped microscopic germ called a "spirochete." When this germ enters a human body through a scratch or even an irritated area of mucous membrane in the reproductive tract or elsewhere, it will cause a sore. This sore is only slightly painful, and for this reason, it may be dismissed as not being serious enough to require medical care. It heals very slowly, and is round with a raised border that causes it to look a bit like a paper punch has been used to make it. The sore may be on the skin in the genital area where it can be easily seen, or it can develop internally, where it may go unnoticed.

Because this lesion is not too bothersome, and if it happens to be inside a woman's vagina, she will probably not even know it is there. Syphilis, therefore, is often neglected and left untreated. When untreated, the germ will slowly migrate through the bloodstream or body tissues to any part of the body where it lies dormant. Years later, a crippling form of arthritis may develop, a serious brain infection causing permanent loss of normal mental functioning can occur, or a baby born to an untreated syphilitic mother is almost certain to have serious birth defects. The other results are too many to list. The important fact is that syphilis can be cured. It needs careful, long-term follow-up, but it is completely curable.

Herpetic VD

A fairly new venereal disease is called "herpetic VD." It is caused by one of several viruses that also cause cold sores or fever blisters about the mouth and nose. Some authorities believe it has become a problem in the reproductive tract because of the fairly widespread practice of oral sex. At any rate, it is painful and it is almost untreatable. The ulcerations it causes can be cauterized with chemicals, but this is painful and may not cure it after all. As with most infections caused by viruses, however, the body does tend to fight it and recover its health.

Vaginal Infections

There are two common vaginal infections that are not usually spread through sexual intercourse, though they may be. They are caused by microorganisms called yeast and Trichomonas. Both of these infections can be easily picked up in a bathtub or from swimming. They commonly occur after long or intensive treatment with antibiotics. They produce a vaginal discharge that causes severe itching and burning. Since the urethra and urinary bladder are very close to the vagina, there may be a bladder infection as well.

Treatment of these diseases is best recommended by your physician. He can prescribe medication to be inserted in the vagina and may order oral medication to completely cure them. Though men rarely have any symptoms of these infections, they may carry the organisms. A husband and wife can bounce this sort of infection back and forth between them without any other sexual exposure. In such cases, oral treatment is necessary for both spouses.

It is unfortunate that one needs to include negative topics in a book such as this. Teaching our children about sex ought to be positive and happy. In our Western world, however, these tragedies are reality. We do have incest, abortions, and venereal disease, and you parents need to know and understand these issues.

The happy side to such information is that, in most instances, you can prevent these problems from happening to your children. Your awareness of the possibility of such tragic episodes in their lives can make you watchful and protective. Through your information and responsibility, you may teach your children more effectively. Your positive attitude will invite them to come to you before they become involved in something that could be harmful to them. This positive life cycle can be transferred to your children as they grow so that they, too, will benefit from healthy attitudes, accurate information, and a sense of responsibility.

—From Grace H. Ketterman, M.D., *How to Teach Your Child About Sex*. Old Tappan, N.J.: Fleming H. Revell, 1981.

FOR FURTHER READING:

Busch, Phyllis S. *What About VD?* School Book Service, 1976.

Chiappa, Joseph A., and Forish, Joseph J. *The VD Book*. New York: Holt, Rinehart and Winston, 1977.

VIOLENCE

PARENTS ARE IN A POSITION to do far more good or evil to their children than preacher or teacher or anyone else. Only if parents abandon this opportunity do children find their chief influences in others, particularly their peers. But such abandoning responsibility is in itself an act of violence comparable to turning away from the shouts of help coming from a drowning child in a river.

Not much at all of the violence parents practice on their children can be discussed here. We will not be able to go into the "battered-baby syndrome" even though this mass epidemic in the United States in the last decade is one of the striking examples in which the United States populace is far more violent than our European neighbors. All that will be discussed here are a few of the ways in which parents stunt the moral growth of their children. The evidence will be taken from *The Psychology of Moral Behavior* by Derek Wright, a summary of the research that has been done on this subject, mainly in the last generation.

An essential point to begin with is the fact that it is becoming clear that parents do largely control the moral growth of their children and so can make a decision on just what they want to produce: "Perhaps the most fundamental policy decision that parents concerned with their children's morality have to make is whether they wish them to grow into morally autonomous persons or moral replicas of themselves. The natural process of development would seem to be towards such autonomy; but parents have it in their power to further or to retard this development." The biblical imperative to love falls precisely in this category of moral autonomy: we do not know what situations others will face and so we cannot reasonably know what loving is going to mean for them. Thus the Christian standard, in Augustine's words, is "love and do as you please," the meaning being that one who loves will decide from within himself to do what is loving. Parents who inhibit the ability to love, which means to be free to find what loving means in each new situation, are doing violence to their children.

The most important thing a parent can do is to give his child a feeling of self-esteem, of self-worth, which comes from love, acceptance, and support. One study of delinquents and nondelinquents showed that "those who at the later age (16) had not become delinquent, presented a much more favorable picture of themselves at the earlier (age 12) testing." This suggests that parents who harp on bad qualities and continually suggest their children will turn out bad are practic-

ing violence on them, helping to make them become that way.

A similar way in which parents can have negative effects on their children is by demanding a particular level of achievement as necessary for real acceptance. This is legalism, and its effects are disastrous morally as St. Paul suggests (Romans 7:7–11). Wright reports that one experiment produced the conclusion that "children whose parents put great emphasis upon achievement at school cheated more in tests of achievement." For the bright student this is perhaps not the case, for pressure may bring out harder work. But for the majority, for average and poor students, the need to relieve the parental pressure to succeed can easily drive them to cheat. Driving a child to cheat in order to escape intolerable pressure is one of the commonest forms of psychological violence parents practice.

Finally, a brief comment needs to be made on the general atmosphere that tends to breed the frustrated and aggressive character: "Delinquent subjects saw their parents as unhappily married and frequently quarrelling, and their own relationships to their parents tended to be characterized by mutual rejection.... The more delinquent subjects saw their parents, and especially their fathers, as generally unjust and inconsistent." It may be that these conditions are rather difficult to change, but they are not inevitable, people can change with help. Thus when such conditions as these are perpetrated by parents, they are not only doing violence to themselves but are driving their children in a direction that will produce substantial misery to themselves as well as to many others. To the extent, therefore, that parents do not seek help to rectify these conditions, they are guilty of psychological violence, cutting into their children every day of their lives.

This very brief survey of psychological

violence is meant mainly as an instigation to further thought rather than as a comprehensive survey or analysis. Hopefully readers of these lines will have their minds joggled sufficiently to begin to ponder the way they treat those who are under their power. Usually we act as we do because we think that is the proper way to carry out our responsibilities. For most people the psychological violence they perform is not recognized, not intended, and not accepted as injurious if it is recognized.

The major problem is that those in power are usually ignorant of the immediate and long-term effects of their actions on the psychological and spiritual make-up of their victims. In addition, the images of man that are presupposed by many parents, teachers, and so on, are far from the biblical picture and thus the goals that are sought for children are un-Christian. Clearly this is the topic for a whole other treatise and so the few words said here can only hint at it.

In sum, it often happens that people with personal power over others exercise it in such a way that they are perpetrators of psychological violence which produces one or many of the following characteristics: lack of self-esteem; fear of failing; diminished curiosity, imagination, and creativity; rigidity; inability to learn; lack of love; inability to resist temptation; frustration; aggressiveness and a propensity for committing violence; right on up to the deeper neurotic or psychotic characteristics.

—From Peter W. Macky, *Violence: Right Or Wrong?* (pp. 121–123) Waco, Tex.: Word Books, 1973.

FOR FURTHER READING:

O'Neill, Dan. *The Mark of Cain.* Snohomish, Wash.: Omega Publishing Co., 1979.

Sider, Ronald J. *Christ and Violence.* Scottdale, Pa.: Herald Press, 1979.

Tournier, Paul. *The Violence Within.* New York: Harper and Row Publishers, 1978.

VOCATION AND WORK

CHOOSING A VOCATION is one of man's most significant and far-reaching decisions. Our choice of occupation determines how we will spend at least one-third of our waking hours, for this is the minimum amount of time that most people spend at work during their adult lives. Our work determines our income and this, in turn, affects one's standard of living and place of residence. The kind of work that we do and the success of our careers have an influence on the type of people we have for friends, on our status in the community, on the kind of relationships we have with our families (the homelife of a busy pastor will likely be very different from that of an office worker or traveling salesman), on our general satisfaction with life (it is hard to be really happy if you hate your job), and on our emotional well-being and feelings of self-worth. Even the church that a person attends is related to his work. There are exceptions, of course, but studies have shown that business executives and professional people tend to affiliate with Episcopalian and Presbyterian while the Baptist church is frequently the choice of "workingmen."

The selection of an occupation has added importance for the Christian. When we acknowledge that Christ is Lord, we must turn over our whole lives—including our working lives—to His control. It becomes crucial, then, that our choice of an occupation be in accordance with divine will, and that our daily work be done diligently "as unto Christ" (Ephesians 6:5, 6).

In view of the social, psychological and theological importance of work, the choice of a vocation should be made with great care and deliberation. Too often, however, the decision is made in a haphazard and hurried fashion. Parents, teachers, friends, and others in our society expect occupational decisions to be made early. Thus, at a time when they are inexperienced, idealistic, and struggling with the problems of adolescence, young people have the added responsibility of choosing from an almost unlimited number of career possibilities. Is it surprising that so many end up dissatisfied and frustrated with their jobs? For perhaps vast numbers of people, work does not offer any challenge but is, instead, a boring drudgery which must be endured—for life.

To help people avoid this unhappy situation and make wise occupational choices, vocational guidance counseling has become more and more prominent within recent years. Industries, governmental agencies, private employment organizations, and schools have hired specialists who are trained to help individuals choose, prepare for, embark on, and adjust to an occupation. These vocational counselors are thoroughly familiar with the occupational world and have the ability to administer and interpret psychological tests, the results of which can be of great help to the job seeker. Rarely, however, do professional people consider the will of God in one's choice of work. It is here that the church leader can play a special role. He cooperates with the professional vocational counselor, but adds a dimension which is uniquely Christian. His concern extends not only to those who are trying to choose a vocation, but also to those who are frustrated in their jobs, or struggling with decisions about education, or for some reason unable to work, or facing the boredom of retirement.

Vocational Counseling Techniques

Whenever one person talks with another about a career choice, vocational counseling is, to some extent, taking place. Whether the counseling is of this informal nature or more professional in character, it involves three basic aspects: being familiar with the world of work, knowing the counselee, and guiding in the making of decisions.

Knowing the World of Work

What would you really like to accomplish in your life work? If you ask this question, people usually give one or more of the following answers: "to help people," "to get personal success in terms of money or fame," or "to express myself in some way" (as in writing or art). To achieve goals such as these, a lot of people apparently think that they must enter a profession. This is highly unrealistic and for many will lead to severe disappointment. In one survey, for example, it was found that 80 percent of high school counselees had been encouraged by their counselors (and probably by their parents) to prepare for a professional career. However, qualifications for a profession are high, and only about 20 percent of teenagers can eventually be accommodated by the professions, so it is clear that 60 percent had overly high aspirations and eventually were forced to lower their sights and enter less prestigious positions.

This kind of disappointment can be prevented if the counselor knows something about the world of work and the requirements for various occupations. But this is not an easy task. Literally thousands of job opportunities are available, and even the professional guidance counselor cannot keep fully abreast of all developments in the field. How, then, can the pastor, Sunday School teacher, or other church leader help the occupation seeker? The answer is twofold: show him where to get information, and suggest the questions that he should ask about different jobs.

Sources of Information. Two of the best places to get occupational information are in the school guidance office and the local library. Frequently these places contain occupational information files, books describing various vocations, catalogs and brochures describing training or educational opportunities, and relevant government publications. In the United States, for example, the government produces several helpful publications, including the *Occupational Outlook Handbook*, the *Occupational Guides* and the *Dictionary of Occupational Titles*. The latter, usually referred to as the DOT, is the most complete source of information. Published in several volumes, it is a massive compilation which describes thousands of jobs and categorizes them into seven major occupational groupings:

professional and managerial occupations
clerical and sales occupations
service occupations
agricultural, fishery, forestry and kindred occupations
skilled occupations
semiskilled occupations
unskilled occupations

A second source of information is the people who live in the community who are willing to talk about their work. A good way to learn about the insurance business, for example, is to talk with an insurance salesman. While such interviews can be helpful, they are time-consuming and limited by the availability of resource people.

Third, information is often available from trade unions and professional organizations. When someone asks me for information about the profession of psychology, for example, I usually suggest that they write to the American Psychological Association and request a booklet entitled *A Career in Psychology*. Many other organizations provide similar occupational literature.

Type of Information. When one has located the depository of information, what sort of things does he look for as he tries to find out about jobs? This will vary from situation to situation. Some occupations are rare or obscure and we need to ferret out a great deal of information. Other fields of work are well known and the counselee may only want to uncover one or two pertinent facts.

If some member of the church is interested in vocational guidance, we can perform a useful service by telling him where vocational information is available, and then meeting with him to discuss his findings. This collection of information is only a part of vocational guidance, but it can be a significant and important part.

Knowing the Counselee

There are many reasons why people choose to enter a specific occupation. The opinions of parents are very important—especially with younger people—but in addition there are the influence of friends or teachers, the interest that comes from hobbies and extracurricular activities, the glamour and prestige that are associated with different occupations (being a surgeon sounds much more attractive than being a used-car salesman), the information that describes various careers, and the student's evaluation of his own abilities and potentialities.

One of the guidance counselor's biggest tasks is to help the counselee get a more realistic appraisal of himself. The professional vocational counselor would probably conduct an interview and give a number of tests in order to get this information. But even without skills in psychological testing, the church leader can help the counselee to evaluate himself in the following areas:

General Ability. A lot of people may want to be physicians but not many people are smart enough to handle the rigorous requirements of medical school. In vocational counseling we must try to help the counselee set his aspirations in accordance with his ability. Usually this will involve slowing down someone whose goals are unrealistically high, but occasionally we must encourage capable people who have set their sights too low. The student's grades are often a good indication of his ability and of his potential for performance in later schooling.

Specific Abilities. Most of us have special abilities in at least one or two areas and these should be considered in vocational planning. Some people, for example, are mechanically inclined—they can fix anything. Others have unusual musical ability or a special way of getting along with people. Equally important are a person's noticeable weaknesses. A person who can't throw a ball obviously would be ill-advised if we encouraged a career in baseball.

Personality Traits. People with equal intellectual ability are not equally suited for the same occupations. Some are shy and withdrawn; others are outgoing. Some like a lot of change; others prefer life to be more orderly and routine. Some are cheerful, impulsive, active or critical, while others might be less cheerful, prone to plan carefully, and more lethargic and accepting. Personality differences such as these are very important in vocational choice and adjustment. The person who wants to be a missionary had better be flexible, accepting and able to get along with people, for example, or he is heading for trouble.

Interests. Our likes and dislikes are also important in career choice. While tests give a good summary of such interests, it can also be helpful to reflect on our preferences and jot these down on a piece of paper. As a start, we might ask how we spend our spare time and money. This is an excellent barometer of one's values and gives a good clue to one's interests. It should be emphasized that the counselee should try to identify his own real interests and not simply reflect on the suggestions and aspirations of his parents or teachers.

Spiritual State. The person who is deeply committed to Christ and wanting to serve Him in all aspects of life, will approach vocational counseling with different aspirations than will the non-Christian or the half-hearted believer. The Christian counselor would certainly want to ascertain the counselee's spiritual state, therefore, and at some time discuss the believer's responsibility to spend his life in service to Christ and in the place of His choosing.

Other Factors. Certain occupations are closed to people on the basis of sex, age, physique, health, lack of training or other similar issues. In spite of civil rights legislation, color of skin still seems to be a barrier to success in some occupations and, in others, citizenship is a deterrent. In some states, for example, a non-American cannot get a license to teach or practice his profession—regardless of his competence or quality and place of training. In most denominations, women cannot be ordained as ministers; and no mission society will accept candidates who are physically unhealthy. Individual differences such as these must be considered in vocational planning.

Guidance in the Decision Process

It would be convenient if the counselor could analyze the world of work, appraise the counselee's characteristics, and then announce the one perfect occupation. Such a goal is, of course, impossible. Even if we could attain complete knowledge of the job market and of an individual's traits, it is unlikely that we would come up with one "perfect job." For most people several occupations could be satisfying, but none is likely to be perfect in all respects.

The work of the counselor, therefore, is to help the counselee acquire the needed information and to guide as he uses this to make his vocational decision. In the words of one writer,

> ... we need to help young people learn how to make decisions which are, on the one hand, appropriate for them, and on the other hand, realistic and flexible. This means that they need to know what alternative courses of action are open to them; what the consequences and risks of choosing each of them are; and how these factors relate to their own system of values. They need to become aware that the ultimate responsibility for making choices rests with them, but that we stand ready to help them in the decision making process.... We need to (and indeed must) "motivate" adolescents to make the choices, educationally and vocationally, which are feasible for them at their stage of development.

—From Gary Collins, *Effective Counseling.* Carol Stream, Ill.: Creation House, 1972.

FOR FURTHER READING:

Bachhuber, Thomas D. *When Your Son Or Daughter Plans for the Future.* St. Meinrad, Ind.: Abbey Press, 1979.

Bradley, John. *Christian Career Planning.* Portland, Ore.: Multnomah Press, 1977.

Hummel, Dean L., and McDaniels, Carl. *How to Help Your Child Plan a Career.* Washington: Acropolis Books, 1979.

Riddell, Jim, and Whitehurts, Melvin. *Career Decision Making.* Nashville: Broadman Press, 1979.

VOMITING

SPITTING AND VOMITING are common in infants. If an infant vomits whole feedings, he may need a change in formula. The doctor will recommend one that he can digest more easily. A baby who vomits with force, drawing his legs upward because of stomach cramps, should be seen by a doctor immediately.

Sometimes children vomit as a result of eating when they are angry, tired, or overexcited. If a youngster vomits more than once in a short period of time, it may mean that he is suffering from indigestion or that he is coming down with an illness. He should be put to bed. If there is fever, the doctor should be called.

After a siege of vomiting a child should be given only what he can digest most easily: at first small amounts of water or sips of weak tea sweetened with saccharin, followed by fruit juices; then sips of milk; later plain crackers or cereal, and applesauce. When he manages to keep these down, he can gradually be given his regular diet.

—From *The New Encyclopedia of Child Care and Guidance.* Garden City, N.Y.: Doubleday & Co., 1968.

W

WEANING

The Time for Weaning. Children vary a great deal in the time they are ready to give up breast or bottle, and there is no reason to be in a hurry about it. Some are weaned by the time they are a year old. Many continue to get much of their milk by sucking until well into the second year. Some wean themselves overnight; usually it is done gradually. Around a year of age, children are very sensitive to being separated from their mothers, and it is easy to see why nursing is associated with mother. The child of 12 to 18 months who still wants to suck, especially at bedtime, may need extra reassurance and would be especially upset if deprived of it. Later, he'll probably give it up more gracefully.

Help your child in this gradual process by offering him liquids in a cup for some months before you expect him to give up bottle or breast. Don't worry if he doesn't drink all the milk you offer him. If you're inclined to worry, you may worry about whether weaning will mean that the child gets less milk. Be assured that many children at this age drink less than a quart of milk a day, yet are well nourished because their diet as a whole is adequate.

Worrying mothers often defeat their purpose, anyhow. They go along with nursing for months and months. Suddenly one day they decide that the child is too old for this sort of thing, and throw all the bottles away, or abruptly withdraw the breast. In this way, despite their initial indulgence, they end by

forceful and sudden weaning. An earlier start, and more gradual reduction would have been less upsetting.

—From *Your Child From 1 to 6.* Washington: U.S. Department of Health, Education and Welfare, 1969.

FOR FURTHER READING:

Forrer, Gordon R. *Weaning and Human Development.* Roslyn Heights, N.Y.: Libra Pubs., 1969.

WORKING MOTHERS

OUR SOCIETY attaches inordinate importance to economic success. All too often it is used as a gauge of personal worth. Money is often the driving force behind one of the most common and troublesome role conflicts in marriage: the working wife.

The image of the woman who never takes a job outside the home but devotes her entire life to caring for her husband and children is becoming a romantic fiction. "Thirty-five is when the average married American woman reenters the working world. Census figures show she can then expect to be part of the work force for the next twenty-four years or more" (Gail Sheehy, *Passages*, p. 379).

Lois Wladis Hoffman reports that "Women give 'money' as their major reason for working" ("The Decision to Become a Working Wife," *Family Roles and Interaction,* Jerold Heiss, ed. Chicago: Rand McNally, 1968, p. 237). Robert O. Blood, Jr. confirms this finding with his observation. "Economic necessity is the chief reason for working given by working wives. However, 'necessity' is a slippery term in an advertising-saturated culture. Nevertheless, in general, the lower the husband's income, the greater the necessity for the wife to supplement it. And the greater the necessity for her paid activity, the less resentment for the loss of her unpaid services at home" (Blood, "The Effect of the Wife's Employment on the Husband Wife Relationship," *Family Roles and Interaction,* p. 258).

The actual amount of money available to the family does not make as much difference as the standard of living the family attempts to maintain, which is usually set by those around them. Hoffman notes that "Women are motivated to work when they define their husband's income as inadequate . . . and will go to work to maintain their standard of living, or will also take employment to achieve the level of those around them" (Hoffman, pp. 236–237).

A man stood up in one of our large seminars and asked a question about money. He remarked that with the economy and inflation the way they are, both husband and wife have to work, not because they want to but because of necessity. Their schedules are full and time together is limited. He asked, "How can we make family principles work and build a real family time?" And said, "Our financial situation affects these other things."

A woman agreed, "What he's talking about is very real. A lot of us here at the seminar are really struggling with that. How practical is the whole idea of 'Seek ye first the kingdom of God and all these other things will be added'?"

Finances become the identified source of a lot of other problems. We're getting more and more to the place where we expect to live at a certain level of affluence, and in order to do what we think we need those two incomes. How much of that is in the economy, or how much is in the fact that we've had this era of prosperity and believe we should always be able to live at this luxury level?

The choice of life-style is the issue. Some people who are living at an income level of $15,000 to $20,000 per year are saying, "If we had another $5,000 or $10,000 we could really do something," while other people are earning $10,000 to $13,000 or less, and live economically all the time, no matter what. It's a matter of recognizing that Parkinson's law applies to money too "Work expands so as to fill the time available for its completion." You won't have any more money to spend no matter how much you make.

Economic pressures can propel your family into a variety of crises. If raising your standard of living is your only motivation for working as a wife, perhaps you need to choose a more frugal life-style. Though money is the most common reason given for a wife to work, that can produce a number of other kinds of crises in the marriage.

For instance, "Is the financial motivation related to a feeling that the father is a failure? If so, the mother's employment could symbolize his failure for the whole family. On the other hand, the mother's employment could be part of cooperative planning and perceived as a symbol of family unity. Perhaps the working mother is paying penance for her poor management and extravagance. Or, she might want an independent income because of marital difficulties or simply out of a desire for autonomy in an otherwise close and congenial relationship" (Hoffman, p. 238).

Blood reports that "Dual-income couples

quarrel more frequently than one-income couples. When conflict occurs in working-wife families, it does not spread randomly over all aspects of marriage. For instance, there is no increase in difficulties over in-laws, friendships, or sexual or religious matters. Almost all the significant differences are concentrated in the 'domestic-economic' field. Dual-income couples quarrel over money not because of the extra income but in spite of it" (Blood, pp. 263–264).

If any of these problems are plaguing you, can you act to resolve them? Will you affirm that your marriage is more important than the standard of living you are pursuing? Will you affirm that God has a way for you to have a rich and satisfying marriage relationship, even if you are both working?

What kinds of commitments will you make to bring those affirmations to reality? Perhaps some of the income from the second job could be invested in regular evenings and weekends together. Perhaps you need to plan carefully for using your holiday and vacations for the maximum benefit of the whole family, including children. Possibly you could use one of the many programs available in churches and communities for marriage communication training.

These plans of action will not work out the same for every family. The secret is to work on them together.

—From J. Allan Petersen, *Conquering Family Stress.* Wheaton, Ill.: Victor Books, 1978.

FOR FURTHER READING:

Curtis, Jean. *Working Mothers.* New York: Simon & Schuster, Inc., 1977.

Greenleaf, Barbara K., and Schaffer, Lewis A. *Help: A Handbook for Working Mothers.* New York: Berkley Publishing Corp., 1980.

Norris, Gloria, and Miller, Jo Ann. *The Working Mother's Complete Handbook.* New York: E.P. Dutton, 1979.

Scott, Niki. *The Balancing Act: A Handbook for Working Mothers.* Fairway, Kans.: Andrews and McMeel, Inc., 1978.

Index